FAMILY LAW: THE ESSENTIALS

FAMILY LAW: THE ESSENTIALS

William P. Statsky

WEST PUBLISHING COMPANY

Minneapolis/St. Paul   New York   Los Angeles   San Francisco

☐ Production Credits

Text design: Roz Stendahl, Dapper Design

Cover image: *Lofting Model,* bronze, 1991. Sculptor: Paul T. Granlund. Represented by Premier Gallery, Minneapolis. Sculpture photography: Stan Waldhauser.

Copyediting: Patricia Lewis

Composition: Parkwood Composition Service, Inc.

☐ Photo Credit

180 Georgia Office of Child Support

☐ WEST'S COMMITMENT TO THE ENVIRONMENT

In 1906, West Publishing Company began recycling materials left over from the production of books. This began a tradition of efficient and responsible use of resources. Today, 100% of our legal bound volumes are printed on acid-free, recycled paper consisting of 50% new fibers. West recycles nearly 27,700,000 pounds of scrap paper annually—the equivalent of 229,300 trees. Since the 1960s, West has devised ways to capture and recycle waste inks, solvents, oils, and vapors created in the printing process. We also recycle plastics of all kinds, wood, glass, corrugated cardboard, and batteries, and have eliminated the use of polystyrene book packaging. We at West are proud of the longevity and the scope of our commitment to the environment.

West pocket parts and advance sheets are printed on recyclable paper and can be collected and recycled with newspapers. Staples do not have to be removed. Bound volumes can be recycled after removing the cover.

Production, Prepress, Printing and Binding by West Publishing Company.

 PRINTED ON 10% POST CONSUMER RECYCLED PAPER

British Library Cataloguing-in-Publication Data. A catalogue record for this book is available from the British Library.

COPYRIGHT ©1997   By WEST PUBLISHING COMPANY
                                  610 Opperman Drive
                                  P.O. Box 64526
                                  St. Paul, MN 55164-0526

04 03 02 01 00 99   8 7 6 5 4 3

Library of Congress Cataloging-in-Publication Data

Statsky, William P.
     Family law : the essentials / William P. Statsky.
       p. cm.
     Includes index.
     ISBN 0-314-20226-9 (soft : alk. paper)
     1. Domestic relations—United States.   I. Title.
    KF505.S833   1997
346.7301'5—dc20   96-24086
[347.30615]   CIP

For my own domestic relations: Pat, Jess, Gabe, Joe, Brenda, Rich, Clara, Bob, Matthew, Stan, Ann, Ann, Ann, et al.

SUMMARY TABLE OF CONTENTS

CONTENTS

CHAPTER □ 6

Separation Agreements: Legal Issues and Drafting Options   79

CHAPTER □ 7

Child Custody   137

CHAPTER □ 11
Tax Consequences of Separation and Divorce   234

CHAPTER □ 12
The Legal Rights of Women   251

CHAPTER □ 13
Illegitimacy and Paternity Proceedings   266

CHAPTER □ 14
The Legal Status of Children   281

Property and Earnings   283

Domicile   283

Estates   283

Education   284

Neglect and Abuse   284

Delinquency   284

Summary   285

Key Chapter Terminology   288

CHAPTER □ 15
Adoption   289

Introduction   289

Kinds of Adoption   290

Agency Adoption   290

Independent/Private Adoption   290

Black Market Adoption   292

Who May Be Adopted?   292

Who May Adopt?   293

Adoption Procedure   294

Jurisdiction and Venue   294

Petition   294

Notice   295

Consent   295

Involuntary Termination of Parental Rights   297

Placement   299

Can Children Divorce Their Parents?   299

Challenges to the Adoption Decree   300

Baby Richard   300

Baby Jessica   303

Consequences of Adoption   303

Confidentiality   304

Equitable Adoption   305

Wrongful Adoption   305

Summary   310

Key Chapter Terminology   310

CHAPTER □ 16
Surrogacy and the New Science of Motherhood   311

Introduction   313

Definitions   313

Methods of Surrogate Parenting   313

Agreements   313

Reasons for Choosing Surrogate Parenting Agreements   314

Major Arguments for and against Surrogate Parenting   314

Supporting Arguments   314

Opposing Arguments   315

Issues in State Law   315

Adoption Laws   315

Paternity Laws   315

Custody Issues   315

Contractual Duties   316

State Regulation   316

Uniform Status of Children of Assisted Conception Act   317

Summary   320

Key Chapter Terminology   321

CHAPTER □ 17
Torts   322

Classification of Torts   322

Intentional Torts against Property   322

Intentional Torts against the Person   322

Unintentional Tort: Negligence   322

Intrafamily Torts   322

Wrongful Life, Wrongful Birth, Wrongful Pregnancy   324

Derivative Actions   325

Loss of Consortium   325

Loss of Services   326

Nonderivative Actions   326

Alienation of Affections   327

Criminal Conversation   327

Enticement of Spouse   327

Abduction or Enticement of a Child   327

Seduction   328

Vicarious Liability of Family Members   328

Summary   329

Key Chapter Terminology   330

GLOSSARY □ 331

INDEX □ 349

BY THE SAME AUTHOR:

Case Analysis and Fundamentals of Legal Writing, 4th ed. St. Paul: West Publishing Company, 1995 (with J. Wernet)

Essentials of Paralegalism, 2d ed. St. Paul: West Publishing Company, 1993

Essentials of Torts. St. Paul: West Publishing Company, 1994

Family Law, 4th ed. St. Paul: West Publishing Company, 1996

Inmate Involvement in Prison Legal Services: Roles and Training Options for the Inmate as Paralegal. American Bar Association, Commission on Correctional Facilities and Services, 1974

Introduction to Paralegalism: Perspectives, Problems and Skills, 4th ed. St. Paul: West Publishing Company, 1992

Legal Desk Reference. St. Paul: West Publishing Company, 1990 (with B. Hussey, Michael Diamond, & R. Nakamura)

The Legal Paraprofessional as Advocate and Assistant: Roles, Training Concepts and Materials. Center on Social Welfare Policy and Law, 1971 (with P. Lang)

Legal Research and Writing: Some Starting Points, 4th ed. St. Paul: West Publishing Company, 1993

Legal Thesaurus/Dictionary: A Resource for the Writer and Computer Researcher. St. Paul: West Publishing Company, 1985

Legislative Analysis and Drafting, 2d ed. St. Paul: West Publishing Company, 1984

Paralegal Employment: Facts and Strategies for the 1990s, 2d ed. St. Paul: West Publishing Company, 1993

Paralegal Ethics and Regulation, 2d ed. St. Paul: West Publishing Company, 1993

Torts: Personal Injury Litigation, 3d ed. St. Paul: West Publishing Company, 1995

Rights of the Imprisoned: Cases, Materials and Directions. Indianapolis: Bobbs-Merrill Company, 1974 (with R. Singer)

What Have Paralegals Done? A Dictionary of Functions. National Paralegal Institute, 1973

PREFACE

Say it isn't true. A recent *New York Times* story reported that a well-known divorce attorney was giving out pens to prospective clients that said, "Sue Someone You Love." This is not the image the legal profession wishes to project to the public. Yet newspapers, magazines, and talk shows do seem to give the impression that our society is in a litigation frenzy: "Son Sues to Divorce His Mother," "Wife Demands Half of Husband's Medical Practice in Divorce Settlement," "Surrogate Mother Refuses to Turn Over Baby," "Live-in Lover Seeks Palimony."

Our goal in this book is to sort through the headlines in order to find an accurate picture of the state of family law today and the role of the attorney-paralegal team within it. We are living in an era of great change in the practice of family law. The primary focus of the family law practitioner is no longer adultery and who gets the house. No-fault divorce has made marriage relatively easy to dissolve. The women's movement has helped bring about major shifts in determining what property can be split after a divorce and how to split it. The country has declared war on the "deadbeat" parent who fails to pay child support. Major new enforcement mechanisms have been designed to find these parents and make them pay. To the surprise of many, courts have come to the aid of unmarried fathers seeking to undo the adoption of their children. Science and technology have unleashed new concepts of motherhood and parentage. The law has not been able to keep pace with the scientific revolution taking place in the test tube and in the womb.

In short, there is a lot to talk about! It's a fascinating time to study family law.

CHAPTER FORMAT

Each chapter includes features designed to assist students in understanding the material:

☐ A chapter outline at the beginning of each chapter provides a preview of the major topics discussed in the chapter.

☐ Tables are used extensively to clarify concepts and present detailed information in an organized chart form.

☐ Assignments ask students to apply major principles discussed in the chapters.

☐ A chapter summary at the end of each chapter provides a concise review of the main concepts discussed.

☐ Selected terms are defined in the margin next to the text to which the terms are relevant.

☐ Key terms are printed in boldface type the first time they appear in the text. A list of key terms also appears at the end of each chapter to help students review important terminology introduced in that chapter.

SUPPLEMENTS

☐ An **Instructor's Manual/Test Bank** contains competencies, answers to selected assignments, and teaching suggestions, as well as 30–40 multiple choice and essay questions per chapter.

□ **State Supplements** specific for Texas, California, New York, and Florida provide discussions of key differences in state law. These can be purchased at a discount shrinkwrapped with the text.

□ West's **Paralegal Video Library** includes *The Drama of the Law II* and *I Never Said I Was a Lawyer*, among other videos. Available to qualified adopters.

□ **WESTLAW**®, West's on-line computerized legal research system, offers students hands-on experience with a system commonly used in law offices. Ten hours are free to qualified adopters.

□ **WESTMATE**® **Tutorial** is an interactive software that introduces students to WESTLAW capabilities off-line.

□ **Strategies and Tips for Paralegal Educators,** a pamphlet by Anita Tebbe of Johnson County Community College, offers specific teaching ideas to instructors to aid students in reaching their educational goals.

ACKNOWLEDGMENTS

I wish to thank the following people at West who were most helpful in the emergence of this book: Elizabeth Hannan, Patricia Bryant, and Matthew Thurber.

I also wish to thank users of *Family Law*; Third Edition who responded to a survey, giving us helpful feedback for this Essentials version.

Also helpful were the reviewers for *Family Law*, Fourth Edition whose valuable suggestions were incorporated into parts of this Essentials version:

□ Philip A. Augustino
Erie Community College, NY

□ John DeLeo
Central Pennsylvania Business School

□ Ann M. Dobmeyer
Bay Path College, MA

□ Patrick J. Faucheux
Gulf Coast Community College, FL

□ Merle B. Hamre
Southern College, FL

□ Kenneth Hill
Durham Technical Community College, NC

□ Richard Hill
University of Houston—Downtown, TX

□ Norman W. Holt II
Daytona Beach Community College, FL

□ William L. Koleszar
Denver Business College, CO

□ Maryanne Manley
The American Institute, AZ

□ Robert E. Nowak
Queens College, NY

□ Jill H. O'Connor
Sacred Heart University, CT

□ Rebecca Parker
Arapahoe Community College, CO

William P. Statsky
San Diego, California

The Scope of a Family Law Practice

▰▰▰ The Scope of Family Law

A major theme of family law is the disintegration of the family. To work in an office where family law is practiced, you need compassion, flexibility, skill, and, above all, an ability to handle a wide diversity of problems. While some cases are straightforward and "simple," many are not. A veteran attorney recently observed that a family law practice required everyone "to become an expert in many fields of law and not just one."[1]

Assume that you are a paralegal working for Karen Smith, an attorney in your state. One of the office's clients is Susan Miller who lives out of state. The attorney receives the following telegram from Ms. Miller:

2/7/97

Karen Smith:

I am leaving the state in a week to come live with my mother. She will help me move everything so that we can start a new life. I must see you as soon as I arrive. Yesterday my husband called from his business. He threatened me and the children. I will bring the twins with me. I don't know where my oldest boy is. He is probably with his father getting into more trouble.

Susan Miller

A checklist is provided below of many of the questions that are potentially relevant to the case of Susan Miller. As a paralegal, you might be asked to conduct preliminary interviews and field investigation on some of the questions. Others may require legal research in the law library. Many of the technical terms in this list will be defined later. Our goal here is simply to demonstrate that the scope of the law covered in a family law practice can be very broad.

Criminal Law

☐ Has Mr. Miller committed a crime? What kind of threats did he make? Did he assault his wife and children?

---

1. John Greenya, *Family Affairs: Seven Experts in Family Law Discuss Their Experiences . . .*, 9 The Washington Lawyer 23, 31 (November/December 1994).

□ Has he failed to support his family? If so, is the nonsupport serious enough to warrant criminal action against him?

□ Even if he has committed a crime, would it be wise for Ms. Miller to ask the district attorney to investigate and prosecute the case?

□ Is there any danger of further criminal acts by her husband? If so, what can be done, if anything, to prevent them? Can she obtain a restraining order to keep him away?

□ Is Ms. Miller subject to any penalties for taking the children out of state?

Divorce/Separation/Annulment Law

□ What does Ms. Miller want?

□ Does she know what her husband wants to do?

□ Does she have grounds for a divorce?

□ Does she have grounds for an annulment? (Were the Millers validly married?)

□ Does she have grounds for a judicial separation?

□ Does Mr. Miller have grounds for a divorce, annulment, or judicial separation against his wife?

Law of Custody

□ Does Ms. Miller want permanent custody of all three children? (Is she the natural mother of all three? Is he their natural father? Are there any paternity problems?) Will Mr. Miller want custody? What is the lifestyle of the parent or parents seeking custody? Is joint custody an option?

□ If she does not want a divorce, annulment, or judicial separation, how can she obtain legal custody of the children?

□ Does she want anyone else to be given temporary or permanent custody of any of the children (e.g., a relative)? Will such a person make a claim for custody *against* Ms. Miller?

□ If she wants custody, has she jeopardized her chances of being awarded custody by taking the children out of state?

Support Law

□ Is Mr. Miller adequately supporting his wife? Or, is she supporting him?

□ Is he adequately supporting the three children? Do they have any special medical or school needs? If so, are these needs being met?

□ Are the children now covered under Mr. Miller's health insurance policy? Is Ms. Miller covered? Is there a danger that the policy will be changed?

□ Can Ms. Miller obtain a court order forcing him to support them while she is deciding whether she wants to terminate the marital relationship?

□ If she files for divorce, annulment, or judicial separation, can she obtain a temporary support order while the case is in progress?

□ If she files for divorce, annulment, or judicial separation and *loses*, can she still obtain a support order against him?

□ Does Mr. Miller have assets (personal property or real property) against which a support order can be enforced? Is there a danger he might try to hide or transfer these assets?

□ If he cannot be relied upon for support and she cannot work, does she qualify for public assistance such as Aid to Families with Dependent Children (AFDC)?

☐ Would she be entitled to more support in the state she is coming from or in this state?

☐ Is Mr. Miller supporting any other children such as from a previous marriage? If so, how would this affect his duty to support the three he had with Ms. Miller?

Contract/Agency Law

☐ While she is living apart from her husband, can she enter into contracts with merchants for the purchase of food, clothing, furniture, medical care, prescriptions, transportation, and other necessaries and make *him* pay for them? Can she use his credit?

☐ Has she already entered into such contracts?

☐ Can he obligate her on any of his current debts?

☐ Has she ever worked for him or otherwise acted as his agent?

☐ Has he ever worked for her or otherwise acted as her agent?

☐ Have the children (particularly the oldest child) entered into any contracts under their own names? If so, who is liable for such contracts? Can they be canceled or disaffirmed?

Real and Personal Property Law

☐ Do either or both of them own any real property, e.g., land? If so, how is the real property owned? How is title held? Individually? As tenants by the entirety? Who provided the funds for the purchase?

☐ What rights does she have in his property?

☐ What rights does he have in her property?

☐ What is his income? Can his wages be garnished? Is he in a profit-sharing plan at work? What pension or other retirement rights does he have? Is she entitled to a share of these assets?

☐ What other personal property exists—cars, bank accounts, stocks, bonds, furniture? Who owns this property?

Corporate Law/Business Law

☐ What kind of business does Mr. Miller have? Is it a corporation? A partnership? A sole proprietorship? If the parties separate and obtain a divorce, will Ms. Miller be entitled to a share of the business as part of the division of marital property?

☐ What are the assets and liabilities of the business?

☐ Is there a danger that Mr. Miller or his business might go into bankruptcy? If so, how would this affect her rights to support and to a share of the marital property?

Tort Law

☐ Has he committed any torts against her (e.g., assault, conversion)?

☐ Has she committed any torts against him?

☐ Has either parent committed any torts against their own children?

☐ Have the children (particularly the oldest) damaged any property or committed any torts for which the parents might be liable?

Civil Procedure/Conflict of Law

☐ If a court action is brought (e.g., divorce, custody, separate maintenance), what court would have jurisdiction? A court in this state? A court in the state where he resides?

☐ How can service of process be made?

☐ If she sues and obtains a judgment in this state, can it be enforced in another state?

Evidence Law

☐ What factual claims will Ms. Miller be making, e.g., that Mr. Miller has hidden money that could be used to support the family?

☐ What testimonial evidence (oral statements of witnesses) exists to support her claims?

☐ How much of this evidence is admissible in court?

☐ How much of the admissible evidence is likely to be believed by a judge or jury?

☐ What documentary evidence should be pursued, e.g., marriage and birth certificates, records of purchases?

☐ Whose depositions should be taken, if any?

☐ What claims will Mr. Miller make against Ms. Miller? What evidence is he likely to use to support these claims? What objections can be made to this evidence?

Juvenile Law

☐ Can a dependency or child neglect petition be brought against Mr. Miller? Against Ms. Miller?

☐ Why is she upset about her eldest son? Has he committed any "acts of delinquency"?

☐ Is he a Person in Need of Supervision (PINS) or a Child in Need of Supervision (CHINS)?

☐ If he has damaged anyone else's property, can a parent be financially responsible for the damage?

Tax Law

☐ Have Mr. Miller and his wife filed joint tax returns in the past?

☐ Are there any refunds due (or money owed) on past returns?

☐ In a property settlement following a divorce or separation, what would be the most advantageous settlement for Ms. Miller from a tax perspective?

☐ What arrangement might Mr. Miller seek in order to obtain the best tax posture? What is negotiable? What will he be willing to give up in order to obtain his tax objectives? Will he, for example, cooperate in allowing her to have sole custody of the children in exchange for her cooperation in ensuring that his alimony payments are deductible?

Estate Law

☐ Do they both have their own wills? If so, who are the beneficiaries? If there is no divorce, can he leave Ms. Miller out of his will entirely?

☐ Who receives their property if they die without a will?

☐ Are there any life insurance policies on Mr. Miller's life, with Ms. Miller or the children as beneficiaries? If so, is he allowed to change these beneficiaries?

Professional Responsibility/Ethics

☐ Is Mr. Miller represented by counsel? If so, can we contact Mr. Miller directly, or must all communications to him be made through his attorney?

If he is not yet represented, are there limitations on what we can and cannot say to him?

☐ If Ms. Miller can find her eldest son, can she simply take him away from her husband when the latter is not around? Would this be illegal? What is the ethical obligation of an attorney whose client is about to do something illegal?

Miscellaneous

☐ Can Mr. Miller be forced to pay her legal fees that grow out of present and future difficulties together?

☐ Can she be forced to pay his legal fees?

▰▰▰▰ PARALEGAL ROLES

The purpose of this book is to examine many of the above questions that could arise in a case such as *Miller v. Miller*. More specifically, we will examine such questions in the context of paralegal roles in assisting a family law attorney. Here are two overviews of these roles.

Job Description

SOURCE: Colorado Bar Association, Legal Assistant Committee.

Family law legal assistants may perform all or part of the following tasks:

A. Screen Prospective Clients by Telephone Interviews

B. Commencement of Action

1. Initial interview with client to obtain information for pleadings.

2. Prepare initial pleadings, including petition, summons and waiver of service, affidavit as to children, and response.

3. Draft correspondence with clients, courts, and other attorneys.

4. Arrange for service of process.

C. Temporary Orders

1. Prepare motions for temporary orders or temporary injunctions.

2. Notice and set hearings.

3. Assist in settlement negotiations.

4. Draft stipulations for temporary orders after negotiations.

D. Financial Affidavits

1. Work with clients in gathering and compiling financial information.

2. Analyze income and expense information provided by client.

3. Work with accountants, financial advisers, brokers, and other financial experts retained by client.

4. Retain appraisers for real estate, business and personal property.

5. Prepare financial affidavits.

E. Discovery

1. Prepare discovery requests

2. Assist clients in gathering documents and data to respond to discovery requests.

3. Prepare responses to discovery requests.

4. Organize, index, and summarize discovered materials.

F. *Settlement Negotiations*

1. Assist attorney in analysis of proposed settlements.

2. Research legal questions and assist in drafting briefs and memoranda.

3. Assist in drafting separation agreements.

G. *Hearings*

1. Notice and set final orders hearing.

2. Research legal questions and assist in drafting briefs and memoranda.

3. Assist in preparation of trial exhibits and trial notebook.

4. Arrange for expert witnesses and assist in preparing witnesses and clients for trial.

5. Attend hearings.

6. Prepare decree.

H. *Post Decree*

1. Prepare documents for transfers of assets.

2. Arrange for filing and recording of transfer documents.

3. Review bills for tax-deductible fees and prepare opinion letters to client.

4. Draft pleadings for withdrawal from case.

I. *Special Projects*

1. Develop forms for gathering information from client.

2. Maintain files on the following: separation-agreement provisions, current case law, resource materials for clients, and experts in various fields (e.g., custody, evaluation, business appraisals, etc.).

FAMILY LAW FOR PARALEGALS

Y. Spiegel, *Family Law for Paralegals* 6 THE JOURNAL 7 (Sacramento Association of Legal Assistants, June 1986).

The role of a legal assistant in a family law practice is exciting and varied. Whereas all areas of law can be interesting, the opportunities for client contact, full involvement and case responsibility in family law make it a truly satisfying area of specialty. Family law affords tremendous scope for helping people in a very basic change in their lives. With the divorce rate at roughly 50 percent, there are few families who haven't been touched in some way by the problems and trauma of a court action. Our job as legal assistants can be to smooth the way through this difficult time for the client, making the experience kinder, easier to understand, more efficient, and hopefully, less expensive. Divorce is not the only area covered in family law. Adoption, grandparent visitation issues, and emancipation of minors also come under this topic. . . .

The teamwork between attorney and legal assistant is crucial to the success of a paralegal working in the family law area. Your skills and interests, as well as the degree of trust and communication between you and your boss will determine the tasks that you will be assigned. If there is good communication and rapport between you as team members, the clients will come to rely on both of you in handling the case, and your participation will be invaluable.

In my office the attorney conducts the initial interview with the client. This is primarily done to establish the attorney/client bond, which is crucial to the successful processing of the case. Any general questions which the client has about the dissolution process, as well as discussing strategy, fees and expectations are all done at this stage. If there is an immediate need for temporary orders, such as restraining orders or temporary custody or support, the attorney will begin the information gathering process by taking detailed notes of the client's situation. The initial interview is usually concluded by inviting me into the office to be introduced as the "paralegal who will be assisting me with your case." This gives me the authority to contact the client on behalf of the attorney to gather more detailed information, and to answer the client's questions as to general procedure. I find that the clients are, for the most part, pleased to know that a paralegal will be working on their case. I am usually more accessible than the attorney to answer their questions, or to convey information, and they are billed at a lower rate for my time.

It is usually my responsibility to draft the opening documents. These include the summons, petition, and the income and expense forms. With the recent adoption of the Agnos income and expense forms, this job has become quite critical. The Agnos forms are complicated and in some instances intimidating, and clients often need a lot of assistance in filling them out. I find that often our women clients don't understand that the forms are meant to demonstrate "need" for support. They spend all their time trying to make their income on the form come out even with their expenses, and that is usually impossible. It is often my job to tell them that if they don't show the court any evidence of the need for support, the judge won't order any. I am also responsible for drafting mediation counseling stipulations, property declarations and even orders to show cause and motions for pendente lite relief. I rely on notes from the attorney, as well as my own interviews with the client to obtain facts necessary to create the pleadings. The attorney then reviews the documents for accuracy and obtains the signature of the client. When the documents are filed, I see that the papers are served on the client's spouse and keep the client informed of subsequent developments.

Discovery plays an important role in family law. Over the years my office has developed a set of family law interrogatories on our word processor, which can be modified and used to flush out the details of the community, quasi-community, and separate property. Any real property or pension plans must be appraised for their value as community property, and this is also the responsibility of the legal assistant. Building a strong working relationship with the various legal support personnel, such as appraisers, actuaries, deposition reporters, mediation and rehabilitation counselors, process servers, and photocopy services is essential. These people trust and respect my role as professional and as a representative of my office, and often go out of their way to assist us in emergencies because of the relationship which we have built over the years.

Preparing and arranging the service of deposition notices is another important part of family law practice which falls within the scope of the paralegal's responsibility. After the transcript of the deposition has come back from the reporter, it is my job to index and summarize it for the attorney's use in trial preparation. Comparing the bank account dates, numbers, balances and other descriptions of property with the opposing party's previous descriptions is an important part of establishing the full extent of community or separate property interest and achieving an equal division.

Child custody and visitation is often the most traumatic aspect of a family law case. Parents who are separating are often terrified of what the effect will be on their children, and are frequently afraid that dividing their households will result in loss of closeness and opportunities for quality parenting time. Fortunately, California courts lean heavily in favor of joint custody whenever feasible. Mediation counseling programs have been set up in Sacramento, Yolo, and Solano counties and elsewhere to assist parents in working out arrangements for custody and visitation with the assistance of trained facilitators. The agreements they work out are then presented as stipulations to the court. Wherever possible, a judge will not hear a motion for custody or visitation until the parties have been to mediation. This is practical and beneficial, since the mediation session is often the first time that the parties have been able to sit down and actually *listen* to each other since their problems began. It also provides a beginning for the future cooperation that they will have to achieve to be separated parents with children in common. It is my job as legal assistant to prepare the mediation counseling stipulation, to see that it is signed by all parties and attorneys, to make sure that it is filed with the court, and then arrange contact between the mediator and the parties.

If the parties are unable to settle their disputes (and we try very hard to settle every family law case without the necessity of a trial) then I draft a trial brief setting out the facts, the history of the case, the contested and uncontested issues, our proposal for an equal division of property, and a memorandum setting forth the applicable law. Updated income and expense and property declarations must be filed along with the trial brief, and any appraisals or actuarial analyses of pension funds must also be updated as of the time of trial.

Before the day of the trial, I contact the client to make sure that he or she is psychologically prepared to go, and make arrangements with the client for last minute prepping by the attorney. I organize the file to make all exhibits and necessary documents fingertip-accessible to the attorney trying the case, and I subpoena any witnesses who may be needed. It is very hard to get a firm court date because of case congestion, and the client must be assisted in dealing with the resulting anxiety and inconvenience. If the case does go to trial, I often go along to help my boss keep organized with respect to the documents, take notes as to areas of inquiry to be explored, run emergency errands, and keep the witnesses organized.

When the judgment is prepared, either by stipulation in the form of a marital settlement agreement, or by reducing a decision by the trial court to judgment form, I often draft the first document for review by the attorney and client. Keeping track of dates, such as deadlines for appeal, and eligibility for final judgment is also my responsibility. Preparing transfer deeds and noticing pension plans of the divorced spouse's interest are some of the wrap-up details.

As the family law case progresses, a paralegal becomes intimately familiar with the client's life and affairs. You are in a unique position to offer comfort and guidance to people in deep transition. While the legal professional's role should never be confused with that of a therapist or psychiatrist, your positive attitude and sensitivity to the client's situation can make a big difference in how they experience the adjustment to what amounts to an entirely new life. Over the past six years in a practice which is predominantly devoted to family law, I have watched hundreds of clients pass through this difficult change in their lives, heal their wounds, and create more successful and satisfying lifestyles. This is a very rewarding part of my job.

While I have had to skip over many areas of a legal assistant's responsibilities in the area of family law, I have tried to give you a sense of some of the duties that a paralegal may have. Your particular tasks will be assigned by the attorney. Short of giving the client legal advice and appearing as their representative in court, there is tremendous scope for the utilization of paralegals in a family law practice.

SUMMARY

Family law encompasses a wide variety of legal problems. In addition to the obvious areas of divorce, custody, and support, the family law practitioner must know something about criminal law, contract law, corporate and business law, property law, tort law, civil procedure law, evidence law, juvenile law, tax law, estate law, etc.

The paralegal's role depends on the working relationship he or she develops with the supervising attorney. In general, many paralegals conduct interviews; draft pleadings (e.g., summons, petition); draft correspondence; prepare income and expense statements; arrange for service of process; prepare temporary orders (e.g., a restraining order, temporary child custody and support order); gather financial information; arrange for appraisals; prepare discovery requests; digest and index discovery transcripts; conduct legal research; subpoena witnesses; prepare for hearings; help organize the trial notebook; provide general assistance at trial (e.g., take notes of testimony, run emergency errands); and prepare post decree documents (e.g., final judgment, transfer of title).

BREACH OF PROMISE TO MARRY, THE HEART BALM STATUTE, AND CONTRACTS RESTRAINING MARRIAGE

BREACH OF PROMISE TO MARRY

Over 100,000 engagements are broken each year. This can be a costly experience. In some cities "traditional weddings can cost as much as $50,000 or $100,000, and as the wedding day approaches, less and less of the expense of the event can be recovered if the event is canceled." In New York City, for example, a caterer and hotel may be allowed to charge for services and rooms that cannot be rebooked when canceled with less than six months notice.[1] When faced with such costs, some victims of broken engagements look for a way to sue. Can they sue for breach of **contract** or, more specifically, breach of promise to marry?

For centuries, one of the sacred principles in law has been the stability of contracts. An organized society depends on the faithful performance of contractual commitments. Hence courts are available to force parties to abide by their contracts. In the business world, thousands of contracts are made every hour. Merchants invest large amounts of money and other resources in reliance on these contracts. Consequently, the law will not allow a merchant to avoid performing its contract simply because it is now having second thoughts about the agreement reached or because it can now obtain a better deal elsewhere. But does the sacred principle of contractual stability apply to broken promises

> **Contract** An agreement that a court will enforce.

---

1. Keith Bradsher, *Modern Tale of Woe: Being Left at the Altar,* New York Times, March 7, 1990, at B8.

to marry? Should courts be used to force parties to honor such contracts? Before answering these questions, let's review the major components or elements of a contract:

Elements of a Contract

☐ There must be an offer.

☐ There must be an acceptance of the offer.

☐ There must be **consideration.** (Consideration is something of value that is given or exchanged, e.g., an exchange of money for services, an exchange of promises to do something or to refrain from doing something.)

☐ The parties must have the **capacity** to enter a contract.

☐ Some contracts must comply with the **Statute of Frauds.**

Consideration
Something of value that is exchanged between the parties.

Capacity   The legal power to do something. Minors, for example, do not have the capacity to enter a contract that can be enforced against them if they wish to walk away from it.

Statute of Frauds   The requirement that certain kinds of contracts be in writing in order to be enforceable.

EXAMPLE John, age thirty-four, has been dating Mary, an independently wealthy woman of thirty-three. She proposes, John accepts, and they both agree on a wedding date. The next day Mary changes her mind and tells John that he no longer wants to marry him. Does a contract exist that is enforceable by John against Mary? Each of the elements needs to be examined:

1. *Offer.* Mary offered to marry John.

2. *Acceptance.* John agreed to marry her (he accepted her offer).

3. *Consideration.* Something of value was exchanged by both parties; they both exchanged *promises* to marry each other. This mutual *exchange of promises* was the consideration for the contract.

4. *Capacity.* There was no indication that either John or Mary lacked the capacity to enter the contract. For example, when the offer was accepted, neither was a minor, and neither appeared to be mentally incapable of understanding the nature of the agreement.

5. *Writing.* Mutual promises to marry do *not* have to be in writing to be enforceable; the Statute of Frauds does not apply to this kind of contract.

All of the requirements for a contract, therefore, appear to have been met. Does John have a **cause of action** against Mary? Years ago, the answer was yes. The suit for breach of promise to marry was referred to as a **heart balm action.**

The tide has begun to turn against heart balm actions in many states, however. These states have passed **heart balm statutes** such as the following:

Cause of Action   An allegation of facts that gives a party a right to judicial relief.

Heart Balm Action   An action based on a broken heart, e.g., breach of promise to marry, alienation of affections.

Heart Balm Statute   A statute (sometimes called an anti–heart balm statute) that abolishes heart balm actions.

§ 100   Breach of contract to marry shall not constitute an injury or wrong recognized by law, and no action, suit or proceeding shall be maintained therefor.

These statutes were enacted for a number of reasons. The emotions involving a refusal to marry are usually so personal, intense, and possibly bitter that a court did not appear to be a proper setting to handle them. Furthermore, many feel that engaged persons should be allowed to correct their mistakes without fear of a lawsuit. As one judge said, the ''courtroom scene'' should not be ''transposed into a grotesque marketplace whose wares would be the exposure of heart-rending episodes of wounded pride, which should be best kept private rather than public.'' Courts were also afraid of being flooded with breach-of-promise lawsuits, particularly by unscrupulous ''gold diggers and blackmailers'' who use the threat of publicity to force a settlement.[2]

Another criticism of heart balm actions is the difficulty of designing an appropriate **remedy** for the aggrieved party. In the business world, one of the possible remedies for a breach of contract is **specific performance.** For the mar-

Remedy   The method or means by which a court or other body will enforce a right or compensate someone for a violation of a right.

Specific Performance   A remedy for breach of contract that forces the wrongdoing party to complete the contract as promised.

---

2. *Prosser & Keeton on Torts,* 929 (5th ed. 1984).

riage contract that is breached, the remedy of specific performance would mean that the court would force the reluctant party to go through with the marriage contract. The obviously unacceptable concept of a compulsory marriage under these circumstances led many states to abolish the cause of action altogether. Another possible remedy is the payment of **damages** caused by the breach. But what should the damages be, and are the problems involved in calculating them so great that we should abolish heart balm actions altogether? Many states have concluded that the remedy of damages is as inappropriate as specific performance and have therefore abolished the action.

Damages Money paid because of a wrongful injury or loss to person or property.

ASSIGNMENT 2.1

Assume that you live in a state where heart balm actions can be brought. Dan asks Carol to marry him. Carol says yes. The date is set for the wedding. Two weeks before the wedding, Carol learns that Dan has just married Linda. At the time Dan was engaged to Carol, Carol was already married to Bill, but Dan did not know this. Carol was in the process of divorcing Bill and hoped the divorce would be finalized before her marriage to Dan. Carol wanted to wait until the divorce was final before telling Dan about the prior marriage and divorce. Dan did not learn about any of this until after his marriage to Linda. When Carol's divorce to Bill became final, she sued Dan. The cause of action stated in Carol's complaint against Dan is breach of promise to marry. Should Carol be allowed to bring this action? Why or why not?

Assume that a woman lives in a state where it is still possible to sue for breach of promise to marry. Today even these states would not grant her the remedy of specific performance if she won. No court will order a marriage to occur. What then does a court victory mean? What can she recover? What are her damages?

1. **Compensatory damages.** For example:
   - Out-of-pocket expenses. Money spent by the plaintiff in purchasing a trousseau, renting a hall, purchasing rings, etc.
   - Loss of income. The plaintiff may have lost income by leaving a job in order to marry the defendant.
   - Physical and mental health deterioration due to worry, publicity, and humiliation.
   - Injury to the plaintiff's reputation and chances of obtaining a new marriage proposal.
   - Destroyed financial expectations. If the defendant was wealthy and the plaintiff was poor, the plaintiff has obviously lost a great deal in terms of potential standard of living. Note, however, that most states will *not* allow damages for this kind of loss.

2. **Aggravated damages.** For example:
   - Sexual intercourse due to seduction.
   - Pregnancy, miscarriage.
   - An unusual degree of publicity and resulting humiliation.

3. **Punitive damages.** For example:
   - Deceit. The defendant never intended to marry the plaintiff in spite of the promise made.
   - Malice. The defendant wanted to hurt and humiliate the plaintiff, or the defendant recklessly disregarded the impact of the breach of promise.

Compensatory Damages Money to restore the injured party to the position he or she was in before the injury or loss; money to make the aggrieved party whole.

Aggravated Damages Money paid to cover special circumstances that justify an increase in the amount paid.

Punitive Damages (also called Exemplary Damages) Money paid to punish the wrongdoer and to deter others from similar wrongdoing.

Mitigating Circumstances Facts that in fairness justify a reduction in damages because of the conduct of the aggrieved party.

4. **Mitigating circumstances.** For example:

- Plaintiff never loved the defendant. Plaintiff was trying to marry for money only.
- Plaintiff was unchaste before meeting the defendant.
- Defendant broke the promise to marry, but with some sensitivity to the feelings of the plaintiff.

At one time, juries returned very high verdicts against defendants in breach-of-promise actions, e.g., $250,000. More recently, however, the trend has been toward smaller verdicts. Some states will limit damage awards to out-of-pocket losses, e.g., the cost of wedding preparation, and will not compensate the victim for more speculative harm such as that caused by humiliation.

▰▰▰ Interviewing and Investigation Checklist

In a State That Allows Suits for Breach of Promise to Marry
(C = client; D = defendant)

Legal Interviewing Questions

1. On what date did you and D first agree to be married?

2. Where were you at the time of this agreement? Were you in this state? If not, what state?

3. How old were you at the time? How old was D?

4. What specific language did D use when he or she promised to marry you? What specific language did you use when you accepted? (Try to obtain exact quotations.)

5. Who were the first people you told? Did you and D tell them together?

6. Was a date set for a wedding? If so, what date? If not, why not?

7. Were any preparations made, e.g., church selected or caterer ordered?

8. Did D send you any letters ("love letters") about the engagement? Did you send D any?

9. Did D ever repeat his or her promise to marry you? If so, under what circumstances?

10. What other actions did D take to indicate to you that D wanted to marry you? How much time did you spend together? Did you live together? (Where? How long?) Did you talk about children? Did you meet each other's parents?

11. When did you first learn that D no longer wished to marry you? What specifically was said and done?

12. What reason did D give?

13. What did you say or do when you learned about this? Did you give any indication to D that you did not want to marry D? Were you angry? How were your feelings expressed?

14. Was there anything about *your* life prior to the time that D promised to marry you that D did not know but which D now feels you should have revealed, e.g., information about a prior marriage, your age, your prior sex life?

15. What expenses did you incur to prepare for the wedding (e.g., clothes, church, rings)?

16. Were you employed before the engagement? Did you leave your job? How did the cancellation of the marriage affect your job, if at all?

17. Describe your standard of living before the cancellation, e.g., kind of dwelling, car, travel, entertainment interests, etc.

18. Describe D's standard of living.

19. If D had married you, describe what you think your financial standing and standard of living would have been.

20. Describe the effect of D's breach of promise on your physical and mental health, e.g., did you lose any sleep, were there any special mental problems?

21. When D broke the promise to marry you, who knew about it? Was there any publicity?

22. Were you humiliated? Describe the reasons why.

23. Since D broke the engagement, have you dated others? When they find out about the broken engagement, what is their reaction? Do you think your chances of marrying in the future are diminished because of D's breach of promise? Why?

24. Did you have sexual relations with D? Were you seduced by D? Did D impregnate you? (If so, inquire into pregnancy problems, abortion, miscarriage, delivery, etc.)

—Continued

—Continued

25. Do you have any reason to believe that at the time D promised to marry you, D never intended to fulfill this promise? Explain.

26. Do you have any reason to believe D wanted to hurt you? Explain.

27. Could D say that you never loved D?

28. Did D ever give you any gifts?

29. On what date did you receive each gift? Was it before or after the engagement?

30. What were D's exact words when D gave you each gift? What did you say to D?

31. When did each gift come into your possession?

32. Answer questions 28–31 for any gifts you gave D.

33. Did you or D receive any shower gifts or wedding gifts from others before the engagement was broken? Explain.

Possible Investigation Tasks

☐ Try to contact people who may have heard about D's promise to marry C. Obtain witness statements.

☐ Help C locate all letters from D.

☐ Locate all receipts of expenses resulting from wedding preparations. If not available, contact merchants and others to whom money was paid in order to obtain new receipts or copies.

☐ Obtain financial records, e.g., bank statements, to show C's financial worth and standard of living before the engagement was broken. Try to obtain the same kind of records for D.

☐ Obtain medical records to document the physical and mental strain C experienced when D broke the promise to marry, e.g., hospital records, doctor bills.

☐ Determine what kind of publicity, if any, accompanied the news that D broke the engagement, e.g., newspaper clippings.

☐ Attempt to determine whether D had broken any other marriage engagements.

☐ Draft an inventory of every gift in any way connected with D's relationship with C. For each gift, identify the donor, donee, date of gift, kind and value of gift, circumstances surrounding the gift, present location of the gift, etc.

FRAUD

Where a heart balm statute exists, some plaintiffs have tried to get around it by bringing a *tort* cause of action for **fraud** rather than the breach-of-contract cause of action.

Elements of the Tort of Fraud

(Sometimes called misrepresentation or deceit)

☐ There must be a *false* statement of present fact by the defendant (D).

☐ The D must *know* that it is false.

☐ The D must *intend* that the plaintiff (P) rely upon the statement.

☐ The P must *rely* on the statement of the D and be reasonable in so relying.

☐ The P must suffer *harm* due to the reliance.

Fraud Knowingly making a false statement of present fact with the intention that the plaintiff rely on the statement. The plaintiff's reasonable reliance on the statement harms him or her.

Here is an example of how a fraud cause of action might be based on a case of a broken engagement: D told P that he wanted to marry P. At the time D made this *statement*, it was *false* because D never wanted to marry P. D *knew* that the statement was a lie and *intended* to use the statement to get P to do something (e.g., lend D money, have sexual relations with D). P believed that D wanted to marry her and *relied* on D's statement (e.g., by giving D money, by having sex with D). P suffered *harm* because of this reliance (e.g., lost funds, humiliation, unwanted pregnancy).

Can such a fraud cause of action be brought in a state that has abolished the breach-of-contract cause of action? The question is whether the legislature intended the heart balm statute to eliminate *both* causes of action even though the act may specifically mention only the contract action. Some states allow the fraud action. Others have said that the heart balm statute eliminates both the contract *and* the tort action.

On July 4, 1987, in your state, Jim Smith asked Linda Jones to marry him. Jim has a middle-class background, while Linda is independently wealthy. Linda told Jim she had never loved any other man in her life. This was not true, but she felt that unless she told this to Jim, he would never have proposed to her. On July 25, 1987, Linda told Jim that she would marry him, but on August 19, 1987, she informed him that she had changed her mind. Jim is very upset. On October 4, 1989, he filed suit against her. What causes of action might be possible? Explain the elements of each.

INTENTIONAL INFLICTION OF EMOTIONAL DISTRESS

Intentional Infliction of Emotional Distress Intentionally causing severe emotional distress by extreme or outrageous conduct.

Another tort action some plaintiffs have tried to bring is **intentional infliction of emotional distress.** The plaintiff must overcome the burden of establishing that the heart balm statute does not bar this action as well. If this can be done, the next step is to prove that he or she was the victim of particularly shocking conduct by the defendant. For example, a man knows his fiancée is emotionally unstable because she is a former mental patient. He proposes marriage for the sole purpose of humiliating her by changing his mind just after she makes elaborate, public, and expensive wedding plans. A state might conclude that this is sufficiently outrageous and shocking conduct. A more common change-of-mind case, on the other hand, would probably not be enough for this tort.

Review the facts of Assignment 2.2. Could Jim sue Linda for intentional infliction of emotional distress?

▇▇▇▇ THE PROBLEM OF GIFTS

Irrevocable That which cannot be revoked or recalled.

Donor/Donee The *donor* is the person who gives a gift. The *donee* receives it.

It is not commonly known that once a gift is made, it is **irrevocable**—the **donor** cannot reclaim the gift from the *donee*. For a gift to be irrevocable in this way, all of the elements of a gift must be present:

Elements of an Irrevocable Gift

□ There must be a *delivery* of the property.[3]

□ The transfer must be *voluntary.*

□ The donor must intend to relinquish *title* and *control* of what is given.

□ There must be *no consideration* (e.g., payment by the donee).

□ The donor must intend that the gift take effect *immediately;* there must be a *present* intention to give an *unconditional* gift.

□ The donee must *accept* the gift.

If Pat says to Bill, "I'll give you my car next year," no gift has been given. There was no intent that an immediate transfer occur; hence, there was no delivery. If Pat says to Bill, "You have borrowed my pen; maybe I'll give it to you tomorrow," again there is no gift since there was no intent by Pat to relin-

---

3. The delivery of the gift of a house or of the contents of a safe deposit box can be accomplished by a symbolic act such as giving the donee the key to the house or box.

quish her title and dominion over the pen now. This is so even though Bill already had possession of the pen.

Suppose that Pat says to Bill, "I'll give you this desk if it rains tomorrow." No gift has occurred because a condition exists that must be fulfilled before the gift becomes effective, i.e., it must rain tomorrow. There is no present intention to relinquish title and dominion. Suppose that Frank and Judy exchange engagement rings after they both agree to be married. One or both of them then change their minds. Did a legally binding gift occur? It appears that all of the elements of a binding gift existed, so either Frank or Judy can refuse to return the ring. Yet, should we not *infer* a condition that the parties intended the gift to be binding only if the marriage took place? They never explicitly said this to each other, but it is reasonable to infer that this is what they had in mind. This is what they would have intended if they had thought about it. Courts often find that such an *implied intention* exists, thereby forcing a return of premarital gifts.

Examine the following sequence of events:

January 1, 1995:	Mary and Bob meet.
January 2, 1995:	On a date at a restaurant, Bob gives Mary a bracelet.
March 13, 1995:	Mary and Bob become engaged; they exchange rings. The marriage date will be November 7, 1995.
March 26, 1995:	This is Mary's birthday; Bob gives Mary a new car.
June 5, 1995:	Bob and Mary change their minds about marriage.

Bob wants the bracelet, ring, and car back. When Mary refuses, Bob sues her, contending in court that the elements of a gift were not present when he gave Mary the items, because he intended her to keep them only if they married. Should the court infer this condition of marriage? The answer depends on Bob's intention *at the time* he gave each of the items to Mary.

The exchange of rings poses the least problem. When both parties break the engagement, most courts would agree that a condition of marriage was implied and force the return of the rings. At the time the bracelet was given, however, the parties were not engaged. A jury might conclude that Bob's intent was to please Mary, but not necessarily to win her hand in marriage. The bracelet was given the day after they met when it is unlikely that marriage was on anyone's mind. It would be rare, therefore, for a court to rule that the gift of the bracelet was conditional and force Mary to return it.[4] The birthday gift of the car is the most troublesome item. Again the central question is, what was Bob's intent at the time he gave her the car? Mary would argue that no condition of marriage was attached to the gift. She would say that a birthday gift would have been given whether or not they were engaged. Bob, on the other hand, would argue that the extraordinary cost of a new car is strong evidence that it would not have been given as a birthday gift unconnected with the impending marriage. His argument is probably correct. Do you agree?

What further facts would you seek in order to assess whether the car was a gift in the case of Bob and Mary above?

ASSIGNMENT 2.4

---

4. On the other hand, the facts show that two months after the bracelet was given, the parties became engaged. This short time period does raise the possibility, however slight, that marriage *was* on Bob's mind when he gave Mary the bracelet, i.e., that the gift was conditional. More facts would be needed in order to determine whether this argument has merit.

Suppose that Bob unilaterally broke the engagement without any plausible reason or justification. In such a situation, many courts would consider Bob a wrongdoer who should not be able to profit from his wrong by reclaiming any of the gifts. In such courts, the donor can have the conditional gifts returned only if the engagement ended by mutual agreement or if the *donee* broke the engagement without justification.

Third parties, e.g., relatives and friends, often send gifts in contemplation of the coming marriage. When the marriage does not take place, these parties can force a return of the gifts since courts almost always will conclude that such gifts were conditional.

Earlier we saw that some states passed heart balm statutes that abolished the cause of action for breach of promise to marry. Some of these statutes are worded so broadly that courts might interpret them to mean that *any* cause of action growing out of a broken engagement will not be allowed, including a cause of action to obtain the return of conditional gifts.

ASSIGNMENT 2.5

Examine the following sequence of events:

February 13, 1995:	Jim says to Bob, "Please introduce me to Joan. I want to meet her because I know that she is the girl I want to spend the rest of my life with." Bob does so. Jim is so happy that he gives Bob a gold wristwatch and says to him, "I want you to have this. Thanks for being my friend. I want you to wear this watch to my wedding some day."
March 1, 1995:	Joan brings Jim home to meet her mother. When the evening is over, Jim gives Joan's mother an expensive family Bible.
June 23, 1995:	Jim loans Joan $1,000 to pay a medical bill of Joan's youngest brother, giving her one year to pay back the loan without interest.
July 23, 1995:	Joan pays back the $1,000.
September 5, 1995:	They agree to marry. The wedding date is to be February 18, 1996. On the day that they agree to marry, Jim gives Joan a diamond bracelet, saying, "I want you to have this no matter what happens."
December 14, 1995:	They both agree to break the engagement.

Jim asks Bob for the wristwatch back. Bob refuses. Jim asks Joan's mother for the Bible back. The mother refuses. Jim asks Joan for one month's interest at 10 percent on the $1,000 loan and also asks for the bracelet back. Joan refuses both requests. Can Jim obtain any of these items from Bob, the mother, or Joan?

■■■ CONTRACTS RESTRAINING MARRIAGE

In this section we consider contracts of private parties that have the effect of restraining marriage. The state, of course, also restrains the formation of marriages through regulations on obtaining licenses, blood tests, etc. The legality of these regulations will be considered later.

The law looks with disfavor on attempts to limit the right to marry, even with the consent of the person subject to the limitation. Not all restrictions, however, are invalid. A distinction must be made between a *general restraint* on marriage and a *reasonable limitation* on marriage.

GENERAL RESTRAINT

Consider the following situations:

☐ In exchange for a large sum of money to be given to her by her father, Mary agrees never to marry.

☐ As John goes off to war, Jane says, "It is you that I want to marry, and even if you don't want to marry me, even if you marry someone else, even if you die, I promise you that I will never marry anyone else as long as I live." John leaves without promising to marry Jane.

A **general restraint on marriage** is a total or near total prohibition against marriage and is unenforceable. Mary's father cannot sue her to hold her to her agreement never to marry, nor can Jane be sued by John for breach of her promise should she marry someone other than him. People may decide on their own never to marry, but no court will force them to abide by that decision.

The John/Jane agreement is unenforceable for another reason. You will recall that for a contract to exist, there must be consideration. Jane's consideration was her promise never to marry anyone but John. John, however, gave no consideration in exchange. Hence, Jane's promise is unenforceable because she received no consideration; there was no contract to breach.

REASONABLE LIMITATION

A **reasonable limitation on marriage** is one that (1) is a partial rather than a general prohibition, (2) serves what the court feels is a useful purpose, and (3) is not otherwise illegal. Consider the following situations:

☐ John enters a contract in which he promises that he will never marry a woman who is not of his religious faith.

☐ Mary enters a contract in which she promises never to marry anyone who has a criminal record.

☐ Jane enters a contract in which she promises that she will not marry before she turns eighteen, and that she will obtain the permission of her parent if she decides to marry between the ages of eighteen and twenty-one.

☐ Linda enters a contract in which she promises that she will not marry until she completes her college education.

Assume that John, Mary, Jane, and Linda received consideration (e.g., cash) in exchange for their promises. Are the promises enforceable? If John, Mary, Jane, and Linda later decide to marry contrary to their promises, can they be forced through litigation to return whatever consideration they received? Not all states will answer this question in the same way, but generally the answer is yes. The restraints on marriage to which they agreed are enforceable. All of the restraints are *partial:* they do not totally prohibit marriage or come near such a total prohibition. All of the restraints arguably serve a *useful purpose:* to protect a person or a valuable tradition. Do you agree? There is no *illegality* evident in any of the restraints, e.g., no one is being asked to refrain from marriage in order to engage in adultery or fornication (which are crimes in some states). Hence, all of the restraints could be considered reasonable limitations on one's right to marry and are enforceable in most states.

Suppose schoolteachers sign a contract containing a clause that they will quit if they marry. This is not a general restraint on marriage, but is it enforceable as a reasonable limitation? Is there a useful or beneficial purpose to the restriction? Many courts have said yes, although this conclusion has been criticized. Can you see any useful purpose in forcing a teacher to resign under these circumstances? Do not answer this question by saying that people should be forced to do what they have agreed to do. Answer it on the basis of whether you think any person, tradition, value, etc., is being protected by holding the teacher to his or her contract.

Thus far we have been examining *contracts* that restrain marriage. Suppose, however, that the attempted restriction on marriage came as a condition attached to a *gift* rather than through a contract. For example:

Bequest A gift of personal property in a will.

☐ In Bob's will, he promises to give $100,000 to Fran so long as she remains unmarried. When Bob dies, Fran is not married. She is given the **bequest** of $100,000. One year later, Fran marries. Bob's estate brings a suit against Fran to have the money returned.

☐ John has a deed drafted that states, "I convey all my property to my widowed sister, Joan, to be owned and used by her until she remarries, at which time all remaining property shall go to the Red Cross."

The same rules on marriage restrictions should apply to such gifts as apply to contracts. If a person is going to lose a substantial gift upon marriage, the gift obviously operates to restrain marriage. In theory, the same rules do apply. In fact, however, some courts are more inclined to find the restrictions to be reasonable (and hence enforceable) when gifts are involved than when the restraint is embodied in a contract.

ASSIGNMENT 2.6

Closely examine each of the following situations. Determine which restraints on marriage, if any, are enforceable. Give specific reasons you think the restraint is or is not enforceable.

a. John is married to Brenda. John enters a contract with Brenda's father stating that if children are born from the marriage and if Brenda dies before John, John will never remarry. In exchange, John is given the father's large farm to live on for life rent-free. Children are born, and Brenda does die first. John marries Patricia. Brenda's father then sues to evict John from the farm. Does John have a defense to this suit?

b. Joan enters a contract with her aunt stating that she will not have children before she turns twenty-one. In exchange, Joan is given a sum of money. Before she turns twenty-one, Joan has a baby (out of wedlock). The aunt sues Joan for breach of contract. Does Joan have a defense?

c. Fred enters a contract with his father in which the father agrees to pay for Fred's entire medical education if Fred agrees to marry a doctor or a medical student if he decides to marry. When Fred becomes a doctor, he marries Sue, an electrician. The father sues Fred for the cost of the medical education. Does Fred have a defense?

d. Bill and Jean are not married. They live together, sharing bed and board. They enter a contract by which Jean promises to continue to live with Bill and to care for him. Bill agrees to place $500 per month in a bank account for Jean so long as she carries out her promise. Jean cannot receive the money until Bill dies. Also, if she marries before Bill dies, she forfeits the right to all the money in the account. After living with Bill for twenty years, Jean leaves him to marry Tom. Can Jean sue Bill to recover $120,000 (plus interest), the amount in the account at the time she married Tom?

SUMMARY

When two people promise to marry each other, a contract is created so long as the parties have the legal capacity to enter a contract, and the elements of a valid contract exist—offer, acceptance, and consideration. Years ago, if one of the parties refused to enter the marriage, and thereby breached the contract, the other party could bring a heart balm cause of action for breach of promise to marry. Some states, however, have enacted heart balm statutes that abolish this contract action because of the difficulty of assessing damages, the danger of blackmail, and the inappropriateness of trying to force someone to enter a marriage he or she no longer wants.

Fraud is an alternative cause of action a plaintiff might try to bring against a defendant who reneges on a promise to marry. The elements of fraud are as follows: a deliberately false statement of present fact by the defendant, intent to have the plaintiff rely on the statement, actual reliance by the plaintiff on the statement, and resulting harm. Not all states, however, allow a fraud suit. They have interpreted the heart balm statute as abolishing both the contract action and the fraud action. Another possibility is the tort of intentional infliction of emotional distress, but it, too, might not be permitted in a state with a heart balm statute.

In states where a suit is possible, the usual remedy is for the plaintiff to seek compensatory damages. The damage award may be increased by aggravated damages for special circumstances, or by punitive or exemplary damages intended to punish the defendant and deter others from similar conduct. Mitigating circumstances, on the other hand, will decrease the award.

When a planned marriage does not occur, any gifts that have already been exchanged are irrevocable, provided all the elements of a gift exist: delivery, voluntary transfer, intent to relinquish title and control, no consideration, intent to have the gift take effect immediately, and acceptance by the donee. If, however, a court concludes that the donor would not have made the gift except for the anticipation of marriage, the gift is considered conditional and thus must be returned. Some states, however, will reach this result only if the engagement was broken by the donee without justification.

A contract that imposes a total or a near total prohibition on marriage is an unenforceable, general restraint on marriage. On the other hand, contracts that impose reasonable limitations on one's right to marry can be enforceable.

■■■■ KEY CHAPTER TERMINOLOGY

Contract
Consideration
Capacity
Statute of Frauds
Cause of Action
Heart Balm Action
Heart Balm Statute
Remedy
Specific Performance

Damages
Compensatory Damages
Aggravated Damages
Punitive Damages
Mitigating Circumstances
Fraud
Intentional Infliction of
  Emotional Distress

Irrevocable
Donor
Donee
General Restraint on Marriage
Reasonable Limitation on
  Marriage
Bequest

3 ANTENUPTIAL AGREEMENTS AND COHABITATION AGREEMENTS

KINDS OF AGREEMENTS

We need to distinguish between different kinds of agreements that can be entered by adult parties living together. They are summarized in Exhibit 3.1. Our main concerns in this chapter are the antenuptial agreement and the cohabitation agreement. We will consider the others later in the book.

ANTENUPTIAL AGREEMENTS

A major function of an antenuptial agreement is to define rights and obligations during the contemplated marriage as well as upon the termination of the marriage by divorce or death. Why, you might ask, would two individuals about to enter the blissful state of marriage discuss such matters as "who gets what" if there is a divorce? The kinds of people who tend to make antenuptial agreements:

☐ are older
☐ have substantial property of their own
☐ have an interest in a family-run business
☐ have children and perhaps grandchildren from prior marriages

Such individuals may want to make clear that the new spouse is not to have any claim on designated property, or that the children of the former marriage have first claim to property acquired before the second marriage.

An awareness of the large number of marriages that end in divorce causes some people, particularly men and women who have separate careers and have lived together before marriage, to seek a measure of advance protection through an antenuptial agreement.

□ **EXHIBIT 3.1 Kinds of Agreements**

KIND	DEFINITION	EXAMPLE
Cohabitation Agreement	A contract made by two individuals who intend to stay unmarried indefinitely that covers financial and related matters while living together, upon separation, or upon death.	Ed and Claire meet at a bank where they work. After dating several years, they decide to live together. Although they give birth to a child, they do not want to be married. They enter an agreement that specifies what property is separately owned and how they will divide property purchased with joint funds in the event of a separation.
Antenuptial Agreement (also called prenuptial or premarital agreement)	A contract made by two individuals who are about to be married that covers support, property division, and related matters in the event of the death of one of the parties or the dissolution of the marriage by divorce or death.	Jim and Mary want to marry. Each has a child from a prior marriage. Before the wedding, they enter an agreement that specifies the property each brings to the marriage as separate property. The agreement also states that neither will have any rights in this property; it will go to the children from their prior marriages.
Post-nuptial Agreement	A contract made by two individuals while they are married that covers financial and related matters. The parties may have no intention of separating. If they have this intention, the agreement is called a separation agreement.	While happily married, George and Helen enter an agreement whereby George lends Helen $5,000 at 5% interest. She is to make monthly payments of $300. (To make this loan, George uses money he recently inherited from his mother.)
Separation Agreement	A contract made by two married individuals who have separated or are about to separate that covers support, custody, property division, and other terms of their separation.	Sam and Jessica have separated. In anticipation of their divorce, they enter an agreement that specifies how their marital property will be divided, who will have custody of their children, and what their support obligations will be. Later they will ask the divorce court to approve this agreement.

Changing lifestyles, skyrocketing divorce rates and increased awareness about prenuptial agreements have prompted more middle-aged, middle income and young professionals to clamor for such protection from their soon-to-be-spouses. Matrimonial lawyers across the country say they are doing double or triple the number of prenuptial agreements compared to the volume during the previous five to ten years.[1]

Parties, however, cannot completely reshape the nature of their marital status through a contract. While antenuptial agreements are favored by the courts, there are limitations and requirements we need to explore.

VALID CONTRACT

States differ on the requirements for a valid antenuptial contract. (For a general overview of the elements of a contract, see the beginning of chapter 2.) In most states the Statute of Frauds requires the contract to be in writing. The

---

1. Nance, *Prenuptial Pacts: "Till Some Breach Doth Them Part,"* 1 National Law Journal at 26 (November 7, 1988).

"It's a prenuptial agreement silly! I'm asking you to *marry* me!"

SOURCE: Mark Hannabury, 90 CASE AND COMMENT 34 (March–April 1985).

parties must have legal capacity to enter a binding contract and must sign voluntarily. Fraud or duress will invalidate the agreement. An additional requirement in a few states is that the contract be notarized.[2]

DISCLOSURE OF ASSETS

One of the main objectives of an antenuptial agreement is to take away rights that spouses would otherwise have in each other's assets. This is done by a **waiver** of such rights. For a waiver to make sense, you must have knowledge of the other person's assets. This raises a number of questions:

Waiver Giving up a right or privilege by explicitly rejecting it or by failing to take appropriate steps to claim it at the proper time.

☐ Do the parties have a duty to make a disclosure of their assets to each other before signing the antenuptial agreement?
☐ If so, how detailed must this disclosure be?
☐ Can the parties waive their right to have this disclosure?

Most states require disclosure, but allow parties to waive their right to receive it. Of course, a party is not entitled to disclosure if he or she already has knowledge of the other party's wealth. When disclosure is required, states differ on how much disclosure is necessary. Some insist on a full and frank disclosure. In other states, it is enough to provide a general picture of one's financial worth. Careful attorneys will always try to provide maximum disclosure in order to

---

2. In most states, the consideration for the contract is the marriage itself. Section 2 of the Uniform Premarital Agreement Act, however, provides that the agreement "is enforceable without consideration." 9B *Uniform Laws Annotated* § 2 (1987).

rebut a later claim by a spouse that he or she did not know the scope of the other spouse's wealth when the antenuptial agreement was signed. Furthermore, such attorneys will make sure the assets that are disclosed are not undervalued. Often the agreement includes a clause that says full disclosure has been made. This clause, however, is not always controlling, particularly if it can be shown that the party was tricked or forced into signing the entire agreement.

FAIRNESS AND UNCONSCIONABILITY

A few states require the agreement to be fair to both parties. There was a time when society viewed women as vulnerable and in need of special protection. There was almost a presumption that a woman's prospective husband would try to take advantage of her through the antenuptial agreement. Courts that took this view of the status of women tended to scrutinize such agreements to make sure they were fair to the prospective spouse.

The women's movement has helped change this perspective. There is a greater degree of equality between the sexes. Consequently, if a woman makes a bad bargain in an antenuptial agreement, most courts are inclined to force her to live with it so long as:

- □ there was adequate disclosure of the other's assets,
- □ there was no fraud or duress,
- □ there was an opportunity to seek advice from independent counsel or financial advisers, and,
- □ there is no danger of her becoming a public charge and going on welfare because of how little the antenuptial agreement provided.

Of course, the same is true of males of modest means who later regret signing antenuptial agreements with relatively wealthy women.

Courts do not want to see spouses become destitute as a result of what they gave up in an antenuptial agreement. The agreement is **unconscionable** and therefore unenforceable to the extent that it has this consequence. The agreement may have been fair and reasonable at the time the parties signed it before the marriage. But circumstances may substantially change by the time the parties separate or divorce.

Unconscionable
Shocking to the conscience; substantially unfair.

EXAMPLE Norm and Irene enter an antenuptial agreement in which they waive all rights they have in each other's separate property. In the event of a divorce, the agreement provides that Norm will pay Irene support of $2,000 a month for two years. A year before the parties divorce, Irene is diagnosed with cancer. She will need substantially more than $2,000 a month for support. Norm has resources to pay her more than what the antenuptial agreement provides. If he doesn't do so, Irene will need public assistance.

To avoid this unconscionable result, a court will be inclined to disregard the antenuptial agreement and order Norm to pay Irene additional support. The enforceability of this part of the agreement will be judged as of the date of the separation or divorce, not the date the agreement was signed.

ASSIGNMENT 3.1

Do you think that women should be treated differently than men on the issue of whether an antenuptial agreement should be enforced? Do women have enough equality in today's society to require them to live with agreements that, in hindsight, they shouldn't have made? Why or why not?

Careful attorneys advise their clients to give their prospective spouses sufficient time to study and think about the antenuptial agreement before signing. Waiting until the morning of the wedding to bring up the idea of an antenuptial agreement is not wise. This late notice does not necessarily prove that the surprised spouse acted involuntarily when he or she signed. Nevertheless, an attorney recently warned that "Eve-of-wedding prenups give rise to cries of foul later."[3]

PUBLIC POLICY

Public Policy The principles inherent in the customs, morals, and notions of justice that prevail in a state. The foundation of public laws. The principles that are naturally and inherently right and just.

Care must be taken to avoid provisions in an antenuptial agreement that are illegal because they are against **public policy.** For example, the parties cannot agree in advance that neither will ever make a claim on the other for the support of any children they might have together. The livelihood of children cannot be contracted away by such a clause. So, too, it would be improper to agree never to bring a future divorce action or other suit against the other side. It is against public policy to discourage the use of the courts in this way, since legitimate grievances might go unheard.

ASSIGNMENT 3.2

Are the following provisions in an antenuptial agreement legal? Explain why or why not.

a. A clause designating how much support one spouse will receive from the other during the marriage.

b. A clause stating that the husband will never have to wash the dishes.

c. A clause stating that the children from a prior marriage will not live with the parties.

d. A clause stating that any children born to the couple will not attend formal services of any religion.

e. A clause stating a minimum number of times that the parties will engage in sexual intercourse per month.

Very often the antenuptial agreement will specify alimony and other property rights in the event of a divorce. Many courts once considered such provisions to be against public policy because they *facilitate* (or encourage) *divorce.* The theory is that a party will be more inclined to seek a divorce if he or she knows what funds or other property will be available upon divorce, particularly, of course, if the financial terms upon divorce are favorable. Most courts, however, are moving away from this position. Divorces are no longer difficult to obtain in view of the coming of no-fault divorce laws. There is less pressure from society to keep marriages together at all costs. A spouse who wants a divorce can obtain one with relative ease and probably does not need the inducement of a favorable antenuptial agreement to end the marriage. Hence,

---

3. Harriet Cohen, *The "Do's and Don'ts" of Family Law Practice,* 40 The Practical Lawyer 25, 26 (April 1994).

most (but by no means all) courts uphold provisions in antenuptial agreements that provide a designated amount of alimony or, indeed, that provide no alimony in the event of a divorce.

As indicated, however, this approach is not taken in all states. Some courts refuse to enforce *any* antenuptial agreement that tries to define rights in the event of a divorce. They will enforce only non-divorce clauses such as one covering the disposition of property upon death. Other courts distinguish between an alimony-support clause and a property-division clause in an antenuptial agreement. When the parties eventually divorce and one of them tries to enforce the antenuptial agreement, such courts are more likely to enforce the property-division clause than the alimony-support clause.

ASSIGNMENT 3.3

a. The property division clause in the antenuptial agreement of George and Jane provides that in the event of a divorce George will receive $750,000 and Jane will receive all other property acquired during the marriage. Is this clause legal?

b. Assume that George and Jane live in a community property state where it is legal for the parties to agree to treat community property as separate property so that each is no longer entitled to 50 percent of that property. The property-division clause in their antenuptial agreement provides that in the event of a divorce, all community property will be treated as separate property and will go to the party who has title to the property at the time of the divorce. Is this clause legal?

Death clauses in antenuptial agreements are less controversial. Parties often agree to give up the rights they may have (e.g., dower, page 42) in the estate of their deceased spouse. If the antenuptial agreement is not otherwise invalid, such terms are usually upheld by the courts.

The **Uniform Premarital Agreement Act,** which has been adopted in about a fourth of the states, has a very liberal view of what the parties can cover in an antenuptial agreement:

Uniform Premarital Agreement Act, 9B Uniform Laws Annotated § 3 (1987)

(a) Parties to a premarital agreement may contract with respect to:

(1) the rights and obligations of each of the parties in any of the property of either or both of them whenever and wherever acquired or located;

(2) the right to buy, sell, use, transfer, exchange, abandon, lease, consume, expend, assign, create a security interest in, mortgage, encumber, dispose of, or otherwise manage and control property;

(3) the disposition of property upon separation, marital dissolution, death, or the occurrence or nonoccurrence of any other event;

(4) the modification or elimination of spousal support;

(5) the making of a will, trust, or other arrangement to carry out the provisions of the agreement;

(6) the ownership rights in and disposition of the death benefit from a life insurance policy;

(7) the choice of law governing the construction of the agreement; and

(8) any other matter, including their personal rights and obligations, not in violation of public policy or a statute imposing a criminal penalty.

(b) The right of a child to support may not be adversely affected by a premarital agreement.

◼◼ Interviewing and Investigation Checklist

Factors Relevant to the Validity of the Antenuptial Agreement
(C = client; D = defendant/spouse)

Legal Interviewing Questions

1. On what date did you begin discussing the antenuptial agreement?

2. Whose idea was it to have an agreement?

3. On what date did you first see the agreement?

4. Who actually wrote the agreement?

5. Did you read the agreement? If so, how carefully?

6. Did you understand everything in the agreement?

7. Describe in detail what you thought was in the agreement.

8. Did you sign the agreement? If so, why?

9. Were any changes made in the agreement? If so, describe the circumstances, the nature of each change, who proposed it, etc.

10. Do you recall anything said during the discussions on the agreement that was different from what was eventually written down?

11. Was anyone present at the time you discussed or signed the agreement?

12. Where is the agreement kept? Were you given a copy at the time you signed?

13. Before you signed the agreement, did you consult with anyone, e.g., attorney, accountant, relative?

14. If you did consult with anyone, describe that person's relationship, if any, with D.

15. What were you told by the individuals with whom you consulted? Did they think it was wise for you to sign the agreement? Why or why not?

16. How old were you when you signed the agreement? How old was D?

17. How much did you know about D's background before you agreed to marry? What generally did you think D's wealth and standard of living were?

18. How did you obtain this knowledge?

19. While you were considering the antenuptial agreement, describe what you specifically knew about the following: D's bank accounts (savings, checking, trust), insurance policies, home ownership, business property, salary, investments (e.g., stocks, bonds), rental income, royalty income, inheritances (recent or expected), cars, planes, boats, etc. Also, what did you know about D's debts and other liabilities? For each of the above items about which you had knowledge, state how you obtained the knowledge.

20. When did you first learn that D owned (_____) at the time you signed the agreement? (Insert items in parentheses that C learned about only after the agreement was signed.)

21. Do you think you were given an honest accounting of all D's assets at the time you signed? Why or why not?

22. Do you think the agreement you signed was fair to you and to the children you and D eventually had? Why or why not?

Possible Investigation Tasks

☐ Obtain copies of the antenuptial agreement and of drafts of the agreement, if any, reflecting changes.

☐ Contact and interview anyone who has knowledge of or was present during the discussions and/or signing of the agreement.

☐ Try to obtain bank records, tax records, etc., that would give some indication of the wealth and standard of living of D and of C at the time they signed the antenuptial agreement.

☐ Prepare an inventory of every asset that C *thought* D owned at the time the agreement was signed, and an inventory of every asset your investigation has revealed D *in fact* owned at the time of the signing.

ASSIGNMENT 3.4

a. Pretend you are about to be married. Draft an antenuptial agreement for you and your future spouse. You can assume anything you want (within reason) about the financial affairs and interests of your spouse-to-be and yourself. Number each clause of the agreement separately and consecutively. Try to anticipate as many difficulties as possible that could arise during the marriage and state in the agreement how you want them resolved.

b. After your instructor makes note of the fact that you have drafted an agreement, you will be asked to exchange agreements with another member of the class. You are to analyze the agreement written by your classmate. Go through each numbered clause in the agreement and determine whether it is valid or invalid. When you cannot apply a

standard, in whole or in part, because you need more facts, simply list the factual questions to which you would like answers in order to be able to assess the validity of the clause in question.

▰▰▰ SAMPLE ANTENUPTIAL AGREEMENT

**Antenuptial Agreement
7 West's Legal Forms, 2d
§ 14.12, pp. 285–293.**

THIS AGREEMENT made and executed [*date*], by and between [*Independent party*] of _____ , (hereinafter referred to as ''_____''), and [*Dependent party*] of _____ , (hereinafter referred to as ''_____''), both hereinafter collectively referred to as the parties;

WITNESSETH:

WHEREAS, the parties have represented to each other that each is single and legally free to marry; and

WHEREAS, the parties presently contemplate marriage to each other, such marriage to be solemnized in the near future; and

WHEREAS, the parties have fully and completely disclosed the nature and approximate value of all of their presently existing assets, liabilities and income to each parties' satisfaction on their respective schedules annexed hereto; and

WHEREAS, each party recognizes that certain interests, rights, and claims may accrue to each of them in the property and interests of the other as a result of their marriage; and

WHEREAS, the parties desire to define and agree to certain obligations arising out of their marriage to each other and to fix, limit and determine the interest, rights and claims that may accrue to each of them in the property and estate of the other by reason of their marriage to each other and to accept the provisions of this Agreement in lieu of and in full discharge, settlement and satisfaction of any and all interest, rights and claims that otherwise each might or could have under the law, in and to the property and estate of the other, in the event of the parties' separation or dissolution of marriage.

WHEREAS, each party enters into this Prenuptial Agreement (hereinafter referred to as the ''Agreement'') with full knowledge of the extent and approximate present value of all the property and estate of the other, and of all the rights and privileges in and to such property and estate which may be conferred by law upon each in the property and estate of the other by virtue of their marriage but for the execution of this Agreement, to each parties' satisfaction; and

WHEREAS, [*Independent party*] has had the benefit of independent legal advice prior to the execution of this Agreement from [*name*], Esq. of _____ and

WHEREAS, [*Dependent party*] has had the benefit of independent legal advice prior to the execution of this Agreement from [*name*], Esq. of _____ and

NOW, THEREFORE, in consideration of the foregoing and intending to be legally bound hereby, the parties mutually agree as follows:

1. *Disclosure of Facts.* The parties hereby acknowledge that, to their mutual satisfaction, each has had the opportunity to ascertain, has been informed by a full and frank disclosure by the other, and is fully acquainted with and aware of the approximate assets, liabilities, income and general financial circumstances of the other; that each has ascertained and weighed all of the facts, conditions and circumstances likely to influence his or her judgment in all matters embodied herein; that each has given due consideration to all such matters and questions, and clearly understands and consents to all the provisions contained herein; and that each has had the opportunity to have or has in fact had the benefit and advice of independent counsel of his or her own choice and is willing to accept the provisions of the Agreement in lieu of all other rights each may have.

—Continued

Antenuptial Agreement—*Continued*

2. *Effect of Agreement.* After the solemnization of the marriage between the parties, each of them shall separately retain all rights in his or her own separate property now owned and more fully set forth in Schedules "A" and "B" annexed hereto (collectively referred to herein as "the Property", or "Property"). Each party shall have the absolute and unrestricted right to dispose of their said separate property free from any claim that may be made by the other by reason of their marriage, and with the same effect as if no marriage had been consummated between them.

The aforesaid schedules list the Property of [*Independent party*] and [*Dependent party*], respectively, as same is now constituted. Each party shall separately retain all rights to the said Property in its present form and in any other form which is traceable to same, including any appreciation in the value of the Property as a direct or indirect result of the contribution or efforts of either party or due to market factors, except as may be herein contained to the contrary. Any property acquired by either party after the marriage, except for such property which has been specifically excepted in this Agreement and which has not been commingled with joint or otherwise marital property, shall be divided between the parties upon separation or divorce as provided hereinafter. The further effects of this Agreement are as more specifically set forth and detailed in the following provisions.

3. *Release of Marital Rights.* Except as otherwise stated herein, the parties hereby waive, relinquish and release any and all claims and rights either may have ever had, presently has, or may in the future acquire, with respect to the Property listed on the other party's schedule annexed hereto, including any and all property that is traceable and acquired, in whole or in part, from the proceeds derived from the Property and any appreciation or accretion in the value thereof attributable, directly or indirectly, to the efforts or contributions of either party, or due to market factors. This provision shall apply whether the claims and rights arise as a result of the parties' separation or dissolution of marriage.

4. *Parties' Understanding of Rights Waived.* It is the intention of the parties that the disposition of the Property referred to in this agreement be deemed a disposition of this property that would fully satisfy any claims either party may have against the other including each parties' rights to equitable distribution under [*state statute*], together with any amendments thereto, or then existing [*state*] law. Further rights waived by this Agreement are as more specifically set forth and detailed in the following provisions.

5. *General Statement of Intentions.* While in no way limiting or restricting the understanding of the parties, the provisions or effect of this Agreement, the parties generally state their intentions for this Agreement as follows:

a. This is the fourth marriage for [*Independent party*] and the second marriage for [*Dependent party*]. While the parties fully intend to commit themselves to achieving a successful long-term marriage, each party is personally aware of the practicalities and realities of life, together with the time and the financial and emotional cost involved in the unfortunate event of a legal proceeding concerning the parties' separation or dissolution. Each party intends by entering into this Agreement to minimize the time, financial and emotional cost involved in the event of a future separation or dissolution of marriage between them.

b. [*Independent party*] has seven (7) children from two (2) prior marriages. [*Dependent party*] has three (3) children from her prior marriage. While acknowledging that each is assuming a new status and relationship relative to the other's children, the parties intend by entering into this Agreement to provide that each shall continue to be responsible for any parental or legal obligations of support each may have with respect to their own children and in no event shall either party be responsible, now or in the future, for any such parental or legal obligations of support with respect to the other party's children.

c. The parties each have retirement plans either through their employer or self-procured. The parties intend by entering into this Agreement that neither party shall acquire any rights at any time, and in whatever form and nature, to the other's said retirement benefits.

d. While the parties agree to maintain a joint bank account to be funded with marital income and used for the maintenance and acquisition of marital assets, the parties intend to also maintain separate bank accounts which shall be funded with pre-maritally acquired or otherwise separate property money to be used by them at their discretion, which money shall not be commingled with the assets or financial accounts of the other.

—*Continued*

Antenuptial Agreement—*Continued*

6. *Rights to Separate Property.* Each party shall keep and retain sole ownership, enjoyment, control and power of disposal of all the Property listed on their respective schedules annexed hereto, and all increments thereto, free and clear of any interest, rights or claims of the other except as may be otherwise set forth in this Agreement.

7. *Property Acquired during the Marriage.* Nothing contained in this Agreement shall be construed to preclude any rights either party may have in the event of the parties' separation or dissolution of marriage in those assets which are acquired during the marriage, including wedding gifts, and not otherwise specifically exempted or excepted by any other provision contained herein.

8. *Waiver of Spousal Support.* The parties represent that each is presently employed. [*Independent party*] is employed by _____ and [*Dependent party*] is employed by _____ . Each party is entering the marriage financially independent and self-sufficient with assets totalling approximately the same in value. In the event the parties separate or the marriage is dissolved, each party understands and agrees to waive, relinquish and release the other from any duty or obligation to support the other in any fashion or manner whatsoever, which duty or obligation to support such other party may otherwise have arisen but for this Agreement, and no claim or demand for such support shall be made, now or in the future. In the event of and at such time as a separation or dissolution of marriage is sought by either party, and it appearing that the financial circumstance of either party has changed to such a degree that such party can sufficiently demonstrate that he or she would be left without a means of support, destitute or a public charge, or at a standard of living far below that which the party enjoyed before the marriage, as a result of this Agreement, then, and in that event, the party who is not left in any of the foregoing circumstances agrees to provide support to the other in an amount not to exceed $_____ per month and not for a period of time exceeding _____ years.

9. *Waiver of Support Obligation to Other Party's Children.* The parties acknowledge and understand that each presently has unemancipated children from a prior marriage. To the extent that the parties' marriage creates any rights or obligations to support or otherwise provide for the other party's children in any form, at any time whatsoever, the parties each agree that in the event of a separation or dissolution each waives any and all rights or claims that could be made against the other for the support of their children.

10. *Insurance.* In the event the parties separate or the marriage contemplated is dissolved, the parties mutually agree that neither shall be responsible for maintaining any policy of insurance for the benefit of the other. Said policy(ies) of insurance shall include, without limitation, health, life and automobile, etc.

11. Property Rights in Event of Death. The parties understand that this Agreement makes no provision for apportionment of property rights in the event of either party's death. The parties each agree to prepare and execute a Last Will and Testament to resolve any and all such issues that may arise in this regard.

12. *Dedication of Income.* The parties specifically make no delineation as to the precise use of their income, except to state that it is their general intention to pool their income for their mutual benefit, for the purpose of maintaining their agreed-upon lifestyle and for the accumulation of marital assets. For purposes of this provision, retirement income shall at no time be deemed income, but shall instead be deemed separate property.

13. *Non-incurrence of Debt.* The parties represent, warrant and covenant that neither has heretofore incurred any debt, charge, obligation or liability whatsoever for which the other, their legal representatives or either party's property or estate is or may become liable, nor will either party incur such debt, charge, obligation or liability without first providing the other with reasonable notice thereof and obtaining the other's written consent. Each party agrees to indemnify and hold the other harmless of loss, expenses (including reasonable attorney fees) and damages in the event that a claim is made upon the other arising out of or in connection with a breach by either party of the representations, warranties and covenants of this paragraph.

14. *Equitable Distribution.* The parties acknowledge and understand that each enters into the marriage with the same approximate total value of assets. The parties further acknowledge and understand that they intend to pool their financial resources in a joint effort to acquire various and, at present, undetermined assets such as real estate, financial investment accounts, together with other marital assets. In the event of the parties' separation or marriage dissolution, each understands and agrees that all such acquired property shall

—*Continued*

Antenuptial Agreement—*Continued*

be forthwith distributed amicably between them or, in the event the parties cannot agree, liquidated with the net proceeds derived from the liquidation to be evenly distributed between them. Net proceeds shall be defined as the sales price or total liquidated value of any asset less any and all liens and encumbrances, together with any actual gains tax, realtor's and/or broker's commissions, attorney fees and any other reasonable and necessary costs of the liquidation.

15. *Disclosure of Assets, Liability and Income and Voluntary Waiver of Further Discovery.* The parties acknowledge and represent to each other that they have made a full, fair and complete disclosure to the other as to the nature and approximate value of their assets, liabilities and income as presently constituted as per their respective schedules annexed hereto, and that each accepts the said disclosures to their satisfaction. The parties represent and acknowledge that based upon the foregoing representations each freely, knowingly, voluntarily and without undue influence, coercion, fraud or duress waives further discovery relative to the nature and value of the other's assets, liabilities and income.

16. *Inheritances or Gifts from Third Parties.* Notwithstanding any provision herein contained to the contrary, any and all property acquired during the marriage by either party by way of gift or inheritance from a third party shall be deemed the separate property of the party so acquiring it including, but not limited to, any income or other usufruct thereon, increments, accretions, or increases in value of such assets at any time thereto, whether due to market conditions or the services, skills, or efforts of either party, and that all such property shall be kept separate and not commingled with joint or otherwise marital property. To the extent that any such property is commingled or not kept separate from marital property, it shall be deemed joint property. Any assets acquired by the parties jointly during the marriage by way of gift or inheritance from a third party shall be deemed joint property acquired during the marriage the distribution of which, in the event of the parties' separation or dissolution of marriage, shall be governed by Paragraph 14 hereof.

17. *Interspousal Transfers, Devises and Bequests by and between the Parties.* Notwithstanding any provision herein contained to the contrary, any other rights acquired by either party by virtue of any transfer or conveyance of property between the parties during their lifetime, or by devises or bequests made by either party for the benefit of the other pursuant to a Last Will and Testament, shall not be limited or restricted in any way.

18. *Waiver of Right to Share in Retirement Benefits.* The parties hereby waive, relinquish and release any and all claims and rights either may have ever had, presently has, or may in the fugure acquire, in and to any and all retirement benefits titled in the other party's individual name. Specifically, [*Independent party*] waives, relinquishes and releases any and all claims and rights she may have in the past acquired or may in the future acquire in and to [*Dependent party*]'s Civil Service Retirement Plan and agrees to execute any and all documents necessary to give full force and effect to this provision.

19. *Attorney Fees.* The parties acknowledge, understand and agree that in the event of any court proceeding of and concerning their marital relationship or dissolution thereof, that each party shall pay and be responsible for payment of their own respective attorney fees and all ancillary costs incurred in connection with any such proceeding.

20. *Timing of Execution.* The parties recognize and understand that this Agreement is being executed _____ days prior to their scheduled wedding date of [*date*]. The parties acknowledge that each has had sufficient opportunity prior to executing this Agreement to consult with counsel, to reschedule the wedding date if necessary, and/or to not proceed with the marriage, but each nonetheless agrees that the timing of the execution of this Agreement relative to their wedding date has no effect upon their decision to execute same. Both parties further waive their right to argue at any time in the future that they had insufficient time to make an informed and calculated decision to execute same. The parties further represent that this Agreement has been discussed between them for a period of _____ prior to the date hereof, and it is only as a result of their deliberations and thoughtful consideration of the provisions herein contained that the Agreement is being executed at this time.

21. *Voluntary Execution.* The parties each acknowledge and represent that this Agreement has been executed by each of them free from persuasion, fraud, undue influence, or economic, physical or emotional duress of any kind whatsoever asserted by the other party or by other persons.

—Continued

Antenuptial Agreement—*Continued*

22. *Independent Counsel.* The parties acknowledge that each has procured and has been advised as to all aspects of this Agreement by independent counsel of their own choice or has had ample opportunity to procure and seek the advice of counsel but has expressly waived that right. Each party is satisfied that he or she has freely negotiated the contents hereof free from the persuasion or influence of the other party or any third party.

23. *Incorporation of the Agreement.* This Agreement shall be offered in evidence in any proceeding instituted by either of the parties in any court of competent jurisdiction in which a determination of the status of the parties' relationship is sought and shall, subject to the approval of the court, be incorporated in any order or judgment rendered in that action.

24. *Non-merger.* Notwithstanding its incorporation into an order or judgment entered by a court of competent jurisdiction, the provisions of this Agreement shall not merge with, but shall survive, such judgment in its entirety, in full force and effect, except as may be invalidated by a court of competent jurisdiction.

25. *Validity and Enforceability of Agreement.* The parties further agree that this contract is valid and enforceable in any action that may hereafter be commenced by either party that may require the use of this Agreement as evidence to demonstrate the parties' understanding of any issues addressed herein.

26. *Severability.* Should any provision of this Agreement be held invalid or unenforceable by any court of competent jurisdiction, all other provisions shall nonetheless continue in full force and effect, to the extent that the remaining provisions are fair, just and equitable.

27. *Modification of Waiver.* No modification of waiver of any terms of this Agreement shall be valid unless in writing and executed by the parties hereto.

28. *Situs.* The laws of [*state*] shall govern the execution and enforcement of this Agreement.

29. *Necessary Documents.* Each party shall, upon the request of the other, execute, acknowledge, and deliver any instruments appropriate or necessary to carry into effect the intentions and provisions of this Agreement.

30. *Consideration.* The consideration for this Agreement is the mutual promises herein contained and the marriage about to be solemnized. If the marriage does not take place, this Agreement shall be in all respects and for all purposes null and void.

31. *Entire Agreement.* This Agreement contains the entire agreement and understanding of the parties, and no representations or promises have been made except as to those set forth herein.

32. *Binding Effect.* This Agreement shall be binding upon and inure to the benefit of the parties and their respective heirs, executors and administrators.

33. *Effective Date of Agreement.* This Agreement shall become effective upon the date the parties are married.

34. *Effective Date of Executory Provisions.* The executory provisions contained in this Agreement shall become effective at such time as the parties shall become legally separated pursuant to a written separation agreement or cease living together as husband and wife, or are divorced pursuant to a judgment of divorce entered by a court of competent jurisdiction.

35. *Waiver of Right to Jury Trial.* The parties waive and release all rights to a trial by jury in any suit, action or proceeding in any court, and in any jurisdiction for the determination of any dispute or controversy arising out of this Agreement for the enforcement of any of the provisions hereof.

IN WITNESS WHEREOF, the parties have signed, sealed and acknowledged this Agreement on the day and year first above written.

_____ DATED: _____

[*Name*]

_____ DATED: _____

[*Name*]

State of_____)
)   ss:
County of _____)

—Continued

Antenuptial Agreement—*Continued*

BE IT REMEMBERED that on this _____ day of _____ , Nineteen Hundred and Ninety _____ , before me the subscriber, a Notary Public of _____ , personally appeared _____ and _____ , who, I am satisfied, are the persons in the foregoing Agreement named, to whom I first made known the contents thereof, and thereupon they acknowledged that they signed, sealed and delivered the same as their voluntary act and deed, for the uses and purposes therein expressed.

_____
Notary Public

▆▆▆▆ COHABITATION AGREEMENTS

Compare the following two situations:

Jim hires Mary as a maid in his house. She receives weekly compensation plus room and board. For a three-month period Jim fails to pay Mary's wages, even though she faithfully performs all of her duties. During this period, Jim seduces Mary. Mary sues Jim for *breach of contract* due to nonpayment of wages.

Bob is a prostitute. Linda hires Bob for an evening but refuses to pay him his fee the next morning. Bob sues Linda for *breach of contract* due to nonpayment of the fee.

The result in the second situation is clear. Bob cannot sue Linda for breach of contract. A contract for sex is not enforceable in court. Linda promised to pay money for sex. Bob promised and provided sexual services. This was the consideration he gave in the bargain. But sex for hire is illegal in most states. In fact, **fornication** and **adultery** are crimes in some states even if no payment is involved. Bob's consideration was **meretricious** sexual services and, as such, cannot be the basis of a valid contract.

The result in the first situation above should also be clear. Mary has a valid claim for breach of contract. Her agreement to have a sexual relationship with Jim is incidental and, therefore, irrelevant to her right to collect compensation due her as a maid. She did not sell sexual services to Jim. There is no indication in the facts that the parties bargained for sexual services or that she engaged in sex in exchange for anything from Jim, e.g., continued employment, a raise in pay, lighter work duties. Their sexual involvement with each other is a **severable** part of their relationship and should not affect her main claim. Something is severable when what remains after it is removed can survive without it. (The opposite of severable is essential or indispensable.)

Now we come to a more difficult case:

Dan and Helen meet in college. They soon start living together. They move into an apartment, pool their resources, have children, etc. Twenty years after they entered this relationship, they decide to separate. Helen now sues Dan for a share of the property acquired during the time they lived together. At no time did they ever marry.

The fact that Dan and Helen never married does not affect their obligation to support their children, as we shall see in chapter 8. But what about Dan and

Fornication Sexual relations between unmarried persons or between persons who are not married to each other.

Adultery Sexual relations between a married person and someone other than his or her spouse.

Meretricious Pertaining to unlawful sexual relations; vulgar or tawdry.

Severable Removable without destroying what remains.

Helen themselves? They **cohabited** and never married. They built a relationship, acquired property together, and helped each other over a long period of time. Do they have any support or property rights in each other now that they have separated?

Cohabited Lived together as husband and wife whether or not they were married.

This is not an academic question. The Bureau of the Census says that between 1970 and 1993 the number of "unmarried-couple households" in America increased by 600 percent—from 523,000 to 3.5 million. This category consists of two unrelated adults of the opposite sex who share a housing unit (see Exhibit 3.2). Furthermore, an additional 1.5 million households consist of two unrelated adults of the same sex.[4]

For years, the law has denied any rights to an unmarried person who makes financial claims based upon a period of cohabitation. The main reasons for this denial are as follows:

□ To grant financial or property rights to unmarried persons would treat them as if they were married. Our laws favor the institution of marriage. To recognize unmarried relationships would denigrate marriage and discourage people from entering it.

□ Sexual relations are legal and morally acceptable within marriage. If the law recognizes unmarried cohabitation, then illicit sex is being condoned. The relationship is not much different from prostitution.

These two arguments are still dominant forces in many states. In 1976, however, a major decision came from California: *Marvin v. Marvin* 18 Cal. 3d 660, 134 Cal. Rptr. 815, 557 P.2d 106 (1976). This case held that parties living together would not be denied a remedy in court upon their separation solely because

□ **EXHIBIT 3.2 Unmarried-Couple Households**

YEAR	TOTAL NUMBER OF MARRIED COUPLES	TOTAL NUMBER OF UNMARRIED COUPLES	NUMBER OF THESE UNMARRIED COUPLES WITH CHILDREN UNDER 15 YEARS OF AGE	RATIO OF UNMARRIED COUPLES PER 100 MARRIED COUPLES
1993	54,199,000	3,510,000	1,236,000	6
1990	56,112,000	2,856,000	891,000	5
1985	51,114,000	1,983,000	603,000	4
1980	49,714,000	1,589,000	431,000	3
1970	44,593,000	523,000	196,000	1

SOURCE: Arlene Saluter, *Marital Status and Living Arrangements,* Table D, Current Population Reports, P20-478, U.S. Bureau of the Census (May 1994).

---

4. These are not all homosexual-couple households. The count includes some couples who are not cohabiting, e.g., those that include a roommate, a boarder, or a paid employee. In the future, the Bureau will use a new category of "unmarried partner," which is a person who is not related to the householder, who shares living quarters, and who has a close personal relationship with the householder.

they never married. Although all states have not followed *Marvin*, the decision has had a major impact in this still-developing area of the law.

The parties in *Marvin* lived together for seven years without marrying.[5] The plaintiff alleged that she entered an oral agreement with the defendant that provided (1) that he would support her, and (2) that while "the parties lived together they would combine their efforts and earnings and would share equally any and all property accumulated as a result of their efforts whether individual or combined." She further alleged that she agreed to give up her career as a singer in order to devote full time to the defendant as a companion, homemaker, housekeeper, and cook. During the seven years that they were together, the defendant accumulated in his name over $1 million in property. When they separated, she sued for her share of this property.

The media viewed her case as an alimony action between two unmarried "ex-pals" and dubbed it a **palimony** suit. Palimony, however, is not a legal term. The word *alimony* should not be associated with this kind of case. Alimony is a court-imposed obligation of support that grows out of a failed marital relationship. There was no marital relationship in the *Marvin* case.

One of the first hurdles for the plaintiff in *Marvin* was the problem of "meretricious sexual services." The defendant argued that even if a contract did exist (which he denied), it was unenforceable because it involved an illicit relationship. The parties were not married but were engaging in sexual relations. The court, however, ruled that

> "[A] contract is unenforceable only *to the extent* that it *explicitly* rests upon the immoral and illicit consideration of meretricious sexual services. . . . The fact that a man and woman live together without marriage, and engage in a sexual relationship, does not in itself invalidate agreements between them relating to their earnings, property, or expenses." *Marvin v. Marvin*, 557 P.2d at 112, 113.

The agreement will be invalidated only if sex is an express condition of the relationship. If the sexual aspect of their relationship is severable from their agreements or understandings on earnings, property, and expenses, the agreements or understandings will be enforced. An example of an *un*enforceable agreement would be a promise by a man to provide for a woman in his will in exchange for her agreeing to live with him and bear his children. This agreement is *explicitly* based on a sexual relationship. Thus sex in such a case cannot be separated from the agreement and is *not* severable.

The next problem faced by the plaintiff in *Marvin* was the theory of *recovery*. The main reason married parties have financial rights in each other is their *marital status*, which gives rise to duties imposed by law. What about unmarried parties? The *Marvin* court suggested several theories of recovery for such individuals:

- ☐ Express contract
- ☐ Implied contract
- ☐ Quasi contract
- ☐ Trust
- ☐ Partnership

Palimony A nonlegal term for payments made by one nonmarried party to another after they cease living together, usually because they entered an express or implied contract to do so while they were cohabiting.

---

5. The parties were Michelle Marvin and Lee Marvin, the famous actor. Although they never married, Michelle changed her last name to Marvin.

☐ Joint venture
☐ Putative spouse doctrine

Before we examine these theories, three points need to be emphasized. First, as indicated earlier, not all states agree with the *Marvin* doctrine that there are circumstances when unmarried cohabiting parties should be given a remedy upon separation. Second, the above list of seven remedies is not exhaustive. The *Marvin* court recognized that new theories may have to be developed to achieve justice in particular situations. Third, all of the theories will be to no avail, even in states that follow *Marvin*, if it can be shown that "meretricious sexual services" were at the heart of the relationship and cannot be separated (are not severable) from the other aspects of the relationship.

EXPRESS CONTRACT

In an express cohabitation agreement or contract, the parties expressly tell each other what is being "bargained" for, e.g., household services in exchange for a one-half interest in a house to be purchased, or companion services (nonsexual) in exchange for support during the time they live together. There must be an offer, acceptance, and legal consideration. The latter is the exchange of promises. While this is the cleanest theory of recovery, it is often difficult to prove. Rarely will the parties have the foresight to commit their agreement to writing, and it is equally rare for witnesses to be present when the parties make their express agreement. Ultimately the case will turn on which party the court believes.

IMPLIED CONTRACT

Another remedy is to sue under a theory of **implied contract,** also called an *implied in fact contract.* This kind of contract exists when a reasonable person would conclude that the parties had a tacit understanding that they had a contractual relationship even though its terms were never expressly discussed. Consider the following example:

Implied Contract A contract that is not created by an express agreement between the parties but is inferred as a matter of reason and justice from their conduct and the surrounding circumstances.

> Someone delivers bottled milk to your door daily, which you never ordered. You consume the milk every day, place the empty bottles at the front door, exchange greetings with the delivery person, never demand that the deliveries stop, etc.

At the end of the month when you receive the bill for the milk, you will not be able to hide behind the fact that you never expressly ordered the milk. Under traditional contract principles, you have entered an "implied contract" to buy the milk, which is as binding as an express contract. Unless the state has enacted special laws to change these principles, you must pay for the milk.

In the case of unmarried individuals living together, we must similarly determine whether an implied contract existed. Was it clear by the conduct of the parties that they were entering an agreement? Was it obvious under the circumstances that they were exchanging something? Did both sides expect "compensation" in some form for what they were doing? If so, an implied contract existed, which can be as enforceable as an express contract.

QUASI CONTRACT

A **quasi contract** is also called an *implied in law contract.* Although called a contract, it is a legal fiction since it does not involve an express agreement and

Quasi Contract A contract created by law to avoid unjust enrichment.

we cannot reasonably infer that the parties had an agreement in mind. The doctrine of quasi contract is simply a device designed by the courts to prevent **unjust enrichment.**[6] An example might be a doctor who provides medical care to an unconscious motorist on the road. The doctor can recover the reasonable cost of medical services under a quasi contract theory even though the motorist never expressly or impliedly asked for such services. Another example might be a man who arranges for a foreign woman to come to this country to live in his home and provide domestic services. If she came with the expectation of being paid and if what she provided was not meretricious, the law might obligate him to pay the reasonable value of her services, less the value of any support she received from him during the time they were together. The court's objective would be to avoid unjust enrichment. A court might reach a similar result when unmarried cohabitants separate.

TRUST

A **trust** is another option to consider. At times, the law will hold that a trust is implied. Assume that Tim and Sandra, an unmarried couple, decide to buy a house. They use the funds in a joint account to which both contribute equally. The deed to the house is taken in Tim's name so that he has legal title. On such facts, a court will impose an implied trust for Sandra's benefit. She will be entitled to a half-interest in the house through the trust. A theory of implied trust might also be possible if Sandra contributed services rather than money toward the purchase of the property. A court would have to decide what her interest in the property should be in light of the nature and value of these services.

Another example of a trust that is imposed by law is called a **constructive trust.** Assume that a party obtains title to property through fraud or an abuse of confidence. The funds used to purchase the property come from the other party. A court will impose a constructive trust on the property if this is necessary to avoid the unjust enrichment of the person who obtained title in this way. This person will be deemed to be holding the property for the benefit of the party defrauded or otherwise taken advantage of.

PARTNERSHIP

A court might find that an unmarried couple entered the equivalent of a **partnership** and thereby acquired rights and obligations in the property involved in the partnership.

JOINT VENTURE

A **joint venture** is like a partnership, but on a more limited scale. A court might use the joint venture theory to cover some of the common enterprises entered into by two unmarried individuals while living together, e.g., the purchase of a home. Once a joint venture is established, the parties have legally enforceable rights in the fruits of their endeavors.

Unjust Enrichment Receiving property or benefit from another when in fairness and equity the recipient should make restitution of the property or provide compensation for the benefit even though there was no express or implied promise to do so.

Trust A legal entity that exists when one person holds property for the benefit of another.

Constructive Trust A trust created by operation of law against one who has obtained legal possession of property (or legal rights to property) through fraud, duress, abuse of confidence, or other unconscionable conduct.

Partnership A voluntary contract between two (or more) persons to use their resources in a business or other venture, with the understanding that they will proportionately share losses and profits.

Joint Venture An express or implied agreement to participate in a common enterprise in which the parties have a mutual right of control.

---

6. In a suit that asserts the existence of a quasi contract, the amount of recovery awarded a victorious plantiff is measured by what is called *quantum meruit,* which means "as much as he deserves."

PUTATIVE SPOUSE DOCTRINE

In limited circumstances, a party might have the rights of a **putative spouse.** This occurs when the parties attempt to enter a marital relationship, but a legal *impediment* to the formation of the marriage exists, e.g., one of the parties is under age or is married to someone else. If at least one of the parties is ignorant of this impediment, the law will treat the "marriage" as otherwise valid. Upon separation, the innocent party might be entitled to the reasonable value of the services rendered while together, or a share of the property accumulated by their joint efforts.

Putative Spouse A person who reasonably believed he or she entered a valid marriage even though there was a legal impediment that made the marriage unlawful.

ASSIGNMENT 3.5

a. Helen Smith and Sam Jones live together in your state. They are not married and do not intend to become married. They would like to enter a contract that spells out their rights and responsibilities. Specifically, they want to make clear that the house in which they both live belongs to Helen even though Sam has done extensive remodeling work on it. They each have separate bank accounts and one joint account. They want to make clear that only the funds in the joint account belong to both of them equally. Next year they hope to have or adopt a child. In either event, they want the contract to specify that the child will be given the surname, "Smith-Jones," a combination of their own last names. Draft a contract for them. Include any other clauses you think appropriate, e.g., on making wills, the duration of the contract, on the education and religion of children.

b. Tom and George are gay. They live together. George agrees to support Tom while the latter completes engineering school, at which time Tom will support George while the latter completes law school. After Tom obtains his engineering degree, he leaves George. George now sues Tom for the amount of money that would have been provided as support while George attended law school. What result?

c. Richard and Lea have lived together for ten years without being married. This month, they separated. They never entered a formal contract, but Lea says that they had an informal understanding that they would equally divide everything acquired during their relationship together. Lea sues Richard for one-half of all property so acquired. You work for the law firm that represents Lea. Draft a set of interrogatories for Lea that will be sent to Richard in which you seek information that would be relevant to Lea's action.

▄▄▄ Interviewing and Investigation Checklist

Factors Relevant to the Property Rights of Unmarried Couples

Legal Interviewing Questions

1. When and how did the two of you meet?

2. When did you begin living together?

3. Why did the two of you decide to do this? What exactly did you say to each other about your relationship at the time?

4. Did you discuss the living arrangement together? If so, what was said?

5. What was said or implied about the sexual relationship between you? Describe this relationship.

6. What was your understanding about the following matters: rent, house purchase, house payments, furniture payments, food, clothing, medical bills?

7. Did you agree to keep separate or joint bank accounts? Why?

8. What other commitments were made, if any? For example, was there any agreement on providing support, making a will, having children, giving each other property or shares in property? Were any of these commitments put in writing?

9. Did you ever discuss marriage? If so, what was said by both of you on the topic?

10. What did you give up in order to live with him or her? Did he or she understand this? How do you know?

11. What did he or she give up in order to live with you?

12. What other promises were made or implied between you? Why were they made?

—Continued

—*Continued*

13. How did you introduce each other to others?

14. Did you help each other in your businesses? If so, how?

15. What were your roles in the house? How were these roles decided upon? Through agreement? Explain.

16. Did he or she ever pay you for anything you did? Did you ever pay him or her? Explain the circumstances.

17. If no payment was ever made, was payment expected in the future? Explain.

18. Were the two of you "faithful" to each other? Did either of you ever date others? Explain.

19. Did you use each other's money for any purpose? If so, explain the circumstances. If not, why not?

Possible Investigation Tasks

☐ Obtain copies of bank statements, deeds for property acquired while the parties were together, loan applications, tax returns, etc.

☐ Interview persons who knew the parties.

☐ Contact professional housekeeping companies to determine the going rate for housekeeping services.

■■■■ SAMPLE COHABITATION AGREEMENT

Cohabitation Agreement
W. Mulloy, West's Legal Forms, 2d
§ 3.54, pp. 225–229 (1983).

I
Intention of the Parties

_____and _____declare that they are not married to each other, but they are living together under the same roof, and by this agreement intend to protect and define each other's rights pertaining to future services rendered, earnings, accumulated property and furnishings and other matters that may be contained herein. It is expressly set forth herein that the consent of either party to cohabit sexually with the other is not a consideration, either in whole or in part, for the making of this agreement. It is further expressly set forth herein that the general purpose of this agreement is that the earnings, accumulations and property of each party herein shall be the separate property of the person who earns or acquires said property, and shall not be deemed community property, joint property, common law property or otherwise giving the non-earning or non-acquiring party an interest in same.

II
Representations to the Public

It is agreed that should either or both of the parties to this agreement represent to the public, in whatever manner, that they are husband and wife, that said representation shall be for social convenience only, and shall in no way imply that sexual services are a consideration for any party of this agreement, nor shall it imply that sexual cohabitation is taking place.

III
Property, Earnings, and Accumulations

It is agreed that all property of any nature or in any place, including but not limited to the earnings and income resulting from the personal services, skill, effort, and work of either party to this agreement, whether acquired before or during the term of this agreement, or acquired by either one of them by purchase, gift or inheritance during the said term, shall be the separate property of the respective party, and that neither party shall have any interest in, and both parties hereby waive any right or interest he or she may have in the property of the other.

IV
Services Rendered

It is agreed that whatever household, homemaking, or other domestic work and services that either party may contribute to the other or to their common domicile shall be voluntary, free, and without compensation, and each party agrees that work of this nature is done without expectation of monetary or other reward from the other party.

—Continued

Cohabitation Agreement—*Continued*

V
Debts and Obligations

It is agreed that all debts and obligations acquired by either party which is to the benefit of that party shall be the debt or obligation of that party only, and that the other shall not be liable for same. Should one party be forced to pay a debt rightfully belonging to and benefitting the other, the other promises to reimburse, indemnify and hold harmless the one who has paid said debt or obligation.

Those debts and obligations which are to the benefit of both parties, such as utilities, garbage, local telephone service, rent, and renter's insurance shall be paid in such sums and in such proportion by each party as shall be mutually agreeable.

VI
Money Loaned

All money, with the exception of mortgage or rent payments, transferred by one party to the other, either directly or to an account, obligation, or purchase of the other, shall be deemed a loan to the other, unless otherwise stated in writing. This shall include such things as downpayments on a home or vehicle, and deposits in either party's separate bank account.

VII
Rented Premises

It is agreed that should the parties share rented premises, said rented premises shall "belong" to the person who first rented the same, and should the parties separate, the second one shall leave taking only such belongings as he or she owned prior to moving in or purchased while living together.

If the parties both rent the premises from the beginning, then it is agreed that they will have a third person flip a coin to see who "owns" the premises, and the winner will have the option to remain while the loser leaves.

VIII
Rent or Mortgage

It is agreed that the parties may split the rent or mortgage payments in whatever proportion they choose, each contributing such sum as is mutually agreeable. It is also agreed that if one party contributes to the mortgage payment of a premises belonging to or being purchased in the name of the other party, that such contribution shall be deemed rent only, and shall be non-refundable and shall not create in the person who is living in the premises owned or being purchased by the other, any interest in said property or in the equity therein.

IX
Business Arrangements

A. It is agreed that should one party hereto contribute services, labor, or effort to a business enterprise belonging to the other, that the party contributing said services, labor or effort shall not acquire by reason thereof any interest in, ownership of, or claim to said business enterprise, nor shall said person be compensated in any way for said services, labor, or effort, unless the terms of said compensation are expressly agreed to by both parties.

B. Should the parties share services, labor or effort in a jointly owned business enterprise the relative interests of each party shall be apportioned according to a separate partnership agreement, or, if there is no express agreement, then in proportion that each contributed thereto.

C. It is agreed that the business known as _____ is the individual and separate business of [*Name of Owner*], and is not to be deemed a jointly owned business of both parties.

X
Separate Accounts

In conformity with the intentions of the parties set forth herein, both parties agree to maintain separate bank accounts, insurance accounts (except "renter's" insurance to insure the contents of an apartment, house, etc., which the parties may jointly hold), tax returns, credit accounts, credit union accounts, medical accounts, automobile registration and own-

—Continued

Cohabitation Agreement—*Continued*

ership, and deeds to property, and to make all purchases of personal property, including furniture, appliances, records, books, works of art, stereo equipment, etc., separate, in order to avoid confusion as to the ownership of same, and also in order to avoid nullifying the general intent of this agreement.

XI
Duration of This Agreement

This agreement shall remain in effect from the date the parties start cohabiting until either party leaves or removes himself or herself from the common domicile with the intention not to return, or until they marry, or until they make a new written agreement that is contrary to the terms of this agreement.

XII
Attorney Fees and Costs

Each party agrees to act in good faith with the provisions of this agreement, and should one party breach the agreement or fail to act in good faith therewith, such party agrees to pay to the other such attorney fees and costs as may be reasonable in order to properly enforce the provisions herein.

XIII
No Common Law Marriage Intended

Even though the parties hereto are cohabiting under the same roof and may give the appearance of being married, or from time to time represent to the public that they are husband and wife, they do not intend by such acts to acquire the status of "common law" marriage, and expressly state herein that this is not an agreement to marry, that they are not now married, and that they understand they are not married to each other during the term of this agreement.

XIV
Waiver of Support

Both parties waive and relinquish any and all rights to "alimony," "spousal support," or other separate maintenance from the other in the event of a termination of their living together arrangement.

Dated: _____

_____
[*Name and Signature of Party*]

_____
[*Name and Signature of Party*]

Witnesses:

_____

_____

Notary Public:

_____ (SEAL)

My commission expires _____

■■■■ SUMMARY

The four main kinds of agreements parties enter before and after marriage are cohabitation agreement, antenuptial agreement, post-nuptial agreement, and separation agreement. An antenuptial agreement is a premarital contract that defines certain rights and obligations during marriage and upon the termination of marriage by death or divorce. To be enforceable, the agreement must meet the requirements for a valid contract, must be based on disclosure of assets, must not be unconscionable, and must not be against public policy.

A cohabitation agreement is a contract between two unmarried parties covering financial and related matters while they live together, upon separation, or upon death. Some states will enforce such agreements so long as they are not based solely on meretricious sexual services, or so long as the sexual aspect of their agreement is severable from the rest of the agreement. When one party sues the other for breaching the agreement, the media's misleading phrase for the litigation is palimony suit.

If the aggrieved party cannot establish the existence of an express or implied cohabitation contract, other theories might be used by the court to avoid the unfairness of one of the parties walking away from the relationship with nothing. These theories include quasi contract, trust, partnership, joint venture, and the putative spouse doctrine.

■■■■ KEY CHAPTER TERMINOLOGY

Cohabitation Agreement	Fornication	Quasi Contract
Antenuptial Agreement	Adultery	Unjust Enrichment
Post-nuptial Agreement	Meretricious	Trust
Separation Agreement	Severable	Constructive Trust
Waiver	Cohabited	Partnership
Unconscionable	*Marvin v. Marvin*	Joint Venture
Public Policy	Palimony	Putative Spouse
Uniform Premarital Agreement Act	Implied Contract	

THE FORMATION OF CEREMONIAL MARRIAGES AND COMMON LAW MARRIAGES

Marriage is a coming together for better or for worse, hopefully enduring and intimate to the degree of being sacred. It is an association that promotes a way of life, not causes; a harmony in living, not political faiths; a bilateral loyalty, not commercial or social projects. Yet it is an association for as noble a purpose as any involved in our prior decisions. *Griswold v. Connecticut,* 381 U.S. 479, 486, 85 S. Ct. 1678, 1682, 14 L. Ed. 2d 510 (1965)—Justice Douglas.

Intestate Dying without leaving a valid will.

Forced Share A designated share of a deceased spouse's estate that goes to the surviving spouse despite what the will of the deceased spouse gave the surviving spouse.

Dower A widow's right to the lifetime use of one-third of the land her deceased husband owned during the marriage.

Curtesy A husband's right to the lifetime use of all the land his deceased wife owned during the marriage (if issue were born of the marriage).

■■■■ RAISING THE MARRIAGE ISSUE

A client is not likely to walk into a law office and ask, "am I married?" The existence of a marriage becomes an issue when the client is trying to obtain some other objective, such as seeking:

□ A divorce (you can't divorce someone to whom you are not married)

□ Pension benefits as the surviving spouse of a deceased employee

□ Social security survivor benefits through a deceased spouse

□ Worker's compensation death benefits as the surviving spouse of an employee fatally injured on the job

□ Assets as the spouse of a deceased person who died **intestate**

□ Assets under a clause in a will that gives property "to my wife" or "to my husband"

□ A **forced share** of a deceased spouse's estate

□ **Dower** or **curtesy** rights

□ Entrance to the United States (or avoidance of deportation) as a result of being married to a U.S. citizen

☐ The right to assert in a criminal case the **privilege for marital communications,** also called the husband-wife privilege

REGULATING WHO CAN MARRY

Marital status may be achieved through one of two possible methods: ceremonial marriage or common law marriage. As we shall see in the next section, however, many states have abolished common law marriage.

The United States Supreme Court has held that marriage is a fundamental right. Consequently, a state is limited in its power to regulate one's right to marry. For example, a state cannot prohibit **miscegenation.** Nor can it withhold a marriage license pending proof that child-support payments (from an earlier marriage) are being met, and proof that any children due such payments are not likely to become public charges. Only "reasonable regulations that do not significantly interfere with decisions to enter into the marital relationship may legitimately be imposed" *Zablocki v. Redhail*, 434 U.S. 374, 386, 98 S. Ct. 673, 681, 54 L. Ed. 2d 618 (1978). The United States Supreme Court held in *Zablocki* that the restriction based on child-support payments was not reasonable.

States have imposed two major kinds of requirements for entering marriage: (1) technical or formal requirements for ceremonial marriages, e.g., obtaining a license, and (2) more basic requirements relating to the intent and capacity to marry that apply to both ceremonial and common law marriages, e.g., being of minimum age to marry, and not being too closely related to the person you want to marry. The latter requirements will be discussed in chapter 5. Here our focus is primarily on the technical or formal requirements.

CEREMONIAL MARRIAGE

The requirements for a **ceremonial marriage,** found within the statutory code of your state, usually specify the following:

☐ Marriage license

☐ Ceremony performed by an authorized person (Exhibit 4.1)

☐ Witnesses to the ceremony (Exhibit 4.1)

☐ Waiting period

☐ Physical examination of the two parties

☐ Recording of the license in a designated public office following the ceremony

Not all states have the same requirements, and some may impose additional ones.

Privilege for Marital Communication One spouse cannot disclose in court any confidential communications that occurred between the spouses during the marriage. (This privilege does not apply when the spouses are suing each other.)

Miscegenation Mixing the races. The marriage or cohabitation of persons of difference races.

Ceremonial Marriage A marriage that is entered in compliance with the statutory requirements, e.g., obtaining a marriage license, having the marriage performed (i.e., solemnized) by an authorized person.

ASSIGNMENT 4.1

Identify all of the requirements for a ceremonial marriage in your state. Interview someone who was married in your state in order to determine whether all the requirements for a ceremonial marriage were met. You may interview your spouse or a married relative, friend, classmate, etc. Before you conduct the interview, draft a checklist of questions necessary to determine if the marriage is in compliance with state requirements. (These should be questions that could be part of a manual.) Make notes of the interviewee's answers. For all answers, ask the interviewee if any documents or other evidence exists to substantiate (or corroborate) information given. Hand in to your instructor a written account of the interview (including the questions you asked). Remember that one of the primary characteristics of such written work products should be specificity; the details of names, addresses, dates, who said what, etc., can be critical.

□ **EXHIBIT 4.1**
Authorization to
Celebrate or Witness a
Marriage

Number _____ .

To _____ , authorized to celebrate (or witness) marriages in the state of _____ , greeting:

You are hereby authorized to celebrate (or witness) the rites of marriage between _____ , of _____ , and _____ , of _____ , and having done so, you are commanded to make return of the same to the clerk's office of _____ within ten days under a penalty of fifty dollars for default therein.

Witness my hand and seal of said court this _____ day of _____ , anno Domini _____ .

_____ Clerk.

By _____ Assistant Clerk.

Number _____ .

I, _____ , who have been duly authorized to celebrate (or witness) the rites of marriage in the state of _____ do hereby certify that, by authority of a license of corresponding number herewith, I solemnized (or witnessed) the marriage of _____ and _____ , named therein, on the _____ day of _____ , at _____ , in said state.

Suppose that the technical requirements for a ceremonial marriage have been violated. What consequences follow?

Assume, for example, that a statute requires a ten-day waiting period between the date of the issuing of the license and the date of the ceremony. Joe and Mary want to marry right away and find a minister who marries them on the same day they obtained the license. What result? Are they validly married? In most states, the marriage is valid even when there has been a failure to comply with one of the requirements discussed in this chapter for a ceremonial marriage. In such states, noncompliance with the requirements for a ceremonial marriage cannot later be used as a ground for annulment or divorce. Keep in mind, however, that we are *not* discussing age or relationship requirements that involve the *legal capacity* of parties to marry nor are we discussing requirements relating to *intent to marry*. Violations of such requirements can indeed be grounds for annulment or divorce, as we will see in the next chapter.

While noncompliance with technical requirements does not affect the validity of a marriage in most states, other consequences may result. The parties, for example, might be prosecuted for perjury if they falsified public documents in applying for the marriage. The person who performed the marriage ceremony without the authority to do so may be subjected to a fine. Other sanctions similar to these might also apply.

ASSIGNMENT 4.2

Suppose that a statute in a state provides as follows:

§ 10 No marriage shall be invalid on account of want of authority in any person solemnizing the same if consummated with the full belief on the part of the persons so married, or either of them, that they were lawfully joined in marriage.

George and Linda read a newspaper article stating that five of seven ministers connected with the Triple Faith Church in their state had been fined for illegally performing marriage ceremonies. A week later, they are married by Rev. Smith, who is in charge of Triple Faith

Church but who has no authority to marry anyone. Can the validity of their marriage be called into question under § 10?

☐ **Note on Proxy Marriage** Some states sanction a **proxy marriage** in which the ceremony takes place with one or both parties being absent (e.g., the groom is overseas). A third-party agent must be given the authority to act on behalf of the missing party or parties during the ceremony.

▄▄▄ COMMON LAW MARRIAGE

When parties enter a valid **common law marriage,** the marriage is as valid as a ceremonial marriage. Children born during a common law marriage, for example, are legitimate. To end such a marriage, one of the parties must die, or they both must go through a divorce proceeding in the same manner as any other married couple seeking to dissolve a marriage.

Most states have abolished common law marriages. Thirteen states and the District of Columbia still recognize them (see Exhibit 4.2). Even in states that have abolished common law marriages, however, it is important to know something about them for the following reasons:

1. Parties may enter a common law marriage in a state where such marriages are valid and then move to another state that has abolished such marriages. Under traditional **conflict of law** principles, as we shall see, the second state may have to recognize the marriage as valid. In our highly mobile society, parties who live together should be aware that if they travel through states that recognize common law marriages for vacations or for other temporary purposes, one of the parties might later try to claim that they entered a common law marriage in such a state.

2. It may be that your state once recognized common law marriages as valid, but then, as of a certain date, abolished all such marriages for the future. A number of people may still live in your state who entered valid common law marriages before the law was changed, and hence, their marriages are still valid.

What conditions must exist for a valid common law marriage in states that recognize such marriages? Not all states have the same requirements. Generally, however, the following conditions must be met.

Common Law Marriage

☐ The parties must have legal capacity to marry.

☐ There must be an intent to marry and a present agreement to enter a marital relationship—to become husband and wife to each other. (Some states require an express agreement; others allow the agreement to be inferred from the manner in which the man and woman relate to each other.)

☐ The parties must actually live together as husband and wife, i.e., there must be cohabitation.

☐ There must be an openness about the relationship; the parties must make representations to the world that they are husband and wife. (See interviewing questions in checklist below.)

A popular misconception about common law marriages is that the parties must live together for seven years before the marriage becomes legal. These is no such time requirement.

Common Law Marriage The marriage of two people who agree to be married, cohabit, and hold themselves out as husband and wife even though they do not go through a ceremonial marriage.

Conflict of Law An inconsistency between the laws of different legal systems such as two states or two countries.

☐ **EXHIBIT 4.2   Common Law Marriage**

STATE	VALID IN STATE?	RECOGNIZED IF CURRENTLY VALID WHERE CONTRACTED?	STATE	VALID IN STATE?	RECOGNIZED IF CURRENTLY VALID WHERE CONTRACTED?
Alabama	Yes	Yes	Montana	Yes	Yes
Alaska	Not after 1/1/64	Yes	Nebraska	Not after 1923	Yes
Arizona	No	Yes	Nevada	Not after 3/29/43	Yes
Arkansas	No	Yes	New Hampshire	No	Yes
California	Not after 1895	Yes	New Jersey	Not after 1/12/39	Yes
Colorado	Yes	Yes	New Mexico	No	Yes
Connecticut	No	*	New York	Not after 4/29/33	Yes
Delaware	No	Yes	North Carolina	No	Yes
Dist. of Columbia	Yes	Yes	North Dakota	No	Yes
Florida	Not after 1/1/68	Yes	Ohio	Yes	Yes
Georgia	Yes	Yes	Oklahoma	Yes	Yes
Hawaii	No	Yes	Oregon	No	Yes
Idaho	Yes	Yes	Pennsylvania	Yes	Yes
Illinois	Not after 6/30/05	*	Rhode Island	Yes	*
Indiana	Not after 1/1/58	*	South Carolina	Yes	Yes
Iowa	Yes	Yes	South Dakota	Not after 7/1/59	*
Kansas	Yes	Yes	Tennessee	No	Yes
Kentucky	No	Yes	Texas	Yes	Yes
Louisiana	No	*	Utah	No	Yes
Maine	No	*	Vermont	No	*
Maryland	No	Yes	Virginia	No	Yes
Massachusetts	No	Yes	Washington	No	Yes
Michigan	Not after 1/1/57	Yes	West Virginia	No	Yes
Minnesota	Not after 4/26/41	*	Wisconsin	Not after 1913	*
Mississippi	Not after 4/5/56	*	Wyoming	No	Yes
Missouri	Not after 3/3/21	*			

*Legal status unclear.
SOURCE: U.S. Department of Labor, Women's Bureau.

In some states, the courts are reluctant to find all these elements present in a particular case. Common law marriages may be disfavored by the court *even in a state where such marriages are legal*. It is too easy to fabricate a claim that the parties married by common law, particularly after one of them has died.

▇▇▇▇ **Interviewing and Investigation Checklist**

Factors Relevant to the Formation of a Common Law Marriage between C (Client) and D (Defendant)

Legal Interviewing Questions

1. On what date did you first meet D?

2. When did the two of you first begin talking about living together? Describe the circumstances. Who said what, etc.?

—Continued

—Continued

3. Did you or D ever discuss with anyone else your plans to live together?

4. On what date did you actually move in together? How long have you been living together?

5. In whose name was the lease to the apartment or the deed to the house in which you lived?

6. Do you have separate or joint bank accounts? If joint, what names appear on the account?

7. Who pays the rent or the mortgage?

8. Who pays the utility bills?

9. Who pays the food bills?

10. Since you have been living together, have you filed separate or joint tax returns?

11. Have you ever made a written or oral agreement that you and D were going to be married?

12. Why didn't you and D have a marriage ceremony?

13. Did you ever introduce each other as "my husband" or "my wife"?

14. Name any relatives, neighbors, business associates, friends, etc., who think of you and D as husband and wife.

15. Did you and D ever discuss making individual or joint wills? Do you have them? Did you contact any attorneys about them? If so, what are their names and addresses?

16. Did you and D ever separate for any period of time? If so, describe the circumstances.

17. Did you and D ever have or adopt any children? If so, what last name did the children have?

18. On insurance policies, is either of you the beneficiary? How is the premium paid?

19. During your life with D, what other indications exist that the two of you treated each other as husband and wife?

20. Have the two of you ever spent significant time in Alabama, Colorado, District of Columbia, Georgia, Idaho, Iowa, Kansas, Montana, Ohio, Oklahoma, Pennsylvania, Rhode Island, South Carolina, or Texas? (See Exhibit 4.2.) If so, describe the circumstances.

Possible Investigation Tasks

☐ Obtain a copy of the lease or deed.

☐ Obtain copies of bills, receipts, tax returns, etc., to determine how the names of C and D appear on them.

☐ Obtain copies of any agreements between C and D.

☐ Interview anyone C indicates would think of C and D as husband and wife.

☐ Obtain birth certificates of children, if any.

Two situations remain to be considered: *conflict of law* and *impediment removal*.

CONFLICT OF LAW

Bill and Pat live in State X, where common law marriages are legal. They enter such a marriage. Then they move to State Y, where common law marriages have been abolished. A child is born to them in State Y. Bill is injured on the job and dies. Pat claims worker's compensation benefits as the "wife" of Bill. Will State Y recognize Pat as married to Bill? Is their child legitimate?

The law of State X is inconsistent with the law of State Y on the validity of common law marriages. A conflict of law problem exists whenever a court must decide between inconsistent laws of different legal systems. In deciding which law to choose, a court is guided by various conflict of law principles. In the case of marriages, the traditional "conflicts" principle is that the validity of a marriage is governed by the law of the place where the parties entered or contracted it.

Pat and Bill's marriage was contracted in State X, where it is valid. Since the marriage was valid where it was contracted, State Y will accept the marriage as valid (even though it would have been invalid had they tried to enter it in State Y). Pat is married to Bill and their child is legitimate. (In chapter 5, we will discuss the problem of parties moving to another state *solely* to take advantage of its more lenient marriage laws and returning to their original state after the marriage.)

IMPEDIMENT REMOVAL

In 1969 Ernestine enters a valid ceremonial marriage with John. They begin having marital troubles and separate. In 1975 Ernestine and Henry begin living together. Ernestine does not divorce John. She and Henry cohabitate and hold each other out as husband and wife in a state where common law marriages are valid. Except for the existence of the 1969 marriage to John, it is clear that Ernestine and Henry would have a valid common law marriage. In 1981 John obtains a divorce from Ernestine. Henry and Ernestine continue to live together in the same manner as they had since 1975. In 1989, Henry dies. Ernestine claims death benefits under the Worker's Compensation Act as his surviving "wife." Was she ever married to Henry?

Impediment A legal obstacle that prevents the formation of a valid marriage or other contract.

Ernestine and Henry never entered a ceremonial marriage. Until 1981 a serious **impediment** existed to their being able to marry: Ernestine was already married to someone else. When the marriage was dissolved by the divorce in 1981, the impediment was removed. The issue is (1) whether Ernestine and Henry would be considered to have entered a valid common law marriage at the time the impediment was removed, or (2) whether at that time they would have had to enter a *new* common law marriage agreement, express or implied. In most states, a new agreement would not be necessary. An earlier agreement to marry (by common law) will carry forward to the time the impediment is removed so long as the parties have continued to live together openly as husband and wife. Accordingly, Ernestine automatically became the wife of Henry when the impediment of the prior marriage was removed, since she and Henry continued to live together openly as husband and wife after that time. As one court puts it:

> It is not to be expected that parties once having agreed to be married will deem it necessary to agree to do so again when an earlier marriage is terminated or some other bar to union is eliminated. *Matthews v. Britton*, 303 F.2d 408, 409 (D.C. Cir. 1962).

In the states that reach this conclusion, it makes no difference that either or both of the parties knew of the impediment at the time they initially agreed to live as husband and wife.

ASSIGNMENT 4.3

Examine the following sequence of events:

☐ Ann and Rich meet in State Y where they agree to live together as husband and wife forever. They do not want to go through a marriage ceremony, but they agree to be married and openly represent themselves as such. State Y does not recognize common law marriages.

☐ Rich accepts a job offer in State X, where common law marriages are legal, and they both move there.

☐ After three years in State X, Rich and Ann move back to State Y. One year later, Rich dies. In his will, he leaves all his property "to my wife." Ann is not mentioned by name in his will.

☐ From the time they met until the time of Rich's death, they lived together as husband and wife, and everyone who knew them thought of them as such.

Can Ann claim anything under the will? State Y provides tax benefits to "widows." Can Ann claim these benefits?

ASSIGNMENT 4.4

Vivian Hildenbrand and Tom Hildenbrand began living together in Oregon in 1975 and continuously did so until Tom's death in 1984. During this time, pursuant to mutual agreement, they cohabited and held themselves out as husband and wife, but never went through a marriage ceremony. They purchased real property in their joint names as husband and wife. On four different occasions, they went on vacation fishing trips to a resort in Idaho, where they registered as husband and wife, held themselves out as such, and lived together during their stay. Two trips in 1977 were of three days' duration each. Two trips were of seven day's duration each, one in 1978 and one in 1979. Oregon does not recognize common law marriages; Idaho does.

Tom Hildenbrand died in an on-the-job accident while he was working for the Oregon XYZ Chemical Company. Vivian claims Oregon worker's compensation benefits. The state Worker's Compensation Board denies these benefits on the ground that she was not his wife. What is her argument?

☐ **Note on Putative Marriages** In chapter 3 we saw that some courts will treat unmarried parties as putative spouses for purposes of providing limited rights (page 37). Only a few states recognize putative marriages, however, and the requirements for establishing them are very strict:

> A putative marriage is one which has been contracted in good faith and in ignorance of some existing impediment on the part of at least one of the contracting parties. Three circumstances must occur to constitute this species of marriage: (1) There must be bona fides. At least one of the parties must have been ignorant of the impediment, not only at the time of the marriage, but must also have continued ignorant of it during his or her life. (2) The marriage must be duly solemnized. (3) The marriage must have been considered lawful in the estimation of the parties or of that party who alleges the bona fides. *United States Fidelity & Guarantee Co. v. Henderson*, 53 S.W.2d 811, 816 (Tex. Civ. App. 1932).

An example might be a woman who goes through a marriage ceremony in good faith and does not find out until after her "husband" dies that he never even tried to obtain a divorce from his first wife who is still alive. In the few states that recognize putative marriages, such a woman would be given some protection, e.g., she would be awarded the reasonable value of the services she rendered or a share of the property the parties accumulated during the relationship.[1] Note, however, that only the innocent party can benefit from the putative marriage. If the woman had died first in our example, her bigamist "husband" could not claim benefits as her putative spouse.

HOMOSEXUAL "MARRIAGES"

Can a man marry a man? Can a woman marry a woman? Traditional marriage statutes neither specifically prohibit nor approve same-sex marriages. Such marriages, however, have been denied by the courts on the theory that marriage has always been thought to involve a man and a woman.

---

1. Some states have enacted the Uniform Marriage and Divorce Act, which provides in section 209 that "Any person who has cohabited with another to whom he is not legally married in the good faith belief that he was married to that person is a putative spouse until knowledge of the fact that he is not legally married terminates his status and prevents acquisition of further rights. A putative spouse acquires the rights conferred upon a legal spouse, including the right to maintenance following termination of his status, whether or not the marriage is prohibited (Section 207) or declared invalid (Section 208). If there is a legal spouse or other putative spouses, rights acquired by a putative spouse do not supersede the rights of the legal spouse or those acquired by other putative spouses, but the court shall apportion property, maintenance, and support rights among the claimants as appropriate in the circumstances and in the interests of justice."

Denmark is one of the few countries of the world that has specifically authorized same-sex marriages. The parties, however, do not have all the rights of traditional marriages. For example, they cannot adopt minor children.

Proponents of same-sex marriages in America have attempted a number of strategies—all without success:

1. *Equal protection.* Since individuals of the opposite sex can marry, why treat gay individuals differently? Is this unequal treatment unconstitutional? Thus far the courts have said no. (See, however, the discussion of the *Baehr* case below.)

2. *Fundamental right to marry.* The Supreme Court has said that there cannot be unreasonable restrictions on the right to marry since this is a fundamental right. (*Zablocki*, page 43) No court, however, has yet held that the prohibition against same-sex marriages is unreasonable.

3. *Common law marriage.* If gay people cannot enter ceremonial marriages, can they enter a common law marriage if all of the conditions for such a marriage are present, e.g., open cohabitation, intent to marry? No. Where this theory has been used, the courts have still insisted on a man-woman relationship.

4. *Putative spouse doctrine.* Here the parties acknowledge a legal impediment to the marriage but argue that they had a good-faith belief that they were legally married. Courts, however, have said that homosexuals could not possibly have such a good-faith belief.

In many states, homosexual conduct among adults is a crime even if it is consensual. The United States Supreme Court has held that it is constitutional for states to impose criminal penalties for such conduct. *Bowers v. Hardwick*, 478 U.S. 186, 106 S. Ct. 2841, 92 L. Ed. 2d 140 (1986). Such states obviously have little sympathy for the argument that homosexuals should be allowed to marry.

Suppose that one of the parties is a transsexual (an individual, usually a man, who has had a sex-change operation). Can such an individual marry a man? Most courts would not permit the marriage, arguing that both parties to the marriage must have been *born* members of the opposite sex. A few courts, however, take the opposite position and allow such marriages.

A number of other special circumstances need to be considered in this area of the law:

☐ Two homosexuals can enter a *Marvin*-type contract in which they agree to live together and share property acquired during the relationship. The major issue (as in a heterosexual relationship) is whether sexual services were an integral and inseparable part of the agreement. If so, as we saw in chapter 3, the contract will not be enforced.

☐ In some states a gay adult can adopt another gay adult.

☐ Assume that two lesbians live together. One is artificially inseminated and bears a child. In a few states, the other lesbian may be able to adopt the child, who then has two legal parents of the same sex.

☐ In the above situation, if the other lesbian does not adopt the child and the adults separate, can the other lesbian be granted visitation rights? If the women entered a *co-parenting agreement* in which they agreed to raise and support the child together, would such an agreement be enforceable? In the absence of adoption, it is unlikely that a court would be sympathetic to the lesbian seeking visitation rights or asserting other parental rights under a co-parenting agreement.

☐ Some universities have refused to allow gay student couples to live in *married* student housing, even if they can prove they are financially and domestically interdependent. The universities took the position that they had no authority to recognize unmarried couples.

☐ Several large corporations (e.g., Levi Strauss & Co. and Lotus Development Corp.) have recently begun offering health coverage and other benefits to partners of their homosexual employees. The Levi plan applies to any worker who lives and shares finances with an unmarried lover.

☐ Rent-control laws in New York City limit the right of a landlord to evict "the surviving spouse of the deceased tenant or some other member of the deceased tenant's family who has been living with the tenant." In a highly publicized case, the New York State Court of Appeals ruled that a man whose male lover died of AIDS was a "family" member of the deceased within the meaning of this law and therefore was entitled to remain in the apartment. *Braschi v. Stahl*, 74 N.Y.2d 201, 543 N.E.2d 49, 544 N.Y.S.2d 784 (1989).

☐ A few cities allow same-sex couples to acquire some of the rights of married couples. To do so, they must register as **domestic partners.** This allows them health benefits, hospital visitation rights, bereavement leave from work, etc. In San Francisco, domestic partners are defined as two adults who have chosen "to share one another's lives in an intimate and committed relationship of mutual caring, who live together, and who have agreed to be jointly responsible for basic living expenses incurred during the Domestic Partnership." They sign a Declaration of Domestic Partnership (see Exhibit 4.3). If they want to end this new legal relationship, they must file a Notice of Termination with the county clerk. New York City has a similar program (see Exhibit 4.4).

Domestic Partners
Two persons of the same sex who live together in an intimate relationship, who register with the government as domestic partners, and who thereby acquire limited rights enjoyed by a traditional married couple.

As indicated, however, no state has taken the drastic step of legalizing same-sex marriages. But in 1993, a thunderbolt came from Hawaii when the Hawaii Supreme Court wrote the controversial opinion of *Baehr v. Lewin*, 74 Haw. 645, 852 P.2d 44 (1993). While this opinion did not hold that same-sex couples have a fundamental right to marry, it did say that the denial of this right *might* constitute the denial of the equal protection of the law under the Hawaii Constitution.

The *Baehr* case is still in litigation. The case arose when three same-sex couples sued the state after they were denied a marriage license. The trial court dismissed the case on the ground that the Hawaii Revised Statutes (HRS) does not authorize same-sex marriages. The couples then appealed to the Supreme Court of Hawaii, which wrote the *Baehr v. Lewin* decision.

The couples raised two main constitutional arguments before the Supreme Court of Hawaii: privacy and equal protection. Here is a summary of these arguments and how the court responded to them:

☐ *Privacy argument.* There is a right to privacy in the Hawaii Constitution; this right is also implicit in the United States Constitution. Section 6 of the Hawaii Constitution explicitly says, "The right . . . to privacy is recognized." The Fourteenth Amendment of the United States Constitution guarantees "due process of law," which the courts have interpreted to include a right

☐ **EXHIBIT 4.3   San Francisco Declaration of Domestic Partnership**

SAN FRANCISCO

DECLARATION OF

DOMESTIC PARTNERSHIP

We declare under penalty of perjury:

1. We have an intimate, committed relationship of mutual caring;

2. We live together (see definition on the other side of this page);

3. We agree to be responsible for each other's basic living expenses (see definition on the other side of this page) during our domestic partnership; we also agree that anyone who is owed these expenses can collect from either of us;

4. We are both 18 or older;

5. Neither of us is married;

6. Neither of us is related to the other as a parent, brother or sister, half brother or sister, niece, nephew, aunt, uncle, grandparent or grandchild;

7. Neither of us has a different domestic partner now;

8. Neither of us has had a different domestic partner in the last six months (this last condition does not apply if you had a partner who died; if you did, cross this out).

We declare under penalty of perjury under the laws of the State of California that the statements above are true and correct.

Signed on _____, 19____ in _____

Signature _____   Print Name _____

Signed on _____, 19____ in _____

Signature _____   Print Name _____

YOU MUST ALSO FILL OUT THE OTHER SIDE OF THIS FORM

DECLARATION OF DOMESTIC PARTNERSHIP

☐ **EXHIBIT 4.3   San Francisco Declaration of Domestic Partnership—***Continued*

1. Definitions:

"Live together" means that the two of you share a place to live. You don't both have to be on the rental agreement or deed. It is okay if one or both of you has a separate place somewhere else. Even if one of you leaves the place you share, you still live together as long as the one who left intends to return.

"Basic living expenses" means the cost of basic food and shelter. It also includes any other expense which is paid by a benefit you or your partner gets because of the partnership. For example, if you get health insurance from your job, and the insurance covers your partner, you will be responsible for medical bills which the insurance does not pay. You don't have to split basic living expenses to be domestic partners. You just have to agree to provide these things for your partner if he or she can't provide for him or herself.

2. Address: Each of you should fill in your mailing address here:

Name _____

Address _____

City, State & Zip Code _____

Name _____

Address _____

City, State & Zip Code _____

3. The Last Step: To finish setting up a domestic partnership, you must EITHER:

(1) File this form with the San Francisco County Clerk; or
(2) Sign this form in front of a Notary Public and have the Notary fill in the notarization at the bottom of this page.

To be able to file this form with the County Clerk, one of you must work in San Francisco OR both of you live together in San Francisco (see explanation below).

[ ] Check here to state that one of you works in San Francisco.
[ ] Check here to state that you live together in San Francisco.

You don't have to check either space if you finish setting up your domestic partnership by getting this Declaration notarized.

4. Notarization: Use only if you do not file the Declaration with the county clerk

State of _____

County of _____ ss.

On this ____ day of _____ in the year 19 ___, before me _____ personally
appeared _____, personally known to me (or proved to me on the basis of satisfactory evidence) to be the persons whose names are subscribed to this instrument, and acknowledged that they executed it.

_____
Notary Public

□ **EXHIBIT 4.4   New York City's Executive Order Regarding Domestic Partnership**

Executive Order No. 123

August 7, 1989

BEREAVEMENT LEAVE FOR CITY EMPLOYEES

WHO ARE MEMBERS OF A DOMESTIC PARTNERSHIP

WHEREAS, there have been significant changes in our society resulting in diverse living arrangements among individuals and an expanded concept of what constitutes a family unit; and

WHEREAS, many of these living arrangements involve long-term committed relationships between unmarried persons; and

WHEREAS, the death of one individual in such a relationship, or the death of that individual's parent or child or other relative residing in the household, would have a profound personal impact upon the other individual in such a relationship;

NOW, THEREFORE, by the power vested in me as Mayor of the City of New York, it is hereby ordered:

Section 1. Bereavement Leave Established. Bereavement leave for all City employees is hereby established in the event of the death of a "domestic partner", as defined in Section 2, or the death of a parent or child of such domestic partner, or the death of a relative of such domestic partner residing in the household, and shall be afforded in accordance with existing rules and regulations and the terms of this Executive Order.

Section 2. Domestic Partnerships Defined. Domestic partners are two people, both of whom are 18 years of age or older and neither of whom is married, who have a close and committed personal relationship involving shared responsibilities, who have lived together for a period of one year or more on a continuous basis at the time of registration, and who have registered as domestic partners and have not terminated the registration in accordance with procedures to be established by the Department of Personnel of the City of New York.

Section 3. Registration. The Department of Personnel of the City of New York is directed to establish procedures and develop forms for the registration and termination of domestic partnerships. The Department of Personnel shall not register a domestic partnership if either member is currently a member of another domestic partnership or was previously a member of another domestic partnership and less than one year has expired since the termination of that domestic partnership.

Section 4. Effective Date. This Order shall take effect immediately.

Edward I. Koch

M A Y O R

to privacy. The first question is whether the right to privacy in the state or federal constitution establishes a fundamental right of same-sex couples to marry. The *Baehr* court concluded neither the United States Constitution nor the Hawaii Constitution can be interpreted to contain a fundamental right of same-sex couples to marry. The right to privacy does not extend this far.

□ *Equal protection argument.* A state government can regulate marriage such as by writing statutes establishing who is eligible to marry and what rights married couples have in each other's property. But there are limits on the ability of a state to write such statutes. A state can't pass a statute that violates the constitution. Did Hawaii do that here? Section 5 of the Hawaii Constitution contains the state's equal protection clause. It says, "No person shall be . . . denied the equal protection of the laws, nor be denied the enjoyment of the person's civil rights or be discriminated against in the exercise thereof because of race, religion, sex, or ancestry." This section prohibits the state from passing statutes that discriminate against any person in the exercise of his or her civil rights on the basis of sex. The Hawaii Revised Statutes (HRS) discriminates on the basis of sex. It denies same-sex couples access to the marital status and its concomitant rights and benefits. The question then becomes whether the HRS violates the equal protection clause in § 5 of the Hawaii Constitution.

Whenever a court is deciding whether discrimination in a statute is unconstitutional because of an alleged denial of equal protection, it applies a test or standard. There are two main tests: the rational basis test and the strict scrutiny test. The **rational basis test** says that the discrimination in the statute is constitutional if the statute rationally furthers a legitimate state interest. On the other hand, the more-difficult-to-meet **strict scrutiny test** presumes that the statute is unconstitutional unless the state shows compelling state interests that justify the discrimination, and also shows that the statute is narrowly drawn to avoid unnecessary abridgments of constitutional rights. The strict scrutiny test is often applied when the discrimination encroaches on a fundamental right or is against what is called a "suspect class" such as race. (The word "suspect" derives from the conclusion that certain kinds of discrimination create classifications that are inherently suspect or questionable.)

The court had to decide which of these tests to apply in determining whether the HRS unconstitutionally denies same-sex couples the equal protection of the law. The court concluded that the strict scrutiny test should govern. Hence when this case is sent back to the circuit court for a new trial, the Department of Health must show that there are compelling state interests that justify the discrimination against same-sex couples in the HRS and that this statute is narrowly drawn to avoid unnecessary abridgments of constitutional rights.

As indicated, the case is still in litigation. It is unclear whether same-sex marriages will ultimately be legitimized in Hawaii. If they are, however, it is unlikely that the other forty-nine states will do likewise. These states fear, however, that they might be asked to recognize and enforce such marriages within their own boundaries.

Here is how this could happen. Assume that further litigation in *Baehr v. Lewin* ultimately leads to the right of same-sex couples to marry in Hawaii. Ted and Bob enter such a marriage. They then move to Ohio where they continue to live. Bob dies. Ted now goes to an Ohio court and asks for a share of Bob's estate as his "spouse." Or assume that they decide to separate. They go to an Ohio court to ask for a "divorce" and an order dividing their property. The traditional rule, as we have seen, is that the validity of a marriage is determined by the law of the state in which the marriage was entered or contracted. If this rule is applied, must Ohio recognize the validity of the Hawaii marriage even though it considers such marriages void and against its public policy? The problem is further compounded by the **Full Faith and Credit Clause** of the United States Constitution. Would this Clause *require* Ohio to give full recognition to the Hawaii marriage, especially if a Hawaii court renders a judgment that a particular marriage entered in Hawaii is valid? Such questions have no clear answers. The problem has not yet arisen because no state has sanctioned

Full Faith and Credit Clause Article IV of the *United States Constitution* provides that "Full Faith and Credit shall be given in each State to the public Acts, Records, and judicial Proceedings of every other State."

same-sex marriages. Will Hawaii be the first and thereby force other states to confront these questions? This is an area in which we can expect the creation of a good deal of new law—and controversy.

SUMMARY

Many material benefits derive from being married, particularly when a spouse dies, e.g., social security and pension benefits. To claim these benefits, one must establish the existence of a valid ceremonial marriage or, in states that allow them, a valid common law marriage.

States differ on the requirements that must be fulfilled to enter a ceremonial marriage. In many states, the requirements include obtaining a license, waiting a designated period of time, going through a physical examination, having the ceremony performed by an authorized person, having witnesses to the ceremony, and recording the license in the proper public office. Yet in most states, the failure to comply with such requirements is not a ground for an annulment.

In states where common law marriages are still possible, the requirements are a present agreement to enter a marital relationship, living together as husband and wife (cohabitation), and an openness about living together as husband and wife. As with ceremonial marriages, the parties must have the legal capacity to marry and must intend to marry. The latter conditions will be considered in chapter 5.

The validity of a marriage is governed by the state in which it was entered or contracted. Hence if a couple enters a common law marriage in a state where it is valid, but moves to a state where such marriages have been abolished, the latter state will recognize the marriage as valid.

Occasionally an impediment exists to an otherwise valid common law marriage, e.g., one of the parties is still married to someone else. If the impediment is removed while the parties are still openly living together, a valid common law marriage will be established as of the date of the removal.

Same-sex marriages are invalid in every American state. No legislature has passed a statute recognizing them, and all of the arguments made in court to force recognition have been unsuccessful. In some states, however, homosexuals have achieved limited rights in this area, e.g., to enter contracts governing nonsexual aspects of living together, to adopt a gay adult, and to register as "domestic partners" for purposes of being entitled to bereavement leave upon the death of one of the partners. If a state changes its law to allow same-sex marriages, the question then becomes whether the Full Faith and Credit Clause will require the other states to recognize marriages from that state. Thus far we do not have a clear answer to this question.

KEY CHAPTER TERMINOLOGY

Intestate
Forced Share
Dower
Curtesy
Privilege for Marital
  Communications

Miscegenation
Ceremonial Marriage
Proxy Marriage
Common Law Marriage
Conflict of Law
Impediment

Domestic Partners
Rational Basis Test
Strict Scrutiny Test
Full Faith and Credit Clause

ANNULMENT

ANNULMENT, DIVORCE, AND LEGAL SEPARATION

When discussing an **annulment**, it is technically incorrect to refer to an "annulled marriage." The word "marriage" means the legal union of two people as husband and wife. If reasons (i.e., grounds) exist to substantiate the initial *illegality* of the union, then no marriage ever existed in spite of the license, the ceremony, consummation, and perhaps even children. Frequently, you will see the phrase, "suit to annul a marriage." Technically, it would be more accurate to use the phrases, "suit to annul an attempted marriage" or "suit to declare the validity or invalidity of a marriage," but these phrases are not used. Instead we continue to refer to the annulment of marriages.

A **divorce**, on the other hand, is a dissolution of a marriage that once validly existed. In a divorce there is something to dissolve; in an annulment, there is simply a judicial statement or declaration that no marital relationship existed between the parties at the outset.

A **legal separation** (also called a judicial separation) gives the parties permission to end their "bed and board" relationship and live separately. They are still legally married. If they want to remarry, they must obtain a divorce.

THE VOID/VOIDABLE DISTINCTION

Certain grounds for annulment will render the marriage void, while other grounds will render it only voidable. *Void* means the marriage is invalid whether or not any court declares its invalidity. *Voidable* means the marriage is invalid only if a court declares that it is invalid.

Annulment A declaration by a court that a valid marriage never existed.

Divorce A declaration by a court that a marriage has been dissolved so that the parties are no longer married to each other.

Legal Separation A declaration by a court that parties can live separately and apart even though they are still married to each other.

Voidable Marriage A marriage that is invalid only if someone challenges it and a court declares it invalid.

Assume that two individuals have a **voidable marriage,** but that they die without anyone bringing an annulment action or challenging their marriage in any way. The practical effect of this inaction is that the entire world treats the marriage as if it were valid. In effect, there is no practical difference between a marriage that complies with all the legal requirements and a voidable marriage that no one ever challenges. If, however, an annulment action *is* brought and a court declares a voidable marriage to be invalid, the invalidity generally "relates back" to the time when the parties tried to enter the marriage. The invalidity does not begin on the date the court declares the marriage invalid.

Void Marriage A marriage that is invalid whether or not a court declares it so.

A **void marriage** is considered **void ab initio.** Technically, if a marriage is void, there is no need to bring a court action to seek a declaration that it is invalid. Nevertheless, parties will usually want a court declaration in order to remove any doubt that the marriage is invalid.

Void ab Initio Invalid from the very beginning.

States use different terminology to describe the proceeding:

- □ Action for annulment
- □ Suit to annul
- □ Libel for annulment
- □ Action for declaration of invalidity
- □ Action for a judgment of nullity
- □ Action for declaratory judgment (i.e., for a court pronouncement) that the marriage is invalid
- □ Action to affirm the validity of a marriage

■■■■ WHO CAN SUE?

As we study each of the grounds for annulment, one of the questions we must ask is, who can be the plaintiff to bring the annulment action? The wrongdoer (i.e., the party who knowingly did the act that constituted the ground for the annulment) is *not* always allowed to bring the action. This party may lack **standing** to bring the action. If the *innocent* party refuses to bring the action, it may be that the marriage can never be annulled. In such cases, the wrongdoing party, in effect, is prevented (sometimes called **estopped**) from getting out of what might clearly be an invalid marriage. Such a marriage is sometimes referred to as a *marriage by estoppel.* The wrongdoing party has **dirty hands** and should not be allowed to "profit" from this wrongdoing through a court action granting an annulment. When will a wrongdoing party be estopped from bringing an annulment action? The answer often depends on whether the marriage is void or voidable.

Standing The right to bring a case and seek relief from a court.

Estopped Prevented from asserting a right or a defense because it would be unfair or inequitable to do so.

Dirty Hands Wrongdoing or other inappropriate behavior that would make it unfair or inequitable to allow a person to assert a right or a defense he or she would normally have.

Grounds Acceptable reasons for seeking a particular result.

■■■■ OVERVIEW OF GROUNDS FOR ANNULMENT

There are essentially two kinds of **grounds** for annulment. First we examine those that relate to a party's *legal capacity* to marry:

- □ Preexisting marriage
- □ Improper relationship by blood or by marriage
- □ Nonage
- □ Physical disabilities

Second, we will turn to those that focus on whether a party with legal capacity to marry formed the requisite *intent* to marry:

- □ Sham marriages

□ Mental disabilities

□ Duress

□ Fraud

■■■■■ GROUNDS RELATING TO THE LEGAL CAPACITY TO MARRY

PRIOR EXISTING MARRIAGE (BIGAMY)

Here we will consider both the criminal and the civil consequences of **bigamy.**

CRIME   Entering a second marriage or even attempting to enter such a marriage when the first marriage has not ended by death, annulment, or divorce is a felony in most states. **Polygamy**[1] or *bigamy* is a crime.

In some states, if a spouse has disappeared for a designated number of years, he or she will be presumed dead. This presumption is the foundation for what is called the **Enoch Arden defense,** which will defeat a bigamy prosecution following a second marriage. States may differ on the elements of the Enoch Arden defense, e.g., the length of the disappearance, the requirement of diligence in trying to locate the missing spouse before remarrying, etc.

ANNULMENT: THE CIVIL ACTION   Our next concern is the existence of a prior undissolved marriage as a ground for an annulment of a second (attempted) marriage. In most states, a bigamous marriage is void; in only a few states is it voidable.

When a claim is made in an annulment proceeding that a second marriage is invalid because of a prior undissolved marriage, one of the common responses or defenses to this claim is that the *first* marriage was never valid or that this earlier marriage ended in a divorce or annulment. Yet marriage records, particularly old ones, are sometimes difficult to obtain, and for common law marriages, there simply are no records. Consequently, proving the status of a prior marriage can be a monumental task. Was it properly contracted? Was it dissolved? To assist parties in this difficult situation, the law has created a number of **rebuttable presumptions,** such as:

□ A marriage is presumed to be valid.

□ When there has been more than one marriage, the latest marriage is presumed to be valid.

The effect of the second presumption is that the court will treat the first marriage as having been dissolved by the death of the first spouse, by divorce, or by annulment. Note, however, that the presumption is *rebuttable,* which means that the party seeking to annul the second marriage can attempt to rebut (i.e., attack) the presumption by introducing evidence (1) that the first spouse is still alive, or (2) that the first marriage was *not* dissolved by divorce or annulment. The presumption favoring the validity of the latest marriage is so strong, however, that some states require considerable proof to overcome or rebut it.

Bigamy   Entering or attempting to enter a second marriage when a prior marriage is still valid.

Polygamy   Having more than one spouse at the same time, usually more than two.

Enoch Arden Defense The presumption that a spouse is dead after being missing for a designated number of years.

Rebuttable Presumption   A presumption is an assumption of fact that can be drawn when another fact or set of facts is established. The presumption is rebuttable if a party can introduce evidence to try to show that the assumption is false.

---

1. Polygamy often means having more than one *wife* at the same time. Polyandry means having more than one *husband* at the same time.

Finally, we need to consider the impact of *Enoch Arden* in annulment cases. We have already looked at Enoch Arden as a defense to a criminal prosecution for bigamy. We now examine the consequences of Enoch Arden on the second marriage in a civil annulment proceeding. Paul marries Cynthia. Cynthia disappears. Paul has not heard from her for fifteen years in spite of all his efforts to locate her. Paul then marries Mary in the honest belief that his first wife is dead. Mary does not know anything about Cynthia. Suddenly Cynthia reappears, and Mary learns about the first marriage. Mary immediately brings an action against Paul to annul her marriage to him on the ground of a prior existing marriage (bigamy). The question is whether Paul can raise the defense of Enoch Arden. Can Paul contest the annulment action against him by arguing that he had a right to presume that his first wife was dead? States differ in their answer to this question. Here are some of the different approaches:

☐ Enoch Arden applies only to criminal prosecutions for bigamy; the presumption of death does not apply to annulment proceedings.

☐ Enoch Arden does apply to annulment proceedings; the missing spouse is presumed dead. The second marriage is valid and cannot be annulled even if the missing spouse later appears.

☐ Enoch Arden does apply to annulment proceedings; the missing spouse is presumed dead. If, however, the missing spouse later appears, the second marriage can be annulled. Hence, the Enoch Arden defense is effective only if the missing spouse stays missing.

▉▉▉ Summary of Ground for Annulment: Prior Existing Marriage

Definitions: Entering a marriage despite the existence of a prior valid marriage that has not been dissolved by divorce, annulment, or the death of the first spouse.

Void or voidable: In most states, the establishment of this ground renders the second marriage void.

Who can sue: In most states, either party to the second marriage can bring the annulment action on this ground; both have standing.

Major defenses:

1. The first spouse is dead or presumed dead (Enoch Arden).

2. The first marriage was not validly entered.

3. The first marriage ended by divorce or annulment.

4. The plaintiff has "dirty hands" (available in a few states).

Is this annulment ground also a ground for divorce? Yes, in some states.

CONSANGUINITY AND AFFINITY LIMITATIONS

Consanguinity
Relationship by blood.

Affinity Relationship by marriage.

There are two ways that you can be related to someone: by **consanguinity** and by **affinity.**

Examples of a marriage of individuals related by consanguinity would be:

☐ Father marries his daughter.

☐ Sister marries her brother.

Examples of a marriage of individuals related by affinity would be:

☐ Man marries his son's former wife.

☐ Woman marries her stepfather.

State statutes prohibit certain individuals related by consanguinity or related by affinity from marrying. Violating these prohibitions can be a ground for annulment of the marriage.

States generally agree that certain relationships involve **incest**: marriage of parent and child, brother and sister, grandparent and grandchild, etc. Some disagreement exists on whether this is also true of cousin-cousin marriages and affinity relationships.

The *crime* of incest is committed mainly by designated individuals related by consanguinity. Surprisingly, however, the crime can also be committed in some states by designated individuals related by affinity.

Incest Sexual intercourse between two people who are too closely related to each other as defined by statute.

☐ **Notes on Consanguinity and Affinity**

1. Assume that a prohibition to a marriage exists because of an affinity relationship between the parties. What happens to the prohibition when the marriage ends by the death of the spouse who created the affinity relationship for the other spouse? Can the surviving spouse *then* marry his or her in-laws? (For example, John is the father-in-law of Mary, who is married to John's son Bill. After Bill dies, John marries Mary.) Some states allow such marriages, while others maintain the prohibition even after the death of the spouse who created the affinity relationship for the other spouse.

2. The Uniform Marriage and Divorce Act (§ 207) would prohibit all marriages between ancestors and descendants, brother-sister marriages, and adopted brother-sister marriages; it would permit first-cousin marriages and all affinity marriages.

3. States differ on whether two adopted children in the same family can marry.

4. As indicated above, the Supreme Court has held that marriage is a fundamental right and only ''reasonable regulations'' that interfere with the decision to enter a marriage can be imposed. (*Zablocki*, page 43). It is anticipated that some of the rules mentioned above regarding who can marry will be challenged as unreasonable regulations—particularly the rules prohibiting the marriage of individuals related by affinity.

**■■■■ Summary of Ground for Annulment:
Prohibited Consanguinity or Affinity Relationship**

Definition: State statutes provide that persons lack the legal capacity to marry if they are related by consanguinity (blood) or by affinity (marriage) in the manner specified in those statutes.

Void or voidable: In most states, the prohibited marriage is void.

Who can sue: Either party can be the plaintiff in the annulment action; both have standing.

Major defenses:

   1. The parties are not prohibitively related by blood or marriage.

2. The spouse who created the affinity relationship for the other spouse has died (this defense is available only for affinity relationships and only in some states).

Is this annulment ground also a ground for divorce? Yes, in most states.

NONAGE

In order to marry, a party must be a certain minimum age. Marrying below that age constitutes the ground of **nonage**. The minimum age may differ, however, depending upon whether:

   ☐ Parental consent exists.

Nonage Below the required minimum age to enter a designated relationship or to perform a particular task.

☐ The female is already pregnant.

☐ A child has already been born out of wedlock.

In some states, a court may have the power to authorize a marriage of parties under age even if a parent or guardian has refused to consent to the marriage. In these states, the court will consider such factors as the maturity of the parties, their financial resources, whether children (to be born or already born) would be illegitimate if the marriage were not authorized, etc. Still another variation found in some states is that the courts have the authority to require that underage individuals go through premarital counseling as a condition of their being able to marry.

At one time, states imposed different age requirements for males and females. This has been changed either by statute or by a court ruling that this kind of sex discrimination is unconstitutional.

▮▮▮ Summary of Ground for Annulment: Nonage

Definition: At the time of the marriage, one or both of the parties was under the minimum age to marry set by statute.

Void or voidable: In most states, the marriage is voidable.

Who can sue: Usually, only the underaged party is allowed to bring the annulment action. In some states, the parent or guardian of the underaged party also has standing.

Major defenses:

  1. The parties were of the correct statutory age at the time of the marriage.

  2. The underaged party affirmed or **ratified** the marriage by cohabitation after that party reached the statutory minimum age.

  3. The wrong party is bringing the suit.

  4. Even though the parties failed to obtain parental consent as specified in the statute, the absence of this consent is not a ground for annulment. (Note, however, that this defense is available only in some states.)

Is this annulment also a ground for divorce? Yes, in some states.

PHYSICAL DISABILITIES

The major physical incapacities or disabilities mentioned in marriage statutes are communicable venereal disease and incurable **impotence.** While several other physical problems are sometimes involved (e.g., epilepsy and pulmonary tuberculosis in advanced stages), most of the litigation centers on venereal disease and impotence.

As indicated in chapter 4, states often have a statutory requirement that parties contemplating marriage go through a medical examination as a condition of obtaining a marriage license. A major objective of this exam is to determine whether either or both of the parties have communicable venereal disease. Suppose that either or both of the parties do have such a disease at the time of their marriage. It may be that the medical exam failed to show this, or that they failed to take the exam (and entered a common law marriage in a state where such marriages are valid), or that they were able to falsify the results of the medical exam. States differ as to the consequences of marrying where one or both of the parties have the disease. While the marriage is valid in most states, in several states the marriage is not valid, and a ground for annulment can arise as a result. Furthermore, a state may make it a crime knowingly to marry or have sexual intercourse with someone who has an infectious venereal disease.

Issues related to a discussion of impotence include:

☐ Inability to **copulate**—incurable

Ratified Approved retroactively by agreement, conduct, or inaction that should be interpreted as approval. The noun is *ratification.*

Impotence The inability to have sexual intercourse, often due to an inability to achieve or maintain an erection.

Copulate To engage in sexual intercourse.

☐ Inability to copulate—curable

☐ **Sterility**

☐ Refusal to have sexual intercourse

Sterility Inability to have children; infertile.

In most states, only the first situation—an incurable inability to copulate—is a ground for annulment. The standard for incurability is not the impossibility of a cure; rather, it is the present unlikelihood of a cure. The standard for copulation is the ability to perform the physical sex act naturally, without pain or harm to the other spouse. The "mere" fact that a spouse does not derive pleasure from the act is not what is meant by an inability to copulate. The *refusal* to copulate is not an inability to copulate, although the refusal is sometimes used as an indication of (i.e., as evidence of) the inability to copulate. In most states, it makes no difference whether the inability is due to physical (organic) causes or to psychogenic causes, nor does it matter that the person is impotent only with his or her spouse. If normal coitus is not possible with one's spouse, whatever the cause, the ground exists.

It is a defense to an annulment action that the party seeking the annulment knew of the party's impotence at the time of the marriage and yet still went through with the marriage. Also, continued cohabitation (living as husband and wife) long after the party learned of the other partner's impotence may constitute the equitable defense of **laches** and thus bar the annulment action.

Laches Waiting an unreasonably long time to bring a suit or assert a right.

☐ **Note on Testing for AIDS**

Some states require their officials to tell marriage applicants that the state will provide testing for human immunodeficiency virus (HIV). Rejecting the offer will not in itself lead to a denial of the license. At one time, however, Illinois mandated that the "medical examination shall include tests to determine whether either of the parties to the proposed marriage has been exposed to human immunodeficiency virus (HIV) or any other identified causative agent of acquired immunodeficiency syndrome (AIDS)" ILL. REV. STAT. ch. 40, § 204(b). The requirement was eventually repealed. Large numbers of people avoided the test by traveling to neighboring states to obtain a marriage license:

> During the first 6 months of legislatively mandated premarital testing for human immunodeficiency virus in Illinois, 8 of 70,846 applicants for marriage licenses were found to be seropositive, yielding a seroprevalance of 0.011%. The total cost of the testing program for 6 months is estimated at $2.5 million or $312,000 per seropositive individual identified. Half of the reported seropositive individuals reported a history of risk behavior. During the same period, the number of marriage licenses issued in Illinois decreased by 22.5%, while the number of licenses issued to Illinois residents in surrounding states increased significantly. We conclude that mandatory premarital testing is not a cost-effective method for the control of human immunodeficiency virus infection. Turnock and Kelly, *Mandatory Premarital Testing for Human Immunodeficiency Virus: The Illinois Experience,* 261 Journal of the American Medical Association 3415 (June 15, 1989).

▮▮▮ Summary of Ground for Annulment: Physical Disabilities (Impotence)

Definition: The incurable inability to copulate without pain or harm to the spouse.

Void or voidable: Voidable.

Who can sue: Either party; both have standing.

Major defenses:

1. The impotence is curable.

2. The nonimpotent party knew of the other's impotence at the time of the marriage.

3. Statute of limitations or laches (plaintiff waited too long to bring this annulment action).

Is this annulment ground also a ground for divorce? Yes, in some states.

HOMOSEXUAL "MARRIAGES"

Since people of the same sex cannot legally marry, annulment can never be an issue, since there is no accepted marital union to annul. See the earlier discussion of homosexual "marriages" in chapter 4.

▆▆▆ GROUNDS RELATING TO THE INTENT TO MARRY

SHAM MARRIAGES

An essential element of a marriage contract is the intent to enter a marriage. With this in mind, examine the following "marriages":

☐ Dennis and Janet enter a marriage solely to obtain permanent resident alien status for Dennis, who is not a U.S. citizen. Janet is a citizen. Dennis wants to use his marriage status to avoid deportation by immigration officials.

☐ Edna dares Stanley to marry her following a college party. After a great deal of laughing and boasting, they go through all the formalities (obtaining a license, having the blood test, etc.) and complete the marriage ceremony.

☐ Frank and Helen have an affair. Helen becomes pregnant. Neither wants the child to be born illegitimate. They never want to live together but decide to be married solely for the purpose of having the child born legitimate. They agree that the child will live with Helen.

☐ Robin and Ken have been dating for a number of months. They decide to get married "just to try it out." They feel this is a modern and rational way of determining whether they will want to stay together, forever. Both fully understand that there will be "no hard feelings" if either of them wants to dissolve the marriage after six months.

All four of the above couples go through all the steps required to become married. To any reasonable outside observer of their outward actions, nothing unusual is happening. They all intended to go through a marriage ceremony; they all intended to go through the outward appearances of entering a marriage contract. Subjectively, however, they all had "hidden agendas."

According to traditional contract principles, if individuals give clear outward manifestations of mutual assent to enter a contract, the law will bind them to their contract even though their unspoken motive was *not* to enter a binding contract. Most courts, however, apply a different principle to marriage contracts than to other contracts. The first three couples above engaged in totally **sham** marriages. The parties never intended to live together as husband and wife; they had a limited purpose of avoiding deportation, displaying braggadocio, or "giving a name" to a child. Most courts would declare such marriages to be void and would grant an annulment to either party so long as the parties did not **consummate** their union or otherwise cohabit *after* the marriage. Suppose, however, that the couples in these three cases lived together as husband and wife even for a short period after the marriage. Most courts would be reluctant to declare their marriage void. The subsequent **cohabitation** would be some evidence that at the time they entered the marriage they *did* intend to live as husband and wife. The central question is, what intention did the parties have at the time they entered the marriage? Did they intend to be married or not? It is, of course, very difficult to get into their heads to find out what they were

Sham Pretended, false, empty.

Consummate To engage in sexual intercourse for the first time as spouses.

Cohabitation Living together as husband and wife whether or not the parties are married.

thinking. Hence, the law must rely on objective conduct as evidence of intent. If parties cohabit after marriage, this is certainly some evidence that they intended to be married at the time they appeared to enter a marriage contract.

In the first three hypothetical cases, assume that the couples did not cohabit after they entered the marriage. Most courts would, therefore, find that at the time they entered the marriage contract, they did not have the intention to be married, i.e., to assume the duties of a marriage. Again, it should be pointed out, however, that some courts apply a *different* rule and would hold that the marriage is valid whether or not cohabitation followed the marriage ceremony—so long as the parties went through all the proper procedures to be married.

What about the fourth hypothetical case, in which the parties entered a *trial marriage?* The fact that the parties cohabited is evidence that they did intend to be married at the time they entered the marriage contract. Most courts would find that this marriage is valid and deny an annulment to anyone who later claims that the parties never intended to assume the marital status. It cannot be said that they married in jest or that they married for a limited purpose. The fact that they did not promise to live together forever as husband and wife does not mean that they lacked the intent to be married at the time they entered the marriage.

▄▄▄ Summary of Ground for Annulment: Sham Marriage

Definition: The absence of an intention to marry in spite of the fact that the parties voluntarily went through all the formalities of a marriage.

Void or voidable: Void.

Who can sue: Either party; both have standing.

Major defense: The parties did have the intention to marry at the time they entered the marriage ceremony. A major item of evidence that this intention existed is that they cohabited after the ceremony. (NOTE: in some states, the annulment will be denied if the parties went through all the outward formalities of the marriage no matter what their unspoken objective was.)

Is this annulment ground also a ground for divorce? Usually not.

Elaine is twenty years old, and Philip, a bachelor, is seventy-five. Philip asks Elaine to marry him. Philip has terminal cancer and wants to die a married man. He and Elaine know that he probably has less than six months to live and that he will spend the rest of his life in a hospital bed. Under their arrangement, she does not have to continue as his wife after six months if he is still alive. They go through all the formal requirements to be married. On the day after the marriage ceremony, Elaine changes her mind and wants to end the marriage. Can she obtain an annulment?

ASSIGNMENT 5.1

MENTAL DISABILITIES

Two related reasons have been attributed to the existence of *mental disability* as a ground for annulment. First, it is designed to prevent people from marrying who are incapable of understanding the nature of the marriage relationship. Second, it is designed to prevent or at least discourage such individuals from reproducing, since it is argued that many mentally ill parents are likely to be poor parents and their children are likely to become public charges.

Mental disability has been very difficult to define. The various state statutes use different terms to describe this condition: insane, idiot, weak-minded, feebleminded, unsound mind, lack of mental capacity, imbecile, lunatic, incapable of consenting to a marriage, mentally ill or retarded, legally incompetent, mental defective, etc. One court provided the following definition:

> While there has been a hesitancy on the part of the courts to judicially define the phrase "unsound mind," it is established that such term has reference to the mental capacity of the parties at the very moment of inception of the marriage contract. Ordinarily, lack of mental capacity, which renders a party incapable of entering into a valid marriage contract, must be such that it deprives him of the ability to understand the objects of marriage, its ensuing duties and undertakings, its responsibilities and relationship. There is a general agreement of the authorities that the terms "unsound mind" and "lack of mental capacity" carry greater import than eccentricity or mere weakness of mind or dullness of intellect. *Johnson v. Johnson,* 104 N.W.2d 8, 14 (N.D. 1960).

Not all states would agree with every aspect of this definition of mental disability, although in general it is consistent with the definitions used by most courts.

Suppose that a person is intoxicated or under the influence of drugs at the time the marriage contract is entered. In most states, this, too, would be a ground for annulment if the alcohol or drugs rendered the person incapable of understanding the marriage contract.

While the issue of mental health usually arises in annulment actions—when someone is trying to dissolve the marriage—it also becomes relevant in some states at the license stage. Before a state official can issue a license to marry, he or she may be required by statute to inquire into the prior mental difficulties, if any, of the applicants for the license, e.g., to ask whether either applicant has ever been in a mental institution. At one time, the license to marry in these states could be denied to any mentally disabled person unless that person was sterilized or the woman involved in the proposed marriage was over forty-five years old. (For more on sterilization, see page 258.) It is generally conceded, however, that these license restrictions have been ineffective in preventing the marriage of people with serious mental problems. They are also of questionable constitutionality in view of the *Zablocki* opinion (page 43).

Whenever the mental health question arises (at the license stage or as part of an annulment proceeding), it is often very difficult to prove that the "right" amount of mental illness is present. All individuals are presumed to be sane unless the contrary has been demonstrated. Suppose that someone was once committed to a mental institution and, upon release, seeks to be married. Surely, the fact of prior institutionalization does not conclusively prove that the person is *presently* incapable of understanding the marriage contract and the marriage relationship at the time he or she attempts to marry.

Lucid Interval A period of time during which a person has the mental capacity to understand what he or she is doing.

Assume that a person is mentally disabled but marries during a brief period of mental health before relapsing again to his or her prior state of mental disability. The marriage took place during what is called a **lucid interval,** and many states will validate such a marriage if there was cohabitation. Furthermore, some states will deny the annulment if the parties cohabited during a lucid interval at any time *after* the marriage was entered even if one or both parties was not "lucid" at the time of the marriage. The problems of trying to prove that any "interval" was "lucid" can be enormous, however.

☐ **Notes on Mental Illness**

1. A state may have one standard of mental illness that will disable a person from being able to marry, another standard that will disable a person from being able to enter an ordinary business contract, and still another standard that will disable a person from being able to write a will.

2. Mental illness is, of course, also relevant in criminal proceedings where the defense of *insanity* is often raised in an attempt to relieve a defendant of criminal responsibility for what was done. Within criminal law, a great debate has always existed as to the definition of insanity. The M'Naghten "right-wrong" test is as follows: "at the time of the committing of the act, the party accused was laboring under such a defect of reason, from disease of the mind, as not to know the nature and quality of the act he was doing, or if he did know it that he did not know he was doing what was wrong." 10 Clark & F. 200, 8 Eng. Rep. 718 (1843). The Durham "diseased mind" test is as follows: "an accused is not criminally responsible if his unlawful act was the product of mental disease or mental defect." *Durham v. United States,* 214 F.2d 862, 874–75 (D.C. Cir. 1954). See also *United States v. Brawner,* 471 F.2d 969 (1972). The *Model Penal Code* test is as follows: "A person is not responsible for criminal conduct if at the time of such conduct as a result of mental disease or defect he lacks substantial capacity either to appreciate the criminality (wrongfulness) of his conduct or to conform his conduct to the requirements of the law." § 4.01.

■■■ **Summary of Ground for Annulment: Mental Disability**

Definition: The inability to understand the marriage contract and the duties of marriage at the time the parties attempt to enter the marriage due to mental illness, the influence of alcohol, or the influence of drugs.

Void or voidable: Voidable in most states.

Who can sue: In some states, only the mentally ill person (or his or her parent or guardian) can sue for the annulment. In other states, only the mentally healthy person can sue. In many states, either can sue; both have standing.

Major defenses:

1. The person was never mentally disabled.

2. The marriage occurred during a lucid interval.

3. After the marriage began, there was a lucid interval during which the parties cohabited.

4. The plaintiff has no standing to bring this annulment action.

Is this annulment ground also a ground for divorce? Yes, in most states, if the mental disability arises after the marriage commences.

DURESS

If someone has been forced to consent to marry, it clearly cannot be said that that person had the requisite *intent* to be married. The major question of **duress** is what kind of force will be sufficient to constitute a ground for annulment. Applying physical force or threatening its use is clearly sufficient. If an individual is faced with a choice between a wedding and a funeral, and chooses the wedding, the resulting marriage will be annulled as one induced by duress. The same is true if the choice is between bodily harm and marriage. Suppose, however, that the choice does not involve violence or the threat of violence. The most common example is as follows:

> George is courting Linda. They have had sexual relations several times. Linda announces that she is pregnant. Linda's father is furious at George and threatens to "turn him in" to the county district attorney to prosecute him for the crimes of seduction and bastardy. (If Linda is underage, the charge of statutory rape may be involved as

Duress Coercion; acting under the pressure of an unlawful act or threat.

well.) Furthermore, Linda and her father will sue George in the county civil court for support of the child. On the other hand, no criminal prosecution will be brought and no civil action will be initiated if George agrees to marry Linda. George agrees, and the "shotgun wedding" promptly takes place. After the wedding, it becomes clear that Linda was not pregnant; everyone made an honest mistake. George then brings an action to annul the marriage on the ground of duress.

Here the threat is of criminal prosecution and of bringing a civil support action. If such threats are made *maliciously*, they will constitute duress and be a ground for annulment. The threat is malicious if it has no basis in fact. If the threats are made in the good-faith belief that the court action could be won, they are not malicious; no annulment action can be based on them.

In most states, marriages induced by duress are voidable rather than void, but only the innocent party will have standing to bring the annulment action on that ground. If, however, this innocent party voluntarily cohabited with the "guilty" party (i.e., the one who did the coercing) after the effects of the duress have worn off, then the annulment action will be denied on the theory that the marriage has been ratified.

ASSIGNMENT 5.2

Do you think that any of the following marriages could be annulled on the ground of duress?

a. Rita married Dan after Dan threatened to kill Rita's second cousin if she did not marry him. The only reason Rita married Dan was to save her cousin's life.

b. Tom married Edna after Tom's very domineering father ordered him to marry her. Tom had been in ill health lately. Tom married Edna solely because he has never been able to say no to his father.

c. Paula married Charles after Paula's mother threatened suicide if Paula would not marry him. Paula married Charles solely to prevent this suicide.

■■ Summary of Ground for Annulment: Duress

Definition: The consent to marry was induced by (a) physical violence, or (b) threats of physical violence, or (c) malicious or groundless threats of criminal prosecution, or (d) malicious or groundless threats of civil litigation.

Void or voidable: Voidable in most states.

Who can sue: The party who was coerced.

Major defenses:

1. There was no physical violence or threat of it.

2. The plaintiff did not believe the threat of violence and hence was not coerced by it.

3. There was no threat of criminal prosecution or of civil litigation.

4. The threat of criminal prosecution or of civil litigation was not malicious; it was made in the good-faith belief that it could be won.

5. This is the wrong plaintiff (e.g., this plaintiff has "dirty hands" and lacks standing since this is the party who used duress).

6. The plaintiff freely cohabited with the defendant after the effect of the duress had gone (ratification).

Is this annulment ground also a ground for divorce? Yes, in some states.

FRAUD

The theory behind **fraud** as a ground for annulment is that if a party consents to a marriage where fraud is involved, the consent is not real. A party does not have an *intent to marry* if the marriage has a foundation in fraud. The party intends one thing and gets another! Generally, for this ground to succeed, the defendant must intentionally misrepresent or conceal an important fact and the person deceived must reasonably rely upon this fact in the decision to enter the marriage.

Not every fraudulent representation will be sufficient to grant an annulment. As one court put it:

> . . . [T]he fact that a brunette turned to a blond overnight, or that the beautiful teeth were discovered to be false, or the ruddy pink complexion gave way suddenly to pallor, or that a woman misstated her age or was not in perfect health, would lead no court to annul the marriage for fraud. Ryan & Granfield, *Domestic Relations*, 136 (1963).

What kind of fraud *is* ground for an annulment? Most courts have used an **essentials test:** The fraud must involve the essentials of the marital relationship, usually defined as those aspects of the marriage that relate to sex and children. For example, a man misrepresents his intent to have children. This would clearly go to the essentials of the marriage.

A much broader definition of fraud (making annulment easier to obtain on this ground) is the **materiality test:** The fraud must be material, meaning ''but for'' the fraudulent representation (whether or not it relates to sex and children) the person deceived would not have entered the marriage. Fewer courts use the materiality test than those that continue to insist on the essentials test.

Although, in theory, the essentials test is usually deemed to be the stricter of the two tests, in reality, the two tests often overlap and are frequently applied inconsistently by the courts. If children have been born from the union, for example, courts often strain the application of the tests in order to deny the annulment since preserving the marriage may be the only way to legitimize the children in some states. Also, if the marriage has never been consummated, courts tend to be more liberal in finding fraud. Oddly, a few courts treat an unconsummated marriage as little more than an engagement to be married.

The state of mind of the deceiving party is critical. In most states there must be an *intentional misrepresentation* of fact or an *intentional concealment* of fact. Consider the following methods by which false facts are communicated:

Fraud Knowingly making a false statement of present fact with the intention that the plaintiff rely on the statement. The plaintiff's reasonable reliance on the statement harms him or her.

▓▓▓ Forms of Communication

1. Just before their marriage, Joe tells Mary that he is anxious to have children with her. In fact, he intends to remain celibate after their marriage.

1. Joe's statement about children is an *intentional misrepresentation* of fact.

2. Joe says nothing about his planned celibacy since he knows that if he tells Mary, she will not marry him. He says nothing about children or celibacy, and the subject never comes up prior to their marriage.

2. Joe's silence is an *intentional concealment* of fact.

3. Joe does not tell Mary that he intended to remain celibate because he incorrectly assumed that Mary already knew.

3. Joe's silence is an *innocent* (or *good-faith*) *nondisclosure* of fact.

4. Just before their marriage, Joe tells Mary that since he is physically unable to have sexual intercourse, he will have to stay celibate. To his surprise, Joe later finds out that he is not impotent.

4. Joe's statement is an *innocent* (or *good-faith*) *misrepresentation* of fact.

5. One hour after Joe marries Mary, he gets on a bus and disappears forever. They never had sexual intercourse before or after marriage, and never discussed the subject.

5. From Joe's conduct we can draw an *inference* that at the time he married Mary, he probably never intended to consummate the marriage.

Generally, only the first, second, and fifth forms of communication mentioned in the above chart will support an annulment on the ground of fraud. *Innocent nondisclosure* or *innocent misrepresentation* will not be sufficient in most states. It should be pointed out, however, that in some states the innocence of the communication is not relevant so long as the other elements of fraud are present.

▰▰▰▰ Summary of Ground for Annulment: Fraud

Definition: The intentional misrepresentation or concealment of a fact that is essential or material to the marriage and that the person deceived reasonably relies on in the decision to enter the marriage.

Void or voidable: Voidable in most states.

Who can sue: The innocent party only.

Major defenses:

1. The fraud was not about an essential fact.

2. The fraud was not material: the plaintiff did not rely on the fraud in his or her initial decision to marry.

3. The fraud arose after the marriage was entered (again, no reliance).

4. The plaintiff may have relied on the fraud, but he or she was unreasonable in doing so.

5. After plaintiff discovered the fraud, he or she consummated the marriage or otherwise cohabited with the fraudulent party (ratification).

6. The misrepresentation or nondisclosure was innocent—made in good faith with no intention to deceive.

7. This plaintiff has no standing to bring the annulment action since the plaintiff was the deceiver.

8. This plaintiff has "dirty hands" (e.g., in a case involving fraud relating to pregnancy, the plaintiff had premarital sex with the defendant).

Is this annulment ground also a ground for divorce? Yes, in a few states.

□ Note on Church Annulment

The Roman Catholic Church has its own separate system of annulment. The Church does not recognize divorce. The only way to terminate a marriage (other than by death of one of the parties) is through a Church annulment. This will allow a Catholic to remarry in the church, to receive Communion, and to participate in all the other sacraments. Theoretically this participation is denied to a Catholic who remarries without obtaining a Church annulment—even if he or she obtains a civil annulment. Just as the Church does not recognize civil annulments, the state does not recognize Church annulments. The two proceedings are separate.

The Church defines an annulment as "a declaration by a competent tribunal of the Church that what had the appearance of marriage was in fact invalid according to canon law." The annulment, or *declaration of nullity,* is "granted as a result of some impediment or on various grounds related to defective consent or lack of form. The most frequent ground for marriage nullity is *defective consent,* especially lack of due discretion and lack of due competence." Huels, *The Pastoral Companion: A Canon Law Handbook for Catholic Ministry,* 259 (1986). [emphasis added] To determine whether grounds for annulment exist according to *canon law,* the following questions are critical:

> First, when [the couple] said their vows, did both partners freely accept and clearly understand the lifelong commitment they were making? And secondly, at that time, did both partners have the personal capacity to carry out consent, to form a community of life with the chosen partner? *Catholic Update,* UPD 100 (St. Anthony Messenger Press, 1980).

The annulment procedure includes a formal hearing presided over by a tribunal judge. An advocate presents the case of the petitioner seeking the annulment. Also present is a "defender of the bond" who monitors the proceeding to ensure that rights are protected and Church law properly observed. The hierarchy in Rome has criticized American bishops for allowing too many church annulments. Over 50,000 annulments are granted each year in the 119 dioceses of the United States. This constitutes 80 percent of the annulments granted by the Church worldwide.

■■■■■ CONFLICT OF LAW

The conflict of law question requires us to compare the law of two states. The law that exists where the parties were married (the *state of celebration*) must be compared with the law that exists where the parties now live (the state of **domicile** or **domiciliary state**). The question arises as follows:

> Jim and Jane marry in State X where their marriage is valid. They then move to State Y. If they had married in State Y, their marriage would not have been valid. Jim sues Jane in State Y for an annulment. What annulment law does the court in State Y apply—the law of State X or the law of State Y?

State "X" is the state of celebration or the state of contract, i.e., the state where the parties entered the marriage contract. State "Y" is the domiciliary state, i.e., the state where the parties are now domiciled. State "Y" is also called the **forum** state. In this case the domiciliary state happens to be the same as the forum state.

To place this problem in a concrete perspective, assume that Jim dies **intestate.** Assume further that he has children from a prior marriage, but had no children with his second spouse. Under the intestacy laws of most states, his spouse and children receive designated portions of his estate. If there is no spouse, the children obviously have more of an estate to share. Hence, it is in the interest of the children to claim that Jane cannot be the surviving spouse of Jim because they were never validly married. The success of this claim may depend on which law applies—that of State X or State Y.

Before examining the question of what law applies, we need to keep in mind the public policy favoring marriages. Legislatures and courts tend to look for reasons to validate a marriage, rather than to create circumstances that make it easy to invalidate it. This is all the more so if the parties have lived together for a long time and if children are in the picture. We have already seen that the law has imposed a presumption that a marriage is valid. The public policy favoring marriage, however, is not absolute. Other public policies must also be taken into account. The conflict of law rules are a product of a clash of public policies.

General Conflict of Law Rule in Annulment Actions   If the marriage is valid in the state of celebration (even though it would have been invalid if it had been contracted in the domiciliary state), the marriage will be recognized as valid in the domiciliary state *unless* the recognition of the marriage would violate some strong public policy of the domiciliary state.

Thus, in the case of Jim and Jane above, the general rule would mean that State Y would apply the law of State X unless to do so would violate some strong public policy of State Y. Assuming that no such policy would be violated, the annulment would be denied, since the marriage was valid in the state of celebration, State X. Assuming, however, that a strong public policy is involved, State Y would apply its own law and grant the annulment.

What do we mean by a strong public policy, the violation of which would cause a domiciliary state to apply its own marriage law? Some states say that if the marriage would have been *void* (as opposed to merely voidable) had it

Domicile   The place where a person has been physically present with the intent to make that place a permanent home; the place to which one intends to return when away.

Domiciliary State   The state where a person is domiciled. (This person is referred to as the domiciliary.)

Forum   (1) The place where the parties are presently litigating their dispute. (2) A court or tribunal hearing a case.

Intestate   Die without leaving a valid will.

been contracted in the domiciliary state, then the latter state will not recognize the marriage even though the state of celebration recognizes the marriage as valid. In other words, it is against the strong public policy of a domiciliary state to recognize what it considers a void marriage even though other states consider the marriage valid.

A marriage that the domiciliary state would consider bigamous or incestuous is usually not recognized. In such cases, the domiciliary state will apply its own marriage law and grant the annulment even though the marriage may have been valid in the state of celebration. When other grounds for annulment are involved, states differ as to whether they, as domiciliary states, will apply their own marriage law or that of the state of celebration.

MARRIAGE-EVASION STATUTES

Suppose that a man and woman live in a state where they cannot marry, e.g., they are underage. They move from their domiciliary state to another state *solely* for the purpose of entering or contracting a marriage since they can validly marry under the laws of the latter state, e.g., they are not underage in this state. They then move back to their domiciliary state. If an annulment action is brought in the domiciliary state, what law will be applied? The marriage law of the domiciliary state or that of the state of celebration? If the annulment action is brought in the state of celebration, what law will be applied? Again the conflict of law question becomes critical because the annulment will be granted or denied depending upon which state's marriage law governs. Note that the man and woman went to the state of celebration in order to *evade* the marriage laws of the domiciliary state. Several states have enacted *marriage-evasion* statutes to cover this situation. In such states, the choice of law depends upon the presence or absence of an intent to evade. The statute might provide that the domiciliary state will refuse to recognize the marriage if the parties went to the state of celebration for the purpose of evading the marriage laws of the domiciliary state to which they returned. It is sometimes very difficult to prove whether the parties went to the other state with the intent to evade the marriage laws of their domiciliary state. It may depend on circumstantial evidence such as how long they remained in the state of celebration, whether they returned to their initial domiciliary state or established a domicile in another state altogether. The interviewing and investigation checklist below is designed to assist you in collecting evidence on intent:

▬▬ Interviewing and Investigation Checklist

Factors Relevant to the Intent to Evade the Marriage Laws[2]

Legal Interviewing Questions

1. How long have the two of you lived in State Y?
2. Why didn't you marry in State Y?
3. When did you decide to go to State X?
4. Have you or D ever lived in State X?
5. Do you or D have any relatives in State X?
6. Were you or D born in State X?
7. On what date did you and D go to State X?
8. Did you sell your home or move out of your apartment in State Y?
9. When you left State Y, did you intend to come back?
10. After you arrived in State X, when did you apply for a marriage license?

2. See also the interviewing and investigation checklist for establishing domicile, page 208.   *—Continued*

—*Continued*

11. On what date were you married?

12. While you were in State X, where did you stay? Did you have all your clothes and furniture with you?

13. Who attended the wedding ceremony in State X?

14. Did you and D have sexual relations in State X?

15. Did you or D work in State X?

16. How long did you and D stay in State X?

17. Did you and D vote or pay taxes in State X?

18. Did you and D open a checking account in any bank in State X?

19. Where did you and D go after you left State X?

Possible Investigation Tasks

☐ Obtain copies of all records that tend to establish the kind of contact the parties had with State X, e.g., motel receipts, bank statements, rent receipts, employment records.

☐ Interview friends, relatives, and associates of the parties to determine what light they can shed on the intent of the parties in going to State X.

Thus far our main focus has been on marriages that are valid in the state of celebration but invalid and annullable in the domiciliary state if they had been contracted in the latter state (see Exhibit 5.1). Suppose, however, that the marriage was invalid in the state of celebration. The parties then move to a new state where they establish a domicile. If they had been married in their new domicile state, their marriage would have been valid. An annulment action is brought in their new domicile state (Exhibit 5.2).

Our question now becomes, if a marriage is invalid where contracted, can it ever be considered valid in any other state? Will a present domiciliary state validate a marriage that is invalid according to the law of the state of celebration? Surprisingly, the answer is often yes. In some states, a domiciliary state will deny an annulment of a marriage that would have been valid if contracted in the domiciliary state but that is clearly invalid in the state where it was actually contracted. Such states take this position, in part, because of the public policy (and indeed the presumption) favoring the validity of marriages.

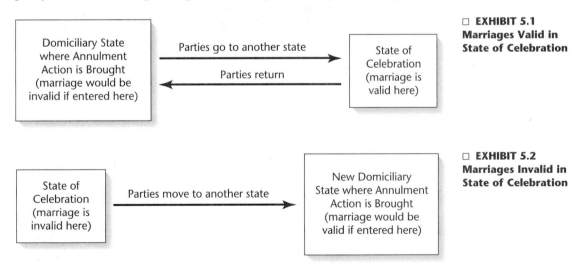

☐ **EXHIBIT 5.1**
Marriages Valid in State of Celebration

☐ **EXHIBIT 5.2**
Marriages Invalid in State of Celebration

■ CONSEQUENCES OF AN ANNULMENT DECREE

In theory, an annulled marriage never existed. The major question that always arises as a result of this theory is: What effect does the annulment have on events occurring after the "marriage"?

The old rule was that once a marriage was declared invalid, the declaration "related back" to the time the parties attempted to enter the marriage. This relation-back doctrine meant that the annulment decree was retroactive. The doctrine, when strictly applied, resulted in some very harsh consequences. Children born to parents before their marriage was annulled were, in effect, born out of wedlock and were illegitimate. Suppose that a woman lives with a man for forty years before their marriage is annulled. She would not be entitled to any alimony or support payments since a man has no duty to support someone who was never his wife! Clearly, these were unfair consequences, and all states took steps to offset them. What follows is an overview of the present law in this area.

LEGITIMACY OF CHILDREN
FROM AN ANNULLED MARRIAGE

Legitimize To formally declare that children born out of wedlock are legitimate.

With few exceptions, states have passed statutes that **legitimize** children from an annulled marriage. Some of the statutes, however, are not absolute, e.g., the statute might say that the children are legitimate only if one or both of the parents honestly believed that their marriage was valid when they entered it, or the statute might legitimize all the children born from an annulled marriage *except* when the annulment was granted on the ground of a prior existing marriage (bigamy).

ALIMONY AND DISPOSITION OF PROPERTY ACQUIRED
BEFORE THE MARRIAGE WAS ANNULLED

In some states, alimony cannot be awarded in annulment proceedings. In other states, however, statutes have been passed that allow alimony in such actions. This includes temporary alimony pending the final outcome of the action and permanent alimony following the annulment decree. It may be, however, that alimony will be denied to the "guilty" party, e.g., the party who committed the fraud or who forced the other party to enter the marriage.

Another limitation on alimony in some states is that only defendants can receive it. By definition, the plaintiff seeking the annulment is saying that no marriage ever existed. A few courts say that it is inconsistent for the plaintiff to take this position and also to ask for alimony.

Where alimony is authorized, attorney fees might also be awarded. If so, the spouse able to pay, usually the husband, must pay the fees of the attorney for the other spouse in defending or initiating the annulment action.

Suppose it is clear in a particular state that alimony cannot be awarded in the annulment action. Courts have devised various theories to provide other kinds of relief such as allowing a party to bring a suit on a theory of *quasi contract* to prevent *unjust enrichment*. Under this theory, the party may be able to recover the reasonable value of the goods and services provided during the relationship. Other theories that might allow a division of property acquired during the relationship include *partnership*, *joint venture*, and *putative spouse*. For a discussion of these theories, see chapter 3 where we discussed similar theories to obtain relief for parties who cohabited but never married.

PROBLEMS OF REVIVAL

Bob is validly married to Elaine. They go through a valid divorce proceeding, which provides that Bob will pay Elaine alimony until she remarries. One year later, Elaine marries Bill; Bob stops his alimony payments. Two years later, Elaine's marriage to Bill is annulled.

In this case, what is Bob's obligation to pay alimony to Elaine? Several possibilities exist:

☐ Bob does not have to resume paying alimony; his obligation ceased forever when Elaine married Bill; the fact that the second marriage was annulled is irrelevant.

☐ Bob does not have to resume paying alimony; *Bill* must start paying alimony if the state authorizes alimony in annulment actions.

☐ Bob must resume paying alimony from the date of the annulment decree; the annulment of the second marriage *revived* his earlier alimony obligation.

☐ Bob must resume paying alimony for the future and for the time during which Elaine was married to Bill; the annulment *revived* the original alimony obligation.

The last option is the most logical. Since the technical effect of an annulment decree is to say that the marriage never existed, this decree should be retroactive to the date when the parties entered the marriage that was later annulled. While the last option is perhaps the most logical of the four presented, it is arguably as unfair to Bob as the first option is unfair to Elaine. States take different positions on this problem. Most states, however, adopt the second or third option mentioned above.

CUSTODY AND CHILD SUPPORT

When children are involved, whether considered legitimate or not, courts will make temporary and permanent custody decisions in the annulment proceeding. Furthermore, child-support orders are inevitable when the children are minors. Hence the fact that the marriage is terminated by annulment usually has little effect on the need of the court to make custody and child-support orders (see chapters 7 and 8).

INHERITANCE

If a spouse dies **testate,** he or she can leave property to the surviving spouse. Suppose, however, that the marriage is annulled before the spouse died and that the will was never changed. In most states, an annulment (or a divorce) automatically revokes gifts to a surviving spouse unless the will specifically says otherwise.

Testate Die leaving a valid will.

Assume that one of the spouses of the annulled marriage dies *intestate.* In this event, the state's intestacy laws operate to determine who inherits the property of the deceased. The intestacy statute will usually provide that so much of the deceased's property will go to the surviving spouse, so much to the children, etc. If the marriage has already been annulled, there will be no surviving spouse to take a spouse's intestate share of the decedent's estate. An annulment (as well as a divorce) terminates mutual intestate rights between the former spouses.

SOCIAL SECURITY
AND WORKER'S COMPENSATION BENEFITS

Earlier we discussed the problem of revival in connection with alimony payments. The same problem exists with respect to certain statutory entitlement benefits. Suppose, for example, that Jane is entitled to social security or worker's compensation benefits following the death of her husband, Jim. Assume that these benefits will cease if and when she remarries. Jane then marries Tom, and the benefits stop. The marriage with Tom is subsequently annulled, however. Are the benefits now revived on the theory that Jane was never married to Tom? Case law is split on this question with some cases holding that the benefits do revive, and others concluding the opposite.

CRIMINAL LAW CONSEQUENCES

Ed marries Diane. He leaves her without obtaining a divorce. He now marries Claire. This marriage is then annulled. He is charged with the crime of bigamy. Can he use the defense that his marriage with Claire was annulled and therefore he was never married to Claire? Most of the cases that have answered this question have said that the subsequent annulment is *not* a defense to the bigamy charge.

INTERSPOUSAL IMMUNITY IN TORT ACTIONS

Interspousal Tort Immunity One spouse cannot sue another for designated torts that grow out of the marriage relationship.

As we shall see in chapter 17, spouses may have the benefit of an **interspousal tort immunity** that prevents certain kinds of tort litigation between spouses. For example, assume George assaults his wife, Paulene, in a state where the immunity applies. She would not be able to sue him for the tort of assault. (She might be able to initiate a *criminal* action against him for the crime of assault and battery, but she could not bring a *civil* assault action against him.) An annulment of the marriage would not change this result. Even if George's marriage with Paulene was later annulled, she would still not be able to bring this tort action against him for conduct that occurred while they were together. The annulment does not wipe out the impact of the interspousal tort immunity.

PRIVILEGE FOR MARITAL COMMUNICATIONS

At common law, one spouse was not allowed to give testimony concerning *confidential communications* exchanged between the spouses during the marriage. The details of this prohibition will be explained in chapter 10. For now, our question is as follows:

> Sam is married to Helen. Their marriage is annulled. A year later Sam is sued by a neighbor who claims that Sam negligently damaged the neighbor's property. The alleged damage was inflicted while Sam was still married to Helen. At the trial, the neighbor calls Helen as a witness and asks her to testify about what Sam told her concerning the incident while they were still living together. According to the privilege for marital communications, Helen would be prohibited from testifying about what she and her husband told each other during the marriage. Their marriage, however, was annulled so that in the eyes of the law they were never married. Does this change the rule on the privilege? Can Helen give this testimony?

The answer is not clear; few cases have considered the issue. Of those that have, some have concluded that the annulment does not destroy the privilege, while others have reached the opposite conclusion.

TAX RETURN STATUS

A husband and wife can file a joint return so long as they were married during the taxable year. Suppose, however, that after ten years of marriage and ten years of filing joint returns, the marriage is annulled. Must the parties now file *amended* returns for each of those ten years? Should the returns now be filed as separate returns rather than joint ones, again on the theory that the annulment meant the parties were never validly married? According to the Internal Revenue Service, Publication 504, *Tax Information for Divorced or Separated Individuals*, p. 1 (1990 Edition):

> You are considered unmarried for the whole year [if you have] . . . obtained a decree of annulment which holds that no valid marriage ever existed. You also must file amended returns claiming an unmarried status for all tax years affected by the annulment not closed by the [three year] statute of limitations.

■■■■■ SUMMARY

A divorce is a termination of a valid marriage. An annulment is an acknowledgment that the parties were never married, whether they lived together (and acted as if they were married) for thirty minutes or for thirty years after the "marriage" ceremony. To obtain an annulment, a party must establish grounds, and must have standing. Two categories of grounds exist: grounds relating to the legal capacity to marry, and grounds relating to the intent to marry. Some of these grounds will render the marriage void, while others will render it voidable.

There are four grounds relating to the legal capacity to marry:

1. *Prior existing marriage.* At the time of the marriage, a prior marriage had not been terminated.

2. *Consanguinity and affinity.* The parties married in violation of a prohibition against the marriage of certain individuals who are already related to each other.

3. *Nonage.* A party was underage at the time of the marriage.

4. *Physical disabilities.* A party had a specified disease or was impotent at the time of the marriage.

There are four grounds relating to the intent to marry:

1. *Sham marriage.* The parties never intended to live together as husband and wife.

2. *Mental disability.* At the time of the marriage, a party was incapable of understanding the nature of the marriage relationship.

3. *Duress.* A party was forced into the marriage.

4. *Fraud.* A party intentionally misrepresented or concealed certain facts from the other party that were either essential to the marriage or were material to the decision to enter the marriage.

Under conflict of law principles:

1. A marriage will be considered valid in a domiciliary state if (a) the marriage is valid according to the state where it was contracted, and (b) recognizing the validity of the marriage would not violate any strong public policy of the domiciliary state. If both conditions are met, the domiciliary state will deny the annulment even though the marriage could have been annulled if it had been contracted in the domiciliary state.

2. Generally, if a marriage would have been void had it been contracted in the domiciliary state, the latter state will not apply the law of the state of celebration where the marriage is valid.

3. Some states have statutes that invalidate marriages contracted in other states solely to evade the domiciliary state's marriage laws.

4. Some states have statutes that invalidate marriages contracted in their own state solely to evade the marriage laws of other states.

5. Some states will validate a marriage contracted in another state (even though the marriage is invalid in the state where it was contracted) so long as the marriage would have been valid if it had been contracted in the state where the parties are now domiciled. In effect, this state will deny the annulment even though the state of celebration would have granted it.

In an annulment proceeding, the court must award custody of the children and provide for their support. Children born from an annulled marriage are usually considered legitimate. If the state does not allow alimony, the court may use a theory such as quasi contract to divide property acquired during the time the parties were together.

Suppose a divorced spouse remarries and thereby loses certain benefits granted by the divorce. But the second marriage is annulled. States do not always agree on whether the divorce benefits are revived. Revival issues might also arise in cases that involve inheritance, bigamy, tort liability, evidence, and income tax status.

◼◼◼ KEY CHAPTER TERMINOLOGY

Annulment

Divorce

Legal Separation

Voidable Marriage

Void Marriage

Void ab Initio

Standing

Estopped

Dirty Hands

Grounds

Bigamy

Polygamy

Enoch Arden Defense

Rebuttable Presumption

Consanguinity

Affinity

Incest

Nonage

Ratified

Impotence

Copulate

Sterility

Laches

Sham

Consummate

Cohabitation

Lucid Interval

Duress

Fraud

Essentials Test

Materiality Test

Domicile

Domiciliary State

Forum

Intestate

Legitimize

Testate

Interspousal Tort Immunity

SEPARATION AGREEMENTS: LEGAL ISSUES AND DRAFTING OPTIONS

Chapter 6 begins our comprehensive study of the separation agreement. Parts of chapter 7 (on child custody), chapter 8 (on child support), and chapter 11 (on taxation) also cover important dimensions of the separation agreement. Chapter 6, however, examines the document as a whole, setting the stage for the other chapters. Our focus throughout will be on the nature of the separation agreement, the drafting options available, and the response of a court *when the parties are not able to reach an agreement.*

▅▅▅▅ SEPARATION AGREEMENTS AND LITIGATION

The negotiation and drafting of the **separation agreement** are among the most important and difficult tasks of the family law practitioner. (For an overview of the kinds of agreements parties can enter before and during marriage, see Exhibit 3.1 in chapter 3.) Generally, a divorce is contemplated by both parties when they enter a separation agreement. This, however, is not always the

Separation Agreement
A contract by two married individuals who have separated or are about to separate that covers support, custody, property division, and other terms of their separation.

case. Occasionally, separation agreements are written by parties who never divorce and hence never remarry.

Separation agreements find their way into court in the following kinds of situations:

☐ One party sues the other for breach of contract, i.e., for violation of the separation agreement; the plaintiff in this suit wants the separation agreement enforced.

☐ The parties file for a divorce and ask the court either (1) to approve the terms of the separation agreement or (2) to approve the terms *and* to incorporate them into the divorce decree so that the decree and the agreement become merged.

☐ After the divorce, one of the parties brings a suit to set aside the separation agreement, e.g., because it was induced by fraud.

The law encourages parties to enter separation agreements. So long as certain basic public policies (to be discussed below) are not violated, the law gives a great deal of leeway to the parties to resolve their difficulties and, in effect, to decide what their relationship will be on such vital matters as alimony, property division, custody and visitation of the children, etc. The role of the lawyer and paralegal is to assist the client in this large endeavor.

A high priority of the family law practitioner must always be to avoid litigation, since it is often extremely time-consuming, expensive, and emotionally draining on everyone involved. The marital breakdown of the parties was probably a most painful experience for the entire family. Litigation tends to remind the parties of old sores and to keep the bitterness alive. While a separation agreement will not guarantee harmony between the spouses, it can help keep their disputes on a constructive level.

■■■■ NEGOTIATION FACTORS

An effective separation agreement is achieved through bargaining or negotiation by the parties on their own or, more commonly, through lawyers representing them. What is an effective, separation agreement? Obviously, this will vary according to individual circumstances. Nevertheless, some general observations can be made about the characteristics of an effective separation agreement:

■■■■ Characteristics of an Effective Separation Agreement

1. *Comprehensive.* It covers all major matters. Should a problem arise months or years later, the parties will not have to say, "We never thought of that when we drafted the agreement."

2. *Fair.* If the agreement is not fair to both sides, it may be unworkable, which will force the parties into expensive and potentially bitter litigation. Hence the worst kind of legal assistance a law office can provide is to "outsmart" the other side into "giving up" almost everything. Little is accomplished by winning the war, but losing the peace. "You gain no advantage in depriving your ex-spouse of what he/she is entitled to. Remember, your ex-spouse has the ability to make your life miser-

able." Mississippi State Bar, Family Law Section, *Consumers Guide to Divorce,* 4 (1990).

3. *Accurate.* The agreement should accurately reflect the intentions of the parties. What they orally agreed to do in formal or informal bargaining sessions should be stated in the written agreement.

4. *Legal.* Certain things can and cannot be done in a separation agreement; the agreement must not attempt to do anything that is illegal.

5. *Readable.* The agreement should be written in language that the parties can understand without having to hire or rehire an attorney every time a question arises.

▬▬▬ CHECKLISTS FOR THE PREPARATION OF A SEPARATION AGREEMENT

Before an intelligent separation agreement can be drafted, a great deal of information is needed. First of all, a series of detailed lists should be compiled on the following items:

□ All prior agreements between husband and wife, e.g., antenuptial agreement, loan agreement

□ All property held by the husband in his separate name

□ All property held by the wife in her separate name

□ All property in one person's name that really "belongs" to the other

□ All property held jointly—in both names

□ All property acquired during the marriage

□ All contracts during the marriage for the sale of real property

□ All insurance policies currently in force

□ All debts currently outstanding, with an indication of who incurred each one

□ All income from any source earned by the husband

□ All income from any source earned by the wife

□ Projected future income of both parties, e.g., salary, dividends, interest, pension rights, royalties, loans that will be repaid, future trust income, expected inheritance

□ All present and projected living expenses of the husband

□ All present and projected living expenses of the wife

□ All present and projected living expenses of the children

In addition to such lists, the following data should be collected:

□ Names and addresses of both spouses and of the children

□ Data on all prior litigation, if any, between the parties

□ Name and address of present attorney of other spouse

□ Names and addresses of prior attorneys, if any, retained by either party

□ Copies of tax returns filed in prior five years

□ Character references (if needed on questions of custody or credibility)

□ Names and addresses of individuals who might serve as arbitrators or mediators

□ Documentation of prior indebtedness

□ Copy of will(s) currently in force, if any

The interrogatories in the next section focus on obtaining information from the *opposing* spouse and are also designed to identify critical information needed to negotiate and draft a separation agreement.

Here is a checklist covering individual clauses of a separation agreement. The checklist is an overview of topics that need to be considered by the parties and that we will consider in chapters 6, 7, 8, and 11. Some of the headings in the checklist are commonly used in the separation agreement itself.

1. *Alimony:*

□ Who pays

□ How much

- ☐ Method of payment
- ☐ Frequency of payment
- ☐ Whether it terminates on the remarriage or the death of either spouse
- ☐ Whether it fluctuates with income of payor
- ☐ Whether it is modifiable
- ☐ Security for payment
- ☐ Method of enforcement
- ☐ Tax consequences

2. *Child support:*
   - ☐ Who pays
   - ☐ How much (check the mandatory child support guidelines)
   - ☐ Whether amount of child support is modifiable
   - ☐ Method of payment
   - ☐ Security for payment
   - ☐ Frequency of payment
   - ☐ Whether it terminates when a child reaches a certain age
   - ☐ Whether it terminates if the child is otherwise emancipated
   - ☐ Day care expenses
   - ☐ Education expenses covering private schools, college, etc.
   - ☐ Tax consequences

3. *Custody:*
   - ☐ Which parent obtains custody and what kind, e.g., sole custody, joint custody, split custody
   - ☐ Visitation rights of noncustodial parent
   - ☐ Visitation rights of others, e.g., grandparent
   - ☐ Summer vacations and special holidays
   - ☐ Transportation expenses
   - ☐ Permissible removal of child from the state on a temporary or permanent basis
   - ☐ Changing the last name of the child
   - ☐ Consultation on all major

educational and medical decisions
   - ☐ The child's participation in religious activity

4. *Health expenses (custodial parent and children):*
   - ☐ Medical
   - ☐ Dental
   - ☐ Drugs
   - ☐ Special needs
   - ☐ Expenses that are not covered by insurance

5. *Insurance:*
   - ☐ Life
   - ☐ Health
   - ☐ Automobile
   - ☐ Disability
   - ☐ Homeowner's

6. *Estate documents:*
   - ☐ Wills that are already in existence (individual or mutual)
   - ☐ Changes to be made in existing wills
   - ☐ Trust accounts for children

7. *Debts still to be paid:*
   - ☐ Incurred by whom
   - ☐ Who pays

8. *Inventory of personal property:*
   - ☐ Cash
   - ☐ Joint and separate bank accounts (savings, checking, certificates of deposit, etc.)
   - ☐ Stocks, bonds, and other kinds of securities
   - ☐ Motor vehicles
   - ☐ Art works
   - ☐ Household furniture
   - ☐ Jewelry
   - ☐ Rights to receive money in the future, e.g., retirement pay, stock options, royalties, rents, court judgment awards

9. *Inventory of real property:*
   - ☐ Residence
   - ☐ Vacation home
   - ☐ Business real estate

☐ Tax shelters

☐ Leases

10. *Income tax returns*

11. *Attorney fees and court costs*

12. *Incorporation of separation agreement into divorce decree (merger)*

13. *Arbitration*

14. *What happens to agreement if parties reconcile*

■ UNCOVERING FINANCIAL ASSETS: INTERROGATORIES

Gaining access to all the personal and financial information needed to negotiate a separation agreement or to prepare for trial is not always easy. In fact, one of the major reasons separation agreements are later challenged is that one of the parties did not have or was not given a complete inventory of the other spouse's financial assets before signing. Later, in chapter 10, we will examine discovery devices that are designed to obtain this kind of information. One of the devices is **interrogatories,** which can be particularly effective when seeking financial assets.

The comprehensive set of interrogatories in Exhibit 6.1 are part of a law office's strategy to uncover facts. Reading them will give you a good idea of the kind of information that is the foundation of effective negotiation and drafting of a separation agreement. Without answers to these questions *prior* to negotiation, an attorney would, in most cases, be unable to negotiate and draft the agreement competently.

Interrogatories A written set of factual questions sent by one party to another before a trial begins.

■ THE BEGINNING OF THE SEPARATION AGREEMENT

On the assumption that the law firm now has a comprehensive picture of the assets of the client and of the opposing spouse (see interrogatories in Exhibit 6.1), we turn to the separation agreement itself.

Exhibit 6.2 on page 97 presents some sample introductory clauses often found in separation agreements. It is good practice in the drafting of a separation agreement to number each paragraph separately (1, 2, 3, etc.) after the introductory clauses, and to use headings for each major topic, e.g., alimony, custody.

A number of issues relating to the introductory clauses in Exhibit 6.2 need to be discussed:

☐ **Public policy and collusion**

☐ **Capacity to contract**

☐ **Duress and fraud**

☐ **Consideration**

PUBLIC POLICY AND COLLUSION

The agreement in Exhibit 6.2 on page 97 between Fred and Linda Jones is careful to point out that a separation has already occurred. When parties are still living together despite their decision to separate, the law operates on the assumption that there is still hope. By definition, a separation agreement attempts to provide *benefits* to the parties in the form of money, freedom, etc. The very existence of such an agreement is viewed as an *inducement* to obtain a divorce unless the parties have already separated or are about to do so shortly. A separation agreement between two parties who are still living together and

(text continues on page 96)

☐ **EXHIBIT 6.1   Interrogatories**

The plaintiff, requests that the defendant answer under oath, in accordance with Section _____ , the following interrogatories:

NOTE: Questions concerning marriage and children pertain to the other party to this suit, unless otherwise indicated. Where a question or part of a question is inapplicable, indicate same.

1. State your full name, age, residence and post office address, home telephone number, social security number, business addresses and business phone numbers.

2. State:
    (a) The names, birth dates and present addresses of all children born or adopted during the marriage, indicating whether any children are emancipated, and who has legal custody of each unemancipated child.
    (b) Whether any dependent child is in need of unusual or extraordinary medical or mental care or has special financial needs, giving a detailed description of the condition which requires such care and the treatment required, to the best of your knowledge, including, but not limited to:
        (i)   Nature of treatment;
        (ii)   Name of treating doctors and/or other professionals;
        (iii) Cost of care; and
        (iv)   Estimated length of treatment.

3. As to yourself state:
    (a) Your present health;
    (b) Whether you have any need of unusual or extraordinary medical care or special financial needs;
    (c) Educational background, giving all schools attended and years of attendance, any degrees conferred, as well as any special training courses and employment skills;
    (d) If you were married at the time you attended school or any special training course, indicate whether your spouse contributed to the cost of your education and/or support and living expenses and the amount thereof, and, if your spouse did not contribute to these, who paid for your education and/or support and living expenses;
    (e) If you own or have been granted a license to practice any profession or other occupation in this or any other state, indicate the nature of such license(s) and the approximate monetary value of each license.

4. If you have any disability(ies) which at any time renders or rendered you unable to perform work or limits or limited your ability to perform work, either now, in the past, or in the future, state:
    (a) The nature of the disability(ies);
    (b) The name and address of each treating physician for the past ten years for said disability(ies);
    (c) The frequency of said treatment;
    (d) The cost of said treatment;
    (e) The nature of said treatment;
    (f) The method of payment for said treatment, including the name of the payor.
        *Attach any medical reports concerning the disability(ies).

PRIMARY AND MARITAL RESIDENCES

5. State your primary residence addresses for the past five (5) years, up to the present time, indicating periods of residence at each address.

6. If you are not currently residing with your spouse, state the names, ages and relationship to you of those persons with whom you reside at the above address, either on a permanent or periodic basis.

7. If your primary residence is rented or leased, state:
    (a) The monthly rental and term of the lease or agreement;
    (b) To whom the rental is paid, including name and address;
    (c) Whether any other persons are contributing to rental payments, the amount of the contribution, and the names of any such persons.
        *Attach copies of cancelled rent checks for the last twelve (12) months and a copy of your lease or rental agreement.

8. If your present primary residence is owned by you, state:
    (a) The date the residence was acquired;
    (b) From whom it was purchased;
    (c) The purchase price;
    (d) The amount of the downpayment;

Continued

☐ **EXHIBIT 6.1** Interrogatories—*Continued*

(e) The source of the downpayment, showing contribution by both spouses, as well as any other persons;

(f) The amount of the original mortgage(s);

(g) The amount of the mortgage(s) as of the date of the separation of the parties;

(h) The amount of the mortgage(s) at the present time if different from (f) or (g) above;

(i) The name and address of the mortgagee(s) and the mortgage number(s), if any;

(j) The market value of the property at the time of the separation of the parties;

(k) The present market value of the property, if different from (j) above;

(l) The tax basis of the property when acquired;

(m) The adjusted tax basis of the property at the time of the separation of the parties;

(n) The current adjusted tax basis, if different from your answer to (m) above;

(o) The nature and dollar amount of any liens or other encumbrances on the property not indicated in previous answers;

(p) The current assessed valuation assigned the property for real property taxation purposes.

*Attach copies of closing statements, deeds, appraisals, as well as the most recent bill or bills for real estate taxes.

9. If the residence referred to in question 8 above is not the "marital residence," then supply the same information as requested in questions 8(a) through 8(p) above for the "marital residence."

*Attach copies of closing statements, deeds, appraisals, as well as the most recent bill or bills for real estate taxes.

10. Who has been paying the mortgage and/or tax payments from the date of the separation of the parties?

OTHER REAL ESTATE

11. If you have an interest in any real property other than indicated in the previous section, for each such piece of real property, state:

(a) Street address, county, and state where the property is located;

(b) Type of property, deed references, and the nature of your interest in the property (full or partial; type of tenancy; restraints on alienation);

(c) Zoning of the property;

(d) Date property was acquired;

(e) From whom it was purchased;

(f) The amount of the downpayment;

(g) The source of the downpayment, showing the contribution of both spouses and others;

(h) The amount of the original mortgage(s);

(i) The purchase price;

(j) The amount of the mortgage(s) as of the date of the separation of the parties;

(k) The amount of the present mortgage(s);

(l) The name and address of the mortgagee(s) and the mortgage number(s), if any;

(m) The present market value of the property;

(n) The nature and dollar amount of any liens or other encumbrances on the property that are not listed in a previous answer;

(o) The names and addresses of all co-owners and the nature of their interest in the property;

(p) Itemize all operation expenses, including but not limited to taxes, mortgage payments, insurance, fuel oil, gas, electric, water and maintenance;

(q) The present assessed valuation assigned the property for real property taxation purposes;

(r) The exact nature and extent of your interest, if not listed in question 11(b);

(s) The tax basis of the property when acquired;

(t) The adjusted tax basis at the time of the separation of the parties;

(u) The names and mailing addresses of all tenants and occupants and the annual and/or monthly rental paid by each, and their relationship to you (e.g., relative, friend) if any;

(v) The source and amount of any income produced by the property, if not previously indicated.

*Attach copies of the closing statements, deeds, and appraisals.

12. If you have sold or otherwise disposed of any real property in which you have had an interest within the last ten (10) years, state for each property, in detail, the same information as asked in interrogatory 11 above.

*Attach copies of each closing statement and deed.

Continued

☐ **EXHIBIT 6.1 Interrogatories—*Continued***

13. If you have executed any contracts to buy or sell real property within the last ten (10) years, indicate the location of the property, terms of the sale, and whether you were the purchaser or seller, and the name of the other party or parties.

　　*Attach a copy of each such contract.

14. If you are the holder of an interest in any real property not disclosed in a previous interrogatory, state for each:
    (a) The type of such property (whether real or personal);
    (b) The location of such property;
    (c) The date acquired;
    (d) The net monthly rental to you from each piece of property;
    (e) The gross monthly rental to you from each piece of property;
    (f) The present value of such property.

INCOME AND EMPLOYMENT

15. State the names, addresses, and telephone numbers of all employers for the last ten (10) years and give the dates of such employment, position held, salary, other compensation, and reason for termination.

16. As to your present employment, state:
    (a) Name and address of your employer;
    (b) Type of work performed, position held, and nature of work or business in which your employer is engaged;
    (c) Amount of time you have been employed in your present job;
    (d) Hours of employment;
    (e) Rate of pay or earnings, gross and net average weekly salary, wages, commissions, overtime pay, bonuses, and gratuities.

    　　*Attach copies of all evidence of above payments, including pay stubs, W-2 forms, etc. for the past twelve months.

17. State what benefits your employer provides for you and/or your family inclusive but not limited to all of the following. Include a brief description of the benefit and whether your family is a beneficiary of the particular benefit:
    (a) Health insurance plan;
    (b) Life insurance;
    (c) Pension, profit sharing, or retirement income program;
    (d) Expense and/or drawing accounts;
    (e) Credit cards (include reimbursement for business expenses placed on your personal credit cards);
    (f) Disability insurance;
    (g) Stock purchase options;
    (h) Indicate whether you are required to pay for all or any part of the benefits listed in this interrogatory and the amount of those payments and/or contributions.

18. If you are furnished with a vehicle by any person, employer, or other entity, state:
    (a) The year, make, model, and license number;
    (b) The name and address of the legal owner;
    (c) The name and address of the registered owner;
    (d) The date you were furnished with such vehicle or replacement vehicle;
    (e) The amount paid for gas, repairs, maintenance, and insurance costs by you personally and by anyone other than yourself. Indicate whether you are reimbursed directly or indirectly for the expenses paid by you personally.

    　　*If this vehicle is leased, attach a copy of said lease.

19. Describe any other property or other benefit furnished to you as a result of your present employment.

20. State and itemize all deductions taken from your gross weekly earnings or other emoluments, including but not limited to taxes, insurance, savings, loans, pensions, profit sharing, dues, and stock options.

21. State if you have an employment contract with any company, corporation, partnership, and/or individual at the present time or at any time during the last three (3) years. If there is or was such a contract of employment, state the terms thereof, or if written, attach a copy hereto.

Continued

22. As a result of your employment at any time during the marriage, are you entitled to receive any monies from any deferred compensation agreement? If so, for each agreement state:
    (a) The date such agreement was made, or if in writing, executed. If written, attach a copy.
    (b) The parties making or executing such agreement.
    (c) The amount you are to receive under such deferred compensation agreement and when you are to receive same. Attach copies of evidence of such payment.

23. State whether you have filed federal, state, and/or local income tax returns during the last five (5) years. If so, indicate the years during which they were filed and whether federal, state, or local.
    *Attach copies of all returns filed during the past five (5) years.

24. State in which bank savings account or checking account your salary, bonus, or other compensation is deposited, giving the name of the bank, branch, and account number. If said salary, bonus, or other compensation checks are cashed or negotiated rather than deposited, indicate the name and branch of the bank(s) or other institutions where said checks are regularly cashed or negotiated.

25. State whether you have received or are receiving any form of compensation, monetary or otherwise, from any work and/or services performed for other individuals, companies, corporations, and/or partnerships outside the business in which you are regularly engaged. If so, state:
    (a) The name and address of the individual, company, corporation, and/or partnership from whom you are receiving or have received such compensation during the last five (5) years;
    (b) The amount of the compensation received;
    (c) The nature of the services rendered by you for said compensation.
    *Attach copies of all 1099 forms covering "miscellaneous income" received as a result of such work and/or services during the last five (5) years.

26. State whether your salary or other compensation will increase during the next year and/or contract period as a result of any union contract and/or employment contract, or as the result of any regular incremental increase, or as a result of a promotion you have received that is not yet effective.

27. Itemize all income benefits and other emoluments not already included in your answers to the preceding interrogatories, including but not limited to any other sources of income such as pensions, annuities, inheritances, retirement plans, social security benefits, military and/or veteran's benefits, lottery prizes, bank interest, dividends, showing the source, amount, and frequency of payment of each. Indicate whether each income benefit and/or other emolument is taxable or nontaxable.

SELF-EMPLOYMENT

28. If you are self-employed or conduct a business or profession as a sole proprietor, partner, or corporation, state the type of entity it is. (For purposes of this question, a corporation includes any corporation in which your interest exceeds twenty percent (20%) of the outstanding stock).

29. If a partnership, list the names and addresses of all partners, their relationship to you, and the extent of their interest and yours in the partnership.
    *Attach copies of any partnership agreements in effect at any time during the last five (5) years and all partnership tax returns filed during this period.

30. If a corporation, list the names and addresses of all directors, officers, and shareholders and the percentage of outstanding shares held by each. If any of the foregoing people are related to you, indicate the relationship.
    *Attach copies of all corporate tax returns filed by the corporation during the past five (5) years.

31. State whether you have had an ownership interest(s) in any other corporation, partnership, proprietorship, limited venture, or other business during the course of the marriage. If so, state:
    (a) The nature of such interest(s);
    (b) The market value of such interest(s);
    (c) The position held by you with respect to such interest(s) including whether you were an officer, director, partner, etc.;
    (d) The date of acquisition of your interest(s) and the market value of said interest(s) when acquired;
    (e) The value of said interest(s) on the date of your marriage if such interest(s) were acquired before your marriage;
    (f) The date of termination of your ownership interest, if terminated;

Continued

□ **EXHIBIT 6.1   Interrogatories—*Continued***

(g) The total sale price of the business enterprise, if sold or transferred;

(h) The amount of the compensation received by you and the form of the compensation if other than cash or negotiable instrument as a result of the sale or transfer;

(i) The terms of each agreement of sale or transfer;

(j) The income received by you from the business during the last year prior to the sale or transfer.

32. State for each business, partnership, corporation, or other business entity in which you have an interest, the following:

   (a) The amount of your contribution to the original capitalization;

   (b) The amount of your contribution for any additional capitalization or loans to the business entity;

   (c) The source from which monies were taken for capitalization and/or loans;

   (d) The market value of the business entity at the time of the separation of the parties;

   (e) The present market value of the business entity if different than (d) above;

   (f) The market value of your share of the business entity at the time the separation of the parties if different than (d) above;

   (g) The present market value of your share of the business entity if different than (f) above;

   (h) The market value of your share of the total value of the business entity at the time of your marriage;

   (i) Amount of loans and/or reimbursement of capitalization paid you by the business entity at any time during the past five (5) years; indicate the amount received, the date received, and the disposition of the proceeds;

   (j) The present amount maintained in the capital account;

   (k) The name and address of all banks or other institutions in which the business entity has or has had, during the past five (5) years, checking, savings, or other accounts, the account numbers of each account, the amount presently contained in each, the amount contained in each at the time of the separation of the parties, and the amount contained in each six (6) months prior to the separation of the parties. If an account was closed prior to the time periods mentioned in this question, that is, prior to six (6) months before the separation of the parties, indicate the amounts in each such account for a three (3) year period prior to the closing account. State the destination of the amount in the account when closed;

   (l) The total value of your capital account;

   (m) The total value of all accounts receivable;

   (n) The dollar value of all work in progress;

   (o) The appreciation in the true worth of all tangible personal assets over and above book value;

   (p) The total dollar amount of accounts payable;

   (q) A list of all liabilities.

33. State the name and address of the following:

   (a) All personal and business accountants consulted during the last five (5) years;

   (b) All personal, business, or corporate attorneys consulted during the past five (5) years;

   (c) Your stockbroker(s);

   (d) Your investment advisor(s).

PERSONAL ASSETS

34. Itemize all accounts in banks or other institutions, time deposits, certificates of deposit, savings clubs, Christmas clubs, and checking accounts in your name or in which you have an interest presently or have had an interest during the past five (5) years, stating for each:

   (a) The name and address of each depository;

   (b) The balance in those accounts as of the date of the separation of the parties;

   (c) The present balance;

   (d) The balance four (4) months prior to the separation of the parties;

   (e) If there is any difference between your answers to (b), (c), and (d) above, specify when the withdrawals were made, who received the benefit of the withdrawals, who made the withdrawal, and where the proceeds of the withdrawals went;

   (f) The name and address in which each account is registered, account numbers, and the present location and custodian of the deposit books, check registers, and certificates.

   *Attach copies of the monthly statements of such accounts for the past five (5) years and copies of savings account books or savings books and check registers.

Continued

35. State whether you have a safe deposit box either in your name individually, or in the name of a partnership, corporation, or other business entity to which you have access, stating the following:
    (a) The location of the box and box number.
    (b) The name in which it is registered and who, in addition to yourself, has access to the box;
    (c) List the contents of said box in which you claim an interest.

36. If you have any cash in your possession or under your control in excess of one hundred dollars ($100), specify:
    (a) The amount of the cash;
    (b) Where it is located;
    (c) The source of said cash.

37. For each vehicle of any nature in which you have any interest, including, but not limited to, automobiles, trucks, campers, mobile homes, motorcycles, snowmobiles, boats, and airplanes, state:
    (a) The nature of each vehicle;
    (b) Your interest therein;
    (c) The name in which the vehicle is registered;
    (d) The make, model, and year of each;
    (e) The price paid, the date acquired, and the source of the funds used;
    (f) The principal operator of the vehicle since its purchase;
    (g) The present location of the vehicle;
    (h) The name and address of any co-owners;
    (i) The present value of the vehicle.

38. State whether you own any horses or other animals with a value in excess of two hundred fifty dollars ($250). If so, state:
    (a) The date of purchase, the purchase price, and the source of the funds used;
    (b) The type of animals;
    (c) The market value of the animals at the time of the separation of the parties;
    (d) Their present market value if different from (c);
    (e) The names and addresses of any co-owners and the percentage of their interest.

39. List all household goods, furniture, jewelry, and furs with a value in excess of two hundred fifty dollars ($250), in which you have an interest, stating for each:
    (a) The nature of each;
    (b) Your interest therein;
    (c) The price paid, the date acquired, and the source of the funds used;
    (d) The present value of the asset;
    (e) Whether the asset is "marital property," "separate property," or "community property." If you claim the asset is separate property, state your reasons therefor.

40. State whether you own or have an interest in any collections or hobbies, including but not limited to art, stamps, coins, precious metals, antiques, books, and collectibles with an aggregate value in excess of two hundred fifty dollars ($250). If so, state:
    (a) The nature of each;
    (b) Your interest therein and the interest of any co-owners. Also state the names and addresses of all co-owners and their relationship to you;
    (c) A complete itemization of each such collection, showing the price paid, the date acquired, and the source of the funds used;
    (d) The present value of each element of the asset (an "element" means a unit capable of being sold by itself);
    (e) If owned prior to the marriage, the value of each such element at the time of the marriage.

41. State whether you are receiving or are entitled to receive any royalty income. If so, state:
    (a) The basis for such income, including the nature of any composition, copyright, work, or patent from which such income arose;
    (b) The amount of such income during the past five (5) years;
    (c) The terms of any agreement in relation to such composition, copyright, work, or patent.
    *Attach copies of any royalty statement or other invoice verifying such income.

42. State whether you have any legal actions pending for money damages, or whether you are entitled to receive any legal settlements or insurance recoveries. If so, state:
    (a) The amount of money you are demanding in your pleadings, or to which you are entitled as an insurance recovery or legal settlement;

Continued

☐ **EXHIBIT 6.1 Interrogatories—*Continued***

(b) The court in which the action is or was pending, the caption of the case, and the index or docket number;

(c) Whether any other person has an interest in the insurance recovery, legal settlement, or pending action and, if so, state their name, address, and the nature of their interest;

(d) The circumstances resulting in your becoming entitled to the insurance recovery or legal settlement, or the circumstances leading to the commencement of the legal action.

43. State whether you have any HR10 or IRA arrangements. If so, state:
(a) The date of the creation of each such plan;
(b) The amounts contributed by you or on your behalf to each such plan;
(c) The current value of your account under each such plan.

44. State whether you are entitled to receive, or have received during the past five (5) years any gambling awards or prizes, indicating the nature thereof, the amount, when you are to receive the same, and the date you became entitled to the award or prize.

45. State the names and addresses of all persons who owe you money if not indicated in previous interrogatories. Also state as to each:
(a) The amount thereof;
(b) When said sum is due;
(c) The nature of the transaction that entitled you to receive the money and when the transaction took place.

STOCK ASSETS

46. Itemize all shares of stock, securities, bonds, mortgages, and other investments, other than real estate revealed in previous interrogatories, stating for each:
(a) Identity of each item indicating the type and amount of shares;
(b) Whose name they are registered in, the names of any co-owners, their interest therein, and their relationship to you;
(c) The source of the monies from which you purchased the item;
(d) The original price of each item;
(e) The market value at the time of the separation of the parties;
(f) The present market value of each item if different from (e) above;
(g) The amount of any dividends or other distribution received;
(h) The present location and custodian of all certificates or evidences of such investments.
*Attach hereto monthly statements of these securities for the past five (5) years.

47. State whether any of the shares of stock owned by you and listed in any of your previous answers to interrogatories is subject to any cross purchase or redemption agreement. If so, state:
(a) The date of such agreements;
(b) The parties to such agreements;
(c) The event that will bring about the sale or transfer under the agreement;
(d) The sale price under the agreement.

48. Itemize all shares of stock, securities, bonds, mortgages, and other investments, other than real estate and business entities previously listed in your name or in which you have an interest, which you have sold in the last five (5) years, stating for each:
(a) The identity of each item indicating the type and amount of shares;
(b) Whose name they were registered in, including the names of any co-owners, their interest therein, and their relationship to you;
(c) The source of the monies from which you purchased each item;
(d) The original price of each item and date of purchase;
(e) The market value at the time of the separation of the parties;
(f) The amount of dividends or other distribution received;
(g) The date each was sold or transferred;
(h) To whom each was sold or transferred;
(i) The amount received for each such sale or transfer;
(j) The disposition and destination of the proceeds of said sale;
(k) If applicable, the value of each such item at the time of your marriage.

49. Itemize all shares of stock, securities, bonds, mortgages, and other investments purchased by you but held nominally by third persons, stating for each:
(a) The manner in which the person is holding said investment;

Continued

(b) The identity of each item as to type and amount of shares;

(c) Whose name they are registered in, including the names of any co-owners, their interest therein, and their relationship to you;

(d) The source of the monies from which you purchased each item;

(e) The original price of each item;

(f) The market value at the time of the separation of the parties;

(g) The present market value of each item;

(h) The value, if applicable, at the time of your marriage;

(i) The present location and custodian of all certificates or evidence of such investments;

(j) The amount of dividends or other distribution received.

*Attach hereto monthly statements of these securities for the past three (3) years.

50. Are you the holder of any mortgages, accounts receivable, notes, or other evidence of indebtedness not indicated in your answer to previous interrogatories? If so, for each such instrument, state:

(a) The type of instrument;

(b) The date of maturity of such instrument;

(c) The amount of interest payable to you under such instrument;

(d) The nature of the sale or transaction (including the type of merchandise sold) from which the said instrument arose;

(e) The date the instrument was acquired by you.

51. State whether you have any money invested in any business ventures not answered in previous interrogatories. For each such investment, state:

(a) The nature of such investment;

(b) Your share of the interest therein;

(c) The original cost of such investment and the source of monies used for said investment;

(d) The amount of income yielded from the said investment;

(e) The present value of said investment.

52. If, during the course of your marriage, you have received any inheritances, state:

(a) From whom you inherited;

(b) The nature and amount of the inheritance;

(c) The disposition of any of the assets of the inheritance, tracing them to the time of the separation of the parties;

(d) The value of the inheritance at the time of the separation of the parties;

(e) The present value of the inheritance.

53. State whether you expect to receive any future inheritances. If so, state:

(a) From whom you expect to inherit;

(b) The nature and amount of inheritance.

54. State whether you have, during the last five (5) years, sold or transferred any interest in personal property valued in excess of two hundred fifty dollars ($250), and for each such sale or transfer, state:

(a) The nature of the property;

(b) The date of the sale or transfer;

(c) The method of transfer;

(d) The name and address of each purchaser or person receiving title;

(e) The amount received for said transfer or sale;

(f) The disposition of the proceeds of said sale or transfer.

55. State whether you have made any gift of any money or other personal property to friends, relatives, or anyone else during the past five (5) years of a value in excess of two hundred fifty dollars ($250). If so, state:

(a) The name and address of said person and the relationship of that person to you;

(b) The nature and value of the gift or the amount of money given;

(c) The date each gift was given;

(d) The reason for such gift.

TRUSTS

56. State whether you are the grantor, beneficiary, or holder of a power of appointment for any trust created by you, the members of your family, or any other persons or corporations. If so, state:

Continued

□ **EXHIBIT 6.1 Interrogatories—*Continued***

(a) The date of the trust instrument;

(b) The name of the settlor of each trust;

(c) The name of the beneficiary(ies) of each trust;

(d) The present amount of each trust corpus;

(e) The amount of the trust corpus at the time of the separation of the parties;

(f) The amount of the trust corpus at the time of your marriage, if applicable.

(g) Any restrictions on alienation to which such corpus is subject;

(h) The terms of each trust instrument;

(i) The income earned by the trust during the past five (5) years.

   *If there is a trust instrument, attach a copy hereto. If the trustee has rendered an accounting during the past five (5) years attach a copy hereto.

57. List any and all property, assets, or other things of a value in excess of two hundred fifty dollars ($250) that you hold in trust for anyone, stating as to each:

(a) The description of the property, its location, the name and address of the person for whom you hold same, and his or her relationship to you;

(b) The conditions or terms of the trust, including the amounts you are paid as commissions or other compensation for holding such property;

(c) How such property was acquired by you and whether you paid any part of the consideration therefor.

58. List all property or other things of value of any nature or kind with a value in excess or two hundred fifty dollars ($250) that is held in trust for you or that is in the care or custody of another person, corporation, or entity for you, stating for each:

(a) The nature of the property or other thing of value, its location, and custodian;

(b) The name and address of the trustee, if different than above;

(c) The conditions or terms of the trust;

(d) How such property or other thing of value was acquired and who paid the consideration therefor;

(e) The original cost;

(f) The value at the time of the separation of the parties;

(g) The present value if different than (f) above.

   *Attach copies of any trust instruments or writings evidencing the above.

INSURANCE

59. List each life insurance policy, annuity policy, disability policy, or other form of insurance not disclosed in a previous interrogatory, stating for each:

(a) The name and address of the insurance company;

(b) The policy number;

(c) The type of policy;

(d) The name and address of the owner of the policy;

(e) The name and address of the present beneficiary of the policy;

(f) If there has been a change of beneficiary in the last five (5) years, give the date of each change and the name and address of each former beneficiary;

(g) The date the policy was issued;

(h) The face amount of the policy;

(i) The annual premium and the name and address of the person paying the premium currently and for the past five (5) years;

(j) The cash surrender value of said policy;

(k) If any loans have been taken out against the policy, the date of each such loan, the person making such loan, the amount of the loan, and the purpose for which the proceeds were utilized;

(l) If said policy has been assigned, the date of the assignment, the name and address of each assignee;

(m) The present custodian of the policy;

(n) If any policy is supplied by an employer, whether it is a condition of employment and under what conditions it terminates.

60. State whether you have surrendered, transferred, or in any way terminated any form of insurance policy for the last five (5) years. If so, state:

(a) The name and address of the insurance company;

Continued

☐ **EXHIBIT 6.1 Interrogatories—*Continued***

    (b) The number of the policy;

    (c) The type of policy;

    (d) The name and address of the last or current owner of the policy;

    (e) The name and address of the last or present beneficiary of the policy;

    (f) The face amount of the policy;

    (g) The cash surrender value of the policy at present or just prior to its being surrendered, transferred, or terminated;

    (h) The person transferring, surrendering, or terminating said policy;

    (i) If any cash was realized from the said transfer, termination, or surrender, the amount realized and for what purposes the proceeds were used.

PENSION AND DISABILITY

61. State whether you are entitled to any pension, profit sharing, or retirement plan. If so, state:

    (a) The nature of the plan;

    (b) The name and address of the entity or person providing the plan;

    (c) Whether your interest in the plan is vested and, if not, the date and conditions under which the plan will vest;

    (d) Whether the plan is contributory or noncontributory and, if contributory, the amount you contributed during the marriage;

    (e) The amount you earned in the plan during the marriage;

    (f) If you have the right to withdraw any monies from the plan, how much money you may withdraw and when;

    (g) If you have withdrawn or borrowed any monies from the plan, indicate when and how much was borrowed and whether the money must be returned or repaid;

    (h) If there are any survivor benefits, give a brief description thereof.

    *Attach copies of all writings concerning the plan(s) in your possession or which are readily available from your employer or pension payor.

62. If you are entitled to any disability benefits, state:

    (a) The nature of the disability;

    (b) The dollar amount of the award;

    (c) The date of payment of the award;

    (d) Whether there are any survivor benefits, giving a brief description thereof;

    (e) Whether any benefits or awards are presently being claimed by you, litigated, or are being reviewed, indicating the amount thereof if not included above.

EXPENSES

63. Itemize your average monthly expenses in detail [see chart below]. If any of the expenses include support of any other person outside your immediate family, set forth the name and address of such person, and the portion of each expense attributable to each such person supported. (NOTE: All weekly expenses must be multiplied by 4.333 to obtain the monthly expense.) If certain expenses are paid by your employer, spouse, or another party, so indicated by footnoting.

         *   *   *   *   *

MONTHLY BUDGET EXPENSE FOR
interrogatory 63

Food _____	Dentists _____
Clothing _____	Orthodontists _____
Mortgage(s) _____	Psychiatrists _____
Property taxes _____	Attorney fees _____
Rent _____	Drugs _____
Utilities _____	Hair care _____
Fuel oil _____	Dry cleaners _____
Telephone _____	Laundry _____
Garbage collection _____	Veterinarian _____
Water _____	Newspapers _____
Plumbing _____	Magazines _____
Electrician _____	Insurance _____
Doctors _____	Homeowner _____

Continued

☐ **EXHIBIT 6.1   Interrogatories—Continued**

Renter _____	Camp _____
Automobile _____	Household improvements _____
Life _____	Household repairs _____
Hospitalization _____	Apartment maintenance _____
Floater _____	Garden maintenance _____
Umbrella _____	Pool maintenance _____
Disability _____	Termite/pest service _____
Other _____	Tree service _____
Professional dues _____	Water softener _____
Club dues _____	Furniture & appliances _____
Babysitters _____	Furnishings _____
Domestics _____	Contributions _____
Burglar alarm service _____	Vacations _____
Voluntary support payments _____	Christmas presents _____
Court-ordered support payments _____	Chanukah presents _____
Past Due Installment Obligations	Other presents _____
Credit cards _____	Entertainment _____
Auto loans _____	Misc. spending money _____
Personal loans _____	Cable TV _____
Charge accounts _____	Emergencies _____
Credit card fees _____	
Education _____	DETAIL ALL OTHER EXPENSES
Allowances _____	BELOW:
Sports & hobbies _____	
Dancing lessons _____	_____
Music lessons _____	
Sport lessons _____	_____
Auto expenses _____	
Gas _____	_____
Maintenance _____	
Commuting _____	_____
Parking _____	
License & registration _____	_____
Transportation _____	

TOTAL MONTHLY EXPENSES _____

64. State whether anyone contributes to your support, income, or living expenses who has not been included in your answers to a previous interrogatory. If so, state:
    (a) Their names and address;
    (b) Their relationship to you;
    (c) The amount of support, income, or living expenses received by you during the last five (5) years and the frequency of said support, income, or living expenses;
    (d) The reason for said support;
    (e) The nature of said support.

LIABILITIES

65. Set forth a list of all credit card balances, stating:
    (a) The name of the obligor;
    (b) The total amount due at the present time and the amount due at the time of the separation of the parties;
    (c) The minimum monthly payment;
    (d) The name in which the card is listed and the names of all persons entitled to use the card;
    (e) The exact nature of the charges for which the money is owed;
    (f) Who incurred each obligation.

    *Attach copies of all credit card statements for the past twelve (12) months.

66. Set forth in detail any outstanding obligations, including mortgages, conditional sales contracts, contract obligations, promissory notes, or government agency loans not included in your answers to any previous interrogatories, stating for each:

Continued

☐ **EXHIBIT 6.1   Interrogatories—*Continued***

    (a) Whether the obligation is individual, joint, or joint and several;
    (b) The names and addresses of each creditor, and their relationship to you;
    (c) The form of the obligation;
    (d) The date the obligation was incurred;
    (e) The consideration received for the obligation;
    (f) A description of any security given for the obligation;
    (g) The amount of the original obligation;
    (h) The date of interest on the obligation;
    (i) The present unpaid balance of the obligation;
    (j) The date and the amount of each installment repayment due;
    (k) An itemization of the disposition of the funds received for which the obligation was incurred.

67. List all judgments outstanding against you or your spouse not included in your answer to a previous interrogatory, and for each state:
    (a) The names of the parties and their respective attorneys;
    (b) The courts in which the judgments were entered and the index or docket number assigned to each case;
    (c) The amount of each judgment.

68. If there is a wage execution, judgment, or order to pay out of income and earnings, state:
    (a) How much is taken from your earnings each week;
    (b) The name and address of obligors, and their relationship to you;
    (c) The balance due.

69. State the nature of any lien or security interest not indicated in your answer to a previous interrogatory to which any of the assets listed by you in previous interrogatories are subject, indicating for each:
    (a) The name and address of the holder thereof;
    (b) The holder's relationship to you;
    (c) The amount and frequency of the payments you make thereon;
    (d) The balance due.

MISCELLANEOUS

70. If any money, property, and/or asset was acquired by you either before the marriage or after the separation of the parties, state for each with a value in excess of two hundred fifty dollars ($250) the following:
    (a) The nature of the property;
    (b) The date acquired;
    (c) The source of the acquisition;
    (d) Your interest therein;
    (e) The present market value.

71. If any other money, property, or assets described in the above interrogatory was sold, transferred, or disposed of, state for each:
    (a) The manner of the disposition;
    (b) The date of the disposition;
    (c) To whom sold, transferred, or disposed and their relationship to you;
    (d) The amount received.

72. List all gifts received by you from your spouse with a value in excess of one hundred dollars ($100), giving for each:
    (a) The date received;
    (b) The nature of the gift;
    (c) The market value of the gift when given, and currently.

73. List all gifts received by you from your family, your spouse's family, or any other party or entity, with a value in excess of one hundred dollars ($100), giving for each:
    (a) The name of the donor and the relationship of the donor to you;
    (b) The date received;
    (c) The nature of the gift;
    (d) The market value of the gift when given, and currently.

74. If you have prepared a financial statement of your assets and liabilities, either individually or for any business in which you have an interest within the past five (5) years, state:

Continued

☐ **EXHIBIT 6.1   Interrogatories—*Continued***

   (a) The dates of all such statements;

   (b) The name and address of the person, firm, company, partnership, corporation, or entity for whom they were prepared;

   (c) The name and address of all persons who worked on the preparation of such statements.

      *Attach copies of all such statements.

75. State what counsel fees you have paid or agreed to pay for services rendered in connection with the separation of the parties.

76. State whether you have made application for any loans with any lending institutions, individuals, companies, or corporations during the past five (5) years. If so state for each:

   (a) The name and address of the lending institution, individual, company, or corporation;

   (b) The date of the application;

   (c) The amount of the loan;

   (d) Whether your application was approved or denied.

      *Attach a copy of all such loan applications.

77. List any gift made by you in excess of two hundred fifty dollars ($250) within the past five (5) years. For each such gift, state:

   (a) The name of the donee;

   (b) The reason for the gift;

   (c) The amount of the gift.

(text continued from page 83)

who intend to remain together indefinitely might be declared unenforceable. It would be the equivalent of one spouse saying to another, "If you leave me now, I'll give you $25,000." The agreement is invalid because it is **conducive to divorce.** This is against **public policy.**

Another kind of illegal agreement is an attempted "private divorce." Suppose a husband and wife enter the following brief separation agreement:

> "We hereby declare that our marriage is over and that we will have nothing to do with each other henceforth. As we part, we ask nothing of each other."

Assume further that this agreement is not shown to anyone. To permit parties to make such a contract would be to enable them to divorce themselves without the involvement of a court. At the time the parties attempted to enter this contract, it may have seemed fair and sensible. Suppose, however, that months or years later, the wife finds herself destitute. If she sues her husband for support or alimony, he cannot defend the action by raising her contract commitment not to ask anything of him. If either of them later tries to marry someone else, he or she will have no defense against a charge of bigamy.

A more serious kind of illegal agreement between husband and wife involves **collusion.** An example would be a plaintiff in a divorce action who falsely asserts that the defendant deserted her on a certain date, and the defendant falsely admits to this or remains silent even though he knows that the assertion is false. Their *collusive* objective is usually to *facilitate* the granting of the divorce. Before no-fault divorce became part of our legal system (see chapter 9), this kind of falsehood was common. Another example is a clause in a separation agreement providing that if either party later seeks a divorce, the other party promises not to appear or not to raise any defenses to the divorce action even if the parties know that such defenses exist. Such an agreement would be invalid because it is collusive, improperly inducing divorce.

The rule that separation agreements are invalid if they are conducive to divorce has been criticized as unrealistic since it is difficult to imagine a mu-

---

Conducive to Divorce
Tending to encourage or contribute to divorce.

Public Policy   The principles inherent in the customs, morals, and notions of justice that prevail in a state. The foundation of public laws. The principles that are naturally and inherently right and just.

Collusion   (1) An agreement to commit fraud. (2) An agreement between a husband and wife in a divorce proceeding that one or both will lie to the court to facilitate obtaining the divorce.

Separation Agreement

THIS AGREEMENT is entered on this _____day of _____ , 19 ___ , by Fred Jones (referred to in this agreement as the Husband), residing at _____ , and by Linda Jones (referred to in this agreement as the Wife), residing at _____ .

Witnesseth:

WHEREAS, the parties were married on _____ , 19 ___ in the state of _____ _____ , city of _____ , and

WHEREAS, _____ children were born of this marriage: (here list each child with dates of birth)

WHEREAS, as a result of irreconcilable marital disputes, the parties have been voluntarily living apart since _____ , 19 ___ which both parties feel is in their own best interests and that of their children, and

WHEREAS, both parties wish to enter this agreement for the purpose of settling all custody, support, and property rights between them, and any other matter pertaining to their marriage relationship, and

WHEREAS, both parties acknowledge that they have had separate and independent legal advice from counsel of their own choosing on the advisability of entering this agreement, that they have not been coerced or pressured into entering the agreement, and that they voluntarily decide to enter it.

NOW THEREFORE, in consideration of the promises and the mutual commitments contained in this agreement, the parties agree as follows:

> [the full text of the agreement goes here in numbered paragraphs; sample agreements are found at the end of this chapter.]

□ **EXHIBIT 6.2**
Sample Introductory Clauses in a Separation Agreement

tually acceptable separation agreement involving future divorce that does *not* in some way facilitate or encourage the parties to go through with the divorce. Nevertheless, courts continue to watch for improper facilitation and collusion. The coming of no-fault divorce has lessened a court's inclination to invalidate a separation agreement for these reasons. Since divorce has been made much easier to obtain because of no-fault grounds, courts are more reluctant to try to save the marriage at all costs and more willing to let the separation agreement be the vehicle through which the parties confront the inevitable. This is not to say that courts will no longer be concerned with collusion and agreements that are conducive to divorce. These prohibitions are still on the books. The atmosphere, however, has changed with no-fault. Most of the court decisions on these prohibitions were decided before the arrival of no-fault. It is questionable how willing courts are to follow all of those decisions today.

Below are a series of clauses sometimes found in separation agreements with comments on how the courts have treated the issues of divorce facilitation and collusion raised by the clauses.

"The wife agrees that she will file for a divorce against the husband within three months."

"None of the terms of this separation agreement shall be effective unless and until either of the parties is granted a divorce."

The first clause is invalid; a party cannot promise to file for a divorce. The clause does not merely encourage divorce, it makes it almost inevitable. The second clause appears to be as bad as or worse than the first. Neither of the parties will obtain any of the benefits in the separation agreement unless one of them obtains a divorce. Arguably, this clause encourages one of the parties to file for divorce and the other party to refrain from contesting the divorce. Oddly, however, the courts have not interpreted the second clause in this way. It *is* legal to condition the entire separation agreement on the granting of a divorce. The logic of this result is not entirely clear, but the courts so hold.

> "The wife agrees that if the husband files for divorce, she will not raise any defenses to his action."
>
> "In the event that the wife travels to another state to file for divorce, the husband agrees to go to that state, appear in the action, and participate therein."

The first clause is collusive. If a party has a defense, it is improper to agree not to assert it. Even if you are not sure whether you have a defense, it is collusive to agree in advance to refrain from asserting whatever defense you *might* have. Courts consider this as improper as an agreement to destroy or to conceal important evidence.

The second clause is more troublesome. Here the parties are clearly contemplating an out-of-state divorce, perhaps because they both realize that they would have difficulty establishing the grounds for divorce in their own state. Such **migratory divorces** were once quite common. Is a clause conducive to divorce if it obligates the defendant to appear in the foreign divorce action? Some states think that it is and would invalidate the agreement. Other states, however, would uphold the agreement.

Migratory Divorce A divorce obtained in a state to which one or both parties traveled before returning to their original state.

ASSIGNMENT 6.1

Determine whether any of the following clauses improperly facilitate divorce or are collusive.

a. "In the event that the wife files a divorce action, the husband agrees not to file any defenses to said action if and only if it is clear to both parties that the husband has no defense."

b. "In the event that the wife files a divorce action, the husband will pay in advance all expenses incurred by the wife in bringing said action."

c. "In the event that the wife files for a judicial separation, for separate maintenance, or for an annulment, the husband agrees to cooperate fully in the wife's action."

CAPACITY TO CONTRACT

There was a time in our history when the very thought of a wife entering a contract with her husband was anathema. A married woman lacked the *capacity to contract* with her husband. At common law, the husband and wife were one, and "the one" was the husband! You cannot make a contract with yourself. This rule, of course, has been changed. A wife can enter a contract with her husband (although the Internal Revenue Service and the husband's creditors are often suspicious of such contracts, especially when the result is to place property purchased by the husband in the name of the wife). A woman is no longer denied the right to enter a separation agreement (a contract) with a man simply because she is his wife.

Today, the major question of capacity involves mental health. A separation agreement is invalid if either party lacked the capacity to understand the agreement and the consequences of signing it. The traditional test is as follows: The person must understand the nature and consequences of his or her act at the time of the transaction. This understanding may not exist due to insanity, mental retardation, senility, temporary delirium due to an accident, intoxication, drug addition, etc.

DURESS AND FRAUD

In the excerpt from the Jones separation agreement in Exhibit 6.2, you will note that several times at the beginning of the agreement the parties mention that they are entering it "voluntarily." According to traditional contract principles, if a party enters a contract because of **duress,** it will not be enforced. Suppose that a wife is physically threatened if she does not sign the separation agreement. Clearly, the agreement would not be valid. The husband could not sue her for breaching it or attempt to enforce it in any other way.

Of course, simply because the separation agreement says that the parties enter it "voluntarily" does not necessarily mean that no duress existed. A spouse could have been forced to say the agreement was signed "voluntarily." But to have the agreement say that it was "voluntarily" signed is at least *some* indication (however slight) that no duress existed, although an **aggrieved** party can introduce evidence to the contrary.

During discussions and negotiations, if a spouse lies about a major asset that he or she possesses, the separation agreement must be set aside for **fraud.** If the spouse fails to disclose or undervalues major assets, many courts will again invalidate the agreement unless its terms are deemed to be fair to the other spouse.

Suppose that after signing the separation agreement, a party becomes destitute or near-destitute. Some courts will intervene and not allow him or her to suffer the consequences of a bad bargain in the separation agreement, even if there was no clear evidence of duress or fraud. At one time, many courts presumed that a husband took unfair advantage of his wife unless he demonstrated otherwise. These courts did not allow the husband to treat his wife **at arm's length** as he would a competitor in a commercial transaction. The women's movement has helped change this attitude. Courts no longer so blatantly protect women. Both sides will be forced to live with the agreement they signed, particularly if there was full disclosure of assets, no duress or fraud, both had the opportunity to seek independent advice before they signed, and neither is about to become a public charge.

The last WHEREAS clause in the beginning of the Jones separation agreement in Exhibit 6.2 states that both Fred and Linda had the benefit of separate legal advice on the advantages and disadvantages of signing the agreement. As indicated, this fact can be very significant in a court's deliberation on whether to set the agreement aside on a ground such as duress. It is relatively difficult to challenge the validity of a separation agreement that was signed after both sides had the benefit of their own attorney—even though the spouse with most of the resources may have had to pay for both attorneys.

CONSIDERATION

Contracts must be supported by **consideration** to be valid. The separation agreement is a set of promises by the parties of what they will do. The exchange of these promises (some of which may have already been performed, at least in part, at the time the agreement is signed) is the consideration for the separation agreement. A wife's promise to relinquish all claims she may have

Duress Coercion; acting under the pressure of an unlawful act or threat.

Aggrieved Injured or wronged; the person injured or wronged.

Fraud Knowingly making a false statement of present fact with the intention that the plaintiff rely on the statement. The plaintiff's reasonable reliance on the statement harms him or her.

At Arm's Length As between two strangers who are looking out for their own self-interests. At a distance; without trusting the other's fairness; free of personal bias or control.

Consideration Something of value that is exchanged between the parties, e.g., an exchange of promises to do something or to refrain from doing something.

against her husband's estate when he dies is an example of her consideration to him. A husband's promise to transfer to his wife full title to land he solely owns is an example of his consideration to her.

We have already seen, however, that certain kinds of consideration are improper. A couple, for example, cannot exchange promises that one party will file for divorce and the other party will refrain from asserting any defenses he or she might have. Such consideration is illegal because it is conducive to divorce, and may be collusive.

Perhaps the main consideration in the separation agreement involves the separation itself. A husband and wife have the right to live with each other as husband and wife, i.e., the right of cohabitation. By reason of the separation agreement, the parties promise each other that they will never again claim this cohabitation right.

ALIMONY PAYMENTS AND PROPERTY DIVISION: INTRODUCTION

Alimony The amount of money or other property paid in fulfillment of a duty to support one's spouse after a separation or divorce.

Property Division The distribution of property accumulated by spouses as a result of their joint efforts during the marriage. (Sometimes referred to as a **property settlement**.)

Arrears Payments that are due but have not been made. (Also called **arrearages**.)

Outstanding Unpaid.

Discharged Released; forgiven so that the debt is no longer owed.

We now begin our coverage of **alimony** and **property division**. These two concepts are sometimes confused. A separation agreement (or a court opinion) may refer to a property division but mean *both* support and property division. In part, the confusion may be due to the fact that in the minds of the husband and wife, there is not always a clear distinction between these two concepts.

Exhibit 6.3 presents some major consequences of the distinction between alimony and property division. These consequences must be understood before examining the options available to the parties in drafting those clauses of the separation agreement that cover alimony and property division.

EFFECT OF BANKRUPTCY

Under most forms of bankruptcy, citizens can eliminate all or most of their debts in order to make a fresh start. If a husband has fallen behind on his obligation under a separation agreement or a divorce decree, all **arrears** constitute a debt to his wife. Each time an alimony payment becomes due, a new debt is created. All **outstanding** obligations under a property division agreement are also debts. When a debtor goes into bankruptcy, some of his or her debts are **discharged**. Which ones? The Bankruptcy Act of Congress provides as follows:

> A discharge . . . does not discharge an individual debtor from any debt . . . to a spouse, former spouse, or child of the debtor, for alimony to, maintenance for, or support of such spouse or child, in connection with a separation agreement, divorce decree or other order of a court of record. . . . 11 U.S.C.A. § 523(a)(5).

Hence, debts in the nature of spousal or child support survive bankruptcy; they are not discharged. Property division debts, however, are treated differently. In general, they also are not dischargeable. But under two special circumstances, they *are* dischargeable: first, the spouse who owes the obligation (the debtor) proves that he or she does not have enough assets to pay the property division debt plus all his or her other legitimate debts, *or* second, the debtor proves that the benefit of discharging the property division debt outweighs the harm or detriment that this discharge would cause the other spouse.[1]

---

1. 11 U.S.C.A. § 523 (a)(15): An individual debtor will not be discharged from any non-support debt incurred by the debtor in the course of a divorce or separation or in connection with a separation agreement unless:

☐ **EXHIBIT 6.3   Alimony and Property Division Terms of a Separation Agreement**

EFFECT OF BANKRUPTCY

Alimony	*Property Division*
If the spouse with the obligation to pay alimony goes into bankruptcy, his or her obligation to pay alimony is *not* discharged. All unpaid or delinquent alimony debts are still owed.	Under certain circumstances, a spouse may be able to discharge his or her property division debt through bankruptcy.

EFFECT OF REMARRIAGE AND DEATH

Alimony	*Property Division*
If the person receiving alimony remarries, the alimony payments stop unless the separation agreement specifically provides otherwise. If the person paying alimony remarries, the alimony payments to the first spouse must continue unless a court provides otherwise. If the husband or wife dies, alimony payments cease unless the separation agreement specifically provides otherwise.	Remarriage or death of either party does not affect the terms of the property division. All remaining obligations under the property division must be fulfilled regardless of remarriage or death.

AVAILABILITY OF CONTEMPT

Alimony	*Property Division*
If a party fails to fulfill an alimony obligation and falls into arrears, the power of the court to punish for contempt can be used as an enforcement device if the separation agreement has been incorporated and merged into a later divorce decree.	If either party fails to fulfill the obligations under the property division, states differ on whether the contempt power of the court can be used as an enforcement device. Many states say that it cannot.

THE COURT'S POWER TO MODIFY TERMS

Alimony	*Property Division*
If the alimony terms of the separation agreement later prove to be seriously inadequate, the court sometimes has the power to modify those terms in order to require more alimony to be paid.	If either party later becomes dissatisfied with the terms of an otherwise valid property division, the court will rarely, if ever, modify those terms.

FEDERAL INCOME TAX TREATMENT

Alimony	*Property Division*
Alimony payments are includible in the gross income of the payee and are deductible for the payor.	Transfers of property incident to a divorce are not reportable as income by the transferee nor deductible by the transferor. The basis of the property in the hands of the transferee is the same as the transferor's basis.

This has a number of practical consequences. Assume that the husband is in serious financial difficulties and that bankruptcy is a possibility (a fact that must be carefully investigated by the lawyer and paralegal representing the wife).

Footnote 1, continued.

(A) the debtor does not have the ability to pay such debt from income or property of the debtor not reasonably necessary to be expended for the maintenance or support of the debtor or a dependent of the debtor and, if the debtor is engaged in a business, for the payment of expenditures necessary for the continuation, preservation, and operation of such business; or (B) discharging such debt would result in a benefit to the debtor that outweighs the detrimental consequences to a spouse, former spouse, or child of the debtor. . . .

The wife may be advised in the negotiation stage of the separation agreement to accept a small property division in exchange for a high amount of alimony. In the event that a bankruptcy does occur, she does not want to take the risk that he will be able to prove to the Bankruptcy Court that he fits within one of the two special circumstances that allow a discharge of property division debts. If he can, she loses everything still owed under the property division, whereas the alimony debt always survives the bankruptcy.

EFFECT OF REMARRIAGE AND DEATH

Normally, a spouse will want to stop paying alimony in the event that the receiving spouse remarries. But alimony that ends upon the receiving spouse's remarriage can be an incentive *not* to remarry. To offset this, at least to some extent, the separation agreement might provide that alimony payments will continue after the remarriage of the receiving spouse, but at a lower amount.

If the paying spouse remarries, his or her alimony obligation continues unless modified by a court.

If either party dies, alimony payments cease, unless the separation agreement specifically provides otherwise. The separation agreement, for example, could provide that the alimony payments will continue after the death of the husband at which time the wife would collect the alimony from his **estate** or from a trust fund set up by him. Furthermore, the husband might take out a life insurance policy payable on his death to his wife. This, in effect, continues some measure of support for the wife after he dies. Absent such provisions, the death of the paying spouse terminates the alimony obligation in most states.

Estate All the property left by the deceased. After being used to pay debts, this property is distributed to those entitled under the will or the intestacy laws.

The situation is entirely different with respect to property division commitments; they continue no matter who dies or remarries. For example, as part of a property division (having nothing to do with support), John agrees to pay Mary $25,000. After John has paid Mary $1,000 of this amount, he dies. Mary can make a claim against John's estate for $24,000. If Mary died after John paid the $1,000, her estate could require John to pay the remaining $24,000 to it (i.e., to Mary's estate) for distribution according to Mary's will or according to the laws of intestacy. The same is true if either party remarries. The funds or other property owed under the property division clauses of the separation agreement remain due and owing no matter who remarries.

AVAILABILITY OF CONTEMPT

When one of the parties breaches a term of the separation agreement, ensuing legal action may depend upon whether the agreement is incorporated and merged into a subsequent divorce decree. If it is not, the regular breach-of-contract remedies are available, e.g., suit for damages, suit to rescind the contract. The sanctions for **contempt** (e.g., fine, prison) are *not* available. To some extent, the picture changes if the divorce decree incorporates and merges with the separation agreement. Alimony provisions *can* be enforced by the contempt powers of the court when incorporation and merger have occurred. States differ on whether the property division terms of a separation agreement can also be enforced by contempt. Many states say that it cannot. The sanction of contempt, however, is usually available when a party has violated a specific court order to transfer property.

Contempt Obstructing or assailing the authority or dignity of the court such as by intentionally violating a court order.

COURT'S POWER TO MODIFY TERMS

Courts will not modify an alimony term unless the ex-spouse is about to become a public charge or is facing serious financial difficulties due to a change of circumstances since the time he or she signed the separation agreement containing the original alimony term. A property division term, on the other hand, is rarely, if ever, modifiable by a court.

FEDERAL INCOME TAX TREATMENT

The federal tax implications of alimony and property division in a separation agreement will be treated in detail in chapter 11.

DISTINGUISHING BETWEEN ALIMONY AND PROPERTY DIVISION

As you can see, it can make a great deal of difference whether a term of a separation agreement is classified as alimony or as property division. The classification hinges on the intent of the parties at the time they entered the separation agreement. For example, did the parties intend a five-year annual payment of $50,000 to be alimony or property division? Unfortunately, it is often difficult to answer this question. As indicated earlier, the parties may either be confused about the distinction or pay no attention to it. At a later date, however, when the parties realize the importance of the distinction (e.g., at tax time or when bankruptcy occurs), they will probably make conflicting claims about what their intentions were. It is the court's job to turn the clock back to when they were negotiating the separation agreement and determine what their intent was at that time. In making this determination, the court will consider a number of factors:

- ☐ Labels used in the agreement
- ☐ Contingencies
- ☐ Method of payment
- ☐ The nature of what is transferred

Usually, none of these factors is conclusive by itself. All of them must be considered. One of the factors may clearly indicate an intent that a term is alimony. If, however, the other factors clearly suggest that the term is part of the property division, the court may conclude that it is the latter. Unhappily, the factors often point in opposite directions.

LABELS USED IN THE AGREEMENT   Sometimes the separation agreement will explicitly label a provision as "alimony" or as a "property settlement" or "property division." These labels, however, do not always control. For example, suppose that an annual payment of $10,000 given to the wife is labeled "Property Division." If it is otherwise clear to the court that this money was in the nature of support, the court will classify it as alimony in spite of the label.

CONTINGENCIES   Terms that are **contingent** on the occurrences of certain events are often interpreted as alimony rather than as a property division, e.g., $10,000 a year to the wife until she remarries or dies. The presence of such contingencies suggests an intent to provide support while needed rather than an intent to divide property.

Contingent
Conditional; dependent on something that may not happen.

METHOD OF PAYMENT   A term may provide a single *lump-sum payment* (e.g., $10,000), *periodic payment* (e.g., $10,000 a year), or a *fluctuating payment* (e.g., $10,000 a year to be increased or decreased depending upon earnings in a particular year). Single lump-sum payments often suggest a property division. Periodic and fluctuating payments often suggest alimony.

THE NATURE OF WHAT IS TRANSFERRED   A conveyance of property other than cash (e.g., a house, a one-half interest in a business) often suggests a property division. Cash alone, however, usually suggests alimony.

Again, these are only guides. All of the circumstances must be examined in order to determine the intent of the parties. It may be that a court will conclude that a transfer of a house was intended as alimony or support. The court might also conclude that a single lump-sum payment was intended as alimony. While a court will be inclined to rule otherwise in these examples, specific proof of intent will control.

ALIMONY

We will now examine individual clauses in the separation agreement, starting with alimony. Keep in mind, however, that no individual clause of a separation agreement can be fully understood in isolation. The negotiation process involves a large variety of factors. A party may agree to a term in the agreement not so much because that term in and of itself gives the party what he or she wants, but rather because the party decided to concede that term in order to gain another term, e.g., a wife may accept a lower alimony provision in exchange for the husband's agreement to the term giving her sole custody of their child. This is the nature of the bargaining process.

Alimony, as we have seen, is the amount of money or other property paid in fulfillment of a duty to support one's spouse after a separation or divorce. (Later, in chapter 11 on taxation, we will see that the Internal Revenue Service uses a broader definition of alimony to determine when it is deductible.) While the parties are still married, the payments are sometimes referred to as *spousal support* or as *separate maintenance*. The word *alimony* is more commonly used when the divorce has occurred or is imminent.

Traditionally, it was the husband's duty to support the wife. Today, however, the duty is mutual in the sense that it will be imposed on the party who has the resources for the benefit of the party in need. To impose the duty only on a man would amount to unconstitutional sex discrimination in violation of the Equal Protection Clause of the U.S. Constitution and in violation of many state constitutions. In the vast majority of situations, however, it is the woman who is the recipient of support through a separation agreement and/or through a court order.

First, we will examine some of the major negotiating options that must be considered in drafting the support provisions of the separation agreement. Then, we turn to how a court will handle spousal support if the parties have not been able to negotiate an agreement.

SUPPORT PROVISIONS IN A SEPARATION AGREEMENT

PERIODIC PAYMENTS OR LUMP SUM? In a few states, it is illegal for a husband and wife to agree on a lump-sum payment in satisfaction of the support duty. In most states, however, it is permissible. From the perspective of the recipient, collectibility is an important factor in deciding whether to seek a single lump-sum alimony payment. The wife may find it safer to take the lump-sum payment now rather than hassle with installment or periodic payments if there is any likelihood that the husband will fall behind in his payments. It can be expensive and psychologically draining to have to go after a delinquent husband.

FIXED OR FLUCTUATING PERIODIC PAYMENTS? If periodic payments are agreed to, a number of questions need to be considered and resolved. Should the payments have a fixed dollar amount, e.g., $300 per week? On what day of the month or week is each payment due? Another major option is the flexible periodic payment. The amount of the payment may fluctuate up or down depending upon the income of the husband, of the wife, or of both. An alimony payment of 25 percent of the husband's gross earnings, for example, provides an automatic fluctuating standard.

MEDICAL AND DENTAL EXPENSES Does the alimony payment cover medical, dental, or mental health expenses (e.g., psychiatrist)? If not, do the parties want to include a term in the separation agreement on how these expenses are to be covered? They must also consider the tax consequences of paying these expenses.

LIFE INSURANCE Even though the duty of support usually ends at the death of the **payor** or of the **payee,** the parties might agree that the support payments will continue after the payor dies. If so, one way to do this is through a life insurance policy on the life of the party with the support duty. The beneficiary would be the other spouse and/or the children. If a life insurance policy already exists, the parties may decide to include a term in the separation agreement that requires a spouse to continue paying the premiums, to increase the amount of the policy, to name the other spouse as the irrevocable beneficiary, etc. The agreement should also specify whether an existing policy remains in force if either side remarries. If no life insurance policy exists, the parties need to decide whether to take one out.

Payor One who makes a payment of money or is obligated to do so.

Payee One to whom money is paid or is to be paid.

MODIFICATION The separation agreement may contain a clause that the terms of the agreement shall not be modified unless both parties agree in writing to do so. Will a court honor such a clause? The answer is no where children are involved. As we shall see later, judges will change custody and child support clauses when they feel the best interest of the children warrants it. This is so whether or not the separation agreement is later incorporated and merged into the divorce decree.

What about the *alimony* term of the separation agreement? Will a court modify this term if the separation agreement has been incorporated and merged into the divorce decree even though the agreement has a no-modification clause? States differ on their answer to this question. Some state courts *will* modify the alimony term if a change of circumstances since the divorce decree justifies it, e.g., the payee is about to become destitute. We will return to the subject of modification later in this chapter.

TERMINATION OF SUPPORT PAYMENTS   The circumstances that will terminate the support obligation should be explicitly spelled out in the separation agreement. For example, it might say that payments end when:

☐ The payee dies.

☐ The payor dies.

☐ The payee remarries. (If the second marriage is later annulled, states differ on whether the original support obligations of the first husband revive. See chapter 5.)

☐ The payee commits adultery or fornication.

☐ The payee fails to abide by the custody terms of the separation agreement.

☐ The payee competes with the payor in business. (In most states, however, such a term will *not* be enforced since a payee's support payments cannot be conditioned on something that is not reasonably related to the marriage relationship.)

Of course, the separation agreement can provide the opposite. It may state, for example, that the support payments will *continue* when:

☐ The payor dies. (The payor's estate would then have the obligation to continue the support payments. Life insurance is often used as a method of continuing support payments after the payor's death.)

☐ The payee remarries. (Rather than continue the support payments in full after the payee remarries, the separation agreement usually provides for a reduced support payment. Some payors fear that if the total support payment ends upon remarriage, the payee will have little incentive to remarry. It should be pointed out, however, that a few states forbid support payments to continue after the payee remarries.)

The termination of alimony payments does not affect arrears, i.e., unpaid back payments. All delinquent payments that accrued before the support obligation terminated must be paid. If they terminated upon the death of the husband, for example, all payments he failed to make before he died can be enforced against his estate.

Escrow   Property is delivered by one person to another who will hold it until a designated condition or contingency occurs; then the property is delivered to the person for whose benefit the escrow was established.

Surety Bond   An obligation by a guarantor to pay a second party if a third party defaults in its obligation to the second party.

SECURITY   When a payor fails to make a support payment, the payee can sue, but this is hardly an adequate remedy. Litigation can be expensive, lengthy, and emotionally draining. Preferable would be a term in the separation agreement that provides *security* to the payee for the performance of the support obligation. This security can be provided in a number of forms:

1. Escrow. The payor deposits a sum of money with an escrow agent, e.g., a bank, with instructions to pay the payee a designated amount of money in the event that the payor falls behind in a payment.

2. Surety bond. The payor gives the payee a surety bond. The payor pays premiums to the surety company. The surety company guarantees that if the payor fails to fulfill the support obligation, the company will fulfill it up to the amount of the bond.

3. Annuity. The payor purchases an annuity contract that provides a fixed income to the payee (annuitant) in the amount of the support obligation.

4. Trust. The payor transfers property (e.g., cash) to a trustee (e.g., a bank) with instructions to pay a fixed income to the payee (the beneficiary) in the amount of the support obligation.

The last two forms of security do not depend upon a breach by the payor of the support obligation clause of a separation agreement in order to come into effect.

COURT-ORDERED ALIMONY
IN THE ABSENCE OF A SEPARATION AGREEMENT

How will a court decide the question of support if the parties have not been able to reach agreement on the matter? The major factors considered by the court are outlined in Exhibit 6.4. (In some states, these factors are spelled out in the statutory code.) Once a court decides to grant alimony, it will consider many of the same options discussed above, e.g., whether the amount should fluctuate, whether security should be provided.

Annuity A fixed sum payable to an individual at specified intervals for a limited period of time or for life.

Trust A method of holding property by which legal title is given to one party (the trustee) for the benefit of another (the beneficiary).

Rehabilitative Alimony Alimony for a limited time until the payee can go to school or pursue employment on the way to becoming financially self-sufficient. (Also known as *durational maintenance*.) Designed to combat the notion that alimony is a permanent pension.

☐ **EXHIBIT 6.4 Factors a Court Will Consider in the Alimony Decision**

1. **The Needs of the Payee**
   ☐ The traditional general guideline is that alimony should enable the payee to maintain substantially the same standard of living enjoyed during the marriage.
   ☐ The payee's needs may vary according to his or her age and health.
   ☐ Most courts will provide a lower alimony award, or none at all, if the person requesting alimony has independent income and property. They will consider all resources of the payee, e.g., the expectation of inheritances.
   ☐ Most courts consider the payee's current employability. The presence of young children, of course, substantially limits the employment prospects of parents with custody.
   ☐ Many states authorize a court to grant **rehabilitative alimony,** which generally covers a limited period of time. In other states, however, the alimony award is granted for an indefinite period until modified by court order.
2. **The Length of the Marriage**
   ☐ Courts are very reluctant to grant significant alimony for a marriage of a short duration, e.g., under two years.
3. **The Ability of the Payor to Pay**
   ☐ The age and health of the payor.
   ☐ The payor's standard of living during and after the marriage.
   ☐ The payor's present and anticipated debts and other financial obligations.
   ☐ The voluntariness of the payor's financial condition. A husband, for example, cannot voluntarily enter a state of poverty by quitting a high-paying job solely to avoid alimony. The focus is not simply on the payor's present resources. The test is the payor's "earning capacity." (A similar issue arises when the parties confront the property division. One spouse cannot destroy or *dissipate* the property accumulated during the marriage and thereby prevent the other spouse from obtaining his or her fair share.)
4. **Marital Fault**
   ☐ In most states, marital fault of the payee will *not* disqualify him or her from receiving alimony, although it can sometimes be taken into consideration in determining the amount of the alimony award.
   ☐ In some states, however, only if the payee was granted the divorce based on the payor's fault will the payee be entitled to alimony.
   ☐ In a few states, if the payor is found at fault, his or her alimony obligation may be increased.
5. **Other Factors**
   ☐ Some courts say that a factor in the award of alimony is the contribution (financial or otherwise) of the payee in helping the payor generate assets during the marriage. This factor, however, is more relevant to property division. Yet, as indicated, some courts tend to blur the distinction between alimony and property division.
   ☐ The court's decision on property division is sometimes a factor in awarding alimony. A court may be inclined to give a lower alimony award if it feels that the payee has been given "a good deal" in the property division. Some courts take the position that the adequacy of a support award can be determined only after the marital assets have been divided—again supporting the view that no single item in a separation agreement or court decree should be examined in isolation.

■■■■■■ PROPERTY DIVISION: GENERAL PRINCIPLES

CATEGORIZING PROPERTY

A property division should be based on a fair allocation of the property accumulated by the spouses during the marriage due to their joint efforts. Whether the property division is agreed to by the parties or imposed by a court in the absence of agreement, the following preliminary questions must be examined:

1. What kind of property do the parties have?
2. How was the property acquired?
3. How is the property held? Who has title?

Real Property Land and anything permanently attached to the land.

Personal Property Movable property; any property other than real property.

WHAT KIND OF PROPERTY DO THE PARTIES HAVE? **Real property** can include a main home, a vacation home, land and building used in a business, condominium, etc. **Personal property** consists of cars, boats, cash, stocks, bonds, royalties, furniture, jewelry, art objects, books, records, clothes, photographic equipment, sports equipment, pets, business supplies (inventory), credits, accounts receivable, exclusive options to buy, insurance policies, etc.

Later we will examine three categories of assets that have generated considerable controversy in recent years: future pensions, professional degrees, and the goodwill of a business or profession.

In Vitro Fertilization The surgical removal of a woman's eggs and their fertilization with a man's sperm in the laboratory.

☐ **Note on Embryos as "Property"** Assume that a woman is unable to conceive because damaged tubes prevent her eggs from reaching the womb. The eggs can be removed surgically, fertilized with her husband's sperm in the laboratory **(in vitro fertilization),** and reimplanted in the uterus at a later time during a normal ovulation cycle, hopefully to mature to a healthy fetus. Billig, *High Tech Earth Mothering,* 9 DISTRICT LAWYER 57 (July/August 1985). The procedure is known as an embryo transplant. In chapter 16 we will examine the question of what happens when the implantation is made in a "rented womb" of a surrogate mother. Here our concern is the "property" status of the embryos themselves.

What happens if the woman and her husband separate and file for divorce *before* the embryo is reimplanted in her? An embryo can be frozen between fertilization and implantation. What is the status of the *frozen embryo?* Who "owns" it? Is the embryo "property" to be divided upon divorce? Does the court have to decide its "custody"? Should the embryo be treated as potential life? When does life begin? Is the embryo a potential child?

The problem arises when the parties disagree about what should be done with the embryo. Suppose the husband wants it destroyed because he does not want to become the father of a child with his soon-to-be-ex-wife, but she wants the embryo kept alive so that a reimplantation can be attempted in her at a later time. Can he be forced to be a father against his will? Is this question any different from whether a man can force the woman he impregnates to have an abortion because he does not want to become a father? The courts have held that a man cannot force a woman to have an abortion. Is this any different from whether he can force a doctor to destroy a frozen embryo?

Definitive answers to such questions do not exist. Medical technology is moving much faster than the development of law and ethics in our society. The experts are at loggerheads:

> "We're talking about four-celled embryos—they haven't developed into organs or anything. They are too rudimentary; . . . therefore, they can't really be harmed, and there should be no requirement that unwanted embryos be saved."

"Obviously, embryos are not property. These entities should not be defined as being property in terms of being able to be bought and sold. They are potential beings and declaring the embryos as property comes up to the threshold of crossing the barrier of assaulting the value of a potential person."

Curriden, *Frozen Embryos,* American Bar Association Journal 69–70 (August 1980).

More than 5,000 in vitro fertilization babies have been born in this country, and more than 20,000 "frozen embryos" remain in storage in laboratories across the United States. Clearly, there is a need for legislatures and courts to provide guidance on their status.

A major breakthrough came in 1992 with the Tennessee case of *Davis v. Davis,* 842 S.W.2d 588 (Tenn. 1992). Junior Lewis Davis sought a divorce from his wife, Mary Sue Davis. The parties were able to agree on all terms of dissolution, except one: who was to have "custody" of the seven "frozen embryos" (also referred to as preembryos) stored in a Knoxville fertility clinic that had attempted to assist the Davises in achieving a much-wanted pregnancy during a happier period in their relationship. Mary did not want to use the "frozen embryos" herself, but wanted authority to donate them to a childless couple. Junior was adamantly opposed to such donation and wanted the "frozen embryos" discarded. When the Davises signed up for the IVF program at the Knoxville clinic, they did not execute a written agreement specifying what disposition should be made of any unused embryos that might result from the cryopreservation process. Nor were there any Tennessee statutes to guide the court on what to do in this situation.[2]

The Tennessee Supreme Court established its own guidelines on what to do when the parties cannot agree. The party wishing to avoid procreation should ordinarily prevail, assuming the other party has a reasonable possibility of achieving parenthood by means other than use of the preembryos in question. If no other reasonable alternatives exist, then the argument in favor of using the preembryos to achieve pregnancy should be considered. However, if the party seeking control of the preembryos intends merely to donate them to another couple, the objecting party has the greater interest and should prevail.

Junior Lewis Davis was "ecstatic" over this ruling. "I think this is a great step for men regarding our biological rights," he said.[3]

HOW WAS THE PROPERTY ACQUIRED? Real and personal property can be acquired in a variety of ways:

☐ As a gift to one of the spouses

☐ As a gift to both of the spouses

☐ As a **bequest** to one or both spouses

☐ As a **devise** to one or both spouses

☐ Through **intestate succession**

☐ Through funds from the salary of one of the spouses

☐ Through funds from the salaries of both of the spouses

Timing is important. When did the party or parties receive the property? Was it brought into the marriage or was it acquired during the marriage? If the

Bequest A gift of personal property in a will.

Devise A gift of real property in a will.

Intestate Succession Obtaining the property from a deceased who died without leaving a valid will. The persons entitled to this property are identified in the statute on intestate distribution.

2. Louisiana has a statute entitled "Human Embryos." It forbids the intentional destruction of a cryopreserved IVF embryo and declares that disputes between parties should be resolved in the "best interest" of the embryo. 1986 La. Acts R.S. 9:121 et seq. Under the Louisiana statute, unwanted embryos must be made available for "adoptive implantation."

3. Mark Curriden, *No Forced Fatherhood,* 78 American Bar Association Journal 35 (September 1992).

property was separately owned before the marriage, was its value increased due to mutual efforts during the marriage?

HOW IS THE PROPERTY HELD? WHO HAS TITLE? Property can be held in a number of ways:

1. *Legal title in name of one spouse only.* The title to the property is in the name of only one of the parties. This could be because the property was purchased with the funds of that one spouse. Or, it may be that the property was purchased with the funds of one spouse but placed in the name of the other spouse (perhaps in the hope of insulating the property from the claims of the creditors of the spouse who purchased the property). Finally, title may be in the name of one spouse even though both contributed funds for its purchase.

2. *Joint tenancy.* In a **joint tenancy,** each joint tenant has an equal right to possess the entire property. They do not each own a piece of the property; each joint tenant owns it all. When one joint tenant dies, his or her interest passes to the surviving joint tenants by the **right of survivorship.**

3. *Tenancy by the entirety.* Under a **tenancy by the entirety,** each spouse has a right of survivorship, as with any joint tenancy.

4. *Tenancy in common.* In a **tenancy in common,** all parties have a right to possession of the property, but their share in the property may not be equal. There is no right of survivorship. When one tenant dies, the property goes to whomever the deceased designated by will, or to the heirs of the deceased by intestate succession if the deceased died without leaving a valid will. Hence, a major distinction between (1) a joint tenancy and a tenancy by the entirety and (2) a tenancy in common is that the property of a deceased tenant passes through the estate of that tenant only in the case of a tenancy in common. In the other tenancies, the property passes immediately to the surviving tenant(s) by **operation of law.**

5. *Community property.* The following information is taken from Clark, *The Law of Domestic Relations in the United States,* 512–515 (2d ed., Practitioner's Edition 1987):

> [Nine] states have adopted **community property** as a means of providing equitably for the property interests of married persons.* [Most of the other states in the country are generally classified as *common law property* states.] The principle underlying community property is that the efforts of both spouses are instrumental in contributing to the welfare of the family, and that therefore property acquired by either spouse during the marriage, with certain exceptions, should belong to both spouses. Community property was originally a Spanish institution and was enacted first in those states whose law was influenced by Spanish law, spreading later to other states. . . .
>
> [C]ommunity property . . . arises when the spouses are married and includes property acquired by either spouse during the marriage, except property acquired by gift, devise or inheritance to one spouse only.† Property which does not fall within the definition of community property is characterized as **separate property** of the spouse

---

*These are Arizona, California, Idaho, Louisiana, Nevada, New Mexico, Texas, Washington, and Wisconsin. 4A R. Powell, Real Property § 625[2] (Rev.ed.1982).

†Id. at § 625.2[1]. The Uniform Marital Property Act § 4, 9A Unif.L.Ann. 29 (Supp.1985) defines marital property in substantially the same way. Under that Act the parties may by agreement vary the manner in which property is held. Uniform Marital Property Act § 3, 9A Unif.L.Ann. 28 (Supp. 1985) Community property states permit this also.

Joint Tenancy Property that is owned equally by two or more persons with the *right of survivorship.*

Right of Survivorship When one owner dies, his or her share goes to the other owners; it does not go through the estate of the deceased owner.

Tenancy by the Entirety A joint tenancy held by a husband and wife.

Tenancy in Common Property owned by two or more persons in shares that may or may not be equal, with no right of survivorship.

Operation of Law Automatically because of the law. (A result occurs by operation of law when it happens because the law mandates the result, not because a party agrees to produce the result.)

Community Property Property in which each spouse has a one-half interest because it was acquired during the marriage, regardless of who earned it or who has title to it. **Common law property** is property owned by the spouse who earned it.

Separate Property Property totally owned by one spouse; noncommunity property.

who has acquired it. The difficulty of applying this ostensibly simple definition to the many forms in which property is acquired has led to the development of a rebuttable presumption that property acquired by either spouse during the marriage, whether title is taken in the name of either spouse or of both, is community property.* The presumption may be rebutted if it can be proved that the funds with which the property was acquired were the separate funds of one of the spouses.

In most community property states the parties may by agreement vary the usual rules. They may agree that all property acquired by either of them is separate property, or that it is all community property, or they may agree on the characterization of particular items of property.

Some examples indicate the difficulties of determining whether particular property is community or separate property. Thus veterans' education benefits have been held to be separate property when they were earned before marriage, but paid after marriage, even though the statute provided for increased benefits for dependents, including spouses. There is a conflict in the decisions concerning damages for personal injury. The Texas authorities classify such damages as separate property, but they hold that the medical expenses and loss of earnings recovered in such a suit are community property. Other courts hold that the entire recovery is community property. Where property is purchased before marriage but paid for in part after marriage out of community funds, its classification as community or separate varies among the community property states. Some would characterize it as separate property, some as separate or community depending upon when title vested, and some would apply complex calculations to establish the proportion of separate to community funds going into the purchase.

The diversity in characterization of property as community or separate, and the differences between the community property states and the common law states, have created difficult questions of the conflict of laws. An early case, *Saul v. His Creditors,*[†] established the rule that when the marriage occurred in a common law state, where the parties were then domiciled, but they later became domiciled in the community property state, property acquired after the change in domicile had the status of community property. California has carried this a step further by enacting a statute creating the institution of **quasi-community property.** . . . Quasi-community property is divisible on divorce in the same fashion as community property.

Quasi-Community Property Property acquired by the spouses when they lived in a non-community property state before moving to a community property state. If they had acquired it in a community property state, it would have been community property.

The right to manage and control community property is a subject for differing statutory provisions among the various community property states. Traditionally the husband alone had this power. The United States Supreme Court, in *Kirchberg v. Feenstra,*[‡] was presented with an Equal Protection Clause challenge to the former Louisiana statute which made the husband the "head and master" of the community and gave him the power to convey community property without the wife's consent. The Court held that such gender-based classifications cannot stand in the absence of proof that they further some important governmental interest. Finding no such interest in this case, the Court held that the statute violated the [Equal Protection Clause of the] Fourteenth Amendment. Within the constitutional limit so laid down, the states have provided for management and control by each spouse, have required the consent of both spouses for certain transfers of community property, and have authorized joint management of at least some forms of community property. The obvious analogy here is to the law of partnership, since the spouses owe each other **fiduciary** duties of good faith and fair treatment in dealing with community property, as do partners with respect to partnership property.

Fiduciary Pertaining to good faith, loyalty, trust, and candor; pertaining to the obligation to protect another's interest and to provide fair treatment.

---

*There may be other presumptions, such as the statutory presumption in California that where a single family residence is acquired by husband and wife as joint tenants, it is community property.

[†]Mart. (N.S.) 569, 16 Am.Dec. 212 (La. 1827).

[‡]450 U.S. 455, 101 S. Ct. 1195, 67 L. Ed. 2d 428 (1981).

WHAT PROPERTY IS DIVIDED AND WHO GETS WHAT?

The general rule in community property states and in common law property states is that property acquired by a party *before the marriage* is deemed to be the separate property of that party and therefore not divisible upon divorce unless both parties agree to divide it. The same is usually true of property obtained solely by one spouse through gift or inheritance during the marriage, e.g., from a relative of that spouse. During the marriage, however, such property will undoubtedly increase in value. This **appreciation** may be deemed to be divisible property regardless of the manner in which the property was acquired or when it was acquired.

Appreciation An increase in the value of property.

All other property obtained during the marriage is potentially divisible upon divorce, depending upon the special laws of individual states.

After identifying which property is divisible, the next question is how the division is made. In community property states like California, the division is usually 50/50 unless the parties agree otherwise in a separation agreement. In common law property states, courts have considerably more discretion. If the parties cannot agree on how to divide marital assets, the goal of the court in a common law property state is to achieve an **equitable distribution** (see Exhibit 6.5). The court will weigh a number of factors such as:

Equitable Distribution The fair, but not necessarily equal, division between former spouses of property acquired during the marriage.

☐ Who earned the asset

☐ What the other spouse did to contribute to the household while the asset was being earned

☐ Any interruption of personal career or educational opportunities of either spouse (especially the one who stayed at home with the kids)

☐ The length of the marriage

☐ The desirability of keeping the marital home for use as a residence for any dependent

☐ Any intentional dissipation of marital assets

☐ Any other factor necessary to do equity and justice to the parties

☐ **EXHIBIT 6.5   Property Division upon Divorce**

KIND OF PROPERTY	COMMON LAW PROPERTY STATES	COMMUNITY PROPERTY STATES
Property acquired before marriage	This is separate property. All of it goes to the spouse who acquired it unless he or she agrees otherwise.	This is separate property. All of it goes to the spouse who acquired it unless he or she agrees otherwise.
Property acquired by one spouse during marriage by gift or inheritance	This is separate property. All of it goes to the spouse who acquired it unless he or she agrees otherwise.	This is separate property. All of it goes to the spouse who acquired it unless he or she agrees otherwise.
Property acquired during marriage other than by gift or inheritance	If the spouses cannot agree, each gets a fair (equitable) share, which may or may not be equal.	50/50 split between the spouses unless they agree otherwise.
Increased value (appreciation) of separate or community property that occurs during marriage	If the spouses cannot agree, each gets a fair (equitable) share of the amount of the appreciation, which may or may not be equal.	50/50 split of the amount of the appreciation between the spouses unless they agree otherwise.

In a common law property state that applies the principle of equitable distribution, most courts will seek a property division that reflects the proportionate contribution made by each spouse. Often a court will presume that the division should be equal unless the factors listed above would suggest a different allocation. A major theme in this area of family law is the recognition of the contribution made by the stay-at-home spouse to the acquisition and growth (i.e., appreciation) of marital assets. It is often clear, for example, that a husband would not be able to earn $150,000 a year, study the stock market, and buy two homes out of his salary if he also had to stay home to care for the three kids and worry about the washing machine that is not working! Since permanent alimony is becoming less common, courts use property division as the primary vehicle of achieving "equity and justice."

Once the decision is made on how to divide the property in a community property state or in a common law property state, the next concern is to identify the most *practical* way to accomplish the division. A 50/50 split or a 60/40 split of cash is easy. Not so for the division of homes, vehicles, and businesses. They can't be conveniently chopped up. Sometimes it is practical to sell an asset and divide the proceeds according to the allocation that applies. When this is not practical, other options are negotiated and/or ordered by the court:

☐ The wife will keep the house, and the husband will keep the car and his business.

☐ The wife will live in the house, but the husband will retain a designated amount of the equity in the house, which must be paid to him if the house is sold.

☐ The wife receives $25,000 as a lump-sum payment, and the husband receives everything else.

Many factors can play a role in the negotiations. For example, the wife may agree to a lower property division in exchange for the husband's agreement to let her have custody of the children. She may agree to a higher alimony award in exchange for a relatively lower property division out of fear that he is on the brink of bankruptcy (in which the property division debts, but not the alimony debts, might be discharged). He may be able to convince her to take more alimony and less property so that he can take advantage of the alimony tax deduction. She may agree even though she must pay taxes on the alimony received. They both know that his higher income would cause the same money to be taxed at a higher rate. He may find ways to compensate her for this in other terms of the separation agreement.

UNLAWFUL DISSIPATION

As we saw when discussing alimony, a spouse cannot avoid a support obligation by voluntarily becoming poor. The amount of the obligation will be based on earning capacity, not necessarily actual earnings. A similar principle is at work in the property division. One spouse cannot squander—**dissipate**— marital property so that there is nothing left to divide in the separation agreement. If dissipation occurs, a court will try to make the victim whole by awarding him or her an amount equivalent to the dissipation. This award will come from the separate property of the spouse who committed the dissipation or from this spouse's share of the marital property. For example, assume the

Dissipate Waste, destroy, or squander.

marital assets of Ted and Helen are $50,000 in a joint checking account and a home with an equity of $200,000. They live in a state that divides marital property equally. Two months before the divorce, Helen goes to Las Vegas and gambles away the entire $50,000 in the checking account. She has dissipated a marital asset. The divorce court would have granted Ted $25,000 of the checking account funds. Since this is no longer possible, the court will look to other available assets. Instead of granting Ted a 50 percent interest in the home ($100,000), it will grant him a 62.5 percent interest ($125,000) as a way to compensate him for Helen's dissipation. If needed to compensate Ted for his loss, the court could reach any available separate property belonging to Helen.

PENSIONS, DEGREES, AND GOODWILL

Three recent areas of contention involving property division are pensions, professional degrees (or occupational licenses), and the goodwill of a business. Until fairly recently, parties negotiating a separation agreement did *not* include these items in their bargaining. They were either considered too intangible or were simply assumed to belong to one of the parties separately, usually the husband. Litigation and legislation, however, have forced drastic changes in these views. As a result, the negotiations for a separation agreement now regularly take account of these items in one way or another.

DIVIDING A PENSION   Many workers are covered by **pension** plans at work. Employer-sponsored plans may be financed entirely by the employer or by the employer with employee contributions. There are two main kinds of pension plans, the **defined-benefit plan** and the **defined-contribution plan.**

> □ **Defined-Benefit Plan**   The amount of the benefit is fixed, but not the amount of contribution. The formula for such plans usually gears the benefits to years of service and earnings (e.g., a benefit of $10 a month for each year of employment) or a stated dollar amount.

> □ **Defined-Contribution Plan**   Each employee has his or her own individual account. The amount of contribution is generally fixed, but the amount of the benefit is not. Such plans usually involve profit-sharing, stock-bonus, or money-purchase arrangements where the employer's contribution (usually a percentage of profits) is divided among the participants based on the individual's wages and/or years of service and accumulations in the individual's pension account. The eventual benefit is determined by the amount of total contributions and investment earnings in the years during which the employee is covered.

Vested   Fixed so that it cannot be taken away by future events or conditions; accrued so that you now have a right to present or future possession or enjoyment.

Qualified Domestic Relations Order   A court order that allows a nonemployee to reach pension benefits of an employee or former employee to satisfy a support or other marital obligation to the nonemployee.

Alternate Payee   A nonemployee entitled to receive pension benefits of an employee or former employee pursuant to a Qualified Domestic Relations Order.

Accumulated benefits in these plans are not **vested** until the employee has a nonforfeitable right to receive the benefits, whether or not the employee leaves the job before retirement.

Can pension benefits be divided upon divorce? Assume that a wife stayed home to care for the children while her husband worked. Is she entitled to any of his pension benefits? The question is important because retirement benefits may be the largest portion of the marital estate in many marriages.

Yes, it is possible for a spouse, an ex-spouse, or a child to receive some or all of these pension benefits if the court so directs in a special order called a **Qualified Domestic Relations Order (QDRO).** Any one of these individuals can become an **alternate payee** under the plan. If the parties cannot agree in their separation agreement on how to divide pension benefits, a judge can issue a QDRO to enforce an obligation of child support (see chapter 8), alimony, or other marital property right of the alternate payee. Before this dramatic change in the law became effective in 1984, individuals other than the employee could not demand that pension benefits be paid directly to them. QDROs have now made this practice commonplace. Exhibit 6.6 provides an example of a typical QDRO provided by an employer as guidance to its employees in drafting proposed QDROs to be signed by a judge. The example assumes that the alternate payee will receive one-half of the employee's pension benefits. It is certainly possible for a different allocation to be ordered, however.

How much does the nonemployee receive from the employee's pension fund? What amount or percentage will be ordered in the QDRO? The parties can negotiate this in their separation agreement. If they cannot reach an agree-

---

□ **EXHIBIT 6.6   Qualified Domestic Relations Order (QDRO)**

This sample QDRO is provided by Apex Company, Inc., to its employees as an example of an order the company will treat as a QDRO through a separate court order or as part of the divorce decree itself. The company does not give individual tax advice or advice about the marital property rights of either party.

1. Pursuant to Section 414(p) of the Internal Revenue Code, this qualified domestic relations order ("Order") assigns a portion of the benefits payable in the Apex Company, Inc. Annuity Plan ("the Plan") from _____[Member's Name]_____ (Member No. _____) to _____[Spouse's Name]_____ in recognition of the existence of his/her marital rights in _____[Member's Name]_____ retirement benefits.

2. The Member in the Plan is _____[Member's Name]_____ , whose last known mailing address is _____ , Social Security No. _____ .

3. The Alternate Payee is _____[Spouse's Name]_____ , whose last known mailing address is _____ , Social Security No. _____ .

[Use the following paragraph if the Member is not already receiving retirement benefits:]

4. Apex Company, Inc. is hereby ORDERED to assign a portion of the accumulations so that each party as of the date of the assignment has a retirement account of approximately the same value. The date of assignment is _____ .

[Use the following paragraph if the Member is already receiving retirement benefits:]

4. Apex Company Inc. is hereby ORDERED to make monthly payments equal to one-half of the amount payable to _____[Member's Name]_____ directly to _____[Spouse's Name_____ . These direct payments to _____[Spouse's Name]_____ shall be made beginning after the date of this order and ending at _____[Member's Name]_____ 's death.

5. This qualified domestic relations order is not intended to require the Plan to provide any type or form of benefits or any option not otherwise provided by the Plan, nor shall this Order require the Plan to provide for increased benefits not required by the Plan. This Order does not require the Plan to provide benefits to the Alternate Payee that are required to be paid to another Alternate Payee under another order previously determined to be a qualified domestic relations order.

6. All benefits payable under the Apex Company, Inc. Annuity Plan other than those payable to _____[Spouse's Name]_____ shall be payable to _____[Member's Name]_____ in such manner and form as he/she may elect in his/her sole and undivided discretion, subject only to plan requirements.

7. _____[Spouse's Name]_____ is ORDERED AND DECREED to report any retirement payments received on any applicable income tax return. The Plan Administrator of Apex Company, Inc. is authorized to issue the appropriate Internal Revenue Form for any direct payment made to _____[Spouse's Name]_____ .

8. While it is anticipated that the Plan Administrator will pay directly to _____[Spouse's Name]_____ the benefit awarded to her, _____[Member's Name]_____ is designated a constructive trustee to the extent he receives any retirement benefits under the Plan that are due to _____[Spouse's Name]_____ but paid to _____[Member's Name]_____ . _____[Member's Name]_____ is ORDERED AND DECREED to pay the benefit defined above directly to _____[Spouse's Name]_____ within three days after receipt by him.

_____   _____
[NAME OF COURT]   [NAME OF JUDGE]

ment, the court will decide. It is possible for an alternate payee to receive up to 100 percent of the employee's pension benefits.

Employees and employers do not like QDROs—the former because they had thought their pension could never be touched by anyone, and the latter because of the extra administrative burden imposed. During negotiations, the employee will usually try to get the other side to accept some other benefit in lieu of asking the court for a QDRO. If, however, nothing else of comparable value is available, dividing pension benefits through a QDRO is unavoidable. (In chapter 8, we will consider a similar device called a Qualified Medical Child Support Order—QMCSO—that covers health insurance for children.)

A great deal depends on the *value* of the employee's pension plan. Without knowing this value, the negotiations are meaningless. Yet determining value can be a complex undertaking, often requiring the services of actuarial and accounting specialists. Value will depend on factors such as:

□ Type of pension plan

□ Amount contributed to the plan by the employee and by the employer

□ How benefits are determined, e.g., when they accrue or are vested

□ Age of employee

□ Employee's earliest retirement date

□ Employee's life expectancy

Present Value The amount of money an individual would have to be given now to produce or generate a certain amount of money in a designated period of time.

Often the parties must calculate the **present value** of a benefit. Assume that at the beginning of the year you become entitled to $1,000 at the end of the year. On January 1, you are *not* given $1,000; you are given the present value of $1,000. The present value of $1,000 is $909.09 if we assume that you could invest $900.09 in a local bank (or in some other investment entity) at 10 percent interest. When a benefit is distributed, what is actually received may be the present value of the benefit, calculated in this way. If a 10 percent rate of interest is too high in today's market, the parties will have to assume a lower interest percentage and a higher present value. At 5 percent interest, for example, the present value of $1,000 is $952.38. (If you brought $952.38 to a bank offering 5 percent interest, at the end of the year you would have $1,000 in your account.)

A number of companies have been formed that help parties value pensions. One such company is Legal Economic Evaluations, Inc., whose application is presented in Exhibit 6.7.

ASSIGNMENT 6.2

Find a friend or relative who works at a place where he or she is covered by a pension. Assume that you work at an office where your friend or relative is a client who is seeking a divorce in which one of the issues is the division of pension benefits. (If you are covered by an employee pension plan, use yourself as the client in this assignment.)

Your supervisor asks you to do two things. First, obtain as much information as you can about the client's pension, e.g., the kind of plan it is, when benefits become available. Second, obtain an employer-approved copy of a sample QDRO. Ask the client to call the personnel office at work in order to speak to the "plan administrator" (the person in charge of administering the pension plan) and request the information and the sample.

Prepare a report that summarizes the plan's features, pointing out whatever you think will be relevant to later negotiations on dividing the pension benefits. (You can change the name of your friend or relative.) Attach the copy of the sample QDRO to your report.

☐ **EXHIBIT 6.7 Pension Valuation Form**

**LEGAL
ECONOMIC
EVALUATIONS, INC.**
1000 Elwell Court, #203
Palo Alto, CA 94303
(415)969-7682

PENSION VALUATION

ATTORNEY INFORMATION

Name _____   Today's Date ____ / ____ / ____
Name of Firm _____ Representing: ☐ Petitioner's Spouse
Street _____   ☐ Pensioner
City, State & Zip Code _____   ☐ Both
Telephone Number (   ) _____ How Did you Hear of Us? _____

CASE INFORMATION

(For Faster Service, please collect the information below and call one of our Economists at (800)221-6826 or (800)648-9900 inside California.)

Pensioner Name _____ Gender M F Birthdate ____ / ____ / ____
Employer _____ Occupation _____
Date of Employment ____ / ____ / ____   Date Entered Plan ____ / ____ / ____   Termination Date ____ / ____ / ____
Spouse Name _____   Birthdate ____ / ____ / ____
Date of Marriage ____ / ____ / ____

If the pensioner is already receiving benefits, how much are they ($ ____) and when did they begin (____ / ____ / ____)?
Have you enclosed a copy of the pension plan booklet? ☐ Yes
Have you enclosed the pensioner's most recent benefits statement? ☐ Yes
Is there any other recent correspondence regarding pension benefits? ☐ Yes ☐ No   If so, please enclose a copy.
If no information regarding benefit amounts is available, please list the pensioner's salary for the last five years below:
(Also state any other relevant information below.)

_____
_____
_____
_____

In addition to the present value of the pension, do you wish us to show the spouse's net interest based on the ratio of service during marriage to total plan service (also known as the "Time Rule" or "Coverture Percentage")?
☐ Yes ☐ No

BILLING

☐ Enclosed is a check for $100 payable to Legal Economic Evaluations, Inc.
  Please mail remittance and this completed form to the above address.

M3

DIVIDING A DEGREE

Bill and Pat are married in 1973. While Bill goes through college, medical school, and internship to become a doctor, Pat works full-time to support the two of them. On the day he obtains his license to practice medicine, they decide to divorce. During the long years of Bill's education, they have accumulated almost no property. Pat earns $25,000 a year at her job. Since she is fully capable of supporting herself, the court decides that she should receive no alimony. They have no children.

Many would consider it an outrage that Pat walks away from the marriage with nothing. She is not eligible for alimony, and there is no tangible property to divide. He walks away with a professional degree and a doctor's license ready to embark on a lucrative career. Courts have slowly come to the realization that the supporting spouse should be given a remedy in such a situation.

In our example, what financial factors are involved?

1. The amount Pat and/or her family contributed to Bill's support while he was in school

2. The amount Pat and/or her family contributed to the payment of Bill's education expenses

3. The amount Bill would have contributed to the marriage if he had worked during these years rather than gone to school

4. Any increased earnings Pat would have had if she had taken a different job, e.g., by moving to a different location

5. Any increased earnings Pat would have had if she had continued her education rather than working to support Bill through his education

6. The increased standard of living Pat would have enjoyed due to Bill's expected high earnings if they had stayed married

7. The share of his increased earnings to which Pat would have been entitled if they had stayed married

Restitution An equitable remedy in which a person is restored to his or her original position prior to the loss or injury. Restoring to the plaintiff the value of what he or she parted with.

Some courts will consider only items (1) and (2) in providing Pat with a remedy. As a matter of equity, she is entitled only to **restitution**—a return of what she and/or her family contributed while Bill was acquiring his degree and license. Such courts do not consider a degree and license to be divisible property. They are personal to the holder. Under this view, it logically follows that she is not entitled to a share of his increased earnings as a result of the degree and license. All of the above items (1–7) are taken into consideration in deciding the question of *spousal support.* Increased earnings as a result of the degree and license are taken into consideration because one of the factors in an alimony or maintenance decree is the spouse's ability to pay. The problem, however, is that the wife may not be eligible for alimony because of her own employability. Nor can equity be done by giving the wife a generous share of tangible property since no such property may have been accumulated due to the fact that the husband had high educational expenses and little or no income of his own. In such situations, one minimal remedy is a direct award for items (1) and (2) above, which again amounts to little more than restitution. A few courts, however, will deny even this remedy, taking the position that the wife, in effect, was making a gift of her money and other resources to the husband during his education.

A growing number of cases, however, have ruled that the degree and license *do* constitute divisible marital property and that more than restitution is called for. They take the position that it is unconscionable for one spouse to walk away with nothing while the other enjoys the fruits of their joint labor and hardship. The degree and license are the product of a joint investment. It is unrealistic to think that the sacrificing spouse was making a gift of time and money to the other spouse who studied for the degree and license. In one case, for example, the divorce court concluded that the wife was entitled to an equitable portion of her husband's medical license since it was achieved through the mutual sacrifice and effort of both spouses. The trial court held that the license had a present value of $188,000 and awarded the wife 40 percent of this amount, payable in eleven yearly payments.

Frank and Elaine are married in your state. Both work at low-paying jobs at a fast-food restaurant. Elaine wishes to become a paralegal, and Frank would like to become an electrician. A local institute has a one-year paralegal training program and a nine-month electrician training program. Frank and Elaine decide that only one of them can go to school at a time. Frank volunteers to let Elaine go first, keeping his job at the restaurant to support them both while she is at the institute. A month before Elaine is scheduled to graduate, Frank has a serious accident at the restaurant. He will not recover fully from his injury or be able to go to school for at least five years. When Elaine is graduated, she obtains a good job as a paralegal. The parties seek a divorce a month after graduation. There are no children from the marriage, and no tangible property to divide. In the divorce proceeding, Frank tells the court that the only asset that can be divided is Elaine's paralegal certificate. He asks the court to award him a percentage of the earnings that Elaine will have during the next five years as a paralegal. What should the court do?

DIVIDING A BUSINESS   When a divorce occurs, one of the assets to be divided may be a business acquired during the marriage or at least developed during this time even if one of the parties had the business before the marriage. The business could be a large corporation, a small sole proprietorship, a partnership, a law practice, a medical practice, etc. Business appraisers are often hired to place a value on the business. In addition to plant and equipment, a number of intangible items must be valued, e.g., patents, trademarks, employment agreements, copyrights, securities, and goodwill.

Many standard business documents[4] must be collected when valuating a business. For example:

- [ ] Federal, state, and local income tax returns for the last five years
- [ ] Annual and interim financial statements
- [ ] Bank statements
- [ ] Depreciation schedules
- [ ] Articles of incorporation and bylaws or partnership agreements, including amendments
- [ ] Minutes of meetings of shareholders and directors
- [ ] Buy/sell agreements of shareholders or partners, including amendments
- [ ] Loan applications
- [ ] W-2 statements (or the equivalent) for the highest paid employees
- [ ] Leases
- [ ] Production schedules
- [ ] Inventory reports
- [ ] Management reports
- [ ] Billing records

One aspect of a business that is sometimes particularly difficult to evaluate is its **goodwill.** Because of goodwill, the company is expected to have earnings beyond what is considered normal for the type of business involved. Individuals providing services, such as accountants and lawyers, may also have goodwill:

Goodwill   The favorable reputation of a business that causes it to generate additional business.

---

4. Part of the following list comes from Business Valuation Research, Inc., of Seattle, Washington.

If you are a lawyer facing divorce, it is open season on your practice. . . . Like it or not, law practices and lawyer's goodwill are assets. That you can't sell your practice doesn't mean it has no value. And there are almost no legal limits on the methods an appraiser may use in assigning a value to a law practice. . . . One approach is called the excess earnings method. An appraiser looks at published surveys to find the average income for a lawyer of your experience and type of practice, then compares your earnings with the average. If your earnings are higher than the average, the increment is said to be attributable to goodwill. If your ability to attract clients and collect substantial fees from them brings you more income than you would earn working for an average salary, you have built real goodwill. Gabrielson & Walker, *Surviving Your Own Divorce*, 76, 77 CALIF. LAWYER (June 1987).

If goodwill was developed during the marriage, the spouse who stayed at home may be deemed to have contributed to it (as well as to the rest of the business). In community property states, spouses have a 50/50 interest in the portion of the business (including goodwill) that materialized during the marriage. In other states, the court might reach a different equitable allocation.

The fact that a business (with or without goodwill) is a divisible part of the marital estate does not necessarily mean that upon divorce the business must be sold so that the proceeds can be physically divided. The separation agreement may provide, for example, that the husband gives the wife $150,000 in exchange for the release of any interest that the wife may have in his business. Or vice versa, if she is the one primarily responsible for the business. Similarly, a court may order such an exchange if the parties are not able to agree on dividing the business in their separation agreement.

■■■■■ INSURANCE

A number of questions must be considered by the parties:

☐ What kinds of insurance do the parties now have?

☐ How have the insurance premiums been paid?

☐ Following the separation, what will happen to the policies?

☐ Is there a need for additional insurance?

Several different kinds of insurance policies could be in effect at the time the parties draft the separation agreement:

☐ Life insurance

☐ Homeowners' insurance

☐ Hospitalization or other medical insurance

☐ Liability insurance (for business)

☐ Car insurance

☐ Umbrella insurance

Each kind of policy should be carefully identified with notations as to how much the premiums are, who has paid them, who the beneficiaries are, whether the beneficiaries can be changed and, if so, by whom, etc. Unfortunately, parties often neglect such important details. Insurance policies can be as crucial as other "property" items that must be divided or otherwise negotiated as part of the separation agreement. The parties may opt to leave the policies as they are with no changes. This is fine if it is a conscious decision of *both* parties after *all* the facts are known about each policy, the tax consequences are explained, and the economic advantages and disadvantages of the various ways of handling each policy are discussed.

As we have seen, one spouse usually has no obligation to support the other spouse or the children after the payor spouse dies. The latter, however, may want to assume this obligation voluntarily. Life insurance on the payor's life, with the beneficiaries being the other spouse and/or the children, is a common way of doing this. If such a life insurance policy already exists, then the payor may agree to keep it effective (e.g., pay the premiums) after the separation. The payee and children, however, may not gain much protection from such an agreement if the payor can change the beneficiaries. Hence, as part of the bargaining process, the payee may ask that the designation of the beneficiaries be made irrevocable.

■■■■ DEBTS

The parties must discuss how to handle:

☐ Debts outstanding (i.e., unpaid) at the time the separation agreement is signed

☐ Debts incurred after the separation agreement is signed

A great variety of debts may be outstanding:

☐ Debts between the spouses (e.g., a loan made by one spouse to the other during the marriage)

☐ Business debts incurred by the husband

☐ Family debts incurred by the husband

☐ Business debts incurred by the wife

☐ Family debts incurred by the wife

☐ Business or family debts incurred by both the husband and wife (i.e., the debts are in both names so that there is **joint and several liability** on the debts, meaning that a creditor could sue the husband and wife *together* on the debt, or could sue *either* the husband or the wife for payment of the whole debt).

> **Joint and Several Liability** More than one person is legally responsible. They are responsible together and individually for the entire amount.

The parties must decide who is going to pay what debts, and the separation agreement should specifically reflect what they have decided.

The extent to which the parties are in debt is relevant to (1) the necessity of using present cash and other resources to pay these debts, (2) the availability of resources to support spouse and children, and (3) the possibility of bankruptcy now or in the immediate future. As for the husband's personal or business debts, for example, the wife should not take the attitude that such debts are "his problem." His bankruptcy might cause her to lose whatever he still owes her under the property division agreement. (As we have seen, however, a bankruptcy would not discharge alimony and child support obligations. See Exhibit 6.3.)

As to future debts (i.e., those incurred after the separation agreement is signed), the normal expectation of the parties is that they will pay their own debts. (A cautious spouse, however will often cancel all joint credit cards.) Except for the obligations that arise out of the separation agreement itself, the parties are on their own. A clause should be inserted in the agreement providing that each party promises not to attempt to use the credit of the other.

■■■■ TAXES

In chapter 11 we will discuss the tax consequences of separation agreements. Our focus here is on the question of who pays the taxes and who will be able to take advantage of certain tax benefits. The following are the kinds of situations the parties need to anticipate:

☐ If the Internal Revenue Service (IRS) assesses a tax deficiency and penalty for a prior year during which the parties filed a joint return, who pays the deficiency and penalty?

☐ If the parties file their last joint return in the current tax year, and then, many months later, the IRS assesses a tax deficiency and penalty on that last tax return, who pays this deficiency and penalty?

☐ In the year in which the separation agreement is signed, if the parties file separate returns, with whose resources are each person's taxes paid?

☐ In the current year and in future years, who takes the tax deduction for the payment of interest on the mortgage and for the payment of property taxes on the home where the children and custodial parent continue to live?

☐ In the current year and in future years, who takes the tax exemption for each of the dependent children?

☐ What happens to any tax refunds for the current tax year and for any prior year?

Indemnify To compensate another for any loss or expense incurred.

Often, the husband will agree to a clause in the separation agreement that he will **indemnify** the wife against any tax deficiencies and penalties that may arise out of the joint returns filed in any year during their marriage. Under such a clause, he will have to pay the entire deficiency and penalty for which they both may be jointly and severally liable. Similarly, the parties must also agree on how tax refunds, if any, are to be divided. Such refunds are usually payable by government check to both of the parties. Two signatures are required to sign such checks. Finally, years after a particular return is filed, the IRS might institute an audit. It is a good idea to insert a clause in the separation agreement that both parties agree to cooperate with each other in responding to the issues raised during any possible audits in the future.

There are laws on who can receive the tax benefits of exemptions and deductions from alimony, interest payments, and property-tax payments. The parties do not have total freedom in deciding who can use these tax benefits. The point, however, is that one of the parties will be entitled to the benefits. This is an economic advantage that should be taken into consideration in the overall evaluation of who is getting what from the separation agreement. The parties make a big mistake when they fail to take account of such matters. The separation agreement may specify a dollar amount to be transferred pursuant to a support clause or a property division clause. If, however, all the tax factors have not been considered, the parties may later be surprised by the discrepancy between such stated dollar figures and the *real* amounts that they receive and pay out.

■■■ WILLS

The parties must consider a number of questions involving wills and estates:

☐ Do the spouses already have wills naming each other as beneficiaries? If so, are these wills to be changed? In most states, a divorce automatically revokes gifts to a surviving spouse unless the will specifically says otherwise. Nevertheless, the parties may want to make this explicit in their separation agreement and also cover the period between separation and the issuance of the final divorce decree.

☐ Have they named each other as **executor** of their estates? If so, is this to be changed?

☐ Is the husband going to agree to leave his wife and/or children something in his will? If so, and this requires a change in his will, when is this change to be made?

☐ Is either spouse mentioned as a beneficiary in the will of a relative of the other spouse? If so, is this likely to be changed?

When a spouse dies, the surviving spouse has important rights in the property of the deceased spouse, sometimes in spite of what the latter intended or provided for in a will. Assume that a spouse dies **testate** leaving nothing to the surviving spouse. In most states, a surviving spouse who is dissatisfied with a will can **elect against the will** and receive a **forced share** of the deceased's property. This share is often the same share that the surviving spouse would have received if the deceased had died **intestate.**

The separation agreement should specify what happens to the right to elect against a will and similar rights such as **dower** and **curtesy.** The normal provision is that each side *releases* all such rights in the other's property.

◼◼ MISCELLANEOUS PROVISIONS

A number of other items need to be considered:

LEGAL EXPENSES

One spouse is often ordered by the court to pay the attorney fees of the other in a divorce action. The parties may want to specify this in the separation agreement itself. They should consider not only the legal costs (counsel fees, filing fees, etc.) of a potential divorce, but also the legal costs incurred in connection with the preparation of the separation agreement itself. Of course, if both have adequate resources of their own, the parties may agree that they will pay their own legal bills.

NONMOLESTATION CLAUSE

Most separation agreements contain a **nonmolestation clause,** in which both parties agree, in effect, to leave each other alone. Specifically, they will not try to live with the other person, interfere with each other's lifestyle, or bother each other in any way.

◼◼ MODIFICATION OF THE SEPARATION AGREEMENT

Generally, a court has no power to alter the terms of a valid contract. A separation agreement is a contract. Can its terms be modified? Clearly, the parties to any contract can mutually agree to modify its terms. But can the court *force* a modification on the parties when only one party wants it?

The answer may depend on which terms of the separation agreement are in question. *Property division* terms, as indicated earlier, are rarely modifiable (see Exhibit 6.3). *Child custody* and *child support* terms, however, are almost always

Executor The person designated in a will to carry out the terms of the will and handle related matters.

Testate Die leaving a valid will.

Elect against the Will To obtain a designated share of a deceased spouse's estate in spite of what the latter provided or failed to provide for the surviving spouse in a will.

Forced Share The share of a deceased spouse's estate the surviving spouse receives in spite of what the deceased provided or failed to provide for the surviving spouse in a will.

Intestate Die without leaving a valid will.

Dower The right of a widow to the lifetime use of one-third of the land her deceased husband owned during the marriage.

Curtesy The right of a husband to the lifetime use of all the land his deceased wife owned during the marriage (if issue were born of the marriage).

Nonmolestation Clause A clause in an agreement that the parties will not bother each other.

modifiable according to the court's perception of the best interest of the child (see chapters 7 and 8). The area of greatest controversy concerns *alimony* or *spousal-support* terms.

First, consider two extreme and relatively rare circumstances where the court can modify spousal-support terms:

☐ The separation agreement itself includes a provision allowing a court to modify its terms.

☐ The needy spouse has become so destitute that he or she will become a public charge unless a modification is ordered.

If neither of these situations exists, can the court order a modification of the spousal-support terms of the separation agreement? This involves two separate questions. Does the court have the power to modify, and if so, when will it exercise this power?

THE POWER TO MODIFY

In a few states a court has no power to modify a spousal-support term unless the parties have agreed in the separation agreement to allow the court to do so. Most states, however, will allow their courts to modify a separation agreement even if it expressly says that modification is not allowed. A number of theories have been advanced to support this view. Some states hold that the separation agreement is merely advisory to the court and that as a matter of public policy, the court cannot allow the question of support to be determined solely by the parties. The state as a whole has an interest in seeing to it that this sensitive question is properly resolved. What the parties have agreed upon will be a factor in the court's determination, but it will not be the controlling factor. Other states advance the theory of merger. When a court accepts the terms of a separation agreement, it can *incorporate* and *merge* them into the divorce decree. The agreement loses its separate identity. The question is not whether the separation agreement can be modified, but whether the decree can be modified. Courts are much less reluctant to modify their own decrees than they are to modify the private contracts of parties. Under the merger doctrine, the contract no longer exists. Suppose, however, that a court incorporates but does *not* merge the separation agreement into the decree. Here the court simply refers to the separation agreement in its decree and usually approves the spousal-support terms the parties agreed to. Since there is no merger, the separation agreement remains as an independent—and nonmodifiable—contract.

THE EXERCISE OF THE POWER TO MODIFY

Assuming the court has the power to modify spousal-support orders, when will the court use it? The general rule is that a modification will be ordered only when there has been a substantial change of circumstances of a continuing nature that is not due to voluntary action or inaction of the parties. Furthermore, some courts limit the exercise of their modification power to periodic or ongoing alimony payments; they will not modify a *lump-sum* support award.

Tom and Mary enter a separation agreement that is approved, incorporated, and merged by the court in its divorce decree. Tom is required to pay Mary $750 a month alimony. Assume that Tom comes to the court a year later seeking a decrease, and/or Mary comes seeking an increase.

Unfortunately, courts are not always consistent as to when they will allow a modification in such a case. Consider the following circumstances:

1. *The ex-husband becomes sick and earns substantially less.* Most courts would modify the decree to lessen the amount he must pay—at least during the period when his earning capacity is affected by the illness.

2. *The ex-husband suddenly starts earning a great deal more.* The ex-wife will usually not be able to increase her alimony award simply because her ex-husband becomes more wealthy than he was at the time of the divorce decree. The result might be different if she can show that the *original* alimony award was inadequate due to his weaker earning capacity at that time.

3. *The ex-wife violates the terms of the separation agreement relating to the visitation rights of the ex-husband/father.* Some courts feel that alimony payments and visitation rights are interdependent. If the ex-wife interferes with the father's visitation rights with the children, these courts will reduce or terminate her alimony. For such a result, however, the interference must be substantial.

4. *The ex-wife engages in "immoral" conduct, e.g., has a live-in lover.* When the ex-husband finds out about the lover, his concern is that his alimony payments are being used to support his ex-wife's lover. Most states will not reduce the alimony payments for this reason. In the states that will, the ex-wife's affair usually must be flagrant and ongoing.

5. *The ex-husband wants to retire, change jobs, or go back to school.* When his income is reduced in this way, the courts will consider a downward modification of the alimony obligation only if the proposed change in lifestyle is made in good faith and not simply as a way to avoid paying the original amount of alimony. A rich executive, for example, cannot "drop out" and become a poor farmer. Such an executive, however, may be able to take a lower paying job if this is required for his health.

6. *The ex-husband remarries.* In most states, his alimony obligation to his first wife is not affected by his remarriage. A few states, however, will consider a reduction if it is clear that he cannot meet the burden of supporting two families, particularly when there are children from the second marriage.

7. *The ex-wife remarries.* If the ex-wife remarries, most courts will terminate his alimony obligation unless the parties agreed in the separation agreement that alimony would continue in some form after she remarried.

8. *The ex-husband dies.* Alimony ends on the death of the ex-husband unless the separation agreement provides for its continuance and/or the divorce decree imposes his obligation on the ex-husband's estate.

ASSIGNMENT 6.4

Karen and Jim obtain a divorce decree that awards Karen $500 a month in alimony "until she dies or remarries." A year after the divorce decree becomes final, Karen marries Paul. Jim stops the alimony payments. A year later, this marriage to Paul is annulled. Karen now wants Jim to resume paying her $500 a month alimony and to pay her $6,000 to cover the period when she was "married" to Paul ($500 × 12). What result?

 ARBITRATION AND MEDIATION

Many separation agreements contain a clause providing that disputes arising in the future about the agreement shall be subject to **arbitration.** Normally, a

Arbitration The process of submitting a dispute to a third party outside the judicial system who will render a decision that resolves the dispute.

professional arbitration organization, such as the American Arbitration Association, is specified as the arbitrator who will resolve the dispute. A professional group, however, is not necessary. The parties may select a mutually trusted friend or associate as the arbitrator. The agreement should specify who the arbitrator will be and who will pay the arbitration expenses.

Mediation The process of submitting a dispute to a third party outside the judicial system who will help the parties reach their own resolution of the dispute. The mediator will not render a decision that resolves the dispute.

An alternative to arbitration is **mediation.** In arbitration, the parties agree in advance to abide by the decision rendered by the arbitrator. A mediator, however, does not make a decision. He or she tries to guide the parties to reach a decision *on their own* in much the same manner as a labor mediator tries to assist union and management to reach a settlement. If mediation does not work, the parties either agree to submit the dispute to an arbitrator or are forced to litigate it in court.

■ RECONCILIATION

What happens if the parties become reconciled to each other after they execute the separation agreement but before they divorce? They certainly have the power to cancel or rescind their contract so long as both do so voluntarily. If it is clear that they want to cancel, no problem exists. Legally, the separation agreement goes out of existence. The problem arises when the parties say nothing about the separation agreement after they reconcile and resume cohabitation. Sometime thereafter the parties separate again, and one of them tries to enforce the separation agreement while the other argues that it no longer exists. Courts handle the problem in different ways:

□ The reconciliation will cancel the alimony or spousal-support terms of the separation agreement, but will not cancel the property division terms.

Executory Unperformed as yet.

□ The reconciliation will cancel the **executory** terms of the separation agreement, but will not cancel the executed (already performed) terms.

Reconciliation usually means the full and unconditional resumption of the marital relationship; occasional or casual contact will not suffice. The intent must be to abandon the separation agreement and to resume the marital relationship permanently.

■ Interviewing and Investigation Checklist

Have the Parties Reconciled?

Legal Interviewing Questions

1. On what date did you both sign the separation agreement?

2. When did you stop living together?

3. Where did you both live when you were separated?

4. Was the separation bitter? Describe the circumstances of the separation.

5. After you signed the separation agreement, when did the two of you have your first contact? Describe the circumstances.

6. Have the two of you had sexual intercourse with each other since the separation agreement was signed? How often?

7. Did you ever discuss getting back together again? If so, describe the circumstances, e.g., who initiated the discussion, was there any reluctance?

8. During this period, did the two of you abide by the terms of the separation agreement? Explain.

9. Did you move in together? If so, where did you both stay? Did one of you give up a house or apartment in order to live together?

10. Did you discuss what to do with the separation agreement?

11. Did the two of you assume that it was no longer effective?

—Continued

—Continued

12. After you came together again, did either of you continue abiding by any of the terms of the separation agreement?

13. Did either of you give back whatever he or she received under the terms of the separation agreement?

14. When you resumed the relationship, did you feel that the reunion was going to be permanent? What do you think your spouse felt about it?

15. Did either of you attach any conditions to resuming the relationship again?

16. What have the two of you done since you came together again to indicate that you both considered each other to be husband and wife, e.g., both sign joint tax returns, make joint purchases, spend a lot of time together in public, etc.?

17. Have you separated again? If so, describe the circumstances of the most recent separation.

Possible Investigation Tasks

☐ Interview people who know the plaintiff (P) and defendant (D) well to find out what they know about the alleged reconciliation.

☐ Obtain any documents executed after the separation agreement was signed that may indicate the extent to which P and D did things together during this time, e.g., rent receipts with both of their names on them, opening or continuing joint checking or savings accounts.

ASSIGNMENT 6.5

Tom and Mary execute a separate agreement on February 17, 1978, in which they mutually release all rights (dower, curtesy, right of election, etc.) in each other's estate. They ceased living together on February 2, 1978. On March 13, 1978, Tom moves out of the city. On the next day, he makes a long distance call to Mary in which he says, "This is ridiculous. Why don't you come live with me? You know I still love you." Mary answers, "I guess you're right, but if we are going to live together again, I want you to come back here." Tom then says, "I'm sure we can work that out." They agree to meet next week to discuss it further. Before they meet, Tom dies. Tom's will makes no provision for Mary. Mary now seeks a forced share of his estate, electing against his will. What result? At the time of Tom's death, he was still married to Mary.

▄▄▄▄ SAMPLE SEPARATION AGREEMENTS

Sample Separation Agreement—Equitable Distribution State
7 West's Legal Forms, rev. 2d ed.
§ 10.4, pp. 486–495.

THIS AGREEMENT, made and entered into this _____ day of _____ , 199__, by and between:

_____ , residing at _____ (hereinafter referred to as "Wife", and collectively with "Husband" as "the parties"),

-and-

_____ , residing at _____ (hereinafter referred to as "Husband", and collectively with "Wife" as "the parties").

Witnesseth:

WHEREAS, the parties were married on *[date]*, and said marriage still subsists; and

WHEREAS, the parties have one child between them; namely, _____ , born on *[date]*; and

WHEREAS, irreconcilable differences having arisen between the parties, they have been and intend to continue living separate and apart; and

WHEREAS, in light of the parties' separation, they hereby desire to enter into an agreement dealing with the care and custody of their child, and to define their respective financial and property rights, together with all other rights, remedies, privileges and obligations

—Continued

Sample Separation Agreements—*Continued*

which have arisen out of their marriage. The parties agree that their future relations shall be governed and fully prescribed by the terms of this agreement (hereinafter referred to as "the Agreement"); and

WHEREAS, the parties have disclosed to the other's satisfaction the nature and value of all of their presently constituted assets, liabilities and income; and

WHEREAS, Wife having been represented by the law firm of _____ with offices located at _____ , and Husband having knowingly and voluntarily waived his right to counsel; and

NOW, THEREFORE, in consideration of the mutual promises, covenants, agreements and terms herein contained it is agreed by and between the parties as follows:

Article I
Custody and Visitation

1.1   *Custody and Visitation.*   The parties' child, *[name]*, shall primarily reside with Wife, and Husband shall have reasonable visitation as may be agreed upon between the parties, including holidays, vacations and weekends. Husband shall be responsible for *[name]*'s pick-up and drop-off for all visitations.

1.2   *Alienation of Affections.*   It is expressly understood and agreed by the parties that neither shall do anything to alienate the child's affection for or color the child's attitude toward the other. The parties shall cooperate in every way to help the child better adjust to the circumstances as they now and may in the future exist. The parties agree to conduct themselves in a manner that shall be in the child's best interests, and neither shall do anything that shall adversely affect the child's morals, health and welfare.

Article II
Support, Maintenance and Education of Unemancipated Child

2.1   *Child Support.*   Commencing on the effective date of this Agreement (see Article 9.20), Husband agrees to pay to Wife the sum of _____ ($ _____) Dollars per week as and for *[name]*'s child support until the marital home is sold. Thereafter, Husband's obligation shall be reduced to _____ ($ _____) Dollars per week. Husband's said child support obligation shall terminate upon *[name]*'s emancipation as determined by then existing law.

2.2   *Health Insurance and Unreimbursed, Uncovered Health-Related Expenses.*   Wife agrees to provide health insurance coverage for the child as provided through her employment until such time as the child is emancipated or ineligible to receive benefits under Wife's health insurance plan. The parties shall be responsible for all of the child's unreimbursed, uncovered health-related expenses, including, without limitation, medical, dental, optometric, ophthalmologic, orthodontic, psychological, etc., ___ % by Wife and ___ % by Husband. In the event Wife is no longer eligible to provide health insurance in this regard through her employment, then Husband shall provide same through his employment. In the event neither party is eligible or able to provide health insurance in this regard through their employment, then the parties shall obtain independent health insurance, the cost of which shall be apportioned between the parties, ___ % by Wife and ___ % by Husband.

2.3   *Post-Secondary School Education.*   The parties agree to contribute toward the child's post-secondary school education costs and expenses; including, without limitation, tuition, room, board, miscellaneous school fees, books, transportation, and any related costs and expenses, in accordance with their respective abilities to pay.

2.4   *Life Insurance.*   The parties agree that Husband shall maintain any and all policy(ies) of life insurance as maintained during the marriage for the child's benefit, naming Wife as irrevocable trustee thereof. Husband's obligation to maintain such life insurance shall abate upon the child's emancipation. Husband agrees to name Wife as the policy(ies) owner and to provide Wife with the original policy, together with proof of premium payment, on an annual basis.

Article III
Spousal Support and Maintenance

3.1   *Alimony.*   Each party hereby waives, now and forever, notwithstanding any possible foreseeable or unforeseeable changed circumstances, the right to receive alimony or any other form of spousal support from the other.

—Continued

Sample Separation Agreements—*Continued*

3.2 *Insurance.*   Neither party shall have any obligation to provide or maintain any form of insurance for the other's benefit; such insurance to include, without limitation, health, life, automobile, disability, homeowner's etc., and neither shall have any obligation to pay any of the other's unreimbursed, uncovered health-related expenses.

Article IV
Equitable Distribution

4.1 *Marital Home.*   The parties acknowledge that during the marriage they were vested with title, as tenants by the entirety, to premises located at _____ ("the premises"). Contemporaneously with the execution of this Agreement, Husband agrees to convey all of his right, title and interest in and to the said premises to Wife by tendering to her a fully executed Bargain and Sale Deed with Covenants against Grantor's Acts, Affidavit of Title and Affidavit of Consideration, together with any additional documents necessary to accomplish his conveyance. Wife shall thereafter own the premises and the entire contents thereof free and clear of any and all claims to same by Husband. Wife shall be responsible for all carrying and utility costs for the premises and both parties shall be equally responsible for the cost of any reasonable and necessary repairs and maintenance until the marital home is sold. In the event the sale of the premises results in a capital gains tax consequence, the parties agree to be equally responsible to pay same.

4.2 *Automobiles.*   The parties agree that each shall retain ownership of the automobile presently in their possession. Wife agrees to transfer title to the _____ automobile to Husband; however, Wife shall receive the entirety of any proceeds received in connection with the presently pending insurance claim concerning same. With respect to the leased _____ automobile, at such time as the lease expires or the automobile is turned in, the parties shall be equally responsible for any possible charges assessed in connection therewith. The parties understand and acknowledge that each shall continue to be responsible for any and all obligations with respect to their respective said automobiles including, without limitation, costs of maintenance and repairs, license, registration, insurance and any miscellaneous charges in connection therewith.

4.3 *Bank and Financial Accounts.*   The parties each hereby waive, release and relinquish any and all right, title and interest either may have in and to the other's separately titled bank and financial accounts; including, without limitation, checking, savings, certificates of deposit, money markets and financial investment accounts of whatever kind and nature, and neither shall make any claim against the other's property now or in the future. Any bank accounts maintained during the marriage for the benefit of the parties' child shall remain the property of the child and neither party shall adversely affect same.

4.4 *Retirement Plans, 401(k)s, IRAs and Deferred Savings Plans.*   The parties each hereby waive, release and relinquish any and all right, title and interest either may have in and to the other's pension or profit-sharing plan(s), 401(k), IRA account(s), or any other such retirement benefit of like kind and character, and neither shall make any claim to the other's said property, now or in the future. The parties agree to retain possession and ownership of such property as same is presently titled.

4.5 *Stocks and Bonds.*   The parties agree to mutually waive, release and relinquish any and all right, title and interest either may have to any stocks, stock plans and bonds presently in either party's name. The parties agree to retain possession and ownership of such property as same is presently titled.

4.6 *Personal Effects.*   The parties represent and acknowledge that each party's tangible personal effects such as clothing and jewelry, etc., have been previously distributed between them to their mutual satisfaction.

4.7 *Assets Not Specifically Mentioned Herein.*   To the extent any asset acquired during the parties' marriage is not specifically mentioned or distributed herein, the parties agree to divide and distribute same at a future date.

4.8 *Assets Acquired Subsequent to Execution of This Agreement.*   The parties agree that any asset of whatever kind and nature acquired by any possible means and titled in their individual name or in the name of another shall forever hereafter remain their separate property and shall not be subject to distribution, equitable or otherwise, in any possible future proceeding concerning the status of the parties' marriage.

—Continued

Sample Separation Agreements—*Continued*

Article V
Marital Debt

5.1 *Marital Debt.* The parties represent that there are no joint debts for which either may be liable. In the event there are any joint debts not specifically mentioned herein, at such time as they may become known, the parties shall be equally responsible for paying same. The parties agree to each be responsible for paying any debt heretofore or hereafter acquired in their individual names and neither shall seek any contribution from the other toward the payment of same. In the event either party may be called upon by a creditor of the other to satisfy a debt of the other, the indebted party shall promptly defend, indemnify and hold the other harmless from the creditor's actions.

5.2 *Credit Accounts.* To the extent that either party may presently have in their possession credit cards or credit/financial account access cards, which credit was obtained in the name of the other, each agrees to immediately refrain from using such cards at any time now and in the future, and to this end each further agrees to surrender same to the appropriate titled party forthwith.

Article VI
Taxes

6.1 *Tax Returns.* The parties agree to file income tax returns for the years 199 ___ and 199 ___ based upon the most beneficial tax consequences to both of them. Any refunds which may be received in the future by either party and any liabilities, including underpayment of tax, penalties, interest, etc., incurred in connection with any joint income tax return previously or to be filed by the parties shall be shared and/or borne equally by the parties. Wife shall be permitted to take all tax deductions relative to the marital premises on her 199 ___ and subsequent year tax returns.

6.2 *Child Dependency Exemption.* Wife shall be entitled to claim the child as a dependent on her Federal, State, and any other income tax returns.

Article VII
Counsel and Litigation Fees and Costs

7.1 The parties understand and agree that each shall assume and be responsible for the payment of their own attorney's fees and costs incurred in connection with the negotiation and preparation of this Agreement, and each agrees to defend, indemnify and hold the other harmless from any obligation that may have arisen in connection with their said attorney's fees and costs.

Article VIII
Reconciliation

8.1 *Reconciliation.* Subject to any possible superseding written agreement between the parties, notwithstanding the parties' possible reconciliation, all provisions contained in this agreement, executory or not, shall nonetheless be binding upon the parties and each shall have an affirmative obligation to fulfill their respective obligations to each other as defined herein.

Article IX
Miscellaneous Provisions

9.1 *Independent Legal Representation.* The parties acknowledge that each has had the opportunity to be represented by independent counsel with respect to the negotiation, drafting and execution of this Agreement. Wife has been represented by _____ , with offices at _____ and Husband, notwithstanding his opportunity to do so, Husband has freely, voluntarily and without coercion, duress or undue influence waived his right to be represented by independent counsel at all stages during the negotiation, drafting and entry into this Agreement. The parties represent and acknowledge that each understands all of the legal and practical effects of this Agreement, and with this understanding, each signs same voluntarily, of their own free will, and without any undue influence, fraud, coercion or duress of any kind whatsoever exercised upon either of them by any person.

9.2 *Non-Molestation and Interference.* The parties agree that neither will molest, malign, disturb, or interfere with the other or the other's relatives in any manner whatsoever during the period of their separation. Each shall be free from interference, direct or indirect, by the other, and be entitled to live his or her life as if single and unmarried to the other.

—Continued

Sample Separation Agreements—*Continued*

9.3   *Voluntary Execution.*   The parties acknowledge and represent that this Agreement is fair and reasonable under the circumstances and that it is not the result of any fraud, duress or undue influence exercised by either party or any third party upon either of them, and that each executes same voluntarily and of their own free will.

9.4   *No Bar to Divorce; No Merger.*   Nothing in this Agreement shall be construed as a relinquishment by either party of their right to prosecute or defend any suit to dissolve the instant marriage in any court of proper jurisdiction. It is further specifically understood and agreed that the provisions of this Agreement relating to the equitable distribution of the parties' property are accepted by each party as a final settlement for all purposes whatsoever. Should either of the parties obtain a decree, judgment or order of separation or dissolution of marriage in any other state, county or jurisdiction, each of the parties to this Agreement hereby consents and agrees that this Agreement and all of its covenants shall not be affected in any way by any such separation or dissolution of marriage and that nothing in any such decree, judgment, order or further modification or revision thereof shall alter, amend or vary any term of this Agreement, whether or not either or both of the parties should remarry, it being understood by and between the parties that this Agreement shall survive and shall not be merged into any judicial decree, judgment or order of separation or dissolution of marriage.

9.5   *Further Assurances.*   Each of the parties, from time to time, at the request of the other, shall execute, acknowledge and deliver to the other any and all further instruments and take such steps which may be reasonably required to give full force and effect to the provisions of this Agreement.

9.6   *Waiver of Claims against Estate, etc.*   Except as may be herein contained to the contrary, upon the effective date of this Agreement each party may dispose of his or her property in any way, and each party waives, relinquishes and releases any and all rights he or she may now have or may hereinafter acquire under the present or future laws of any jurisdiction to share in the property or estate of the other as a result of the marital relationship including, but not necessarily limited to, dower, curtesy, equitable distribution, statutory allowances, widower's and/or widow's allowance, homestead rights, right to take by intestate distribution, right to take against the Last Will and Testament of the other, right to act as administrator(trix) or executor(trix) of the other's estate, or any community property rights whatsoever.

9.7   *Waiver of Further Discovery.*   The parties acknowledge their understanding of each party's right to obtain and take advantage of the panoply of discovery tools available to litigants in a court proceeding including, but not necessarily limited to, interrogatories, depositions, requests to produce, an examination of the books and records of the other party, and the procurement of independent valuations of the assets possessed and/or controlled by the other, etc., prior to the execution of this Agreement. Each party expressly represents and agrees that he or she is sufficiently familiar with the income and assets of the other and hereby knowingly, freely and voluntarily waives his or her right to further utilize the foregoing discovery tools for purposes of negotiating the terms and conditions of this Agreement. The parties further acknowledge that without the benefit of full and complete discovery, neither party has been given advice concerning the fairness and/or equitable nature of the parties' settlement. The parties nonetheless deem the instant Agreement fair and reasonable under the circumstances.

9.8   *Negotiated Settlement.*   The parties acknowledge that the settlement terms reflected in this Agreement represent a compromise and negotiated settlement, and that each has actively participated with the assistance of independent counsel in the preparation of this Agreement or has had the opportunity to retain such counsel.

9.9   *Mutual Releases.*   Except as may be herein contained to the contrary, each party hereby releases and discharges, and by this Agreement does for himself or herself, and his or her legal heirs, representatives, executors, administrators, and assigns, release and discharge the other of and from all causes of action, claims, rights or demands whatsoever, in law or in equity, in which either party ever had or now has against the other, except for any and all causes of action for dissolution of marriage and/or post-judgment enforcement applications to a court of competent jurisdiction.

—Continued

Sample Separation Agreements—*Continued*

9.10   *Entire Understanding.*   This Agreement contains the entire understanding of the parties. There are no representations, warranties, covenants or undertakings other than those as expressly set forth herein.

9.11   *Modification or Waiver.*   A modification or waiver of any of the provisions of this agreement shall be effective when and only if made in writing and executed with the same formality as this Agreement. The failure of either party to insist upon strict performance of any of the provisions of this Agreement shall not be construed as a waiver of any subsequent default of the same or similar nature.

9.12   *Situs.*   The place(s) of execution of this Agreement shall have no bearing on the law governing its interpretation, it being understood and agreed by both parties that the Agreement shall be construed and governed in accordance with the laws of the *[State/ Commonwealth]*, exclusive of conflicts of law principles. Additionally, the drafting of this Agreement by the attorneys for Wife shall have no bearing on the interpretation of same.

9.13   *Survivorship.*   This Agreement shall inure to the benefit of both parties, their heirs and assigns forever and shall be binding upon said parties, their heirs and assigns forever except as otherwise stated herein.

9.14   *Review of Agreement.*   The parties acknowledge that each has read and reviewed this Agreement in its entirety, with their respective counsel, prior to signing.

9.15   *Agreement as Evidence.*   This Agreement may be offered into evidence by either party in any action or proceeding of any nature in which the same may be material or relevant.

9.16   *Article and Sub-part Headings.*   The headings of the several articles and subdivisions of this Agreement are inserted solely for the convenience of reference and shall have no further meaning, force or effect.

9.17   *Communication Information.*   For so long as any provision contained herein remains unfulfilled, each party agrees to keep the other informed of his or her residence and telephone number or of such other places or telephone numbers where he or she may readily receive communications.

9.18   *Severability.*   Should any provision of this Agreement be held invalid or unenforceable by any court of competent jurisdiction, all other provisions shall nonetheless continue in full force and effect.

9.19   *Non-collusion.*   The parties represent and acknowledge that there have been no collusive agreements whatsoever made either orally or in writing, or any representations made by one party to the other with respect to the procurement of a decree dissolving the parties' marriage, or with respect to restraining or inhibiting the other from contesting or litigating any pending or future matrimonial action or compliance application incident to the enforcement of the terms of this Agreement.

9.20   *Effective Date of Agreement.*   The effective date of this Agreement shall be the date on which same is fully executed by both parties.

IN WITNESS WHEREOF, the parties have hereunto set their hands the day and year written below their respective names.

Signed, Sealed and Delivered in
the Presence of:

_____   _____

AS TO *[NAME]*   *[NAME]*

DATED: _____   DATED: _____

_____   _____

AS TO *[NAME]*   *[NAME]*

DATED: _____   DATED: _____

—Continued

Sample Separation Agreements—*Continued*

[STATE/COMMONWEALTH] OF _____)

)   SS.

COUNTY OF _____)

    BE IT REMEMBERED that on this _____ day of _____ , 199___ , before me, the subscriber, a _____ , personally appeared *[Name of Party]*, who, I am satisfied, is the person named in the foregoing Agreement, to whom I first made known the content thereof, and thereupon she acknowledged that she signed, sealed and delivered the same as her voluntary act and deed, for the uses and purposes therein expressed.

_____

[STATE/COMMONWEALTH] OF _____)   SS.

)

COUNTY OF _____)

    BE IT REMEMBERED that on this _____ day of _____ , 199___ , before me, the sub-scriber, a _____ , personally appeared [Name of Party], who, I am satisfied, is the person named in the foregoing Agreement, to whom I first made known the content thereof, and thereupon he acknowledged that he signed, sealed and delivered the same as his voluntary act and deed, for the uses and purposes therein expressed.

_____

Sample Separation Agreement—Community Property State

California Judicial Council Form Manual
3-99 to 3-82 (Jan. 1988)

I.   We are Waldo P. Smedlap, hereafter called Husband, and Lydia T. Smedlap, hereafter called Wife.[1] We were married on October 7, 1978 and separated on December 5, 1979. Because irreconcilable differences have caused the permanent breakdown of our marriage,[2] we have made this agreement together to settle once and for all what we owe to each other and what we can expect from each other. Each of us states here that nothing has been held back, that we have honestly included everything we could think of in listing the money and goods that we own; and each of us states here that we believe the other one has been open and honest in writing this agreement. And each of us agrees to sign and exchange any papers that might be needed to complete this agreement.

    Each of us also understands that even after a Joint Petition for Summary Dissolution is filed, this entire agreement will be cancelled if either of us revokes the Dissolution Proceeding.[3]

II. Division of Community Property[4]

    We divided our community property as follows:

    1. Husband transfers to Wife as her sole and separate property:
       A. All household furniture and furnishings located at her apartment at 180 Needlepoint Way, San Francisco.[5]
       B. All rights to cash in savings account #08-73412-085 at Home Savings.
       C. All cash value in life insurance policy #798567 Sun Valley Life Insurance, insuring life of Wife.
       D. All retirement and pension plan benefits earned by Wife during marriage.
       E. 2 U.S. Savings Bond Series E.
       F. Wife's jewelry.
       G. 1972 Chevrolet 4-door sedan, License No. EXL 129.

[1] *Wherever the word Husband appears anywhere in this agreement, it will stand for Waldo P. Smedlap; wherever the word Wife appears, it will stand for Lydia T. Smedlap.*

[2] *This means that there are problems in your marriage which you think can never be solved.* **Irreconcilable differences** *are the only legal grounds for getting a* **Summary Dissolution.**

[3] *This means that the property agreement is a part of the divorce proceedings. If either of you decides to stop the Dissolution proceedings by turning in a* **Notice of Revocation of Summary Dissolution,** *this entire agreement will be cancelled.*

[4] *Community property is property which you own as a couple. If you have no community property, replace part II with the simple statement,* "**We have no community property.**"

[5] *If furniture and household goods in one apartment are to be divided, then they may have to be listed item by item.*

2. Wife transfers to Husband as his sole and separate property:
   A. All household furniture and furnishings located at his apartment on 222 Bond Street, San Francisco.
   B. All retirement and pension plan benefits earned by Husband during the marriage.
   C. Season tickets to Golden State Terriers Basketball games.
   D. 1 stereo set.
   E. 1 set of Jack Nicklaus golf clubs.
   F. 1 RAC color television.
   G. 1973 Ford station wagon License No. EPX 758.
   H. 1 pet parrot named Arthur, plus cage and parrot food.
   I. All rights to cash in Checking Account #1721-319748-07, Bank of America.

III. Division of Community Property (Debts)[6]

1. Husband shall pay the following debts and will not at any time hold Wife responsible for them:
   A. Mister Charge account #417-38159 208-094.
   B. Debt to Dr. R. C. Himple.
   C. Debt to Sam's Drugs.
   D. Debt to U.C. Berkeley for college education loan to Husband.[7]

2. Wife shall pay the following debts and will not at any time hold Husband responsible for them:
   A. Cogwell's charge account #808921.
   B. Debt to Wife's parents, Mr. and Mrs. Joseph Smith.
   C. Debt to Green's Furniture.
   D. Debt to Dr. Irving Roberts.

IV. Waiver of Spousal Support[8]
Each of us waives any claim for spousal support now and for all time.

V. Dated: _____ Dated: _____

_____   _____
       Waldo P. Smedlap   Lydia T. Smedlap

[6]If you have no unpaid debts, replace part III with the simple statement, **"We have no unpaid community obligations."**

[7]A general rule for dividing debts is to give the debt over to the person who benefited most from the item. In the sample agreement, since the Husband received the education, you could agree that he should pay off the loan.

[8]In this clause you are giving up the right to have your spouse support you.

ASSIGNMENT 6.6

Two members of the class will role-play in front of the rest of the class a negotiation session involving a husband and wife who want to enter a separation agreement. The spouses are representing themselves. They have two children, ages two and three. Each member of the class (including the two role-players) will draft a separation agreement based upon the understandings reached at the negotiation session. The role-players can make up the facts as they go along, e.g., names of the parties, addresses, kinds of assets involved. Use the checklist on pages 81–83 as an overview of the topics to be negotiated. In the negotiation session, the role-players should not act hostile toward each other. They should be courteous but anxious to protect their own rights. Finally, they should not leave any matters hanging—everything discussed should result in some form of agreement through the process of bargaining and compromise.

■■■■■ SUMMARY

A major goal of the law office is to prepare an effective separation agreement that will avoid litigation. The first step is the collection of extensive information, particularly financial information pertaining to everyone involved. Elaborate checklists can be helpful in this effort, as well as detailed interrogatories sent to the other spouse.

For a separation agreement to be valid, the parties must have the capacity to contract. The agreement must not violate public policy by inducing the parties to divorce, and it must not be the product of collusion, duress, or fraud. Finally, the consideration for the agreement must be proper.

The separation agreement should clearly distinguish alimony from property division. The distinction can be relevant in a number of areas, e.g., the effect of bankruptcy, the effect of remarriage and death, the availability of enforcement by contempt, the power of the court to modify terms, and federal tax treatment. The distinction is not simply a matter of labels. The question is, what did the parties intend?

In negotiating alimony, the parties should consider a number of factors, e.g., method of payment, coverage, relationship to child support, modification, termination, and security. The principal focus of the court will be the needs of the recipient, the length of the marriage, and the ability of the payor to pay. In most states marital fault is not relevant.

In negotiating property division, the first step is to categorize all the property to be divided as personal or real. What resources were used to acquire it? How is title held? The division that is made depends on the bargaining process and on whether the parties live in a community property state or in a common law property state. Pension assets can be divided, particularly through a Qualified Domestic Relations Order (QDRO). Businesses are also divisible, including their goodwill. Not all states agree, however, as to whether a license or degree can be divided.

The parties need to consider the continuation of insurance policies, debts incurred before and after the separation agreement is signed, the payment of taxes, whether wills need to be changed, the payment of counsel fees, and the need for a nonmolestation clause.

Child custody and child support terms of a separation agreement are modifiable by a court, unlike property division terms. Spousal-support terms are often modifiable, particularly if the separation agreement has been incorporated and merged into the divorce decree.

When problems arise that involve an interpretation of the separation agreement, the parties may decide to submit the controversy to arbitration or mediation in lieu of litigation. If the parties reconcile and resume cohabitation after they sign the separation agreement, the spousal-support terms (but not the property division terms) are automatically canceled in some states. In others, both support and property division terms are canceled if they are executory.

■■■■■ KEY CHAPTER TERMINOLOGY

Separation Agreement	Payor	Quasi-Community Property
Interrogatories	Payee	Fiduciary
Conducive to Divorce	Escrow	Appreciation
Public Policy	Surety Bond	Equitable Distribution
Collusion	Annuity	Dissipate
Migratory Divorce	Trust	Pension
Duress	Rehabilitative Alimony	Defined-Benefit Plan
Aggrieved	Real Property	Defined-Contribution Plan
Fraud	Personal Property	Vested
At Arm's Length	In Vitro Fertilization	Qualified Domestic Relations
Consideration	Bequest	Order (QDRO)
Alimony	Devise	Alternate Payee
Property Division	Intestate Succession	Present Value
Property Settlement	Joint Tenancy	Restitution
Arrears	Right of Survivorship	Goodwill
Arrearages	Tenancy by the Entirety	Joint and Several Liability
Outstanding	Tenancy in Common	Indemnify
Discharged	Operation of Law	Executor
Estate	Community Property	Testate
Contempt	Common Law Property	Elect against the Will
Contingent	Separate Property	Forced Share

Intestate   Nonmolestation Clause   Mediation
Dower   Arbitration   Executory
Curtesy

CHILD CUSTODY

7

▬▬▬ KINDS OF CUSTODY

Few issues in family law are as emotionally draining as child custody. In divorce cases, judges sometimes tell the parties, "I can dissolve the marriage, but I cannot dissolve the family." A party can be an ex-spouse, but cannot be an ex-parent.[1] A major premise of the law of child custody is that it is important to try to preserve as much of the parental-child relationship as possible after the original family unit has disintegrated due to divorce. Before examining how this is done, we need to understand some basic custody terminology.

☐ **Legal Custody** Legal custody is the right and the duty to make the decisions about raising a child, e.g., decisions on the child's health, education, religion, and discipline. While married and living together, both parents have legal custody of their children. Upon divorce or separation, if both parents continue to make the major decisions together about the health, education, religion, and discipline of the child, they are sharing legal custody, a situation known as joint custody, or joint legal custody.

☐ **Physical Custody** Physical custody simply refers to the parent with whom the child lives. If a court awards custody to one parent only, that parent is called the **custodial parent.** The other is the **noncustodial parent,** who usually has visitation rights.

☐ **Sole Custody** Sole custody exists when one parent has both legal custody and physical custody. The other parent has visitation rights. About 70 percent of all custody decisions today are sole-custody arrangements.[2]

---

1. Unless, of course, there has been a termination of parental rights because of severe parental unfitness or a consent to adoption. See chapter 15.
2. Some states distinguish between *sole physical custody* (child resides full-time with one parent) and *sole legal custody* (one parent makes all the decisions on health, education, and welfare). In Texas, the person with primary responsibility for decisions on the child's upbringing is called the *managing conservator*. A child can have joint managing conservators.

□ **Joint Custody** Joint custody means that each parent shares legal custody (joint legal custody) and/or shares physical custody (joint physical custody) over alternating, but not necessarily equal, periods of time. These arrangements are sometimes referred to as shared custody, shared parental responsibility, shared parenting, or co-parenting. Bird's-nest custody is joint custody where the child remains in a single home and each parent moves in and out during alternate periods of time.

□ **Split Custody** Split custody has two meanings. First, it refers to an arrangement in which one parent has legal custody, with physical custody going to each parent in alternating periods when the child lives with him or her. Second, it refers to a situation involving more than one child. Each parent receives sole custody of at least one child with visitation rights to the other children. This second definition is also referred to as *divided custody.*

None of these categories is static. One kind of custody arrangement may eventually evolve into another kind, either by formal agreement or by informal mutual understanding. For example, one side may have sole custody, but because of circumstances (e.g., illness or job change), visitation becomes so extensive that the parents end up with the equivalent of a joint-custody arrangement.

■ SEPARATION AGREEMENT

CUSTODY

In negotiating the custody term of a separation agreement, the parties must consider many circumstances:

□ The kind of custody they want.

□ The age and health of the child.

□ The age and health of the parents. Which parent is physically and mentally more able to care for the child on a day-to-day basis?

□ The parent with whom the child has spent the most time up to now. With whom are the emotional attachments the strongest?

□ Which parent must work full-time?

□ The availability of backup assistance, e.g., from the grandparents or close friends who can help in emergencies.

□ The availability of day-care facilities.

□ How will the major decisions on the child's welfare be made, e.g., whether to transfer schools, whether to have an operation? Must one parent consult the other on such matters? Is joint consent ever needed?

□ The religious upbringing of the child.

□ The child's surname. Can the name be changed if the mother remarries?

□ Can the child be moved from the area?

□ Who would receive custody if both parents died?

□ If disputes arise between the parents concerning custody, how are they to be resolved? Arbitration? Mediation?

□ What happens if one parent violates the agreement on custody? For example, the custodial parent interferes with the visitation rights of the noncustodial parent. Can the latter stop paying alimony?

□ Mutual respect. Do the parties specifically agree to encourage the child to love both parents?

In recent years, *joint custody* has received a good deal of attention. Advocates of this option claim that it is psychologically the most healthy alternative for the child. It arguably produces less hostility between parents, less hostility between child and individual parent, less confusion in values for the child, less sexual stereotyping of parental roles (one parent "works," the other cares for the children), less manipulation of the child by one or both parents, less manipulation of one or both parents by the child, etc. Others, however, argue that the decision on joint custody should be approached with great caution since it will work only in exceptional circumstances. The parents have just separated. By definition, therefore, they are not able to cooperate in the manner called for by a joint-custody arrangement. A recent study of 700 divorce cases in Massachusetts concluded that couples with joint legal custody are more than twice as likely to reopen lawsuits over child-care arrangements than couples where only one parent had custody.[3]

The following factors are relevant to a decision on whether joint custody will work. Any one of these factors might tip the scale *against* its feasibility.

1. Is each parent fit and suitable as a custodial parent?

2. Do both parents agree to joint custody, or is one or both opposed?

3. Have the parents demonstrated that they are able to communicate at least to the extent necessary to reach shared decisions in the child's best interest?

4. Is there geographical proximity so that there will be no substantial disruption of the child's schooling, association with friends, religious training, etc.?

5. Do the parents' homes present similar environments, or will the child be confronted with vastly different or potentially disruptive environmental changes when moving between the two homes of his or her parents?

6. Is there any indication that the psychological and emotional needs and development of the child will suffer due to the joint custodial arrangement?

7. Does each parent have a work schedule and home routine that is compatible with the child's needs so that either can assume full parental duties when with the child?

8. Is joint custody in accord with the child's wishes or does the child have strong opposition to such an arrangement?

VISITATION

In negotiating visitation rights in a separation agreement, a number of details must be worked out:

☐ When can the noncustodial parent have the child visit? Alternating weekends? School vacations? Holidays? Which ones? How much advance notice is needed if additional time is desired?

☐ At what time is the child to be picked up and returned?

☐ Can the noncustodial parent take the child on long trips? Is the consent of the custodial parent needed?

☐ Can the custodial parent move out of the area even though this makes visitation more burdensome and costly?

---

3. The Wall Street Journal, July 15, 1991 at p. B1; The Compleat Lawyer, 13 (Fall 1991).

    □ Who pays the transportation costs, if any, when the child visits the non-custodial parent?

    □ Is the noncustodial parent required to be available for visits? Will it be a violation of the separation agreement if he or she does *not* visit? Or, is visitation at the sole discretion of the noncustodial parent?

    □ When the noncustodial parent decides not to visit at a given time, must he or she notify the custodial parent in advance, or attempt to?

    □ Do any third parties have visitation rights, e.g., grandparents?

    □ If disputes arise between parents on visitation, how are they resolved? Arbitration? Mediation?

    □ What happens if one of the parties violates the agreement on visitation?

    □ Does this breach justify nonperformance by the other party of another term of the separation agreement, e.g., alimony payments?

There are two major choices in selecting visitation times. The parties can simply state in their separation agreement that visitation will be at "reasonable" times to be mutually agreed upon by the parties in the future, with adequate advance notice to be given by the noncustodial parent when he or she wants visitation. Alternatively, the agreement can spell out precise times for visitation. The following article advocates the latter position in cases where both parents have relatively stable work schedules.

"FIXING DEFINITE SCHEDULES"
By Fain
The Matrimonial Strategist 2 *(May 1983).*

The traumatic and emotional issues that often dominate determination of custody and visitation . . . rights of parents of minor children continue to provoke much litigation. This has perhaps been measurably improved by constructive mediation efforts that have now been initiated by many courts of this country.

As much as it would be preferable to maintain a degree of flexibility in allowing parents to agree on reasonable visitation rights, it is the opinion of most family-law practitioners that it is more important to fix visitation or shared physical custody rights as specifically as possible. . . . This will minimize friction and ensuing disputes between parents who are frequently in a hostile posture to begin with. When visitation rights are set down with particularity, it is more likely that arguments will be discouraged, and less likely that the custodial parent will attempt to limit or defeat the noncustodial parent's visitation rights.

Problems Can Arise
In certain situations, though, specifying visitation rights . . . can lead to problems for parents and child. For example, if a non-custodial parent has an occupation or job with defined hours during the week and regular vacations every year, specificity is fine. But, if the non-custodial parent has an occupation or profession which frequently requires travel, or in which the work requirements do not permit vacations to be planned in advance, specifying rigid visitation rights can often lead to conflict. Such situations should be resolved by tailor-made provisions in the separation agreement.

It is clear that regularity and consistency of visits . . . is better for children because it promotes stability and security of the children's lives, as well as for the parents. However, as with all theories of custody and visitation, even these theories are now being challenged, as exemplified by the continued stress on joint legal and physical custody arrangements. . . .

In a typically traditional visitation arrangement the following schedule has been found reasonably effective in agreements. As with all example clauses, it should be varied or modified by the attorneys and parties to comport with the facts and circumstances of a given case.

SAMPLE VISITATION SCHEDULE:
CUSTODY AND VISITATION RIGHTS

Custody of the minor children, Jane X and Joe X, is awarded *Wife.*

    I. **Husband** shall have the children with him at the following times:

      A. Regular Visitation:

        1. On alternate weekends from seven (7:00)

p.m. Friday to seven (7:00) p.m. Sunday, commencing Friday, _____ , 19XX.

2. The entire month of **July,** 19XX, the entire month of **August,** the following year, and alternating July and August in subsequent years.

B. Holidays and Special Days:

1. Lincoln's Birthday, 19XX, from seven (7:00) p.m. the day before said holiday to seven (7:00) p.m. the day of said holiday, and thereafter on alternate years.

2. Washington's Birthday, 19XX, from seven (7:00) p.m. the day before said holiday to seven (7:00) p.m. the day of said holiday, and thereafter on alternate years.

3. Memorial Day, 19XX, from seven (7:00) p.m. the day before said holiday to seven (7:00) p.m. the day of said holiday, and thereafter on alternate years.

4. Independence Day, 19XX, from seven (7:00) p.m. the day before said holiday to seven (7:00) p.m. the day of said holiday, and thereafter on alternate years.

5. Labor Day, 19XX, from seven (7:00) p.m. the day before said holiday to seven (7:00) p.m. the day of said holiday, and thereafter on alternate years.

6. Columbus Day, 19XX, from seven (7:00) p.m. the day before said holiday to seven (7:00) p.m. the day of said holiday, and thereafter on alternate years.

7. Veterans Day, 19XX, from seven (7:00) p.m. the day before said holiday to seven (7:00) p.m. the day of said holiday, and thereafter on alternate years.

8. Thanksgiving Day, 19XX, from seven (7:00) p.m. the day before said holiday to seven (7:00) p.m. the day of said holiday, and thereafter on alternate years.

9. Christmas 19XX, the first week of the Christmas school vacation, commencing seven (7:00) p.m. the last day of school before the vacation and ending at eleven (11:00) a.m. Christmas Day to five (5:00) p.m. New Year's Day, and thereafter on alternate years.

10. Christmas Day, 19XX, the second week of Christmas school vacation, commencing eleven (11:00) a.m. Christmas Day to five (5:00) p.m. New Year's Day, and thereafter on alternate years.

11. The entire Easter school vacation in the year 19XX, including Easter Sunday, commencing seven (7:00) p.m. the last day of school before the vacation and ending at seven (7:00) p.m. the day before school resumes, and thereafter during the Easter vacation on alternate years.

12. On the children's birthdays in the year 19XX, and thereafter on alternate years.

13. Every Father's Day.

14. On Husband's birthday

15. Religious Holidays (where applicable):

> a. Good Friday of 19XX, from noon (12:00) p.m. to six (6:00) p.m. of said day, and thereafter on alternate years, or
>
> b. The first day of the Jewish Holidays of Yom Kippur, Rosh Hashannah and Passover during 19XX, commencing at five (5:00) p.m. on the eve of each such day and terminating at seven (7:00) p.m. on such day, and thereafter on alternate years.

II. **Wife** shall have the children with her on the holiday and special days listed in Clause I-B in the years alternate to the years in which Husband has the children with him pursuant to Clause I-B; Wife shall also have the children on every Mother's Day and on Wife's birthday.

[*Editor's Note: A common variation would be to split the holidays between Husband and Wife and have them switch halves in alternate years. Another suggested addition if the children are young is Halloween in alternating years.*]

III. Priorities:

The rights of Wife under Clause II shall override the regular visitation rights of Husband set forth in Clause I-A, in the event of conflict between Clause I-A and Clause II, except that Husband shall not be limited in his right to take the children out of the Home-City area during the period set forth in Clause I-A2 above, even though Wife shall thereby be deprived of the right she would otherwise have under Clause II to have the children with her during said period. In the event of conflict between Clause I-B and Clause II, the rights of Husband under Clause I-B shall override the rights of Wife under Clause II.

[*Editor's Note: The significance of Clause III cannot be overrated. A key function of any drafter is to avoid argument over meaning and intention. A provision establishing a hierarchy of clauses will help avoid problems.*]

ASSIGNMENT 7.1

Richard and Helen Dowd have been married for six years. They are both computer consultants who work out of their home. They have one child, Kevin, aged four. Recently, they decided to separate. Draft a joint-custody agreement for them. Assume that both want to be active in raising Kevin.

COURT-ORDERED CUSTODY: THE CHILD'S PERSPECTIVE

When they brought the sword before him, he said, "Cut the living child in two, and give half to one woman and half to the other." 1 Kings 3:24–25 (NAB)

When parents cannot agree on custody, the courts must resolve the matter. Judges, forced into the role of King Solomon, say that child custody is one of the most painful issues they face. In a custody battle, it is often difficult for a court to force parents to focus on the best interest of the child rather than on their own hostility toward each other.

In a few states, parties are *required* to go through a parenting class for divorcing parents. For example, Tarant County, Texas, has a four-hour seminar on how parents can help their children cope with separation and visitation. Using video and role-playing, the seminar emphasizes the emotional harm that fighting parents can continue to inflict on their children.

Most courts have guidelines they distribute to the parties on the effect of divorce on children. Sometimes these guidelines are made part of the court's custody decree. Before examining how courts make the custody decision, we should examine some of these guidelines. The following (written on the assumption that the mother is awarded custody) are used in Wisconsin:

GUIDELINES
Dade County Family Court Counseling Service Staff, Madison, Wisconsin.

Relation toward Children

Although the court does have the power to dissolve the bonds of matrimony, the court does not have the power to dissolve the bonds that exist between you as parents and your children. Both of you, therefore, are to continue your responsibility to emotionally support your children. You are to cooperate in the duty and right of each other to love those children. By love, the court means the training, the education, the disciplining and motivation of those children. Cooperation means to present the other party to the children with an attitude of respect either for the mother or for the father. Neither of you should in any way downplay, belittle or criticize the other in the presence of those children because you may emotionally damage your children and/or you may develop a disappointment or hatred in the minds of those children for the party that attempts to belittle or demean the other in the presence of those children. It is of utmost importance you both recognize your children's right to love both parents without fear of being disloyal to either one of you.

In support of this admonition, the courts have drafted written guidelines on your future conduct relating to the best interest of your children. I sincerely urge that you preserve them, periodically read them and always be guided by them.

Guidelines for Separated Parents

As you know, your children are usually the losers when their parents separate. They are deprived of full-time, proper guidance that two parents can give—guidance and direction essential to their moral and spiritual growth.

It is highly desirable that you abstain from making unkind remarks about each other. Recognize that such remarks are not about a former spouse but are about a parent of your children. Such comments reflect adversely upon the children.

It is urged that both parties cooperate to the end that mutual decisions concerning the interest of the children can be made objectively. Parents should remember that the mother who has custody should urge the children to find time to be with the father and encourage them to realize that their father has affection for them and contributes to their support. The father should recognize that his plans for visitation must be adjusted from time to time in order to accommodate the planned activities of the child. Visitation should be a pleasant experience rather than a duty. Cooperation in giving notice and promptness in maintaining hours of visitation are important to avoid ruffled feelings.

Although there is probably some bitterness between you, it should not be inflicted upon your children. In every child's mind there must and should be an image of two good parents. Your future conduct with your children will be helpful to them if you will follow these suggestions.

i. *Do Not's*

a. Do not poison your child's mind against either the mother or father by discussing their shortcomings.

b. Do not use your visitation as an excuse to continue the arguments with your spouse.

c. Do not visit your children if you have been drinking.

ii. *Do's*

a. Be discreet when you expose your children to [anyone] with whom you may be emotionally involved.

b. Visit your children only at reasonable hours.

c. Notify your spouse as soon as possible if you are unable to keep your visitation. It's unfair to keep your children waiting—and worse to disappoint them by not coming at all.

d. Make your visitation as pleasant as possible for your children by not questioning them regarding the activities of your spouse and by not making extravagant promises which you know you cannot or will not keep.

e. Minimize the amount of time the children are in the care of strangers and relatives.

f. Always work for the spiritual well-being, health, happiness and safety of your children.

iii. *General*

a. The parent with whom the children live must prepare them both physically and mentally for the visitation. The children should be available at the time mutually agreed upon.

b. If one parent has plans for the children that conflict with the visitation and these plans are in the best interests of the children, be adults and work out the problem together.

c. Arrangements should be made through visitation to provide the mother with some time "away" from the family. She needs the time for relaxation and recreation. Upon her return, she will be refreshed and better prepared to resume her role as mother and head of the household. Therefore, provide for extended periods of visitation such as weekends and vacations.

Bill of Rights for Children in Divorce Action

1. The right to be treated as important human beings, with unique feelings, ideas and desires and not as a source of argument between parents.

2. The right to a continuing relationship with both parents and the freedom to receive love from and express love for both.

3. The right to express love and affection for each parent without having to stifle that love because of fear of disapproval by the other parent.

4. The right to know that their parent's decision to divorce is not their responsibility and that they will live with one parent and will visit the other parent.

5. The right to continuing care and guidance from both parents.

6. The right to honest answers to questions about the changing family relationships.

7. The right to know and appreciate what is good in each parent without one parent degrading the other.

8. The right to have a relaxed, secure relationship with both parents without being placed in a position to manipulate one parent against the other.

9. The right to have the custodial parent not undermine visitation by suggesting tempting alternatives or by threatening to withhold visitation as a punishment for the children's wrongdoing.

10. The right to be able to experience regular and consistent visitation and the right to know the reason for a cancelled visit.

Many courts force parents into **mediation** to try to construct a workable custody plan they both can support. The mediator is a private counselor or a trained government employee who meets with the parents to try to help them reach agreement. The mediator does not force a decision on them. While he or she may ultimately recommend a custody/visitation arrangement to the court, the primary objective of mediation is to pressure the parents to reach their own agreement, which they can take before the judge for approval.

Mediation The process of submitting a dispute to a third party (other than a judge) who will help the parties reach their own resolution of the dispute.

■■■■■ PARENT VS. PARENT: CONSIDERATIONS IN THE CUSTODY DECISION

First, we consider the custody decision when the dispute is between the two *biological parents* who cannot agree on custody. The standard used by the court is the **best interest of the child.** In the vast majority of cases, the court will award sole custody to *one* of the parents and give visitation rights to the other. Earlier, we examined other kinds of custody such as joint custody. As indicated, there is considerable debate on the feasibility of a joint-custody decree. Unless the parties mutually agree to try joint custody, it is unlikely that a court will order it. The primary focus of the following discussion, therefore, will be on the kind of custody that is most commonly awarded: sole custody.

Contested Disputed; challenged. If the parties agree, the matter is *uncontested.*

Guardian Ad Litem A special guardian appointed by the court to represent the interests of another.

In a **contested** custody case of this kind, the main participants are the mother and her lawyer against the father and his lawyer. (The parent with all or most of the financial resources will often be ordered to pay the reasonable attorney fees of the other parent.) In most states, the court has the power to appoint *separate* counsel for the child. A **guardian ad litem** is an individual (often a lawyer) who is appointed to represent the interests of a third party— here, the child. This lawyer is to act independently of the other lawyers in the case.

How does the court decide who receives custody? What factors go into the decision? Earlier in this chapter you found a list of factors that parties negotiating a separation agreement must consider in arriving at a mutually acceptable custody arrangement. A court will usually consider these same factors in rendering a custody decision when the parties have not been able to reach agreement, or in deciding whether to approve a custody arrangement that they have agreed upon.

- ☐ **Court discretion**
- ☐ **Stability**
- ☐ **Availability**
- ☐ **Emotional ties**
- ☐ **Legal preferences**
- ☐ **Morality and lifestyle**
- ☐ **Religion**
- ☐ **Wishes of the child**
- ☐ **Expert witnesses**

THE COURT'S DISCRETION

Of necessity, trial judges are given great discretion in making the custody decision. There are no rigid formulas that can be followed. The standard is very broad: the best interest of the child. Inevitably, the judge's personal views and philosophy of life help shape his or her concept of what is in the best interest of a child, e.g., views on the traditional family, alternate lifestyles, working women, child discipline. Of course, a judge would never admit that he or she is following his or her own personal views and philosophy; judges are supposed to be guided by "the law" and not by their individual biases. In reality, however, they are guided by both.

STABILITY

By far the most important consideration is stability. There is almost a presumption that it is in the best interest of the child to award custody to the parent who will cause the least amount of disruption to the disintegrating life of the child. The loss of a household with two functioning parents is a shattering experience for most children. They will need as much stability as possible in their living arrangement, schooling, religious practice, access to relatives and friends, participation in cultural heritage, etc. While their lives will never be the same again, a court will want to know how each parent proposes to maintain maximum stability and continuity in these areas.

AVAILABILITY

Which parent will be available to spend the time required to respond to the day-to-day needs of the child? There is a danger that the child will feel abandoned and responsible for the divorce. To offset this danger, it is important that at least one of the parents be available to the child to provide reassurance and comfort. The court will want to know which parent in the past:

- ☐ Took the child to doctor's appointments
- ☐ Met with teachers
- ☐ Took the child to church
- ☐ Helped with homework
- ☐ Attended school plays with the child
- ☐ Involved the child in athletic activities
- ☐ Arranged and attended birthday parties
- ☐ Changed diapers
- ☐ Stayed up with the sick child during the night

Then the court will want to know what *plan* each parent has for the future as to these needs. The health, age, and employment responsibilities of each parent are obviously relevant to this plan.

Immediately after the separation, it is common for one of the parents to have temporary custody. Upon filing for divorce, the court may formally order a temporary-custody arrangement (with visitation rights) pending the final court proceeding, which may take place months later. During this interval, the court will inquire into the amount and kind of contact each parent had with the child. Again, the above list of questions becomes important, particularly with respect to the parent who moved out. How much time has this parent spent with the child? Have letters and gifts been sent? What about visits and telephone calls? To what extent has this parent gone out of his or her way to be with the child?

EMOTIONAL TIES

Closely related to time availability is the emotional relationship that has developed in the past between a parent and child and the future prospects for this development. Which parent has been sensitive or insensitive to the psychological crisis that the child has experienced and will probably continue to experience because of the divorce? Of particular importance is the extent to which one parent has tried and succeeded in fostering the child's love for the *other* parent. A qualification to become a custodial parent is the ability and inclination to cooperate in arranging visitations by the other parent. Hence, a major issue will be which parent can separate his or her own needs and lingering bitterness from the need of the child to maintain emotional ties with both parents. (Children who have been pressured by one parent to be hostile toward the other might suffer from what is called the **parental alienation syndrome.**)

Parental Alienation Syndrome   A disorder suffered by some children at the center of a custody dispute. They idealize one parent while expressing hatred for the other, even though the relationship with both parents was relatively positive before the dispute.

A number of other factors are relevant to the emotional needs of the child:

☐ The level of education of the parent

☐ The psychological health of the parent: Has the parent been in therapy for any reason? Has it been helpful? What is the parent's attitude about seeking such help? Positive? Realistic? Does the parent think that the *other* parent is the only one who needs help?

☐ The stability of the parent's prior work history

☐ Views on discipline, TV watching, studying, religious activities, cleaning the child's room, etc.

☐ How siblings get along in the home

☐ General home and neighborhood environment: Cramped apartment conditions? Residential area? Easy accessibility to school, friends, and recreational facilities?

Also, does the parent seeking sole custody plan to move from the area? If so, into what kind of environment? How will the proposed move affect the other parent's ability to visit the child? Depending upon the circumstances of the case, a court might award custody to a parent on condition that he or she *not* move out of a designated area without the consent of the other parent.

LEGAL PREFERENCES

Tender Years Presumption   Young children are better off living with their mother than with their father.

Until the 1850s, fathers had a near-absolute right to the custody of their children. Following this period, most states adopted the **tender years presumption.** The court presumed that a young child's best interest was to be with its mother. This presumption was justified on the basis of biological dependence, socialization patterns, and tradition. "There is but a twilight zone between a mother's love and the atmosphere of heaven, and all things being equal, no child should be deprived of that maternal influence." *Tuter v. Tuter*, 120 S.W.2d 203, 205 (Mo. App. 1938). A very strong case had to be made against the mother to overcome the presumption, e.g., proof that the mother was unfit.

Within the last twenty years, more and more fathers have been seeking sole custody. They have argued that it is unconstitutional for a court to give preference to one parent over the other solely on the basis of sex. Recent courts have tended to agree and have been granting custody to fathers in increasing numbers. Some states have passed statutes that specifically outlaw the use of sex-based presumptions in custody cases. Yet courts continue to grant custody to mothers in the overwhelming number of cases. A 1990 study of divorce in nineteen states conducted by the National Center for Health Statistics found that:

☐ Mothers were awarded sole custody in 71 percent of the cases.

☐ Fathers were awarded sole custody in 8.5 percent of the cases.

☐ Custody was shared in 15.5 percent of the cases.

☐ Custody was awarded to other relatives or friends in 5 percent of the cases.

Most of the judges now sitting on the bench grew up with full-time moms at home. Some experts feel it is difficult for these judges to accept the notion of giving sole custody to working fathers. But new judges are on the way. It "will take a generation of judges who are brought up by, or married to career women" before there is more sympathy for granting custody to working parents—particularly fathers.[4]

In place of the tender years presumption, many courts have substituted a **primary caregiver presumption** by which the court presumes that custody should go to the parent who has been the primary person taking care of the child over the years. This, of course, usually means that the mother continues to receive sole custody in most cases since she is usually the one who stays home to care for the child. Even when both the mother and father work outside the home, the mother is more likely to be awarded custody as the primary caregiver or caretaker. Some, therefore, have argued that this presumption is simply the tender years presumption in disguise.

Primary Caregiver Presumption The primary person who has taken care of the child should have custody.

One preference favored the father: it was presumed to be in the best interest of older boys to be placed with their fathers. Today, very few courts even mention this presumption. Although it has not been as controversial as the tender years presumption, it is subject to the same criticisms.

A less controversial presumption is that brothers and sisters are best kept together with the same parent whenever possible. Finally, courts widely accept the idea that the preference of older, more mature children as to their own custody should be given great, though not necessarily controlling, weight.

MORALITY AND LIFESTYLE

"A judge should not base his decision upon [a] disapproval of the morals or other personal characteristics of a parent that do not harm the child. . . . We do not mean to suggest that a person's associational or even sexual conduct may not be relevant in deciding a custody dispute where there is compelling evidence that such conduct has a significant bearing upon the welfare of the children." *Wellman v. Wellman*, 104 Cal. App. 3d 992, 998, 164 Cal. Rptr. 148, 151–52 (1980).

Is it possible to separate the private morality (particularly sexual morality) of parents from the welfare of their children? If a parent engages in what the community considers immoral conduct, can we presume (conclusively presume?) that this parent is unfit and that it is in the best interest of the child to be placed with the other parent? In *Stanley v. Illinois*, 405 U.S. 645, 92 S. Ct. 1208, 31 L. Ed. 2d 551 (1972), the United States Supreme Court held that a state cannot presume that a father is unfit simply because he never married the mother of his illegitimate child. Such a father must be given a hearing to determine his *actual* fitness or unfitness. This theme has carried over into child-custody cases where there is a trend in favor of the principle that immoral conduct in itself is not a sufficient basis to deny custody unless the conduct adversely affects the welfare of the child, as suggested by the above quotation from *Wellman v. Wellman*. Suppose, for example, a parent has a live-in lover. In

---

4. Jan Hoffman, *Divorced Fathers Make Gains in Battles to Increase Rights*, New York Times, April 26, 1995, at p. A11.

most states, this fact will not automatically disqualify the party from custody unless there is some evidence that the living arrangement is detrimental to the child such as by causing the child embarrassment or exposing the child to ridicule from peers.

What happens if one of the parents seeking custody is homosexual? Some courts would never grant custody to a gay parent, especially if the other parent follows a more traditional lifestyle. Other courts, however, take a different view. They will want to know whether:

☐ The gay parent has a live-in lover.

☐ The parent's sexual activities are open and obvious to the child.

☐ The child is psychologically able to handle the parent's homosexuality.

☐ The child's social life will be adversely affected. (For example, will the child be teased by classmates?)

These courts will award custody of the child to a gay parent if all of the factors point to a healthy home environment for the child and there is no evidence that the homosexuality will have an adverse impact on the child. At one time, there was fear that a parent's homosexuality would cause the child to be homosexual. Many studies have rejected this conclusion, particularly since a child's sexual preferences are developed during its infancy and very early years. This is usually well before the homosexual parent seeks custody. It must be acknowledged, however, that a gay parent has a substantial uphill battle in gaining custody (or in keeping custody if the homosexuality is revealed only after the parent has been awarded custody). Gay parents have been most successful in winning custody when the heterosexual parent is either no longer available or is demonstrably unfit. In such cases, the homosexual parent wins by default unless his or her conduct is so offensive that the court will grant custody to neither biological parent.

RELIGION

Under our Constitution, a court cannot favor one religion over another or prefer organized religion over less orthodox forms of religious beliefs. To do so could amount to an unconstitutional "establishment" of religion. The state must remain neutral. In the law of custody, the question is what effect the practice of religion is likely to have on the child, not which religion is preferable or correct according to the judge's personal standards, or according to the standards of the majority in the community, or according to "respectable" minorities in the community. The court will want to know what religion, if any, the child has practiced to date. Continuity is highly desirable. Also, will the practice of a particular religion tend to take the child away from other activities? For example, will the child be asked to spend long hours in door-to-door selling of religious literature and hence be unable to attend regular school? If so, the court will be reluctant to award custody to the parent who would require this of the child.

ASSIGNMENT 7.2

When Helen married John, she converted from Catholicism to his religion, Judaism. Neither Helen nor John was a very religious person, however. To a moderate extent, their two children were raised in the Jewish faith. The couple divorced when the children were ages four and five. Because of John's job, he could not be the sole custodian of the

children. Hence he agreed that Helen receive sole custody. But he asked the court to order Helen to continue raising the children in the Jewish faith.

a. Under what circumstances do you think a court can grant this request so that, in effect, John will be granted *spiritual custody* of the children even though physical custody and legal custody (in all matters except religion) will be granted to Helen?

b. Suppose that Helen returns to her original religion and starts taking the children to Catholic Mass. What options does John have?

WISHES OF THE CHILD

Older children are almost always asked where they would want to live. Courts are understandably reluctant, however, to ask young children to take sides in custody disputes. If this becomes common practice, there would be an incentive for both parents to pressure the child to express preferences. If, however, the court is convinced that the child is mature enough to state a rational preference and that doing so would not harm the child, evidence of such a preference will be admissible. Great caution must be used in questioning the child. The judge may decide to speak to the child outside the formal courtroom (with the lawyers but not the parents present), or the judge may allow a professional (e.g., child psychologist, social worker) to interview the child at home.

EXPERT WITNESSES

Psychologists, psychiatrists, social workers, and other experts can be called as expert witnesses by either parent to testify on the child's home environment and emotional development, the mental stability of the parents, the suitability of various custody plans, etc. Either parent, or the guardian at litem for the child, can make a motion that the court order a custody evaluation by an expert. An example of a custody-evaluation report by such an expert is provided in Exhibit 7.1.

> ☐ **Note on Frozen Embryos** A husband and wife participate in *in vitro fertilization* resulting in an embryo that is frozen for later implantation. Before this can occur, the parties file for divorce. What is the status of the frozen embryo? Is it "property" to be divided between the parties? Does the court have to make a "custody" decision? See the discussion on page 108.

■■■■■ COURT DECISION ON VISITATION

Courts want to preserve as much of the child's relationship with both parents as possible. Hence, visitation rights are almost always granted to the noncustodial parent even if they must be exercised in the presence of third parties (*supervised visitation*). Failing to grant such rights would be a step in the direction of terminating the parental rights of that parent (see Chapter 15). Moreover, as indicated earlier, one of the criteria that a court will use in awarding sole custody to a parent is whether the latter will cooperate in the exercise of visitation rights by the other parent. Custodial parents who fail to provide such cooperation are sometimes dealt with harshly by the court, e.g., terminating spousal support, transferring custody to the other parent, contempt orders. It is never permissible, however, for the noncustodial parent to terminate child support payments in retaliation for the custodial parent's violation of visitation rights.

Whenever possible, the court will favor frequent and regular visitation by the noncustodial parent, e.g., every other weekend, alternating holidays, sub-

(text continues on page 154)

□ **EXHIBIT 7.1 Sample Custody Evaluation by an Expert**

Psychiatric Custody Evaluation

August 25, 1981

Honorable James K. O'Brien
Supreme Court of New York
New York County
60 Centre Street
New York, New York 10007

Re: Johnson v. Johnson
Docket No. M-3784-81

Dear Judge O'Brien:

This report is submitted in compliance with your court order dated June 9, 1981, requesting that I conduct an evaluation of the Johnson family in order to provide the court with information that would be useful to it in deciding which of the Johnson parents should have custody of their children Tara, Elaine, and Charles.

My findings and recommendations are based on interviews conducted as itemized below:

July 6, 1981—Mrs. Carol Johnson and Mr. Frank Johnson, seen jointly	2 hours
July 7, 1981—Mr. Frank Johnson	1 hour
July 11, 1981—Mrs. Carol Johnson	1 hour
July 13, 1981—Tara Johnson	1 1/2 hours
July 14, 1981—Mr. Frank Johnson	1 hour
July 20, 1981—Mrs. Carol Johnson	1 hour
July 21, 1981—Charles Johnson	3/4 hour
Elaine Johnson	3/4 hour
July 22, 1981—Tara Johnson	1/2 hour
Mrs. Carol Johnson and Tara Johnson, seen jointly	1/2 hour
July 24, 1981—Mrs. Carol Johnson	1 hour
July 27, 1971—Mrs. Carol Johnson and Mr. Frank Johnson, seen jointly	1 hour
Aug. 3, 1981—Elaine Johnson	3/4 hour
Aug. 4, 1981—Tara Johnson	1/4 hour
Mr. Frank Johnson and Tara Johnson, seen jointly	1/2 hour
Aug. 10, 1981—Tara Johnson	
Mr. Frank Johnson and Mrs. Carol Johnson, seen jointly	3/4 hour
Aug. 11, 1981—Tara Johnson	
Elaine Johnson	
Charles Johnson	
Mrs. Carol Johnson and Mr. Frank Johnson, seen jointly	3/4 hour
Aug. 14, 1981—Tara Johnson	
Elaine Johnson	
Charles Johnson	
Mrs. Carol Johnson and Mr. Frank Johnson, seen jointly	1 hour
	16 hours

In addition, on Aug. 16, 1981, Mr. and Mrs. Johnson were seen together for the purpose of my presenting these findings and recommendations to them. This interview lasted two hours, bringing to 18 the total number of hours spent with the Johnson family in association with this evaluation.

Continued

☐ **EXHIBIT 7.1　Sample Custody Evaluation by an Expert—*Continued***

Mr. Frank Johnson, an airline pilot, is 43 years old. His first wife died soon after the delivery of Tara, who is now 16 years of age. He married Mrs. Carol Johnson when Tara was 2 years old. Mrs. Johnson, a housewife, who was formerly an elementary school teacher, is now 40. Her first marriage ended in divorce. A child of this relationship died soon after birth. There are two children of the Johnson marriage: Elaine, 11 and Charles, 7. Mrs. Johnson adopted her stepdaughter Tara in July 1980. In October 1980, Mr. Johnson initiated divorce proceedings because he felt that his wife no longer respected him and that she was a poor mother for the children, especially his daughter Tara. However, Mr. and Mrs. Johnson are still occupying the same domicile.

Both parents are requesting custody of all three children. It is this examiner's recommendation that Mr. Frank Johnson be granted custody of Tara and that Mrs. Carol Johnson be granted custody of Elaine and Charles. The observations that have led me to these conclusions will be divided into four categories: 1) Mr. Frank Johnson's assets as a parent, 2) Mr. Frank Johnson's liabilities as a parent, 3) Mrs. Carol Johnson's assets as a parent, and 4) Mrs. Carol Johnson's liabilities as a parent. Following these four presentations I will comment further on the way in which my observations brought about the aforementioned recommendations. Although much information was obtained in the course of the evaluation, only those items specifically pertinent to the custody consideration will be included in this report.

Mr. Frank Johnson's Assets as a Parent

Mr. Frank Johnson is Tara's biological father. The special psychological tie that this engenders is not enjoyed by Mrs. Carol Johnson and Tara. It is not the genetic bond per se that is crucial here; rather, it is the psychological attachment that such a bond elicits. Mr. Johnson had already started to develop a psychological tie with Tara while his first wife was pregnant with her. He was actually present at her birth and assumed an active role in her rearing—almost from birth because of the illness and early death of his first wife. This situation prevailed until the time of his marriage to Mrs. Johnson when Tara was 2 years of age. Although Mrs. Johnson has been Tara's primary caretaker since then, Mr. Johnson's early involvement with Tara during these crucial years of her development contributes to a very strong psychological tie between them that has continued up to the present time.

My observations have convinced me, and both parents agree, that at this time, Tara has a closer relationship with her father than her mother. Her relationship with Mrs. Johnson at this time is characteristically a difficult one in that there are frequent battles and power struggles. Although Tara is not completely free of such involvement with her father, such hostile interaction is far less common. In my interviews with Mr. Johnson and Tara, I found her to be far more friendly with him than I observed her to be with Mrs. Johnson in my joint interviews with them.

In every interview, both alone and in joint sessions with various members of the family, Tara openly and unswervingly stated that she wished to live with her father: "I want to live with my father. I am closer to him." "When I was younger, my mother did more things; but since I'm older, my father does more things." "My father listens to what I say; my mother doesn't."

Mr. Johnson and Tara both utilize a similar method of communication. Neither feels a strong need to give confirmation of examples to general statements that they make, and they are therefore comfortable with one another. Mrs. Johnson, on the other hand, is much more specific in her communications and this is a source of difficulty, not only in her relationship with Tara, but in her relationship with her husband as well.

All five family members agree that Mr. Johnson spends significant time with Charles, involved in typical father-son activities, sports, games, etc. It is also apparent that Charles has a strong masculine identification and this arose, in part, from his modeling himself after his father.

Mr. Frank Johnson's Liabilities as a Parent

Mr. Johnson states that he would not have involved himself in the custody evaluation conducted by this examiner if he had to contribute to its financing. Accordingly, Mrs. Johnson assumed the total financial obligation for this evaluation. I conclude from this that with regard to this particular criterion for comparing the parents, Mr. Johnson's position is less strong than Mrs. Johnson's.

On many occasions Mr. Johnson made general comments about his superiority over his wife with regard to parental capacity. For example, "She's a very poor mother," "She neglects the children," and "If you had all the information you would see that I'm a better parent." However, it was extremely

Continued

□ **EXHIBIT 7.1 Sample Custody Evaluation by an Expert—*Continued***

difficult to elicit from Mr. Johnson <u>specific</u> examples of incidents that would substantiate these statements. I not only considered this to be a manifestation of Mr. Johnson's problem in accurately communicating, but also considered it to be a deficiency in his position. One cannot be convinced of the strength of such statements if no examples can be provided to substantiate them.

In the hope that I might get more specific information from Mr. Johnson I asked him, on at least three occasions, to write a list of specifics that might help corroborate some of his allegations. He came to three subsequent interviews without having written anything in response to my invitation. I consider such failure to reflect a compromise in his motivation for gaining custody of the three children. When he did finally submit such a list it was far less comprehensive than that which was submitted by Mrs. Johnson and in addition, the issues raised had far less significance, e.g., "She's late once in a while," "She's sometimes forgetful," and "She doesn't like playing baseball with Charles."

Although I described Mr. Johnson's communication problem as a factor supporting his gaining custody of Tara, I would consider it a liability with regard to his gaining custody of Elaine and Charles. Tara (possibly on a genetic basis) communicates in a similar way and so, as mentioned, is comfortable with her father when they communicate. Elaine and Charles, however, appear to be identifying with their mother with regard to communication accuracy. Accordingly, intensive exposure to Mr. Johnson might compromise what I consider a healthier communicative pattern.

Mr. Johnson's profession as an airline pilot has not enabled him to have predictable hours. Not only is his schedule variable, but there are times when he is required to work on an emergency basis. All three children agree that Mrs. Johnson is more predictably present. Mr. Johnson's irregular schedule is not a significant problem for Tara who, at 16, is fairly independent and would not suffer significantly from her father's schedule. The younger children, however, are still in need of predictability of parental presence and Mr. Johnson has not demonstrated his capacity to provide such predictability. In my final interview with Mr. Johnson he stated that he would change his work pattern to be available to his children during non-school hours. Mrs. Johnson was very dubious that this could be arranged because his job does not allow such flexibility. Both parents agreed, however, that it had not occurred in the past and that such predictability was not taking place at the time of this evaluation.

Both Charles and Elaine stated that they wanted to live with their mother and not live with their father. Charles stated, "I want to be with my mother. I'd be alone when my father goes to work." Elaine stated, "I want to live with my mother. I'm closer to my mother. I'm not as close to my father."

In a session in which I was discussing his future plans with Mr. Johnson, he stated that he was considering moving to California because he could earn more money there by supplementing his income with certain business ventures that he had been invited to participate in. He stated also that he would still move even if he were only to be granted custody of Tara. Although I appreciate that a higher income could provide Mr. Johnson's children with greater financial flexibility, I believe that the disadvantages of such a move would far outweigh its advantages from their point of view. Specifically, the extra advantages they might enjoy from such a move would be more than offset by the even greater absence of their father who, his liabilities notwithstanding, is still an important figure for them.

In an interview in which I discussed with Mr. Johnson how he would react to the various custodial decisions, he was far more upset about the prospect of losing Tara than he was about the possibility of losing Charles and Elaine. In fact, he appeared to be accepting of the fact that Elaine would go to her mother. Although somewhat distressed about the possibility of Charles' living with his mother, he did not show the same degree of distress as his wife over the prospect of losing the younger two children.

Mrs. Carol Johnson's Assets as a Parent

Mrs. Carol Johnson was far more committed to the custody evaluation than her husband. As mentioned, she was willing to make the financial sacrifices involved in the evaluation. I consider this to be a factor reflecting greater motivation than her husband for gaining custody of the children. Mrs. Johnson is more available to the children during non-school hours than her husband and this is one element in her favor regarding gaining custody, especially of the younger children. Mrs. Johnson is a more accurate and clearer communicator than her husband and this is an asset. As mentioned, the younger children do not seem to have been affected by their father's communication difficulty. Having them live with him might result in their acquiring this maladaptive trait.

During her pregnancy with Elaine, Mrs. Johnson suffered with toxemia and associated high blood pressure and convulsions. Most physicians generally discourage women with this disorder from becoming pregnant again because it is genuinely life endangering. However, Mrs. Johnson did wish to have a third child, primarily because her husband, she states, was so desirous of having a son. Her pregnancy

Continued

☐ **EXHIBIT 7.1   Sample Custody Evaluation by an Expert—Continued**

with Charles was complicated by the exacerbation of a preexisting asthmatic condition from which she states that she almost died. A less maternal woman would not have become pregnant again.

Elaine stated on many occasions, and in every interview, both alone and with other family members, that she wished to live with her mother: "I'm closer to my mother," "She's home more than my father," "They call my father to do things at work all the time," and "My mother has more feelings for me than my father."

Charles also, both in individual session and in joint interviews, emphatically stated that he wished to live with his mother: "I want to stay with my mother because she doesn't work as much as my father." "If you get sick the father might not know what to do, but the mother does." "My mother knows how to take care of me." "She doesn't work that much." "She reads me books more than my father."

On one occasion Mr. Johnson stated: "Carol is closer to Elaine than I am. They are similar. They're both sore losers. Both get emotional if they don't have their way." Mrs. Carol Johnson agrees that she and her daughter Elaine have these traits, but not to the degree described by her husband. Although there are certainly negative elements regarding the reasons why Mr. Johnson sees Elaine to be closer to his wife, this statement is an admission of his recognition of this preference of Elaine for her mother. The situation is analogous to Mr. Johnson's involvement with Tara. They are closer to one another, yet maladaptive and undesirable factors are contributing to the closeness.

Mrs. Carol Johnson's Liabilities as a Parent

Tara is not Mrs. Johnson's biological daughter. Although she has raised Tara from her infancy, as if she were her own biological child, and although she has adopted her, Mrs. Johnson is at a certain disadvantage regarding the development of a strong psychological parent-child tie. As mentioned, I believe that a biological relationship increases the strength of the psychological bond. Accordingly, Mrs. Johnson is at a disadvantage when compared to Mr. Johnson regarding this aspect of the custody consideration.

Mrs. Johnson and Tara have a poor relationship at this point. In my interviews with Mrs. Johnson and Tara I found the latter to view her mother scornfully and to be openly resentful of her authority. On one occasion Tara said: "She has a lot of nerve telling me what to do." Were this an isolated statement, it would probably not have much significance. However, all agreed that it epitomized her general attitude toward her mother. Although some of the scornful attitude Tara exhibits toward her mother can be viewed as age-appropriate, I believe the extent goes beyond what is to be expected for teen-agers.

Mrs. Johnson cannot provide Charles with the same kind of father model and father-type involvement that her husband can. Although she claims an interest in sports and a greater degree of facility than the average woman, it is still clear that her husband has been far more involved in this type of activity with his son than has Mrs. Johnson.

Mr. Johnson accuses Mrs. Johnson of being excessively punitive and too strong a disciplinarian. Mrs. Johnson claims that her husband is too lax with the children and does not implement proper disciplinary measures. I believe that it is most likely that Mrs. Johnson is a little too punitive and that Mr. Johnson is a little too lenient. However, neither parent exhibits these difficulties to a degree that would be significantly injurious to the children, nor would I consider this to be a factor compromising either of their capacities as parents. It is probable, however, that these differences are playing a role in Tara's antagonism to her mother and her gravitating toward her father.

In every interview, both individual and joint, Tara openly stated that she wished to live with her father. "I would be very unhappy if the judge made me go with my mother." "He can't make me live with my mother. I'd run away to my father if he did."

Conclusions and Recommendations

Weighing the above factors as best I can, I believe that the evidence is strongly in favor of Mr. Johnson being given custody of Tara. I believe, also, that the above evidence strongly supports the conclusion that Elaine should be given to Mrs. Johnson. Although there are certain arguments supporting Mr. Johnson's gaining custody of Charles, I believe that these are greatly outweighed by arguments in favor of Mrs. Johnson's gaining custody. Were the court to conclude that Tara would be better off living with Mrs. Johnson, I believe that there would be a continuation of the present hostilities, and this could be disruptive to the healthy psychological development of the younger children—if they were exposed to such hostile interactions over a long period. I believe that if Mr. Johnson were to be granted custody of Elaine and Charles it is most likely that they would suffer psychological damage. All things considered, I believe he is the less preferable parent for the young children and, if they had to live with him, they would suffer emotional deprivations that could contribute to the development of psychiatric disorders.

Richard A. Gardner, M.D.

SOURCE: R. Gardner, M.D., *Family Evaluation in Child Custody Litigation*, 318–25 (1982).

(text continued from page 149)

stantial summer vacation time. When the custody battle is between two relatively fit parents, the court is even more inclined to grant greater visitation rights to the loser so long as the court is convinced that the losing parent had the proper motivation in seeking custody.

An essential component of successful visitation in most cases is physical proximity between the child and the noncustodial parent. A great deal of litigation has centered on the right of the custodial parent to move the child substantial distances away. Some courts flatly forbid such moving. A few states have statutes that cover this problem. For example:

Minn.Stat.Ann. § 518.175(3) (1969)   The custodial parent shall not move the residence of the child to another state except upon the order of the Court or with the consent of the non-custodial parent, when the non-custodial parent has been given visitation rights by the decree.

In extreme cases, the court might order the custodial parent to post a bond to secure compliance with the visitation rights of the noncustodial parent.

In most states, the decision on whether to allow the custodial parent to move is based on what is in the best interest of the child. In an important recent decision, the New York Court of Appeals laid out the factors a court will take into consideration. *In the Matter of Tropea,* ____ N.E.2d ____ , 1996 WL 137476 (NY). The court said:

> [W]e hold that each relocation request must be considered on its own merits with due consideration of all the relevant facts and circumstances and with predominant emphasis being placed on what outcome is most likely to serve the best interests of the child. While the respective rights of the custodial and noncustodial parents are unquestionably significant factors that must be considered . . . , it is the rights and needs of the children that must be accorded the greatest weight, since they are innocent victims of their parents' decision to divorce and are the least equipped to handle the stresses of the changing family situation.
>
> Of course, the impact of the move on the relationship between the child and the noncustodial parent will remain a central concern. Indeed, even where the move would leave the noncustodial parent with what may be considered "meaningful access," there is still a need to weigh the effect of the quantitative and qualitative losses that naturally will result against such other relevant factors as the custodial parent's reasons for wanting to relocate and the benefits that the child may enjoy or the harm that may ensue if the move is or is not permitted. Similarly, although economic necessity or a specific health-related concern may present a particularly persuasive ground for permitting the proposed move, other justifications, including the demands of a second marriage and the custodial parent's opportunity to improve his or her economic situation, may also be valid motives that should not be summarily rejected, at least where the overall impact on the child would be beneficial. While some courts have suggested that the custodial spouse's remarriage or wish for a "fresh start" can never suffice to justify a distant move (see, e.g., *Elkus v. Elkus,* 182 A.D.2d 445), such a rule overlooks the value for the children that strengthening and stabilizing the new, post-divorce family unit can have in a particular case.
>
> In addition to the custodial parent's stated reasons for wanting to move and the noncustodial parent's loss of access, another factor that may well become important in a particular case is the noncustodial parent's interest in securing custody, as well as the feasibility and desirability of a change in

custody. Obviously, where a child's ties to the noncustodial parent and to the community are so strong as to make a long-distance move undesirable, the availability of a transfer of custody as a realistic alternative to forcing the custodial parent to remain may have a significant impact on the outcome. By the same token, where the custodial parent's reasons for moving are deemed valid and sound, the court in a proper case might consider the possibility and feasibility of a parallel move by an involved and committed noncustodial parent as an alternative to restricting a custodial parent's mobility.

Other considerations that may have a bearing in particular cases are the good faith of the parents in requesting or opposing the move, the child's respective attachments to the custodial and noncustodial parent, the possibility of devising a visitation schedule that will enable the noncustodial parent to maintain a meaningful parent-child relationship, the quality of the lifestyle that the child would have if the proposed move were permitted or denied, the negative impact, if any, from continued or exacerbated hostility between the custodial and noncustodial parents, and the effect that the move may have on any extended-family relationships. Of course, any other facts or circumstances that have a bearing on the parties' situation should be weighed with a view toward minimizing the parents' discomfort and maximizing the child's prospects of a stable, comfortable and happy life.

Like Humpty Dumpty, a family once broken by divorce, cannot be put back together in precisely the same way. The relationship between the parents and the children is necessarily different after a divorce and, accordingly, it may be unrealistic in some cases to try to preserve the noncustodial parent's accustomed close involvement in the children's everyday life at the expense of the custodial parent's efforts to start a new life or to form a new family unit. In some cases, the child's interests might be better served by fashioning visitation plans that maximize the noncustodial parent's opportunity to maintain a positive nurturing relationship while enabling the custodial parent, who has the primary child-rearing responsibility, to go forward with his or her life. In any event, it serves neither the interests of the children nor the ends of justice to view relocation cases through the prisms of presumptions and threshold tests that artificially skew the analysis in favor of one outcome or another.

Rather, we hold that, in all cases, the courts should be free to consider and give appropriate weight to all of the factors that may be relevant to the determination. These factors include, but are certainly not limited to each parent's reasons for seeking or opposing the move, the quality of the relationships between the child and the custodial and noncustodial parents, the impact of the move on the quantity and quality of the child's future contact with the noncustodial parent, the degree to which the custodial parent's and child's life may be enhanced economically, emotionally and educationally by the move, and the feasibility of preserving the relationship between the noncustodial parent and child through suitable visitation arrangements. In the end, it is for the court to determine, based on all of the proof, whether it has been established by a preponderance of the evidence that a proposed relocation would serve the child's best interests.

———

Another issue that is occasionally litigated is whether *third parties*, e.g., grandparents, stepparents, can be given rights of visitation. Factors considered by the court in deciding this question include:

□ The language of the statute in the state that governs who can visit. A court will want to know if it has statutory power to grant visitation rights to third parties.

□ Whether the custodial parent objects to granting the visitation rights. And if so, why.

□ Whether the child has lived with the third party for a substantial period of time in the past or has otherwise formed close emotional ties with the third party.

The best interest of the child is again the standard the court will use if it has the power to grant visitation rights to anyone other than biological parents. Even when the power exists, however, it is rarely used except in situations such as the following:

> The father dies soon after the divorce in which the mother was given sole custody of the child. The paternal grandparents are granted visitation rights. The child had a warm relationship with these grandparents in the past. If visitation is not allowed, the child may lose all contact with the father's side of the family.

> A stepparent has been supporting his wife's child by a prior marriage. When the stepparent and mother divorce, he seeks visitation rights, even though he never adopted the child. Visitation rights are granted if the stepparent had a close relationship with the child while together, and it would be very disruptive to end the relationship abruptly.

■■■■■ THE NEW "TERROR WEAPON"

> "I had to face the fact that for one year [during the exercise of unsupervised visitation rights by the father], I sent my child off to her rapist." [5]

> "For many parents engaged in seriously contested child custody disputes, false allegations of child abuse have become an effective weapon for achieving an advantage in court." [6]

In alarming numbers, parents are being accused of sexually abusing their children, usually during visitation. The issue can also arise during an initial custody proceeding where one parent claims that the other committed sex abuse during the marriage, and hence should not be granted custody, or should not be granted visitation rights in unsupervised settings.

The level of bitterness generated by this accusation is incredibly high. It is the equivalent of a declaration of total war between the parties. The chances of reaching a settlement or of mediating the custody dispute—or anything else that is contested—often vanish the moment the accusation is made. Protracted and costly litigation is all but inevitable.

Nor does litigation always resolve the matter. Assume that a mother with sole custody is turned down when she asks a court to terminate the father's right to visit the child because of an allegation of child abuse. The court finds the evidence of abuse to be insufficient and orders a continuation of visitation. Unable to accept this result, the mother goes underground out of desperation and a total loss of faith in the legal system. She either flees with the child, or she turns the child over to sympathetic third parties who agree to keep the

---

5. Szegedy-Maszak, *Who's to Judge,* New York Times Magazine, 28 (May 21, 1989).
6. Gordon, *False Allegations of Abuse in Child Custody Disputes,* 2 Minnesota Family Law Journal 225 (1985).

child hidden from the authorities. The child might be moved from one "safe house" to another to avoid detection. This underground network consists of a core of dedicated women who at one time were in a similar predicament or who are former child-abuse victims themselves.

If the mother remains behind, she is hauled back into court. If she refuses to obey an order to produce the child, she faces an array of possible sanctions, including imprisonment for civil contempt or even prosecution for criminal kidnaping. Unfortunately, the media have an excessive interest in cases of this kind. Once reporters and cameras become involved, a circus atmosphere tends to develop.

Attorneys can find themselves in delicate situations. The first question they face is whether to take the case. When an alleged child abuser—usually the father—seeks representation, the attorney understands the father's need for a vigorous defense. What if he didn't do it? Yet attorneys tend to place cases of this kind in a different category. Many need to believe in his innocence before they will take the case. According to a prominent matrimonial attorney, "I have a higher duty to make sure some wacko doesn't get custody of his child." Before proceeding, therefore, the attorney might ask him to:

□ Take a lie detector test

□ Take the *Minnesota Multiphasic Personality Index test* (**MMPI**), which may be able to reveal whether someone has a propensity to lie and is the kind of person who statistically is likely to be a child abuser

□ Be evaluated by a knowledgeable psychologist or psychiatrist.

Some attorneys have even insisted that the father undergo hypnosis as a further aid in trying to assess the truth of the allegation.

Attorneys representing the mother face similar concerns. Is she telling the truth? Is she exaggerating, knowingly or otherwise? Is she trying to seek some other strategic advantage from the father, e.g., more financial support? (Custody blackmail?) What advice should the attorney give her when she first reveals the charge of sexual abuse, particularly when the evidence of abuse is not over-whelming? Should she be advised to go public with the charge? As indicated, the consequences of doing so—and of not doing so—can be enormous. Bitter litigation is almost assured. What if the attorney talks her out of going public with the charge in order to settle the case through negotiation, "and a month or two later something terrible happens?" Faced, therefore, with a need to know if the accusation is true, the attorney may ask *her* to go take a polygraph test or an MMPI test, or to undergo an independent evaluation by a psychologist or psychiatrist.

Other attorneys disagree with this approach. They do not think that clients should be subject to such mistrust by their own attorney. And they fail to see much value in some of the devices used to assess the truth. Some typical comments from such attorneys are that professionals "trained in sexual abuse are wrong very often"; "Frankly I trust my horse sense more than I trust psychiatrists"; and "There is no research that says the polygraph or MMPI is of any use." [7]

Of course, attorneys for both sides will have to interview the child. This can be a very delicate task. There is a danger of emotional damage every time the

---

7. Fisk, *Abuse: The New Weapon,* The National Law Journal, 20 (July 17, 1989).

child is forced to focus on the events in question. Even though children are generally truthful, many are susceptible to suggestion and manipulation. Very often, the charge is made that the child has been "brainwashed" into believing that abuse did or did not occur. Clearly, the child needs protection. A separate attorney (guardian at litem) is usually appointed by the court to represent the child in the litigation. Guidelines may exist in the state on who can interview the child and in what setting. Trained child counselors are commonly used. Using special, anatomically correct dolls, the counselor will ask the child to describe what happened. These interviews are usually videotaped. When the time comes for a court hearing, the judge will often interview the child outside the courtroom, e.g., in the judge's chambers without either parent present.

■ BIOLOGICAL PARENT VS. PSYCHOLOGICAL PARENT

Thus far our main focus has been the custody dispute where the main combatants are the two biological parents. Suppose, however, that the dispute is between one biological parent and a third party such as a/an:

- □ Grandparent
- □ Other relative
- □ Stepparent (who never adopted the child)
- □ Foster parent (who is temporarily caring for the child at the request of the state)
- □ Neighbor
- □ Friend

Assume that the other biological parent is out of the picture because he or she has died, has disappeared, or does not care. The third party is usually someone with whom the child has established close emotional ties. Frequently, the child has lived with the third party for a substantial period of time. This may have occurred for a number of reasons:

- □ The biological parent was ill, out of the state, out of work, etc.
- □ The biological parent was in prison.
- □ The state asked the third party to care for the child temporarily.
- □ The child could not stay at home because of marital difficulties between the biological parents.
- □ The biological parent was in school for substantial periods of time.
- □ The biological parent once considered giving the child up for adoption.

Psychological Parent
An adult who is not legally responsible for the care of a child, but who has formed a substantial emotional bond with the child.

Third parties who have formed such emotional ties with a child are referred to as **psychological parents.** See Goldstein, Freud, and Solnit, *Beyond the Best Interests of the Child* (1979).

There are two main schools of thought among courts when the custody dispute is between a biological parent and a psychological parent:

1. It is in the best interest of the child to be placed with its biological parent (this is a strong presumption).

2. It is in the best interest of the child to be placed with the adult who will provide the most wholesome, stable environment.

The emphasis of the first approach is on parental rights: unless you can show that the biological parent is *unfit*, he or she has the right to custody. The emphasis of the second approach is on the child's needs. Most states follow the first approach. In these states, the question is not whether the biological parent or the psychological parent can provide the best home for the child. The question is whether it is clear that placement with the biological parent would be harmful to the child. While the child may suffer some damage if his or her relationship with the psychological parent is severed, this does not necessarily overcome the biological parent's overriding right to have the child. The law is very reluctant to take children away from their natural parents because of a determination that someone else could do a better job raising them.

In practice, courts sometimes tend to blur the two approaches listed above. While maintaining allegiance to the doctrine of parental rights, the court might still undertake a comparison between the benefits to the child of living with the biological parent, as opposed to the benefits of living with the psychological parent. When the benefits to be derived from the latter are overwhelming, the court might be more inclined to find unfitness in the biological parent or to conclude that giving custody to the biological parent would be detrimental to the child. The interpretation of the evidence can be very subjective. There is often enough data to support any conclusion the court wants to reach. A person's mistakes in raising children can be viewed either as an inability to be a competent parent or as an inevitable component of the nearly impossible job of parenting in today's society.

ASSIGNMENT 7.3

Make up a fact situation involving a custody dispute between a biological parent and a psychological parent. Make it a close case. Include facts that would strongly favor each side. Now write a memorandum in which you discuss the law that would apply to your case. Assume that you are working for the office that represents the psychological parent.

◼◼◼◼ MODIFICATION OF THE CUSTODY ORDER BY THE STATE THAT ISSUED THE ORDER

In this section we consider the modification of a custody order by the *same* state that issued the order. Later we will examine the special jurisdiction problems that arise when a party with a custody order from one state tries to have it modified in another state. While our discussion will focus on the two biological parents, the same principles apply no matter who is given custody by the original order.

Two reasons justify a court in modifying its own custody order:

☐ There has been a significant change in circumstances since the original order, or

☐ Relevant facts were not made available to the court at the time of its original order.

In either situation, new facts are now before the court. The question becomes whether it is in the best interest of the child for the court to change its mind and award custody to the other parent. Given the disruption of such a change, the answer is no, unless the new facts *substantially* alter the court's perception of the child's welfare. For example:

☐ The custodial parent has been neglecting or abusing the child.

☐ The custodial parent has moved from the area, contrary to the court's order, thus making visitation extremely difficult or impossible.

☐ The custodial parent has adopted an unorthodox lifestyle that has negatively affected the child's physical or moral development (or there is a danger that this lifestyle will have this effect).

It is not enough that the custodial parent has experienced hard times such as sickness or loss of a part-time job since the original order. Nor is it enough to show that mistakes have been made in raising the children. To justify a modification, the adverse circumstances or mistakes must be (1) ongoing, (2) relatively permanent, (3) serious, and (4) detrimental to the children.

ASSIGNMENT 7.4

a. Make up a fact situation involving a case in which sole custody was granted to one parent, but the other parent is now seeking a modification. Make it a close case. Include facts that support a modification and facts that support a continuation of the status quo. Now write a memorandum in which you discuss the law that would apply to your case. Assume that you are working for the office that represents the party who wants to prevent the other side from modifying the order.

b. Read Exhibit 7.2 containing an affidavit in support of a motion to modify a custody decree. Do you think the court should reconsider the custody order as requested? What further facts, if any, would you like to have?

■■■■■ JURISDICTIONAL PROBLEMS AND CHILD SNATCHING

Earlier we discussed the modification of a child-custody order by the state that issued the order. Suppose, however, that a party tries to have the order modified by *another* state. Consider the following sequence:

Dan and Ellen are divorced in New York where they live. Ellen receives custody of their child. Dan moves to Delaware. During a visit of the child in Delaware, Dan petitions a Delaware court for a modification of the New York custody order. Ellen does not appear in the Delaware proceeding. Dan tells the Delaware court a horror story about the child's life with Ellen in New York. The Delaware court modifies the New York order on the basis of changed circumstances, awarding custody to Dan.

Or worse:

While their child is in a New York school yard, Dan takes the child out of the state without telling Ellen. Dan petitions a Delaware court for a modification of the custody order. If he loses, he tries again in Florida. If he loses, he tries again in another state until he finds a court that will grant him custody.

The latter situation involves what has been commonly called *child snatching*. The parent "grabs" the child and then "shops" for a favorable forum **(forum shopping)**. For years the problem reached epidemic proportions.

Forum Shopping
Seeking a court that will be favorable to you. Traveling from court to court until you find one that will provide a favorable ruling.

Courts are caught in a dilemma. When a custody order is made, it is not a final determination by the court. Custody orders are always modifiable on the basis of changed circumstances that affect the welfare of the child. This rule is designed to help the child by making the court always available to protect the child. But if an order is not final, it is not entitled to *full faith and credit* by another state, i.e., another state is not required to abide by it. Hence, other states are free to reexamine the case to determine whether new circumstances warrant

☐ **EXHIBIT 7.2 Affidavit in Support of a Motion to Modify the Custody Decree**

AFFIDAVIT IN SUPPORT
Index No. 3

STATE OF NEW YORK ⎱
COUNTY OF _____ ⎰ ss.

_____ , being duly sworn, deposes and says:

1. I am the defendant herein. This affidavit is submitted in support of an application for reconsideration of the decision of the court made in this action on _____ , 19 ___ , insofar as custody of my children is concerned.

2. Custody of the children has been awarded to my ex-wife, plaintiff. I did not contest her claim in the divorce. When I reported this to the children, they became extremely upset. My son told me that he did not want to live with his mother and that he felt it was unfair for a boy of his age to be forced to live with a parent contrary to his desires. My daughter had a similar reaction.

3. I tried to convey the situation to the Court by an informal application of reconsideration, on the strength of simple notes written to the Court by my children. My attorney advised me that the Court would not alter its determination.

4. I love my children very much. A history of prior proceedings between my wife and myself indicates that she had been awarded custody of the children under a Family Court order several years ago. At that time, she lived with the children in our house in Peekskill. I paid support, as directed for the children and my wife, and for the upkeep of the house. About two years ago my wife ousted my son from the house and sent him to live with me. At that time, I occupied a small apartment in Peekskill so that I could be near the children. I would see them quite often and would take them to school on many mornings. When my son came to me, I made room for him and we lived together until my daughter came to live with us about a year ago. We made room for her. My wife made no objections to the children living with me and made no attempts to get them to come back to her. While we all lived in my small apartment, my wife continued to live in the Peekskill house all by herself. I continued paying the upkeep on the house, although my wife permitted it to fall into a state of deteriorating disrepair. I contributed to her support.

5. I took care of my children as best I could. They were grown and attended school most of the day. In the evening we enjoyed a family life. We were together on the week-ends. There were many week-ends when their mother would not attempt to spend any time with them. My son stayed away from the Peekskill house. My daughter visited there with her mother on occasion. I know that on many occasions my wife stayed away from the Peekskill house for days at a time.

6. I have devoted my non-working hours to my children. I altered my schedule so that I would see them off to school each morning when I was not away from the City. If I was to be away, I would arrange adult supervision. I worked with my children on their homework and on anything else where they sought my participation. We shopped together and played together. My children were encouraged to maintain their friendships and to bring their friends to our home. Because of cramped quarters, my children would often visit with their friends and I encouraged them to maintain relationships with companions of their respective ages. I shared their problems and their joys. I tried to set responsible examples for them. My son had demonstrated to me that he is growing into a responsible young man who aspires to attend Massachusetts Institute of Technology. I am proud of his seriousness and of his healthy outlook in times like this. I have tried to maintain a closely knit family between my children and myself so that they should know the advantages of love, companionship, and security. I know that they did not find any such relationship at their mother's bosom.

7. My children have revealed to me that they were wrong in not having made a definite choice during this interview with the court on the matter of their preference of a home. I understand that they will still love their mother and I have not attempted to sway them from that plateau. They told me that they wanted the court to decide the problem for them and that they had hoped that they could be the force which could solve the rift between plaintiff and myself. They were unaware that at the time of the interview, my wife's prayer for divorce had already been granted. My son told me that he indicated to the court that he preferred to live with me although he did not state, unequivocally, that he did not desire to live with his mother.

8. I gather from my children's reaction and from what they have told me that they misunderstood what was required of them during their interview with the court. I submit that another interview should be granted if the court feels that my children's affidavits are insufficient to establish their desires. Had I not seen the effect of the custody decision on my children and had they not indicated their grief over it, I would sit back and abide by the will of the court.

9. I seriously question my wife's fitness as our children's custodian. She voluntarily relinquished their custody, as aforesaid. Under adverse living conditions (cramped quarters), my children have thrived and demonstrated a progression toward adulthood. I believe that my wife's having been competitive instead of being cooperative with the children operated to compromise their welfare. I believe that using the children as a pawn has lost our children's respect. I feel that my pleasures must be subservient to the welfare of my children. They deserve as real a home as can be possible under the circumstances. They are entitled to eat a meal in peace and one which shows concern in its preparation. I believe that the children deserve some security in the knowledge that they have the genuine care and love of a parent. I believe that they cannot get this from their mother.

10. WHEREFORE, I respectfully pray that this application be granted and that upon reconsideration I be awarded custody of my children.

[Signature]

_____

SOURCE: Marino, J., McKinney's Forms, Form 14:24B and Form 14:33A West Publishing Co. (1976).

a modification. To maintain flexibility, states require very little to trigger its jurisdiction to hear a custody case, e.g., the domicile or mere presence of the child in the state along with one of the parents. The result is chaos: scandalous child snatching and unseemly forum shopping.

The question, therefore, is how to cut down or eliminate child snatching and forum shopping without taking away the flexibility that courts need to act in the best interest of the child. Two major statutes need to be discussed:

☐ The *Uniform Child Custody Jurisdiction Act*

☐ The *Parental Kidnaping Prevention Act*

UNIFORM CHILD CUSTODY JURISDICTION ACT (UCCJA)

In 1968 the **Uniform Child Custody Jurisdiction Act (UCCJA)** was issued by the National Conference of Commissioners on Uniform Laws. This conference proposes laws for adoption by the various state legislatures. When first proposed, only a small number of states adopted the UCCJA. But after a top-rated television program (*60 Minutes*) gave national exposure to the problem, many of the states fell in line.

Two important questions are covered in the UCCJA:

☐ When does a court in the state have the power or jurisdiction to make the *initial* decision on child custody?

☐ When will a court modify a custody order of another state?

A goal of the UCCJA is to "avoid jurisdictional competition and conflict with courts of other states in matters of child custody which have in the past resulted in the shifting of children from state to state with harmful effects on their well-being" (§ 1).

JURISDICTION TO MAKE THE INITIAL CHILD-CUSTODY DECISION

The foundation of the UCCJA is § 3, which specifies the conditions that must exist for a court to hear a child-custody case. Without one of these conditions being present, the court will have no jurisdiction to decide the case. Any *one* of the following four conditions will be sufficient to confer such jurisdiction:

1. *Home state.*

Home State The state where a child has lived for at least six consecutive months, or since birth if the child is less than six months old.

   ▪ This is the **home state** of the child at the time the case is brought. A home state is where the child has lived for at least six consecutive months (or since birth if the child is less than six months old). These time periods can include temporary absence from the state. *Or*

   ▪ This state was the home state of the child (as defined above) within six months of the commencement of the custody suit, but the child is now being kept out of state and at least one parent or person claiming the right to custody still lives in this state.

2. *Significant connection/substantial evidence.* Even though this is not the home state of the child, it is in the best interest of the child for this state to take jurisdiction because:

   ▪ The child and parents, or the child and at least one person claiming custody, have a significant connection with this state, *and*

   ▪ There is substantial evidence in this state concerning the child's present or future care, protection, training, and personal relationships.

3. *Physical presence/abandonment/emergency.* Even though this is not the home

state of the child and even though there is not significant connection with or substantial evidence in this state, the state can still take jurisdiction if:

- The child is physically present in the state and has been abandoned, *or*
- The child is physically present in the state and an emergency exists because the child has been subjected to or threatened with mistreatment, abuse, neglect, etc.

4. *No other state has jurisdiction.* Even though this is not the home state of the child, even though there is no significant connection with or substantial evidence in this state, and even though there is no abandonment or emergency, this state can still take jurisdiction if:

- It is in the best interest of the child for this state to take jurisdiction, and no other state would have jurisdiction under any of the conditions substantially similar to those listed above: (1) No other state is the home state. (2) There is no significant connection with or substantial evidence in another state. (3) The child is not physically present in another state faced with abandonment or an emergency. *Or*
- It is in the best interest of the child for this state to take jurisdiction, and another state has declined to accept jurisdiction because this state is the more appropriate forum to determine custody.

Section 8(a) of the UCCJA also has a *"clean hands"* provision. A court can decline to exercise jurisdiction if the petitioner for custody has "wrongfully taken the child from another state or has engaged in similar reprehensible conduct" and it is "just and proper" for the court to decline jurisdiction under the circumstances.

Thus, simply because a court has jurisdiction to take a custody case, it will not necessarily use that jurisdiction. In addition to refusing jurisdiction in a case where the petitioner has **dirty hands,** a court can also decline to use its jurisdiction if it is clear under the circumstances that another state would be a more convenient forum to resolve the custody dispute (§ 7). For example, it may be possible for *two* states to have a significant connection with the parties. Substantial evidence on the child's welfare may exist in *both* states. One of these states, however, could decline to exercise its jurisdiction because the other state has a *more* significant connection and *more* substantial evidence. The UCCJA, therefore, encourages states to defer to the most convenient and appropriate state available.

Dirty Hands Wrong-doing or other inappropriate behavior that would make it unfair or inequitable to allow a person to assert a right or a defense he or she would normally have.

Fred and Jane were married in Ohio on January 1, 1980. On March 13, 1980, they had a child, Bob. From the first day of their marriage, however, they began having marital difficulties. On July 4, 1980, Fred moved to Kentucky. Bob continued to live with his mother in Ohio. By mutual agreement, Fred can occasionally take the child to Kentucky for visits. After a scheduled one-day visit on November 5, 1980, Fred decides not to return the child. He keeps Bob until November 1, 1981, when he returns him to Jane. Fred then joins the Army. When he returns on October 6, 1985, he discovers that Jane has been beating Bob.

Assume that both Ohio and Kentucky have adopted the UCCJA. Under § 3 and § 8(a) of the UCCJA, which state would have jurisdiction to determine the custody of Bob on the following dates:

April 4, 1980
November 6, 1980
January 1, 1981
September 1, 1981
October 6, 1985

JURISDICTION TO MODIFY A CUSTODY ORDER OF ANOTHER STATE

Thus far we have examined the jurisdiction of a state to make an *initial* custody order. We have addressed the questions of when does a court have jurisdiction to decide the custody question for the first time, and if more than one state has jurisdiction, which is the most convenient forum? We now turn to the question of *modification:* when does one state have jurisdiction to modify a custody order of another state? Section 14 of the UCCJA governs:

> A court in this state (where a modification is being sought) can modify the custody order of another state only if:
>
> (i) The state that issued the custody order no longer appears to have jurisdiction under conditions substantially similar to § 3 (i.e., it is no longer the home state, or it no longer has significant connection/substantial evidence, or the child is not physically present in the state faced with abandonment or an emergency), *or,* the state has declined to assume jurisdiction to modify its own custody order. And,
>
> (ii) This state (where a modification is being sought) has jurisdiction under § 3 (i.e., it is the home state, or it has significant connection/substantial evidence, or the child is physically present in the state faced with abandonment or an emergency).

For example, before a California court can modify a New York custody order, the California court must first determine whether New York would now have jurisdiction under § 3 (or under provisions substantially similar thereto), *and* whether California now has jurisdiction under § 3.

Again, however, even though a state has jurisdiction to modify the order of another state, the state may decline to exercise this jurisdiction. Section 8(b) is the dirty hands provision for modification cases:

> Unless required in the interest of the child, the court shall not exercise its jurisdiction to modify a custody decree of another state if the petitioner, without consent of the person entitled to custody, has improperly removed the child from the physical custody of the person entitled to custody or has improperly retained the child after a visit or other temporary relinquishment of physical custody. If the petitioner has violated any other provision of a custody decree of another state the court may decline to exercise its jurisdiction if this is just and proper under the circumstances.

ASSIGNMENT 7.6

Reread the facts in Assignment 7.5. Assume that in 1981, an Ohio court awarded custody of Bob to Jane. On October 10, 1985, Fred asks a Kentucky court to grant him custody. Assume further that both Ohio and Kentucky have adopted the UCCJA. Can Kentucky modify?

Exhibit 7.3 shows the form used to file a declaration under the UCCJA.

PARENTAL KIDNAPING PREVENTION ACT (PKPA)

Not all states had adopted the UCCJA by 1980, and some states that did adopt it changed several of its key provisions. This meant that there were still opportunities for forum shopping. To combat this, Congress passed the **Parental Kidnaping Prevention Act (PKPA)** to give added clout to the anti-child snatching movement. Congress was concerned that the lack of nationwide consistency in state custody laws contributed to a tendency of parties "to frequently resort to the seizure, restraint, concealment, and interstate transportation of children, the disregard of court orders, excessive relitigation of cases, obtaining of conflicting orders by the courts, . . . and interstate travel and communication

☐ **EXHIBIT 7.3 Declaration under Uniform Child Custody Jurisdiction Act (UCCJA)**

ATTORNEY OR PARTY WITHOUT ATTORNEY *(Name and Address)*:	TELEPHONE NO.:	*FOR COURT USE ONLY*

ATTORNEY FOR *(Name)*:

SUPERIOR COURT OF CALIFORNIA, COUNTY OF

STREET ADDRESS:

MAILING ADDRESS:

CITY AND ZIP CODE:

BRANCH NAME:

CASE NAME:

DECLARATION UNDER **UNIFORM CHILD CUSTODY JURISDICTION ACT (UCCJA)**	CASE NUMBER:

1. **I am a party** to this proceeding to determine custody of a child.
2. *(Number)*: _____ minor children are subject to this proceeding as follows:
   (Insert the information requested below. The residence information must be given for the last FIVE years.)

a. Child's name		Place of birth	Date of birth	Sex
Period of residence	**Address**	**Person child lived with** *(name and present adress)*		**Relationship**
to present				
to				
to				
to				
to				

b. Child's name		Place of birth	Date of birth	Sex
☐ Residence information is the same as given above for child a. *(If NOT the same, provide the information below.)*				
Period of residence	**Address**	**Person child lived with** *(name and present address)*		**Relationship**
to present				
to				
to				
to				
to				

c. ☐ Additional children are listed on Attachment 2c. *(Provide requested information for additional children on an attachment.)*

(Continued on reverse)

Form Approved by the
Judicial Council of California
MC-150 [Rev. January 1, 1987] [Cor. 1/2/87]
DECLARATION UNDER
UNIFORM CHILD CUSTODY JURISDICTION ACT (UCCJA)
Civil Code, § 5158
Probate Code, §§ 1510(f), 1512

□ **EXHIBIT 7.3   Declaration under Uniform Child Custody Jurisdiction Act (UCCJA)—*Continued***

SHORT TITLE:	CASE NUMBER:

3. Have you participated as a party or a witness or in some other capacity in another litigation or custody proceeding, in California or elsewhere, concerning custody of a child subject to this proceeding?
   [ ] No   [ ] Yes   *(If yes, provide the following information:)*

   a. Name of each child:

   b. Capacity of declarant: [ ] party   [ ] witness   [ ] other *(specify)*:
   c. Court *(specify name, state, location)*:

   d. Court order or judgment *(date)*:

4. Do you have information about a custody proceeding pending in a California court or any other court concerning a child subject to this proceeding, other than that stated in item 3?
   [ ] No   [ ] Yes   *(If yes, provide the following information:)*

   a. Name of each child:

   b. Nature of proceeding: [ ] dissolution or divorce   [ ] guardianship   [ ] adoption   [ ] other *(specify)*:

   c. Court *(specify name, state, location)*:

   d. Status of proceeding:

5. Do you know of any person who is not a party to this proceeding who has physical custody or claims to have custody of or visitation rights with any child subject to this proceeding?
   [ ] No   [ ] Yes   *(If yes, provide the following information:)*

a. Name and address of person	b. Name and address of person	c. Name and address of person
[ ] Has physical custody [ ] Claims custody rights [ ] Claims visitation rights	[ ] Has physical custody [ ] Claims custody rights [ ] Claims visitation rights	[ ] Has physical custody [ ] Claims custody rights [ ] Claims visitation rights
Name of each child	Name of each child	Name of each child

I declare under penalty of perjury under the laws of the State of California that the foregoing is true and correct.
Date:

▶

. . . .   _____
(TYPE OR PRINT NAME)   (SIGNATURE OF DECLARANT)

6. [ ]   Number of pages attached after this page:

> NOTICE TO DECLARANT: You have a continuing duty to inform this court if you obtain any information about a custody proceeding in a California court or any other court concerning a child subject to this proceeding.

MC-150 [Rev. January 1, 1987]   **DECLARATION UNDER**   **Page two**
  [Cor. 1/2/87]   **UNIFORM CHILD CUSTODY JURISDICTION ACT (UCCJA)**

that is so expensive and time consuming." To remedy this problem, Congress enacted the PKPA.

The PKPA addresses the question of when one state *must* enforce (without modification) the custody decree (or visitation order) of another state. Phrased another way, when must one state give *full faith and credit* to the custody decree of another state? In answering this question, the PKPA adopts many of the principles of the UCCJA. The essential question is whether the state that rendered the custody decree had jurisdiction to do so based on provisions very similar to § 3 of the UCCJA, discussed earlier. First, this state must have had jurisdiction according to its own laws. Additionally, one of the following conditions must be met as of the time the state rendered its custody decree:

> "(A) such state (i) is the home State of the child on the date of the commencement of the proceeding, or (ii) had been the child's home State within six months before the date of the commencement of the proceeding and the child is absent from such State because of his removal or retention by a contestant or for other reasons, and a contestant continues to live in such State;
>
> "(B)(i) it appears that no other State would have jurisdiction under subparagraph (A), and (ii) it is in the best interest of the child that a court of such State assume jurisdiction because (I) the child and his parents, or the child and at least one contestant, have a significant connection with such State other than mere physical presence in such State, and (II) there is available in such State substantial evidence concerning the child's present or future care, protection, training, and personal relationships;
>
> "(C) the child is physically present in such State and (i) the child has been abandoned, or (ii) it is necessary in an emergency to protect the child because he has been subjected to or threatened with mistreatment or abuse;
>
> "(D)(i) it appears that no other State would have jurisdiction under subparagraph (A), (B), (C), or (E), or another State has declined to exercise jurisdiction on the ground that the State whose jurisdiction is in issue is the more appropriate forum to determine the custody of the child, and (ii) it is in the best interest of the child that such court assume jurisdiction; or
>
> "(E) the court has continuing jurisdiction. . . ."

In these circumstances, the custody order shall be given full faith and credit by another state. Another state "shall not modify" it. Once a court has proper jurisdiction to render a custody decree, this jurisdiction continues so long as this state remains the residence of the child *or* of any party claiming a right to custody.

Congress also made available to the states the *Federal Parent Locator Service,* which will help to locate an absent parent or child for the purpose of enforcing laws on the unlawful taking or restraint of a child or for the purpose of making or enforcing a child-custody determination. Previously, this service has been used mainly in child-support cases (see chapter 8).

■■■■■ CHILDREN ABROAD: SPECIAL PROBLEMS

The following material deals with child abduction over international borders. As we have seen, parental kidnaping within the United States can lead to complex jurisdictional problems. These problems multiply when the child is taken out of the country.

LOCATING A MISSING CHILD ABROAD
United States Department of State,
Office of Citizens Consular Services, Washington,
D.C.

The resolution of child custody disputes is a private legal matter in which the Department of State may not properly intervene. Our role is limited to questions concerning the welfare and whereabouts of the American citizen children abducted by one parent and transported to a foreign jurisdiction and the issuance of passports to children who are the subject of custody disputes.

Consular Welfare/Whereabouts Search
When a child has been abducted by a parent, the American embassy or consulate can conduct a welfare/whereabouts check for the child. Under this procedure, the consular officer attempts to locate the child and ascertain the child's state of health. The consular officer will endeavor to either personally interview the child or enlist the services of local authorities to determine the child's health and welfare. The consular officer may begin by contacting local authorities to verify the child's entry and/or residence in the country. When the child is located, the consular officer may telephone the parent/guardian abroad or speak directly to the child. A personal visit to the child by the consular officer may be requested by the parent in the United States. If difficulty ensues when the parent/guardian refuses the consular officer access to the child, local officials, family services agencies or police authorities may be requested to determine the child's well-being. A report of the child's condition is then relayed to the requesting parent. If the welfare/whereabouts check convinces the consular officer that the child may have been abused or if evidence provided by the parent in the U.S. such as police reports, medical records or school records supports allegations of child abuse, the consular officer will make strong representations to the local authorities for a thorough investigation and, if necessary, request the removal of the child into the protective custody of the local courts or child welfare service. Consular officers cannot, however, take custody or force the return of the child to the deprived parent in the United States.

ONE POSSIBLE SOLUTION: THE HAGUE CONVENTION
International Parental Child Abduction, 3d ed.,
United States Department of State, Bureau of Consular
Affairs (1989).

The most difficult and frustrating element for most parents whose child has been abducted abroad is that U.S. laws and court orders are not directly enforceable abroad. Each sovereign country has jurisdiction within its own territory and over persons present within its border, and no country can force another to decide cases or enforce laws within its confines in a particular way. Issues that have to be resolved between sovereign nations can only be handled by persuasion, or by international agreement.

The increase in international marriages since World War II increased international child custody cases to the point where 23 nations, meeting at the Hague Conference on Private International Law in 1976, agreed to seek a treaty to deter international child abduction. Between 1976 and 1980, the United States was a major force in preparing and negotiating the Hague Convention on the Civil Aspects of International Child Abduction. The Convention came into force for the United States on July 1, 1988, and applies to abductions or wrongful retentions that occurred on or after that date.

Thirty-seven countries have now ratified the Hague Convention, and other countries are working toward ratification. Call or write Citizens Consular Service to learn which countries have joined.

What Is Covered by the Convention
The countries that are parties to the Convention have agreed with each other that, subject to certain limited exceptions, a child wrongfully removed or retained in one of these countries shall promptly be returned to the other member country where the child habitually resided before the abduction or wrongful retention. The Convention also provides a means for helping parents to exercise visitation rights abroad.

There is a treaty obligation to return an abducted child below the age of 16 if application is made less than one year from the date of wrongful removal or retention. After one year, the court is still obligated to order the child returned unless the person resisting return demonstrates that the child is settled in the new environment. A court may refuse to order a child returned if there is a grave risk that the child would be exposed to physical or psychological harm or otherwise placed in an intolerable situation. A court may also decline to return the child if the child objects to being returned and has reached an age and degree of maturity at which the court can take account of the child's views. Finally, the return of the child may be refused if the return would violate the fundamental principles of human rights and freedoms of the country where the child is being held.

SUMMARY

Legal custody and physical custody can be given to one parent (sole custody) or to both parents (joint custody). In negotiating custody and visitation terms of a separation agreement, many factors need to be considered, such as the age and health of the parents and child, the emotional attachments of the child, the work schedules of the parents, etc. If negotiations fail and the parties cannot agree, litigation is necessary. This can be a stressful experience, not only for the parents, but also for the person caught in the middle—the child.

The court has considerable discretion in resolving a custody battle between two biological parents according to the standard of the best interest of the child. It will consider a number of relevant factors such as stability in the child's life, including cultural continuity, availability to respond to the child's day-to-day needs, emotional ties that have already developed, etc. At one time, courts applied evidentiary guidelines such as the presumption that a child of tender years is better off with his or her mother. Today, many courts reject such presumptions, although fathers continue to complain that the mother is still given an undue preference.

The moral values and lifestyles of the parent seeking custody are generally not considered by the court unless they affect the welfare of the child. If the parents practice different religions, the court cannot prefer one religion over another, but can consider what effect the practice of a particular religion will have on the child. If the child is old enough to express a preference, it will be considered. Often the court will also consider the testimony of expert witnesses.

The court will generally favor liberal visitation rights for the noncustodial parent. Occasionally, such rights will be granted to individuals other than biological parents, e.g., grandparents. One of the most distressing issues in this area is the charge by the custodial parent that the child has been sexually molested during visitation. This may lead to a denial of visitation or to visitation only when supervised by another adult, usually a professional.

When the custody battle is between a biological parent and a nonparent (often called a psychological parent), the biological parent usually wins unless he or she can be shown to be unfit.

Occasionally, it is in the best interest of the child for a court to modify an earlier custody decision because of changed circumstances. Frantic parents will sometimes engage in forum shopping and child snatching in order to find a court that will make a modification order. To cut down on this practice, two important laws have been enacted: the state Uniform Child Custody Jurisdiction Act, and the federal Parental Kidnaping Prevention Act. When the child has been taken to a foreign country, the aid of the Hague Convention on Child Abduction might be enlisted.

KEY CHAPTER TERMINOLOGY

Legal Custody
Physical Custody
Custodial Parent
Noncustodial Parent
Sole Custody
Joint Custody
Split Custody
Mediation

Best Interest of the Child
Contested
Guardian ad Litem
Parental Alienation Syndrome
Tender Years Presumption
Primary Caregiver Presumption
MMPI
Psychological Parents

Forum Shopping
Uniform Child Custody Jurisdiction Act (UCCJA)
Home State
Dirty Hands
Parental Kidnaping Prevention Act (PKPA)

8 CHILD SUPPORT

▬▬▬▬ SEPARATION AGREEMENT

When the parties are negotiating the child support terms of a separation agreement, they need to consider a wide range of factors:

☐ According to state guidelines, what is the minimum amount of child support that must be paid to the custodial parent? Do the parties want to exceed the minimum?

☐ What standard of living was the child accustomed to during the marriage?

☐ Do the providers of support have the financial resources to maintain this standard of living?

☐ What are the tax considerations? Unlike alimony, child support payments are not deductible by the provider (see chapter 11). Consequently, the provider or payor may try to convince the other parent to agree to a lower child support payment in exchange for a higher alimony payment in order to take advantage of the deduction. Alimony payments, unlike child support payments, are taxable to the recipient. Hence, the alimony recipient (payee) will usually want some other benefit to compensate for the increased taxes that will result from agreeing to the higher alimony and lower child support payments, e.g., some extra benefit in the property division terms of the separation agreement.

☐ On what day is each payment to be made?

☐ How many payments are to be made? One covering everyday expenses and a separate one covering large, emergency expenses, e.g., hospitalization?

☐ Will there be security for the payments, e.g., a trust account, an escrow account that can be used in the event of nonpayment?

☐ Is the child to be covered by medical insurance? If so, who pays the premiums?

☐ When the provider dies, is his or her estate obligated to continue payments? If so, must the provider's will so state?

☐ Is the child to be the beneficiary of a life insurance policy on the life of the provider? If so, how much, who pays the premiums, and can the beneficiaries be changed by the provider? Does the payment of premiums (and hence the insurance coverage) end when the child reaches the age of majority?

☐ Is there an escalation clause? Do the support payments fluctuate with the income of either of the parents?

☐ Do the support payments fluctuate with the income of the child, e.g., summer jobs, inheritance?

☐ Do they fluctuate in relationship to the Consumer Price Index?

☐ Do the payments end or change when the child reaches a certain age, marries, moves out of the house, or becomes disabled?

☐ What educational expenses will be covered by the provider? Tutors, preparatory school, college, graduate/professional school, room, board, books, transportation, entertainment expenses while at school, etc.?

☐ When the child is away at school, does the provider have to continue sending child support payments to the custodial parent?

☐ Do school payments go to the custodial parent or directly to a child away at school?

☐ If disputes arise between the parents concerning child support payments, what happens? Arbitration? Mediation?

There are limits, however, on what the parties can agree to in their separation agreement. They cannot, for example, absolve one or both from the obligation to pay child support, nor can they agree to an amount less than what state guidelines require if more is needed for the child's support than what they provide in their agreement.

■■■■■ INITIAL DECISION BY A COURT

Often the first request of the custodial parent is to ask the court to issue a temporary order for child support while the divorce litigation is pending (**pendente lite**). Later, a permanent support order will be part of the final divorce decree. We turn now to an examination of how the court makes these preliminary and permanent child support decisions.

Pendente Lite While the litigation is going on.

JURISDICTION TO ORDER CHILD SUPPORT

A court must have **personal jurisdiction** (sometimes called *in personam jurisdiction*) over the noncustodial parent from whom child support is being sought. This usually means that this parent must be served with process (service of process) while physically in the state. When child support is sought in a divorce proceeding, service of process occurs when the following documents are delivered to the defendant: a copy of the divorce complaint or petition and a summons to appear in court at a designated time to answer the complaint. In the vast majority of cases, the defendant is a resident of the state, so it is relatively easy to obtain personal jurisdiction over him or her. If such a defendant is difficult to find within the state, alternative methods of service are usually available, e.g., publishing a notice of the litigation in a newspaper.

Problems arise, however, if the defendant is a nonresident of the state. If personal jurisdiction is not obtained over such a defendant, then a child support

Personal Jurisdiction The power of a court to render a decision that binds an individual defendant.

order rendered by the state is invalid and cannot be enforced. A different result is reached if the issue before the court is whether the parties can be divorced. Personal jurisdiction over a nonresident is *not* necessary for the court to grant a divorce so long as one of the spouses is domiciled in the state. Later, we will consider the enforceability of a decree that divorces the parties (see chapter 10). Here our focus is the enforceability of a child support decree.

Domicile The place where a person has been physically present with the intent to make that place a permanent home.

> Ted and Wilma are married in New York. They have one child. Wilma takes the child and moves to California where she establishes a **domicile.** Wilma files for divorce in California. Ted remains in New York. He has never been in California and therefore is not served in California. The California court grants the divorce and orders Ted to pay child support.

The support order in the California court is invalid since California never had personal jurisdiction over Ted. The divorce itself, however, is valid since Wilma was domiciled in California. Personal jurisdiction over the defendant is not necessary for a court to have the power to terminate a marriage. Domicile of one of the spouses is sufficient. The parties have a **divisible divorce.** The part of the divorce that dissolved the marriage is enforceable (because of the presence of the plaintiff's domicile in California). The part of the divorce that ordered child support is not enforceable (because of the absence of personal jurisdiction over the defendant in California).[1]

Divisible Divorce A divorce decree that is enforceable in another state only in part.

How, then, does a court acquire personal jurisdiction over a nonresident defendant? The defendant, of course, can always consent to a court's assertion of personal jurisdiction by agreeing to appear in the court and fully litigate all the issues in the case. Can personal jurisdiction be obtained in the absence of such consent?

Long Arm Statute A law that gives a state court personal jurisdiction over a nonresident based on his or her purposeful contact with the state.

Most states have what is called a **long arm statute** that enables a state to acquire jurisdiction over nonresident defendants who have sufficient purposeful contact with the state so that it is fair and reasonable for the state to resolve (i.e., adjudicate) the disputes involved. Not all contacts will be sufficient to confer personal jurisdiction through the long arm statute, however. In the situation above involving Ted and Wilma, for example, the fact that Ted may often call or write his child in California is not sufficient to confer personal jurisdiction on a New York state resident. Nor would it be sufficient if Ted originally had custody of the child and agreed to send the child to California to live with its mother. Suppose, however, that Ted often visited the child in California, arranged for the child to attend a certain school in California, and opened a bank account for the child in California. Of course, if Ted is personally served with process while physically in California, the latter state would acquire personal jurisdiction over him for purposes of rendering a child support order. The question is whether personal jurisdiction can be acquired in the absence of such service. Did he have enough contact with California to make it fair and reasonable for him to be forced to defend a child support action in California? The answer is *probably yes*. The courts are still developing standards for determining when a nonresident defendant has sufficiently minimal contacts with a state for the purpose of acquiring personal jurisdiction through a long arm statute. Each case must be decided on its own facts. When Ted visited the child in California and arranged for a school and a bank account there, he in

---

1. As we will see in chapter 10, a *spousal*-support order and a property division order also require personal jurisdiction over any defendant against whom such orders are sought to be enforced. The only order that does not require personal jurisdiction of the defendant is the dissolution order itself, which simply requires the domicile of the plaintiff.

effect took advantage of the services of the state of California. He arguably became purposefully involved with the state. It therefore seems fair and reasonable to expect him to come to California and litigate the child support issue.

It again must be emphasized, however, that the law does not inevitably point to this result. The United States Supreme Court has not yet given us clear guidelines on when a long arm statute can validly confer personal jurisdiction over a nonresident in a family law case of this kind. See *Kulko v. Superior Court,* 436 U.S. 84, 98 S. Ct. 1690, 56 L. Ed. 2d 132 (1978).

WHO PAYS CHILD SUPPORT?

The traditional rule was that only the father had the legal duty to support his children. Today, each parent has an equal duty of support regardless of who has custody and day-to-day control of the children. The essential question is, who has the ability to pay? The mother, the father, or both? In practice, it is usually the father who is ordered to pay. He is the one who often controls most of the financial resources. Furthermore, the prejudice of the traditional rule still lingers in the minds of many judges.

What about a stepparent (someone who has married one of the natural parents)? If the stepparent has adopted the child formally or equitably (see chapter 15), there is a duty to support the child even after the marriage ends in divorce. Without adoption, however, most states say that the stepparent has no duty of support unless he or she has agreed otherwise.

STANDARDS TO DETERMINE AMOUNT OF SUPPORT

A child has many needs that must be paid for: shelter, food, clothing, education, medical care, transportation, recreation, etc. A court will consider a number of factors in determining the amount of child support. These factors are quite similar to what the parties must assess on this issue in their separation agreement:

☐ State guidelines—the most important (see discussion below).

☐ Standard of living enjoyed by child before the separation or divorce.

☐ Child's age.

☐ Child's own financial resources, e.g., from a trust fund set up by a relative, from part-time employment.

☐ Financial resources of custodial parent.

☐ Financial resources of noncustodial parent.

☐ Earning potential of both parents.

☐ Child's need and capacity for education, including higher education.

☐ Financial needs of noncustodial parent.

☐ Responsibility of noncustodial parent to support others, e.g., a second family from a second marriage.

Note that marital fault is not on the list. Which parent was at fault in "causing" the divorce is not relevant and should not be considered in assessing the need for child support.

Since 1987 every state has been under a federal mandate to adopt **child support guidelines** for the determination of child support by its courts.[2] The guidelines establish a rebuttable presumption on the amount of child support that should be awarded. A judge is required to use this amount unless to do so would be inequitable to the parties or the child.

Child Support Guidelines A required method of determining the amount of child support that must be paid.

---

2. 42 U.S.C.A. § 667; 45 C.F.R. §§ 302.52, 302.56.

While the guidelines are not the same in every state, many states have based their guidelines on the *Income Shares Model,* which operates on the principle that the children should receive the same proportion of parental income that they would have received had the parents lived together. Studies have shown that individuals tend to spend money on their children in proportion to their income, and not solely on need. Child support is calculated as a *share* of each parent's income that would have been spent on the children if the parents and children were living in the same household. The calculation of these shares is based on the best available economic data on the amount of money ordinarily spent on children by their families in the United States. This amount is then adjusted to the cost of living for a particular state.

Exhibits 8.1 and 8.2 provide further information on how this amount is calculated in one particular state, South Carolina.

☐ **EXHIBIT 8.1   South Carolina Schedule of Basic Child Support Obligations**

Important: These figures are *not* child support payments to be made by either parent. They are the amounts of child support to be contributed by *both* parents. An individual parent's share of this amount must be computed by use of the formula found on the Child Support Obligation Worksheet [Exhibit 8.2].

MONTHLY COMBINED GROSS INCOME	ONE CHILD	TWO CHILDREN	THREE CHILDREN	FOUR CHILDREN	FIVE CHILDREN	SIX CHILDREN
500.00	50	50	50	50	50	50
550.00	57	58	58	59	60	60
600.00	94	95	96	97	98	99
650.00	123	124	126	127	128	130
700.00	151	154	155	157	159	160
750.00	159	183	185	187	189	191
800.00	168	216	218	221	223	225
850.00	176	248	251	254	257	259
900.00	185	270	284	287	290	293
950.00	194	282	317	320	324	327
1000.00	202	295	349	353	357	360
1050.00	211	307	364	385	390	394
1100.00	219	320	378	418	423	427
1150.00	228	332	393	434	456	461
1200.00	236	344	408	450	488	494
1250.00	245	357	422	466	506	527
1300.00	253	369	437	483	523	560
1350.00	261	381	450	498	539	577
3250.00	518	751	886	979	1061	1135
3300.00	522	756	891	985	1067	1142
3350.00	525	761	897	991	1074	1149
5250.00	665	959	1125	1243	1347	1442
5300.00	670	966	1133	1252	1357	1452
5350.00	675	973	1141	1261	1367	1463
7250.00	843	1213	1420	1569	1701	1820
7300.00	847	1219	1427	1577	1710	1829
7350.00	852	1225	1435	1585	1718	1839
9250.00	999	1441	1693	1871	2028	2170
9300.00	1002	1446	1699	1877	2035	2177
9350.00	1006	1451	1705	1884	2042	2185
11250.00	1127	1629	1916	2117	2295	2456
11300.00	1130	1633	1921	2123	2302	2463
11350.00	1133	1637	1927	2129	2308	2469

If the obligor's income and corresponding number of children fall into a shaded area, compute the support obligation using obligor's income only.

□ **EXHIBIT 8.2 South Carolina Child Support Obligation Worksheet**

_____)
Name of Plaintiff   )
                        vs.   )   File Number
_____)   **Child Support Obligation**
Name of Defendant   )
)   **Worksheet A**

	Father	Mother

1. **Monthly Gross Income** ...._____   _____

2. Monthly Alimony (this action)
   a. To be received ....+_____   +_____
   b. To be paid ....−_____   −_____

3. Other monthly alimony or child
   support paid (if having priority over   **Combined Monthly Adjusted Gross Income**
   this action ....−_____   −_____

4. **Adjusted Monthly Gross Income** ...4(F)_____ + 4(M)_____   = 4(C)
                                                                                4(F) + 4(M) = 4(C)

Number of Children to be supported by Order in this Action: ☐

5. Basic Combined Child Support Obligation (Gross)
   (from Schedule, using Combined Monthly Adjusted Gross Income (Line (4C)) ....5(C)_____

	Father	Mother

6. Adjustments to Basic Child Support
   Obligation
   a. Health insurance premium (portion
      covering children only) ....+_____   +_____
   b. Work-related child care costs
      (net of tax credit) ....+_____   +_____

   Total adjustments to Basic Combined
   Child Support Obligation ....6(F)_____ + 6(M)_____   = 6(C) + _____

7. **Total Combined Monthly Child Support Obligation (Net)** ....7(C)
                                                                                5(C) + 6(C) = 7(C)

	Father	Mother

8. Proportional share of combined monthly
   adjusted gross income ....8(F)_____ %   8(M)_____ %
                                          4(F)/4(C) = 8(F)   4(M)/4(C) = 8(M)

9. Gross child support obligation of
   individual parent (monthly) ....9(F)_____   9(M)_____
                                          7(C) × 8(F) = 9(F)   7(C) × 8(M) = 9(M)

**Complete Items 10–11 _for Non-Custodial
Parent Only_**

   Non-Custodial Parent is (check one):   Father ☐   Mother ☐

10. Credit for adjustments to basic
    combined child support obligation   10(F)_____   10(M)_____
    (from item 6(F) or item 6(M)) .... (same as item 6(F))   (same as item 6(M))

11. **_Net Child Support to be paid
    to custodial parent_** ....11(F)_____   11(M)_____
                                          9(F) − 10(F) = 11(F)   9(M) − 10(M) = 11(M)

Worksheet Prepared by:

Date: _____   _____

                                       For: Father ☐   Mother ☐

COMPUTATION OF CHILD SUPPORT [see Exhibit 8.2]   A South Carolina court can determine a total child support obligation in line 7 of Worksheet A by adding the basic child support obligation (line 5), health insurance (line 6a), and work-related child care costs (line 6b).

The total child support obligation is divided between the parents in proportion to their income. Line 8 calculates each parent's proportional share of combined monthly adjusted gross income. After the adjustments of line 10, line 11 computes the net child support to be paid to the custodial parent.

A monetary obligation is computed for each parent. The guidelines presume that the custodial parent will spend that parent's share directly on the child in that parent's custody. In cases of joint custody or split custody where both parents have responsibility of the child for a substantial portion of the time, there are provisions for adjustments. Line 11 reflects that portion of the calculated total child support obligation to be paid by the parents.

A number of computer companies have devised software for lawyers who need to calculate child support under state guidelines (see Exhibit 8.3).

COST OF COLLEGE   A good deal of litigation has centered on the issue of educational expenses, particularly higher education. Does a divorced parent have a duty to send his or her child to college? Arguments *against* imposing this duty are as follows:

☐ A parent's support duty is limited to providing the necessities to the child, e.g., food, shelter, clothing. College is not a necessity; it is a luxury.

☐ A parent's support duty terminates when the child reaches the age of majority in the state, e.g., eighteen. A child in college will be over the age of majority during some or most of the college years.

☐ Children of parents who are still married have no right to force their parents to send them to college. Why should children of divorced parents have the right to be sent to college?

Some states, however, have rejected these arguments and have required the divorced parent to pay for a college education as part of the child support

☐ **EXHIBIT 8.3   Advertisement for Software That Calculates Child Support Payments**

payments if the parent has the ability to pay and the child has the capacity to go to college. Arguments supporting this position:

☐ In today's society, college is not a luxury. A college degree, at least the first one, is a necessity.

☐ A parent's duty to provide child support does not terminate in all cases when the child reaches majority. For example, a physically or mentally handicapped child may have to be supported indefinitely. Some courts take the position that the support duty continues so long as the child's need for support continues, i.e., so long as the child remains dependent. This certainly includes the period when the child is in college.

☐ It is true that married parents have no obligation to send their children to college. But there is a strong likelihood they will do so if they have the means and their children have the ability. When the court requires a divorced parent to send his or her children to college, the same tests are applied: ability to pay and capacity to learn. Thus, the court, in effect, is simply trying to equalize the position of children of divorced parents with those of married parents.

THE SECOND FAMILY Another area of controversy concerns the noncustodial parent's responsibility of supporting others. Should the amount of child support be less because this parent has since taken on the responsibility of supporting a second family? Suppose there is a remarriage with someone who already has children and/or they have additional children of their own. The old view was that the parent's primary responsibility was to the first family. No adjustment would be made because the parent has voluntarily taken on additional support obligations. Many courts, however, no longer take this hard line. While they will not permit the parent to leave the first family destitute, they will take into consideration the fact that a second family has substantially affected the parent's ability to support the first. Given this reality, an appropriate adjustment will be made. It must be emphasized, however, that not all courts are this understanding. Some continue to adhere to the old view.

Jim and Carla have one child, George, who is two years old at the time they seek a divorce. By mutual agreement, Carla will have custody of George. When the issue of child support arises in the divorce proceeding, Carla asks the court to take into consideration the fact that Jim has already announced his engagement to a rich widow. Carla feels that this should prompt the court to require Jim to make higher child support payments. Should it? Would it make any difference if Carla were the one about to marry a wealthy new spouse? Would this affect the amount of child support that Jim should pay?

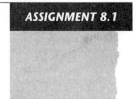

ASSIGNMENT 8.1

■■■■■■ MODIFICATION OF CHILD SUPPORT ORDERS

The standard rule is that a child support order can be modified on the basis of a substantial change of circumstances that has arisen since the court granted the order, assuming, of course, that the court has personal jurisdiction over the parent from whom a modification is sought. The changed circumstances must be serious enough to warrant the conclusion that the original award has become inequitable, e.g., the child's welfare will be jeopardized if the child support award is not increased due to an unexpected illness of the child, requiring costly medical care. Alternatively, the child support award can be decreased if it is clear that the need no longer exists at all or to the same degree—e.g., if the child has died, acquired independent resources, moved out on his or her own. A recent federal law allows the parties to request a review of a child support order every three years to make sure that it complies with the guidelines.

Frequently, the custodial parent claims that child support should be increased because the noncustodial parent's ability to pay has increased since the time of the original order, e.g., by obtaining a much better paying job. This is a ground to increase child support only when it is clear that the original decree was inadequate to meet the needs of the child. At the time of the original decree, a lesser amount may have been awarded because of an inability to pay more *at that time*. Hence, a later modification upward is simply a way for the court to correct an initially inadequate award. Since many initial awards *are* inadequate, courts are inclined to grant the modification.

Arrearage Payments that are due but have not been made (also called **arrears**).

Note that we have been discussing the modification of *future* child support payments. What about **arrearages?** Can a court modify a delinquent obligation? There was a time when courts were sympathetic to requests by delinquent obligors to forgive past due debts, particularly when the court was convinced that future obligations would be met. Congress changed this in 1986 when the Bradley Amendment banned retroactive modification of child support arrearages.[3]

What happens when the noncustodial parent seeks a modification downward because he or she can no longer afford the amount originally awarded? If the circumstances that caused this change are beyond the control of the parent, e.g., a long illness, the courts will be sympathetic. Suppose, however, that the change is voluntary. For example:

> At the time of a 1990 child support order, Dan was a fifty-year-old sales manager earning $120,000 a year. The order required him to pay his ex-wife $3,000 a month in child support. In 1991, Dan decides to go to evening law school. He quits his job as a sales manager and takes a part-time job as an investigator earning $10,000 a year. He then petitions the court to modify his child support payments to $250 a month.

In many courts, Dan's petition would be denied because he has not lost the *capacity* to earn a high salary. Self-imposed poverty is not a ground to reduce child support in such courts. Other courts are not this dogmatic. They will grant the modification petition, if:

☐ The child will not be left in a destitute condition, and,

☐ The petitioner is acting in good faith.

The court will want to know whether a legitimate change-of-career or change-of-lifestyle is involved. Is it the kind of change that the party would probably have made if the marriage had not ended? If so, the court will be inclined to grant a modification downward, so long as the child is not seriously harmed thereby. On the other hand, is the parent acting out of *bad faith* or malice, e.g., to make life more miserable for the custodial parent? If so, the modification request will be denied.

---

3. This prohibition does not apply for any period during which there was a pending petition to modify child support, but only from the date that notice of the petition was given to the other party. 42 U.S.C.A. § 666(a)(9).

We saw in chapter 6 that separation agreements are often sloppily written in that they fail to distinguish between property division terms (which are not modifiable by a court) and support terms (which are). For example, suppose that the parties agree to give the "wife the exclusive use of the marital home until the youngest child reaches the age of twenty-one." Is this a division of property or a child support term? If it is the former, then the husband cannot modify it on the basis of changed circumstances (e.g., her remarriage). If it is a child support term, then a modification is possible. Most courts would interpret the above clause as a child support term since it is tied to a period of time when the child would most likely need support. Yet a court *could* rule the other way. Needless litigation often results from poor drafting.

---

a. What standards apply to a request to modify child support payments in your state?

b. Sara pays her ex-husband, Harry, $800 a month in child support under a 1995 court order that granted custody to Harry but gave liberal visitation rights to Sara. Due to continuing bitterness, Harry refuses to allow Sara to see their child. Sara then petitions the court to reduce her child support payments. How should her request for a modification be handled?

ASSIGNMENT 8.2

Assume the same facts as Assignment 8.1 except that Jim does not announce his marriage to the rich widow until after the initial child support order is made in the divorce proceeding. Once the marriage occurs, Carla asks the court to modify the order by increasing the amount paid for child support. What result? Would it make any difference if Carla were the one to marry a wealthy new spouse? Can Jim ask the court to modify his child support payments downward?

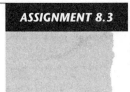

ASSIGNMENT 8.3

In a 1989 divorce decree, Frank was ordered to pay $1,000 a month in child support to his former wife, Irene, who was granted custody of their child. He makes all of his payments in 1989. When he loses his job on January 1, 1990, however, he can afford only $500 a month, which he now pays every month. In June of 1990, he asks a court to modify the child support order to $500 a month. Assume that the court agrees that he can pay only $500 a month and modifies the order to this effect on July 1, 1990. By the end of 1990, what is the total amount of child support payments that he would be legally obligated to make in 1990?

ASSIGNMENT 8.4

■■■■■■ ENFORCEMENT OF CHILD SUPPORT ORDERS

Nonpayment of child support has reached epidemic proportions. Every year billions of dollars go uncollected. The Census Bureau found that in 1991:

☐ 11.5 million families with children had a parent living outside the home (this represents almost one-third of all families with children);

☐ 9.9 million families (out of the 11.5 million total) consist of women with custody, and 1.6 million consist of men with custody;[4]

---

4. Since more than 85 percent of custodial parents are mothers, in our discussion we will often refer to the delinquent parent/obligor as the father, although there is still a significant number of cases in which the delinquent parent is the mother.

□ 6.2 million custodial parents had child support court awards or child support agreements with the noncustodial parent; 5.3 million custodial parents had neither;

□ $17.7 billion in child support was ordered, but only $11.9 billion was paid;

□ 50 percent of the 6.2 million parents with child support awards or agreements received the full payment, 25 percent received partial payment, and 25 percent received nothing.

Predictably, there has been a dramatic increase in the number of families enrolled in the main public assistance program for families: Aid to Families with Dependent Children (AFDC). Many families are on AFDC because of parents who fail to pay child support. In response to the crisis, Congress added Title IV-D to the Social Security Act[5] to encourage the creation of enforcement agencies, remedies, and procedures throughout the country. In each state, an agency now exists whose function is to carry out the mandate of Title IV-D by providing new enforcement tools that can be used along with the more traditional ones. The agencies have different names, e.g., Child Support Enforcement Branch or Division, Office of Recovery Services, Child Support and Paternity Unit. Collectively, they are all known as **IV-D agencies.** They assist AFDC recipients, as well as non-AFDC recipients, although the latter may be charged a nominal fee for the services provided. Exhibit 8.4 shows one state's application for child support enforcement services.

If a woman receives AFDC, she must **assign** or transfer her support rights to the state IV-D agency or other county welfare agency that attempts to collect support from the father. This simply means that she gives the agency the right to keep any support money that it collects on her behalf. This money is then used to offset the AFDC money she receives on an ongoing basis for herself

IV-D Agency A state agency that attempts to enforce child support obligations.

Assign To transfer rights or property.

(text continues on page 183)

---

5. 42 U.S.C.A. §§ 651–665.

☐ **EXHIBIT 8.4 Massachusetts Application for Child Support Enforcement Services**

**Massachusetts Department of Revenue
Child Support Enforcement Division**

**Application for
Child Support Enforcement Services**

● ● ● ●

Absent Parent Background and Financial Information:

---

a. Is the absent parent currently married? Yes ☐ No ☐ Don't Know ☐
(If no or don't know, skip to question #b.)
What is his or her spouse's name? _____
Does his or her spouse work? Yes ☐ No ☐ Don't Know ☐
   If yes, where does she or he work, if you know? _____
   What is her or his income $ _____ per _____ Don't Know ☐
                                         (Week, Month or Year)

b. If not married, does the absent parent share his or her household with another adult?
Yes ☐ No ☐ Don't Know ☐

c. Does the absent parent have any children who are not also your children?
Yes ☐ No ☐ Don't Know ☐

If yes, please list their names and ages here, along with the name of the adult with whom they live.

Name	Age	Living With:
_____	_____	_____
_____	_____	_____

d. Is the absent parent providing support for children who are not also your children?
Yes ☐ No ☐ Don't Know ☐
If yes, how much is he/she paying? $ _____ per _____ Don't Know ☐
                                              (Week, Month or Year)

e. To your knowledge, does the absent parent have any of the following sources of income?

Type of Income	Amount (if known)		Week/Month/Year
Worker's compensation	$ _____	per	_____
Unemployment compensation	_____		_____
Social Security retirement (over 62, green check)	_____		_____
Other pension	_____		_____
Social Security disability (green check)	_____		_____
Supplemental Security Income (SSI) (gold check)	_____		_____
Other disability	_____		_____
Welfare	_____		_____
Veteran's benefits	_____		_____
Commissions	_____		_____
Trust income	_____		_____
Rental income (from houses/apartments he or she owns)	_____		_____
Annuities	_____		_____
Interest income	_____		_____
Dividend income	_____		_____

f. To your knowledge, does he or she have—or has he or she ever had in the last three years:

	Yes	No	When	Amount
Royalties	☐	☐	19____	$ _____
Severance pay	☐	☐	19____	_____
Capital gains	☐	☐	19____	_____
Prizes and awards	☐	☐	19____	_____
Lottery winnings	☐	☐	19____	_____
Gambling winnings	☐	☐	19____	_____
Bonuses	☐	☐	19____	_____

Continued

☐ **EXHIBIT 8.4 Massachusetts Application for Child Support Enforcement Services—*Continued***

g. Does the absent parent:

Own any houses or other real estate? Yes ☐ No ☐ Don't Know ☐

If yes, please describe and indicate location if you can. _____

_____

Own any motor vehicle? Yes ☐ No ☐ Don't Know ☐

If yes, for each vehicle, please identify the model, color, state where it is registered, and license plate number, if you can.

_____

_____

Own a boat? Yes ☐ No ☐ Don't Know ☐

If yes, please indicate the registration number, if you can. _____

Where is it moored? _____

            City or Town   State

Own any stocks or bonds? Yes ☐ No ☐ Don't Know ☐

If yes, please use a separate sheet of paper to identify the name and address of the absent parent's stock broker and list any stocks and/or bonds owned by the absent parent if that information is available to you. Indicate the name of the company, the number of shares, and the date the stock was purchased, if possible.

Have any bank accounts? Yes ☐ No ☐ Don't Know ☐

List the name(s) of the bank(s), location(s), and type(s) of account(s) if that information is available to you.

Bank Name	Location	Type of Account
_____	_____	_____

If you need additional space, please continue on a separate piece of paper.

Have any credit cards? Yes ☐ No ☐ Don't Know ☐

If yes, please list the names of the companies and account numbers if that information is available to you.

Credit Company	Account Number
_____	_____
_____	_____
_____	_____

Have any outstanding loans? Yes ☐ No ☐ Don't Know ☐

If yes, please identify the name of the bank(s) or financial institution(s), location(s) and account number(s).

Lending Institution	Location	Account Number
_____	City/Town State	_____
_____	City/Town State	_____

h. Have you ever filed a joint income tax return with the absent parent? Yes ☐ No ☐

If yes, for which state(s) and for what year(s)?

    State   Tax Years

_____ 19 ___ to 19 ___ If you filed a joint *federal* return, for what years? 19 ___ to 19 ___

i Does the absent parent have any disabilities or handicaps? Yes ☐ No ☐ Don't Know ☐

j. Does the absent parent have a driver's license? Yes ☐ No ☐ Don't Know ☐

If yes, from what state? _____ What is the license number? _____ Don't Know ☐

k. Does the absent parent have any trade or commercial licenses? Yes ☐ No ☐ Don't Know ☐

If yes, what sort of license is it? _____

From what state was it issued? _____

l. Has the absent parent ever belonged to any labor unions? Yes ☐ No ☐ Don't Know ☐

If yes, enter the name of the union, local number, city and state.

_____

Continued

☐ **EXHIBIT 8.4 Massachusetts Application for Child Support Enforcement Services—*Continued***

m. Does the absent parent go by any other names or aliases? Yes ☐ No ☐ Don't Know ☐

If yes, please identify. _____

n. Has the absent parent ever been a member of the armed forces? Yes ☐ No ☐ Don't Know ☐

If yes, what branch of service? _____

___/___/___   ___/___/___   _____   _____

Date Entered   Date Discharged   Service Number   Last Duty Station

o. What high school, trade school and/or college did the absent parent attend? Please indicate the name and address of each school, the dates attended and the degree earned.

Name	Address	Dates of Attendance	Degree
_____	_____	_____	_____
_____	_____	_____	_____

Please attach an additional piece of paper if you need more space.

p. Does the absent parent have a criminal record?

Yes ☐ No ☐ Don't Know ☐ If yes, in which state? _____

q. Please identify the names and addresses of as many of the absent parent's past employers as you can. (Do not include the most recent employer which you have already identified earlier.)

Name	Address
_____	_____
_____	_____

Please attach an additional piece of paper if you need more space.

r. What are the names of the absent parent's parents? (Please indicate their names even if they are deceased.)

Father's Name	Mother's Maiden Name
Street or P.O. Box	Street or P.O. Box
City State Zip	City State Zip
( )	( )
Telephone	Telephone

s. Please provide the names and addresses of others who might know the whereabouts of the absent parent.

Name	Relationship	Phone
Street or P.O. Box	City State	Zip
Name	Relationship	Phone
Street or P.O. Box	City State	Zip

SOURCE: Massachusetts Department of Revenue Child Support Enforcement Division.

(text continued from page 180)

and her children. If she fails to cooperate in assigning these rights, her share of the AFDC benefits can be terminated, and the AFDC benefits of her children can be sent to some other responsible adult who will agree to make them available for the children.

One of the valuable services provided by the state IV-D agency is its attempt to keep careful records on when the noncustodial parent pays and fails to pay child support. The availability of this data helps to keep the pressure on. Furthermore, many IV-D agencies can be quite persistent in going after the noncustodial parent through automatic billing, telephone reminders, delinquency notices, etc. Other enforcement tools are also available through the IV-D agency as outlined below.

A new *federal* agency was created to coordinate, evaluate, and assist state IV-D agencies—the Office of Child Support Enforcement within the U.S. Department of Health and Human Services.

But, first things first. A very large number of noncustodial parents simply disappear. Problem number one is to *find* the noncustodial parent in order to obtain a child support order, and/or in order to enforce it. Another service provided by the IV-D agency is its **State Parent Locator Service** (SPLS). At the national level, there is a comparable **Federal Parent Locator Service** (FPLS) that operates through the Office of Child Support Enforcement. The FPLS can be very helpful if the search for the parent involves more than one state.

The starting point in the search is the custodial parent who is asked to provide the following leads to the state IV-D agency on the whereabouts of the noncustodial parent:

☐ Social security number (check old state and federal tax returns, hospital records, police records, bank accounts, insurance policies, credit cards, loan applications, pay slips, union records, etc.)

☐ Last known residential address

☐ Current or recent employer's name and address

☐ Prior employers' names and addresses

☐ Place of birth

☐ Names and addresses of relatives and friends

☐ Local clubs and organizations to which he once belonged

☐ Local banks, public utilities, and other creditors he may have had or now has

The State Parent Locator Service of the IV-D agency will use the leads provided by the custodial parent to try to locate the noncustodial parent. (See Exhibit 8.4) It will check the records of other state agencies for a current address, e.g., Department of Motor Vehicle Registration, Unemployment Compensation Commission, Tax Department, and prisons. If the noncustodial parent has moved to another state, the IV-D agency in that state can be asked to provide comparable search services, or the Federal Parent Locator Service can be asked to help. The latter can also search the records of federal agencies for leads, e.g., Internal Revenue Service, Department of Defense, Selective Service Commission, National Personnel Records Center, Veterans Administration, and Social Security Administration.

Once the noncustodial parent is located, the next step is to secure a child support order against him. A paternity proceeding may be needed to establish the obligation of support. (Paternity is discussed in chapter 13.) If the parent has moved to another state, URESA (the Uniform Reciprocal Enforcement of Support Act) and UIFSA (the more recent Uniform Interstate Family Support Act) can be used by a custodial parent in one state to obtain and enforce a child support (or alimony) order in another state without ever having to travel to the latter state. URESA and UIFSA are discussed in chapter 10.

The court has the following enforcement options available to it:[6]

☐ **Civil contempt proceeding**

☐ **Execution**

---

6. Some of these options also apply to the enforcement of alimony obligations. See chapter 10.

- ☐ Prosecution for criminal nonsupport
- ☐ Income withholding
- ☐ License denial or revocation
- ☐ Tax Refund Intercept Program (TRIP)
- ☐ Unemployment compensation intercept
- ☐ Qualified Domestic Relations Order (QDRO)
- ☐ Qualified Medical Child Support Order (QMSCO)
- ☐ Credit bureau referral ("credit clouding")
- ☐ Posting security
- ☐ Protective order

In our discussion of these options the person obligated to make child support payments will be referred to as the **obligor.**

CIVIL CONTEMPT PROCEEDING

Contempt of court exists when the authority or dignity of the court is obstructed or assailed. The most glaring example is an intentional violation of a court order. There are two kinds of contempt proceedings, civil and criminal, both of which can lead to the jailing of the offender. The purpose of a *civil contempt* proceeding is to compel future compliance with the court order, whereas the purpose of a *criminal contempt* proceeding is to punish the offender.[7] Criminal contempt in child support cases is rare because of the cumbersome nature of any criminal proceeding.

When civil contempt occurs in child support cases, the offender is jailed until he agrees to comply with the court order. Suppose, however, that the offender has no resources and thus cannot comply. In effect, such a person would be imprisoned because of his poverty. This is illegal. Imprisonment for debt is unconstitutional because it amounts to a sentence for an indefinite period beyond the control of the offender. To bypass this constitutional prohibition, a court must determine that the offender has the *present ability* to pay the child support debt but simply refuses to do so. Such an individual is in control of how long the sentence will be. In effect, the keys to jail are in his own pocket. Release occurs when he pays the child support debt.

In addition to jailing the obligor, most courts have the power to order the less drastic sanction of imposing a fine when the obligor is found to be in civil contempt.

EXECUTION

Once an obligor fails to pay a judgment ordering child support, the sheriff can be ordered to seize the personal or real property of the obligor in the state. All of this occurs through a **writ of execution.** Its initial effect is to create a **lien** on the property that prevents the obligor from disposing of it. The property seized can then be sold by the sheriff. The proceeds from this *forced sale* are used to pay the judgment and the expenses of the execution. Not all property of the obligor, however, is subject to execution in every state. Certain property, e.g., clothes and cars, may be exempt from execution.

Obligor   Someone who is legally obligated to another. The latter is the *obligee.*

Contempt   Obstructing or assailing the authority or dignity of the court.

Writ of Execution   A document directing a court officer to seize the property of someone who lost a judgment, sell it, and pay the winner of the judgment.

Lien   An encumbrance or claim on property imposed for the payment of a debt.

---

7. Homer Clark, *The Law of Domestic Relations in the United States,* § 18.3, p. 390 (Practitioner's Ed. 2d 1987).

Suppose that the obligor moves to another state after failing to pay a child support order. To answer the question of whether the mother can go to the obligor's new state and seek execution or other enforcement remedies against him there, see page 232, where there is a discussion of when one state must give full faith and credit (i.e., enforce) to the court order of another state.

PROSECUTION FOR CRIMINAL NONSUPPORT

In most states, the willful failure to support a child is a *state* crime for which the obligor can be prosecuted. (In 1992, willful nonpayment of support for a child residing in another state became a *federal* crime.) There must be an ability to provide support before the obligor can be tried and convicted of *criminal nonsupport* or desertion. The range of punishment includes probation, fine, and imprisonment. Except for relatively wealthy offenders, imprisonment is seldom an effective method of enforcing child support. Most obligors are wage earners, and once they are jailed, their primary source of income obviously dries up. One way out of this dilemma is for the judge to agree to suspend the imposition of the jail sentence on condition that the obligor fulfill the support obligation, including the payment of arrearages. The obligor would be placed on *probation* under this condition.

The threat of prosecution has encouraged some delinquent obligors to come forward. Several states have launched highly publicized amnesty programs (see Exhibit 8.5).

INCOME WITHHOLDING

Income withholding is a mandatory, automatic deduction from the obligor's income when he falls behind in child support payments. Wages of an employee are the most common example of income that is subject to withholding, although other kinds may qualify as well, e.g., commissions, retirement payments. In most cases, a child support order from the court will mandate immediate wage withholding for all current support obligations and for all arrearages unless a better form of payment is agreed to by the parties and approved by the court. Wage withholding is the most effective method of collection available. The amount collected in this way increased from $26 million in 1985 to almost $4 billion in 1992 (see Exhibit 8.6).

□ **EXHIBIT 8.5**
Ad Placed in Sports Section of Local Paper

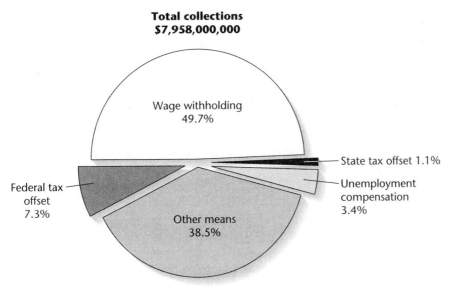

Total collections
$7,958,000,000

Wage withholding
49.7%

State tax offset 1.1%

Federal tax
offset
7.3%

Unemployment
compensation
3.4%

Other means
38.5%

□ **EXHIBIT 8.6 Child Support Collection Methods**

SOURCE: Eleanor Landstreet, *Enforcing Child Support Against the Self-Employed and Nonwage Earners* (Office of Child Support Administration, 1994).

Some employers are irritated by the record keeping involved in income withholding even though they are usually entitled to a small fee for this service. But employers do not have a choice on whether to participate. Furthermore, they can be fined or otherwise sanctioned by the state for subjecting an obligor-employee to any discipline because of income withholding. Exhibit 8.7 outlines government guidelines to employers regarding this matter.

Income withholding is similar to the more traditional **garnishment** process under which a third party, e.g., a bank or employer, who owes the obligor money or other property is ordered by a court to turn it over to a debtor of the obligor, such as the custodial parent. Garnishment, however, is usually less effective than income withholding because of the more cumbersome procedures for instituting garnishment and the restrictions that may exist on how long it can be in effect.

Garnishment A process whereby a debtor's property under the control of another is given to a third person to whom the debtor owes a debt.

Jim is subject to a child support order in your state to pay his ex-wife, Wanda, $900 a month for their fifteen-year-old daughter, Paula. Jim fails to make payments for three months. Wanda then goes to the state IV-D agency to seek help. Income withholding is commenced through Jim's employer, the ABC Truck Company. Six months later, Paula gets married. Jim goes to his supervisor and asks that income withholding terminate because he no longer has a duty to support his daughter. Assume he is correct that a parent does not have to support a child who has been emancipated through marriage. Can the company stop the withholding?

ASSIGNMENT 8.5

LICENSE DENIAL OR REVOCATION

To engage in certain occupations, a person must obtain a license from the state. Examples include plumber, hairdresser, real estate broker, accountant, electrician, teacher, doctor, and lawyer. Many states will deny an initial application for a license, deny an application for a renewal of a license, or revoke the license of a parent who is delinquent in making child support payments. In Maine, for example, revocation notices are sent to parents who are at least

☐ **EXHIBIT 8.7   Wage Withholding for Child Support: An Employer's Guide**

Employer's Guide for Universal Wage Withholding
The following is a brief summary of your legal responsibilties as an employer:

You may already be familiar with wage withholding for child support orders administered by the Child Support Enforcement agency in your State. Now you could be receiving wage withholding orders for almost *every* employee who has a child support order issued against him or her—regardless of whether the case is administered by the State Child Support Enforcement agency or is privately handled through an attorney, a court, or another office; regardless of whether payments are in arrears; and regardless of whether the parent has been regularly paying his or her child support obligation.

In addition to ensuring that child support is received on time, wage withholding has advantages for the employee ordered to pay child support. It offers a clear record that child support payments have been made in full, on time, and as ordered. It is a convenient way for a parent to fulfill a legal responsibility: a parent paying by wage withholding does not have to write checks or take payments to the former spouse, child support office, or court every week or month. Wage withholding avoids missed payments. Employers, such as yourself, also benefit when employees are under less stress and don't have to take time off to resolve child support issues. You will be able to use electronic funds transfer/electronic data interchange technology to transmit wage withholdings, if you choose.

This Guide presents answers to questions that you may have about your responsibilities under Federal wage withholding laws.

How will I know if I have to start withholding child support from an employee's wages?
You will receive a notice that tells you when to begin, how much to deduct, and where to send the money.

How long after I receive the notice do I begin the withholding?
Withholding is to begin no later than the first pay period that occurs 14 days after the mailing date of the order.

The withholding may add administrative fees to my business. May I charge a fee for this service?
If your State law allows, you may collect a fee to help offset your costs. The fee can be deducted each time a payment is withheld. The fee is an additional amount to be deducted from the employee's wages and is not to be deducted from the support payment.

If I don't want to get involved in collecting child support, can I dismiss someone who has a withholding order against his wages?
No. If you refuse to hire, or if you discipline or discharge an employee because of wage withholding for child support, you will be subject to a fine under your State's law.

And if I don't carry out the withholding?
If you fail to withhold child support as specified in the notice, you will be liable for the full amount you should have withheld from the employee's wages.

If the employee tells me the amount to be deducted is wrong, what should I do?
Continue to withhold wages according to the notice. The employee must contest the facts with the withholding agency, not the employer. Until you are notified otherwise by the withholding agency, you should proceed with the withholding as ordered.

Is there a limit to the amount that can be withheld?
The total amount that can be withheld from any employee's paycheck is limited by the Consumer Credit Protection Act unless further limited by State law. The limits provided in the Consumer Credit Protection Act are 50 percent of disposable earnings if an obligated parent has a second family and 60 percent if there is no second family. These limits are each increased by five percentage points (to 55 and 65) if payments are in arrears for a period equal to 12 weeks or more.

Will I be responsible for determining how to apply the Consumer Credit Protection Act limits?
Yes. However, your State Child Support Enforcement agency will help you if you need assistance.

Several of my employees already have garnishments against their paychecks and, if I deduct for child support, the total deducted will be more than allowed under law. How do I handle this?
Withholding for child support takes priority over other legal processes carried out under State law against the same wages. In fact, the only withholding that takes precedence is a prior Federal tax levy. This means that child support must be withheld first, then deductions for other garnishments or attachment orders can be made. If you have any questions, contact your State Child Support Enforcement agency.

How do I know when to stop the withholding?
The withholding remains in effect until you are notified by the withholding agency of *any* changes to the order.

What do I do if the employee quits the job?
You must notify the Child Support Enforcement agency *promptly* when the employee leaves and give the employee's last known home address and the new employer's name and address, if known.

SOURCE: U.S. Department of Health and Human Services, Office of Child Support Administration (June 1994).

ninety days behind. A few states include the revocation of the *driver's* license of a delinquent obligor.

TAX REFUND INTERCEPT PROGRAM (TRIP)

Income tax refunds owed by state and federal tax authorities to obligors can be intercepted and used to fulfill past-due child support obligations. During the first four years of the **Tax Refund Intercept Program** (TRIP), 1.5 million such tax refunds were intercepted for this purpose.

The collection occurs through the state IV-D agency. It is not possible for a woman with four hungry children to call the Internal Revenue Service and ask that it send her the father's refund check. She must first apply to the IV-D agency in the state. A notice (Exhibit 8.8) is then sent to the taxpayer that his tax refund is about to be intercepted to meet the child support debt. If the taxpayer contests the interception, a hearing is held.

UNEMPLOYMENT COMPENSATION INTERCEPT

The unemployment compensation benefits of the obligor can also be intercepted to meet ongoing (not just past-due) child support payments. This method of withholding enables the state IV-D agency to collect at least some support from an unemployed obligor. Nothing is left to chance. Computers at the unemployment compensation agency and at the state IV-D agency communicate with each other to identify delinquent parents who have applied for or who are eligible for unemployment compensation. An investigator from the IV-D agency will then contact the surprised obligor. It may even be possible to intercept benefits across state lines pursuant to reciprocal agreements among cooperating states. (In most states a similar intercept program can reach an obligor's worker's compensation benefits.)

QUALIFIED DOMESTIC RELATIONS ORDER (QDRO)

Qualified Domestic Relations Order A court order that allows a nonemployee to reach pension benefits of an employee or former employee in order to satisfy a marital obligation to the nonemployee.

Very often an obligor will have pension and other retirement benefit plans through his employer. A special court order, called a **Qualified Domestic Relations Order (QDRO)**, allows someone other than the obligor to reach some or all of these benefits in order to meet a support obligation of the obligor, such as child support. The child becomes an *alternate payee* under these plans.[8] This person cannot receive benefits under the plan that the obligor himself would not have been able to receive. For example, if the obligor is not entitled to a lump-sum payment, the child as alternate payee is also subject to this limitation.

QUALIFIED MEDICAL CHILD SUPPORT ORDER (QMCSO)

Many children of a noncustodial parent have no health insurance. Assume that this parent is working for a company that has a group health plan. But the parent either refuses to add the child to the plan, or the insurance company tells the parent that the child is ineligible because he or she does not live with the parent, does not live in the insurer's service area, is not claimed as a dependent on the parent's tax return, or was born to unmarried parents. In 1993 Congress passed a law that made it illegal for insurance companies to use such reasons to

---

8. For an example of a Qualified Domestic Relations Order in which the ex-spouse is the alternate payee seeking support through alimony, see Exhibit 6.6 in chapter 6.

☐ **EXHIBIT 8.8   Notice of Collection of Income Tax Refund**

Department of the Treasury
Internal Revenue Service

If you have any questions, refer to this information:

Date of This Notice: January 4, 1994
Social Security Number: 215-32-2726
Document Locator Number:
Form   Tax Year Ended: 1992

Call:

Sam Jones
999 Peachtree Street
Doraville, CO 99999

or

Write: Chief, Taxpayer Assistance Section
Internal Revenue Service Center

If you write, be sure to attach this notice.

THIS IS TO INFORM YOU THAT THE AGENCY NAMED BELOW HAS CONTACTED US REGARDING AN OUTSTAND-ING DEBT YOU HAVE WITH THEM.

UNDER AUTHORITY OF SECTION 6402(c) OF THE INTERNAL REVENUE CODE, ANY OVERPAYMENT OF YOUR FED-ERAL INCOME TAX WILL BE APPLIED TO THAT OBLIGATION BEFORE ANY AMOUNT CAN BE REFUNDED OR APPLIED TO ESTIMATED TAX. IF YOU HAVE ANY QUESTIONS ABOUT THE OBLIGATION OR BELIEVE IT IS IN ERROR, YOU SHOULD CONTACT THAT AGENCY IMMEDIATELY.

NAME OF AGENCY

DEPT. OF SOCIAL SERVICES
DIV. OF INCOME AND SUPPORT
CHILD SUPPORT ENFORCEMENT
1575 OBLIGATION STREET
TIMBUKTU, CO 92037

CONTACT: CHILD SUPPORT
PHONE: 619-456-9103

Qualified Medical Child Support Order   A court order requiring that a group health plan provide benefits for the child of a parent covered under the plan.

deny coverage to children. A court order can now be obtained to require coverage. It is called the **Qualified Medical Child Support Order (QMCSO).** The child becomes an *alternate recipient* under the health plan. The employer can deduct the cost of adding the child to the plan from the parent's pay.

CREDIT BUREAU REFERRAL ("CREDIT CLOUDING")

An obligor may be warned that a credit bureau (e.g., TRW, Trans Union, CBI-Equifax) will be notified of a delinquency in making child support payments unless the delinquency is eliminated by payment or unless satisfactory arrangements are made to pay the debt. Once the computers of a credit bureau have information on such payment problems, a "cloud" on the obligor's credit rating is created *(credit clouding),* which notifies potential creditors that the obligor may be a bad credit risk. This method of pressuring compliance with child support obligations is particularly effective with self-employed obligors who often don't have regular wages that can be subjected to income withholding or garnishment. Many states now routinely report child support debts to credit bureaus. (See Exhibit 8.9.)

POSTING SECURITY

In some cases, a noncustodial parent may be asked to post security in the form of a bond or other guarantee that will cover future support obligations.

☐ **EXHIBIT 8.9   States Routinely Reporting Child Support Debts to Credit Bureaus as of December 31, 1993**

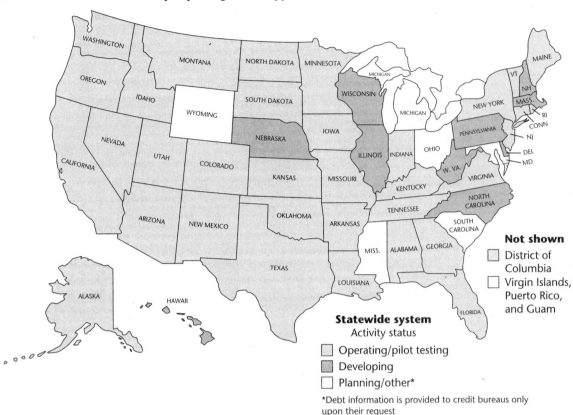

Not shown

☐ District of Columbia

☐ Virgin Islands, Puerto Rico, and Guam

Statewide system
Activity status

☐ Operating/pilot testing

▨ Developing

☐ Planning/other*

*Debt information is provided to credit bureaus only upon their request

SOURCE: 16 *Child Support Report* 3 (Office of Child Support Enforcement, 1994).

PROTECTIVE ORDER

Some men do not react kindly to requests from the mothers of their children that they meet their child support obligations. Occasionally, they may even physically assault the mother or threaten to do so. The police may be called in, although some have complained that the police do not take so-called domestic disputes seriously. Usually, the woman can obtain through the local prosecutor or district attorney a **protective order,** which threatens the man with arrest and jail unless he stays away from the children and their mother.

Protective Order A court order designed to protect a person from harm or harassment.

An unmarried couple lives together. The woman promises the man that she will use birth control, but has no intention of keeping this promise. When a child is born, can the father refuse to support it because of the mother's "fraud"?

ASSIGNMENT 8.6

▬▬ NECESSARIES

A seldom used but still available method for a spouse and child to obtain support is to go to merchants, make purchases of **necessaries,** and charge them to the credit of the nonsupporting husband/father. The latter must pay the bills, whether or not he knows about them or authorizes them so long as:

Necessaries The basic items needed by family members to maintain a standard of living.

☐ They are in fact for necessaries, and,

·   ☐ The husband/father has not already provided them for the family

Since the definition of necessaries is not precise, and since a merchant has difficulty knowing whether a husband/father has already made provision for the necessaries of his family, few merchants are willing to extend credit in these circumstances without express authorization from the husband/father. Some states, however, have eliminated the requirement that there be evidence of a failure of the husband/father to provide necessaries before his credit can be charged.

What are necessaries? Generally, they encompass what is needed and appropriate to maintain the family at the standard of living to which it has been accustomed, e.g., home, food, clothing, furniture, medical care. The educational expenses of minor children are necessaries. A college education, on the other hand, is not in many states.

☐ **Note** Some states have tried to enforce the support obligation through their marriage-formulation statutes. The statute may provide, for example, that no individual will be allowed to enter a marriage if that person has failed to support his or her child in the custody of someone else. The United States Supreme Court has held, however, that such statutes are an unconstitutional interference with the fundamental right to marry. *Zablocki v. Redhail,* 434 U.S. 374, 98 S. Ct. 673, 54 L. Ed. 2d 618 (1978). (See chapter 4.)

◼◼◼ SUMMARY

In negotiating the child support terms of a separation agreement, the parties must consider a number of factors, the most important of which are the state guidelines on child support, the standard of living to which the child was accustomed during the marriage, and the financial resources available for support. A court will consider the same factors in deciding whether to approve what the parties have negotiated.

Before the court can make a child support order, it must have personal jurisdiction over the defendant. This is acquired through in-person service of process or through the long arm statute. The defendant can be the father, the mother, or anyone who has formally adopted the child. Child support orders for future payments can be later modified if changed circumstances are serious enough to warrant it.

The major problem in this area is enforcement: a very large number of noncustodial parents are not making their child support payments. Title IV-D agencies have been established to combat this problem by locating delinquent parents (obligors) and by using new enforcement tools to make them pay what they owe.

In a civil contempt proceeding, an obligor with the present ability to pay can be jailed for nonpayment. A writ of execution can be levied against his property. Other options include criminal prosecution, income withholding, wage garnishment, license revocation, tax-refund intercept, unemployment-compensation intercept, Qualified Domestic Relations Orders, Qualified Medical Child Support Orders, credit clouding, and posting security. If the obligor physically threatens the custodial parent, a protective order can be sought.

In some states, the custodial parent or child can make purchases of necessaries and charge them to the credit of the obligor.

◼◼◼ KEY CHAPTER TERMINOLOGY

Pendente Lite
Personal Jurisdiction
Domicile
Divisible Divorce
Long Arm Statute
Child Support Guidelines
Arrearages
IV-D Agencies

Assign
State Parent Locator Service
Federal Parent Locator Service
Obligor
Contempt
Writ of Execution
Lien
Garnishment

Tax Refund Intercept Program
Qualified Domestic Relations
  Order (QDRO)
Qualified Medical Child Support
  Order (QMCSO)
Protective Order
Necessaries

DIVORCE, JUDICIAL SEPARATION, AND SEPARATE MAINTENANCE

9

▰▰▰▰ DIVORCE: HISTORICAL BACKGROUND

In order to obtain a divorce that dissolves the marital relationship, specified reasons must exit. These reasons, called **grounds,** are spelled out in statutes. The two categories of grounds are no-fault and fault. The major **no-fault grounds** are as follows:

☐ Living apart
☐ Incompatibility
☐ Irreconcilable differences, irretrievable breakdown

The major fault grounds are as follows:

☐ Adultery
☐ Cruelty
☐ Desertion

Although these are the main three, a number of other fault grounds also exist in most states.

For many years, fault grounds were the only grounds for divorce, the premise being that a marriage should not be terminated unless there was evidence of serious wrongdoing by one of the spouses—blame had to be established. Many believed that such stringent divorce laws would help prevent the failure of marriages. In colonial America, it was common to deny the guilty spouse the right of remarriage if a divorce was granted. The payment of alimony was sometimes used to punish the guilty spouse rather than as a way to help the other become reestablished. In short, guilt, wrongdoing, and punishment were

Grounds Acceptable reasons for seeking a particular result.

No-Fault Grounds Reasons for granting a divorce that do not require proof that either spouse committed marital wrongs.

predominant themes of our divorce laws. (Exhibit 9.1 shows how the divorce rate has changed since 1941.)

During this period of fault-based divorce, the system was frequently criticized as irrelevant and encouraging fraud. Over 90 percent of the divorces were **uncontested,** meaning that there was no dispute between the parties. Since both spouses wanted the divorce, they rarely spent much time fighting each other about whether adultery, cruelty, or other fault grounds existed. In fact, parties often flagrantly lied to the courts about the facts of their case in order to quickly establish that fault did exist. While such **collusion** was obviously illegal, the parties were seldom caught. Since both sides wanted the divorce, there was little incentive to reveal the truth. The system also encouraged **migratory divorces,** where one of the parties would "migrate," or travel, to another state solely to take advantage of its more lenient divorce laws. Some of these states gained the reputation of being divorce mills.

Reform was obviously needed. In 1969 California enacted the first no-fault divorce law in the country. Soon other states followed. Today, no-fault grounds (or their equivalent) exist in every state. Some states have eliminated the word "divorce" and replaced it with the word **dissolution** as a symbolic gesture that

Uncontested Not disputed; not challenged.

Collusion An agreement between spouses in a divorce proceeding that one or both will lie to the court to facilitate the obtaining of the divorce.

Migratory Divorce A divorce obtained in a state to which one or both spouses traveled before returning to their original state.

□ **EXHIBIT 9.1**
Number of Divorces and Divorce Rates

YEAR	NUMBER OF DIVORCES	PERCENTAGE CHANGE FROM PREVIOUS YEAR	RATE PER 1,000 TOTAL POPULATION
1992	1,210,000	+ .01	4.7
1991	1,187,000	+ .01	4.7
1990	1,175,000	− .01	4.7
1989	1,186,000	.00	4.8
1988	1,183,000	+ .02	4.8
1987	1,157,000	− .03	4.8
1986	1,192,000	+ .01	5.0
1985	1,172,000	+ .01	4.9
1984	1,156,000	− .005	4.9
1983	1,158,000	− .01	4.9
1982	1,170,000	− .03	5.0
1981	1,213,000	+ .03	5.3
1980	1,182,000	.00	5.2
1979	1,181,000	+ .04	5.3
1978	1,130,000	+ .03	5.1
1977	1,090,000	+ .006	5.0
1976	1,083,000	+ 4.5	5.0
1975	1,036,000	+ 6.0	4.9
1974	977,000	+ 6.8	4.6
1973	915,000	+ 8.3	4.4
1972	845,000	+ 9.3	4.1
1971	773,000	+ 9.2	3.7
1965	479,000	+ 6.4	2.5
1960	393,000	− .5	2.2
1955	377,000	− .5	2.3
1950	385,000	− 3.0	2.6
1946	610,000	+25.8	4.3
1941	293,000	+11.0	2.2

SOURCE: B. Wilson, National Center for Health Statistics. December 17, 1992. See also F. Cox, *Human Intimacy,* 596 (6th ed. 1993)

a new day has arrived. This does not mean, however, that fault grounds have been abolished. Most states have retained them, and oddly enough, at times fault becomes relevant to a court's discussion of a no-fault ground, as we will see in a moment. Yet in the main, fault is largely ignored in current practice, except when child custody and parental fitness are in issue.

■■■■■ NO-FAULT GROUNDS FOR DIVORCE

LIVING APART

Living "separate and apart" is a ground for divorce in many states. The statutes authorizing this ground of **living apart** must be carefully read since slight differences in wording may account for major differences in meaning. The simplest statute authorizes the divorce if the parties have lived separate and apart for a designated period of consecutive time, as outlined below. While this requirement exists in all the statutes, some states impose additional and more restrictive requirements. For example, living separate and apart may have to be pursuant to a court order or a separation agreement, or it may have to be consensual or "voluntary."

Living Apart A no-fault ground of divorce that exists when the spouses live separately for a designated period of consecutive time.

TIME In all states where living apart is a ground, the statute requires that the parties live apart for a designated period of time, ranging from six months to three years. The purpose of the time limitation is, in effect, to force the parties to think seriously about whether a reconciliation is possible.

CONSECUTIVENESS If the parties have separated off and on over a period of time, the living-apart ground is not established, even if the sum total of time the parties were actually separated exceeds the designated time required for separation under the statute. The separated time must be consecutive, and it must continue right up to the time one of the spouses brings the divorce action on the ground of living apart. Hence, if the parties reconcile and resume cohabitation, even if only temporarily, the period of separation will not be considered consecutive. If, following cohabitation, the parties separate again, the requisite consecutiveness of the period of living apart will be calculated as of the time when the most recent cohabitation ended.

CONSENT Several states require that the period of separation be consensual or voluntary on the part of *both* spouses. Thus, if one spouse is drafted into the service or is hospitalized for an extended period of time, the separation is surely not by consent.

Sometimes the *cause* of the separation may be relevant to its voluntariness. Suppose, for example, that Bob deserts his wife Linda and they live apart for a period in excess of that required by the statute. Arguably, the parties did not separate voluntarily; they separated as a result of the *fault* of Bob. Some states will deny the divorce on the ground of living apart because the separation was not voluntary. Others will deny the divorce on this ground only when the plaintiff seeking the divorce is the "guilty" party. Most states, however, will grant the divorce to either party on the basis that voluntariness and marital fault are irrelevant so long as there was a living apart for the requisite period of time.

Interviewing and Investigation Checklist

Divorce on the Ground of Living Apart

Legal Interviewing Questions

1. How long have you lived apart?

2. On what date did you separate?

3. Since that date, what contact have you had with D (defendant)?

4. Have you ever asked D to live with you again? Has D ever asked you?

5. Have you had sexual intercourse with D since you separated?

6. Describe the circumstances of your separation with D.

7. When you separated, did you intend a permanent separation? If so, what indications of this did you give?

8. Did D intend a permanent separation? If so, what indications did D give?

9. What was the condition of your marriage at the time of separation?

10. Did you leave D? Did D leave you? Did you both leave at the same time by mutual agreement?

11. When the separation occurred, did either of you protest? Were you or D dissatisfied with the separation?

12. Since you separated, have either of you asked or suggested that the two of you get back together again? If so, what was the response of the other?

13. Have either of you obtained a judicial separation or a decree of separate maintenance? If so, when? Have you been living separate since that time? Have both of you abided by the terms of the judicial separation or of the maintenance decree?

14. Are you now living separate from D?

15. Since you separated, at what address have you lived? (Same question about D.)

16. Do you and D have a separation agreement?

Possible Investigation Tasks

☐ Collect evidence that the parties have lived separate and apart, e.g., rent receipts from the apartments of the client and of D, copies of separate utility bills.

☐ Obtain witness statements from people aware of the separation.

ASSIGNMENT 9.1

Assume that a statute provides that one of the grounds for divorce is voluntary separation for a period of two consecutive years. This living-apart ground is the only one authorized in the state. Could a divorce be granted on the ground of living apart in the following three situations?

a. Fred and Gail are married. On June 10, 1985, they agree to separate. Fred moves out. On May 15, 1987, when he learns that she is thinking about filing for divorce, he calls Gail and pleads with her to let him come back. She refuses. On July 25, 1987, she files for divorce on the ground of living apart.

b. Tom and Diane are married. On November 1, 1985, Diane deserts Tom. Tom did not want her to go. On March 13, 1986, Tom meets Karen. They begin seeing each other regularly. On June 14, 1986, Tom tells Karen that he hopes he never sees Diane again. On December 28, 1987, Tom files for divorce on the ground of living apart.

c. Bill and Susan are married. For over three years they have been living separate lives due to marital difficulties, although they have continued to live in the same house. They have separate bedrooms and rarely have anything to do with each other. One of them files an action for divorce on the ground of living apart.

As we shall see, many states allow parties to seek a *judicial separation,* which is a court authorization that the parties can live separate lives under specified terms, e.g., alimony, custody order. In some states, this judicial separation can be *converted* into a divorce after a designated period of time. Similarly, a decree of *separate maintenance* can often be converted into a divorce after this period of time.

□ Note on Enoch Arden

When a spouse has disappeared for a certain period of time, the **Enoch Arden defense** presumes that the missing spouse is dead, and in some states, this enables the spouse left behind to remarry without being charged with bigamy or having the second marriage annulled if the missing spouse returns after the statutory period (see chapter 5).

Enoch Arden Defense The presumption that a spouse is dead after being missing for a designated number of years.

Summary of Ground for Divorce: Living Apart

Definition: Living separate and apart for a designated, consecutive period of time. (In some states, the separation must be mutual and voluntary.)

Who can sue: In most states, either party. In a few states, the party at fault cannot bring the divorce action, i.e., the party who wrongfully caused the separation.

Major defenses:

1. The parties have never separated.

2. The parties have not been separated for the period designated in the statute.

3. The parties reconciled and cohabitated before the statutory period was over, i.e., the separation was not consecutive.

4. The separation was not voluntary (this defense is available in only a few states).

5. The agreement to separate was obtained by fraud or duress.

6. The court lacks jurisdiction (see chapter 10).

7. Res judicata (see chapter 10).

8. Statute of limitations or laches.

Is this also a ground for annulment? No.

Is this also a ground for judicial separation? Yes, in many states.

Is this also a ground for separate maintenance? Yes, in many states.

INCOMPATIBILITY

Some states list **incompatibility** as a ground for divorce. Courts often say that "petty quarrels" and "minor bickerings" are not enough to grant the divorce on this ground. There must be such rift or discord that it is impossible to live together in a normal marital relationship. For most of the states that have this ground, fault is not an issue; the plaintiff does not have to show that the defendant was at fault in causing the incompatibility, and the defendant cannot defend the action by introducing evidence that the plaintiff committed marital wrongs. In a few states, however, the courts *are* concerned about the fault of the defendant and the plaintiff.

Incompatibility Such discord exists between the spouses that it is impossible for them to live together in a normal marital relationship.

Suppose that the plaintiff alleges that the parties are incompatible. Can the defendant defend by disagreeing? Do *both* husband and wife have to feel that it is impossible to live together? Assuming that the plaintiff is able to establish that more than "petty quarrels" are involved, most courts will grant the divorce to the plaintiff even though the defendant insists that they can still work it out. Each state's statute, however, must be carefully examined to determine whether this is a proper interpretation.

The ground of incompatibility and the ground of cruelty appear to be rather similar. Even though cruelty is a fault ground while incompatibility is not, the same or similar kind of evidence is used to establish both grounds. The major difference in most states is that for cruelty, unlike incompatibility, the plaintiff must show that the acts of the defendant endangered the plaintiff's physical health.

▆▆▆ Interviewing and Investigation Checklist

Divorce on the Ground of Incompatibility

(This checklist is also relevant to the breakdown ground, discussed next.)

Legal Interviewing Questions

1. Are you and D (defendant) now living together? If not, how long have you been separated?

2. Have you ever sued D or been sued by D for separate maintenance or for a judicial separation? If so, what was the result?

3. Describe your relationship with D at its worst.

4. How often did you argue? Were the arguments intense or bitter? Explain.

5. Did you or D ever call the police?

6. Did you or D receive medical attention as a result of your arguments or fights?

7. Did you or D have a drinking or drug problem?

8. How did D act toward the children? What is your relationship with them?

9. Have you and D had any sexual problems?

10. Do you feel that there is any possibility that you and D could reconcile your differences?

11. Do you think D feels that the two of you can solve your problems?

12. Have you or D ever sought counseling or therapy of any kind?

13. Are you now interested in any such help in order to try to save the marriage? Do you feel it would work? How do you think D feels about this?

Possible Investigation Tasks

☐ Obtain copy of judicial separation judgment, separate maintenance decree, police reports, hospital records, if any.

▆▆▆ Summary of Ground for Divorce: Incompatibility

Definition: The impossibility of two parties being able to continue to live together in a normal marital relationship because of severe conflicts or personality differences.

Who can sue: Either party in most states.

Major defenses:

1. The differences between the parties are only minor.

2. The defendant was not at fault in causing the incompatibility (this defense is *not* available in most states).

3. The court lacks jurisdiction.

4. Res judicata.

5. Statute of limitations or laches.

Is this also a ground for annulment? No.

Is this also a ground for judicial separation? Yes, in many states.

Is this also a ground for separate maintenance? Yes, in many states.

IRRECONCILABLE DIFFERENCES, IRREMEDIABLE BREAKDOWN

Irreconcilable Differences Such discord exists between the spouses that the marriage has undergone an irremediable breakdown.

The newest and most popular version of the no-fault ground for divorce adopted in many states provides that the marriage can be dissolved for **irreconcilable differences** that have caused the *irremediable breakdown* of the marriage. The goal of the legislatures that have enacted this ground has been to focus on the central question of whether it makes any sense to continue the marriage.[1] The statutes often have similar language and content. For example:

---

1. One court phrased the test as follows: "The new statutory test for determining if a marriage is irretrievably broken is simply whether for whatever reason or cause (no matter whose 'fault') the marriage relationship is for all intents and purposes ended, no longer viable, a hollow sham beyond hope of reconciliation or repair." *Ryan v. Ryan*, 277 So. 2d 266, 271 (Fla. 1977).

☐ Discord or conflict of personalities that destroys the legitimate ends of marriage and prevents any reasonable expectation of reconciliation

☐ Irretrievable breakdown of the marriage

☐ Breakdown of marriage to such an extent that the legitimate objects of marriage have been destroyed and there remains no reasonable likelihood that the marriage can be preserved

☐ Substantial reasons for not continuing the marriage

This ground for divorce is obviously quite similar to the incompatibility ground just considered.

What happens if the defendant denies that the breakdown of the marriage is irremediable and feels that marriage counseling would help? In most states, this is simply one item of evidence that the court must consider in deciding whether remediation is possible. It is likely, however, that if one party absolutely refuses to participate in any reconciliation efforts, the court will conclude that the breakdown of the marriage is total even if the other party expresses a conciliatory attitude. Again, the language of individual statutes would have to be examined on this issue.

■■■ Interviewing and Investigation Checklist

Divorce on the Ground of Irremediable Breakdown

Legal Interviewing Questions

1. How long have you been married to D (defendant)? How many children do you have?

2. How does D get along with the children?

3. How often do you and D communicate meaningfully?

4. Does D insult you, ridicule your religion, your political views, your family?

5. Does D do this in front of anyone? Who else knows that D does this? How do they know?

6. Has D ever ridiculed or criticized you to your friends, relatives, or other associates?

7. Do you think that D has ever tried to turn the children against you? If so, how do you know? What specifically have the children or others said or done to make you think so?

8. Does D drink or use drugs? If so, how much, how often, and how has it affected your marriage?

9. Has D ever hit you? If so, describe the circumstances. How often has D done this? Did the children see it? Has anyone else ever seen it?

10. Were there any other major events or scenes that were unpleasant for you? If so, describe them.

11. How would you describe your sexual relationship with D? Has D ever refused your request for sex? Has D ever made any unreasonable sexual demands on you?

12. Has D ever accused you of infidelity?

13. Does D stay away from home often? Does D ever not come home at night?

14. Have you ever had to call the police because of what D did?

15. Has D ever sued you, or have you ever sued D?

16. How often do you fight or argue with D?

17. Is D now living with you? If not, explain the circumstances of the separation.

18. Has D's behavior affected your health in any way? Have you had to see a doctor?

19. Have you seen or have you considered seeing a psychiatrist or some other person in the field of mental health?

20. Have you ever experienced any behavior like this before?

21. How was your health before D started behaving this way?

22. Do you have any difficulty sleeping?

23. Do you have any difficulty doing your regular work because of D?

24. What is D's opinion of you as a spouse?

25. Do you think that you will ever be able to live in harmony with D? Explain why or why not.

—Continued

—Continued

26. Does D think the two of you will ever be able to get back together again? Explain why or why not.

Possible Investigation Tasks

☐ Obtain all of C's (client's) medical records, if any, from doctors, hospitals, etc., that have treated her as a result of what D has done.

☐ If the children are old and mature enough, interview them to see how they viewed D's relationship with C and, specifically, how D treated them.

☐ Obtain police records, if any, resulting from any fights or disturbances.

ASSIGNMENT 9.2   Dan and Helen were married in your state. Helen does not want to be married anymore. She loves Dan and enjoys being his wife, but simply wants to live alone indefinitely. Dan does not want a divorce. Can she obtain a no-fault divorce?

■■■■ Summary of Ground for Divorce: Irreconcilable Differences, Irremediable Breakdown

Definition: The breakdown of the marriage to the point where the conflicts between the spouses are beyond any reasonable hope of reconciliation.

Who can sue: Either party.

Major defenses:

1. The breakdown is remediable.

2. The court lacks jurisdiction.

3. Res judicata.

4. Statute of limitations or laches.

Is this also a ground for annulment? No.

Is this also a ground for judicial separation? Yes, in many states.

Is this also a ground for separate maintenance? Yes, in many states.

■■■■ FAULT GROUNDS FOR DIVORCE

Although fault grounds are less often considered in today's courts, they remain in force. They include:

☐ Adultery   ☐ Desertion

☐ Cruelty   ☐ Others

ADULTERY

Adultery Voluntary sexual intercourse between a married person and someone to whom he or she is not married.

Adultery is voluntary sexual intercourse between a married person and someone to whom he or she is not married. This person is called the **corespondent.** The intercourse is not voluntary, of course, if the defendant is raped or if the defendant is insane at the time. Since direct evidence of adultery is seldom available, circumstantial evidence must be relied upon. Specifically, the plaintiff must prove that the defendant had the *opportunity* and the *inclination* to commit adultery. **Corroboration** is often required to support the plaintiff's testimony.

Co-respondent The person who allegedly had voluntary sexual intercourse with a spouse charged with adultery.

Corroboration Additional evidence of a point beyond that offered by the person asserting the point.

Fornication Sexual intercourse between unmarried persons.

Illicit Cohabitation Fornication between two persons who live together.

☐ **Notes on Sexual Relations as a Crime and as a Tort**

1. In most states adultery (as defined above), fornication, and illicit cohabitation are crimes. **Fornication** is sexual intercourse between unmarried persons. **Illicit cohabitation** is fornication between two individuals who live together. It is rare, however, for the state to prosecute anyone for these crimes.

2. Criminal conversation is a tort brought against a third party who has had sexual intercourse (adultery) with the plaintiff's spouse (see chapter 17).

Criminal Conversation
A tort committed by a person who has sexual relations with the plaintiff's spouse.

CRUELTY

In most marriage ceremonies, the parties take each other "for better or worse." This concept was viewed quite literally early in our history, particularly when the woman was the one claiming to have received too much of the "worse." It was expected that a good deal of fighting, nagging, and mutual abuse would occur within the institution of marriage. The concept of permitting the marriage to be dissolved because of "mere" cruelty or indignities was alien to our legal system for a long time. The change in the law came slowly. When cruelty was allowed as a ground for divorce, the statute would often require that it be "extreme" or "inhuman" before the divorce could be granted. Furthermore, some states limited the ground to actual or threatened *physical* violence. Later, *mental anguish* came to be recognized as a form of cruelty and indignity, but there was often a requirement that the psychological cruelty must result in some impairment of the plaintiff's health. Some courts will accept a minimal health impairment, e.g., a loss of sleep. Other courts require more serious impairment. Whether a court will accept a minimum impairment or will require something close to hospitalization, most courts have insisted on at least some physical effect from the cruelty. Only a few states will authorize a divorce on the ground of cruelty or indignity where the mental suffering does not produce physical symptoms.

Cruelty The infliction of serious physical or mental suffering on another.

DESERTION

Desertion (also called *abandonment*) occurs when (1) one spouse voluntarily leaves another, (2) for an uninterrupted statutory period of time, e.g., two years, (3) with the intent not to return to resume cohabitation, and when (4) the separation occurred without the consent of the other spouse and (5) there was no justification or reasonable cause for the separation. **Constructive desertion** exists when the conduct of the spouse who stayed home justified the other spouse's departure, or when the spouse who stayed home refuses a sincere offer of reconciliation (within the statutory period) from the other spouse who initially left without justification. In effect, the spouse who stayed home becomes the deserter! The spouse who left would be allowed to sue the other spouse for divorce on the ground of desertion.

OTHERS

A number of closely related and sometimes overlapping grounds exist in some states. Here is a partial list (some of which are also grounds for annulment):

- Bigamy
- Impotence
- Nonage
- Fraud
- Duress
- Incest
- Imprisonment for three consecutive years
- Unexplained absence
- Neglect of duty = Support
- Obtaining an out-of-state divorce that is invalid
- Venereal disease or AIDS
- Unchastity
- Pregnancy by someone else at the time of the marriage

☐ Conviction of a serious crime

☐ Insanity; mental incapacity for three years

☐ Habitual drunkenness

☐ Drug addiction

☐ Nonsupport

☐ Treatment injurious to health

☐ Deviate sexual conduct

☐ Any other cause deemed by the court sufficient, if satisfied that the parties can no longer live together

■■■■■ DEFENSES TO THE FAULT GROUNDS FOR DIVORCE

The basic defenses to the fault grounds for divorce may be defined as follows:

☐ Collusion

Parties to a divorce committed fraud on the court by agreeing on a story to be told to the court by one or both parties even though both know the story is untrue.

☐ Connivance

There was a willingness or a consent by one spouse that the marital wrong be done by the other spouse.

☐ Condonation

There was an express or implied forgiveness by the innocent spouse of the marital fault committed by the other spouse.

☐ Recrimination

The party seeking the divorce (the plaintiff) has also committed a serious marital wrong.

☐ Provocation

The plaintiff incited the acts constituting the marital wrong by the other spouse.

These defenses are rarely used today, however, since the fault grounds are themselves seldom used.

☐ Note on Religious Divorces

> When a man hath taken a wife, and married her, and it come to pass that she find no favor in his eyes, because he hath found some uncleanliness in her: then let him write her a bill of divorcement, and give it in her hand, and send her out of his house. Deuteronomy 24:1, (KJV)

A Jewish couple that wants a religious divorce can go to a special court called a *Beth Din* presided over by a rabbi who is aided by scribes and authorized witnesses. There the husband delivers a **get,** or bill of divorcement, to his wife. Fault does not have to be shown. Both the husband and wife must consent to the divorce, but it is the husband who gives the get, and the wife who receives it. In New York, a religious divorce is allowed only if a secular (i.e., civil) divorce or annulment is underway or has already been granted. If a Jewish man has a civil divorce but not a religious divorce, he can still be remarried by a rabbi. But a Jewish woman without a get—even if divorced in a civil court—is called an *agunah,* or abandoned wife, and cannot be remarried by a rabbi. Markoff, *How Couples "Get" a Religious Divorce,* 8 National Law J. (August 15, 1988).

A Moslem divorce is traditionally performed by a husband pronouncing the word **Talak** (I divorce you) three times. The wife need not be present. In some countries, however, the process is more public. In Pakistan, for example, the husband must notify the chairman of an arbitration council that he has pronounced the *Talak.* The council will then attempt to reconcile the parties. If this fails, the divorce becomes absolute

90 days after the husband pronounced the *Talak*. In Egypt, the husband must pronounce the *Talak* in the presence of two witnesses who are usually officers of a special court. *The Religious Effect of Religious Divorces,* 37 Modern Law Review, 611–613 (1974).

▮▮▮▮▮ JUDICIAL SEPARATION

A **judicial separation** is a decree by a court that two people can live separately—from bed and board—while still remaining husband and wife. The decree also establishes the rights and obligations of the parties while they are separated. A judicial separation is also known as a:

- ☐ Legal separation
- ☐ Limited divorce
- ☐ Divorce a mensa et thoro
- ☐ Separation from bed and board
- ☐ Divorce from bed and board

Parties subject to a judicial separation are not free to remarry. The marriage relationship remains until it is dissolved by the death of one of the parties, by annulment, or by an absolute divorce, or a *divorce a vinculo matrimonii,* as the "full" divorce is called.[2]

Perhaps the main function of a judicial separation is to secure support from the other spouse. In this sense, an action for judicial separation is very similar to an action for separate maintenance, to be discussed in the next section. For religious or family reasons, the parties may not wish to end the marriage by obtaining a divorce. If support is needed, a judicial separation is an alternative in many states.

We should distinguish a judicial separation from a *separation agreement.* The latter is a private contract between a husband and wife. The agreement may or may not become part of (i.e., be incorporated and merged in) the judicial separation decree or the absolute divorce decree if one is later sought. Also, it is important that the word "separated" or "separation" be used carefully. Alone, these words mean simply a *physical* separation between the husband and wife. If, however, a court-sanctioned or court-ordered separation is involved, then the reference should be to a *legal* or *judicial* separation.

To obtain a judicial separation, *grounds* must be established in the same manner as grounds must be established to obtain an absolute divorce. In fact, the grounds for judicial separation are often very similar if not identical to the grounds for an absolute divorce, e.g., no-fault grounds such as incompatibility or irretrievable breakdown, and fault grounds such as adultery or cruelty.

In a judicial separation decree, the court can award alimony and can issue custody and child support orders, all of which are enforceable through traditional execution and contempt remedies. If the parties have drafted a separation agreement, the court will consider incorporating and merging the terms of this agreement into the judicial separation decree. The separation agreement, of course, will reflect the wishes of the parties on the critical issues of alimony, property division, child custody, and child support.

After a judicial separation decree has been rendered, the fact that the parties reconcile and resume cohabitation does not mean that the decree becomes inoperative. It remains effective until a court declares otherwise. Hence, a husband who is under an order to pay alimony to his wife pursuant to a judicial

Judicial Separation A declaration by a court that parties can live separate and apart even though they are still married to each other.

---

2. In some community property states (see page 110), the "community estate" is dissolved by a separation from bed and board. See Internal Revenue Service, *Community Property and the Federal Income Tax,* p. 2 (1988 Edition).

separation decree must continue to pay alimony even though the parties have subsequently reconciled and are living together again. To be relieved of this obligation, a petition must be made to the court to change the decree.

The major consequence of a judicial separation decree in many states is its *conversion* feature. The decree can be converted into a divorce—an absolute divorce. In effect, the existence of the judicial separation decree for a designated period of time can become a ground for a divorce.

■■■■■ SEPARATE MAINTENANCE

Separate Maintenance
Court-ordered spousal support while the spouses are separated.

An action for **separate maintenance** (sometimes called an action for *support*) is a proceeding brought by a spouse to secure support. The action is usually filed by wives, but an increasing number of husbands are seeking spousal support by this route. Like the judicial separation decree, a separate maintenance decree does not alter the marital status of the parties; they remain married to each other while living separately. To the extent that both decrees resolve the problem of support, there is very little practical difference between them.

Since the main objective of the separate maintenance action is to reach the property (e.g., cash, land) of the defendant for purposes of support, the court must have personal jurisdiction over the defendant (see chapter 8).

The major ground for a separate maintenance decree is the refusal of one spouse to support the other without just cause. In addition, most states provide that all of the grounds for divorce will also be grounds for a separate maintenance award. Furthermore, in a divorce action, if the court refuses to grant either party a divorce, it usually can still enter an order for separate maintenance.

If the plaintiff refuses a good faith offer by the defendant to reconcile, the plaintiff becomes a wrongdoer, which may justify the defendant in refusing to provide support. If the separate maintenance action is still pending, the plaintiff will lose it. If a separate maintenance decree has already been awarded, the defendant may be able to discontinue making payments under it.

The court determines the amount and form of a separate maintenance award in the same way that it makes the alimony determination in a divorce (see chapter 6). If needed, the court can also make child support and child custody decisions in the separate maintenance action.

Separate maintenance decrees can be enforced in the same manner as alimony awards in divorce decrees, e.g., contempt, execution (see chapters 6, 8, 10).

■■■■■ SUMMARY

The three major court proceedings that can be used when a marriage is in deep trouble are divorce, judicial separation, and separate maintenance. Grounds must exist before parties can use any of these three actions.

There are three major no-fault grounds for divorce: living apart, incompatibility, and irreconcilable differences that cause the irremediable breakdown of the marriage. The major fault grounds for divorce are adultery, cruelty, and desertion. Fault grounds, and the defenses to them, are less commonly used today.

Actions for judicial separation and separate maintenance are primarily designed to secure spousal support in a marriage that will continue to exist, at least for the time being.

■■■■■ KEY CHAPTER TERMINOLOGY

Grounds
No-Fault Grounds

Uncontested
Collusion

Migratory Divorce
Dissolution

Living Apart

Enoch Arden Defense

Incompatibility

Irreconcilable Differences

Adultery

Co-respondent

Corroboration

Fornication

Illicit Cohabitation

Criminal Conversation

Cruelty

Desertion

Constructive Desertion

Connivance

Condonation

Recrimination

Provocation

Get

Talak

Judicial Separation

Separate Maintenance

10 DIVORCE PROCEDURE

KINDS OF DIVORCE

Uncontested Not disputed; not challenged.

Over 90 percent of divorce cases are **uncontested** since the parties are in agreement on the termination of the marital relationship, alimony, property division, child custody, and child support. In such cases, divorce procedure is often relatively simple. If, however, the bitterness of the past has not subsided and agreements have not been reached, the technicalities of procedure can occupy center stage in costly and complicated proceedings.

The following terms are often used in connection with divorce procedure:

☐ **Migratory Divorce** A divorce obtained in a state to which one or both spouses traveled before returning to their original state. The husband and/or wife travels (migrates) to another state in order to obtain a divorce—usually because it is procedurally easier to divorce there. He or she establishes domicile in the state, obtains the divorce, and then returns to the "home" state, where at some point there will be an attempt to enforce the "foreign" divorce judgment. If the domicile was valid, this divorce is entitled to full faith and credit (i.e., it must be enforced) by the home state or any other state.

☐ **Foreign Divorce** A divorce decree obtained in a state other than the state where an attempt is made to enforce that decree. For example, a divorce decree that is granted in Iowa or in France would be a foreign divorce when an attempt is made to enforce it in New York.

☐ **"Quickie" Divorce** A migratory divorce obtained in what is often called a *divorce mill* state, i.e., a state where the procedural requirements for divorce are very slight in order to encourage out-of-state citizens to come in for a divorce and, while there, to spend some tourist dollars.

☐ **Collusive Divorce**   A divorce that results from an agreement or "conspiracy" between a husband and wife to commit fraud on the court by falsely letting it appear that they qualify procedurally or substantively for a divorce.

☐ **Default Divorce**   A divorce granted to the plaintiff because the defendant failed to appear to answer the complaint of the plaintiff. (In most states, the divorce is not granted automatically; the plaintiff must still establish grounds for the divorce.)

☐ **Divisible Divorce**   A divorce decree does two things: (1) dissolves the marital relationship, and (2) resolves the questions of alimony, property division, child custody, and child support. The divorce decree is thus *divisible,* or "dividable" into these two objectives. A *divisible divorce* is a divorce decree granted in one state but enforceable in another state only as to the dissolution of the marriage, not as to support, property division, etc. The other state does not have to give full faith and credit to other parts of the divorce decree. The divorce is divisible because only part of it must be recognized in another state.

☐ **Bilateral Divorce**   A divorce granted by a court when both parties were present before the court.

☐ **Ex Parte Divorce**   A divorce granted by a court when only one party (the plaintiff) was present before the court. The court did not have personal jurisdiction over the defendant.

☐ **Dual Divorce**   A divorce granted to both husband and wife. A court might award the divorce decree to one party only—to the plaintiff or to the defendant, if the latter has filed a counterclaim for divorce against the plaintiff. A dual divorce, however, is granted to *both* parties.

☐ **Uncontested Divorce**   A divorce granted to parties who had no disagreements. The defendant does not appear at the divorce proceeding (see *default divorce* above) or appears without disputing any of the plaintiff's claims.

☐ **Contested Divorce**   A divorce granted after the defendant appeared and disputed some or all of the claims made by the plaintiff at the divorce proceeding.

☐ **Divorce a Mensa et Thoro**   A *judicial separation* (see chapter 9); a *limited divorce.* The parties are not free to remarry since they are still married after receiving this kind of "divorce."

☐ **Limited Divorce**   A *judicial separation;* a *divorce a mensa et thoro.*

☐ **Divorce a Vinculo Matrimonii**   An *absolute divorce.* The parties are no longer married. They are free to remarry.

▬▬▬ DOMICILE

The word *domicile* is often confused with the word *residence.* Many divorce statutes use the word *residence* even though the meaning intended is *domicile.* Except for such oddities, there are distinct differences between the two words:

☐ **Residence**   The place where someone is living at a particular time. A person can have many residences, e.g., a home in the city, plus a beach house, plus an apartment in another state or country.

☐ **Domicile**   The place (1) where someone has physically been (2) with the intention to make that place his or her permanent home, or with no intention to make any other place a permanent home. It is the place to which one would intend to return when away. With rare exceptions, a person can have only one domicile.

It is important to be able to determine where one's domicile is, particularly in our mobile society. Here are two specific reasons why:

□ In most states, a court does not have divorce jurisdiction to dissolve a marriage unless one or both spouses are domiciled in the state where that court sits.

□ Liability for inheritance taxes may depend upon the domicile of the decedent at the time of death.

Emancipated Legally independent of one's parent or legal guardian.

Generally, children cannot acquire a domicile of their own until they reach majority (e.g., eighteen years of age) or become otherwise **emancipated.** In effect, a child acquires a domicile by **operation of law** rather than by choice. The law operates to impose a domicile on the child regardless of what the child may want (if the child is old enough to form any opinion at all). The domicile of a child is the domicile of its parents. If they are separated, the child's domicile is that of the parent who has legal custody.

Operation of Law A result occurs by operation of law when it happens because the law mandates the result, not because a party agrees to produce the result.

An emancipated child and an adult can pick any domicile they want **(domicile by choice)** so long as they are physically present in a place (even if only momentarily) and have the intention to make it their permanent home at the time of their presence there. This intention can sometimes be very difficult to prove. Intention is a state of mind, and the only way to determine a state of mind is by interpreting external acts.

Domicile by Choice A domicile chosen by a person with the capacity to choose.

A person's verbal statements are not necessarily conclusive evidence of his or her state of mind. Suppose, for example, that Bill is domiciled in Ohio and, while visiting California, becomes violently ill. He knows that if he dies domiciled in California, his beneficiaries will pay a lower inheritance tax than if he had died domiciled in Ohio. While lying in a California sick bed just before he dies, Bill openly says, "I hereby declare that I intend California to be my permanent home." This statement in itself fails to prove that Bill was domiciled in California at the time of his death. Other evidence may show that he made the statement simply to give the appearance of changing his domicile and that, if he had regained his health, he would have returned to Ohio. If this is so, then his domicile at death is Ohio in spite of his declaration, since he never actually intended to make California his permanent home.

The following chart seeks to identify some of the factors courts will consider in determining whether the requisite state of mind on intention existed.

■ Interviewing and Investigation Checklist

How to Determine When a Person Has Established a Domicile

Legal Interviewing Questions

1. When did you come to the state?

2. How often have you been in the state in the past? (Describe the details of your contacts with the state.)

3. Why did you come to the state?

4. Was your intention to stay there for a short period of time? A long period of time? Indefinitely? Forever?

5. While you were in the state, did you also have homes elsewhere in the state, and/or in another state, and/or in another country? If so, give details, e.g., addresses, how long you spent at each home, etc.

6. Where do you consider your permanent home to be?

7. Have you ever changed your permanent home in the past? (If so, give details.)

8. Do you own a home in the state? Do you rent a home or apartment? How long have you had the home or apartment? Do you own any other land?

9. Where are you registered to vote?

10. Did you inform the board of elections in your old state that you moved?

11. Where is your job or business?

12. In what state is your car registered?

—*Continued*

—*Continued*

13. What state issued your driver's license?

14. In what states do you have bank accounts?

15. In what states do you have club memberships?

16. In what state do you attend church or synogogue?

17. Did you change your will to mention your new state?

18. When you register at hotels, what address do you give?

19. What is your address according to the credit card companies you use?

20. Where do your relatives live?

Possible Investigation Tasks

☐ Interview persons with whom the client may have discussed the move to the state, e.g., relatives, neighbors, business associates.

☐ Obtain copies of records that would indicate the extent of contact with the state, e.g., state tax returns, bank statements, land ownership papers, leases, hotel receipts, voting records, library cards.

In some states—Florida, for example—it is possible to make a formal declaration, or affidavit, of domicile that is filed with an official government body (Exhibit 10.1).

ASSIGNMENT 10.1

In each of the following situations, determine in what state the person was domiciled at the time of death.

a. While living in Illinois, Fred hears about a high-paying job in Alaska. He decides to move to Alaska, since he is tired of Illinois. He sells everything he owns in Illinois and rents an apartment in Alaska. There he discovers jobs are not easy to find. He decides to leave if he cannot find a job in three months. If this happens, he arranges to move in with his sister in New Mexico. Before the three months are over, Fred dies jobless in Alaska.

b. Gloria lives in New York because she attends New York University. Her husband lives in Montana. Gloria plans to rejoin her husband in Montana when she finishes school in six months. Two months before graduation, her husband decides to move to Oregon. Gloria is opposed to the move and tells him that she will not rejoin him if he does not return to Montana. Her husband refuses to move back to Montana. One month before graduation, Gloria dies in New York.

▰▰▰▰ JURISDICTION

Before discussing the nature of jurisdiction, some definitions that apply to this area of the law must be examined:

☐ **Adversarial Hearing**   Both the plaintiff and the defendant appear at the hearing or other court proceeding to contest all the issues.

☐ **Ex Parte Hearing**   Only one party appears at the hearing or other court proceeding; the defendant is not present.

☐ **Direct Attack vs. Collateral Attack**   Two kinds of challenges or attacks can be made on a judgment: direct and collateral. The difference depends on when the attack is made and on what kind of court proceeding the challenge is raised in. Assume, for example, that Mary goes to a state trial court to sue Ed for child support. He does not appear in the action. Mary wins a judgment. But Ed refuses to pay any child support under the judgment. He believes the trial court lacked personal jurisdiction to render its child support judgment against him. If he raises this challenge to the judgment in a normal appeal immediately after the trial court rendered its judgment, he would be bringing a *direct attack* against the judgment. Suppose, however, that the time for bringing a normal appeal has passed. In the same state or in a different state, Mary brings a separate suit against Ed to enforce the child support judgment. In this new

☐ **EXHIBIT 10.1   Florida Declaration of Domicile**

DECLARATION OF DOMICILE

TO THE STATE OF FLORIDA AND COUNTY OF _____ :

This is my Declaration of Domicile in the State of Florida that I am filing this day in accordance, and in conformity with Section 222.17, Florida Statutes.

I, _____ , was formerly a legal resident of

_____ , and I resided at _____ ,
     City   State   Street and Number

_____ ,

however, I have changed my domicile to and am and have been a bona fide resident of the State of Florida since the _____ day of _____ , 19 _____ . I now reside at _____ _____ , _____ County, Florida, and this statement is to be taken as my declaration of actual legal residence and permanent domicile in this State and County to the exclusion of all others, and I will comply with all requirements of legal residents of Florida.

I understand that as a legal resident of Florida: I am subject to intangible taxes; I must purchase Florida license plates for motor vehicles, if any, owned by me and/or my spouse; I must vote in the precinct of my legal domicile (if I vote), and that my estate will be probated in the Florida Courts.

I was born in the U.S.A.: Yes _____ No _____ Place of Birth: _____

Naturalized citizen—Where: _____ Date _____ No. _____

Permanent Visa: Yes _____ No _____ Date _____ No. _____

Sworn and subscribed before me this _____ day of

_____ , A.D. 19 ____ .

PAUL F. HARTSFIELD, Clerk of Circuit Court

By _____
                Deputy Clerk

_____
                Signature

_____
          (Mailing Address)
      (To be executed and filed with
        Clerk of Circuit Court)

Penalty for perjury—up to 20 years in state prison—(Section 837.01, Florida Statutes)

---

suit, Ed says the child support judgment is invalid because the court that rendered it lacked personal jurisdiction over him. This is a *collateral attack* against the judgment. In general, an attack against a judgment is collateral when it is brought in a court proceeding that is outside the normal appeal process.

☐ **Res Judicata**   When a judgment on its merits has been rendered, the parties cannot relitigate the same dispute (i.e., the same cause of action); the parties have already had their day in court.

☐ **Estop or Estoppel**   Stop or prevent.

☐ **Equitable Estoppel**   Equitable estoppel means that a party will be prevented from doing something because it would be unfair to allow him or her to do it. A party will be *equitably estopped* from attacking the validity of a judgment—even a clearly invalid judgment—when:

■ The party obtained the judgment or participated in obtaining it, *or*

■ The party relied on the judgment by accepting benefits based on it, *or*

■ The party caused another person to rely on the judgment to the detriment of the other person.

☐ **Foreign** Another state or country. A foreign divorce decree, for example, is one rendered by a state other than the state where one of the parties is now seeking to enforce the decree.

☐ **Forum State** The state in which the parties are now litigating a case.

☐ **Full Faith and Credit** Under Article IV of the U.S. Constitution, a valid public act of one state must be recognized and enforced by other states. Hence a divorce granted by a state with proper jurisdiction must be recognized by every other state, i.e., it must be given full faith and credit by other states.

☐ **Service of Process** Providing a formal notice to a defendant that orders him or her to appear in court to answer allegations in claims made by a plaintiff. The notice must be delivered in a manner prescribed by law.

☐ **Substituted Service** Service of process other than by handing the process documents to the defendant in person, e.g., service by mail, service by publication in a local newspaper.

The word **jurisdiction** has two main meanings: a *geographic* meaning and a *power* meaning. A specific geographic area of the country is referred to as the jurisdiction. A Nevada state court, for example, will often refer to its entire state as "this jurisdiction." The more significant definition of the word, which we will examine below, relates to power—the power of a court to resolve a particular controversy. If a citizen of Maine wrote to a California court and asked for a divorce through the mail, the California court would be without jurisdiction (without power) to enter a divorce decree if the husband and wife never had any contact with that state. The issue of how a court acquires the power—the jurisdiction—to hear a divorce case can sometimes be a complicated one, as we will see.

Our study of jursidiction will focus on the different attacks or challenges a party will often try to assert against the jurisdiction of a divorce court. In particular, we will examine the following themes:

> **Jurisdiction** (1) The geographic area over which a particular court has authority. (2) The power of a court to act.

☐ Kinds of jurisdiction
☐ What part of the divorce decree is being attacked
☐ Who is attacking the divorce decree
☐ In what court the divorce decree is being attacked
☐ How jurisdiction is acquired

To a very large extent, the success of a jurisdictional attack on a divorce decree depends on the kind of jurisdiction involved, the part of the divorce decree being attacked, the identity of the person bringing the attack, etc. We now turn to a discussion of these critical factors.

KINDS OF JURISDICTION

1. Subject-matter jurisdiction. The power of the court to hear cases of this kind. A criminal law court would not have subject-matter jurisdiction to hear a divorce case. So too, a divorce decree rendered by a court without subject-matter jurisdiction over divorces is void.

2. In rem jurisdiction. The power of the court to make a decision affecting the **res,** which is a thing, object, or status. In divorce actions, the *res* is the

> **Res** A thing, object, or status.

marriage status, which is "located" in any state where one or both of the spouses are domiciled. A state with in rem jurisdiction because of this domicile has the power to terminate the marriage. (Another kind of jurisdiction is *personal* jurisdiction over the defendant. If a court does not have personal jurisdiction, it will not have the power to grant alimony, child support, or a property division; it can only dissolve the marriage.) A court lacks in rem jurisdiction if it renders a divorce judgment when neither party was domiciled in that state. Such a judgment is not entitled to full faith and credit (see discussion below); therefore, another state is not required to enforce the divorce.

3. **Personal jurisdiction** (also called *in personam jurisdiction*). The power of the court over the person of the defendant. If a court has personal jurisdiction over a defendant, it can order him or her to pay alimony and child support and can divide the marital property. If a court makes such an order without personal jurisdiction, the order can be attacked on jurisdictional grounds; it is not entitled to full faith and credit.

Exhibit 10.2 summarizes the kinds of divorce jurisdiction.

PART OF DIVORCE DECREE BEING ATTACKED

A divorce decree usually accomplishes three objectives:

1. *Dissolves the marriage.* For a court to have jurisdiction to dissolve a marriage, one or both of the spouses must be domiciled in the state. When this is so, the court has in rem jurisdiction, which is all that is needed to dissolve the marriage. Personal jurisdiction of both parties is not needed.

2. *Alimony, child support, and property division.* Alimony, child support, and property division cannot be ordered by the court unless it has personal jurisdiction over the defendant. Hence, it is possible for the court to have jurisdiction to dissolve the marriage (because of domicile) but not have jurisdiction to make alimony, child support, and property division awards (because the plaintiff was not able to take the necessary steps, such as service of process, to give the court personal jurisdiction over the defendant). This is the concept of the *divisible divorce*—a divorce that is effective for some purposes but not for others.

☐ **EXHIBIT 10.2   Kinds of Divorce Jurisdiction**

KIND OF JURISDICTION THE COURT CAN ACHIEVE	HOW THIS KIND OF JURISDICTION IS ACQUIRED	POWER THIS KIND OF JURISDICTION GIVES THE COURT
Subject-matter jurisdiction	A state statute or constitutional provision gives the court the power to hear cases involving the subject matter of divorce.	The court can hear divorce cases.
In rem jurisdiction	One or both of the spouses are domiciled in the state.	The court can dissolve the marriage.
Personal jurisdiction	Process is personally delivered to the defendant—service of process. (Alternatives may include substituted service, the long arm statute, etc.)	The court can order the defendant to comply with alimony, child support, or property division obligations.

(The special problems involved in acquiring jurisdiction to render child custody decisions are discussed in chapter 7.)

3. *Child custody.* On the jurisdictional requirements to make a child custody award, see chapter 7.

PERSON ATTACKING DIVORCE DECREE

1. *The person who obtained the divorce.* A person should not be allowed to attack a divorce decree on jurisdictional grounds if that person was the plaintiff in the action that resulted in the divorce. This person will be estopped in any action to deny the validity of a divorce. The same result will occur if this person helped his or her spouse obtain the divorce or received benefits because of the divorce. (The effect of this rule, sometimes known as *equitable estoppel,* is to prevent a person from attacking a divorce decree that is clearly invalid. Note, however, that a few courts do not follow this rule and *will* allow a person to attack a divorce he or she participated in obtaining earlier.)

2. *The person against whom the divorce was obtained.* If the person now attacking the divorce on jurisdictional grounds was the defendant in the action that led to the divorce and made a personal appearance in that divorce action, he or she will not be allowed to attack the divorce. He or she should have raised the jurisdictional attack in the original divorce action.

If the original divorce was obtained *ex parte* (i.e., no appearance by the defendant), the defendant *will* be able to attack the divorce on jurisdictional grounds, such as the fact that the plaintiff was not domiciled in the state that granted the divorce, or the court that granted the divorce had no subject-matter jurisdiction.

If the person against whom the divorce was obtained has accepted the benefits of the divorce (e.g., alimony payments), many courts will estop that person from now attacking the divorce on jurisdictional grounds.

If the person against whom the divorce was obtained has remarried, he or she will be estopped from claiming that the second marriage is invalid because of jurisdictional defects in the divorce decree on the first marriage. Some states, however, will allow the jurisdictional attack on the divorce if the person making the attack did not know about the jurisdictional defect (e.g., no domicile), at the time.

3. *A person who was not a party to the divorce action.* A second spouse who was not a party to the prior divorce action cannot challenge the validity of that divorce on jurisdictional grounds. This second spouse relied on the validity of that divorce when he or she entered the marriage and should not now be allowed to upset the validity of that marriage by challenging the validity of the divorce.

A child of the parties of the prior divorce action cannot challenge the validity of the divorce on jurisdictional grounds if that child's parent would have been estopped from bringing the challenge.

COURT IN WHICH DIVORCE DECREE IS BEING ATTACKED

Many of the disputes in this area arise when a divorce decree is obtained in one state and brought to another state for enforcement. Is the *forum state* (where enforcement of the divorce decree is being sought) required to give *full faith and credit* to the foreign divorce? The answer may depend on which of the three aspects of the divorce decree a party is attempting to enforce:

1. *The dissolution of the marriage.* If either the plaintiff or the defendant was domiciled in the state where the divorce was granted, every other state must give full faith and credit to the part of the divorce decree that dissolved the marriage. The forum state must decide for itself whether there was a valid domicile in the foreign state. The person attacking the foreign divorce decree has the burden of proving the jurisdictional defect, i.e., the absence of domicile in the foreign state.

2. *Alimony, child support, and property division awards.* If the state where the divorce was obtained did not have personal jurisdiction over the defendant, then that state's award of alimony, child support, and property division is *not* entitled to full faith and credit in another state. Again we see the divisible-divorce concept: only part of the divorce decree is recognized in another state if the court had jurisdiction to dissolve the marriage because of domicile but had no jurisdiction to grant alimony, child support, and a property division due to the absence of personal jurisdiction over the defendant.

3. *Custody award.* See chapter 7.

HOW JURISDICTION IS ACQUIRED

1. *Subject-matter jurisdiction.* The only way a court can acquire subject-matter jurisdiction over a divorce is by a special statute or constitutional provision giving the court the power to hear this kind of case. A divorce decree rendered by a court without subject-matter jurisdiction over divorces is void.

2. *In rem jurisdiction.* All that is needed for a court to acquire in rem jurisdiction is the domicile of at least one of the spouses in the state. The case can proceed so long as reasonable notice of the action is given to the defendant. If the defendant is not domiciled in the state, notice can be by substituted service, e.g., mail, publication of notice in a newspaper.

3. *Personal jurisdiction.* A court can acquire personal jurisdiction over the defendant in several ways:

a. Personal service of process on the defendant in the state. This is effective whether or not the defendant is domiciled in the state.[1]

b. Consent. The defendant can always consent to personal jurisdiction simply by appearing in the action and defending the entire case. But if the defendant is a nondomiciliary, he or she can appear solely to contest the jurisdictional issue without being subjected to full personal jurisdiction. *Any* appearance by a *domiciliary*, however, will confer full personal jurisdiction on the court.

c. Substituted service, e.g., mail, publication in a newspaper. Substituted service of process will confer personal jurisdiction if the defendant is domiciled in the state. For nondomiciliaries, see the following discussion on the long arm statute.

---

1. The United States Supreme Court has said: "Among the most firmly established principles of personal jurisdiction in American tradition is that the courts of a State have jurisdiction over nonresidents who are physically present in the State. The view developed early that each State had the power to hale before its courts any individual who could be found within its borders, and that once having acquired jurisdiction over such a person by properly serving him with process, the State could retain jurisdiction to enter judgment against him, no matter how fleeting his visit." *Burnham v. Superior Court of California,* 495 U.S. 604, 610, 110 S. Ct. 2105, 2110 (1990).

d. Long arm statute. This is used to acquire personal jurisdiction over a defendant who is not domiciled in the state. This defendant must have sufficient minimum contacts with the state so that it is reasonable and fair to require the defendant to appear and be subjected to full personal jurisdiction in the state. What constitutes sufficient minimum contacts to meet this standard has not been answered clearly by the courts. Here are some of the factors that a court will consider, no one of which is necessarily conclusive: the defendant was domiciled in the state at one time before he or she left, the defendant cohabitated with his or her spouse in the state before the defendant left the state, the defendant visits the state, the defendant arranges for schooling for his or her children in the state, etc. In addition to these minimum contacts, the defendant must be given reasonable notice of the action.

e. URESA (Uniform Reciprocal Enforcement of Support Act) and UIFSA (Uniform Interstate Family Support Act) can be used to acquire personal jurisdiction over a defendant. These statutes are discussed later in the chapter.

JURISDICTIONAL ANALYSIS: EXAMPLES

Here are some examples of how divorce jurisdiction is determined:

1. Tom and Mary are married. Both are domiciled in Massachusetts. Mary moves to Ohio, which is now her state of domicile. She obtains a divorce decree from an Ohio state court. The decree awards Mary $500 a month alimony. Tom was notified of the action by mail but did not appear. He has had no contacts with Ohio. Mary travels to Massachusetts and brings an action against Tom to enforce the alimony award of the Ohio court.

☐ **Jurisdictional Analysis**

■ The Ohio court had jurisdiction to dissolve the marriage because of Mary's domicile in Ohio. This part of the divorce decree is entitled to full faith and credit in Massachusetts, i.e., Massachusetts *must* recognize this aspect of the Ohio divorce decree if Massachusetts determines that Mary was in fact domiciled in Ohio at the time of the divorce decree.

■ The Ohio court did not have jurisdiction to render an alimony award since it did not have personal jurisdiction over Tom. This part of the divorce decree is not entitled to full faith and credit in Massachusetts, i.e., the Massachusetts court does not have to enforce the Ohio alimony award.

■ Suppose that Tom had an out-of-state divorce in a state where he alone was domiciled. Suppose further that the divorce decree provided that Mary was *not* entitled to alimony. If this court did not have personal jurisdiction over Mary, she would not be bound by the no-alimony decision even though she would be bound by the decision dissolving the marriage.

2. Bill and Pat are married in New Jersey. Bill brings a successful divorce action against Pat in a New Jersey state court. Bill is awarded the divorce. Pat was not served with process or notified in any way of this divorce action. Bill then marries Linda. Linda and Bill begin having marital difficulties. They separate. Linda brings a support action (separate-maintenance action) against Bill. Bill's defense is that he is not married to Linda because his divorce with Pat was invalid due to the fact that Pat had no notice of the divorce.

☐ **Jurisdictional Analysis**

■ Bill is raising a collateral attack against the divorce decree. He is attacking the jurisdiction of the court to award the divorce because Pat had no notice of the divorce action.

■ Bill is the person who obtained the divorce decree. In most states, he will be estopped from attacking the decree on jurisdictional grounds. Whether or not the court in fact had jurisdiction to render the divorce decree, Bill will not be allowed to challenge it. He relied on the divorce and took the benefits of the divorce when he married Linda. He should not be allowed to attack the very thing he helped accomplish.

3. Joe and Helen are married in Texas. Helen goes to New Mexico and obtains a divorce decree against Joe. Joe knows about the action but does not appear. Helen has never been domiciled in New Mexico. Joe marries Paulene. When Helen dies, Joe claims part of her estate. His position is that he is her surviving husband because the New Mexico court had no jurisdiction to divorce them since neither was ever domiciled there.

□ **Jurisdictional Analysis**

■ Joe was not the party who sought the New Mexico divorce. The divorce proceeding was ex parte. Normally, he would be allowed to attack the divorce decree on the ground that no one was domiciled in New Mexico at the time of the divorce.

■ But Joe relied upon the divorce and accepted its benefits by marrying Paulene. It would be inconsistent to allow him to change his mind now, and it could be unfair to Paulene. Hence, Joe will be estopped from attacking the divorce on jurisdictional grounds.

ASSIGNMENT 10.2

John and Sandra were married in Florida but live in Georgia. Sandra returns to Florida with their two children. John never goes back to Florida. He often calls his children on the phone, and they come to visit him pursuant to arrangements he makes with Sandra. Once he asked his mother to go to Florida to look after the children while Sandra was sick. Sandra files for a divorce in Florida. John does not appear, although he is given notice of the action. (Florida has a long arm statute.) Sandra is granted the divorce and $840 a month in child support. No alimony is awarded. She later travels to Georgia and asks a Georgia court to enforce the child support order, which John has been ignoring. What result?

You cannot go into a United States District Court or any federal court to obtain a divorce. Federal courts do not have subject-matter jurisdiction over divorces. Parties who want to dissolve their marriage must use their local state courts.

Most states require that the plaintiff be a resident of the forum state for a designated period of time before a divorce can be granted, e.g., six weeks, a year. In a few states, it is sufficient that the defendant is a resident even if the plaintiff is not. While the word "residence" is frequently used in the state statutes, the meaning intended by most of the statutes is domicile: one's permanent home where one intends to stay indefinitely. As we saw in the preceding pages, for a court to have jurisdiction to divorce a couple, domicile must exist. The statutes on residency (domicile) state the length of time during which there must be residence (domicile) in the state.

Complaint A pretrial document filed by one party against another that states a grievance, called a cause of action.

Summons A formal notice from the court ordering the defendant to appear and answer the allegations of the plaintiff.

■■■ MISCELLANEOUS PRETRIAL MATTERS

COMPLAINT

The divorce action begins when the plaintiff completes service of process on the defendant by giving him or her the **complaint** (the pleading that states the cause of action for divorce—see Exhibit 10.3) and the **summons** (a document

☐ **EXHIBIT 10.3   The Basic Structure of a Complaint**

STATE OF _____   Caption

COUNTY OF _____

FAMILY COURT BRANCH

Mary Smith, Plaintiff

        v.   Civil Action No. _____

Fred Smith, Defendant

     COMPLAINT FOR ABSOLUTE DIVORCE   Commencement

The plaintiff, through her attorney, alleges:

(1) The jurisdiction of this court is based upon section _____ , title _____ of the State Code (1978).

(2) The plaintiff is fifty years old.

(3) The plaintiff is a resident of the State of _____ , County of _____ . She has resided here for five years immediately preceding the filing of this complaint.

(4) The parties were married on March 13, 1983 in the State of _____ , County of _____ .

(5) There are no children born of this marriage.   Body

(6) The plaintiff and defendant lived and cohabitated together from the date of their marriage until February 2, 1996 at which time they both agreed to separate because of mutual incompatibility. This separation has continued voluntarily and without cohabitation for more than two years until the present time.

(7) Since the separation, the plaintiff has resided at _____ _____ , and the defendant has resided at _____ .

(8) There is no reasonable likelihood of reconciliation.

WHEREFORE, the plaintiff PRAYS: Prayer

(1) For an absolute divorce.   For

(2) For alimony and a division of property.   Relief.

(3) For restoration of her maiden name.

(4) For reasonable attorney's fees and costs.

(5) For such other relief as this Court may deem just and proper.

_____   _____

Linda Stout   Mary Smith, Plaintiff

Attorney for Plaintiff

234 Main St.

_____ , _____ 07237

STATE of _____   Verification

COUNTY of _____

Mary Smith, being first duly sworn on oath according to law, deposes and says that she has read the foregoing complaint by her subscribed and that the matters stated therein are true to the best of her knowledge, information, and belief.

_____

Mary Smith

Subscribed and sworn to before me on this _____ day of _____ , 19 ____

_____

Notary Public

My commission expires _____

Petition Another name for complaint in some states.

In Forma Pauperis As a poor person.

that orders the defendant to appear and answer the complaint—see Exhibit 10.4). The complaint is sometimes called the **petition**. The plaintiff also files the complaint or petition with the court along with the appropriate filing fees. If the plaintiff is poor, he or she can ask the court to waive the fees and proceed **in forma pauperis.**

In some states it is possible to obtain a divorce primarily through the mail without going through elaborate court procedures. Such a divorce is often referred to as a *summary dissolution* or a *simplified dissolution*. The requirements for taking advantage of this option are quite strict. In California, for example, the couple must be childless, married for five years or less, have no interest in real property (other than a lease on a residence), waive any rights to spousal support, etc. Cal. Civil Code § 4550 (1983). In short, there must be very little need for courts, lawyers, and the protection of the legal system. The less conflict

☐ **EXHIBIT 10.4 Divorce Summons**

STATE OF MAINE
CUMBERLAND COUNTY

SUPERIOR COURT
Civil Action, Docket Number _____

A.B., Plaintiff
   of Bath,
   Sagadahoc County,
       v.
C.D., Defendant
   of Portland,
   Cumberland County,

To the Defendant _____ :

The Plaintiff _____ has begun a divorce action against you in this Court. If you wish to oppose the divorce, you or your attorney must prepare and file a written Answer to the attached Complaint within 20 days from the day this summons was served upon you. You or your attorney must file your Answer by delivering it in person or by mail to the office of the Clerk of the Superior Court, Cumberland County Courthouse, 142 Federal Street, Portland, Maine. On or before the day you file your Answer, you or your attorney must mail a copy of your Answer to the Plaintiff's attorney, whose name and address appear below.

IMPORTANT WARNING: IF YOU FAIL TO FILE AN ANSWER WITHIN THE TIME STATED ABOVE, OR IF, AFTER YOU FILE YOUR ANSWER, YOU FAIL TO APPEAR AT ANY TIME THE COURT NOTIFIES YOU TO DO SO, A JUDGMENT MAY IN YOUR ABSENCE BE ENTERED AGAINST YOU FOR THE DIVORCE. IF AN ORDER FOR PAYMENT OF MONEY IS ENTERED AGAINST YOU, YOUR EMPLOYER MAY BE ORDERED TO PAY PART OF YOUR WAGES TO THE PLAINTIFF OR YOUR PERSONAL PROPERTY, INCLUDING BANK ACCOUNTS, AND YOUR REAL ESTATE MAY BE TAKEN TO SATISFY THE JUDGMENT. IF YOU INTEND TO OPPOSE THE DIVORCE, DO NOT FAIL TO ANSWER WITHIN THE REQUIRED TIME.

If you believe you have a defense to the Plaintiff's Complaint or if you believe you have a claim of your own against the Plaintiff, you should talk to a lawyer.

[Seal of the Court]

Dated _____

_____
Name of Plaintiff's Attorney

_____
Address

_____
Telephone

Clerk of Said Superior Court
Served on _____
      Date

_____
Deputy Sheriff

between parties over children, property, and support, the easier it is to obtain a divorce.

A party who represents him or herself in a divorce action (summary or traditional) is proceeding **pro se**.

Pro Se On one's own behalf. Representing oneself.

GUARDIAN AD LITEM

If the husband or wife is a minor or if the defendant is insane at the time of the divorce action, the court may require that the individual be represented by a **guardian ad litem** or *conservator* to ensure that the interests of the individual are protected during the proceeding. In a disputed child-custody case, the state might appoint a guardian ad litem to represent the child.

Guardian ad Litem A special guardian appointed by the court to represent the interests of another.

VENUE

Venue refers to the place of the trial. Within a state, it may be that the divorce action could be brought in a number of different counties or districts because each one of them has or could acquire the necessary jurisdiction. The *choice of venue* is the choice of one county or district among several where the trial could be held. The state's statutory code will often specify the requirements for the selection of venue. The requirements often relate to the residence (usually meaning domicile) of the plaintiff or defendant. For example, the statute might specify that a divorce action should be filed in the county in which the plaintiff has been a resident (meaning domiciliary) for three months preceding the commencement of the action.

Venue The place of the trial. The county, district, or state where the trial is held.

PLEADING

As we have seen, the complaint (or petition) is the **pleading** that states the nature of the action, the fact that the parties are married, the basis of the court's jurisdiction, the grounds for the divorce, the relief sought, etc. (See Exhibit 10.3.) The response of the defendant is stated in the pleading called the **answer** (often referred to as the *response*). In most states, the defendant can **counterclaim** for divorce in his or her answer.

Pleading A formal document that contains allegations and responses of the parties in litigation.

Answer The pleading filed by the defendant that responds to the complaint of the plaintiff.

Counterclaim A claim made by the defendant against the plaintiff.

WAITING PERIOD

Some states have a compulsory *waiting period* or "cooling-off" period (e.g., sixty days) that usually begins to run from the time the divorce complaint is filed. During this period of time, no further proceedings are held in the hope that tempers might calm down, producing an atmosphere of reconciliation.

■ DISCOVERY

Discovery refers to a series of devices designated to assist the parties prepare for trial, particularly in reference to the financial status of the parties. For example, when the plaintiff is the wife who needs alimony, she might use some of the discovery devises to identify her defendant-husband's assets. The standard devices are as follows:

Discovery Steps that a party can take before trial to obtain information from the other side in order to prepare for trial.

□ **Interrogatories** A written set of factual questions sent by one party to another before a trial begins (see page 84).

□ **Deposition** A deposition is an in-person, question-and-answer session conducted outside the courtroom, e.g., in one of the attorney's offices. The person questioned is said to be *deposed*.

☐ **Request for Admissions**   If a party believes that there will be no dispute over a certain fact at trial, it can request that the other party admit (i.e., stipulate) the fact. This will avoid the expense and delay of proving the fact at trial. The party can also be asked to admit that a specific document is genuine. The other party, of course, need not make the admission if it feels that there is some dispute over the fact.

☐ **Mental or Physical Examination**   If the mental or physical condition of a party is relevant to the litigation, many courts can order him or her to undergo an examination. If paternity is at issue, for example, the court might order the husband to undergo a blood-grouping test.

☐ **Request for Production**   One party can ask another to allow the inspection, testing, or copying of documents or other tangible things relevant to the case, e.g., tax returns, credit card receipts, diaries, business records.

ASSIGNMENT 10.3

Pick any well-known married couple in the media. Assume that they are getting a divorce and that you work for the law firm that is representing the wife. You are asked to draft a set of interrogatories meant to elicit as much relevant information as possible about the husband's personal and business finances. The information will be used in the firm's representation of the wife on alimony and property division issues. Draft the interrogatories.

■■■■ PRELIMINARY ORDERS

Obtaining a divorce can be time-consuming even when the matter is uncontested. The court's calendar may be so crowded that it may take months to have the case heard. If the case is contested and some bitterness exists between the parties, the litigation can seemingly be endless. While the litigation is going on (or to use the Latin phrase, **pendente lite**), the court may be asked to make a number of *preliminary* orders (sometimes called temporary orders) that remain in effect only until final determinations are made later:

Pendente Lite   While the litigation is going on.

☐ Granting physical and legal custody of the children

☐ Granting exclusive occupancy of the marital home to the custodial parent

☐ Granting a child support order

☐ Granting alimony

☐ Granting attorney's fees and related court costs in the divorce action

☐ Enjoining (preventing) one spouse from bothering or molesting the other spouse and children

☐ Enjoining a spouse from transferring any property, which might make it unavailable for the support of the other spouse and children

☐ Appointing a receiver over a spouse's property until the court decides what his or her obligations are to the other spouse and children

☐ Enjoining the parties from changing any insurance policies

☐ Ordering an inventory and appraisal of all family assets and debts

☐ Granting control of any business operated by the spouses

☐ Enjoining the defendant from leaving the state or the country

☐ Enjoining either spouse from taking the children out of the state

☐ Enjoining the defendant from obtaining a foreign divorce

For an example of a request for preliminary or temporary orders, see Exhibit 10.5.

☐ **EXHIBIT 10.5 Motion and Affidavit for Temporary Alimony, Maintenance of Support, or Custody of Minor Children**

SUPERIOR COURT OF THE DISTRICT OF COLUMBIA
FAMILY DIVISION
DOMESTIC RELATIONS BRANCH

-

v.   *Plaintiff*   Jacket No. -

-
                                Defendant

MOTION AND AFFIDAVIT

	Note: **FINANCIAL STATEMENT REQUIRED** **FILL OUT AND ATTACH HERETO.**

For ☐ TEMPORARY ALIMONY, MAINTENANCE OR SUPPORT
☐ TEMPORARY CUSTODY OF MINOR CHILDREN

Now comes ☐ Plaintiff   and moves the Court that -
☐ Defendant   (name)

be required to pay such amount as seems just and reasonable for the support and maintenance of

the ☐ Plaintiff (and - minor children) pending the final disposition of this cause (and
☐ Defendant

to award ☐ her the temporary custody of said minor children). Note: *Strike out portions of the preceding that do not apply.*
☐ him

The following facts are submitted in support of the above motion:

1. Marriage:	Date:	Place:	2. Are you agreeable to a reconciliation: ☐ Yes ☐ No

3. Children by this marriage:		Living with			Amounts Contributed to family
Name	Age	Name	Address	Relation	

4. WIFE		5. HUSBAND	
Age:	Married before: ☐ Yes—How terminated? ☐ No	Age:	Married before: ☐ Yes—How terminated? ☐ No
Occupation:	Employer:	Occupation:	Employer:
Living with	Name: Relation: Address:	Living with	Name: Relation: Address:

6. Wife asks for support of self (and _ _ _ _ minor children):	Amount: $ Per: ☐ Week ☐ Month	7. Husband willing to contribute as such support:	Amount: $ Per: ☐ Week ☐ Month
8. Husband's support to family:	Before Separation: $ After Separation: $	9. Previous divorce proceedings between parties. ☐ Yes ☐ No Alimony awarded: ☐ Yes ☐ No	
10. Juvenile Court proceedings: ☐ Yes ☐ No Explain:		11. Remarks	

▬▬ TRIAL

Some states do not permit jury trials in divorce cases. If there is no jury, the judge decides the questions of fact as well as the questions of law. If a jury trial is allowed, the jurors are selected through a procedure known as **voir dire.** During this procedure, the lawyers and/or judge ask questions of prospective jurors to assess their eligibility to sit on the jury.

Voir Dire Jury selection.

The lawyers begin the trial by making opening statements outlining the evidence they intend to try to prove during the trial. The plaintiff's side will usually present its case first. The lawyer will call the plaintiff's witnesses and directly examine them. The other side can cross-examine these witnesses. Physical evidence such as documents are introduced as exhibits. Some evidence may have to be **corroborated,** meaning that additional evidence must be introduced to support the position taken by the party. The plaintiff's side will "rest" its case after presenting all of its witnesses and evidence. The defendant's lawyer then begins his or her case through direct examination of witnesses, introduction of exhibits, etc.

Corroborated
Providing additional evidence of a point beyond that offered by the person asserting the point.

When a party has the burden of proving a fact, the standard of proof is usually a **preponderance of evidence:** the fact finder must be able to say from the evidence introduced and found admissible that it is *more likely than not* that the fact has been established as claimed. Occasionally, however, the law requires a fact to meet a higher standard of proof, e.g., clear and convincing evidence. Who has the burden of proof? In general, the party asserting a fact has the burden of proof on that fact. For example, a spouse who claims that the other spouse has a hidden bank account and physically assaulted the children has the burden of proof on these facts.

Preponderance of Evidence A standard of proof that is met if the evidence shows it is more likely than not that an alleged fact is true or false as alleged.

Within the marriage, there is a **privilege for marital communications,** which prevents one spouse from testifying about confidential communications between the spouses during the marriage. This privilege, however, does not apply to:

Privilege for Marital Communications One spouse cannot disclose in court any confidential communications that occurred between the spouses during the marriage.

□ Criminal proceedings in which one spouse is alleged to have committed a crime against the other or against the children
□ Civil cases between the spouses such as a divorce action

The privilege is limited to cases in which a third party is suing one or both of the spouses and attempts to introduce into evidence what one spouse may have said to another. Such evidence is inadmissible.

A **default judgment** can be entered against a defendant who fails to appear. The plaintiff, however, is still required to introduce evidence to establish his or her case. Unlike other civil proceedings, the default judgment is not automatic.

Default Judgment A judgment rendered when the other side failed to appear.

□ **Note on Alternative Dispute Resolution (ADR)** The following are alternatives to traditional litigation of a family law dispute in court, or at least alternatives that can be attempted before resorting to traditional litigation.

Arbitration

Both sides agree to submit their dispute to a neutral third person who will listen to the evidence and make a decision. This individual is usually a professional arbitrator hired through an organization such as the American Arbitration Association. An arbitration proceeding is not as formal as a court trial. Generally, the decision of an arbitrator is not appealable to a court. If a party is dissatisfied, he or she must go to court and start all over again.

Rent-a-Judge

This is actually another form of arbitration. A retired judge is hired by both sides to listen to the evidence and to make a decision that has no more or less validity than any other arbitrator's decision.

Mediation

Both sides agree to submit their dispute to a neutral third person who will try to help the disputants reach a resolution on their own. In some states, mediation is mandatory; the parties are required to try to work out their differences before final action by the court. The mediator does not render a decision, although occasionally he or she may make suggestions or recommendations to the parties and ultimately to the court. The most common issues that are handled in mediation are custody and visitation arrangements.

Med-Arb

First mediation is tried. Those issues that could not be mediated are then resolved through arbitration. Often, the same person serves as mediator and arbitrator in a Med-Arb proceeding.

REVELATIONS OF A FAMILY LAW MEDIATOR: WHAT GOES ON BEHIND CLOSED DOORS TO HELP DIVORCING COUPLES REACH AGREEMENT?

by Joshua Kadish
Oregon State Bar Bulletin 27 (February/March 1992).

Over the past seven or eight years, I have mediated a substantial number of family law cases. My office mates often inquire, "Just what happens behind those closed doors, anyway?" "What was the loud screaming about, followed by hysterical laughter and silence?" "How do you get these embattled couples to agree on anything if they hate each other so much?" I usually parry these questions with a crafty smile and a muttered, "I have my ways . . ." as I scuttle down the hallway.

Bowing to pressure from various fronts, I have decided that the time has come to tell all. What follows is fiction, which I hope reveals the truth.

Fred and Wilma were a young couple in the process of divorcing. They had significant disagreement about custody of their two children, ages 1½ and 6. Both had consulted with attorneys and, after receiving estimates of the cost of a custody battle, had followed their attorneys' recommendation to at least try mediation. Wilma had called me to set up an appointment, and at the appointed hour I ushered them into my office.

My office is somewhat different from many lawyers' offices. I do have a desk in one corner. Most of the office is given over to a sitting area consisting of a large, comfortable couch and two chairs grouped around a coffee table. I always let the couple enter my office first and seat themselves as they wish. Depend-

ing upon how they arrange themselves, I can get a preliminary idea of how hotly the battle is raging. Some couples will sit together on the couch. Most position themselves as far away from each other as possible. Fred and Wilma put a good deal of distance between themselves.

After we were settled, I spent a few minutes describing mediation to them. First, my job was to remain neutral and to help them reach agreements for themselves. My job was not to reach decisions for them. Second, what transpired in the mediation sessions was confidential and would not later be disclosed in a courtroom. Third, the process was voluntary and anyone was free to terminate the mediation at any time. Fourth, we would consider the interests of their children to be of paramount importance.

Without looking at either one of them, I then asked them to tell me about their current situation while I studiously looked down at my legal pad. I like to see who will start talking first. This gives me a clue about where the balance of power may lie in the relationship. I am always concerned about one party overpowering the other in mediation.

Fred started talking. Speaking angrily, he told me about their 10-year marriage, the two children and Wilma's affair and withdrawal from the marriage. He stated that although he worked hard, he spent more than an average amount of time caring for the children. He felt that in having an affair, Wilma had proved herself to be an unstable person and that he would be a preferable custodial parent. He pointed out that Wilma had worked during the course of the marriage and that parenting duties had been shared between them more or less equally.

During the course of his statement, Wilma had interrupted Fred to point out that although she had had an affair, it occurred after they had separated and that Fred had been emotionally distant and withdrawn from the marriage for a number of years. Her statement ignited a loud argument between them. I let them argue for a minute or two to get a sense of their style of arguing. This argument was a well-rehearsed one which they must have been through a hundred times. As each one spoke, I could see that neither party was listening but was marshaling arguments with which to respond, making sure that his or her position was well defended.

I interrupted the argument by stating that I suspected they had had this argument before. This brought a slightly sheepish smile to both faces. Humor is often useful in easing tension and getting people on another track. I then borrowed an idea from an excellent mediator, John Haynes, and asked each of them to take a few minutes to think about what was the absolute worst outcome they could imagine in mediation. By asking this question, I wanted to get them further off the track they had been racing down and to give them a few minutes to calm down. After a few minutes, I asked each to answer. Fred said he was afraid of losing everything, including his children. Wilma stated that she was afraid of the same thing.

I remarked that it was interesting that they were both afraid of exactly the same thing, specifically a loss of their children to the other party. I then asked whether it would be possible for them to agree that whatever the outcome of mediation was, it would not result in a complete loss of the children to the other person. They both indicated that they would agree to this.

From that point, the atmosphere eased considerably. Both Fred and Wilma had dramatically realized that each was concerned about exactly the same thing. When people realize that they have the same concerns, it makes them feel closer or at least less adversarial. Moreover, they had been able to reach their first agreement. They realized they had a common interest in not becoming estranged from their children and that they could agree this would not be a result of the mediation.

I then asked what the current situation was regarding the children. Fred stated that he had moved out and was living in a small apartment. He was seeing the children every other weekend. However, he emphasized that he was a very involved father and he wanted the children to spend at least half of their time with him on an alternating weekly basis. Wilma thought this would be bad for the children. She wanted them to be at home with her and see Fred every other weekend. She clearly wished to be the primary parent and felt that the children needed a mother's love. She was quite concerned about the children being in Fred's care for more than one overnight at a time. Fred interrupted her to state that he felt he was just as good a parent as she was. Wilma responded by telling an anecdote about Fred forgetting to feed the children lunch about three weeks ago.

Again, I interrupted. Taking a bit of a risk, I asked whether each parent thought the children loved and needed the other parent. Again, each parent responded affirmatively. My asking this question had the effect of derailing the disagreement and again bringing Fred and Wilma back to some common ground of understanding. Most parents will at least admit the children love and need the other parent.

The next task was to help Fred and Wilma learn to listen to each other and to start separating their positions from their interests. I asked them each if they thought they could state what the other person's position was regarding custody and visitation and the reasons for it. Fred thought he could, but when he tried, Wilma felt he was inaccurate. I then asked Wilma to tell him again what she was concerned about, which she did. Fred was then able to repeat Wilma's position back to her. We then reversed the process, and after a couple of tries, Wilma was able to state Fred's concerns back to him.

This is a simple technique known as "active listening" which I borrowed from the field of psychology. It is not too difficult to learn the rudiments, particularly when you are married to a clinical psychologist, as I am. The goal in active listening is to make each person feel understood. There is great power in helping each party feel his or her position is genuinely understood by the other person. In most marital disputes, as one party talks, the other party is not listening, but is preparing arguments to respond to the other. This results in long, well worked out and pointless disputes. Active listening slows the pace down and helps couples improve their communication; if you are assured that you will be listened to, you will be much more likely to be able to listen to another.

At this point Fred and Wilma understood not only each other's positions, but the interests and reasons behind the positions. Wilma was concerned about being separated from the children for too many overnight periods in a row. Fred was concerned about long periods of time going by without seeing the children. I pointed out that although their positions (alternating weekly versus every other weekend visitation) conflicted, their interests did not necessarily conflict. Perhaps it would be possible to work out a schedule where Fred saw the children frequently, but not for a long string of overnights. Perhaps every other weekend visitation with some shorter but frequent mid-week visitations, plus frequent telephone contact would be acceptable.

I then hauled out a blank calendar. Using the calendar as the focus of discussion, we worked out a visitation schedule that seemed acceptable to both of them. During this discussion, I emphasized to them that they were fortunate to have the opportunity to experiment with different patterns of visitation because it is very difficult to sit in a room and decide what will and will not work in the long run. I suggested that they should commit to trying a certain pattern of visitation for perhaps two months and also commit to reviewing it and altering it as indicated by their needs and the children's.

By finally working out a schedule, I was trying to do several things. First, I was trying to show them that in some ways their interests could be meshed. Second, big problems can be broken down into small, manageable pieces. Rather than creating a visitation

schedule which was engraved in stone and would last for the next 20 years, they could try something for two months. Finally, I had introduced the idea of experimentation and flexibility. They could adjust the situation based upon how they and the children actually reacted to the plan.

I ended the session by telling them I would write their agreement in memo form, which they could review with their attorneys. I then asked each of them to comment on the process of the session. Did either of them have any concerns about what had happened? What did they like about the session? What could we do differently next time when we moved to a discussion of financial issues? I try to make people feel that they are in control of the process. Fred and Wilma both stated that they were pleased with the session and surprised that they had been able to reach agreement. Fred asked how I had done it. "I have my ways . . ." I muttered as I ushered them to the door.

DIVORCE JUDGMENT

An **interlocutory** decree (or a *decree nisi*) is one that will not become final until the passage of a specified period of time. In some states, after the court has reached its decision to grant a divorce, an interlocutory decree of divorce will be issued. During the period that this decree is in force, the parties are still married. The divorce decree could be set aside if the parties reconcile.

Interlocutory Not final; interim.

In many states, the parties may not remarry while the trial court's divorce judgment is being appealed. Finally, in a few states, even a final divorce judgment will not automatically enable a party to remarry. The court may have the power to prohibit one or both of the parties from remarrying for a period of time.

An absolute, or final, judgment (as opposed to an interlocutory judgment) will determine whether the marriage is dissolved. If it is, the divorce may be granted to the plaintiff, or to both parties (dual divorce) if both initially filed for the divorce. The judgment will also resolve the questions of alimony, child custody, child support, and property division. (All of this, of course, assumes that the court had proper jurisdiction to make these determinations as outlined earlier in this chapter.) In addition, the judgment will often restore the woman's maiden name, if that is her wish, and determine what the surname of the children will be as part of the custody decision.

Exhibit 10.6 shows a notice of entry of judgment, and Exhibit 10.7 shows a record of dissolution of marriage.

ENFORCEMENT OF DIVORCE JUDGMENT

In chapter 8, we covered the enforcement of child support. Here, our main focus is the enforcement of the alimony portion of a divorce judgment and, to

☐ **EXHIBIT 10.6 Notice of Entry of Judgment**

3-41

ATTORNEY OR PARTY WITHOUT ATTORNEY *(Name and Address):*	TELEPHONE NO.	**FOR COURT USE ONLY**

ATTORNEY FOR *(Name):*

SUPERIOR COURT OF CALIFORNIA, COUNTY OF

STREET ADDRESS:

MAILING ADDRESS:

CITY AND ZIP CODE:

BRANCH NAME:

MARRIAGE OF

PETITIONER:

RESPONDENT:

NOTICE OF ENTRY OF JUDGMENT	CASE NUMBER:

You are notified that the following judgment was entered on *(date):*

1. ☐ Dissolution of Marriage

2. ☐ Dissolution of Marriage — Status Only

3. ☐ Dissolution of Marriage — Reserving Jurisdiction over Termination of Marital Status

4. ☐ Legal Separation

5. ☐ Nullity

6. ☐ Other *(specify):*

Date: Clerk, by _____ , Deputy

— NOTICE TO ATTORNEY OF RECORD OR PARTY WITHOUT ATTORNEY —

Pursuant to the provisions of Code of Civil Procedure section 1952, if no appeal is filed the court may order the exhibits destroyed or otherwise disposed of after 60 days from the expiration of the appeal time.

Effective date of termination of marital status *(specify):*

WARNING: NEITHER PARTY MAY REMARRY UNTIL THE EFFECTIVE DATE OF THE TERMINATION OF MARITAL STATUS AS SHOWN IN THIS BOX.

CLERK'S CERTIFICATE OF MAILING

I certify that I am not a party to this cause and that a true copy of the Notice of Entry of Judgment was mailed first class, postage fully prepaid, in a sealed envelope addressed as shown below, and that the notice was mailed

at *(place):*   California,

on *(date):*

Date: Clerk, by _____ , Deputy

some extent, the property division portion as well.[2] A good deal of this section, however, will also be relevant to child support enforcement.

---

2. While either party can be challenged for failure to abide by alimony and property division orders, it is usually the ex-husband who is in this position. The examples used herein reflect this.

☐ **EXHIBIT 10.7 Record of Dissolution of Marriage**

OREGON DEPARTMENT OF HUMAN RESOURCES
HEALTH DIVISION
Vital Records Unit
**RECORD OF DISSOLUTION
OF MARRIAGE, OR ANNULMENT**

SAMPLE

CO. FILE NO. _____

136-

State File Number

TYPE OR PRINT PLAINLY IN BLACK INK

HUSBAND

1. HUSBAND'S NAME (First, Middle, Last)

2. RESIDENCE OR LEGAL ADDRESS — STREET AND NUMBER — CITY OR TOWN — COUNTY — STATE

3. SOCIAL SECURITY NUMBER (Optional)

4. BIRTHPLACE (State or Foreign Country)

5. DATE OF BIRTH (Month, Day, Year)

WIFE

6a. WIFE'S NAME (First, Middle, Last)

6b. MAIDEN SURNAME

7. FORMER LEGAL NAMES (IF ANY) — (1) — (2) — (3)

8. RESIDENCE OR LEGAL ADDRESS — STREET AND NUMBER — CITY OR TOWN — COUNTY — STATE

9. SOCIAL SECURITY NUMBER (Optional)

10. BIRTHPLACE (State or Foreign Country)

13. DATE OF BIRTH (Month, Day, Year)

MARRIAGE

12a. PLACE OF THIS MARRIAGE - CITY, TOWN OR LOCATION

12b. COUNTY

12c. STATE OR FOREIGN COUNTRY

13. DATE OF THIS MARRIAGE (Month, Day, Year)

14. DATE COUPLE LAST RESIDED IN SAME HOUSEHOLD (Month, Day, Year)

15. NUMBER OF CHILDREN UNDER 18 IN THIS HOUSEHOLD AS OF THE DATE IN ITEM 14

Number _____ ☐ None

16. PETITIONER

☐ Husband ☐ Wife ☐ Both

ATTORNEY

17a. NAME OF PETITIONER'S ATTORNEY (Type/Print)

17b. ADDRESS (Street and Number or Rural Route Number, City or Town, State, Zip Code)

18a. NAME OF RESPONDENT'S ATTORNEY (Type/Print)

18b. ADDRESS (Street and Number or Rural Route Number, City or Town, State, Zip Code)

DECREE

19. MARRIAGE OF THE ABOVE NAMED PERSONS WAS DISSOLVED ON: (Month, Day, Year)

20. TYPE OF DECREE

DISSOLUTION OF MARRIAGE ☐ ANNULMENT ☐

21. DATE DECREE BECOMES EFFECTIVE (Month, Day, Year)

22. NUMBER OF CHILDREN UNDER 18 WHOSE PHYSICAL CUSTODY WAS AWARDED TO

Husband _____ Wife _____
Joint (Husband/Wife) _____ Wife _____
☐ No children

23. COUNTY OF DECREE

24. TITLE OF COURT

25. SIGNATURE OF COURT OFFICIAL

26. TITLE OF COURT OFFICIAL

27. DATE SIGNED (Month, Day, Year)

ORS 432.010 REQUIRED STATISTICAL INFORMATION. THE INFORMATION BELOW WILL NOT APPEAR ON CERTIFIED COPIES OF THE RECORD.

	28. NUMBER OF THIS MARRIAGE—First, Second, etc. (Specify below)	29. IF PREVIOUSLY MARRIED, LAST MARRIAGE ENDED		30. RACE - American, Indian, Black, White, etc. (specify below)	31. EDUCATION (Specify only highest grade completed)	
		By Death, Divorce, Dissolution, or Annulment (Specify below)	Date (Month, Day, Year)		Elementary/Secondary (0–12)	College (1–4 or 5+)
HUSBAND	28a.	29a.	29b.	30a.	31a.	
WIFE	28b.	29c.	29d.	30b.	31b.	

THE PETITIONER OR LEGAL REPRESENTATIVE OF THE PETITIONER IS RESPONSIBLE FOR COMPLETING THE PERSONAL INFORMATION ON THIS FORM AND SHALL PRESENT THIS FORM TO THE CLERK OF THE COURT WITH THE PETITION.
IN ALL CASES THE COMPLETED RECORD SHALL BE A PREREQUISITE TO THE GRANTING OF THE FINAL DECREE

45-5 (2-89)

A number of enforcement options can be used against a delinquent party:

- Civil contempt
- Execution
- Garnishment
- Attachment
- Posting security
- Receivership
- Constructive trust
- Criminal nonsupport
- Qualified Domestic Relations Order (QDRO)
- Qualified Medical Child Support Order (QMCSO)
- Uniform Reciprocal Enforcement of Support Act (URESA)

CIVIL CONTEMPT

A delinquent party who must pay a money judgment, e.g., an alimony order, is called the *judgment debtor*. The person in whose favor the judgment is rendered is the *judgment creditor*. For disobeying the order, the judgment debtor can be held in civil contempt, for which he will be jailed until he complies with the order. This remedy, however, is not used if the judgment debtor does not have the present financial ability to pay the alimony obligation. Inability to pay does not mean burdensome or inconvenient to pay. Using all resources currently available or those that could become available with reasonable effort, he must be able to comply with the alimony order. (Exhibit 10.8 shows an affidavit in support of a motion to punish for contempt.)

Contempt is generally not available to enforce property division orders. The latter are more often enforced by execution, attachment, posting security, receivership, and constructive trust, which are discussed below.

EXECUTION

A judgment is *executed* when the court orders the sheriff to carry it out by seizing the property of the judgment debtor, selling it, and turning the proceeds over to the judgment creditor. This is done pursuant to a **writ of execution.**

Writ of Execution A document directing a court officer to seize the property of someone who lost a judgment, sell it, and pay the winner of the judgment.

Execution is usually possible only with respect to support orders that are *final* and *nonmodifiable*. Such orders can become final and nonmodifiable in two ways:

- In some states, each unpaid installment automatically becomes a final and nonmodifiable judgment of nonpayment to which execution will be available.
- In other states, each unpaid installment does not become a final and nonmodifiable judgment of nonsupport until the wife makes a specific application for such a judgment and one is entered. Execution is available only after the judgment is so entered or docketed.

As we saw in chapter 8, federal law places severe restrictions on the ability of a court to modify child support arrearages retroactively.

GARNISHMENT

Garnishment A process whereby a debtor's property under the control of another is given to a third person to whom the debtor owes a debt.

When **garnishment** is used, the court authorizes the judgment creditor to reach money or other property of the judgment debtor that is in the hands of the third party, e.g., the employer or bank of the judgment debtor.

ATTACHMENT

Property of the judgment debtor is *attached* when the court authorizes its seizure to bring it under the control of the court so that it can be used to satisfy a judgment.

POSTING SECURITY

The court may require the judgment debtor to post a bond, i.e., *post security,* which will be forfeited if he fails to obey the judgment.

RECEIVERSHIP

The court can appoint a *receiver* over some or all the judgment debtor's property to prevent him from squandering it or otherwise making it unavailable to satisfy the judgment.

CONSTRUCTIVE TRUST

The court could impose a trust on property that the judgment debtor conveys to a "friendly" third party (e.g., the judgment debtor's mother) in an effort to make it appear that he no longer owns the property. A **constructive trust** is a trust created by the law, rather than by the parties, in order to prevent a serious inequity or injustice.

Constructive Trust A trust created by operation of law against one who has obtained legal possession of property (or legal rights to property) through fraud, duress, abuse of confidence, or other unconscionable conduct.

CRIMINAL NONSUPPORT

The state can criminally prosecute the judgment debtor for the willful failure to meet his support obligation—*criminal nonsupport.*

☐ **EXHIBIT 10.8 Affidavit in Contempt Proceeding**

SUPREME COURT OF THE STATE OF NEW YORK
COUNTY OF _____

_____ ,
                Plaintiff,
      -against-
_____ ,
                Defendant,

AFFIDAVIT IN SUPPORT OF MOTION
TO PUNISH FOR CONTEMPT

Index No. _____

STATE OF NEW YORK   } ss.:
COUNTY OF _____

_____ , being duly sworn, deposes and says:

That I am the plaintiff in the above entitled action and make this application to punish the defendant for contempt of Court for willfully neglecting and refusing to comply with the Judgment of this Court dated _____ , 19 _____ , directing the defendant, among other things, to pay to the plaintiff the sum of _____ ($ _____) Dollars per week as alimony, plus the sum of _____ ($ _____) Dollars per week per child for the maintenance and support of the infant children _____ , _____ , and _____ , for a total sum of _____ ($ _____) Dollars per week by check or money order at the residence of the plaintiff.

That hereto annexed is a copy of the Judgment of Divorce herein. That the defendant was duly personally served with a copy of said Judgment on the _____ day of _____ , 19 _____ .

That defendant has failed, neglected, and refused to pay me the amounts of money set forth in said Judgment of Divorce during the period commencing _____ , 19 _____ to date.

That the above named defendant has willfully neglected and failed to comply with said Judgment of this Court and he is now in arrears in the sum of _____ ($ _____) Dollars, and no part of which has been paid although duly demanded. That the neglect and refusal of the above named defendant to comply with said Judgment of the Court was calculated to and did defeat, impair, impede, and prejudice the rights and remedies of the above named plaintiff.

That the arrears are computed as follows:

Continued

☐ **EXHIBIT 10.8   Affidavit in Contempt Proceeding—*Continued***

DATE	AMOUNT DUE	AMOUNT PAID	ARREARS
_____	$ _____	$ _____	$ _____
_____	$ _____	none	$ _____
_____	$ _____	$ _____	$ _____
_____	$ _____	none	$ _____
_____	$ _____	none	$ _____
_____	$ _____	$ _____	$ _____
_____	$ _____	none	$ _____
_____	$ _____	$ _____	$ _____
_____	$ _____	none	$ _____
_____	$ _____	$ _____	$ _____
_____	$ _____	none	$ _____

TOTAL ARREARS $ _____

That total arrears are therefore due me in the sum of _____ ($ _____) Dollars.

That it is respectfully submitted that the defendant deliberately does this to defeat and prejudice the rights and remedies of myself and my infant children.

That defendant is employed as a school teacher with the same position that he held at the time of the trial on _____ , 19 ____ , which was only _____ months ago. His income is at least as much as he was earning then, if not more. The defendant is also engaged in private tutoring.

That no order of sequestration has been made herein for the reason that there is no property to sequestrate.

That no bond or security has been given for the payment of said alimony.

That your deponent has been unable to obtain steady employment and is in dire financial straits by reason of the defendant's willful refusal to comply with said Judgment of Divorce.

That no previous application for the relief herein prayed for has been made.

That the reason that an order to show cause herein is requested is that the same is required on an application of this matter by virtue of section 245 of the Domestic Relations Law.

WHEREFORE, an order to show cause is respectfully prayed requiring the defendant to show cause why he should not be punished for contempt for willfully disobeying the Judgment of this Court.

[*Signature*] _____

[*Type Name of Deponent*]

SOURCE: J. Marvins, *McKinney's forms,* 13:131A (1976).

QUALIFIED DOMESTIC RELATIONS ORDER (QDRO)

Under a **QDRO,** the court authorizes the judgment creditor to receive all or a portion of the pension or other retirement benefits that the judgment debtor has available through his employer. The ex-spouse, as judgment creditor, becomes an *alternate payee* under these plans. She cannot, however, receive benefits under the plan that the obligor himself would not have been able to receive. For example, if the obligor is not entitled to a lump-sum payment, the ex-spouse as alternate payee is also subject to this limitation. A child in need of support can also be an alternate payee through a QDRO. For an example of a QDRO, see Exhibit 6.6 in chapter 6.

QUALIFIED MEDICAL CHILD SUPPORT ORDER (QMCSO)

Under a **QMCSO,** a court can require parents to include their children on available group health plans where they work. Insurance companies cannot deny coverage because the child does not live with the parent, does not live in the insurer's service area, is not claimed as a dependent on the parent's tax return, or was born to unmarried parents. The child becomes an *alternate recipient* under the health plan.

UNIFORM RECIPROCAL ENFORCEMENT OF SUPPORT ACT (URESA)

What happens when the defendant leaves the state? As we have seen, a court must have personal jurisdiction over a defendant in order to obtain and enforce an alimony or child support order against him. When the parties no longer live in the same state, the state of the wife or ex-wife may not be able to obtain personal jurisdiction over the husband/father if the latter is not domiciled in the state, or is not physically present in the state (and hence cannot be served with process in the state), or does not have sufficient minimal contacts with the state for the long arm statute to apply. Furthermore, it may be quite impractical for her to travel to the new state of the husband/father to try to find him and obtain a support order against him there.

One remedy in that situation is the *Uniform Reciprocal Enforcement of Support Act* **(URESA).** It authorizes a two-state lawsuit without requiring the aggrieved party to leave her own state. The two states involved are the initiating state and the responding state. The *initiating state* is the state of the *obligee,* the party claiming child support and/or spousal support. The obligee can also be a government agency that wants to be reimbursed for the public assistance it has already paid the obligee(s). The *responding state* is the state of the obligor, the party allegedly owing support.

The obligee starts the process by filing a petition or complaint in a court in the initiating state. The petition identifies the obligor, provides facts that will help locate the obligor, and alleges a support obligation that is currently owed to the obligee.

If the court in the intitiating state determines that further proceedings are warranted, it will send the petition to a court in the responding state. Up to this point, the obligor is not involved. No notice has been sent to the obligor, and there has been no hearing at which the obligor has denied or admitted the support duty.

The responding state now acts to acquire personal jurisdiction over the obligor, e.g., by the service of process on the obligor within the state. The obligee does *not* have to travel to the responding state. The beauty of URESA is that a state official acts on the obligee's behalf in the responding state.

The case against the obligor now proceeds in the court of the responding state. The obligor raises any defenses he may have to the claim that he owes a duty of support to the obligee. Under URESA, the responding state can litigate the question of paternity if it is an issue. Once the court concludes that the duty does exist, it enters a support order against the obligor. The traditional enforcement mechanisms discussed earlier are used where appropriate, e.g., civil contempt, execution, garnishment.

Support payments made by the obligor are sent to the court that issued the order in the responding state. The latter then forwards them to the court in the initiating state, which in turn gives them to the obligee(s).

URESA has been very successful. After some relatively minor revisions, it became known as RURESA: the Revised Uniform Reciprocal Enforcement of Support Act. In 1994 every state had the opportunity to replace RURESA with the Uniform Interstate Family Support Act **(UIFSA).** Though this revision was more substantial, the main features of the interstate collection process remained the same.

█ FULL FAITH AND CREDIT

Assume that an obligee obtains a support judgment in one state and then travels to another state where the obligor now lives (rather than use URESA) to try to enforce the judgment. Can the obligor relitigate the support issue in his state, or is his state required to enforce the earlier judgment against him?

Under the **Full Faith and Credit Clause** of the United States Constitution, one state must give effect to the public acts, e.g., the court judgments, of another state. For example:

> Phyllis obtains a divorce from Bob in Ohio. Bob falls behind in the alimony and child support payments he is obligated to make under the terms of the Ohio divorce judgment. Bob then moves to Kentucky. Phyllis goes to Kentucky to bring a suit against Bob to collect all unpaid installments.

The question is whether Kentucky can relitigate the alimony and child support issues, or whether it must give *full faith and credit* to the Ohio judgment by allowing Phyllis to sue on the Ohio judgment. The answer depends upon the status of the Ohio divorce judgment:

☐ Did the Ohio court have subject-matter jurisdiction over divorce actions?

☐ Did the Ohio court have personal jurisdiction over Bob?

☐ In Ohio, would each unpaid installment (of alimony and child support) be automatically considered a final and nonmodifiable judgment?

If the answer to each of these questions is yes, then the Kentucky court *must* give full faith and credit to the Ohio judgment and permit Phyllis to enforce it against Bob without allowing him to relitigate the alimony and child support obligation. Suppose, however, that no Ohio final judgment exists on unpaid installments until Phyllis makes specific application to an Ohio court for such a judgment and that at the time she brought her Kentucky action, she had not obtained such a judgment. Under these circumstances, a Kentucky court would not be *obliged,* under the Full Faith and Credit Clause, to force Bob to pay all unpaid installments.

Under the doctrine of **comity,** however, a state can decide to give full faith and credit to a foreign judgment even though it is not obliged to do so. It may decide to do so to reduce the burden on an ex-wife seeking back alimony and child support payments. Another example of the application of the comity doctrine involves foreign land decrees. Suppose that as part of the Ohio divorce decree, the Ohio court ordered Bob to transfer title to land he owned in Kentucky to Phyllis. Phyllis then brings an action in Kentucky to force Bob to convey his Kentucky land to her. Generally, a forum state (here, Kentucky) does not have to give full faith and credit to the judgment of a foreign state (Ohio) that affects the title to land in the forum state. The latter state, however, may nevertheless decide to enforce that foreign judgment affecting its land as a matter of comity.

Full Faith and Credit Clause "Full Faith and Credit shall be given in each State to the public Acts, Records, and judicial Proceedings of every other State." Art. IV.

Comity Following the law of another state out of mutual respect, rather than obligation.

█ SUMMARY

A person's residence is the place where he or she is living at a particular time. Domicile is the place where a person has been physically present with the intent to make that place a permanent home; it is the place to which one intends to return when away. In divorce laws, however, the word residence often has the meaning of domicile.

A divorce decree is divisible when only part of it is enforceable. The decree will dissolve the marriage. This part of the decree is enforceable if the court had in rem jurisdiction. If the court also orders alimony, child support, or property division without having personal jurisdiction over the defendant, this part of the decree is not enforceable.

There are times, however, when a party with a valid jurisdictional challenge to a divorce decree will be estopped from bringing the challenge.

Once a court grants a divorce, one of the major concerns of the judgment debtor is how to enforce it. The remedies that are often available include civil contempt, execution, garnishment, attachment, posting security, receivership, constructive trust, prosecution for criminal nonsupport, QDRO, QMCSO, URESA, and UIFSA.

KEY CHAPTER TERMINOLOGY

Uncontested
Migratory Divorce
Foreign Divorce
"Quickie" Divorce
Collusive Divorce
Default Divorce
Divisible Divorce
Bilateral Divorce
Ex Parte Divorce
Dual Divorce
Uncontested Divorce
Contested Divorce
Divorce a Mensa et Thoro
Limited Divorce
Divorce a Vinculo Matrimonii
Residence
Domicile
Emancipated
Operation of Law
Domicile by Choice
Adversarial Hearing
Ex Parte Hearing
Direct Attack
Collateral Attack
Res Judicata

Estoppel
Equitable Estoppel
Foreign
Forum State
Full Faith and Credit
Service of Process
Substituted Service
Jurisdiction
Subject-Matter Jurisdiction
In Rem Jurisdiction
Res
Personal Jurisdiction
Long Arm Statute
Complaint
Summons
Petition
In Forma Pauperis
Pro Se
Guardian ad Litem
Venue
Pleading
Answer
Counterclaim
Discovery
Interrogatories

Deposition
Request for Admissions
Mental or Physical
  Examination
Request for Production
Pendente Lite
Voir Dire
Corroborated
Preponderance of Evidence
Privilege for Marital
  Communications
Default Judgment
Alternative Dispute Resolution
  (ADR)
Interlocutory
Writ of Execution
Garnishment
Constructive Trust
QDRO
QMCSO
URESA
UIFSA
Full Faith and Credit Clause
Comity

11 TAX CONSEQUENCES OF SEPARATION AND DIVORCE

THE ROLE OF TAX LAW IN THE BARGAINING PROCESS

Tax law should play a major role in the representation of divorce clients. Clauses in a separation agreement, for example, may have little relationship to the real world of dollars and cents if their tax consequences are not assessed (and to the extent possible, *bargained for*) before the agreement is signed. Income that once supported one household must now support two (or more) households. Careful tax planning can be of some help in accomplishing this objective.

We need to examine the three major financial components of a separation and divorce: alimony, child support, and property division. In general, the tax law governing these categories is as follows:

☐ The person who pays alimony (the payor) can deduct it.

☐ The person who receives alimony (the recipient or payee) must report it as income.

☐ Child support payments are not deductible to the payor nor reportable as income by the recipient.

☐ Payments pursuant to a property division are not deductible to the payor nor reportable as income by the recipient.

Since alimony is deductible, but child support and property division payments are not, attempts are often made to disguise child support or property division payments as alimony. A major theme of this chapter is to determine when such attempts are legal and when they will be challenged by the Internal Revenue Service (IRS).

Under our *progressive tax system,* every taxpayer does not pay the same tax *rate.* A high-income taxpayer will pay a higher percentage of income as tax than a low-income taxpayer. We refer to these individuals as being in different *tax brackets.* Generally, a deduction is worth more to someone in a high-income bracket than to someone in a lower bracket. The question at the bargaining table is whether the latter will cooperate in allowing the former to take such a deduction. Since a tax advantage to one side may be a distinct tax *dis*advantage to the other side, cooperation will probably be withheld unless something else is offered to offset the disadvantage. To understand the scope of what is negotiable between the parties, we need to understand the fundamentals of tax law and practice in this area.

■ ALIMONY

When certain conditions or tests are met, alimony (or separate-maintenance) payments are deductible to the payor and taxable to the recipient. The payments are:

- ☐ Reported as taxable income on line 11 of the recipient's 1040 return (see Exhibit 11.1), and
- ☐ Deducted from gross income on line 29 of the payor's 1040 return to obtain the latter's **adjusted gross income (AGI)** (refer again to Exhibit 11.1)

Adjusted Gross Income (AGI) The total amount of income received by a taxpayer less allowed deductions.

Since the deduction comes through the determination of adjusted gross income, there is no need to itemize deductions in order to take advantage of it.

Note that line 29 requires the payor to give the name and social security number of the recipient. Failure to do so can result in a $50 penalty fine and a disallowance of the deduction. Providing this information will make it easier for the IRS to check its own records to make sure that the recipient is reporting as income what the payor is deducting as alimony.

Unfortunately, defining alimony can be a complex undertaking. The IRS has its definition *for tax purposes,* and as we shall see, this definition is broader than the traditional notion of alimony as spousal support.

DEDUCTIBLE ALIMONY: THE SEVEN TESTS

When does a payment qualify as alimony for tax purposes?[1] When it meets the seven requirements for alimony listed in Exhibit 11.2. A more thorough discussion of each requirement follows:

- ☐ **Divorce or Separation Agreement**
- ☐ **No Joint Return**
- ☐ **Parties Are Not Members of the Same Household**
- ☐ **Payment in Cash**
- ☐ **No Payment after Death of Recipient**
- ☐ **Payment Is Not Treated as Child Support**
- ☐ **Parties Have Not Exercised Nonalimony Option**

DIVORCE OR SEPARATION AGREEMENT The payment must be to a spouse or former spouse pursuant to and required by a divorce decree or a separation agreement. The decree does not have to be final. A payment ordered

---

1. The rules discussed here on the tax treatment of alimony payments pursuant to a decree of divorce also apply to payments pursuant to a decree of separate maintenance and a decree of annulment. The rules are also limited to payments made after 1984. Different rules apply to payments made before 1985.

☐ **EXHIBIT 11.1   1040 Income Tax Form**

Form **1040**

Department of the Treasury–Internal Revenue Service
U.S. Individual Income Tax Return (T) **1994**

IRS Use Only–Do not write or staple in this space.

For the year Jan. 1–Dec. 31, 1994, or other tax year beginning _____ , 1994, ending _____ , 19 ___   OMB No. 1545-0074

Label
(See
instructions
on page 12.)
Use the IRS
label.
Otherwise,
please print
or type.

L A B E L   H E R E

Your first name and initial	Last name	Your social security number
If a joint return, spouse's first name and initial	Last name	Spouse's social security number
Home address (number and street). If you have a P.O. box, see page 12.	Apt. no.	For Privacy Act and Paperwork Reduction Act Notice, see page 4.
City, town or post office, state, and ZIP code. If you have a foreign address, see page 12.		

Presidential Election Campaign ▶
(See page 12.)

Do you want $3 to go to this fund?
If a joint return, does your spouse want $3 to go to this fund?

Yes | No   Note: Checking "Yes" will not change your tax or reduce your refund.

Filing Status
(See page 12.)

Check only
one box.

1 ☐ Single
2 ☐ Married filing joint return (even if only one had income)
3 ☐ Married filing separate return. Enter spouse's social security no. above and full name here. ▶
4 ☐ Head of household (with qualifying person). (See page 13.) If the qualifying person is a child but not your dependent, enter this child's name here. ▶
5 ☐ Qualifying widow(er) with dependent child (year spouse died ▶ 19 ___). (See page 13.)

Exemptions
(See page 13.)

If more than six
dependents,
see page 14.

6a ☐ Yourself. If your parent (or someone else) can claim you as a dependent on his or her tax return, *do not* check box 6a. But be sure to check the box on line 33b on page 2

b ☐ Spouse

No. of boxes checked on 6a and 6b ___

c Dependents:

(1) Name (first, initial, and last name)	(2) Check if under age 1	(3) If age 1 or older, dependent's social security number	(4) Dependent's relationship to you	(5) No. of months lived in your home in 1994

No. of your children on 6c who:
● lived with you ___
● didn't live with you due to divorce or separation (see page 14) ___
Dependents on 6c not entered above ___

d If your child didn't live with you but is claimed as your dependent under a pre-1985 agreement, check here ▶ ☐

e Total number of exemptions claimed

Add numbers entered on lines above ▶ ___

Income

**Attach
Copy B of your
Forms W-2,
W-2G
1099-R here.**

If you did not
get a W-2, see
page 15.

Enclose, but do
not attach, any
payment with
your return.

7 Wages, salaries, tips, etc. Attach Form(s) W-2 — **7**
8a **Taxable** interest income (see page 15). Attach Schedule B if over $400 — **8a**
b Tax-exempt interest (see page 16). DON'T include on line 8a **8b**
9 Dividend income. Attach Schedule B if over $400 — **9**
10 Taxable refunds, credits, or offsets of state and local income taxes (see page 16) — **10**
11 Alimony received ◀ — **11**
12 Business income or (loss). Attach Schedule C or C-EZ — **12**
13 Capital gain or (loss). If required, attach Schedule D (see page 16) — **13**
14 Other gains or (losses). Attach Form 4797 — **14**
15a Total IRA distributions **15a** ___ b Taxable amount (see page 17) **15b**
16a Total pensions and annuities **16a** ___ b Taxable amount (see page 17) **16b**
17 Rental real estate, royalties, partnerships, S corporations, trusts, etc. Attach Schedule E — **17**
18 Farm income or (loss). Attach Schedule F — **18**
19 Unemployment compensation (see page 18) — **19**
20a Social security benefits **20a** ___ b Taxable amount (see page 18) **20b**
21 Other income. List type and amount–see page 18 ___ — **21**
22 Add the amounts in the far right column for lines 7 through 21. This is your **total income** ▶ — **22**

Recipient reports alimony as income.

**Adjustments
to Income**

Caution: See
instructions . . ▶

23a Your IRA deduction (see page 19) **23a**
b Spouse's IRA deduction (see page 19) **23b**
24 Moving expenses. Attach Form 3903 or 3903-F **24**
25 One-half of self-employment tax **25**
26 Self-employed health insurance deduction (see page 21) **26**
27 Keogh retirement plan and self-employed SEP deduction **27**
28 Penalty on early withdrawal of savings **28**
29 Alimony paid. Recipient's SSN ▶ ___ **29**
30 Add lines 23a through 29. These are your **total adjustments** ▶ — **30**

Payor of alimony reports payments as adjustment to income. You deduct alimony from gross income to obtain your adjusted gross income.

**Adjusted
Gross Income**

31 Subtract line 30 from line 22. This is your **adjusted gross income**. If less than $25,296 and a child lived with you (less than $9,000 if a child didn't live with you), see "Earned Income Credit" on page 27 ▶ — **31**

Cat. No. 11320B   Form **1040** (1994)

A payment qualifies as alimony when:

1. The payment is to a spouse or former spouse under a divorce decree or separation agreement.
2. The parties do not file a joint return with each other.
3. The parties are not members of the same household when the payment is made. (This third requirement applies only if the parties are separated under a decree of divorce or separate maintenance.)
4. The payment is in cash.
5. There is no obligation to make any payment (in cash or other property) after the death of the recipient.
6. The payment is not treated as child support.
7. The parties have not exercised the option of treating qualifying alimony payments as nonalimony.

☐ **EXHIBIT 11.2**
Requirements for Alimony

by an *interlocutory* (interim or nonfinal) decree or a decree *pendente lite* (while awaiting the court's final decree) can also qualify.

Note that there is no specific requirement that the payment of alimony be for the *support* of the recipient, although we normally think of this as the purpose of alimony. *To qualify as alimony, a payment does not have to discharge an obligation of support.* The great attraction of alimony to the payor is its deductibility. The fact that alimony, for tax purposes, is not limited to spousal support is an open invitation to payors to try to fit different kinds of payments under the rubric of alimony to take advantage of this deductibility feature. Later we will examine the extent to which such efforts can succeed.

Finally, if a spouse makes an *additional* payment beyond what is required by the divorce or separation agreement, the additional payment is not alimony for tax purposes.

EXAMPLE 1 A 1994 separation agreement requires Linda to pay her ex-husband, Fred, a total of $1,000 per month in alimony. Assume that this amount fulfills all the requirements of deductible alimony. Hence, Linda can deduct each $1,000 payment and Fred must report it as income. During the last seven months of the year, Linda decides to increase her alimony payments to $3,000 each month in order to cover some extra expenses Fred is incurring.

Linda may *not* deduct the extra $14,000 ($2,000 × 7 months) she voluntarily added, and Fred does not have to report this $14,000 as income on his return. This is so even if state law considers the entire $3,000 payment each month to be alimony. Under *federal tax* law, voluntary alimony payments are not deductible.

NO JOINT RETURN   The parties must not file a joint return with each other at the time the attempt is made to deduct the alimony.

PARTIES ARE NOT MEMBERS OF THE SAME HOUSEHOLD   The *same-household* requirement applies when the parties have been separated under a decree of divorce.[2] (Note that two people living in physically separate rooms

---

2. As indicated earlier, references to a divorce decree include decrees of separate maintenance. See footnote 1.

are still considered part of the same household.) If there is no divorce decree, alimony payments can be deductible even if the parties are still living in the same household, so long as the other requirements for *deductible alimony* are met.

There is a one-month grace period for those separated by divorce. A payment made while the parties are together in the same household can be deductible if one party is preparing to move and does, in fact, move within one month after the payment.

EXAMPLE 2 Jack and Tara live at 100 Elm Street. They are divorced on January 1, 1995. Jack is obligated to pay Tara $500 a month in alimony on the first of each month. He makes his first payment January 1, 1995. He moves out of the Elm Street house on February 15, 1995.

The January 1, 1995, payment is *not* deductible. Since the parties have a divorce decree, they must not be living in the same household at the time of the alimony payment. Jack and Tara were both living at 100 Elm Street—the same household—at the time of that payment. The one-month grace period does not apply since Jack did not move out within a month of this payment. If he had left earlier (e.g., January 29, 1995), the payment *would* have been deductible. Of course, all payments after February 15, 1995 (when they opened separate households) are deductible, if the other requirements for deductible alimony are met.

PAYMENT IN CASH   Only *cash* payments, including checks and money orders, qualify.

EXAMPLE 3 Under the terms of a separation agreement and divorce decree, Bob:
- ☐ Gives Mary, his ex-wife, a car
- ☐ Paints her house
- ☐ Lets her use his mother's house
- ☐ Gives her stocks, bonds, or an annuity contract

The value of these items cannot be deducted as alimony since they are not in cash.

Can cash payments made by the payor to a third party be deducted as alimony?

EXAMPLE 4 Bob sends $1,000 to Mary's landlord to pay her rent. He also sends $800 to Mary's college to cover part of her tuition costs and $750 to Mary's bank to pay the mortgage on the house she owns.

Can Bob deduct any of these payments as alimony, and does Mary have to report them as income? The answer is yes, if the cash payment to the third party is required by the divorce decree or by the separation agreement, or, when not so required, if Mary sends Bob a written request to make the cash payment to the third party. The written request must state that Bob and Mary both intend the payments to the third party to be treated as alimony. If all the other tests for alimony are met, the payment to the third party is deductible by the payor and includible in the income of the recipient on whose behalf the payment is made.

Suppose that the third party is an insurance company.

EXAMPLE 5 Bob pays an annual premium of $1,700 on a life insurance policy on his life with Mary as the beneficiary.

Can he deduct these premiums as alimony? The answer is yes, but only if two conditions are met:

☐ The payor (Bob) is obligated to make these premium payments by the divorce decree or separation agreement.

☐ The beneficiary (Mary) *owns* the policy so that the payor cannot change the beneficiary.

NO PAYMENT AFTER DEATH OF RECIPIENT If the payor is obligated (under the divorce decree or separation agreement) to make payments after the death of the recipient, none of the payments made after *or before* the death of the recipient qualify as alimony. Here the IRS is trying to catch a blatant and improper attempt to disguise property division as alimony in order to take advantage of a deduction.

EXAMPLE 6 Under the terms of a separation agreement, Bob agrees to pay Mary $20,000 a year "in alimony" for ten years. If Mary dies within the ten years, Bob will make the remaining annual payments to Mary's estate. In the sixth year of the agreement, after Bob has paid Mary $120,000 (6 years × $20,000), Mary dies. For the next four years, Bob makes the remaining annual payments totaling $80,000 (4 years × $20,000) to Mary's estate.

All of the payments made by Bob will be disallowed as alimony—the entire $200,000 covering the periods before and after Mary's death. It makes no difference that the separation agreement called the payments "alimony." To qualify as deductible alimony, one of the tests is that the payor must have no liability for payments after the death of the recipient.

Whenever the payor must make payments beyond the death of the recipient, there is a strong suspicion that the payments are really part of a property division arrangement. Most normal debts continue in effect after the death of either party. If, for example, I pay you $3,500 to buy your car, and you die before delivering the car to me, it is clear that your obligation to give me the car survives your death. Your estate would have to give me the car. The same is true of a property division debt. Assume that Bob is obligated under a property division agreement to transfer a house to Mary, his ex-wife. If Bob dies before making this transfer, his estate can be forced to complete the transfer to Mary. Property division debts survive the death of either party. On the other hand, it is very rare for a "real" alimony debt to continue after the death of the recipient. After the recipient dies, he or she does not need alimony!

EXAMPLE 7 At the time of their separation, Mary had a separate career in which she earned a high salary. Bob owned a going business valued at $400,000, which he started when he married Mary. Bob and Mary agreed that she should have a substantial share of this business as part of the property division between them. But Bob does not want to sell the business in order to give Mary her share. In the negotiations, Mary asks for $150,000, payable immediately. Bob agrees that $150,000 is a fair amount, but he doesn't have it. Hence, he counters by offering her $200,000 payable over ten years in $20,000 annual payments to be labeled as "alimony" in their separation agreement. If Mary dies within the ten years, Bob will make the annual payments to Mary's estate. The extra $50,000 is added to offset the fact that Mary will have to wait in order to receive all her money and will have to pay income tax on whatever Bob declares as deductible alimony.

Again, this arrangement will not work. There are ways to disguise property division as alimony, but this is not one of them. The $200,000 can never be deductible alimony since the parties planned to continue the payments after the death of the recipient.

The IRS will reach the same conclusion if the payor agrees to make a substitute payment to a third party on the death of the recipient or a lump-sum payment to the estate of the recipient after his or her death.

PAYMENT IS NOT TREATED AS CHILD SUPPORT   Child support is neither deductible by the payor nor includible in the income of the recipient. But what is child support? This question is easy to answer if the divorce decree or separation agreement specifically designates or fixes a payment (or part of a payment) as child support.

EXAMPLE 8 Under the terms of a divorce decree, Jane must pay Harry $2,000 a month, of which $1,600 is designated for the support of their child in the custody of Harry.

The $1,600 has been fixed as child support. Hence, it is not deductible by Jane nor includible in the income of Harry. This remains true even if the amount so designated varies from time to time.

Suppose, however, payments are made to the parent with custody of the children, but the parties say nothing about child support in their separation agreement, and the divorce decree is equally silent. The payments may even be labeled "alimony." In such a case, the IRS will suspect that the parties are trying to disguise child support payments as alimony in order to trigger a deduction for the payor. The suspicion will be even stronger if the separation agreement or divorce decree states that the payments are to be *reduced* upon the happening of certain events or contingencies that relate to the child's need for support.

EXAMPLE 9 Under the terms of a separation agreement, Bill will pay Grace $2,000 a month, "in alimony," which will be reduced to $800 a month when their child leaves the household and gets a job.

Contingency An event that may or may not occur.

The parties are trying to disguise $1,200 a month as alimony, although it is fairly obvious that this amount is child support. Otherwise, why would the parties reduce the payment at a time when the child would no longer need support? What other reason would the parties have to add such a **contingency?** The device will not work.

☐ **Child Support Improperly Disguised as Alimony** The IRS will conclude that a payment is child support rather than alimony when the amount of the payment is to be reduced:

1. On the happening of a contingency relating to the child, or
2. At a time that can be clearly associated with a contingency relating to the child.

A contingency relates to a child when the contingency depends on an event that relates to that child.

EXAMPLE 10 The separation agreement of Bill and Mary Smith says that an "alimony" payment from Bill to Mary will be reduced by a designated amount when their son, Bob does any of the following:

- ☐ Reaches a specified age (see discussion below on when the reduction is to occur at the age of majority)
- ☐ Attains a specified income level
- ☐ Dies
- ☐ Marries
- ☐ Leaves school
- ☐ Leaves home (temporarily or permanently)
- ☐ Gains employment

Since each of these contingencies depends on an event that obviously relates to the child, no alimony deduction is allowed.

A payor will often want to reduce a payment when the child reaches the age of majority, which is usually 18 under state law. Will the IRS treat this reduction as an indication that alimony is being improperly disguised as child support? From what we have said thus far, one would expect the answer to be an unqualified "yes." But this is not necessarily so. The rule is as follows:

> ☐ **Reduction upon Age of Majority: Presumption of Child Support** The IRS will *presume* that a payment is child support if the reduction is to occur not more than six months before or after the child reaches the age of majority in the state.

Thus, if the reduction is to occur *more* than six months before or after the child reaches the age of majority, it will be treated as an alimony reduction.

EXAMPLE 11 Leo, Elaine, and their son Fred live in a state where the age of majority is 18. Fred was born on March 13, 1972. Leo and Elaine are divorced on January 12, 1980. Under the terms of the divorce decree, Elaine gets custody of Fred, and Leo must pay Elaine $2,000 a month in "alimony" until July 1, 1990, when the monthly payments are reduced to $1,200.

On these facts, the IRS will presume that the amount of the reduction is child support. Fred reaches the age of majority on March 13, 1990, when he turns 18. The reduction occurs on July 1, 1990, four months afterward. Since this reduction occurs "not more than six months . . . after the child reaches the age of majority," the presumption of child support applies.[3] The IRS will presume that the amount of the reduction ($800) is child support.

EXAMPLE 12 Same facts as in Example 11 except that the reduction is to occur on March 13, 1991.

On these facts, the presumption of child support does not apply. The reduction occurs one year after Fred reaches the age of majority, which of course is more than six months. The entire $2,000 can be deductible alimony.

---

3. This presumption can be rebutted by showing that the time at which the payments are to be reduced was determined independently of any contingencies relating to the children. For example, the payment period might be one customarily provided in the state, such as a period equal to one-half the duration of the marriage.

PARTIES HAVE NOT EXERCISED NONALIMONY OPTION Assume that all of the first six tests for determining alimony (see Exhibit 11.2) are met by the parties. As a result, the payor can deduct the payments and the recipient must include them in income. But suppose the parties do *not* want the payments to be deductible/includible. It may be, for example, that both parties are in the same tax bracket and hence neither would benefit significantly more than the other by having the tax alimony rules apply. They can decide to treat otherwise qualifying alimony payments as *nonalimony.* This is done by including a provision in the separation agreement or by asking the court to include a provision in the divorce decree that the payments will *not* be deductible to the payor and will be excludible from the income of the recipient.

The designation of nondeductibility/nonincludibility must be attached to the recipient's tax return for every year in which it is effective.

THE RECAPTURE RULE: FRONT LOADING OF PAYMENTS

A common tactic of a party who wants to try to disguise property division payments as alimony is to make substantial payments shortly after the divorce or separation, i.e., to **front load** the payments.

Front Load To try to disguise alimony as property division by making substantial "alimony" payments shortly after the separation or divorce.

EXAMPLE 13 Jim runs a cleaning business, which he developed during his marriage to Pat. The value of the business is $180,000 on the date of their divorce. During their negotiations for the separation agreement, they both agree that each should receive an equal share of the business, which Jim wants to continue to run after the divorce. They are clearly thinking about a property division. Of course, any payments pursuant to a property division are not deductible. Jim suggests a different route: he will pay Pat $30,000 a year in "alimony" for the first three years after their separation in return for a release of all her interest in the business. To secure this arrangement, Jim gives Pat a lien on the business until he pays the $90,000. For each of the three years, the payor (Jim) takes a $30,000 deduction, and the recipient (Pat) includes $30,000 in her income.

Recapture Rule Tax liability will be recalculated when the parties improperly attempt to disguise property division as alimony by front loading.

We said earlier there is no requirement that alimony be for the support of the recipient. Accordingly, in theory it is not improper to try to disguise property division payments as deductible alimony. But the parties must not go too far. The **recapture rule** is designed to catch parties who have gone too far through excessive front loading. To this end, the rule limits the extent to which large payments made over a relatively short period can qualify as deductible alimony. When the rule applies, its effect is to change the tax treatment of past payments by:

☐ Requiring the payor to remove the deduction previously taken for payments, and hence to include such payments in the calculation of the payor's income, and

☐ Allowing the recipient who previously included the alimony in income (and paid taxes on it) to deduct it from income so that taxes do not have to be paid on it

To apply the rule, let us look at a three-year period, beginning with the first calendar year that a payment qualifies as alimony. (This first year is sometimes referred to as the first *post-separation year,* which is not necessarily the year the parties separated.) The second and third years are the next two calendar years whether or not payments are made during these years.

EXAMPLE 14 Al and Jane were divorced on February 3, 1992. Under the terms of the divorce decree, Jane pays Al the following amounts of "alimony:"

Year	Amount
1992	$60,000
1993	40,000
1994	20,000

To figure the amounts that must be recaptured, if any, use the worksheet in Exhibit 11.3. In our example, $22,500 must be recaptured by Jane, the payor. She must show this amount as income on line 11 of her 1994 return. (Line 11 now says "Alimony received." She must cross out the word "received" and write in the word "recapture," so that 11 will read "Alimony recapture.") Al, the payee, can deduct $22,500 on line 29 of his 1994 return. (Line 29 now says "Alimony paid." He must cross out the word "paid" and write in the word "recapture" so that line 29 will read "Alimony recapture.")[4]

PROPERTY DIVISION

In this section our focus will be the division of property between spouses that fairly accounts for their mutual efforts in obtaining and/or improving the property during the marriage. Before discussing the tax consequences of such a property division, we need to review some basic terminology. The following example (at the top of page 244) will be used to help explain this terminology.

☐ **EXHIBIT 11.3 Recapture Worksheet**

WORKSHEET FOR RECAPTURE OF ALIMONY

Note: Do not enter less than zero on any line.

1. Alimony paid in **2nd year**		$40,000	
2. Alimony paid in **3rd year**	$20,000		
3. Floor	$15,000		
4. Add lines 2 and 3		35,000	
5. Subtract line 4 from line 1			$ 5,000
6. Alimony paid in **1st year**		60,000	
7. Adjusted alimony paid in **2nd year** (line 1 less line 5)	35,000		
8. Alimony paid in **3rd year**	20,000		
9. Add lines 7 and 8	55,000		
10. Divide line 9 by 2	27,500		
11. Floor	$15,000		
12. Add lines 10 and 11		42,500	
13. Subtract line 12 from line 6			*17,500
14. **Recapture alimony.** Add lines 5 and 13			$22,500

*If you deducted alimony paid, report this amount as income on line 11, Form 1040.
 If you reported alimony received, deduct this amount on line 29, Form 1040.

---

4. There are a number of important exceptions to the recapture rule. Regardless of the amount of the payment, the recapture rule does not apply (a) to payments under a temporary support order before the divorce or separation, (b) to payments required over a period of at least three calendar years of a fixed part of the payor's income from a business or property, or from compensation for employment or self-employment, or (c) to payments that end because the payor or recipient dies or the recipient remarries.

EXAMPLE 15 Tom buys a house in 1970 for $60,000. He spends $10,000 to add a new room. In 1981, he sells the house to a stranger for $100,000.

☐ **Transferor** The person who transfers property. Tom is the transferor.

☐ **Transferee** The person to whom property is transferred. The stranger is the transferee.

☐ **Appreciation** An increase in value. Tom's house appreciated by $40,000 (from $60,000 to $100,000). He has made a profit, called a *gain.* The gain, however, is *not* $40,000. See the definition for *adjusted basis* below.

☐ **Depreciation** A decrease in value. If the highest price Tom could have obtained for his house had been $55,000, the house would have depreciated by $5,000.

☐ **Realize** To benefit from or receive. Normally, *income, gain,* or *loss* are realized when they are received. If Tom could sell his house for $100,000, but he decides not to do so, he has not realized any income. He has a "paper" gain only. He does not have to pay taxes on a gain until he has realized a gain, e.g., by actually selling the house.

☐ **Fair Market Value** The price that could be obtained in an open market between a willing buyer and a willing seller dealing *at arm's length.* A sale between a parent and a child will usually not be at fair market value since the fact that they are related will probably affect the price paid. It is possible for a happily married husband and wife to sell something to each other at fair market value, but the likelihood is that they will not. In our example, Tom sold his house for $100,000 to a stranger. There is no indication that the buyer or seller was pressured into the transaction or that either had any special relationship with each other that might have affected the price or the terms of the deal. The price paid, therefore, was the fair market value.

☐ **Basis** The initial capital investment, usually the cost of the property. Tom's basis in his house is $60,000.

☐ **Adjusted Basis** The basis of the property after adjustments are made. The basis is either adjusted upward (increased) by the amount of *capital improvements* (i.e., structural improvements on the property) or adjusted downward. Tom added a room to his house—a structural improvement. His basis ($60,000) is increased by the amount of the capital expenditure ($10,000), giving him an adjusted basis of $70,000.

When Tom sold his house for $100,000, he *realized* income. To determine whether he realized a gain or profit, we need to compare this figure with his adjusted basis. The amount of gain for tax purposes is determined as follows:

SALE PRICE − ADJUSTED BASIS = TAXABLE GAIN
($100,000)   ($70,000)   ($30,000)

Tom must declare this gain of $30,000 on his tax return. Of course, if the sale price had been *less* than the adjusted basis, he would have realized a loss. If, for example, he had sold the house for $65,000, his loss would have been $5,000 ($70,000 − $65,000).

TAX CONSEQUENCES OF A PROPERTY DIVISION

A property division can be in cash or in other property. To illustrate:

CASH: Ex-wife receives a lump sum of $50,000 (or five yearly payments of $10,000) in exchange for the release of any rights she may have in property acquired during the marriage.

OTHER PROPERTY: Ex-wife receives the marital home, and the ex-husband receives stocks and the family business. They both release any rights they may have in property acquired during the marriage.

Cash property divisions rarely pose difficulties unless the parties are trying to disguise property division as alimony in order to take advantage of the deductibility of alimony. We already discussed when such attempts will be unsuccessful. A true property division in cash is a nontaxable event; nothing is deducted and nothing is included in the income of either party. The IRS will assume that what was exchanged was of equal value.

Suppose, however, that property other than cash is transferred in a property division and that the property so transferred had *appreciated* in value since the time it had been acquired by the transferor. Our problem is twofold:

☐ When *appreciated* property is transferred as part of a property division, is any gain or loss realized?

☐ What is the basis of such property in the hands of the transferee?

To examine these questions in concrete terms, let us return to Tom and his house in Example 15. Suppose that instead of selling the house to a stranger, he transfers it to his wife.

EXAMPLE 16 Tom buys a house in 1970 for $60,000. He spends $10,000 to add a new room. In 1981, on the date of his divorce, he transfers the house to his wife, Tara, as part of a property division that they negotiated. Tara releases any rights, e.g., dower, that she may have in his property. On the date of the transfer, the fair market value of the house is $100,000.

Note that all of this occurred before 1984. The law changed in 1984, but in order to understand the change, we need to understand the old law. The first question in Example 16 is whether Tom realized a gain of $30,000 at the time of the transfer to his ex-wife. Prior to 1984, the answer was yes. The United States Supreme Court so held in *United States v. Davis*, 370 U.S. 65, 82 S. Ct. 1190, 8 L. Ed. 2d 335 (1962). Hence, when Tom transferred a $100,000 home to his ex-wife as part of a property division, he received no deduction, since the transfer did not qualify as alimony, and he had to pay tax on his realized gain of $30,000. In answer to the second question, the basis of the property in the hands of Tara, the transferee, was the fair market value of the property at the time of the transfer, here $100,000. What Tara gave Tom (i.e., a release of her rights in his property) was assumed to be equal in value to what she received.

EXAMPLE 17 Same facts as in Example 16. In 1983 Tara sells the home to a stranger for $105,000. Assume that she made no capital improvements in the property since she acquired it from her ex-husband, Tom, in 1981.

Tara has realized a gain of $5,000. When she received the property, her basis was its fair market value, $100,000. Since she did not improve the property, this was her adjusted basis when she sold it in 1983:

SALE PRICE − ADJUSTED BASIS = TAXABLE GAIN
($105,000)   ($100,000)   ($5,000)

Everybody was unhappy about these tax rules—except the transferee, who was delighted to have fair market value as the basis. Transferors complained about being hit twice. "It's bad enough having to turn over property to my ex-wife that I can't deduct. On top of it all, I owe tax to the IRS on the appreciation." The IRS was also unhappy, because many transferors were neglecting to report the gain that resulted from the appreciation. Furthermore, the high basis of the property in the hands of the transferee (i.e., fair market value) meant that the IRS often collected very little tax when the transferee sold the property to someone else. See Example 17.

In 1984 Congress made a radical change in the law, which had the effect of overruling *United States v. Davis.* Under the new law, no gain or loss is recognized upon the transfer of appreciated property, and the adjusted basis in the property of the transferor is carried over to become the transferee's basis.

EXAMPLE 18 Use the same facts as in Examples 16 and 17 except that the date of the divorce, when Tom transferred the house to Tara, is 1985 (rather than 1981), and the date Tara sold the house to a stranger is 1986 (rather than 1983).

The new rules apply. Tom does *not* pay a tax on the appreciation at the time of the transfer to Tara. And the tax picture at the time Tara sells the property is substantially different:

SALE PRICE − ADJUSTED BASIS = TAXABLE GAIN
($105,000)   ($70,000)   ($35,000)

Tara takes over Tom's adjusted basis at the time she receives the property from him—$70,000. This becomes her basis when she sells it to someone else.

Needless to say, it is essential that a spouse know the adjusted basis of the property in the hands of the other spouse before accepting that property as part of a property division. It is meaningless, for example, to be told that property is "worth $150,000" on the market unless you are also told what the adjusted basis of that property is.

These new rules do not apply to every transfer of property between spouses or ex-spouses. We turn now to those that are covered.

PROPERTY TRANSFERS COVERED

In general, the new tax rules governing a property division apply to property transfers that are *incident to a divorce.* A property transfer is incident to a divorce when the transfer:

☐ Occurs within one year after the date on which the marriage ends, *or*
☐ Is related to the ending of the marriage

A property transfer is related to the ending of the marriage *if* it occurs within six years after the date on which the marriage ends *and* is made under a divorce or separation instrument.

A property transfer that is not made under a divorce or separation instrument, or that does not occur within six years after the end of the marriage is *presumed* to be unrelated to the ending of the marriage, unless the parties can show that some business or legal factors prevented an earlier transfer of the property.

EXAMPLE 19 Gabe solely owns a garage and a residence. He and his wife, Janet, are divorced on January 10, 1985. Pursuant to a property division that is spelled out in their separation agreement, Gabe will keep the residence but will transfer the garage to Janet on March 13, 1992.

Was the transfer of the garage incident to a divorce? It did not occur within a year of the ending of the marriage. But was it related to the ending of the marriage? It did not occur within six years of the ending of the marriage. The transfer was made just over seven years after the divorce. We are not told why the parties waited this long after the divorce, but there is no evidence of business or legal factors that prevented an earlier transfer. Hence the IRS will *presume* that the transfer was not related to the ending of the marriage, and the new tax rules discussed above will *not* apply to the transfer.

☐ **Tax Treatment of Payments and Transfers Pursuant to Post-1984 Divorce Agreements and Decrees**

	Payor	**Recipient**
Alimony	Deduction from gross income.	Included in gross income.
Alimony recapture	Included in gross income of the third year.	Deducted from gross income of the third year.
Child support	Not deductible.	Not includible in income.
Property settlement	Not included in gross income. Not deductible.	Not included in gross income. Not deductible; basis for the property is the same as the transferor's basis if the transfer is incident to a divorce.

SOURCE: West's Federal Taxation: Individual Income Taxes, 4–22 (1994).

▬▬▬ LEGAL AND RELATED FEES IN OBTAINING A DIVORCE

Obtaining a divorce can be expensive. In addition to attorney fees, one or both parties may have to hire an accountant, actuary, and appraiser. Only two types of such fees are deductible:

☐ Fees paid for *tax* advice in connection with a divorce

☐ Fees paid to obtain *alimony* included in gross income

Other fees are not deductible. For example, you cannot deduct legal fees paid to negotiate the most advantageous or financially beneficial property division.

Bills from professionals received by a taxpayer should include a breakdown showing the amount charged for each service performed.

EXAMPLE 20

For representation in divorce case $9,000
For tax advice in connection with the divorce   800
Total bill..$9,800
Only $800 is deductible.

EXAMPLE 21

For representation in divorce case $6,500
For services in obtaining alimony 1,200
Total bill...$7,700

Only $1,200 is deductible.

ASSIGNMENT 11.1

John and Carol are divorced on September 1, 1991. Their separation agreement requires John to pay Carol $500 a week for her support until she dies. Use the guidelines of this chapter to answer the following questions that present a number of variations in the case of John and Carol.

a. Carol has an automobile accident. To help her with medical bills, John sends her a check for $900 with the following note: "Here's my monthly $500 payment plus an extra $400 alimony to help you with your medical bills." Can John deduct the entire $900 as alimony?

b. A year after the divorce, Carol has trouble paying her state income tax bill of $1,200. John wants to give her a gift of $1,200 in addition to his regular $500 monthly alimony. He sends $1,200 to the state tax department on her behalf. Can John deduct the $1,200 as alimony?

c. Assume that in the September 1, 1991 divorce, Carol is awarded $1,500 a month in alimony, effective immediately and payable on the first of each month. John makes a payment on September 1, 1991. (He also paid her $1,000 for her support on August 1, 1991, before they went to court.) During all this time, John lived in the basement of their home, which has a separate entrance. He moves into his own apartment in another town on October 25, 1991. Which of the following 1991 payments, if any, are deductible: $1,000 (on August 1), $1,500 (on September 1), and $1,500 (on October 1)?

d. Assume that under the divorce decree, John must make annual alimony payments to Carol of $30,000, ending on the earlier of the expiration of fifteen years or the death of Carol. If Carol dies before the expiration of the fifteen-year period, John must pay Carol's estate the difference between the total amount he would have paid her if she survived, minus the amount actually paid. Carol dies after the tenth year in which payments are made. John now pays her estate $150,000 ($450,000 − $300,000). How much of the $300,000 paid before her death is deductible alimony? How much of the $150,000 lump sum is deductible alimony?

e. Assume that under the terms of the separation agreement, John will pay Carol $200 a month in child support for their only child, Nancy, and $900 a month as alimony. If Nancy marries, however, the $900 payment will be reduced to $400 a month. What is deductible?

f. Assume that under the terms of the separation agreement, John will pay Carol $200 a month as child support for their only child, Nancy, and $900 a month as alimony. While Nancy is away at boarding school, however, the $900 payment will be reduced to $400 a month. What is deductible?

ASSIGNMENT 11.2

a. Greg was born on July 31, 1980. He is the only child of Bill and Karen. Under the terms of their separation agreement, which becomes effective on December 5, 1995, Bill is to have custody of Greg, and Karen is to pay him $4,000 a month in alimony. The agreement specifies that "none of the alimony is to be used for child support." On April 15, 1998, the alimony payment is to be reduced to $2,200 a month. What will be deductible?

b. Millie pays Paul the following amounts of alimony under the terms of her 1987 divorce decree:

Year	Amount
1987	$25,000
1988	4,000
1989	4,000

What amounts, if any, must be recaptured?

c. Under a 1989 separation agreement and divorce decree, Helen transfers a building she solely owns to her ex-husband, Ken, in exchange for his release of any rights he has in other property that Helen acquired during the marriage. The transfer is made on the day of the divorce. Helen had bought the building in 1986 for $1,000,000. In 1987 she made $200,000 worth of capital improvements in the building. Its fair market value on the date she transfers it to Ken is $1,500,000. A week later, however, the market crashes and Ken is forced to sell the building for $800,000. What are the tax consequences of these transactions?

d. Same facts as (c) except assume that all of these transactions occurred before 1984. What are the tax consequences of the transactions?

e. Dan and Karen are negotiating a separation agreement in contemplation of a divorce that they expect to occur within six months of today's date. Karen wants $1,000 a month in alimony, and she wants Dan to pay all of her legal fees. Dan agrees to do so. Assume that there will be no difficulty deducting the $1,000 a month under the alimony rules. Dan would also like to deduct what he pays for her legal fees, which are anticipated to be $12,000, of which $3,000 will be for obtaining alimony from Dan. What options exist for Dan?

▮▮▮▮ SUMMARY

Since a husband and wife are often in different tax brackets, the issue of who receives a tax deduction for a certain payment can be extremely important. Tax consequences, therefore, should be a part of the negotiation process in a separation and divorce.

If seven tests are met, alimony can be deducted by the payor but then must be declared as income by the recipient:

1. The payment must be to a spouse or former spouse and must be required by a divorce decree or separation agreement.

2. The parties must not file a joint return with each other.

3. The parties must not be members of the same household if they are separated under a decree of divorce.

4. The payment must be in cash.

5. The payor must be under no obligation to make payments after the death of the recipient.

6. The payment must not be improperly disguised as child support.

7. The parties must not elect to treat qualifying alimony payments as nonalimony.

If substantial payments are made shortly after a divorce or separation, the IRS will suspect that the parties are trying to disguise nondeductible, property division payments as deductible alimony payments. Such excessive front loading may result in a recalculation of taxes paid in prior years in order to recapture improper deductions for alimony.

In a property division incident to a divorce, property is transferred from one ex-spouse to the other. The property can be cash (e.g., $50,000) or noncash (e.g., a house). When there is a transfer of cash, none of it is deducted by the transferor, and none of it is included in the income of the transferee. When there is a transfer of noncash property that has appreciated in value, the following rules apply:

1. The transferor does not deduct anything.

2. The transferee does not include anything in income.

3. The transferor does not have to pay taxes on the amount of the appreciation.

4. The basis of the property in the hands of the transferee is the same basis that the property had in the hands of the transferor.

A fee paid to your own attorney, accountant, or other professional is deductible if for tax advice in connection with a divorce, or if paid to help you obtain alimony that is included in gross income.

KEY CHAPTER TERMINOLOGY

Adjusted Gross Income (AGI)	Transferor	Realize
Contingency	Transferee	Fair Market Value
Front Load	Appreciation	Basis
Recapture Rule	Depreciation	Adjusted Basis

The Legal Rights of Women

Man is, or should be, woman's protector and defender. The natural and proper timidity and delicacy which belongs to the female sex evidently unfits it for many of the occupations of civil life. The constitution of the family organization, which is founded in the divine ordinance, as well as in the nature of things, indicates the domestic sphere as that which properly belongs to the domain and function of womanhood . . . The paramount destiny and mission of woman are to fulfill the noble and benign offices of wife and mother. This is the law of the Creator. *Bradwell v. Illinois,* 83 U.S. (16 Wall.) 130, 140–41, 21 L. Ed. 442 (1872)

No longer is the female destined solely for the home and the rearing of the family, and only the male for the marketplace, and the world of ideas. *Stanton v. Stanton,* 412 U.S. 7, 15, 95 S. Ct. 1373, 1378, 43 L. Ed. 2d 688 (1975).

▧ THE STATUS OF WOMEN AT COMMON LAW

Today, a married woman would consider it condescending to be told that she has the right to:

☐ Make her own will

☐ Own her own property

☐ Make a contract in her own name

☐ Be a juror

☐ Vote

☐ Bring a suit and be sued

☐ Execute a deed

There was a time in our history, however, when a married woman could engage in none of these activities, at least not without the consent of her husband. For example, she could not bring a suit against a third party unless her husband agreed to join in it. Upon marriage, any personal property that she owned automatically became her husband's. If she committed a crime in the presence of her husband, the law assumed that he forced her to commit it. If she worked outside the home, her husband was entitled to her earnings. In short, at common law, the husband and wife were considered one person, and the one person was the husband![1]

While a great deal has happened to change the status of married women, not all sex discrimination has been eliminated.

Married Women's Property Acts Statutes removing all or most of the legal disabilities imposed on women as to the disposition of their property.

■■■■■ OWNING AND DISPOSING OF PROPERTY

Most states have enacted **Married Women's Property Acts** that remove the disabilities married women suffered at common law. Under the terms of most of these statutes, women are given the right to own and dispose of property in the same manner as men.

ASSIGNMENT 12.1

Mary and Thad are married. Mary is a doctor and Thad is an architect. Before the marriage, Thad incurred a $35,000 debt at a local bank for his own education expenses. He is now in default on the loan. To collect this debt, can the bank reach a vacation home that is solely owned by Mary? Answer this question based on the following assumptions:

a. Mary acquired title to the vacation home as an inheritance from her uncle before she married Thad.

b. Mary acquired title to the vacation home as an inheritance from her uncle during her marriage to Thad.

c. Mary acquired title to the vacation home by buying it from a stranger solely from her own earnings as a doctor during her marriage to Thad.

d. Mary acquired title to the vacation home by buying it from Thad for $1 during the marriage. Thad inherited it from his mother before he married Mary. The sale to Mary was made just before Thad discovered that he was going to default on the bank loan. (See the next section on "Contracts and Conveyances.")

■■■■■ CONTRACTS AND CONVEYANCES

Conveyance The transfer of an interest in land.

Today women have the power to enter into all forms of contracts and **conveyances** in their own names, independent of their husbands. If, however, both spouses own property together, the wife normally must have the consent of her husband—and vice versa—to convey the property to someone else.

What about contracts and conveyances between the spouses? Are there any restrictions on the ability of one spouse to enter into agreements with the other? If they are still living together, they cannot enter a contract concerning one spouse's duty to support the other (although such a contract will be valid after the parties have separated, see chapter 6).

Courts tend to be very suspicious of conveyances of property between husband and wife. Suppose, for example, that a husband transfers all his property into his wife's name, for which she pays nothing, so that when he is sued by his creditors, he technically does not own any assets from which they can satisfy

---

1. An unmarried woman at common law was not as handicapped, since she could own property and enter into contracts in her own name. But she could not vote or serve on juries, and her inheritance rights were limited. H. Clark, *The Law of Domestic Relations in the United States,* § 8.1, p. 498 (Practitioner's Ed. 2d ed. 1987).

their claims. The transfers would be considered fraudulent and would be in-validated by a court.

Two other situations can cause difficulty:

☐ The husband buys property with his separate funds but places the title in his wife's name. (Assume this is not a fraudulent transfer—he is not trying to defraud his creditors.)

☐ The wife buys property with her separate funds but places the title in her husband's name. (Again, assume no intent to defraud her creditors.)

Some courts treat the above two situations differently. In the first, most courts presume that the husband intended to make a gift of the property to his wife. In the second circumstance, however, a few courts do *not* presume a gift of the wife to her husband. Rather, the presumption is that the husband is holding the property in trust for his wife. Arguably, however, this is an unconstitutional discrimination based on sex, and some courts have so held. In these courts, whatever either spouse contributes to the purchase price is considered a gift to the other spouse unless it is clear that they had a different intention.

■■■■■■ DEATH OF THE HUSBAND

DOWER

At common law, when a husband died, the surviving wife was given the protection of **dower,** although not all states defined dower in the same way. In many states, it was the right of a surviving wife to use one-third of all the real estate her deceased husband owned during the marriage.[2] The practical impact of this law was that the husband could not sell or give his property to others without accounting for her dower right. Very often she was paid to "waive her dower rights" so that others could obtain clear title to this property.

Dower The right of a widow to the lifetime use of one-third of the land her deceased husband owned during the marriage.

RIGHT OF ELECTION

Dower has been abolished in most states. In its place, the wife is given a share of her deceased husband's estate, often called a **forced share** because she can elect to take it in place of, and in spite of, what he gives her in his will. In exercising this **right of election,** she usually receives whatever the state would have provided for her if her husband had died **intestate.**

Forced Share The share of a deceased spouse's estate that a surviving spouse elects in lieu of provisions for the latter in the deceased's spouse's will.

Right of Election The right to take a designated share of a deceased spouse's estate in spite of what the latter provided or failed to provide for the surviving spouse in a will.

■■■■■■ NAME

Many women change their surname to that of their husband at the time of marriage. This is done for one of two reasons:

☐ The law of the state gives her a choice on keeping her maiden name or taking her husband's name, and she chooses the latter.

☐ The law of the state gives her a choice that she does not know about; she uses her husband's name simply because that is the custom.

At one time, the law of some states *required* her to use her husband's name. Such laws have either been repealed or are clearly subject to constitutional

Intestate Dying without leaving a valid will.

---

2. Some states imposed the requirement that she die leaving issue capable of inheriting the estate. If the wife died, the surviving husband was protected by **curtesy,** which was the right of a husband to the lifetime use of all the land his deceased wife owned during the marriage (if issue were born of the marriage).

attack since husbands are not required to take the name of their wife and no rational reason exists for the distinction. If she decides not to use her husband's name, she does not have to go through any special steps to exercise this choice. Once she is married, she simply continues using her maiden name, or she starts using a totally new name (other than her husband's). In such states, her legal name is whatever name she uses after her marriage so long as she is not trying to defraud anyone (e.g., to make it difficult for her creditors to locate her), and so long as her use of the name is exclusive and consistent.

Once there has been a divorce, most states permit the woman to request that the court allow her to resume using her maiden name or another name. Some states, however, place restrictions on resuming a maiden name or selecting a new name if there are children of the marriage. Suppose that she makes the request that her child's name be changed to her maiden name or to the name of her new husband. Many courts are reluctant to authorize this change unless it can be shown to be in the best interest of the child.

Independent of marriage or divorce, every state has a statutory procedure that must be used when citizens (male or female) wish to change their name. This *change-of-name* procedure involves several steps, e.g., filing a petition to change one's name in the appropriate state court, stating the reasons for the change, paying a fee to the court, publishing a notice of the court proceeding in a local newspaper. The process is usually not complicated so long as the court is convinced that the name change will not mislead anyone who may need to contact the individual, e.g., police officials, a former spouse, creditors.

▃▃▃ CREDIT

Federal law prohibits discrimination on the basis of sex or marital status in a credit application.[3] Creditors such as banks or department stores that violate this prohibition can be sued and subject to punitive damages. In addition, a successful plaintiff can force the defendant to pay her court costs and reasonable attorney's fees in bringing the suit. Some of the specific prohibitions are as follows:

☐ A creditor cannot refuse to grant a woman an individual account because of her sex or marital status. For example, a woman cannot be required to open a joint account with her husband if she wants her own account and otherwise qualifies for one.

☐ A creditor cannot refuse a woman's request to open an account in her maiden name or in her hyphenated surname with her husband.

☐ A creditor cannot ask a woman for information about her husband or ex-husband unless she is relying on his income in seeking credit.

☐ A creditor cannot ask about a woman's plans to have children. In order to estimate her expenses, however, the creditor may ask how many children she has, their ages, and the cost of caring for them.

☐ A creditor cannot require that a woman disclose income from alimony, child support, or separate maintenance in her application for credit. If, however, she decides to disclose such items, the creditor cannot refuse to consider them. Furthermore, she can be asked how regularly she receives them in order to determine whether they are dependable sources of income.

---

3. Or on the basis of race, color, religion, national origin, or age. 15 U.S.C.A. § 1691.

☐ A creditor cannot require that a woman use a courtesy title (Miss, Ms., or Mrs.) on the application form.

☐ A creditor cannot request a woman's marital status in an application for an individual, unsecured account (such as a bank credit card or an overdraft checking account) where no community property is involved. A creditor cannot discriminate against a woman because of her marital status, but may consider her marital status in deciding whether to extend credit to her if she lives in a state where differences in her marital status may affect the creditor's ability to collect if she defaults, e.g., in a community property state.

☐ A creditor cannot consider a woman's sex as a factor in deciding whether she is a good risk.

▰▰▰ EMPLOYMENT

JOB DISCRIMINATION

There are a good many laws that in theory have eliminated job discrimination against women. The Equal Protection Clause of the United States Constitution provides that:

> No State shall . . . deny to any person within its jurisdiction the equal protection of the laws.

If a state passes a law that treats women differently from men, it will be invalidated unless there is a reasonable purpose for the differentiation. Only *unreasonable* discrimination violates the Constitution. Title VII of the 1964 Civil Rights Act provides that:

> It shall be an unlawful employment practice for an employer . . . to fail or refuse to hire or to discharge any individual, or otherwise to discriminate against any individual with respect to his compensation, terms, conditions, or privileges of employment, because of such individual's . . . sex; . . . 42 U.S.C.A. § 2000e–2(a)(1)(1974).

Again, this does not mean that all sex discrimination in employment is illegal. If men and women are doing the same job in a company but are being paid differently, the practice would be invalid, since they are both performing the same job. Job-related sex discrimination is permitted, however, if sex is a **Bona Fide Occupational Qualification (BFOQ),** meaning that sex discrimination is reasonably necessary to the operation of a particular business or enterprise. For example, it would be proper for a state prison to exclude women from being guards in all-male prisons where a significant number of the inmates are convicted sex offenders. It is reasonable to anticipate that some of the inmates would attack the female guards, creating a security problem. In this instance, the discrimination based on sex (i.e., being a male) in an all-male prison would be a BFOQ. An even clearer example of a BFOQ would be an acting job that required someone to play a mother. On the other hand, a BFOQ does *not* exist simply because customers or co-workers prefer a person of a particular sex to fill a position.

Bona Fide Occupational Qualification Sex discrimination that is reasonably necessary for the operation of a particular business or enterprise.

An employer cannot refuse to hire a woman because of her pregnancy-related condition so long as she is able to perform the major functions necessary to the job. Also, an employer may not terminate workers because of pregnancy, force them to go on leave at an arbitrary point during pregnancy if they are still able to work, or penalize them in reinstatement rights, including credit for previous service, accrued retirement benefits, and accumulated seniority.

Finally, men and women who perform substantially equal work in the same establishment are covered by the Equal Pay Act. This law prohibits employers from discriminating in pay because of sex if the job performed by men and women requires equal skill, effort, and responsibility under similar working conditions. There can, however, be pay differences based on seniority or merit. It is illegal for an employer to retaliate against an employee who files a charge of equal pay discrimination.

SEXUAL HARASSMENT

Sexual harassment is also an unlawful employment practice under Title VII of the Civil Rights Act. Unwelcome sexual advances, requests for sexual favors, and other verbal or physical conduct of a sexual nature constitute sexual harassment when:

☐ Submission to such conduct is either explicitly or implicitly made a term or condition of an individual's employment; or

☐ Submission to or rejection of such conduct by an individual is used as the basis for employment decisions affecting that person; or

☐ Such conduct has the purpose or effect of unreasonably interfering with an individual's work performance or creating an intimidating, hostile, or offensive working environment.

It is not a defense for an employer to say that it did not know that one of its employees engaged in sexual harassment of another employee, or that the harassment took place in spite of an explicit company policy forbidding it. If it *should have known of the harassing conduct,* the employer must take immediate and appropriate corrective action, which usually entails more than merely telling all employees not to engage in sexual harassment.

ENFORCEMENT

The Equal Employment Opportunity Commission (EEOC) is a federal agency with the primary responsibility of enforcing Title VII of the Civil Rights Act. A charge of employment discrimination (see Exhibit 12.1) can be made to the EEOC in its offices throughout the country.

Most states have a *fair employment practices* (FEP) law that also provides protection against sex discrimination in employment. A complaint can be initiated at an EEOC office or at the state or city agency that administers the local FEP law.

The major complaint leveled against the laws outlawing sex discrimination in employment is that they have been very inadequately enforced. The law of discrimination can be complex and confusing. Bringing a discrimination case is usually time-consuming and expensive. Many feel we have a long way to go before the problem is solved.

▬▬▬ SEXUALITY AND REPRODUCTIVE RIGHTS

Topics relevant to a discussion of sexuality and reproductive rights include:

☐ Contraception

☐ Sterilization

☐ Abortion

☐ New routes to motherhood

☐ Lesbianism

☐ **EXHIBIT 12.1 Charge of Discrimination**

CHARGE OF DISCRIMINATION This form is affected by the Privacy Act of 1974; see Privacy Act Statement on reverse before completing this form.	ENTER CHARGE NUMBER ☐ FEPA ☐ EEOC

_____ and EEOC
(State or local Agency, if any)

NAME *(Indicate Mr., Ms., or Mrs.)*	HOME TELEPHONE NO. *(Include Area Code)*

STREET ADDRESS	CITY, STATE AND ZIP CODE	COUNTY

NAMED IS THE EMPLOYER, LABOR ORGANIZATION, EMPLOYMENT AGENCY, APPRENTICESHIP COMMITTEE, STATE OR LOCAL GOVERNMENT AGENCY WHO DISCRIMINATED AGAINST ME *(If more than one list below.)*

NAME	NO. OF EMPLOYEES/MEMBERS	TELEPHONE NUMBER *(Include Area Code)*

STREET ADDRESS	CITY, STATE AND ZIP CODE

NAME	TELEPHONE NUMBER *(Include Area Code)*

STREET ADDRESS	CITY, STATE AND ZIP CODE

CAUSE OF DISCRIMINATION BASED ON *(Check appropriate box(es))* ☐ RACE ☐ COLOR ☐ SEX ☐ RELIGION ☐ NATIONAL ORIGIN ☐ AGE ☐ RETALIATION ☐ OTHER *(Specify)*	DATE MOST RECENT OR CONTINUING DISCRIMINATION TOOK PLACE *(Month, day, year)*

THE PARTICULARS ARE *(If additional space is needed, attached extra sheet(s))*:

■ I also want this charge filed with the EEOC. I will advise the agencies if I change my address or telephone number and I will cooperate fully with them in the processing of my charge in accordance with their procedures.	NOTARY—(When necessary to meet State and Local Requirements)
	I swear or affirm that I have read the above charge and that it is true to the best of my knowledge, information and belief.
I declare under penalty of perjury that the foregoing is true and correct. Date Charging Party *(Signature)*	SIGNATURE OF COMPLAINANT SUBSCRIBED AND SWORN TO BEFORE ME THIS DATE (Day, month, and year)

EEOC FORM 5. PREVIOUS EDITIONS OF THIS FORM ARE OBSOLETE AND MUST NOT BE USED. MAR 84

FILE COPY

The first three topics are discussed below. New routes to motherhood, such as surrogate motherhood, in vitro fertilization, and similar themes, are examined in chapter 16. Legal problems involving homosexuality and lesbianism are covered in chapter 4 on marriage and chapter 15 on adoption.

CONTRACEPTION

Married and unmarried individuals cannot be denied access to contraceptives. "If the right of privacy means anything, it is the right of the *individual,* married or single, to be free from unwarranted governmental intrusion into matters so fundamentally affecting a person as the decision whether to bear or beget a child." *Eisenstadt v. Baird,* 405 U.S. 438, 453, 92 S. Ct. 1029, 1038, 31 L. Ed. 2d 349 (1972).

STERILIZATION

Some states have laws that authorize the forced sterilization of persons legally considered mentally retarded or insane to prevent them from reproducing. Over sixty years ago, the United States Supreme Court decided that a state could legally sterilize a person it termed "feeble-minded." The woman in question was an institutionalized eighteen-year-old who was the daughter of a feeble-minded woman in the same institution; the eighteen-year-old had already had a baby that was feeble-minded. In a well-known passage, Justice Oliver Wendell Holmes said, "Three generations of imbeciles are enough." *Buck v. Bell,* 274 U.S. 200, 208, 47 S. Ct. 584, 585, 71 L. Ed. 1000 (1927). Since forced sterilization is rarely, if ever, practiced today, the courts have not had a chance to rule on the constitutionality of the practice under modern interpretations of the U.S. Constitution. If, however, the United States Supreme Court had such a case before it today, it would probably overrule *Buck v. Bell.*

ABORTION

In the early 1970s, abortion was a crime in every state. It was permitted only when the health of the woman necessitated it (usually to preserve her life) or when special circumstances warranted it, e.g., when the pregnancy was caused by rape or incest.

In 1973 the law was dramatically changed by the landmark case of **Roe v. Wade,** 410 U.S. 113, 93 S. Ct. 705, 35 L. Ed. 2d 147 (1973), in which the United States Supreme Court held that a pregnant woman's *right to privacy* included the right to terminate her pregnancy. The ruling in *Roe* was later modified by the 1992 case of *Planned Parenthood of Southeastern Pennsylvania v. Casey.* Before examining *Casey,* however, we need to look at what *Roe* said.

In *Roe v. Wade,* the Court did not conclude that the right to have an abortion was absolute. The extent of the right depended on the stage of a woman's pregnancy:

1. For the stage prior to approximately the end of the first trimester, the abortion decision and its effectuation must be left to the medical judgment of the pregnant woman's attending physician.

2. For the stage subsequent to approximately the end of the first trimester, the state, in promoting its interests in the health of the mother, may, if it chooses, regulate the abortion procedure in ways that are reasonably related to maternal health.

3. For the stage subsequent to viability, the state in promoting its interest in the potentiality of human life may, if it chooses, regulate, and even proscribe, abortion except where it is necessary, in appropriate medical judgment, for the preservation of the life or health of the mother.

A major theme of *Roe* was that the state should not be regulating abortions until **viability,** unless the regulations were clearly necessary to protect the health of the mother. If this necessity did not exist, the state could not prohibit a woman from obtaining an abortion during the first trimester when a fetus is not viable. *Roe* held that to deny her this right would infringe upon her constitutional right to privacy. Different considerations applied during the next twelve weeks—the second trimester. Between the end of the first trimester and the beginning of the child's viability (a child is usually considered viable after about six months), the state could regulate medical procedures to make sure that abortions are performed safely but could not prohibit abortions altogether. Once the child is viable—during the third trimester—abortions could be prohibited unless they were necessary to preserve the life or health of the mother.

Viability The stage of fetal development when the life of an unborn child may be continued indefinitely outside the womb by natural or artificial life-support systems.

The Court later reinforced *Roe* by holding that a wife may have an abortion without the consent of her husband.

Some limits, however, were upheld. For example, if a poor woman wanted an abortion for nonhealth reasons (i.e., a nontherapeutic abortion), the state was *not required* to pay for it, although a number of states decided to set aside funds for such abortions. Also, if a pregnant minor was living with and dependent on her parents, it was permissible for a state to require that the parents be notified of, and give their consent to, the child's desire to have an abortion—so long as the girl had the opportunity to go to court to try to convince a judge that she was a mature minor and that therefore parental notice and consent were not needed in her particular case.

These restrictions in *Roe,* however, did not significantly limit the number of abortions performed in America—approximately 1.5 million a year. The Supreme Court acknowledged that abortion continued to be "the most politically divisive domestic issue of our time." Some activities argued for a constitutional amendment that would return us to the pre-*Roe* days when states could extensively outlaw abortion. As it became clear that these efforts would not succeed, many wondered whether the appointment of conservatives to the Supreme Court by Presidents Reagan and Bush would lead to an overruling of *Roe* by the Court itself. The burning question of the day was whether there were now enough votes on the Court to abandon *Roe.* The answer came in the opinion of *Planned Parenthood of Southeastern Pennsylvania v. Casey,* 505 U.S. 833, 112 S. Ct. 2791, 120 L. Ed. 2d 674 (1992).

Casey did not overrule *Roe.* Though *Casey* made some important changes, the Court adhered to the essential features of *Roe:*

> It must be stated at the outset and with clarity that *Roe's* essential holding, the holding we reaffirm, has three parts. First is a recognition of the right of the woman to choose to have an abortion before viability and to obtain it without undue interference from the State. Before viability, the State's interests are not strong enough to support a prohibition of abortion or the imposition of a substantial obstacle to the woman's effective right to elect the procedure. Second is a confirmation of the State's power to restrict abortions after fetal viability, if the law contains exceptions for pregnancies which endanger a woman's life or health. And third is the principle that the State has legitimate interests from the outset of the pregnancy in protecting the health of the woman and the life of the fetus that may become a child. These principles do not contradict one another; and we adhere to each. 112 S. Ct. at 2804.

The Due Process Clause of the Fourteenth Amendment declares that no state shall "deprive any person of life, liberty, or property, without due process of law." The basis of a woman's right to terminate her pregnancy is the protection of "liberty" in the Fourteenth Amendment. But every restriction on this liberty is not unconstitutional.

The key test continues to be viability. In *Roe,* the Court used a trimester analysis as a guide in the determination of viability. In *Casey,* the Court decided to reject this analysis as too rigid. In the future, the question of when a child was able to survive outside the womb would be determined by the facts of medicine and science rather than by rigid assumptions of what is possible during the trimesters of pregnancy.

After viability, a state can regulate, and even prohibit, abortion except where abortion is medically necessary to preserve the life of the mother. Before viability, however, a state cannot prohibit abortions. Nor can it place "undue burdens" on the right to seek an abortion. The state can pass laws designed to encourage women to choose childbirth over abortion and laws designed to further her health or safety so long as these laws do not present "substantial obstacles" in the path of her decision to abort a nonviable fetus.

Using these tests, the Court in *Casey* reached the following conclusions about specific laws enacted by the state of Pennsylvania:

□ It is *not* an undue burden on the right to abortion for a state to require (except in a medical emergency) that at least 24 hours before performing an abortion a physician give a woman information about the nature of the procedure, the health risks of abortion and of childbirth, the probable gestational age of her unborn child, available medical assistance for childbirth, methods of obtaining child support from the father, and a list of agencies that provide adoption and other services as alternatives to abortion. Providing this information is not a substantial obstacle because the information allows women to give informed consent to whatever decision they make.

□ It *is* an undue burden on the right to abortion for a state to require, except in a medical emergency, that no physician shall perform an abortion on a married woman without receiving a signed statement from the woman that she has notified her spouse that she is about to undergo an abortion. This is a substantial obstacle because many women may not seek an abortion due to a fear of psychological and physical abuse from their husband if they tell him about their plan to have an abortion. Furthermore, a woman does not need her husband's consent to undergo an abortion. Since he does not have a veto, notifying him about the planned abortion is not necessary.

The *Casey* opinion is not the final word on abortion. The justices in *Casey* did not all agree on how to decide the case. New facts will come before the Court in the future, which will lead to further clarification. As members of the Court are replaced by new justices, we should not be surprised to find more changes. It is still true that abortion is "the most politically divisive domestic issue of our time."

■■■ THE BATTERED WIFE

Consider the following facts:

□ Spousal violence occurs in close to one of every three marriages. Trent, *Wife Beating: A Psycho-Legal Analysis,* Case and Comment 14 (November-December 1979).

□ Almost 2 million women are victims of severe assaults by their male partners each year. Over half of these men beat their wives or girlfriends at least three times a year.

□ One-fifth to one-third of all women will be physically assaulted by a partner or ex-partner during their lifetime.

□ One-third of murdered women are killed by their husbands or lovers.

□ According to a recent poll, 20 percent of all Americans (and 25 percent of college-educated Americans) condone the use of physical violence in marriage. Strong and DeVault, *The Marriage and Family Experience,* 427 (4th ed. 1989); AMA, *Violence Against Women* 7 (1991).

These alarming figures are actually considered low, since partner violence is one of the most underreported crimes in the country. It would be more accurate to *double* the figures we have. Hence, researchers have concluded that the real number of women severely assaulted each year is closer to 4 million.

Historically, the wife was considered the property of her husband in many respects. Hence it is not surprising to find religious and legal approval of his use of physical force against her. Around 1475, for example, Friar Cherubino of Siena compiled the following *Rules of Marriage:*

> When you see your wife commit an offense, don't rush at her with insults and violent blows. . . . Scold her sharply and terrify her. And if this still doesn't work . . . take up a stick and beat her soundly, for it is better to punish the body and correct the soul than to damage the soul and spare the body. . . . Then readily beat her, not in rage but out of charity and concern for her soul, so that the beating will redound to your merit and her good. Quoted in T. Davidson, *Conjugal Crime,* 99 (1978).

Hence, wife beating was acceptable and indeed was considered a duty of the husband. Society even condoned a particular weapon for the deed: a "rod not thicker than his thumb," or a stick that was not too thick to pass through a wedding ring! United States Commission on Civil Rights, *Under the Rule of Thumb: Battered Women and the Administration of Justice* 2 (January 1982).

Eventually, laws were passed outlawing wife beating. Yet the crime continues at an alarming rate today. As indicated, women frequently do not report such violence, particularly when they are still living with their abuser/husband. Furthermore, when a woman does report the incident to the authorities, she often is not taken seriously. Many complain that the police handle violence in a "domestic quarrel" differently, that is, less seriously, from an assault on the street between strangers. Politically active women's groups have campaigned for a change in the attitude and policies of courts, legislatures, and law enforcement agencies. In addition, they have fought for the creation of shelters to which battered women can flee.

If a woman is persistent and desperate enough, her main remedy is to go to court to ask for an **injunction** (see Exhibit 12.2). In this situation, the injunction is to stop abusing the plaintiff and/or her children. Depending on the state, the injunction is called a *restraining order* or a *protective order.* For purposes of obtaining the injunction, **abuse** is often defined as attempting to cause bodily injury or intentionally, knowingly, or recklessly causing bodily injury, or by threat of force placing another person in fear of imminent serious physical harm.

Injunction A court order requiring a person to do or to refrain from doing a particular thing.

In addition to the civil remedy of an injunction, a woman can ask the state to prosecute the defendant for a crime, e.g., assault, aggravated assault, battery, aggravated battery, reckless conduct, disorderly conduct, harassment. Some states have special crimes that are limited to acts committed against a spouse.

☐ **EXHIBIT 12.2 Protective Order**

3-116.3

SUPERIOR COURT OF CALIFORNIA, COUNTY OF	*FOR COURT USE ONLY*
STREET ADDRESS:	
MAILING ADDRESS:	
CITY AND ZIP CODE:	
BRANCH NAME	

PROTECTED PERSON (NAME):

RESTRAINED PERSON (NAME):

EMERGENCY PROTECTIVE ORDER	COURT CASE NUMBER:

1. **THIS EMERGENCY PROTECTIVE ORDER WILL EXPIRE AT 5 P.M. ON:** _____
   (INSERT DATE OF NEXT COURT DAY)

2. Reasonable grounds appear that an immediate danger of domestic violence exists and this order should be issued
   a. AGAINST RESTRAINED PERSON *(name):* _____
   b. WHO must not contact, molest, attack, strike, threaten, sexually assault, batter, telephone, or otherwise harass or disturb the peace of the protected person
   (1) ☐ or the peace of the following family or household members *(names):* _____
   _____
   _____

   c. ☐ WHO must stay away from the protected person at least *(yards):* _____

   d. ☐ WHO must move out and not return to the residence at *(address):* _____

3. ☐ Temporary custody of the following minor children is given to the protected person:

   Children *(names and ages):* _____
   _____

4. ☐ The protected person has been given a copy of this order, the application, and instructions about how to get a more permanent order.

5. Date: _____

6. **Law Enforcement Officer:** .... ▶ _____
   (PRINT NAME)   (SIGNATURE)

   a. Badge No.: _____   b. Incident Case No.: _____

   c. Agency: _____   d. Telephone No.: _____

7. **Service of this order and application on the restrained person was completed as follows:**

	Date	Time	Signature
a. ☐ I orally advised person of contents:	_____	_____	_____
b. ☐ I personally gave person copies:	_____	_____	_____

DESCRIPTION OF RESTRAINED PERSON (fill out what you know)
(1) approximate age: _____   (4) weight: _____   (7) vehicle make: _____
(2) race: _____   (5) hair color: _____   (8) vehicle model: _____
(3) height: _____   (6) eye color: _____   (9) vehicle license No.: _____
(10) other distinguishing features: _____

VIOLATION OF THIS ORDER IS A MISDEMEANOR PUNISHABLE BY A $1000 FINE, SIX MONTHS IN JAIL, OR BOTH. THIS ORDER SHALL BE ENFORCED BY ALL LAW ENFORCEMENT OFFICERS IN THE STATE OF CALIFORNIA.

(See reverse for important notices)

Form Adopted by Rule 1295.95
Judicial Council of California
1295.95 (New July 1, 1988)

Emergency Protective Order
(Domestic Violence Prevention)
WHITE copy to court, CANARY to restrained person, PINK to protected person

Code of Civil Procedure, § 546(b)

In 1994 Congress passed the Violence Against Women Act, which established a federal civil rights cause of action for victims of crimes of violence motivated by gender.[4] This could include wife beating, stalking, rape, and other sexual assaults. Under this Act, a victim can go into a federal court to seek compensatory and punitive damages, injunctive relief, and attorney fees. Later, in chapter 17, we will examine whether the victim of domestic violence can bring a traditional personal injury *tort* action against the abuser in a state court.

Unfortunately, these civil and criminal remedies have not been effective in substantially decreasing the incidence of domestic violence. In fact, many argue that the violence is on the rise.

Some women have taken the extreme step of killing the husband who has been abusing them. Does this killing constitute the crime of murder or manslaughter? In part, the answer depends on when the killing occurs. Compare the predicament of the women in the following two situations. Assume that both women had been physically abused by their husband or boyfriend for years:

> Carol is being physically attacked by her husband, who is coming at her with a knife. As he approaches, Carol shoots him.

> Hours after being beaten by her boyfriend, Helen takes a gun to his bedroom and shoots him while he is asleep.

It is highly unlikely that Carol has committed a crime. She is protected by the traditional defense of *self-defense*. Citizens can use deadly force that they reasonably believe is necessary to protect themselves from imminent death or serious bodily injury.

What about Helen? Unless she can prove temporary insanity, she must establish the elements of self-defense to avoid conviction. But she apparently was not in *imminent* danger at the time she shot her boyfriend. Arguably, for example, she could have left the home while he was sleeping if she felt that he might kill or maim her once he awoke. Women in Helen's situation have been prosecuted for crimes such as manslaughter and murder.

In these prosecutions, a novel argument that is often raised by the woman is the battered wife syndrome or, more broadly, the **battered woman syndrome.** She claims that she acted out of a *psychological paralysis.* A variety of circumstances combined to block all apparent avenues of escape: financial dependence, loneliness, guilt, shame, and fear of reprisal from her husband or boyfriend. Buda & Butler, *The Battered Wife Syndrome,* 23 Journal of Family Law 359 (1984–85). From this state of "learned helplessness," she kills him. This argument is not an independent defense; it is an argument designed to bolster the self-defense argument. More accurately, it is an attempt to broaden the definition of *imminent danger* in self-defense. To a woman subjected to the psychological terror and paralysis of long-term abuse, the danger from her husband or boyfriend is real and close at hand. At any moment his behavior might trigger a flashback in her mind to an earlier beating, causing her to honestly believe that she is in immediate danger.

Prosecutors are not sympathetic to the battered-woman-syndrome argument. They say it is too easy to exaggerate the extent of the abuse and, more importantly, the extent to which the abuse resulted in such a state of paralysis that the wife felt her only way to protect herself—immediately—was to kill her

Battered Woman Syndrome Psychological helplessness because of a woman's financial dependence, loneliness, guilt, shame, and fear of reprisal from her husband or boyfriend who has repeatedly battered her in the past.

---

4. 42 U.S.C.A. § 13981.

husband. Some courts, however, are at least willing to listen to testimony on the syndrome. This has been very helpful for the defendant because when jurors hear this testimony, they are often reluctant to return guilty verdicts even if the traditional elements of self-defense that the judge instructs them to apply do not warrant such a verdict.

ASSIGNMENT 12.2

a. Do you think that a court encourages killing when it allows evidence of the battered woman syndrome to be introduced in trials of women who kill their spouses or boyfriends? Explain why or why not.

b. Do you think it is possible for a battered *man* syndrome to exist? Explain why or why not.

▮▮▮▮▮ MARITAL RAPE

The common law rule was that a husband cannot rape his wife. The "husband cannot be guilty of rape committed by himself upon his lawful wife, for by their mutual matrimonial consent and contract, the wife hath given up herself in this kind unto her husband which she cannot retract." 1 M. Hale, *The History of the Pleas of the Crown* 629 (1736). This view is still the law in some states. Most states, however, allow prosecution if the couple is living apart and a petition has been filed for divorce or separate maintenance. The reluctance of courts and legislatures to allow the criminal law of rape to apply to married couples is in part based on a fear that a wife will lie about whether she consented to sexual intercourse.

▮▮▮▮▮ SUMMARY

Historically, a married woman had very few rights independent of her husband. Today her situation is very different. For example, her right to own and dispose of property and to enter contracts is now equal to that of her husband. There are some restrictions on contracts and conveyances between spouses, e.g., they cannot enter a contract to provide services and support if they are still living together, and they cannot transfer property to each other in order to defraud creditors. However, these restrictions apply equally to husbands and wives.

When a husband dies, his wife has a right of dower in his property. Many states have replaced this with a right to elect a forced share of his estate. In most states the wife is not required to take her husband's surname upon marriage, nor is she required to keep it upon divorce if she used it when married.

An applicant for credit cannot be discriminated against on the basis of sex or marital status. Sex discrimination in employment is illegal unless sex is a bona fide occupational qualification. Salaries cannot be determined on the basis of gender. Cer-

tain forms of pregnancy-related discrimination and sexual harassment are also prohibited. These laws are enforced by the federal Equal Employment Opportunity Commission and by state agencies that administer rules on fair employment practices.

In the area of sexuality and reproductive rights, neither men nor women can be denied access to contraceptives. But they can be subjected to forced sterilization if they are mentally retarded or insane. A state cannot place undue burdens on a woman's right to an abortion before viability.

Wife beating is a major problem in our society in spite of the laws against it and the availability of restraining orders and protective orders to keep the offending husband or boyfriend away. A few women have taken the drastic step of killing their abuser. In such cases, the defense of the battered woman syndrome is sometimes raised within the context of self-defense.

Finally, marital rape is not a crime in every state, although most states allow prosecution if a petition has been filed for divorce or separate maintenance.

■■■■ KEY CHAPTER TERMINOLOGY

Married Women's Property Acts
Conveyances
Dower
Curtesy
Forced Share

Right of Election
Intestate
Bona Fide Occupational Qualifi-
cation (BFOQ)
Roe v. Wade

Viability
Injunction
Abuse
Battered Woman Syndrome

13

ILLEGITIMACY AND PATERNITY PROCEEDINGS

⬛⬛⬛ ILLEGITIMACY

"The status of illegitimacy has expressed through the ages society's condemnation of irresponsible liaisons beyond the bonds of marriage. But visiting this condemnation on the head of an infant is illogical and unjust. Moreover, imposing disabilities on the illegitimate child is contrary to the basic concept of our system that legal burdens should bear some relationship to individual responsibility or wrongdoing. Obviously, no child is responsible for his birth and penalizing the illegitimate child is an ineffectual—as well as an unjust—way of deterring the parent. Courts are powerless to prevent the social opprobrium suffered by these hapless children, but the Equal Protection Clause does enable us to strike down discriminatory laws relating to status of birth where . . . the classification is justified by no legitimate state interest, . . ." *Weber v. Casualty & Surety Co.,* 406 U.S. 164, 175, 92 S. Ct. 1400, 1406, 31 L. Ed. 2d 768 (1972).

Filius Nullius An illegitimate child—"the son [or child] of no one."

At common law, the illegitimate child (still referred to as a *bastard* in many legal texts) was **filius nullius,** the child of nobody. The central disability imposed by this status was that the child born out of wedlock had no right to inherit from either parent. In addition, the child had no right to be supported by the father. Fortunately, the pronounced discrimination that has existed for centuries between the legitimate and the illegitimate child is eroding. This is not to say, however, that the discrimination has completely ended.

INHERITANCE

Intestate Die without leaving a valid will.

Most states have passed statutes permitting an illegitimate child to inherit from its mother when the latter dies **intestate.** Some states have tried to prevent the child from inheriting from its father who dies intestate, but such laws have been declared unconstitutional. *Trimble v. Gordon,* 430 U.S. 762, 97 S. Ct. 1459, 52 L. Ed. 2d 31 (1977). Cf. *Labine v. Vincent,* 401 U.S. 532, 91 S. Ct. 1017, 28 L. Ed. 2d 288 (1971). Yet restrictions on inheritance do exist. For example, assume that an illegitimate child waits until after his or her father dies before declaring that a parent-child relationship existed. Some states would not allow such a child to inherit, insisting that paternity must be determined by a court *before* death as a condition of inheriting from an intestate parent.

TESTATE DISTRIBUTION

Assume that the father of an illegitimate child dies **testate,** and that a clause in the will gives property "to my children" or "to my heirs." If the father has legitimate and illegitimate children living when he dies, the question sometimes arises as to whether he intended the word "children" or "heirs" to include his illegitimate children. To resolve this question of intent, the court must look at all of the circumstances, e.g., how much contact the illegitimate child had with the father at the time the father wrote the will and at the time he died. A surprisingly large number of cases exist in which the court concluded that the illegitimate child was *not* included in the word "children" or "heirs."

Testate Die leaving a valid will.

SUPPORT

There was a time when many state laws did not obligate a father to support his illegitimate children. Such laws have been invalidated as an improper discrimination between legitimate and illegitimate children. Hence, so long as paternity can be established, a father has an equal duty to support all his children.

WRONGFUL DEATH

When a parent dies due to the wrongful act of another, who can sue? Legitimate and illegitimate children have an equal right to bring wrongful death actions against defendants who have caused the death of one or both parents.

WORKER'S COMPENSATION

When a father dies from an injury on the job, the worker's compensation laws of the state permit the children of the deceased to recover benefits. If the state gives a preference to legitimate children over illegitimate children in claiming these benefits, the state is unconstitutionally denying equal protection of the law to the illegitimate children.

SOCIAL SECURITY

Social security laws discriminate against illegitimate children in various phases of the social security system. Some of these discriminatory provisions have been declared unconstitutional, yet others have been allowed to stand. While it is unconstitutional to deny social security survivorship benefits to a child solely because that child is illegitimate, it may be permissible to impose greater procedural burdens on illegitimate children than on legitimate children in applying for benefits. For example, if the law requires that a child be "dependent" on the deceased father as a condition of receiving survivorship benefits, an illegitimate child can be forced to *prove* that he or she was dependent on the father, whereas no such requirement will be imposed on the legitimate child—the law will *presume* that the legitimate child was dependent on the father without requiring specific proof of it.

ARTIFICIAL INSEMINATION

There are three main kinds of **artificial insemination:**

1. Artificial insemination with the semen of the husband (AIH)

Artificial Insemination The impregnation of a woman by a method other than sexual intercourse.

2. Artificial insemination with the semen of a third-party donor (AID)

3. Artificial insemination in which the semen of the husband is mixed (confused) with that of a third-party donor (AIC or CIA)

Children born through AIH are clearly legitimate; the natural father is the mother's husband. States differ as to the legitimacy of the children born through AID and AIC. In some states, such children are illegitimate. Most states, however, provide that the child is legitimate only if the insemination was with the consent of the husband of the mother. This consent also obligates the husband to support the child no matter how the insemination occurred.

■■■■ LEGITIMATION AND PATERNITY

Legitimation confers the status of legitimacy on an illegitimate child. A major reason parties go through legitimation is to clarify and assure rights of inheritance. A **paternity proceeding** is a process by which the fatherhood of a child is determined. In most states, a finding of paternity does not necessarily lead to the legitimation of the child.

Legitimation The steps that enable an illegitimate child to become a legitimate child.

Paternity Proceeding A formal process to determine whether a particular man is the biological father of a particular child.

LEGITIMATION

States have different methods by which illegitimate children can be legitimated:

☐ *Acknowledgment.* The father publicly recognizes or acknowledges the illegitimate child as his. States differ on how this acknowledgment must take place. In some states, it must be in writing and witnessed. In others, no writing is necessary if the man's activities strongly indicate that he is the father of the child, e.g., the father treats the child the same as the children who were born legitimate.

☐ *Marriage.* If the mother and father of the illegitimate child marry, the child is often automatically legitimated.

☐ *Combination of acknowledgment and marriage.* Some states require marriage of the parents and some form of acknowledgment by the father.

☐ *Legitimation proceeding.* A few states have special proceedings by which illegitimate children can be legitimated.

☐ *Paternity proceedings.* Although most paternity proceedings deal with fatherhood only, in a few states a finding of paternity also legitimates the child.

☐ *Legitimation by birth.* In a very few states, all children are legitimate whether or not their parents were married at the time of birth.

As indicated earlier, children of annulled marriages are considered legitimate according to special statutes, even though technically the parents were not validly married at the time the children were born (see chapter 5).

PATERNITY

A major method by which a father is forced to support his illegitimate child is through a paternity proceeding, sometimes called a **filiation** proceeding or a bastardy proceeding. Once fatherhood is determined, the support obligation is imposed. Most paternity proceedings in the country today are instigated by the state to try to recover some of the welfare money paid to custodial parents. In fact, programs such as Aid to Families with Dependent Children require the custodial parent to cooperate in the paternity proceeding.

Filiation (1) A judicial determination of paternity. (2) The relation of child to father.

The starting point in establishing paternity is to obtain detailed facts from the mother. The questionnaire in Exhibit 13.1 has this objective.

The paternity proceeding itself looks a good deal like a criminal proceeding in some states. A warrant is issued for the arrest of the **putative** (i.e., alleged) father, the jury renders a guilty or not guilty verdict, etc. In most states, however, the proceeding is civil rather than criminal.

Putative Alleged or reputed.

The mother (on her own or at the prompting of the welfare department) usually initiates the paternity proceeding, although the child is often also given standing to sue through a specially appointed representative, e.g., a **guardian ad litem.** (Exhibit 13.2 shows an example of a paternity petition.) When the mother brings the action, it is important to know whether the child was made a party to the proceeding and was represented. If not, then in some states, the child will not be bound by the judgment. For example:

Guardian ad Litem A special guardian appointed by the court to represent the interests of another.

> Mary, the mother of Sam, brings a paternity proceeding against Kevin, alleging he is the father of Sam. Sam is not made a party to the proceeding. A guardian ad litem is not appointed for him, and he is not otherwise represented in court. The court finds that Kevin is not the father of Sam. Ten years later, Sam brings his own action against Kevin for support, alleging that he is the son of Kevin.

Is Sam's support action ten years later barred by the defense of **res judicata?** That is, was the fatherhood issue already resolved in the paternity proceeding? States differ in their answer to this question. Many will bar the later suit of the child only if the latter was a party to the earlier case that decided the fatherhood issue. In such states, Sam *would* be able to relitigate the paternity issue against Kevin since he was not represented on his own or through a guardian ad litem in the proceeding ten years earlier.

Res Judicata When a judgment on the merits has been rendered, the parties cannot relitigate the same dispute; they have already had their day in court.

A related question is whether the mother can enter a settlement with the putative father under which she agrees to drop the paternity proceeding in exchange for the defendant's agreement to pay a certain amount for the support of the child and for the mother's expenses in giving birth to the child. In some states, it is illegal to enter into such an agreement. In states where this type of settlement is permitted, the child must be represented and/or the settlement must be approved by the court.

The paternity proceeding requires **personal jurisdiction** over the defendant–putative father (see chapter 10). This generally means that service of process must be made on the defendant in person within the forum state, i.e., the state where the paternity proceeding is being brought. If the defendant is not a resident of the forum state, personal jurisdiction over him may be obtainable under the state's **long arm statute** on the basis of his not having supported his alleged child in the forum state, or on the basis that his in-state acts of intercourse caused the mother's pregnancy.

Personal Jurisdiction The power of a court to render a decision that binds an individual defendant.

Long Arm Statute A law that gives a state court personal jurisdiction over a nonresident based on his or her purposeful contact with the state.

Once the trial on the paternity issue begins, the defendant may be faced with a *presumption of legitimacy*. A child born to a married woman is presumed to be legitimate unless conclusively proven otherwise. This means that if the defendant is the husband of the mother and denies paternity, he must introduce very strong evidence that he is not the father, e.g., evidence that he is sterile. At one time, neither spouse could introduce evidence that he or she had no sexual intercourse around the time of conception (i.e., evidence of nonaccess) if such evidence would tend to "bastardize" or "illegitimize" the child. This was known as **Lord Mansfield's rule.** Hence, if a defendant had not had sexual intercourse with his wife in years, he could not introduce evidence to this effect if it would tend to bastardize the mother's recently born child.

☐ **EXHIBIT 13.1   Paternity Questionnaire**

1. Your full name _____
   Your Social Security number _____
   Your address _____
   Your home phone _____ Your work phone _____
   Your date of birth _____
   With whom are you living: _____

2. List two people who will always know where you live:
   Name _____ Name _____
   Address _____ Address _____
   _____
   Phone _____ Phone _____

3. Give the following information regarding the father of your child:
   Full name _____
   Address _____
   Date of birth _____ Social Security number _____
   Home phone _____ Work phone _____
   Do you have a picture of the father: _____

4. Child's name _____ Child's date of birth _____ Child's sex _____

5. Do you have a picture of the child: _____

6. Does the child look like the father: _____

7. Does the child have the same coloring: _____

8. When and where did you meet the father: _____

9. When did you begin dating the father: _____

10. Did you ever live with the father: _____ If so, where and when: _____
    Landlord _____ Phone _____
    Address _____

11. Others who knew you were living together:
    Name _____ Name _____
    Relationship to you _____ Relationship to you _____
    Address _____ Address _____
    Phone _____ Phone _____

12. When did you first have sexual relations with the father: _____

13. When did you last have sexual relations with him: _____

14. Where was the child conceived? (Where did you get pregnant):
    City _____ County _____ State _____

15. Date father was told that you were pregnant: _____

16. Who told the father that you were pregnant: _____

17. What did he say when he was told you were pregnant: _____
    _____

18. Was a father listed on your child's birth certificate: _____ Did he sign it: _____

19. If no father was listed, explain why the father was not named on the birth certificate: _____

20. Write anything the father said suggesting to you that he is the child's father such as "Isn't our baby cute," or "I am glad you had my baby."
    _____
    _____

21. Did the father sign any papers or write any letters suggesting he is your baby's father: _____

22. What did he sign: _____ Where: _____

23. Did the father offer to help pay for an abortion? If so, briefly explain what he said, when, where, and if anyone else was present: _____
    _____

24. Did the father ever give or offer to give you money for the child? If so, how much and when: _____

25. Did the father ever buy the child gifts? If so, list the gifts and dates given: _____
    _____

Continued

□ **EXHIBIT 13.1 Paternity Questionnaire—*Continued***

26. Did you ever tell anyone that the father of your child is someone other than the man you are naming on this form: _____ If so, whom did you tell: _____

27. What was said (include name of other man named): _____

28. Give the names, addresses, phone numbers of all witnesses who may be called to testify who have:
    a. Seen you and the father together during time of conception (8–10 months prior to birth).
    b. Seen you and the father kissing, necking, petting, or aware of or have knowledge of any intimate relations you had with the alleged father.
    c. Heard the father make a statement to anyone about you getting an abortion or helping pay for an abortion.
    d. Heard the father make a statement to anyone suggesting or admitting he was the father of the child. (Indicate for each witness briefly what his or her testimony would be.)
    Name _____ Phone _____
    Address _____
    Testimony _____
    Name _____ Phone _____
    Address _____
    Testimony _____

29. Answer these questions for the 8th month before the birth (one month pregnant):
    a. Month _____ Year _____
    b. Were you having sex with the father: _____
    c. How frequently did you have intercourse: _____
    d. Did you use birth control on any occasion: _____
    e. Did the father use birth control on any occasion: _____
    f. Did you have sex with any other men during that month: _____
    If so, list their names, addresses, or other information that may be helpful in locating them.
    Name _____ Address _____
    Phone _____
    Name _____ Address _____
    Phone _____

30. Answer these questions for the 7th month before the birth (two months pregnant):
    a. Month _____ Year _____
    b. Were you having sex with the father: _____
    c. How frequently did you have intercourse: _____
    d. Did you use birth control on any occasion: _____
    e. Did the father use birth control on any occasion: _____
    f. Did you have sex with any other men during that month: _____
    If so, list their names, addresses, or other information that may be helpful in locating them.
    Name _____ Address _____
    Phone _____
    Name _____ Address _____
    Phone _____

31. Answer these questions for the 11th month before the birth (two months before you became pregnant):
    a. Month _____ Year _____
    b. Were you having sex with the father: _____
    c. How frequently did you have intercourse: _____
    d. Did you use birth control on any occasion: _____
    e. Did the father use birth control on any occasion: _____
    f. Did you have sex with any other men during that month: _____
    If so, list their names, addresses, or other information that may be helpful in locating them.
    Name _____ Address _____
    Phone _____
    Name _____ Address _____
    Phone _____

32. Answer these questions for the 10th month before the birth (one month before you became pregnant):
    a. Month _____ Year _____
    b. Were you having sex with the father: _____
    c. How frequently did you have intercourse: _____
    d. Did you use birth control on any occasion: _____

Continued

☐ **EXHIBIT 13.1 Paternity Questionnaire—*Continued***

     e. Did the father use birth control on any occasion: _____

     f. Did you have sex with any other men during that month: _____

       If so, list their names and addresses, or other information that may be helpful in locating them.

       Name _____ Address _____

       Phone _____

       Name _____ Address _____

       Phone _____

33. Answer these questions for the 9th month before the birth (the month you became pregnant):

     a. Month _____ Year _____

     b. Were you having sex with the father: _____

     c. How frequently did you have intercourse: _____

     d. Did you use birth control on any occasion: _____

     e. Did the father use birth control on any occasion: _____

     f. Did you have sex with any other men during that month: _____

       If so, list their names, addresses, or other information that may be helpful in locating them.

       Name _____ Address _____

       Phone _____

       Name _____ Address _____

       Phone _____

34. Are you presently married: _____ If so, give name of husband. _____

35. Date of marriage _____ Place of marriage _____

36. Were you married at any time between one year before and one year after the birth of the child? ____

     If so, give name of each husband, date, and place of marriage, and, if applicable, the date and place of divorce or annulment:

     Name _____ Date of marriage _____

     Place _____ Date of divorce/annulment _____

     Name _____ Date of marriage _____

     Place _____ Date of divorce/annulment _____

37. On what date did your last menstrual flow begin before the birth of your child: _____

38. On what date did your last menstrual flow end before the birth of your child: _____

39. Do you have a calendar or other records showing these dates: _____

40. Do you have a diary or other written records of the dates you had intercourse with your child's father: _____

41. Name of doctor who cared for you before the child was born: _____

42. Name of doctor who cared for child after birth: _____

43. Address: _____

44. Circle one: Child premature, overdue, or normal term.

45. Exact due date _____ Birth weight _____

46. Who paid for the birth of the child:

     FHP _____ Medicaid _____ Other (please name) _____

47. Name of hospital in which child was born: _____

_____

State of _____   )

) ss.

County of _____   )

_____ , being duly sworn states that she has read the above document and that the statements contained therein are true to the best of her knowledge.

_____

Signature

_____

Date

Subscribed and sworn to before me this _____ day of _____ , 19 _____ .

_____

Notary Public

Resides at: _____

My Commission Expires: _____

□ **EXHIBIT 13.2 Paternity Petition**

FAMILY COURT OF
COUNTY OF

....

In the Matter of a Paternity Proceeding

_____ Petitioner,

—against—

_____ Respondent,

....

Docket No.
PATERNITY PETITION
(Parent)

TO THE FAMILY COURT:
 The undersigned Petitioner respectfully shows that:
 1. Petitioner resides at _____
 2. Petitioner had sexual intercourse with the above named Respondent (on several occasions covering a period of time beginning on or about the _____ day of _____ , 19 ___ , and ending on or about the _____ day of _____ , 19 ___ , and as a result thereof (Petitioner) became pregnant.
 3. *(a) (Petitioner) gave birth to a (male) (female) child out of wedlock on the _____ day of _____ , 19 _____ , at _____ .
  *(b) (Petitioner) is now pregnant with a child who is likely to be born out of wedlock.
 4. (Respondent) who resides at _____ is the father of the child.
 5. (Respondent) (has acknowledged) (acknowledges) paternity of the child (in writing) (and) (by furnishing support).
 6. No previous application has been made to any court or judge for the relief sought herein (except _____ .)

WHEREFORE, Petitioner prays that this Court issue a summons or warrant requiring the Respondent to show cause why the Court should not enter a declaration of paternity, an order of support and such other and further relief as may be appropriate under the circumstances.

_____
Petitioner

Dated: _____ , 19 _____ .

*Alternative allegations.

The United States Supreme Court recently traced the origin of these rules in its opinion, *Michael H. v. Gerald D,* 109 S. Ct. 2333, 2342–43 (1989):

 The presumption of legitimacy was a fundamental principle of the common law. H. Nicholas, Adulturine Bastardy 1 (1836). Traditionally, that presumption could be rebutted only by proof that a husband was incapable of procreation or had had no access to his wife during the relevant period. *Id.,* at 9–10 (citing Bracton, De Legibus et Consuetudinibus Angliae, bk. i, ch. 9, p. 6; bk. ii, ch. 29, p. 63, ch. 32, p. 70 (1569)). As explained by Blackstone, nonaccess could only be proved "if the husband be out of the kingdom of England (or, as the law somewhat loosely phrases it, *extra quatuor maria* [beyond the four seas]) for above nine months. . . ." 1 Blackstone's Commentaries 456 (Chitty ed. 1826). And, under the common law both in England and here, "neither husband nor wife [could] be a witness to prove access or nonaccess." J. Schouler, Law of the Domestic Relations § 225, p. 306 (3d ed. 1882); R. Graveson & F. Crane, A Century of Family Law: 1857–1957, p. 158 (1957). The primary policy rationale underlying the common law's severe restrictions on rebuttal of the presumption appears to have been an aversion to declaring children illegitimate, see Schouler, *supra,* § 225, at 306–307; M. Grossberg, Governing the Hearth 201 (1985), thereby depriving them of rights of inheritance and succession, 2 Kent's Commentaries 175 (1827), and likely making them wards of the state. A secondary policy concern was the interest in promoting the "peace and tranquillity of States and families," Schouler, *supra,* § 225, at 304, quoting Boullenois, Traité des Status, bk. 1, p. 62, a goal that is obviously impaired by facilitating suits against husband and wife asserting that their children are illegitimate. Even though, as bastardy laws became less harsh, "[j]udges in both [England and the United States] gradually widened the acceptable range of evidence that could be offered by spouses, and placed restraints on the 'four seas rule' . . . [,] the law retained a strong bias against ruling the children of married women illegitimate." Grossberg, *supra,* at 202.

It is obviously very difficult for a husband to deny that he is the father of his wife's child. The harshness of this rule has been criticized. A number of states have either eliminated or substantially limited Lord Mansfield's rule.

The discovery of human blood groups and types has been of great assistance in paternity cases because they:

☐ Can be determined at birth or shortly thereafter
☐ Remain constant throughout an individual's life
☐ Are inherited

In 1981, the United States Supreme Court commented on the operation and effectiveness of blood group tests as follows:

If the blood groups and types of the mother and child are known, the possible and *impossible* blood groups and types of the true father can be determined under the rules of inheritance. For example, a group AB child cannot have a group O parent, but can have a group A, B, or AB parent. Similarly, a child cannot be type M unless one or both parents are type M, and the factor rh' cannot appear in the blood of a child unless present in the blood of one or both parents. . . . Since millions of men belong to the possible groups and types, a blood grouping test cannot conclusively establish paternity. However, it can demonstrate *non-paternity,* such as where the alleged father belongs to group O and the child is group AB. It is a negative rather than an affirmative test with the potential to scientifically exclude the paternity of a falsely accused putative father.

The ability of blood grouping tests to exonerate innocent putative fathers was confirmed by a 1976 report developed jointly by the American Bar Association and the American Medical Association. Miale, Jennings, Rettberg, Sell & Krause, *Joint AMA–ABA Guidelines: Present Status of Serologic Testing in Problems of Disputed Parentage,* 10 Family L. Q. 247 (Fall 1976). The joint report recommended the use of seven blood test "systems"—ABO, Rh, MNS, Kell, Duffy, Kidd, and HLA—when investigating questions of paternity. . . . These systems were found to . . . provide a 91% cumulative probability of negating paternity for erroneously accused Negro men and 93% for white men. . . .

The effectiveness of the seven systems attests the probative value of blood test evidence in paternity cases. The importance of that scientific evidence is heightened because "[t]here are seldom accurate or reliable eye witnesses since the sexual activities usually take place in intimate and private surroundings, and the self-serving testimony of a party is of questionable reliability." Larson, *Blood Test Exclusion Procedures in Paternity Litigation: The Uniform Acts and Beyond,* 13 J. Family L. 713 [1974].

Little v. Streater, 101 S. Ct. 2202, 2206 (1981).

Since 1981 when the preceding commentary was written, the effectiveness of scientific testing has increased significantly. Today newly discovered serologic and statistical methods have made major changes in the law of evidence in this area. A "wider range of genetic tests have come to be admissible, and not merely to demonstrate that it is biologically impossible for a particular man to be the father, but also to show that it is highly probable that a specific man *is* the father." Kay & Kanwischer, *Admissibility of Genetic Testing in Paternity Litigation,* 22 Family L. Quarterly 109, 109–10 (1988). The tests are used to indicate the likelihood or **probability of paternity** of a man who is not excluded by the tests:

The test results will establish whether your client is excluded as being the father of the child; or if not, what is the probability or likelihood of his being the actual father. If the client is excluded by the blood test, then the case has ended and the mother will have to accuse some other man as being the father. If your client is not excluded, the probability or likelihood of his paternity will be mathematically determined. The likelihood that he is the actual father is then compared statistically to that of a fictional man who is assumed to have had sexual intercourse with the mother and who is assumed not to be excluded by the test. These results are expressed in the form of a "paternity index" and in the form of a "probability of paternity." For example, the paternity index would be expressed as (53 to 1) fifty-three to one; that is, the putative father is fifty-three times more likely to have fathered the child than some other man who could have had intercourse with the mother and who would not be excluded by the blood test. The "probability of paternity" is generally expressed in a percentage figure; for example, 98.15%. Neubaum, *Defense of Paternity Cases,* Case & Comment, 38–39 (July–August 1987).

Special testing laboratories have been established to conduct these tests. An example of how one such laboratory operates appears in Exhibit 13.3.

A relatively recent development in the scientific determination of paternity is DNA testing, which is also used in criminal cases. Exhibit 13.4 and the article on page 277 present an overview of the DNA testing process.

□ **EXHIBIT 13.3   Paternity Testing Procedures**

PATERNITY TESTING
Parker Laboratories

Parker Laboratories, provides paternity testing for disputed paternity cases. The tests performed at Parker are ABO, HLA, Rh, MNSs, Duffy, Kidd and Kell. ABO, Rh, MNSs and HLA typing will be performed on all non-excluded cases. The cumulative probability of exclusion (CPE) for these four systems is 97% for Caucasians and 96% for Blacks. Duffy, Kidd and Kell typings are reserved for the non-excluded cases with low likelihoods of paternity. The addition of these three systems provides a CPE of 98% for Caucasians and 97% for Blacks.

If more markers are required, the blood will be sent to a reference laboratory for serum protein and red cell enzyme testing. When combined with the testing performed at the Parker Laboratories, this further testing yields a CPE greater than 99%.

Paternity cannot be proven with 100% certainty. Non-paternity can be proven by obtaining exclusions.

Testing will be performed in duplicate by separate technologists and reviewed by the medical director before mailing. A copy of the final results will be sent to the alleged father's attorney, the mother's attorney and the child's attorney, if any. An explanation of the results will accompany the final reports.

We recommend that the mother, alleged father and child's blood specimens be drawn at the same time and place, preferably at the Parker laboratory, in order that each can serve as witness to the event. At the time an appointment for paternity testing is made, the following information is required:

1. Name of alleged father
2. Name of mother
3. Name and age of child
4. Names, addresses and phone numbers of all attorneys involved

If it is not possible for the parties to come to the laboratory to have specimens drawn, a kit will be sent to the laboratory that will be drawing the blood. However, the Parker Laboratories does not take responsibility for any errors in identification of the blood samples if they are not drawn at our laboratory. The kit will contain all information necessary for the drawing and sending of the blood; e.g., instructions for drawing, identification and consent forms, tubes and labels. A witness must sign the identification and consent forms, check the driver's license of each party and ensure that the tubes are properly labelled. Photographs and fingerprints are required to be taken on all parties.

Specimens must reach Parker Laboratories within 24 hours after being drawn. Federal Express or some other similar air carrier service which delivers within 24 hours is recommended. Blood should arrive at our laboratory before 10:30 a.m. on the day of the scheduled appointment.

If testing is required from a reference laboratory, letters will be sent immediately to all involved attorneys concerning the further testing.

A written report of final test results will be mailed within a two week period in most cases. Phone reports will not be given.

☐ **EXHIBIT 13.4   The DNA Fingerprinting Process**

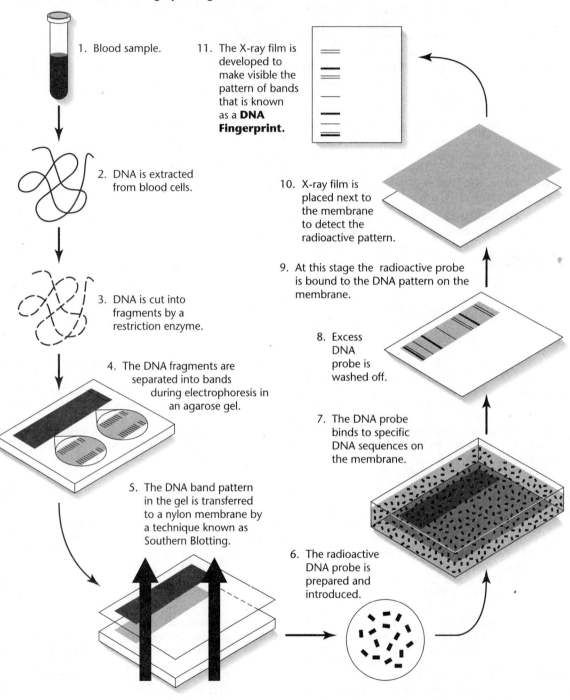

1. Blood sample.

11. The X-ray film is developed to make visible the pattern of bands that is known as a **DNA Fingerprint.**

2. DNA is extracted from blood cells.

10. X-ray film is placed next to the membrane to detect the radioactive pattern.

3. DNA is cut into fragments by a restriction enzyme.

9. At this stage the radioactive probe is bound to the DNA pattern on the membrane.

8. Excess DNA probe is washed off.

4. The DNA fragments are separated into bands during electrophoresis in an agarose gel.

7. The DNA probe binds to specific DNA sequences on the membrane.

5. The DNA band pattern in the gel is transferred to a nylon membrane by a technique known as Southern Blotting.

6. The radioactive DNA probe is prepared and introduced.

SOURCE: *Cellmark Diagnostics,* National L. J., 25 (December 18, 1989).

DNA PROFILING
Establishing Paternity, 64–66, Office of Child
Support Enforcement (3rd ed. 1990).

Use of DNA profiling—a fundamental break-through in the field of identification—has tremendous potential application and impact in parentage testing. This new way of identifying an individual involves a test on actual genetic material known as deoxyribonucleic acid, typically known by its abbreviation, DNA. Two discoverers of the structure of DNA, Dr. James Watson and Dr. Francis Crick, were awarded a Nobel Prize for their work.

DNA, a molecule that carries the body's genetic information, is contained in every living organism in every cell which has a nucleus (over 99 percent of the cells in the human body). Our chromosomes are made of DNA. DNA is the "blueprint of life" and is what determines each person's unique genetic individuality. Each person's characteristics are based upon the order in which the 3 billion building blocks in a person's DNA are linked together. DNA actually consists of two long strands which coil around each other to form a double helix. In many respects, DNA is like a long zipper. The strands are always in exact alignment as determined by the sequence of the constituent building blocks. The strands can be separated, and the sister strands will zip back together in flawless alignment because the building blocks fit together perfectly.

DNA testing is significant because the configuration of DNA is different in virtually every individual, with the exception of identical twins. Although DNA testing is a relatively new achievement, examination of DNA has wide applicability in forensic science and special value in the settlement of disputed paternity matters.

To perform the analysis, DNA is removed intact from the cells. In paternity testing, blood is used because it can easily be obtained in sufficient quantity. In forensic cases, human cells may be obtained from samples of blood, semen, hair roots, or from any other DNA carrying cell in the body. After DNA is removed and purified, it is cut apart at specific sequences in a carefully controlled way using specialized restriction enzymes which act as biological scissors. Electrophoresis is then used.

The DNA fragments are placed at one end of a sheet of gel and exposed to an electrical charge that allows them to move across the gel. The smaller fragments of DNA move more rapidly through the gel than larger fragments causing the DNA to separate into bands by size. Scientists transfer the bands of DNA fragments from the gel onto a nylon membrane. The nylon membrane is heated and gene probes that have been labeled with a small amount of radioactive material are added. A "gene probe" is a shorter section of DNA—perhaps several hundred or several thousand building blocks (or teeth) long from one strand—which will zip up without fail in the right spot on its partner strand.

Typically, several probes are used, each of which identify the alleles of a single DNA locus. The probes attach themselves to specific invisible bands of repetitive DNA. Technicians then place the membrane(s) on film that is sensitive to the radioactive probes allowing them to obtain an image of the repetitive DNA.

The resulting image obtained from the gene probe looks much like the striped bar code which, together with a computer, is used to scan millions of items every day, such as consumer items in a grocery store. Using the bar code analogy, each dark band visible on the bar code reflects where the gene probe has located its correct partner strand, among the millions of fragments generated by the restriction enzymes acting on the individual's DNA.

The chances that two unrelated persons will have the same DNA are 1 in a quadrillion. Even with siblings (except identical twins), the chances are one in 10 trillion. Every bar in the child's code can be attributed to either the mother or the father, with an even split in the number attributionable to each.

The first step in the analysis is to compare the child's code with the mother's and locate all the bars that match up. The remaining bars in the child's code are then compared with those of the alleged father. If the man is, in fact, the father, every remaining bar will match up with one of the father's code. If the man is not the father, very few bars will match.

As the body of scientific data develops, their use as a supplemental test continues, and as quality control procedures and accreditation guidelines are established, the DNA probes may emerge as the most useful approach to confirming or disproving parentage.

One consequence of the effectiveness of all of these tests is that most disputed paternity cases today are resolved on the basis of the tests rather than by trial. Testing can be expensive, however. If the putative father is indigent, the state must pay for the tests. If he refuses to undergo the tests, many states will either force him to be tested or allow the trial court to take his refusal into consideration in making the paternity decision. The strong implication of such a refusal is that he has something to hide. Many states provide state-appointed counsel for the putative father in these proceedings.

ASSIGNMENT 13.1

a. In a paternity action a mother is asked to state with whom she has had sexual intercourse during the period of possible conception. Can she refuse to answer?

b. In a divorce action, the court concludes that Tom is the father of two children born during the marriage and is ordered to pay child support for them. Five years later, a criminal nonsupport case is brought against Tom who admits that he made only two of the child support payments in the five years. During the criminal trial, he contests paternity and asks the court to order blood tests for himself, his ex-wife, and the two children. Assume these tests were not available at the time of the divorce action. What result?

Of course, not every father must be dragged into court in order to establish paternity. Some openly declare paternity even though they do not wish to marry the mother, or may not be able to because she is already married to someone else or because he is already married. In some states, a father in such cases can file a document declaring paternity. In New York, for example, there is a special office within the Department of Social Services where a father can "register" himself as the father by filing an *Instrument to Acknowledge Paternity of an Out of Wedlock Child* (see Exhibit 13.5). This document will ensure that he will receive legal notice of an attempt to adopt the child. Additionally, it will make clear that the child has a right to inherit from the father in the event that the latter dies without leaving a valid will.

Recently, it became even easier for a father to acknowledge paternity. Unmarried fathers are often present in the hospital during or soon after the birth of their child. The federal government now requires every state to establish a program allowing fathers while in the hospital to sign a simple form voluntarily acknowledging paternity. Before being asked to sign, the father will be given information on the child support duties of parents. This acknowledgment will be of considerable help months or years later if he becomes estranged from the mother and refuses to pay child support on the ground that he is not the father.

▬▬▬ SUMMARY

At one time, an illegitimate child had very few rights. This situation has changed, although the discrimination has not been entirely eliminated. An illegitimate child can now fully inherit from his or her father who dies intestate. Some states insist, however, that paternity be established before the parent dies. If the parent dies testate, leaving property "to my children," or "to my heirs," the answer to the question of whether illegitimate children were included in these phrases depends on the intent of the parent.

Legitimate and illegitimate children have the same right to be supported, to bring wrongful-death actions because of the death of a parent, and to receive worker's compensation benefits if the parent dies on the job. To obtain social security benefits, however, an illegitimate child must prove he or she was dependent on a deceased father, whereas the law presumes the dependence of a legitimate child.

In most states, when a child is born through artificial insemination with the semen of a man other than the husband, the latter has a duty to support the child, and the child is considered legitimate if the husband consented to the insemination.

Legitimation can occur in a number of ways: acknowledgment of paternity, marriage of the mother and father, legitimation proceeding, paternity proceeding, etc. In some states, all children are legitimate regardless of whether the mother and father ever married.

☐ EXHIBIT 13.5   Form to Register Paternity

The **Putative Father Registry** is a confidential file maintained in Albany to register fathers of children born out of wedlock.

PURPOSE

The Putative Father Registry was developed to ensure that, if an individual has registered (or has been registered by a court) as the father of a particular child, he will receive legal notice if that child is to be adopted. Additionally, registration provides such a child the right of inheritance in the event of the death of an out of wedlock father. A father may be registered for both purposes provided he follows the instructions in this leaflet.

REGISTRATION

The attached form, called "An Instrument to Acknowledge Paternity of An Out of Wedlock Child," must be filled out in the presence of a witness and signed and notarized before it is returned to the address indicated. Once it is received it will be filed in the Putative Father Registry. The New York State Department of Social Services shall, upon request from any court or authorized agency, provide the names and addresses of persons listed with the registry. The department will not divulge this information to any other party.

The mother and other legal guardian of the child, (if any) will be contacted by registered mail to notify her (them) that a registration has been received.

· ·

INSTRUMENT TO ACKNOWLEDGE PATERNITY OF AN OUT OF WEDLOCK CHILD
(pursuant to Section 4–1.2 of New York Estates, Powers and Trust Law)

I _____ , residing at _____
      NAME OF FATHER   ADDRESS

_____ hereby acknowledge that I am
    TOWN   STATE   ZIP CODE

the natural father of _____ born on _____ in
                       NAME OF CHILD   DATE OF BIRTH

_____ . The natural mother of the child
    TOWN   STATE   ZIP CODE

_____ is _____ who resides
      CHILD'S NAME   NAME OF NATURAL MOTHER

at _____

Witness _____   _____
             SIGNATURE   NATURAL FATHER (SIGNATURE)

           _____
              ADDRESS

           _____
      TOWN   STATE   ZIP CODE

STATE OF NEW YORK
COUNTY OF _____

On the _____ day of _____ _____ , before
        DAY   MONTH   YEAR

me came _____ to me known to be the individual described
             NATURAL FATHER

herein and who executed the foregoing instrument, and acknowledges to me that he executed same.

           _____
              NOTARY PUBLIC

STATE OF NEW YORK
COUNTY OF _____

This instrument must be filed with the New York State Department of Social Services, Putative Father Register, 40 North Pearl Street, Albany, New York 12243, within sixty days after it is completed. The natural mother indicated on this instrument will be sent notification of this acknowledgement within seven days after its filing.

A major function of a paternity proceeding is to establish a father's duty of support. For this purpose, the court must have personal jurisdiction over him. The child should be joined as a party in the proceeding to ensure that the judgment will be binding on the child. If the defendant is married to the mother, he may face a number of evidentiary obstacles at the trial, e.g., the presumption of legitimacy and Lord Mansfield's rule. Traditional blood group testing can help establish the nonpaternity, though not the paternity, of a particular defendant. More modern scientific techniques, however, claim the ability to establish the high probability of paternity.

All states allow a father to file a paternity acknowledgment in the hospital at the birth of his child.

■ KEY CHAPTER TERMINOLOGY

Filius Nullius	Paternity Proceeding	Personal Jurisdiction
Intestate	Filiation	Long Arm Statute
Testate	Putative	Lord Mansfield's Rule
Artificial Insemination	Guardian ad Litem	Probability of Paternity
Legitimation	Res Judicata	DNA Testing

THE LEGAL STATUS OF CHILDREN

▬▬▬ AGE OF MAJORITY AND EMANCIPATION

In most states and for most purposes, an adult is an individual who is eighteen years of age or older. A **minor** is anyone under eighteen. (Note: a person reaches eighteen on the day *before* his or her eighteenth birthday.) At this age, *majority* is achieved. There was a time, however, when the age of majority was twenty-one, and in some states it still is. Furthermore, a person may be a minor for one purpose, but not for another. Hence, one cannot always rely on eighteen as the critical age to determine rights and obligations. Three questions must always be asked:

Minor Someone under the age of majority, which is usually eighteen.

1. What is the individual trying to do, e.g., vote, drink alcohol, drive, enter a contract, avoid a contract?

2. Does the state set a specific age as the minimum for that task or objective?

3. Has the individual been emancipated? If so, does the emancipation mean that the person is no longer a minor for purposes of that particular task or objective?

Emancipation is the loss of a parent's legal control over a child. Children can be emancipated before the age of majority if certain events take place that clearly indicate they are living independently of their parents with the consent of the latter. Such events include marriage, entering military service, abandonment by the parents, an explicit agreement between the parents and the child that the latter can live independently, etc. In some states, a child can apply to a court for an order of emancipation when the consent of the parents cannot be obtained. As we discuss the various rights and obligations of minors, we will see that it is sometimes important to know whether emancipation has occurred.

Emancipation
Becoming legally independent of one's parent or legal guardian.

▬▬▬ CONTRACTS

As a general rule (to which there are exceptions), a minor does not have legal capacity to enter a binding contract. Consequently, a minor has no legal obligation to perform a contract if he or she **disaffirms** it at any time before

Disaffirm To repudiate.

281

reaching majority or within a reasonable time after reaching majority. In effect, such contracts are voidable.

> Tom is fifteen years of age—clearly a minor. He goes to the ABC Truck Co. and purchases a truck. The sales contract calls for a small down payment (which Tom pays) with the remainder to be paid in installments—on credit. Six months later, Tom changes his mind about the truck and decides to take it back to the dealer. The truck is still in good working order.

If Tom were an adult, he would be bound by his contract. Once an adult and a merchant enter into a contract, they both are bound by it. Neither party can rescind a contract simply because of a change of mind. The difference in our example is that Tom is a minor. Most states give minors the right to disaffirm their contracts so long as they do so while they are still minors or within a reasonable time (e.g., several months) after they have reached majority. In Tom's case, this would mean that he is not bound by the contract to buy the truck. He can take it back and perhaps even force the company to return whatever money he paid on it. In some states, however, the merchant can keep all or part of the purchase price paid thus far to cover depreciation resulting from the minor's use of the item.

Why are minors given this right to disaffirm? The objective of the law is to protect young people from their immaturity. Merchants are on notice that if they deal with minors, they do so at their own risk.

This does not mean that every contract of a minor is invalid. If the minor does not disaffirm, the contract is valid and can be enforced against the minor. Similarly, if a minor tries to disaffirm too late, the contract will be enforced. Suppose that Tom tried to disaffirm the truck contract when he was twenty years old in a state where the age of majority is eighteen. It won't work. He must disaffirm *before* he reaches majority or within a *reasonable* time thereafter.

What happens if the minor commits fraud to induce the merchant to enter a contract, e.g., lies about his or her age through a forged birth certificate? Some courts take the position that such wrongdoing by the minor **estops** him or her from being able to disaffirm. Other courts, however, argue that the policy of protecting minors against their own immaturity is so strong that even their own fraud will not destroy their right to disaffirm.

Special statutes have been passed in many states to limit the minor's right to disaffirm, particularly with respect to certain kinds of contracts. In several states, for example, some employment contracts, such as sports and show business contracts, are binding on minors. Similarly, contractual arrangements with banks and other lending institutions cannot be disaffirmed in many states. Finally, when a minor makes a contract with a merchant for **necessaries** such as food or clothing (see chapter 8), the contract can rarely be disaffirmed.

When a guardian has been appointed over a minor and the guardian enters a contract on behalf of that minor, the contract generally cannot be disaffirmed by the minor. Suppose, for example, that a minor is involved in litigation and an offer of settlement is made. A settlement is a contract. If a court appoints a **guardian ad litem** who negotiates a settlement contract on behalf of the minor, which the court finds is fair, the minor cannot later disaffirm the settlement.

Most states have enacted the Uniform Gifts to Minors Act pursuant to which gifts of certain kinds of property, e.g., securities, can be made to minors through custodians of the property. The custodian can sell the property on behalf of the minor. Contracts made by the custodian for this purpose cannot be disaffirmed by the minor.

Estop To be prevented from asserting a right or a defense because it would be unfair or inequitable to do so.

Necessaries The basic items needed by family members to maintain a standard of living.

Guardian ad Litem A special guardian appointed by the court to represent the interests of another.

Suppose that a minor has become emancipated before reaching the age of majority, e.g., by marrying or by being abandoned by the parents. Does this end the child's power to disaffirm? There is no absolute answer to this question. A minor so emancipated may be denied the power to disaffirm in some states, while in others, it will not affect the power.

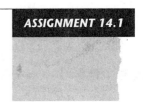

ASSIGNMENT 14.1

George is a wealthy thirteen-year-old who owns an expensive painting. He signs a contract to exchange the painting for a valuable horse owned by Helen, an equally wealthy twelve-year-old. Both George and Helen are represented by their separate attorneys during the negotiations on the contract. Once the contract is signed and the items are exchanged, what rights do George and Helen have? Assume that there are no problems with the quality and condition of the painting and the horse.

PROPERTY AND EARNINGS

A minor can own real property and most personal property in his or her own name. The parents of a minor do not own and cannot dispose of the minor's property. Earnings are an exception. A minor does *not* have a right to keep his or her own earnings. The parent with the duty to support the child has a right to keep the child's earnings. If, however, the child has not yet reached the age of majority but has been emancipated (e.g., by express agreement with the parents, by marriage, by abandonment by the parents), the parents would not be entitled to the child's earnings.

DOMICILE

The **domicile** of a minor is the domicile of the parents—even in some instances when the minor lives in a different state from the parents. With parental consent, however, a minor can acquire his or her own separate domicile. Similarly, if a minor who has not yet reached the age of majority is emancipated, most states give that individual the power to acquire his or her own domicile.

Domicile For adults, domicile is the place where they have been physically present with the intent to make that place a permanent home.

ESTATES

States have specified a minimum age for a person to have the legal capacity to dispose of his or her property by a will. Some states have different minimum ages for the disposition of personal property (e.g., clothes, cash) and of real property (e.g., land). In a few states, the emancipation of the minor by his or her marriage will enable the minor to make a valid will before reaching the minimum age.

If the parent of a minor dies, the court will appoint a guardian over the person and/or estate of the minor. This person is called a general guardian, a guardian of the estate, or a guardian ad litem. It is this guardian's duty to:

☐ Manage the minor's property

☐ Collect funds due the minor

☐ Sell, lease, or mortgage the minor's property (with the approval of the court)

☐ Invest the minor's funds

☐ Pay the minor's debts

☐ Support the minor from the minor's funds

☐ Represent the minor in court when needed

Estate All the assets or property of a person that is available to satisfy that person's obligations.

For such services, the minor must pay the guardian a fee, which might be a percentage of the minor's **estate.** If the guardian is not an attorney and legal services are required, the guardian will hire an attorney on behalf of the minor.

■■■■ EDUCATION

School attendance is compulsory for children up to a designated age, usually sixteen. The school does not have to be public if an alternate private school meets minimum educational standards.

In Loco Parentis Standing in the place of (and able to exercise some of the rights of) parents.

Children at home can be subject to corporal (i.e., physical) punishment by their parents so long as the punishment does not constitute abuse. Teachers are **in loco parentis,** which means that they stand in the place of parents. As such, teachers can also impose corporal punishment on children if reasonably necessary for proper education and discipline. Subjecting children to such punishment is *not* considered cruel and unusual punishment under the Constitution.

A student cannot be expelled or given a long-term suspension from school without being accorded certain procedural rights. For example:

☐ The right to receive written notice of the charges against him or her

☐ The right to a hearing on the charges to determine whether they are valid

☐ The right to an impartial hearing officer. (The latter cannot be directly involved in the matter. For example, the teacher who brought the charges against the student cannot be the hearing officer.)

☐ The right to be represented by counsel at the hearing

☐ The right to present evidence and to confront the accuser at the hearing

If the student is faced with a less severe punishment, such as a short-term suspension, all of these procedural rights are not provided. The student has a right to know the basis of the charges and the right to respond to them, but not necessarily to a hearing with legal representation.

■■■■ NEGLECT AND ABUSE

Neglect The failure to provide support, medical care, education, moral example, or discipline.

Abuse Physically harming a person.

Statutes exist to protect children who have been neglected or abused by their parents. Neglect is often defined as failing to give support, education, medical care, or other care necessary for the child's welfare, e.g., the refusal of a parent to give a child a needed operation, leaving a young child unattended at home for a long period of time. Abuse often involves physical harm inflicted by the parent on the child. (See Exhibit 14.1 for relevant statistics on maltreatment by parents and by others.)

If a court finds that a child has been neglected or abused, a number of options are usually available. Criminal penalties might be imposed. The court may have the power to terminate the parent's parental rights (discussion in chapter 15), or the child may be placed in the custody of the state's child welfare agency for foster care placement.

■■■■ DELINQUENCY

At common law, a minor below the age of seven was incapable of committing a crime—or so the law conclusively presumed. Evidence that such a child was in fact capable of committing a crime was inadmissible. A minor between the ages of seven and fourteen could be guilty of a crime if the prosecutor could show that the minor was mature enough to have formed the criminal intent necessary for the particular crime. A rebuttable presumption existed that a minor between these ages could *not* possess the requisite criminal intent. This simply meant that the court would assume the absence of this intent unless the prosecutor affirmatively proved otherwise. Minors over fourteen were treated and tried the same as adults.

In the early part of this century, a trend developed to remove the stigma of criminality from the misconduct of minors. Juvenile courts were created. Terms such as **juvenile delinquent,** PINS (Person In Need of Supervision), MINS (Minor In Need of Supervision), and CHIPS (Child In Need of Protection and Services) began to be widely used. A juvenile delinquent is a person under a certain age, e.g., sixteen, whose conduct would constitute a crime if performed by an adult. A PINS, MINS, or CHIPS is a person who has committed a so-called *status offense,* which in this context means noncriminal misconduct by a person under a certain age. Examples of such offenses include habitual truancy from school and incorrigibility at home. When a juvenile court decides that a child fits into one of these special categories, it has a number of options, including sending the child home with a warning, institutionalization in a juvenile facility, probation under the supervision of a youth counselor, and **foster home** placement.

While this system of special treatment is now widely used, it has been criticized as too lenient, particularly when the child commits a serious act such as homicide or sexual assault. Experts say that hundreds of children under age twelve commit homicides each year. Anderson, *Grown-up Crime, Boy Defendant,* 75 Amer. Bar Assoc. J. 26, 27 (November 1989). When a child of a specified age is accused of particularly heinous conduct of this kind, most states give a judge discretion in deciding whether the case should be handled in a juvenile court or whether the regular criminal adult courts should take over.

Juvenile Delinquent A young person under a designated age whose conduct would constitute a crime if committed by an adult.

Foster Home A temporary home for a child when his or her own family cannot provide care and when adoption is either not possible at the present time or is under consideration.

□ Notes on the Legal Status of Children

1. Twenty-one has been the traditional minimum voting age, although most states have recently lowered this to eighteen.

2. On the tort liability of a minor, see chapter 17.

3. On the abortion rights of minors, see chapter 12.

■ SUMMARY

The age of majority is eighteen, but a state may impose different age requirements for performing different activities. Emancipation before the age of majority can make a minor eligible for some of these activities.

A number of special laws apply to minors. For example, they have the right to disaffirm contracts they have entered. They can own real and personal property in their own name, but unless they have been emancipated, their parents have a right to keep their earnings. Also, minors cannot acquire their own domicile without parental consent, and in most states, an unemancipated minor is ineligible to make a will. If the parents of a minor die,

the court will appoint a guardian to oversee his or her affairs.

School is compulsory until a designated age. Teachers stand in the place of parents and, as such, can impose reasonable corporal punishment. However, students are entitled to certain procedural rights, e.g., a hearing, if the school wants to expel or suspend them long term.

When a parent neglects or abuses a child, the state has a number of options, e.g., criminal prosecution, foster home placement, and termination of parental rights. A child below the age of seven cannot commit a crime, but one between seven and fourteen can be prosecuted if the state can over-

☐ **EXHIBIT 14.1 Child Abuse and Neglect Cases Reported and Investigated: 1991 and 1992**

[Based on reports alleging child abuse and neglect that were referred for investigation by the respective child protective services agency in each State.]

STATE	1991				1992			
	Population under 18 years old	Number of reports[1]	Number of children subject of a report	Investigation disposition, number of children substantiated[2]	Population under 18 years old	Number of reports[1]	Number of children subject of a report	Investigation disposition, number of children substantiated[2]
United States	**65,142,000**	**1,767,674**	**2,689,193**	**860,261**	**66,166,000**	**1,898,911**	**2,855,691**	**991,758**
Alabama	1,071,000	28,462	43,969	21,334	1,076,000	28,311	43,246	23,265
Alaska	180,000	[3]8,983	8,983	6,252	185,000	[3]9,892	9,892	8,544
Arizona	1,010,000	26,531	44,844	28,091	1,047,000	29,339	51,216	30,556
Arkansas	626,000	15,860	33,520	8,118	629,000	17,250	36,089	7,538
California	8,163,000	302,834	416,757	71,226	8,423,000	326,120	463,090	73,675
Colorado	883,000	31,796	50,874	8,688	909,000	34,409	55,740	9,237
Connecticut	764,000	14,369	22,080	15,957	771,000	14,369	22,080	15,957
Delaware	168,000	4,367	7,941	2,209	172,000	4,586	8,292	2,157
District of Columbia ..	121,000	5,119	9,444	4,046	117,000	5,596	12,093	3,718
Florida	2,998,000	117,887	184,720	82,386	3,106,000	116,403	180,285	88,563
Georgia	1,775,000	40,142	68,057	43,460	1,800,000	51,225	46,192	46,192
Hawaii	288,000	[3]5,017	5,017	2,191	293,000	[3]5,310	5,310	2,277
Idaho	318,000	9,477	19,507	7,103	324,000	12,230	24,020	6,395
Illinois	2,998,000	67,751	117,912	39,572	3,029,000	74,220	131,592	43,433
Indiana	1,465,000	41,954	63,192	33,329	1,461,000	39,233	58,970	30,283
Iowa	725,000	19,025	27,553	8,154	735,000	19,432	28,094	7,834
Kansas	[4]672,000	9,133	[4]19,280	(NA)	678,000	[3]22,079	22,079	11,585
Kentucky	959,000	33,505	52,912	24,469	964,000	35,997	56,438	24,437
Louisiana	1,233,000	25,579	44,612	14,997	1,238,000	26,087	47,893	16,050
Maine	310,000	4,080	9,503	4,373	306,000	4,826	10,177	4,927
Maryland	1,201,000	29,254	46,806	(NA)	1,226,000	30,062	48,699	(NA)
Massachusetts	1,374,000	35,614	58,218	28,048	1,384,000	32,286	52,581	24,601
Michigan	2,484,000	49,074	113,932	26,366	2,509,000	51,601	117,316	25,931

STATE	1991				1992			
	Population under 18 years old	Number of reports[1]	Number of children subject of a report	Investigation disposition, number of children substantiated[2]	Population under 18 years old	Number of reports[1]	Number of children subject of a report	Investigation disposition, number of children substantiated[2]
Minnesota	1,189,000	17,480	26,663	9,948	1,206,000	17,988	27,462	11,217
Mississippi	751,000	14,377	20,138	7,207	748,000	17,528	32,076	10,712
Missouri	1,340,000	46,343	76,249	22,235	1,350,000	49,286	79,493	24,339
Montana	224,000	7,236	[4]11,029	(NA)	226,000	9,691	14,760	5,328
Nebraska	435,000	7,993	17,087	5,841	439,000	7,961	17,029	5,262
Nevada	321,000	12,858	20,573	7,413	338,000	13,914	22,540	7,699
New Hampshire	280,000	6,550	10,480	2,872	280,000	6,755	10,943	917
New Jersey	1,842,000	[3]53,750	53,750	19,489	1,863,000	[3]50,443	50,443	17,499
New Mexico	458,000	[3]18,234	18,234	5,117	469,000	[3]26,969	26,969	6,716
New York	4,366,000	131,476	212,420	55,586	4,422,000	137,779	228,457	92,238
North Carolina	1,643,000	45,315	71,427	24,636	1,662,000	55,411	88,472	29,546
North Dakota	173,000	3,925	6,435	3,262	172,000	4,515	7,565	3,669
Ohio	2,819,000	88,255	144,218	57,934	2,820,000	95,376	148,101	61,327
Oklahoma	845,000	[3]21,328	21,328	8,287	858,000	[3]24,092	24,092	8,063
Oregon	748,000	23,530	37,648	7,961	766,000	25,622	41,506	8,705
Pennsylvania	2,830,000	[3]23,861	23,861	7,986	2,844,000	[3]25,891	25,891	8,419
Rhode Island	230,000	8,844	13,820	5,919	233,000	8,395	12,886	4,931
South Carolina	938,000	18,956	30,978	10,735	945,000	19,712	33,854	11,348
South Dakota	200,000	[3]11,205	11,205	3,826	204,000	[3]10,486	10,486	2,903
Tennessee	1,230,000	[3]29,715	29,715	10,367	1,246,000	[3]31,231	31,231	11,469
Texas	4,969,000	97,676	153,753	58,199	5,072,000	110,937	174,255	62,342
Utah	642,000	14,534	23,254	10,179	654,000	15,910	27,047	10,875
Vermont	145,000	3,175	2,689	1,437	144,000	2,750	3,205	1,498
Virginia	1,539,000	34,067	50,732	13,702	1,562,000	35,880	55,680	14,472
Washington	1,315,000	39,067	59,311	(NA)	1,355,000	39,704	55,836	41,879
West Virginia	437,000	13,888	22,221	(NA)	438,000	12,932	20,949	(NA)
Wisconsin	1,311,000	[3]44,963	44,963	17,657	1,330,000	[3]47,622	47,622	19,213
Wyoming	136,000	3,260	5,379	2,097	138,000	3,268	5,458	2,017

NA Not available. [1]Except as noted, reports are on incident/family based basis or based on number of reported incidents regardless of the number of children involved in the incidents. [2]Type of investigation disposition that determines that there is sufficient evidence under State law to conclude that maltreatment occurred or that the child is at risk of maltreatment. [3]Child-based report that enumerates each child who is a subject of a report. [4]1990 data.

SOURCE: U.S. Department of Health and Human Services, National Center on Child Abuse and Neglect, National Child Abuse and Neglect Data System, Working Paper 2, 1991 Summary Data Component, May 1993; Child Maltreatment—1992, May 1994.

come the presumption that such a child is not old enough to form the necessary criminal intent. A modern tendency is to treat misbehaving children as juvenile delinquents or as persons in need of supervision rather than as defendants in criminal courts.

■ KEY CHAPTER TERMINOLOGY

Minor	Guardian ad Litem	Abuse
Emancipation	Domicile	Juvenile Delinquent
Disaffirm	Estate	Foster Home
Estop	In Loco Parentis	
Necessaries	Neglect	

ADOPTION

■ INTRODUCTION

A number of important terms should be defined and distinguished before discussing the subject of adoption.

☐ **Custody** The control and care of an individual.

☐ **Guardianship** The legal right to the custody of an individual.

☐ **Ward** An individual who is under guardianship.

☐ **Termination of Parental Rights** A judicial declaration that a parent shall no longer have any right to participate in decisions affecting the welfare of the child.

☐ **Adoption** The legal process by which an adoptive parent assumes the rights and duties of a natural (i.e., biological) parent.

☐ **Paternity** The fatherhood of a child.

☐ **Foster Care** A child welfare service that provides shelter and substitute family care when a child's own family cannot care for it. Foster care is designed to last for a temporary period during which adoption is neither desirable nor possible, or during the period when adoption is under consideration.

☐ **Stepparent** A person who marries the natural mother or father of a child, but is not one of the child's natural parents. For example, assume that Ted and Mary marry each other. It is the second marriage for both. Ted has a son, Bill, from his first marriage. Mary has a daughter, Alice, from her first marriage. Ted is the natural father of Bill and the stepfather of Alice. Mary is the natural mother of Alice and the stepmother of Bill. If Alice adopts Bill, she becomes his *adoptive parent;* she will no longer be his stepparent.

Adoption establishes a permanent, legal, parent-child relationship between the child and a person who is not the natural parent of the child. (Approximately 2 percent of children in the country today live with adoptive parents. See Exhibit 15.1.) In many states, an adoption leads to the reissuance of the child's birth certificate, listing the adoptive parent as the "mother" or "father"

CATEGORY	NUMBER IN 1980	NUMBER IN 1990
Children living with both natural parents	39,523,000	37,026,000
Children living with natural mother and stepfather	5,355,000	6,643,000
Children living with adoptive parents	1,350,000	974,000
Children living with natural father and stepmother	727,000	608,000
Unknown	293,000	197,000

SOURCE: *Statistical Abstract of the United States,* Table 79 (1994).

of the child. The relationship is permanent in that only the court can end the relationship by terminating the parental rights of the adoptive parent. Even the divorce or death of the adoptive parent does not end the relationship. Assume, for example, that Tom marries Linda and then adopts her son, Dave, by a previous marriage. If Tom subsequently divorces Linda, he does not cease to be Dave's parent. His obligation to support Dave, for example, continues after the divorce. Similarly, when Tom dies, Dave can inherit from Tom as if he were a natural child of Tom. In this sense, the parent-child relationship continues even after the death of the adoptive parent.

KINDS OF ADOPTION

The three main kinds of adoption are agency adoption, independent adoption, and black market adoption. A fourth, equitable adoption, will be considered later in the chapter.

AGENCY ADOPTION

In an **agency adoption,** the child is placed for adoption by a licensed private or public agency. There are two main circumstances in which such agencies become involved. First, the parent (usually the mother) voluntarily transfers the child to the agency by executing a formal surrender document that relinquishes all parental rights in the child. Second, a court terminates the parental rights of a parent because of abandonment, abuse, or neglect, and asks the agency to place the child for adoption.

INDEPENDENT/PRIVATE ADOPTION

In an **independent adoption** (also called a private adoption), a natural parent places the child for adoption with the adoptive parents, often with the help of an attorney, a doctor, or both. (See Exhibit 15.2 for sample adoption ads.) As with agency adoptions, a court must give its approval to the independent adoption. Furthermore, the state may require an agency to investigate the prospective adoption and file a report, which is considered by the court. It should be noted, however, that in an independent adoption, the level of involvement by the agency is far less extensive and intrusive than in a traditional agency adoption, where the agency supervises the entire process.

Most, but not all, independent adoptions are initiated by a stepparent or by someone who is otherwise already related to the child. Yet many independent adoptions occur when no such relationship exists.

□ **EXHIBIT 15.2**
**Sample ads used
in adoption.**

Here is an example of how an independent adoption might occur:

When Ralph and Nancy Smith discovered that they were infertile, they decided to adopt. Several visits to adoption agencies, however, were quite discouraging. One agency had a long waiting list of couples seeking to adopt healthy, white infants; it was not taking any new applications. Another accepted their application, but warned that the process might take up to five years, with no guarantee that a child would eventually become available. Nationally, hundreds of thousands of women are waiting to adopt a relatively small number of healthy, white infants. The small number of available children is due to the widespread use of abortion and the declining social stigma attached to the single-parent motherhood.

Acting on the advice of a friend, the Smiths then tried the alternative of an independent adoption. They placed personal ads in newspapers and magazines seeking to contact an unwed pregnant woman who would be willing to relinquish her child for adoption. They also sent their résumé and letters of inquiry to doctors, members of the clergy, and attorneys specializing in independent adoptions. In some cities, the yellow pages had listings for attorneys with this specialty. Their efforts were finally successful when an attorney led them to Diane Kline, a seventeen-year-old pregnant girl. The Smiths prepared a scrapbook on their life, which Diane reviewed. She then interviewed the Smiths and decided to allow them to adopt her child. The Smiths paid the attorney's fees, Diane's medical bills, the cost of her psychological counseling, travel expenses, and living expenses related to the delivery of the baby. Diane signed a consent form relinquishing her rights in the baby and agreeing to the adoption by the Smiths, who formally applied to the court for the adoption. A social worker at a local agency investigated the case and made a report to the court, which then issued an order authorizing the adoption.

In this example, the natural mother had personal contact with the adoptive parents. This is not always the case. Independent adoptions can also resemble agency adoptions, where anonymity is more common.

Note that the money paid by the Smiths covered medical, legal, and related expenses. Other payments would be illegal. Assume, for example, that Diane had hesitated about going through with the adoption and the Smiths had offered her $10,000 above expenses. This could constitute illegal *baby buying,* turning an independent adoption into a **black market adoption.** Such a payment to a birth parent, to an attorney, or to anyone is illegal. A person may pay those expenses that are naturally and reasonably connected with the adoption, so long as no cash or other consideration is given to induce someone to participate in the adoption. (The separate but related problems of surrogate motherhood will be considered in the next chapter.)

In some states, independent adoptions are more common than agency adoptions. Critics argue that illegal payments are frequent, and that the lack of safeguards in independent adoptions can lead to disastrous consequences. A dramatic example occurred in 1988 when a New York City attorney was convicted in the battery death of a six-year-old girl who had been placed in his care so that he might arrange an independent adoption. The attorney had kept the child—and then abused her—when prospective adoptive parents failed to pay his fee for the adoption. Proponents of independent adoptions view this case as an aberration and maintain that the vast majority of independent adoptions are legal and are adequately supervised.

BLACK MARKET ADOPTION

Frustration with agency adoptions leads to the alternative of independent adoptions. And frustration with both kinds of legal adoptions leads to *black market adoptions,* which involve a payment beyond reasonable expenses.

An adoption becomes baby buying when the payment is for the placement of the child rather than for reasonable expenses. (See Exhibit 15.6 at the end of this chapter.) The most blatant example is the *baby broker* who financially entices women to give up their children and then charges adoptive parents a large "fee" for arranging the adoption. In 1990, a typical black market adoption cost up to $50,000.

It is difficult to know how many independent adoptions turn into black market adoptions, since the participants have an interest in keeping quiet about the illegal payment. To discourage such payments, some states require the adoptive parent to file with the court a list of all expenditures pertaining to the adoption. This, however, has not stopped black market adoptions, and critics argue that the only way to do so is to eliminate independent adoptions so that all adoptions will be more adequately supervised by traditional public and private agencies.

■■■■■ WHO MAY BE ADOPTED?

In the vast majority of cases, the person adopted (called the adoptee) is a child, usually an infant. Yet in most states it is possible for one adult to adopt another adult as well. The most common reason for this practice is that the adoptive parent wants to give the adopted adult rights of inheritance from the adoptive parent. In effect, the latter is designating an heir.

Suppose, however, that a homosexual wants to adopt his or her homosexual lover. A few courts have allowed it, but most courts would agree with New York in disallowing it. The "sexual intimacy" between such individuals "is utterly repugnant to the relationship between child and parent in our society, and . . . a patently incongruous application of our adoptive laws." *In the Matter of Robert Paul P.,* 63 N.Y.2d 233, 481 N.Y.S.2d 652, 653 (1984).

WHO MAY ADOPT?

The petitioners (i.e., the persons seeking to become the adoptive parents) will be granted the adoption if it is in "the best interest of the child." Such a broad standard gives the judge a good deal of discretion. In addition to relying on the child welfare agency's investigation report, the judge will consider a number of factors, no one of which is usually controlling.

1. *Age of petitioner.* Most states require the petitioner to be an adult. The preference is for someone who is not unusually older than the child. A court would be reluctant, for example, to allow a seventy-five-year-old to adopt an infant, unless special circumstances warranted it.

2. *Marital status of petitioner.* While many states allow single persons to adopt, the preference is for someone who is married. His or her spouse is usually required to join in the petition.

3. *Health of petitioner.* Adoptive parents are not expected to be physically and emotionally perfect. If a particular handicap will not seriously interfere with the raising of the child, it will not by itself bar the adoption.

4. *Race.* Most judges and adoption agencies prefer that the race of the child be the same as that of the adoptive parents. Some states have time periods during which the search for adoptive parents must be limited to adoptive parents of the same race. This obviously limits the number of interracial or transracial adoptions that occur. The problem, however, is that there are not enough same-race adoptive parents available. In 1994 Congress passed the Multiethnic Placement Act, which prohibits states from delaying or denying the placement of a child solely on the basis of race, color, or national origin. If an agency receives federal assistance, it cannot "categorically deny to any person the opportunity to become an adoptive or a foster parent, solely on the basis of the race, color, or national origin of the adoptive or foster parent, or the child, involved; or delay or deny the placement of a child for adoption or into foster care, or otherwise discriminate in making a placement decision, solely on the basis of the race, color, or national origin of the adoptive or foster parent, or the child, involved." 42 U.S.C.A. § 5115a.

5. *Religion.* When possible or practicable, the religion of the adoptive parents should be the same as the religion of the natural parents. Interfaith adoptions, though allowed, are generally not encouraged.

6. *Wishes of the child.* The court will consider the opinion of the prospective adoptee if he or she is old enough to communicate a preference.

7. *Economic status.* The adoptive parents must have the financial means to care for the child. The court will examine their current financial status and prospects for the future in light of the child's support needs.

8. *Home environment and morality.* Everyone's goal is for the child to be brought up in a wholesome, loving home where values are important and where the child will be nutured to his or her potential. Illegal or conspicuously unorthodox lifestyles are frowned upon.

Earlier we saw that most states do not allow the adoption of a homosexual adult by another homosexual. The hesitancy is stronger against a homosexual adopting a child. Even in Denmark where same-sex marriages are now legal, the couple cannot adopt minor children. There are circumstances, however, when a gay *natural* parent will be given custody of his or her child following

Second-Parent Adoption The adoption of a child by a partner (or cohabitant) of a natural parent who does not give up his or her own parental rights.

a divorce. This is usually because the child is old enough to have already established a healthy relationship with this parent, and because the heterosexual natural parent is either absent or unfit. Courts are more reluctant, however, to allow a homosexual to *adopt* a child with whom he or she does not already have a biological relationship. In **second-parent adoptions,** a few states have made an exception. For example, a lesbian applies to adopt the child of her partner who has just given birth via artificial insemination. Most second-parent adoptions, however, involve a heterosexual couple.

ASSIGNMENT 15.1

a. Mary Jones is a Baptist. She wants to place her one-year-old child for adoption. Mr. and Mrs. Johnson want to adopt the child and file the appropriate petition to do so. The Johnsons are Jewish. Mary Jones consents to the adoption. What effect, if any, will the religious differences between Mary Jones and the Johnsons have on their adoption petition? Assume that Mary has no objection to the child's being raised in the Jewish faith.

b. Same facts as in part (a) above except that the Johnsons are professed atheists. Mary Jones does not care.

c. Both Paul and Helen Smith are deaf and mute. They wish to adopt the infant daughter of Helen's best friend, a widow who just died. Can they?

ADOPTION PROCEDURE

A rather elaborate set of procedures exists for adoption; it is not easy to adopt a child. Courts are very concerned about protecting the interests of the child, the natural parents, and the adoptive parents. When the most sought-after babies (i.e., healthy, white infants) are in short supply, the temptation to "buy" a baby on the black market is heightened. One way to try to control this is by increasing procedural safeguards in the process.

JURISDICTION AND VENUE

Subject Matter Jurisdiction The power of the court to hear a particular category or kind of case.

Subject matter jurisdiction refers to the power of the court to hear a particular kind of case. Not every court in a state has subject matter jurisdiction to issue adoption decrees. The state constitution or state statutes will designate one or perhaps two courts that have authority to hear adoption cases, e.g., the state family court or the state juvenile court. There are also specifications for selecting the county or district in which the adoption proceeding must be brought. The selection is referred to as the **choice of venue.** It will usually depend on the residence (or occasionally on the domicile) of one or more of the participants, usually the natural parents, the adoptive parents, or the child.

Choice of Venue The selection of the court to try the case when more than one court has subject matter jurisdiction to hear that kind of case.

PETITION

States differ on the form and content of the adoption **petition** filed by the adoptive parents to begin the adoption proceeding. The petition will contain such data as the names of the petitioners; their ages; whether they are married and, if so, whether they are living together; the name, age, and religion of the child, etc. While the natural parents play a large role in the adoption proceeding, not all states require that they be mentioned in the petition itself. (For an example of the format of a petition, see Exhibit 15.3.)

☐ **EXHIBIT 15.3 Adoption Petition**

FAMILY COURT OF THE STATE OF _____
COUNTY OF _____

In the Matter of the
Adoption by

_____ of _____

a minor having the first
name of

Index No.

PETITION
(Agency)

whose last name is contained
in the Schedule annexed to
the Petition herein.

TO THE FAMILY COURT:

1. (a) The name and place of residence of the petitioning adoptive mother is:
       Name:
       Address:
She is (of full age) (a minor), born on
She is (unmarried) (married to
and they are living together as husband and wife).
Her religious faith is
Her occupation is
and her approximate annual income is $

   (b) The name and place of residence of the petitioning adoptive father is:
       Name:
       Address:
He is (of full age) (a minor), born on
He is (unmarried) (married to
and they are living together as husband and wife).
His religious faith is
His occupation is
and his approximate annual income is $

2. As nearly as can be ascertained, the full name, date and place of birth of the (male) (female) adoptive child are set forth in the Schedule annexed to this Petition and verified by a duly constituted official of an authorized agency.

3. (a) As nearly as can be ascertained, the religious faith of the adoptive child is
   (b) As nearly as can be ascertained, the religious faith of the natural parents of the adoptive child is

4. The manner in which the adoptive parents obtained the adoptive child is as follows:

5. The adoptive child has resided continuously with the adoptive parents since

6. The name by which the adoptive child is to be known is

7. The consent of the above-mentioned authorized agency has been duly executed and is filed herewith. The consent of the natural parents of the adoptive child is not required because

8. No previous application has been made to any court or judge for the relief sought herein.

9. The adoptive child has not been previously adopted.

10. To the best of petitioners' information and belief, there are no persons other than those hereinbefore mentioned interested in this proceeding.

11. WHEREFORE, your petitioners pray for an order approving the adoption of the aforesaid adoptive child by the above named adoptive parents and directing that the said adoptive child shall be regarded and treated in all respects as the child of the said adoptive parents and directing that the name of the said adoptive child be changed as specified in paragraph 6 above and that henceforth (s)he shall be known by that name.

SOURCE: 1 *Guide to American Law,* 103 (1983).

NOTICE

Due process of law requires that both natural parents be given *notice* of the petition to adopt the child by the prospective adoptive parents. (Later when we study the Baby Richard and Baby Jessica cases, we will see the importance of this requirement.) The preferred method of providing notice is to personally serve the natural parents with process within the state where the adoption petition is brought. If this is not possible, the court may allow substituted service, e.g., registered mail.

There was a time when the father of an illegitimate child was not entitled to notice of the adoption proceeding; only the mother of such a child was given notice. The situation has changed, however, due to recent decisions of the United States Supreme Court. While the full scope of the rights of the father of an illegitimate child have not yet been fully defined by the courts, it is clear that he can no longer be ignored in the adoption process. As we shall see, however, there is a difference between a parent's right to notice of the adoption proceeding and the parent's right to prevent the adoption by refusing to consent to it.

CONSENT

Adoption occurs in essentially two ways: with the consent of the natural parents or without their consent. When consent is necessary, the state's statute will usually specify the manner in which the consent must be given, e.g., whether it must be witnessed, whether it must be in writing, whether the formalities for consent differ for agency adoptions as opposed to independent adoptions, whether the consent form must mention the names of the parties seeking to adopt the child, etc. Some states say that the consent is not valid if it is obtained prior to the birth of the child. Many states say that it cannot be obtained until at least seventy-two hours after birth. Once the consent is validly given, the mother has a period of time, e.g., ten days, during which she has the right to change her mind and revoke the consent. See Exhibit 15.4 for an example of a consent form.

Unfit Demonstrating abuse or neglect that is substantially detrimental to a child.

Both natural parents must consent to the adoption unless the parental rights of one or both of them have been formally terminated because of unfitness. An **unfit** parent loses the power to veto the adoption. As indicated earlier, the father of an illegitimate child has a right to present his views on the propriety of the proposed adoption. He must be given notice of the adoption proceeding unless he has abandoned the child. If he has lived with his illegitimate child, supported him or her, or otherwise maintained close contacts with the child, a court will grant him the same rights as the mother. He *will* be allowed to veto the proposed adoption.

Often a child welfare agency will place the child in a foster home. Foster parents cannot prevent the adoption of the child by someone else. The consent of foster parents to the adoption is not necessary. This does not mean that the foster parents can be ignored entirely. When an agency attempts to remove the child from the foster home, many states give the foster parents the right to object to the removal and to present their arguments against the removal. While foster parents may be given a right to be heard on the removal, they cannot veto the adoption of the child.

Once a natural parent consents to the adoption, can the consent be changed, assuming that it was given according to the requisite formalities? When the

□ **EXHIBIT 15.4 Consent Form**

CONSENT TO ADOPTION

We, the undersigned, being the father and mother, respectively, of _____ , who was born on _____ , 19__ , in _____ County, California, and being the persons entitled to the sole custody of said child do hereby give our full and free consent to the adoption of said child by _____ and _____ , his wife, and do hereby relinquish to said persons forever all of our rights to the care, custody, control, services, and earnings of said child.

Each of us hereby promises that, as soon as adoption proceedings are commenced in the state of _____ , we will properly execute any further instruments or papers necessary to effectuate the adoption of said child by said persons.

Each of us hereby authorizes said persons, or either of them, to procure and provide any and all medical, hospital, dental, and other care needed for said child, it being understood by us that said persons have agreed to, and will pay, such expenses without seeking reimbursement from us prior to the adoption of said child.

Each of us fully understand that, upon the signing of this instrument, we have irrevocably relinquished and waived all right to withdraw the consent and authority herein given.

DATED: _____ , 19__ .

_____
[*Name and Signature of Party*]

_____
[*Name and Signature of Party*]

Witnesses:

_____

_____

Notary Public: (SEAL)

_____

My commission expires _____

SOURCE: D. Adams, *California Code Form* (1960).

adoptive decree has been entered, most states will *not* allow the consent to be revoked, but some states permit revocation beforehand if:

1. The court determines that the revocation would be in the best interest of the child.

2. The court determines that the consent was obtained by fraud, duress, or undue pressure.

See Exhibit 15.5 for an example of a notice of hearing on revocation.

INVOLUNTARY TERMINATION OF PARENTAL RIGHTS

It would be illogical to permit a natural parent to prevent the adoption of his or her child by withholding consent if that parent has abandoned the child. Many statutes, therefore, provide that abandonment as well as extreme cruelty, conviction of certain crimes, or willful neglect will mean that the consent of a parent engaged in such conduct is not necessary. The difficulty, however, is the absence of any clear definition of terms such as abandonment or extreme cruelty. Many courts have taken the position that a parent does not lose the right to withhold consent to an adoption unless the parent's conduct demonstrates *a clear intention to relinquish all parental duties*. Nonsupport in itself, for example, may not be enough if the parent has made some effort to see the child, at least occasionally.

☐ **EXHIBIT 15.5   Notice of Hearing on Issue of Revocation of Adoption**

STATE OF NEW YORK
_____ COURT
COUNTY OF _____
ADDRESS _____

In the Matter of the Adoption of

_____
Adoptive Child

} NOTICE OF HEARING ON ISSUE OF REVOCATION
AND DISPOSITION AS TO CUSTODY, PRIVATE
PLACEMENT ADOPTION

PLEASE TAKE NOTICE that the _____ Court, _____ County, New York, on the _____ day of _____ , 19__ at _____ o'clock or as soon thereafter as counsel can be heard, will hear and determine whether the revocation of consent of the parent in the above entitled matter shall be permitted and, in any event, hear and determine what disposition should be made with respect to the custody of said child.

_____
Chief Clerk of the _____ Court

To: _____
Adoptive Parents

_____
Parents

_____ , Esq.
Attorney for Adoptive Parent(s)

_____ , Esq.
Attorney for Parent(s)

_____
Law Guardian

SOURCE: *West's McKinney's Forms, New York* § 22:24 (1986)

As demonstrated in the following checklist, many factors are relevant to the question of whether a parent had the *intention to abandon* or otherwise relinquish all rights in the child. A court will consider all of these factors in combination; no one factor is usually determinative.

▮▮▮ Interviewing and Investigation Checklist

Factors Relevant to Whether an Intent to Abandon the Child Existed

Legal Interviewing Questions

1. How old are you now?

2. With whom is your child living?

3. Is the person who is caring for the child your relative, a friend, a stranger?

4. How did the child get there?

5. How long has the child been there?

6. When is the last time you saw the child?

7. How often do you see your child per month?

8. How many times do you speak to your child on the phone per month?

9. How often do you write to your child?

10. Did you ever say to anyone that you did not want your child or that you wanted your child to find a home with someone else? If so, explain.

11. Did you ever say to anyone that you wanted your child to live with someone else temporarily until you got back on your feet again? If so, explain.

12. Have you ever placed your child in a public or private adoption agency? Have you ever discussed adoption with anyone? If so, explain.

13. Have you ever been charged with neglecting, abandoning, or failing to support your child? If so, explain.

14. Has your child ever been taken from you for any period of time? If so, explain.

—Continued

—*Continued*

15. Have you ever been found by a court to be mentally ill?

16. How much have you contributed to the support of your child while you were not living with the child?

17. Did you give the child any presents? If so, what were they and when did you give them?

18. While your child was not with you, did you ever speak to the child's teachers or doctors? If so, explain how often you did so.

19. Were you on public assistance while the child was not living with you? If so, what did you tell the public assistance workers about the child?

20. How well is the child being treated now?

21. Could anyone claim that the child lived under immoral or unhealthy circumstances while away from you and that you knew of these circumstances?

22. Has the child ever been charged with juvenile delinquency? Has the child ever been declared a person in need of supervision?

Possible Investigation Tasks

☐ Interview relatives, friends, and strangers who knew that the client visited the child.

☐ Interview anyone with whom the client may have discussed the reasons for leaving the child with someone else.

☐ Prepare an inventory of all the money and other property given by the client for the support of the child while the child was living with someone else.

☐ Collect receipts, e.g., canceled check stubs, for all funds given by the client for such support.

☐ Locate all relevant court records, if any, e.g., custody order in divorce proceeding, neglect or juvenile delinquency petitions and orders.

☐ Interview state agencies that have been involved with the child. Determine how responsive the client has been to the efforts of the agency to help the child and the client.

To take the drastic step of ordering an involuntary termination of parental rights, there must be clear and convincing evidence that the parent is unfit. It is not enough to show that the parent has psychological or financial problems, or that there are potential adoptive parents waiting in the wings who can provide the child with a superior home environment. There must be a specific demonstration of unfitness through abandonment, willful neglect, etc.

The parent can be represented by counsel at the termination proceeding. There is, however, no automatic right to state-appointed counsel if the parent cannot afford to pay one. A court must decide on a case-by-case basis whether an indigent parent needs free counsel because of the complexity of the case.

If parental rights are terminated and there are adoptive parents available, a separate adoption procedure will take place. Of course, the parent whose rights have been terminated is not asked to consent to the adoption.

Mary is the mother of two children. She is convicted of murdering her husband, their father. What facts do you think need to be investigated in order to determine whether Mary's parental rights should be terminated?

ASSIGNMENT 15.2

PLACEMENT

Before ruling on a petition for adoption, the court, as indicated, will ask a public or private child welfare agency to investigate the case and make a recommendation to the court. The agency, in effect, assumes a role that is very similar to that of a social worker or a probation officer in many juvenile delinquency cases.

CAN CHILDREN DIVORCE THEIR PARENTS?

No. It is, of course, logically impossible to divorce someone to whom you are not married. The concept of parental divorce was created by the media in

Unemancipated
Legally dependent on one's parent or legal guardian.

the Florida case of *Gregory K. v. Rachel K.* Gregory was an eleven-year-old, **unemancipated** child who asked a court to terminate the rights of his natural mother so that his foster parents could adopt him. Since he was the party who initiated the action, the media described him as a child who wanted to "divorce" his parents. The *trial* court allowed him to bring the action, terminated the parental rights of his mother, and granted the adoption.

The decision sparked considerable controversy. Some hailed it as the beginning of a major child's rights movement, comparing Gregory to the black woman who began the civil rights movement by refusing to sit in the back of the bus. "Gregory is the Rosa Parks of the youth rights movement," according to the chairperson of the National Child Rights Alliance. *Boy Wants "Divorce" from Parents*, American Bar Association Journal, 24 (July 1992). Others were deeply disturbed by the decision. They thought it would open a floodgate of litigation brought by disgruntled children against their parents. A presidential candidate lamented that "kids would be suing their parents for being told to do their homework or take out the trash." *Boy Wins "Divorce" from Mom*, American Bar Association Journal, 16 (December 1992).

Nonage Below the required minimum age to enter a desired relationship or perform a particular task.

Standing The right to bring a case and seek relief from a court.

On appeal, however, the Florida Court of Appeals ruled it was an error for the trial court to allow Gregory to initiate the termination action. A minor suffers the disability of **nonage** and hence does not have **standing** to ask a court to terminate the rights of his or her natural parents. Yet the court agreed that the parental rights of Gregory's mother should be terminated. When Gregory filed his petition, his foster parent simultaneously brought his own petition to terminate the rights of Gregory's natural mother on the ground that she had abandoned him. Foster parents *do* have standing in Florida to bring such petitions, and in this case, the adult's termination petition had merit. Hence, although Gregory eventually got the result he wanted (termination of parental rights plus adoption), the court, in effect, shut the door to comparable actions initiated by children in the future. "Courts historically have recognized that unemancipated minors do not have the legal capacity to initiate legal proceedings in their own names." *Kingsley v. Kingsley*, 623 So. 2d 780, 783 (Fla. Dist. Ct. App. 1993).

CHALLENGES TO THE ADOPTION DECREE

Interlocutory Nonfinal; interim.

In many states, an adoption decree does not become final immediately. An **interlocutory** (temporary) decree of adoption is first issued, which becomes final after a set period of time. During the interlocutory period, the child is placed with the adoptive parents. Since it would be very unhealthy for the child to be moved from place to place as legal battles continue to rage among any combination of adoptive parents, natural parents, and agencies, statutes place time limitations within which challenges to the adoption decree must be brought, e.g., two years.

BABY RICHARD

We turn now to one of the most dramatic cases in the history of family law—the Illinois case of Baby Richard: *In re Petition of Doe*, 159 Ill. 2d 347, 638 N.E.2d 181 (1994). Before the glare of cameras and national media, a four-year-old boy was taken from his adoptive parents and turned over to his natural father, Otakar Kirchner, whom the boy had never met. One newspaper account said the biological father "took physical custody of the sobbing child as he frantically reached for his adoptive mother in front of the house where the boy had lived since he was four days old."[1] The public's reaction was intense. Newspapers, newscasts, and talk shows gave the story extensive coverage. The case was called "nightmarish," "monstrous," "absolutely horrible," "state sanctioned child abuse." The governor of Illinois said that Baby Richard was being "brutally, tragically torn away from the only parents he has ever known." The opinion in *In re Petition of Doe* was written by Justice Heiple. When it was published, he was denounced. One columnist, Bob Greene, was particularly critical. Justice Heiple took the highly unusual step of responding to this criticism in the supplemental opinion he wrote denying a rehearing of the case. He referred to the criticism as "journalistic terrorism."

Baby Boy Janikova (known in the media as Baby Richard) lived for three years with John and Jane Doe, his adoptive parents. The Supreme Court of Illinois then ruled that he had been improperly adopted and ordered him returned. He was four years old by the time the order was finally carried out.

Daniella Janikova and Otakar Kirchner were not married when their son— referred to as Baby Boy Janikova and also as Baby Richard—was born. Otakar was out of the country at the time. Four days after the birth, Daniella consented to have the baby adopted by John and Jane Doe. Daniella made this decision after being told that Otakar was romantically involved with another woman. Daniella did not tell Otakar about the adoption by the Does. In fact, she told him the baby was born dead. Fifty-seven days after the boy's birth, Otakar learned the truth. Within two weeks, he challenged the legality of the adoption on the ground that he did not consent to it. Lengthy litigation and media attention followed. The trial court found that Otakar was unfit because he did not show sufficient interest in the child during the first thirty days of the child's life, and therefore his consent to the adoption was not required. On appeal, the appellate court affirmed, ruling that the adoption was in the best interest of the child. The case was then appealed to the Supreme Court of Illinois. (During the litigation, Daniella married Otakar and, therefore, joined him in seeking to revoke the adoption.)

The Supreme Court reversed. Justice Heiple held that the adoption was invalid because it violated the rights of the natural father. The use of the best-interest-of-the-child standard by the lower court "grossly misstated the law."

EXCERPTS FROM OPINION:

The finding that the father had not shown a reasonable degree of interest in the child is not supported by the evidence. In fact, he made various attempts to locate the child, all of which were either frustrated or blocked by the actions of the mother. Further, the mother was aided by the attorney for the adoptive parents, who failed to make any effort to ascertain the name or address of the father despite the fact that the mother indicated she knew who he was. Under the circumstances, the father had no opportunity to discharge any familial duty.

In the opinion below, the appellate court, wholly missing the threshold issue in this case, dwelt on the best interests of the child. Since, however, the father's parental interest was improperly terminated, there was no occasion to reach the factor of the child's best interests. That point should never have been reached and need never have been discussed.

Unfortunately, over three years have elapsed since the birth of the baby who is the subject of these proceedings. To the extent that it is relevant to assign fault in this case, the fault here lies initially with the

---

1. *Unnecessary Cruelty,* The San Diego Union-Tribune, May 4, 1995, at B-12.

mother, who fraudulently tried to deprive the father of his rights, and secondly, with the adoptive parents and their attorney, who proceeded with the adoption when they knew that a real father was out there who had been denied knowledge of his baby's existence. When the father entered his appearance in the adoption proceedings 57 days after the baby's birth and demanded his rights as a father, the petitioners should have relinquished the baby at that time. It was their decision to prolong this litigation through a lengthy, and ultimately fruitless, appeal.

The adoption laws of Illinois are neither complex nor difficult of application. Those laws intentionally place the burden of proof on the adoptive parents in establishing both the relinquishment and/or unfitness of the natural parents and, coincidentally, the fitness and the right to adopt of the adoptive parents. In addition, Illinois law requires a good-faith effort to notify the natural parents of the adoption proceedings. These laws are designed to protect natural parents in their preemptive rights to their own children wholly apart from any consideration of the so-called best interests of the child. If it were otherwise, few parents would be secure in the custody of their own children. If best interests of the child were a sufficient qualification to determine child custody, anyone with superior income, intelligence, education, etc., might challenge and deprive the parents of their right to their own children. The law is otherwise and was not complied with in this case. . . .

In 1972, the United States Supreme Court, in the case of *Stanley v. Illinois* (1972), 405 U.S. 645, 92 S. Ct. 1208, 31 L. Ed. 2d 551 ruled that unmarried fathers cannot be treated differently than unmarried mothers or married parents when determining their rights to the custody of their children. The courts of Illinois are bound by that decision. Subsequently, in 1990, a unanimous Illinois Supreme Court pointed out that when ruling on parental unfitness, a court is not to consider the child's best interests, since the child's welfare is not relevant in judging the fitness of the natural parent; that only after the parent is found by clear and convincing evidence to be unfit does the court proceed to consider the child's best interest and whether that interest would be served if the child were adopted by the petitioners. *In re Adoption of Syck* (1990), 138 Ill. 2d 255, 276–78, 562 N.E.2d 174. . . .

Many law suits are painful matters. This case is no exception. Capital cases, for instance, demand the forfeiture of the life of the defendant. Damage suits take money away from some people and give it to others. No one ever claimed that both sides walk away from a law suit with smiles on their faces. No member of this court ever entertained any thought that the decision it rendered in this case would be easy to accept by the losing litigants. Such an event would be incredible.

As for the child, age three, it is to be expected that there would be an initial shock, even a longing for a time in the absence of the persons whom he had viewed as parents. This trauma will be overcome, however, as it is every day across this land by children who suddenly find their parents separated by divorce or lost to them through death. It will not be an insurmountable trauma for a three-year-old child to be returned, at last, to his natural parents who want to raise him as their own. It will work itself out in the fullness of time. As for the adoptive parents, they will have to live with their pain and the knowledge that they wrongfully deprived a father of his child past the child's third birthday. They and their lawyer brought it on themselves.

This much is clear. Adoptive parents who comply with the law may feel secure in their adoptions. Natural parents may feel secure in their right to raise their own children. If there is a tragedy in this case, as has been suggested, then that tragedy is the wrongful breakup of a natural family and the keeping of a child by strangers without right. We must remember that the purpose of an adoption is to provide a home for a child, not a child for a home.

ASSIGNMENT 15.3

a. Someone obviously made a major blunder in this case. From infancy, Baby Richard lived with one set of adults. Years later, he is forced to live with other adults. Who does Justice Heiple say is to blame? Why? Which of the following cast of characters do *you* think is to blame and why: the natural mother, her attorney, the natural father, his attorney, the adoptive parents, their attorney, the trial court (that granted the adoption), the appellate court (that said it was in the best interest of the child that he go with the Does), the Supreme Court of Illinois (that gave the child to his natural father)?

b. What do you think of the quality of the legal representation given to the Does by their attorney?

c. In chapter 17 we learned that custody decisions are based on the best interest of the child. Did this case say that the best interest of the child is irrelevant?

d. What do you think could have been done to avoid this tragedy?

e. Is it relevant that Daniella married Otakar and therefore agreed with him that the adoption should be set aside?

f. Justice Heiple said, "It will not be an insurmountable trauma for a three-year-old child to be returned, at last, to his natural parents who want to raise him as their own." Do you agree? If Justice Heiple thought the trauma *would be* insurmountable, would he have ruled differently? Recall that he said the best interest of the child was irrelevant in this case.

g. Rich and Paula Davis are the natural parents of John. Following a divorce, Rich is granted custody of John. Rich illegally takes John to another state, where his girlfriend adopts him. During the adoption proceeding, Rich falsely tells the court that John's mother, Paula, is dead. Paula therefore never receives notice of the adoption proceeding. Years later, after the passing of the statute of limitations, Paula learns about the adoption for the first time. Can she still challenge the adoption? How would this case be decided in Illinois in view of *In re Petition of Doe?*

BABY JESSICA

The Baby Jessica case is another highly publicized example of a biological father successfully challenging an adoption on the basis of the biological mother's lies. Cara Clausen gave birth to Baby Jessica in Iowa. Within days of the birth, she put her up for adoption to Jan and Roberta DeBoer, who took her to Michigan. In the adoption proceedings, Cara lied about who the biological father was. Three weeks later, she had a change of heart and told the biological father, Dan Schmidt, what had happened. He then sought to get Baby Jessica back from the adoptive parents. He argued that he never consented to the adoption and was never found to be unfit. After two and a half years of litigation, the Iowa and Michigan courts nullified the adoption and ordered Baby Jessica returned. See *In re Baby Girl Clausen,* 502 N.W.2d 649 (Mich. 1993); and *In the Interest of B.G.C.,* 496 N.W.2d 239 (Iowa 1992). The federal courts refused to change this result. In *DeBoer v. DeBoer,* 114 S. Ct. 1, 2 (1993), the United States Supreme Court said, "Neither Iowa law, Michigan law, nor federal law authorizes unrelated persons to retain custody of a child whose natural parents have not been found to be unfit simply because they may be better able to provide for her future and her education. '[C]ourts are not free to take children from parents simply by deciding another home appears more advantageous.'"

■■■■ CONSEQUENCES OF ADOPTION

Once the adoption becomes final, the adopted child and the adoptive parents have almost all the rights and obligations toward each other that natural parents and children have toward each other. The major exception involves the death of a relative of the adoptive parent.

EXAMPLE Kevin is the adopted child of Paul. Paul's brother, Bill, dies intestate (i.e., without leaving a valid will). Can Kevin inherit from Bill?

In some states, the answer would be no: an adopted child cannot take an intestate share of a relative of its adoptive parents. Other states do not impose this limitation.

In most other respects, an adopted child is treated the same as a natural child:

☐ Adopted children can take the name of their adoptive parents.

□ The birth certificate can be changed to reflect the new parents.

□ Adopted children can inherit from their adoptive parents (and in a few states can continue to inherit from their natural parents).

□ Adoptive parents have a right to the services and earnings of the adopted children.

□ Adoptive parents must support adopted children.

□ Adopted children are entitled to worker's compensation benefits due to an on-the-job injury of their adoptive parent.

□ If an adoptive parent dies with a will leaving property to "my heirs" or to "my children" or to "my issue," without mentioning any individuals by name, most (but not all) courts are inclined to conclude that the intention of the deceased adoptive parent was to include adopted children as well as natural children within the designation of "heirs," "children," or "issue."

■■■■■ CONFIDENTIALITY

In recent years there has been great controversy over whether adopted children have a right to discover the identity of their natural parents. The traditional answer has been no. Once the adoption becomes final, the record is sealed. The data within it are confidential. Some states, however, have created limited exceptions to this rule. If *good cause* can be shown, access to part of the adoption records may be allowed. For example, an adopted child may need medical information on its natural parents to help treat diseases that might be hereditary. Similarly, the adopted child may need some information about the identity of its natural parents to avoid unknowingly marrying a natural brother or sister. Access to any information in the records is the exception, however, and whenever information is provided, every effort is made to limit it to non-identifying information. The need must be great. Many courts have held that it is not enough for the adopted child to prove that he or she is experiencing emotional distress due to not knowing the identity of his or her natural parents.

Open Adoption An adoption in which the natural parent maintains certain kinds of contact with his or her child after the adoption.

Some independent or private adoptions give the participants the option of maintaining limited contact between the natural parent and the child after the adoption. These are called **open adoptions,** involving face-to-face meetings or an exchange of identifying information. Some believe that such adoptions should be discouraged. Young women "are finding it harder to get on with their lives. . . ." "They start living for the photos that the adoptive parents send them every month." Adoptive parents sometimes "find themselves not only raising a new baby but providing counseling for the birth mother who often finds it difficult to break her bond with the child." The Council of State Governments, *Adoption*, State Government News 31 (September 1989). Not many adoptive parents, therefore, pursue open adoptions. A few states have established a register in which adopted children and natural parents can indicate a willingness to communicate with each other. If both do not register, however, the traditional rule of anonymity prevails.

Recently, Tennessee designed a unique program that seeks to provide a measure of access without violating confidentiality. Adoptees age twenty-one or older can obtain information such as the names and addresses of their birth parents. But the birth mothers have a way to protect themselves. They can file a "contact veto" prohibiting the release of information about them unless the children agree *not* to contact them. A child who violates this veto can be subjected to civil and criminal penalties. The Tennessee program is based on a similar one in Australia where there is only one known case of a child violating the veto. Not everyone, however, is happy with this approach. The president of the National Council of Adoption says "it's a disastrous invasion of privacy."[2]

Exhibit 15.6 provides a state-by-state overview of adoption rules including confidentiality.

ASSIGNMENT 15.4

Under what circumstances, if any, should an adopted child be able to gain access to adoption records?

EQUITABLE ADOPTION

Assume that John Smith enters a contract with Mary Jones to adopt Mary's child, Bill, but fails to perform the contract. Such contracts are occasionally in writing but more often are simply oral understandings between parties who know each other very well. Assume further that John takes custody of Bill, treats him as a member of his family, but never goes through formal adoption procedures as he had promised. John then dies intestate, i.e., without leaving a valid will. Technically, Bill cannot inherit from John because the adoption never took place. This argument will be used by John's natural children to prevent an unadopted child—Bill—from sharing in the estate.

Many feel that it would be unfair to deny the child inheritance benefits simply because the deceased failed to abide by the agreement to adopt. To avoid the unfairness, some courts conclude that such a child was adopted under the doctrine of **equitable adoption** and hence is entitled to the inheritance rights of adopted children. The doctrine is also referred to as *adoption by estoppel;* challengers will be estopped (i.e., prevented) from denying that such a child has been adopted.

Some courts will reach the same result *even if there was no initial agreement to adopt.* If clear evidence exists that the deceased treated the child as his or her own in every way, a court might rule that a contract to adopt was *implied.* When the deceased dies intestate, equitable adoption status will be accorded the child so that he or she will have full inheritance rights from the deceased.

Equitable Adoption
For purposes of inheritance, a child will be considered the adopted child of a person who made a contract to adopt the child but failed to go through the formal adoption procedures.

WRONGFUL ADOPTION

Suppose that an adoption agency misrepresents the mental or physical health of a child or the medical history of the child's birth family. For example, an agency fails to tell prospective adoptive parents that a child had been sexually abused or falsely tells them that the child does not have a genetic disorder. The adoption goes forward. The adoptive parents then discover that the child has severe medical problems. Can they sue the agency for damages covering the increased cost of child rearing? The period for challenging the adoption itself may have passed. Furthermore, the adoptive parents may have bonded with the child and hence do not want to "send him back" even if it were possible to annul or abrogate the adoption. In such cases, some states have allowed the adoptive parents to sue, particularly when they made clear to the agency that

---

2. Tamar Lewin, *Tennessee Is Focus of Debate on Adoptees' Birth Records,* p. A1, The New York Times National Edition (March 18, 1996).

☐ **EXHIBIT 15.6**   **Adoption in America**

	IS INDEPENDENT ADOPTION LEGAL?	CAN A PROFIT-MAKING OR-GANIZATION BE LICENSED TO PROVIDE CHILDREN?	WHAT IS THE LENGTH OF TIME BETWEEN FILING FOR AND FINALIZING AN ADOPTION?	HOW SOON AFTER BIRTH CAN A MOTHER CONSENT TO ADOPTION?	HOW LONG IS SHE GIVEN TO REVOKE HER CONSENT?*
Alabama	Yes‡	Yes	6 months	Anytime	Not specified
Alaska	Yes	Yes	Varies	Anytime	10 days
Arizona	Yes	Yes	6 months	72 hours	No time
Arkansas	Yes	Yes	6 months	24 hours	10 days
California	Yes‡	No	Usually 6–12 months	After hospital discharge‡	Until adoption is filed‡
Colorado	Yes‡	Yes	6 months	Anytime in court	Several days
Connecticut	No	No	1 year after placement	48 hours	20–30 days
Delaware	No	Yes	2–30 days	Anytime once drug-free	Until parental rights ended
D.C.	Yes	Yes	6–12 months	72 hours	10 days
Florida	Yes	No	At least 30 days	Anytime	Not specified
Georgia	Yes‡	No	At least 60 days	Anytime	10 days
Hawaii	Yes	No	Varies (131-day average)	3 days	Until placement
Idaho	Yes	Yes	30 days	Anytime	30 days
Illinois	Yes	Yes	6 months	72 hours	No time
Indiana	Yes	Yes	Varies	State policy: 48 hours	Until adoption is final
Iowa	Yes	Yes	6 months from placement	72 hours	Until parental rights ended
Kansas	Yes	Yes	At least 30 days	Anytime	Until adoption is final‡
Kentucky	Yes‡	Yes	Usually within 180 days	5 days, in court	No time
Louisiana	Yes	Yes	6–12 months	5 days	30 days
Maine	Yes	Yes	Varies, a week to several months	Anytime in probate court	Varies
Maryland	Yes	Yes	2–6 months	15 days	90 days
Massachusetts	No	No	Varies	4 days	No time
Michigan	No	Yes	1 year	Anytime	Until placement‡
Minnesota	No‡	No	At least 3 months	Anytime	10 working days
Mississippi	Yes	Yes	0–6 months	72 hours	No time
Missouri	Yes	Yes	9 months	48 hours	Until adoption hearing
Montana	Yes‡	No	No time set	Anytime	Until adoption is final
Nebraska	Yes‡	Yes	6 months	Varies	No time
Nevada	Yes	No	6 months	72 hours	No time
New Hampshire	Yes	No	At least 6 months	72 hours	Until adoption is final
New Jersey	Yes	No	At least 6 months	72 hours	Not specified
New Mexico	Yes	Yes	90–180 days from placement	72 hours	No time

Continued

☐ **EXHIBIT 15.6   Adoption in America—*Continued***

	IS INDEPENDENT ADOPTION LEGAL?	CAN A PROFIT-MAKING OR-GANIZATION BE LICENSED TO PROVIDE CHILDREN?	WHAT IS THE LENGTH OF TIME BETWEEN FILING FOR AND FINALIZING AN ADOPTION?	HOW SOON AFTER BIRTH CAN A MOTHER CONSENT TO ADOPTION?	HOW LONG IS SHE GIVEN TO REVOKE HER CONSENT?*
New York	Yes	No	6 months	Anytime	0–45 days
North Carolina	Yes‡	Yes	1 year	Anytime	1–3 months
North Dakota	No	Yes	At least 6 months	72 hours	10 days
Ohio	Yes	Yes	6 months	72 hours	Until adoption is final
Oklahoma	Yes	No	6 months	Anytime	30 days
Oregon	Yes	Yes	About 90 days	Anytime	Until placement
Pennsylvania	Yes	Yes	No set time	72 hours	Until adoption is final
Rhode Island	Yes	No	At least 6 months	15 days	1 year
South Carolina	Yes	Yes	90–365 days	Anytime	No time
South Dakota	Yes	Yes	6 months, 10 days	5 days	30-day appeal period
Tennessee	Yes	No	6 months	Anytime	15 days
Texas	Yes	Yes‡	6 months	Anytime	0–60 days
Utah	Yes	Yes	At least 6 months	Anytime once drug-free	Until adoption is final
Vermont	Yes	No	6 months from placement	Anytime	10 days
Virginia	Yes‡	Yes	0–12 months	Anytime; effective in 10 days	Before placement or in court
Washington	Yes	Yes	No set time	Before birth‡	Until adoption is final‡
West Virginia	Yes	Yes	At least 6 months	72 hours	No time
Wisconsin	Yes‡	Yes	At least 6 months	Anytime in court	No time
Wyoming	Yes	Yes	6 months	Anytime	No time‡

	WHAT EXPENSES ARE PROSPECTIVE PARENTS ALLOWED TO PAY?**	WHAT ARE THE LEGAL PENALTIES FOR BABY SELLING AND FOR BABY BUYING?	ARE SEALED RECORDS AVAILABLE TO ADULT ADOPTEES?
Alabama	Not defined by law	Maximum 3 months in jail and/or $100 fine	Yes†
Alaska	Not defined by law; must report all payments to court	No defined penalties; judge decides	Yes
Arizona	Birthmother's medical, legal, and counseling costs; must report to court	6 months to 1.9 years in prison and/or $1,000 to $150,000 fine	No
Arkansas	Birthmother's medical, living, and other costs; must report to court	Felony: 3–10 years in prison	No†
California	Not defined by law; all payments must be reported to court	Misdemeanor: local D.A. decides penalty	No
Colorado	Reasonable expenses approved by court	Felony: 4–16 years in prison and/or up to $750,000 fine	No†

Continued

☐ **EXHIBIT 15.6   Adoption in America—*Continued***

	WHAT EXPENSES ARE PROSPECTIVE PARENTS ALLOWED TO PAY?**	WHAT ARE THE LEGAL PENALTIES FOR BABY SELLING AND FOR BABY BUYING?	ARE SEALED RECORDS AVAILABLE TO ADULT ADOPTEES?
Connecticut	Agency fees, birthmother's medical, living, counseling costs; must report to court	Felony: 1–5 years in prison and/or $5,000 fine	No†
Delaware	Agency fees, birthmother's legal costs; must report to court	No defined penalties; judge decides	No
D.C.	Not defined by law	90 days in jail and/or $300 fine	No
Florida	Not defined by law; must report all payments to court	Felony: maximum 5 years in prison	No
Georgia	Birthmother's medical costs; must report to court	Felony: maximum 10 years in prison and/or $1,000 fine	No
Hawaii	Not defined by law	No defined penalties; judge decides	No
Idaho	Not defined by law	Felony: maximum 14 years in prison and/or $5,000 fine	No†
Illinois	Birthmother's medical and legal costs; must report to court	Felony: 1–3 years in prison and/or $10,000 fine	No†
Indiana	Birthmother's medical, legal, and other court-approved costs	Felony: maximum 2 years in prison and/or $10,000 fine	No†
Iowa	Birthmother's medical and other costs; must report to court	30 days in jail and/or $100 fine	No
Kansas	Not defined by law; must report all payments to court	No defined penalties; judge decides	Yes
Kentucky	Not defined by law; must report all payments to court	6 months in prison and/or $500 to $2,000 fine	No†
Louisiana	Birthmother's medical, legal, and living costs‡; must report to court	Felony: maximum 5 years in prison and/or $5,000 fine	No†
Maine	Not defined by law	No defined penalties; judge decides	No†
Maryland	Birthmother's medical and legal costs	Maximum 3 months in jail and/or $100 fine	No†
Massachusetts	In identified adoption, all of birthparents' adoption-related costs	2½–5 years in jail and/or $5,000 to $30,000 fine	No
Michigan	Agency fees and other court-approved costs	Maximum 90 days in jail and/or $100 fine	No
Minnesota	Agency fees	Maximum 90 days in jail and/or $700 fine	No†
Mississippi	Birthmother's medical and legal costs	Maximum 5 years in prison and/or $5,000 fine	No
Missouri	Not defined by law	Felony: maximum 7 years in prison and/or $5,000 fine	No†
Montana	Not defined by law; must report all payments to court	Maximum fine: $1,000	No
Nebraska	Not defined by law	Maximum 3 months in jail and/or $500 fine	No†
Nevada	Birthmother's medical and necessary living costs; must report to court	1–6 years in prison and/or a maximum $5,000 fine	No†
New Hampshire	Not defined by law	No defined penalties; judge decides	No
New Jersey	Birthmother's medical and reasonable living costs; must report to court	3–5 years in prison and/or $7,500 fine	No†

Continued

☐ **EXHIBIT 15.6 Adoption in America—*Continued***

	WHAT EXPENSES ARE PROSPECTIVE PARENTS ALLOWED TO PAY?**	WHAT ARE THE LEGAL PENALTIES FOR BABY SELLING AND FOR BABY BUYING?	ARE SEALED RECORDS AVAILABLE TO ADULT ADOPTEES?
New Mexico	Not defined by law; must report all payments to court	Maximum fine: $500	No
New York	Birthmother's medical, legal, and other necessary costs	No defined penalties; judge decides	No†
North Carolina	Agency fees	Misdemeanor: court decides penalty	No
North Dakota	Not defined by law; must report all payments to court	Felony: maximum 5 years in prison and/or $5,000 fine	No†
Ohio	Birthmother's medical, legal, and other costs; must report to court	Maximum 6 months in jail and/or $500 to $1,000 fine	No
Oklahoma	Birthmother's medical, legal, and counseling costs; must be approved by court	Minimum 1 year in jail	No
Oregon	Not defined by law; must report all payments to court	No defined penalties; judge decides	No†
Pennsylvania	Birthmother's medical costs; must report to court	Maximum 5 years in prison and/or $10,000 fine	No†
Rhode Island	Not defined by law	No defined penalties; judge decides	Yes‡
South Carolina	Not defined by law; must report all payments to court	Felony: maximum 10 years in prison and/or $10,000 fine	No†
South Dakota	Not defined by law; must report all payments to court	Felony: maximum 2 years in prison and/or $2,000 fine	No†
Tennessee	Birthmother's medical and legal costs; must report to court	Felony: 1–10 years in prison	No†
Texas	Birthmother's medical and legal costs	Felony: 2–10 years in prison and/or $5,000 fine	No†
Utah	Birthmother's medical, legal, and other adoption-related costs	Must forfeit payment and pay $10,000 maximum fine	No†
Vermont	Law specifies only those "directly related to mother's support"; must report to court	No defined penalties; judge decides	No
Virginia	Not defined by law	No defined penalties; judge decides	No
Washington	Birthmother's medical and legal costs	Felony: maximum 5 years in prison and/or $10,000 fine	No
West Virginia	Birthmother's medical and legal costs; must report to court	No defined penalties; judge decides	No
Wisconsin	Birthmother's medical, legal, and counseling costs; must report to court	Felony: maximum 2 years in prison and/or $10,000 fine	No†
Wyoming	Not defined by law	No defined penalties; judge decides	No

SOURCE: © 1989 by the National Committee for Adoption, Inc. From *Adoption Factbook,* available from the Committee at P.O. Box 33366, Wash., D.C. 20033. Note: Adoptions of American Indians are governed by the federal Indian Child Welfare Act, which prevents a mother from signing consent papers until 10 days after birth and allows her to revoke her consent until an adoption is final.

*Assuming no fraud, duress, or coercion is proved. **Living expenses usually include medical, housing, food, travel, and clothing costs. †Information may be obtained through a voluntary state registry or adoption agency. ‡With restrictions or exceptions.

Wrongful Adoption A tort action seeking damages for wrongfully stating or failing to disclose to prospective adoptive parents available facts on the health or other condition of the adoptee that would be relevant to the decision on whether to adopt.

they did not want to adopt a problem child. Their argument is that they would not have adopted the child if they had been presented with all the facts. They cannot expect a guarantee that the child will be perfect. But they are entitled to available information that might indicate a significant likelihood of future medical problems. The failure to provide such information may constitute the tort of **wrongful adoption.**

◼ SUMMARY

There are three main kinds of adoptions. First is an agency adoption, where a child is placed for adoption by a private or public agency. Second is an independent/private adoption, where a natural parent places a child for adoption with the adoptive parents, often through an intermediary such as an attorney and after an investigation by an adoption agency. In such an arrangement, any payment to the natural mother beyond covering her expenses constitutes illegal baby buying. Third is a black market adoption, where illegal payments are made to the natural mother beyond her expenses.

A court will allow an adoption if it is in the best interest of the child. In making this determination, a number of factors are considered: the petitioner's age, marital status, health, race, religion, economic status, home environment, and lifestyle. If the child is old enough, his or her preference will usually be considered.

An adoption must follow strict procedures. The court must have subject matter jurisdiction. Proper venue must be selected. The petition must contain the required information. The natural parents must be notified of the proceeding and must consent to the adoption unless their parental rights have been terminated because of conduct that clearly demonstrates an intention to relinquish parental duties.

(A child does not have standing to petition a court to terminate the parental rights of his or her parent.) Under certain circumstances, a parent will be given the right to revoke an earlier consent to the adoption. An agency investigates the prospective adoptive parents and reports back to the court. An interlocutory decree of adoption is then made by the court, which becomes final within a designated period of time.

Once the adoption becomes final, the adopted child is treated the same as a natural child with respect to inheritance rights, support rights, etc. In a traditional adoption, the records are sealed, and matters such as the identity of the natural parents are kept confidential except in relatively rare circumstances. In an open adoption, there may be varying degrees of contact between a natural parent and the child after the adoption becomes final.

An equitable adoption occurs when a person dies before fulfilling a contract to adopt a child, and when unfairness can be avoided only by treating the child as having been adopted for purposes of inheritance. The failure of an adoption agency to give available information about the health of the prospective adoptee might constitute the tort of wrongful adoption.

◼ KEY CHAPTER TERMINOLOGY

Custody
Guardianship
Ward
Termination of Parental Rights
Adoption
Paternity
Foster Care
Stepparent

Agency Adoption
Independent Adoption
Black Market Adoption
Second-Parent Adoption
Subject Matter Jurisdiction
Choice of Venue
Petition
Unfit

Unemancipated
Nonage
Standing
Interlocutory
Open Adoption
Equitable Adoption
Wrongful Adoption

SURROGACY AND THE NEW SCIENCE OF MOTHERHOOD

16

"Abram's wife Sarai had not borne him any children. But she had an Egyptian slave girl named Hagar, and so she said to Abram, 'The Lord has kept me from having children. Why don't you sleep with my slave girl? Perhaps she can have a child for me.' "
Genesis 16:1–2 (TEV)

"The reproductive capabilities available to assist infertile couples today are astonishing. Pioneering doctors can now remove eggs from a woman, fertilize them in a laboratory, and reinsert them into that same woman or into another woman; regulate the woman's hormone balance to enhance implantation; monitor the gestation of embryo and fetus, and perform surgery on the fetus in some cases. We now have the ability to separate a child's genetic, gestational, and legal parents so that it is possible to have five different individuals contributing to the birth of a single child: egg donor, sperm donor, womb donor or gestator, and the social parents who will raise the child."
Billig, *High Tech Earth Mothering*, 9 *District Lawyer*, 57 (July/August 1985).

"Just as men have the right to sell their sperm and become surrogate fathers, so women should have the right to sell their reproductive services and become . . . surrogate mothers."
Gale, *The Right to Pregnancy by Contract*, New York Times Book Rev. 12 (December 17, 1989).

One of the most dramatic family law issues to emerge in the last twenty years has been surrogate motherhood. An unpregnant woman enters a contract to become pregnant, to give birth to a child, and then to relinquish all parental rights upon birth through adoption. Due to spectacular scientific advances, a variety of methods of becoming pregnant are available (see Exhibit 16.1). Unfortunately, traditional legal principles do not always fit results made available by the innovations of medicine and biology.

When something goes wrong in a surrogacy contract, e.g., the surrogate mother changes her mind about giving up the child, someone inevitably sues.

□ **EXHIBIT 16.1   New Ways to Make Babies**

Artificial Insemination and Embryo Transfer

1. Father is infertile. Mother is inseminated by donor and carries child.

    ● + ♂ = ♀

2. Mother is infertile but able to carry child. Donor of ovum is inseminated by father; then embryo is transferred and mother carries child.

    ○ + ♂ = ♀

3. Mother is infertile and unable to carry child. Donor of ovum is inseminated by father and carries child.

    ○ + ♂ = ♀

4. Both parents are infertile, but mother is able to carry child. Donor of ovum is inseminated by sperm donor, then embryo is transferred and mother carries child.

    ○ + ♂ = ♀

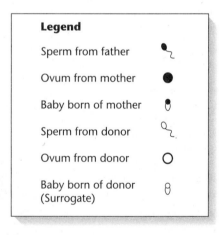

Legend

Sperm from father	♂
Ovum from mother	●
Baby born of mother	♀
Sperm from donor	♂
Ovum from donor	○
Baby born of donor (Surrogate)	♀

In Vitro Fertilization

1. Mother is fertile but unable to conceive. Ovum from mother and sperm from father are combined in laboratory. Embryo is placed in mother's uterus.

    ● + ♂ = ♀

2. Mother is infertile but able to carry child. Ovum from donor is combined with sperm from father.

    ○ + ♂ = ♀

3. Father is infertile and mother is fertile but unable to conceive. Ovum from mother is combined with sperm from donor.

    ● + ♂ = ♀

4. Both parents are infertile, but mother is able to carry child. Ovum and sperm from donors are combined in laboratory.

    ○ + ♂ = ♀

5. Mother is infertile and unable to carry child. Ovum of donor is combined with sperm from father. Embryo is transferred to donor.

    ○ + ♂ = ♀

6. Both parents are fertile, but mother is unable to carry child. Ovum from mother and sperm from father are combined. Embryo is transferred to donor.

    ● + ♂ = ♀

7. Father is infertile; mother is fertile but unable to carry child.

    ● + ♂ = ♀

SOURCE: Strong & DeVault, *The Marriage and Family Experience*, 234 (4th Ed. 1989).

The courts then enter the picture. But what law does a court apply to such a contract? The first instinct of the court is to look to the legislature to determine whether any statutes apply. Until recently, no such statutes existed. Hence the court is forced to write common law to resolve the controversy. (Common law is judge-made law created in the absence of other controlling law such as statutes.) This approach has not been satisfactory. The development of common law is painfully slow, and many feel that it is ill-suited to respond to the rapid developments of science in this area.

Consequently, state legislatures have been under pressure to do something. But the legislatures are not sure what to do. Are new statutes needed? If so, what kind? The following report examines some of the options a legislature should consider.

SURROGATE PARENTING

D. Bennett, *Surrogate Parenting* (1988) (Background Paper 88-2 prepared for the Legislative Counsel Bureau of Nevada)

I. Introduction

In March 1987, the nation's attention focused on a breach of contract battle underway in New Jersey. The contract in question was between Elizabeth and William Stern and Mary Beth Whitehead (now Mary Beth Whitehead-Gould). The Sterns had contracted with Ms. Whitehead in 1985 to act as a surrogate mother. [Under the terms of the contract, Ms. Whitehead was to be artificially inseminated with Mr. Stern's sperm, become pregnant, give birth to a baby, turn it over to the Sterns, and cooperate in the termination of her parental rights. Mrs. Stern would then adopt the baby.] Upon the birth of the baby—known as Baby M in the case—Ms. Whitehead reconsidered and refused to relinquish her parental rights. The Sterns then sued in an attempt to hold Ms. Whitehead to the terms of the contract.

On March 31, 1987, a New Jersey trial court upheld the contract, granted permanent custody to the Sterns, permitted Mrs. Stern to adopt the child, and denied any rights to Ms. Whitehead. On February 3, 1988, the New Jersey Supreme Court approved only the custody portion of the lower court's decision, ruling that surrogate parenting contracts fall under the New Jersey "baby-selling" statutes and are therefore illegal.[1]

The publicity surrounding this case led to a flurry of activity in legislative bodies around the country as pro- and anti-surrogacy groups attempted to sway policymaking bodies to one side or the other. . . .

II. Definitions

Although the term **surrogate parenting** has become widely used since the Baby M case, it can refer to more than one method of achieving parenthood. In addition, the parties involved in a surrogacy contract may not necessarily be limited to a married couple contracting with a single woman. The parties could involve a married surrogate mother, a single father, or single-sex couples. However, for ease of discussion, . . . the terms "married couple," "husband," and "wife" will be used, keeping in mind that a broader definition may apply to these words.

A. Methods

Four general methods of surrogate parenting are recognized. These methods are:

1. *Artificial Insemination by Husband (AIH).* The AIH method is an arrangement in which the surrogate, a woman other than the wife of the sperm donor, is artificially inseminated with the sperm of the husband of a married couple.

2. *In Vitro Fertilization (IVF).* **In vitro fertilization** is a process by which a sperm and an egg are joined in a laboratory and the fertilized egg is implanted in the surrogate.

3. *Artificial Insemination by Donor (AID[1]).* The AID[1] method is a technique in which the surrogate is artificially inseminated with the sperm of a donor other than the contracting male. Such sperm is typically a specimen obtained from a sperm bank.*

4. *Natural Insemination (NI).* The NI method involves a situation where sexual intercourse occurs between the surrogate and the husband of a married couple.

Of the four methods, AIH is the most common and NI is the least. Sometimes, the IVF and AID[1] methods are chosen in surrogate parenting situations, but not as frequently as AIH. . . . Because AIH is the most common method chosen in surrogate parenting agreements, that definition will be applied to the term surrogate parenting in this [discussion].

B. Agreements

The agreement between the surrogate mother and the intended parents takes one of two forms: (1) commercial; or (2) noncommercial. Both agreements involve similar factors. A couple contracts with a woman to bear a child for them. The woman agrees to be artificially inseminated with the husband's sperm, carry the child to term and surrender her parental rights to the biological father upon the birth of the child.

Once the husband has full parental rights to the child [upon birth], the wife (technically the child's stepmother) begins adoption proceedings. Some . . . [states allow] the wife to forgo formal adoption procedures and obtain a substitute birth certificate from

---

1. *In the Matter of Baby M*, 109 N.J. 396, 537 A.2d 1227 (1988).

*AID[2] is a technique in which the *wife* is artificially inseminated with the sperm of a donor other than her husband. Such sperm is also typically a specimen obtained from a sperm bank.

a court of competent jurisdiction. In return, the couple agrees to pay all of the surrogate's medical expenses and other necessary expenses (e.g., maternity clothing).

The difference between a commercial and a noncommercial agreement centers on whether a fee is paid to the surrogate mother. If a fee—usually around $10,000—is paid, then the agreement is considered to be commercial. However, many surrogacy agreements are between family members or friends and do not involve the payment of a fee. These agreements are the noncommercial contracts.

A major argument in the courts and the legislatures involves the nature of this fee. Is it a fee for the surrogate mother's services or is it a fee in exchange for the surrender of her parental rights? . . .

Another factor in surrogacy contracts is the **broker.** Either a private agency or a lawyer, the broker is a third party who coordinates a surrogate parenting agreement. Although a broker receives a fee (in the $10,000–$20,000 range), a broker could be used in both commercial and noncommercial arrangements. However, most arrangements made through a broker include a fee paid to the surrogate mother.

III. Reasons for Choosing Surrogate Parenting Agreements

According to a study of surrogacy recently completed in Wisconsin, the demand for surrogate mothers stems primarily from female infertility. The National Center for Health Statistics estimates that 10 to 15 percent of all married couples are infertile (defined as partners who are sexually active, not using contraception, and unable to conceive after at least one year). The Center excludes the surgically sterile from its statistics. The Wisconsin study also cites evidence that suggests the number of infertile women is on the increase due to the use of intrauterine birth control devices, greater incidence of sexually transmitted diseases, previous abortions and the postponement of childbearing to establish careers. Studies indicate that women who delay having children have a greater risk of being infertile, bearing children with birth defects, and/or being physically impaired. The most common treatments for female infertility are drugs and surgery. Until recently, when these treatments failed, adoption of an unrelated child was the only alternative available.

Couples who want children, but cannot conceive, usually consider adoption. The Wisconsin study noted that, despite a marked increase in the number of live births to single women, fewer unrelated individuals are adopted. Adoption experts believe that the increasing willingness of single mothers to keep their children is a significant factor in limiting the number of infants available for adoption. The stigma once attached to single mothers has diminished. Peers and relatives often encourage single mothers to keep their babies. Medical personnel and social workers are less likely to encourage women to give babies up for adoption.

Laws have changed in recent years to allow single mothers more time to make or revoke a decision to allow adoption. Consequently, couples often cite long waiting periods and other obstacles to adoption (such as the age limit placed on prospective parents) as reasons for seeking surrogate mothers. [R. Roe, *Childbearing by Contract*, 4 (Wisconsin Legislative Bureau, March, 1988).]

Not all couples who contract with a surrogate have failed at adoption. Some couples would rather be childless than adopt an unrelated child. For such families, a genetic link to their child is of primary importance. For example, William Stern lost most of his family in Adolf Hitler's holocaust and wanted a child biologically linked to him. Newspaper interviews of intended fathers confirm the importance some of them place on a biological link when seeking surrogates. One father favored a surrogate birth because "that child will be biologically half-mine" while another father stated that "we believe strongly in heredity."

IV. Major Arguments for and against Surrogate Parenting

A review of the literature on surrogate parenting reveals several common policy positions on each side of this issue.

A. Supporting Arguments

Those who support surrogacy contracts and the regulation of them generally cite the following:

☐ A limitation placed on the fees charged by brokers and the licensing and regulation of brokers will ensure competency, honesty and legitimacy in this process.

☐ Due to the ever-decreasing number of babies available for adoption and the ever-increasing technology in the area of human reproduction, couples who desperately want children will continue to seek out surrogate mothers. Consequently, some form of protection must be provided for the couple, the surrogate mother, and the resulting child.

☐ Proper examination of both couple and surrogate as provided in state law would ensure:

1. That the couple is emotionally and financially ready to bear the responsibility of parenthood.

2. That the couple is truly in need of this service, such as when the wife is unable to carry a child to term.

3. That the woman who will bear the child is emotionally, physically, and psychologically

able to carry the child and to give up her rights to the child at birth.

The majority of surrogate contracts are completed without [controversy]. Only a small percentage of surrogate mothers have refused to surrender the resulting babies. . . .

B. Opposing Arguments

Those people who advocate a ban on surrogacy contracts argue that:

☐ Children will be psychologically damaged when they discover that they were "bought."

☐ Surrogate parenting arrangements are in violation of the Thirteenth Amendment of the United States Constitution, which applies to slavery and can be interpreted to forbid the buying and selling of people.

☐ Surrogate parenting will become another form of economic exploitation of rich people over poor. As exemplified by the Baby M affair, the adoptive couples tend to have an economic and educational advantage over the surrogate. [A] study of potential and existing surrogate mothers also indicates that most of the women are unemployed or on some form of public assistance and only have a high school diploma. Thus, surrogate parenting arrangements will serve to create a class of "womb-sellers."

☐ There are plenty of nonwhite babies, older children, and special needs children available for adoption.

☐ Women will be forced—not because they choose, but because the contract requires—to abort fetuses upon demand or to become pregnant again in the case of a miscarriage.

V. Issues in State Law

According to the Wisconsin study of surrogacy, court decisions and discussions of surrogacy indicated that four existing areas of law affect surrogate parenting agreements. These areas are (1) adoption and termination of parental rights; (2) artificial insemination and legal paternity; (3) child custody; and (4) contracts. . . .

A. Adoption Laws

Two aspects of many state adoption laws may restrict or prevent surrogate parenting agreements. One forbids compensation in exchange for the consent to an adoption, and the other forbids consent to an adoption to be given prior to the birth of the child.

At least 24 states . . . prohibit the payment of compensation for adoptions. Often called **baby-selling** laws, these statutes range from those prohibiting all payments to those allowing payment of certain expenses. Nevada for example, forbids the payment of a fee in return for the mother's agreement to terminate her parental rights of the child.

While surrogacy opponents favor the use of adoption statutes to control it, proponents maintain that modern anti–baby-selling laws predate surrogate parenting and were designed to protect unwed mothers. Under a surrogacy agreement, the intended father is also the biological father; therefore, how can he buy his own child? Also, proponents argue, surrogates have voluntarily agreed to surrender the child. She is not doing so under pregnancy related stress. Finally, the fees are paid primarily to replace lost work time or pain and suffering.

All 50 states . . . have laws that prohibit a mother from granting consent to adoption before a child's birth or for some period of time after birth. Waiting periods range up to as much as 20 days (Pennsylvania). A mother's consent to surrender a newborn for adoption is not valid in Nevada until at least 72 hours after birth.

However, as with baby-selling laws, consent laws were designed to protect unwed mothers. The decisions facing an unwed mother are not like those facing the surrogate mother who has voluntarily chosen to bear children for another couple.

B. Paternity Laws

Paternity laws may also affect surrogate arrangements. Some states retain the common law rule that the husband of a woman who gives birth to a child is presumed to be the father. Courts in many of these states will not admit evidence to the contrary. A majority of states now allow a rebuttal to the presumption of paternity, but place a strict burden of proof on the contending party. . . .

Surrogate supporters argue that paternity laws were designed to protect the child, particularly the rights to inheritance, and were not drafted in anticipation of surrogate parenting arrangements. Rights and duties outlined in surrogate agreements fall on the natural father and would secure the child's rights. Critics point out that paternity determinations are made by courts and do not necessarily give custody to one party or the other.

Paternity laws could also affect surrogate arrangements based on the reliance on artificial insemination. Since most surrogate mothers are artificially inseminated, laws on that subject might be relevant. At least 30 states . . . have laws that presume that the husband of the woman being inseminated is the child's father and that relieves the sperm donor of any legal obligation.

Although some critics approve applying artificial insemination law to surrogate agreements, others find the analogy suspect and open to court challenge.

C. Custody Issues

The traditional basis for custody decisions is a determination of the best interest of the child. The standards for judging the suitability of intended parents include marital and family status, mental and physical health, income and property, any history of child abuse or neglect and other relevant facts. In the case of Baby M, custody of the child was awarded to the Sterns because the court felt it was in the best interest of the child. Ms. Whitehead's divorce after 13 years of marriage and subsequent marriage to the father of her unborn child 2 weeks after the divorce were key factors in the court's decision.

A spokesperson for the National Committee for Adoption objects to surrogate contracts because they are not required to take into account the best interest of the child. Unlike normal adoption proceedings, no one screens intended parents. Currently, surrogacy agreements require nothing more than the financial ability to hire a lawyer and pay the surrogate mother.

Supporters of surrogate agreements argue that intended parents should receive the same treatment as ordinary parents, since the only qualification they lack is the physical ability to have children. Supporters also maintain that surrogate agreements are inherently in the best interest of the child because the intended parents have given much thought to their actions and decided that they truly want a child. Adoption proceedings, on the other hand, were devised to provide a permanent home for a child who otherwise would not have one. In a surrogate agreement, the child's home is provided by contract.

D. Contractual Duties

Existing federal and state contract laws do not address the issues of the surrogate's liability or acceptable remedies in case of breach of contract, nor do they address the responsibilities of the intended parents.

Contracts impose a number of duties on one or both of the intended parents. These duties include the payment of expenses and fees and the assumption of responsibility for the child at birth. If the birth mother performs as agreed, does she have recourse if the other party refuses to pay all or part of the expenses and fees? What happens if the intended parents refuse to take the child? Can the surrogate mother sue the natural father for child support?

Some of these issues are already facing state courts. For example, in Texas, a 24-year-old surrogate mother died of heart failure in her eighth month of pregnancy; and in Washington, D.C., a baby born through a surrogate agreement was diagnosed as having acquired immune deficiency syndrome (AIDS). Now, neither the surrogate mother nor contracting parents want the AIDS baby. These issues were not previously addressed in the contracts.

Enforcement of a surrogate mother's duties are even more difficult. She agrees to be inseminated, bear a child and surrender all parental rights. She is also to refrain from sexual intercourse during the insemination period and has the duty to refrain from activities that may harm the fetus. If medical clauses are included in the contract, what recourse do the intended parents have if the surrogate refuses to follow them? If she refuses the insemination, are any expenses refunded to the intended parents? If the surrogate chooses to have an abortion in the first trimester, which is legally her right, can the intended parents sue for expenses? Can they sue for damages if the surrogate decides to keep the child?

Even if the surrogate agreement clears all other legal hurdles, many questions remain about the responsibilities of each party to the contract.

VI. State Regulation

States differ on how to handle surrogacy contracts:

□ Some states are silent on the subject. No statutes exist, and no cases have yet been litigated in the courts.

□ A few states have outright bans on all commercial and noncommercial surrogacy contracts.

□ Some states prohibit commercial surrogacy contracts.

□ Some states prohibit fees to the surrogate beyond the expenses involved.

□ Some states prohibit fees to an **intermediary,** the person who facilitates the surrogacy arrangement such as by bringing the surrogate and couple together.

□ Some states allow surrogacy contracts, but closely regulate the process including medical and psychological screening, home studies, the payment of fees, time periods within which the surrogate can change her mind, the identification of the legal parents, etc.

In August 1988, the National Conference of Commissioners on Uniform State Laws drafted and approved for use in all state legislatures the **Uniform Status of Children of Assisted Conception Act.** The model act provides two alternatives for consideration by state legislatures: one to regulate surrogate parenting agreements (Alternative A), and the other to ban the agreements (Alternative B).

Alternative A would allow surrogate parenting contracts and provides a regulatory framework. A court hearing would be held at which both parties would be required to submit medical evidence to prove that the would-be mother cannot bear her own child and that the surrogate mother is mentally and physically fit to bear the child. The proposal also would allow the surrogate mother to pull out of the agreement up to 180 days into her pregnancy.

The opposing language in the act (Alternative B) simply bans all surrogate parenting agreements. It does not make any distinction between commercial and noncommercial contracts; all such contracts are void.

Uniform Status of Children of Assisted Conception Act

National Conference of Commissioners on Uniform States Laws (1988)

Section 1. Definitions

In this [Act]:

(1) **"Assisted conception"** means a pregnancy resulting from (i) fertilizing an egg of a woman with sperm of a man by means other than sexual intercourse or (ii) implanting an embryo, but the term does not include the pregnancy of a wife resulting from fertilizing her egg with sperm of her husband.

(2) **"Donor"** means an individual [other than a surrogate] who produces egg or sperm used for assisted conception, whether or not payment is made for the egg or sperm used, but does not include a woman who gives birth to a resulting child.

[(3) **"Intended parents"** means a man and woman, married to each other, who enter into an agreement under this [Act] providing that they will be the parents of a child born to a surrogate through assisted conception using egg or sperm of one or both of the intended parents.]

(4) **"Surrogate"** means an adult woman who enters into an agreement to bear a child conceived through assisted conception for intended parents. . . .

Section 2. Maternity

[Except as provided in Sections 5 through 9,] a woman who gives birth to a child is the child's mother. . . .

Section 3. Assisted Conception by Married Woman

[Except as provided in Sections 5 through 9,] the husband of a woman who bears a child through assisted conception is the father of the child, notwithstanding a declaration of invalidity or annulment of the marriage obtained after the assisted conception, unless within two years after learning of the child's birth he commences an action in which the mother and child are parties and in which it is determined that he did not consent to the assisted conception.

Section 4. Parental Status of Donors and Deceased Individuals

[Except as otherwise provided in Sections 5 through 9:]

(a) A donor is not a parent of a child conceived through assisted conception.

(b) An individual who dies before implantation of an embryo, or before a child is conceived other than through sexual intercourse, using the individual's egg sperm, is not a parent of the resulting child. . . .

Alternative A

Comment

A state that chooses Alternative A should also consider Section 1(3) and the bracketed language in Sections 1(2), 2, 3, and 4.

[Section 5. Surrogacy Agreement

(a) A surrogate, her husband, if she is married, and intended parents may enter into a written agreement whereby the surrogate relinquishes all her rights and duties as a parent of a child to be conceived through assisted conception, and the intended parents may become the parents of the child pursuant to Section 8.

(b) If the agreement is not approved by the court under Section 6 before conception, the agreement is void and the surrogate is the mother of a resulting child and the surrogate's husband, if a party to the agreement, is the father of the child. If the surrogate's husband is not a party to the agreement or the surrogate is unmarried, paternity of the child is governed by [the Uniform Parentage Act]. . . .

Continued

Uniform Status of Children
of Assisted Conception Act—*Continued*

Section 6. Petition and Hearing for Approval of Surrogacy Agreement

(a) The intended parents and the surrogate may file a petition in the [appropriate court] to approve a surrogacy agreement if one of them is a resident of this State. The surrogate's husband, if she is married, must join in the petition. A copy of the agreement must be attached to the petition. The court shall name a [guardian ad litem] to represent the interests of a child to be conceived by the surrogate through assisted conception and [shall] [may] appoint counsel to represent the surrogate.

[(b) The court shall hold a hearing on the petition and shall enter an order approving the surrogacy agreement, authorizing assisted conception for a period of 12 months after the date of the order, declaring the intended parents to be the parents of a child to be conceived through assisted conception pursuant to the agreement and discharging the guardian ad litem and attorney for the surrogate, upon finding that:

   (1) the court has jurisdiction and all parties have submitted to its jurisdiction under subsection (e) and have agreed that the law of this State governs all matters arising under this [Act] and the agreement;

   (2) the intended mother is unable to bear a child or is unable to do so without unreasonable risk to an unborn child or to the physical or mental health of the intended mother or child, and the finding is supported by medical evidence;

   (3) The [relevant child-welfare agency] has made a home study of the intended parents and the surrogate and a copy of the report of the home study has been filed with the court;

   (4) the intended parents, the surrogate, and the surrogate's husband, if she is married, meet the standards of fitness applicable to adoptive parents in this State;

   (5) all parties have voluntarily entered into the agreement and understand its terms, nature, and meaning, and the effect of the proceeding;

   (6) the surrogate has had at least one pregnancy and delivery and bearing another child will not pose an unreasonable risk to the unborn child or to the physical or mental health of the surrogate or the child, and this finding is supported by medical evidence;

   (7) all parties have received counseling concerning the effect of the surrogacy by [a qualified health-care professional or social worker] and a report containing conclusions about the capacity of the parties to enter into and fulfill the agreement has been filed with the court;

   (8) a report of the results of any medical or psychological examination or genetic screening agreed to by the parties or required by law has been filed with the court and made available to the parties;

   (9) adequate provision has been made for all reasonable health-care costs associated with the surrogacy until the child's birth including responsibility for those costs if the agreement is terminated pursuant to Section 7; and

   (10) the agreement will not be substantially detrimental to the interest of any of the affected individuals.

(c) Unless otherwise provided in the surrogacy agreement, all court costs, attorney's fees, and other costs and expenses associated with the proceeding must be assessed against the intended parents.

(d) Notwithstanding any other law concerning judicial proceedings or vital statistics, the court shall conduct all hearings and proceedings under this section in camera. The court shall keep all records of the proceedings confidential and subject to inspection under the same standards applicable to adoptions. At the request of any party, the court shall take steps necessary to ensure that the identities of the parties are not disclosed.

Continued

Uniform Status of Children
of Assisted Conception Act—*Continued*

(e) The court conducting the proceedings has exclusive and continuing jurisdiction of all matters arising out of the surrogacy until a child born after entry of an order under this section is 180 days old. . . .

Section 7. Termination of Surrogacy Agreement

(a) After entry of an order under Section 6, but before the surrogate becomes pregnant through assisted conception, the court for cause, or the surrogate, her husband, or the intended parents may terminate the surrogacy agreement by giving written notice of termination to all other parties and filing notice of the termination with the court. Thereupon, the court shall vacate the order entered under Section 6.

(b) A surrogate who has provided an egg for the assisted conception pursuant to an agreement approved under Section 6 may terminate the agreement by filing written notice with the court within 180 days after the last insemination pursuant to the agreement. Upon finding, after notice to the parties to the agreement and hearing, that the surrogate has voluntarily terminated the agreement and understands the nature, meaning, and effect of the termination, the court shall vacate the order entered under Section 6.

(c) The surrogate is not liable to the intended parents for terminating the agreement pursuant to this section. . . .

Section 8. Parentage under Approved Surrogacy Agreement

(a) The following rules of parentage apply to surrogacy agreements approved under Section 6:

   (1) Upon birth of a child to the surrogate, the intended parents are the parents of the child and the surrogate and her husband, if she is married, are not parents of the child unless the court vacates the order pursuant to Section 7(b).

   (2) If, after notice of termination by the surrogate, the court vacates the order under Section 7(b) the surrogate is the mother of a resulting child, and her husband, if a party to the agreement, is the father. If the surrogate's husband is not a party to the agreement or the surrogate is unmarried, paternity of the child is governed by [the Uniform Parentage Act].

(b) Upon birth of the child, the intended parents shall file a written notice with the court that a child has been born to the surrogate within 300 days after assisted conception. Thereupon, the court shall enter an order directing the [Department of Vital Statistics] to issue a new birth certificate naming the intended parents as parents and to seal the original birth certificate in the records of the [Department of Vital Statistics]. . . .

Section 9. Surrogacy: Miscellaneous Provisions

(a) A surrogacy agreement that is the basis of an order under Section 6 may provide for the payment of consideration.

(b) A surrogacy agreement may not limit the right of the surrogate to make decisions regarding her health care or that of the embryo or fetus.

(c) After the entry of an order under Section 6, marriage of the surrogate does not affect the validity of the order, and her husband's consent to the surrogacy agreement is not required, nor is he the father of a resulting child.

(d) A child born to a surrogate within 300 days after assisted conception pursuant to an order under Section 6 is presumed to result from the assisted conception. The presumption is conclusive as to all persons who have notice of the birth and who do not commence within 180 days after notice, an action to assert the contrary in which the child and the parties to the agreement are named as parties. The action must be commenced in the court that issued the order under Section 6.

Continued

Uniform Status of Children
of Assisted Conception Act—*Continued*

(e) A health-care provider is not liable for recognizing the surrogate as the mother before receipt of a copy of the order entered under Section 6 or for recognizing the intended parents as parents after receipt of an order entered under Section 6. . . .]

[End of Alternative A]

Alternative B

Surrogate Agreements

An agreement in which a woman agrees to become a surrogate or to relinquish her rights and duties as parent of a child thereafter conceived through assisted conception is void. However, she is the mother of a resulting child, and her husband, if a party to the agreement, is the father of the child. If her husband is not a party to the agreement or the surrogate is unmarried, paternity of the child is governed by [the Uniform Parentage Act].] . . .

[End of Alternative B]

ASSIGNMENT 16.1

a. Should surrogacy contracts be banned? If not, what kind of regulation is needed?

b. Do you approve of an advertisement such as the following one placed in the want ad section of the newspaper along with ads for accountants and truck drivers:

"CASH AVAILABLE NOW. Married or single women needed as surrogate mothers for couples unable to have children. Conception to be by artificial insemination. We pay well! Contact the Infertility Clinic today."

c. Do you favor Alternative A or B in the Uniform Status of Children of Assisted Conception Act? Why?

■ SUMMARY

The main methods of achieving surrogate motherhood are artificial insemination and in vitro fertilization. Married couples seek the services of surrogates because of female infertility and the relatively small number of babies available through adoption.

Those who argue that surrogate contracts should be legalized point out that since society cannot stop the practice of surrogacy, it would be better to regulate it to ensure competency and honesty in the process. Those who would ban surrogate contracts denounce the very notion of "buying and selling babies" in an atmosphere of exploitation.

Numerous questions arise as the topic of surrogacy comes before the legislatures of the country. For example, if a surrogate mother is paid as she goes through adoption, has there been a violation of the law that prohibits paying someone to consent to an adoption? Under current paternity laws, is the husband of the surrogate mother presumed to be the father of the child that she is under contract to allow another man to adopt? On the ultimate question of custody, what assurances exist that giving the child to the couple that hires the surrogate mother will always be in the best interest of the child? Also, numerous enforcement questions must be addressed when it becomes clear that one of the parties to the surrogate contract refuses to go along with its terms, or when something happens that is not covered in the terms of the contract, e.g., the surrogate mother gives birth to a baby with AIDS.

State legislatures have handled such questions in different ways, including the following: doing nothing; prohibiting surrogate contracts; permitting such contracts, but regulating them; and finally, giving serious consideration to a new model act called the *Uniform Status of Children of Assisted Conception Act* proposed by the National Conference of Commissioners on Uniform State Laws.

◼◼◼ KEY CHAPTER TERMINOLOGY

Surrogate Parenting

In Vitro Fertilization

Broker

Baby Selling

Intermediary

Uniform Status of Children of Assisted Conception Act

Assisted Conception

Donor

Intended Parents

Surrogate

17 TORTS

■■■■ CLASSIFICATION OF TORTS

Tort A civil wrong that has caused harm to person or property for which a court will provide a remedy.

Torts can be classified as follows:

INTENTIONAL TORTS AGAINST PROPERTY

☐ **Trespass** A wrongful entry on the property of another.

☐ **Conversion** The exercise of dominion or control over someone's property without authorization.

☐ **Nuisance** The use of one's property in such a way as to interfere with someone else's enjoyment of his or her property.

INTENTIONAL TORTS AGAINST THE PERSON

☐ **Assault** The attempt to inflict harmful or offensive contact on a person, placing that person in fear or apprehension of the contact.

☐ **Battery** Harmful or offensive contact with a person.

☐ **False Imprisonment** The detention or restraint of a person without authorization (this tort does not necessarily involve prisons, jails, police, etc.; a person, for example, can falsely imprison his or her neighbor in a garage).

☐ **Malicious Prosecution** Bringing a civil or criminal action against someone for malicious reasons when no reasonable basis or probable cause exists for the action.

☐ **Slander** Oral statements that are false and that injure the reputation of another.

☐ **Libel** Written statements that are false and that injure the reputation of another.

Immunity A defense that prevents someone from being sued for what would otherwise be wrongful conduct.

UNINTENTIONAL TORT: NEGLIGENCE

☐ **Negligence** Injury to person or property caused by a failure to act with reasonable care.

Intrafamily Torts A tort committed by one family member against another.

■■■■ INTRAFAMILY TORTS

Historically, an **immunity** existed for most **intrafamily torts.** This had the effect of rendering tortious conduct nontortious. Courts have always been reluctant to permit tort actions among any combination of husband, wife, and unemancipated child (children are **emancipated** when they are legally independent of their parents or legal guardians). This reluctance is based on the theory that family harmony will be threatened if members know that they can sue each other in tort. If the family carries **liability insurance,** there is also fear that family members will fraudulently try to collect under the policy by fabricating tort actions against each other. Furthermore, courts simply did not want to get involved. According to an 1877 opinion, "it is better to draw the curtain, shut out the public gaze, and leave the parties to forgive and forget." *Abbott v. Abbott,* 67 Me. 304, 307 (1877). At common law, a more technical reason was given for why husbands and wives could not sue each other. The husband and wife were considered to be one person, and that one person was the husband! Hence, to allow a suit between spouses would theoretically amount to one person suing himself. With the passage of the Married Women's Property Acts (see chapter 12) and the enforcement of the laws against sex discrimination, a wife now has her separate identity so that she can sue and be sued like anyone else.

Reform in the law, however, has not meant that intrafamily tort immunity no longer exists. A distinction must be made between suits against the person (such as battery) and a suit against property (such as conversion). For torts *against property,* most states allow suits between spouses and between parent and child. Most states, however, retain the immunity in some form when the suit involves a tort *against the person.* The state of law is outlined in Exhibit 17.1.

□ **EXHIBIT 17.1**
Intrafamily Torts

SPOUSE AGAINST SPOUSE
1. In most states, spouses can sue each other for intentional or negligent injury to their property, e.g., negligence, trespass, conversion.   **2.** In some states, spouses cannot sue each other for intentional or negligent injury to their person—a personal tort action, e.g., negligence, assault, battery.   **3.** Some states permit personal tort actions if the man and woman are divorced or if the tort is covered by liability insurance.   **4.** Some states permit intentional tort actions against the person to be brought by spouses against each other, but continue to forbid negligence actions for injury to the person.
CHILD AGAINST PARENT(S)
1. In all states, a child can sue the parent for intentional or negligent injury caused by the parent to the child's property, e.g., negligence, trespass, conversion.   **2.** In many states, a child cannot sue a parent for intentional or negligent injury caused by the parent to the child's person—a personal tort action, e.g., negligence, assault, battery.   **3.** If the child is emancipated (e.g., married, member of the armed forces, self-supporting), the child in all states can sue the parent for intentional or negligent injury caused by the parent to the child's person, e.g., negligence, assault, battery.   **4.** Some states will permit any child (emancipated or not) to sue the parent for intentional torts causing injury to the person, but continue to forbid actions for negligence causing injury to the person.   **5.** A few states allow the child to sue the parent for all intentional torts causing injury to the person, except where a tort arises out of the parent's exercise of discipline over the child.
OTHER RELATED PERSONS
Brothers and sisters, aunts and uncles, grandparents and grandchildren, and other relatives can sue each other in tort. The restrictions imposed on spouse suits and child suits do not apply to tort actions involving other relatives.

a. Dave knows that he has contagious genital herpes, but does not tell Alice, who contracts the disease from Dave. Can Alice sue Dave for battery? For intentional infliction of emotional distress? For deceit or fraud? Does it make any difference whether the disease was communicated before or after Dave and Alice were married? Does it make any difference that they are now divorced?

b. Jim and Helen live together for a year before they are married. They separate two years after the marriage. While preparing to file for divorce, Helen discovers that she has contracted chlamydia trachomatis, a serious venereal disease that attacks the ovaries. Her reproductive system is permanently damaged. Assume that Jim gave her this disease through intercourse during the marriage. Jim carelessly thought that he was not capable of infecting Helen. Can she sue Jim for negligence?

□ Notes on Intrafamily Crimes and Contracts

1. The state can always *criminally* prosecute one family member for crimes committed against another family member's person or property. There is no intrafamily criminal immunity.

2. To a large extent, it is possible for family members to enter into contracts with each other, e.g., a husband and wife can enter a business partnership with each other, or a father who owns a department store can hire his daughter as president. Since such contracts are legal and enforceable, it follows that the parties can bring *breach-of-contract* actions against each other for alleged violations of these contracts. There is no intrafamily breach-of-contract immunity. Not all contracts among family members, however, are legal. In general, a party cannot enter into a contract to do what the law already requires that party to do. When two parties are happily married, for example, they cannot enter a contract to support each other. They already have this obligation under the law of marriage. Such a contract is said to be "without consideration," and hence unenforceable. On the other hand, business contracts among family members are treated differently. They are almost always enforceable in intrafamily contract actions.

■ WRONGFUL LIFE, WRONGFUL BIRTH, WRONGFUL PREGNANCY

Doctors have been sued in three different kinds of cases for causing the birth of an unwanted child due to negligence, e.g., the doctor made a careless mistake performing a sterilization operation or an abortion.

□ **Wrongful Life** An action by or on behalf of an unwanted deformed or impaired child for its own damages.

□ **Wrongful Birth** An action by parents of an unwanted deformed or impaired child for their own damages.

□ **Wrongful Pregnancy** An action by parents of a healthy child they did not want.

Most states deny a child the right to bring a **wrongful life** case for the anguish of being born deformed. A major reason for this decision is the enormous difficulty of calculating the damages that should be awarded in such a case. According to one court, "The infant plaintiff would have us measure the difference between his life with defects against the utter void of nonexistence, but it is impossible to make such a determination." *Gleitman v. Cosgrove*, 49 N.J. 22, 25, 227 A.2d 689, 692 (1967). Another court was worried that allowing this infant to sue might encourage other infants to sue for being "born into the world under conditions they might regard as adverse. One might seek damages for inheriting unfortunate family conditions; one for being born into a large and destitute family, another because a parent has an unsavory reputation." *Zepeda v. Zepeda*, 190 N.E.2d 849, 858 (Ill. App. 1963).

Wrongful birth cases by parents, on the other hand, have been more successful.

Example A woman contracts German measles early in her pregnancy. Her doctor negligently advises her that the disease will not affect the health of the child. In fact, the child is born with severe defects caused by the disease. If she had known the risks, the woman would have aborted the pregnancy.

States disagree on whether parents can bring a wrongful birth action in such a case. Those that allow it are not reluctant to try to assess the financial and emotional damages of the parents in giving birth to the deformed or impaired child. They can recover their monetary losses attributed to the child's condition and damages for emotional distress.

When the unwanted child is born healthy, a **wrongful pregnancy** action (also called a **wrongful conception** action) by the parents is often allowed. The damages, however, are often limited to the costs of prenatal care and delivery; they rarely extend to the costs of raising the healthy child. The healthy child is usually not allowed to bring the same kind of action in his or her own right.

A pregnant woman has a genetic disease that could lead to the birth of a deformed child. Her doctor negligently fails to diagnose this disease and inform the woman. The child is born deformed with this disease. If she had known of the disease, she would have aborted the pregnancy. Who can bring an action against the doctor for negligence and for what damages?

ASSIGNMENT 17.2

■■■■■ DERIVATIVE ACTIONS

Actions are **derivative** if they are dependent on an underlying wrongful act to someone else. Otherwise, they are nonderivative. The two main derivative actions are loss of consortium and loss of services.

LOSS OF CONSORTIUM

Consortium is the companionship, love, affection, sexual relationship, and services (e.g., cooking, making repairs around the house) that one spouse provides another. There can be a recovery for a wrongful injury to consortium. At one time, only the husband could recover for such a **loss of consortium.** In every state, this view has been changed by statute or has been ruled unconstitutional. Either spouse can now recover for loss of consortium.

The loss-of-consortium action works as follows:

□ Rich and Ann are married.

□ Paul, a stranger, injures Ann by negligently hitting her with his car (or by one of the intentional torts such as battery).

□ Ann sues Paul for negligence. She receives damages to cover her medical bills, lost wages, if any, pain and suffering, punitive damages, if any.

□ Rich then brings a *separate* suit against Paul for loss of his wife's consortium. He receives damages to compensate him for loss or impairment he can prove to the companionship he had with Ann before the accident—to the love, affection, sexual intercourse, and services that she gave him as his wife before the accident.

In his action against Paul, Rich cannot recover for injuries sustained by Ann. Ann must recover for such injuries in her own action against Paul. Paul's liability to Rich is limited to the specific injuries sustained by Rich—loss or impairment of his wife's consortium. If Ann loses her suit against Paul, e.g., because she was contributorily negligent, Rich will *not* be able to bring his consortium suit. To recover for loss of consortium, there must be an underlying successfully litigated tort.

Parties do not have to be married for consortium in one form or another to exist between them. For example:

□ Jim and Rachel are engaged to be married. The defendant negligently injures Rachel before the wedding. Can Jim sue the defendant for loss of consortium?

□ Barbara and Paul are living together; they are not married. The defendant negligently injures Paul. Can Barbara sue the defendant for loss of consortium?

□ Gabe is the son of Bill. The defendant negligently injures Bill. Can Gabe sue the defendant for loss of parental society (*partial consortium*, sometimes called **parental consortium**)?

In the vast majority of states, the answer is *no* to each of these questions. A marriage license is a precondition to a suit for loss of consortium. This conclusion has been criticized. Since the essence of consortium is the emotional commitment and devotion between two people and not the formality of the relationship, a serious interference with this commitment and devotion should be the basis of recovery, according to the critics. The loss suffered by Jim, Barbara, and Gabe is just as real as the loss suffered by a person whose spouse has been injured. Recovery is denied in most states, though.

LOSS OF SERVICES

Suppose that it is the unemancipated child who is injured by the defendant. A parent has a right to services and earnings from the child. In most states, the parent can recover separate damages from the defendant for interference with this right, i.e., for **loss of services.** If, for example, a minor child is crippled by a battery committed by the defendant, the child will be able to recover for the injuries sustained as a result of the battery. The parent can receive *separate* damages due to the fact that the child is no longer able to provide the same services to the home that were possible prior to the accident, e.g., cutting the grass and running errands.

The spouse's claim for damages for loss of consortium rights in the other spouse is *derivative* in that it depends upon the existence of an underlying tort committed by the defendant. The same is true of the parent's claim for damages for loss of services of the child. If the underlying injury was not wrongful or tortious, the parent cannot recover.

■■■■■ NONDERIVATIVE ACTIONS

In many states, a series of nonderivative actions can be brought by one family member because of what the defendant did with or to another family member. These actions consist of the following torts:

☐ Alienation of affections

☐ Criminal conversation

☐ Enticement of spouse

☐ Abduction or enticement of a child

☐ Seduction

To establish any of these causes of action, there is no need to prove an underlying tort; they are torts in their own right. They are nonderivative.

A number of states have passed statutes (sometimes called **heart-balm statutes**) that have abolished some or all of the above tort actions. The actions are not looked upon with favor and are seldom used today even where they have not been abolished.

ALIENATION OF AFFECTIONS

Elements of Alienation of Affections

1. Defendant (e.g., a lover, an in-law) intended to diminish the marital relationship between the plaintiff and the latter's spouse.

2. Affirmative conduct of the defendant in carrying out this intent.

3. Affections between plaintiff and spouse were in fact alienated.

4. Defendant caused the alienation ("but for" the defendant, the alienation would not have occurred, or defendant was a substantial factor in producing the alienation).

CRIMINAL CONVERSATION

Element of Criminal Conversation

Defendant had sex with the plaintiff's spouse (adultery).

ENTICEMENT OF SPOUSE

Elements of Enticement of Spouse

1. Defendant intended to diminish the marital relationship between the plaintiff and the latter's spouse.

2. Affirmative conduct by defendant:
   a. to entice or encourage the spouse to leave the plaintiff's home, *or*
   b. to harbor the spouse and encourage the latter to stay away from the plaintiff's home

3. Plaintiff's spouse left home.

4. Defendant caused the plaintiff to leave home or to stay away ("but for" what defendant did, the plaintiff would not have left or stayed away, or the defendant was a substantial factor in the spouse's leaving or staying away).

ABDUCTION OR ENTICEMENT OF A CHILD

Elements of Abduction or Enticement of Child

1. Defendant intended to interfere with the parent's custody of the child.

2. Affirmative conduct by the defendant:
   a. to abduct or force the child from the parent's custody, *or*
   b. to entice or encourage the child to leave the parent, *or*
   c. to harbor the child and encourage the latter to stay away from the parent's custody.

3. The child left the custody of the parent.

4. Defendant caused the child to leave or to stay away ("but for" what the defendant did, the child would not have left or stayed away, or the defendant was a substantial factor in the child's leaving or staying away).

SEDUCTION

Element of Seduction

The defendant has sex with the plaintiff's minor daughter by force or with the consent of the daughter.

▬▬▬ VICARIOUS LIABILITY OF FAMILY MEMBERS

Vicarious Liability
Being liable because of what someone else has done. Standing in the place of someone else who is the one who actually committed the wrong.

Vicarious liability means that one person is liable solely because of what someone else does. For example, if a trucker negligently hits a pedestrian while making a delivery, the trucker's boss, the *employer*, is liable. The liability is vicarious since it is based on what someone else—the employee—has done.

The person injured could also sue the employee who is directly responsible for the injury. We are all personally liable for our own torts even if someone else is vicariously liable. Often, however, the one directly responsible has minimal resources out of which to satisfy a judgment. The person who is vicariously liable is usually the **deep pocket** who does have such resources.

Deep Pocket The person or organization that probably has sufficient resources to pay damages if a judgment is awarded by the court.

In general, vicarious liability cannot exist among family members. While there are exceptions, the basic principle is that one family member is not liable for the torts of another family member. Thus, a spouse is not liable for the torts committed by the other spouse. Children are not liable for the torts of their parents, and vice versa. For example:

Mary is the ten-year-old daughter of Diane. Mary throws a brick through the window of Jim's hardware store.

Jim must sue *Mary* for the damage done to the store. Her mother is *not* vicariously liable for the tort of her daughter.

The first exception to this rule is fairly limited. A number of states have passed statutes that make parents vicariously liable for the torts of their children, but only up to a relatively modest amount, e.g., $1,000.

In the above example involving Diane and her daughter, note that there was no indication that Diane did anything wrong or improper herself. Suppose, however, that Diane knew that her daughter, Mary, had a habit of throwing bricks into windows. Or assume that Diane was with Mary when she threw the brick at Jim's window. If Diane failed to use reasonable care to control Mary in these circumstances, Diane *would* be liable to Jim. But this would not be a case of vicarious liability. When parents act unreasonably in failing to use available opportunities to control their children, the parents are *independently* liable for **negligence** in a suit brought by the person injured by the child. Since, however, parents are rarely with their children when the latter act mischievously, and rarely know when their children are about to commit specific acts of mischief, it is usually very difficult to prove that the parents negligently failed to control and supervise their children.

Negligence
Unreasonable conduct that causes injury or damage to someone to whom you owe a duty of reasonable care.

ASSIGNMENT 17.3

Jim is the thirteen-year-old son of Harry. Jim takes Harry's car on a joy ride and negligently injures George. Whom can George sue?

The second exception to the rule of no intrafamily vicarious liability is the **family-purpose doctrine,** according to which a defendant will be liable for torts committed by a driver of the defendant's car who is a member of the defendant's family. Not all states have the doctrine, and those that have it do not all agree on its elements. Generally, the elements of the doctrine are as follows:

Elements of Family-Purpose Doctrine

1. Defendant must own the car, or have an ownership interest in it (e.g., co-owner), or control the use of the car.

2. Defendant must make the car available for family use rather than for the defendant's business (in some states, the defendant must make it available for general family use rather than for a particular occasion only).

3. The driver must be a member of the defendant's immediate household.

4. The driver must be using the car for a family purpose at the time of the accident.

5. The driver must have had the defendant's express or implied consent to be using the car at the time of the accident.

The defendant does not have to be the traditional head of the household and does not have to be in the car at the time of the accident. Again, individual states, by case law or by statute, may impose different elements to the doctrine or may reject it entirely.

ASSIGNMENT 17.4

Fred has just bought a used car, but it will not be ready for a week. During the week he is waiting, he rents a car, paying a per-mile charge on it. He tells his family that the car is to be used only to drive to work. One day while the car is at home and Fred is at the supermarket, his child becomes sick. Fred's mother, who is staying with Fred until an opening comes up in a local nursing home, drives the child to the hospital. On the way, she has an accident, injuring the plaintiff. The plaintiff sues Fred for negligence. Apply the five elements of the family-purpose doctrine to determine whether it would apply.

▬▬▬ SUMMARY

There is an immunity for some intrafamily torts, which means that the injured party cannot sue. Courts traditionally have been reluctant to allow suits for intrafamily torts since the courtroom is hardly the best place to resolve family conflicts. But immunity is not the rule in every case. It depends on who the parties are and on what tort has been committed.

Intrafamily torts that damage property (e.g., trespass) are treated differently from torts that injure the person (e.g., battery). Generally, spouses can sue each other for negligent or intentional damage to property. The same is true for such damage caused by the parent to a child's property. There is no immunity for property torts. For torts against the person, in many states, one spouse cannot sue another, and a child cannot sue a parent; immunity does apply to these torts in such states. There are some exceptions to these rules. For example, many

states grant immunity only for negligent injury to the person; thus, any family member can sue another for intentional injury to the person in such states.

If a doctor makes a negligent mistake that results in the birth of a deformed child when the parents had tried to avoid that birth by abortion or sterilization, the parents can bring a wrongful birth action. If the child is born healthy, the parents may be able to bring an action for wrongful pregnancy or for wrongful conception, but the damages are limited. The courts, however, usually do not allow the child to bring his or her own separate wrongful life action.

The two main derivative actions are loss of consortium (covering injury to the companionship, love, affection, sexual relationship, and services that one spouse provides another) and loss of services (covering an interference with the right of parents to the services of their unemancipated child). The main nonderivative actions are alienation of affections, criminal conversation, enticement of a spouse, abduction or enticement of a child, and seduction.

Vicarious liability exists when one person is liable for someone else's tort. Vicarious liability cannot exist among family members, with two major exceptions. First, some states have statutes that impose limited vicarious liability on parents for the torts committed by their children. Second, under the family-purpose doctrine, the owner of a car can be liable for a tort committed by a family member driving the car for a "family purpose."

■■■■ KEY CHAPTER TERMINOLOGY

Tort	Immunity	Loss of Services
Trespass	Intrafamily Torts	Heart-Balm Statute
Conversion	Emancipated	Alienation of Affections
Nuisance	Liability Insurance	Criminal Conversation
Assault	Wrongful Life	Enticement of Spouse
Battery	Wrongful Birth	Abduction
False Imprisonment	Wrongful Pregnancy	Seduction
Malicious Prosecution	Wrongful Conception	Vicarious Liability
Slander	Derivative	Deep Pocket
Libel	Loss of Consortium	Family-Purpose Doctrine
Negligence	Parental Consortium	

GLOSSARY

Abandonment   See Desertion.

Abduction   The unlawful taking away of another.

Absolute Divorce   See Divorce.

Abuse   Physically harming a person.

Abuse of Process   A tort with the following elements: (1) a use of civil or criminal proceedings, (2) for an improper or ulterior purpose, (3) resulting in actual damage. For example, you have someone arrested in order to pressure him to marry your daughter, whom he impregnated. Encouraging marriage is not the purpose of the criminal law.

Acceptance   An assent or acquiescence to an offer.

Accounting   A statement or report on the financial condition or status of a person, company, estate, transaction, enterprise, etc.

Account Receivable   A regular business debt not yet collected.

Acknowledgment   A formal recognition or affirmation that something is genuine.

Actuarial   Pertaining to the calculation of statistical risks, premiums, estate values, etc.

Actuary   A statistician. A person skilled in mathematical calculations to determine insurance risks.

Adjudicate   To decide by judicial process; to judge.

Adjusted Basis   See Tax Basis.

Adjusted Gross Income   The total amount received after making allowed deductions.

Administration   The management and settlement of the estate of a decedent.

Administrative Agency   A part of the executive branch of government whose function is to execute or carry out the law.

Administrator   A person appointed by a court to manage or administer the estate of a deceased, often when no valid will exists. See also Personal Representative.

Adoption   The legal process by which an adoptive parent assumes the rights and duties of the natural (i.e., biological) parent. The latter's parental rights are terminated.

Adoption by Estoppel   See Equitable Adoption, Estopped.

Adultery   Sexual relations between a married person and someone other than his or her spouse.

Adversarial Proceeding   A proceeding in court or at an agency where both parties to a dispute can appear and argue their opposing positions.

Adversary   (1) Involving a dispute between opposing sides who argue their case before a neutral official such as a judge. (2) An opponent.

AFDC   Aid to Families with Dependent Children, a public assistance program.

Affidavit   A written statement of facts given under oath or affirmation.

Affinity   Relationship by marriage rather than by blood.

Affirmative Defense   A defense that raises new facts not in the plaintiff's complaint.

Agency   A relationship in which one person acts for another or represents another by the latter's express or implied authority. See also Administrative Agency.

Aggravated Damages   Money paid to cover special circumstances that justify an increase in the amount paid, e.g., the presence of malice.

Aggrieved   (1) Injured or wronged. (2) The person injured or wronged.

Alienation   The act of transferring property, or title to property.

Alienation of Affections   A tort that is committed when the defendant diminishes the marital relationship between the plaintiff and the latter's spouse.

Alimony   Money or other property paid in fulfillment of a duty to support one's spouse after a separation or divorce. Note, however, that the Internal Revenue Service uses a broader definition of alimony for purposes of determining whether it is *deductible*. See also Rehabilitative Alimony.

Alimony in Gross   Lump-sum alimony.

Allele   One member of a pair or series of genes.

Alternate Payee   A nonemployee entitled to receive pension benefits of an employee or former employee pursuant to a Qualified Domestic Relations Order.

A Mensa et Thoro   See Legal Separation.

American Bar Association   A voluntary, national organization of attorneys.

American Digest System   See Digest. The American Digest System is the most comprehensive digest in existence. It covers almost every court in the country.

...rican Jurisprudence, 2d   A national legal ency-
...pedia.

American Law Reports   A set of reporters that contain selected opinions from many different courts. In
addition, the ALR volumes contain a research paper—
called an *annotation*—that gives a survey of the law
on a particular issue found in the opinion.

Amicus Curiae   Friend of the court. A nonparty to
litigation who gives advice or suggestions to a court
on resolving a dispute before it.

Amnesty   Forgiveness; a general pardon from the
state.

Ancillary   Subordinate; auxiliary, aiding.

Annotated   Organized by subject matter with research references or other commentary.

Annotation   A set of notes or commentaries on
something. The most widely used annotations are
those printed in *American Law Reports*.

Annuity   A fixed sum payable to an individual at specified intervals for a limited period of time or for life.

Annulment   A declaration by a court that a valid
marriage never existed.

Answer   The pleading filed by the defendant that responds to the complaint of the plaintiff.

Antenuptial Agreement   A contract made by two individuals who are about to be married that covers
support, property division, and related matters in the
event of the death of one of the parties or the dissolution of the marriage by divorce or death. Also called
Premarital Agreement and Prenuptial Agreement.
The Uniform Premarital Agreement Act defines a premarital agreement as an agreement between prospective spouses made in contemplation of marriage and
to be effective upon marriage.

Appearance   Formally going before a court.

Appellant   The party bringing an appeal because of
disagreement with the decision of a lower tribunal.

Appellee   The party against whom an appeal is
brought.

Appreciation   An increase in the value of property.

Arbitration   The process of submitting a dispute to
a third party outside the judicial system who will resolve the dispute for the parties.

Arm's Length, At   As between two strangers who
are looking out for their own self-interests. At a distance; without trusting the other's fairness; free of personal bias or control.

Arraignment   Bringing the accused before a court to
hear the criminal charges and to enter a plea thereto.

Arrears, Arrearages   Payments that are due but have
not been made.

Artificial Insemination   The impregnation of a
woman by a method other than sexual intercourse.

Assign   To transfer rights or property to someone.
The noun is *assignment*. The person who makes the
transfer is called the *assignor*. The person who receives
the transfer is called the *assignee* or one of the *assigns*.

Assignee   The person to whom ownership or rights
are transferred. See also Assigns.

Assignment   The transfer of ownership or other
rights.

Assignor   The person who transfers ownership or
rights to another.

Assigns   As a noun, it is a synonym for *assignees,*
who are the persons to whom ownership or other
rights have been or will be transferred. As a verb, it
means to transfer ownership or other rights.

Assisted Conception   A pregnancy resulting from
(1) fertilizing an egg of a woman with sperm of a man
by means other than sexual intercourse, or (2) implanting an embryo. The sperm is not that of her
husband.

At Arm's Length   See Arm's Length.

Attachment   A court authorization of the seizure of
the defendant's property so that it can be used to satisfy a judgment against him or her.

Attorney-Client Privilege   The right of a client to refuse to answer questions that would disclose communications between the client and his or her
attorney. The purpose of the communication must be
the facilitation of legal services from the attorney to
the client. The client can also prevent the attorney
from making such disclosures.

Attorney Work Product   The following material is
protected from discovery: (1) the private memoranda
of an attorney, and (2) mental impressions or personal
recollections prepared or formed by an attorney in anticipation of litigation or for trial.

A Vinculo Matrimonii   See Divorce.

Banns of Marriage   A public announcement of a
proposed marriage.

Basis   See Tax Basis.

Bastardy   Pertaining to a child born before his or her
parents were married, or born to parents who never
married.

Battered Woman Syndrome   Psychological helplessness because of a woman's financial dependence,
loneliness, guilt, shame, and fear of reprisal from her

husband or boyfriend who has repeatedly battered her in the past.

Beneficiary The person named in a document such as a will or insurance policy to receive property or other benefit.

Bequest A gift of personal property in a will.

Betrothal A mutual promise to marry.

BFOQ See Bona Fide Occupational Qualification.

Bias A predisposition to act in a certain way. A preconceived idea of how something should be decided.

Bigamy Entering or attempting to enter a marriage when a prior marriage is still valid.

Bilateral Divorce A divorce granted by a court when both the husband and the wife are present before the court.

Bill A proposed statute offered for passage by the legislature.

Bill for Divorce Petition or complaint for a dissolution of the marriage.

Biological Parent One's natural parent; a parent by blood.

Bird's Nest Custody Joint custody where the child remains in one home and each parent moves in and out during alternating periods of time.

Black Market Adoptions An adoption that involves a payment beyond reasonable expenses in order to facilitate the adoption.

Blue Book See Uniform System of Citation.

Boilerplate Language that is commonly used in a document. It sometimes refers to nonessential language often found in the same kind of document.

Bona Fide Occupational Qualification (BFOQ) Sex discrimination that is reasonably necessary for the operation of a particular business or enterprise.

Book Value The value at which an asset is carried on the balance sheet.

Canon (1) A rule of behavior. (2) A maxim or guideline.

Canon Law Church or ecclesiastical law.

Canons of Ethics Rules that embody standards of conduct. In the legal profession, the canons of ethics are often referred to as a Code of Ethics or as a Code of Professional Responsibility that governs attorneys. The current canons of ethics of the American Bar Association are found within the Model Rules of Professional Responsibility.

Capacity (1) The legal power to do something. (2) The ability to understand the nature and effects of one's actions or inaction.

Capital Improvements Structural improvements on property, as opposed to ordinary maintenance work.

Capitalization The total amount of the various securities issued by a corporation.

Caption of Complaint The heading or beginning of the complaint that contains the name of the court, the names of the parties, their litigation status, and the name of the document, e.g., Complaint for Divorce.

CARTWHEEL A research technique designed to increase the effectiveness of your use of an index in a reference book. The technique helps you identify a large variety of word or phrase substitutes to check in an index.

Case Law The body of law found in court opinions. See Court Opinion.

Cash Surrender Value The amount of money that an insurance policy would yield if cashed in with the insurance company. The amount an insurer will pay upon cancellation of the policy before death.

Cause of Action An allegation of facts that, if proved, would give a party a right to judicial relief. A cause of action is a legally acceptable reason for suing; it is a theory of recovery.

Ceremonial Marriage A marriage that is entered in compliance with the statutory requirements, e.g., obtaining a marriage license, having the marriage performed (i.e., solemnized) by an authorized person.

Challenge for Cause The elimination of a prospective juror during *voir dire*, which is the jury selection process, for a specific reason such as bias.

Chambers A judge's private office.

Chattel See Personal Property.

Chinese Wall Steps taken in an office to prevent a tainted employee from having any contact with a particular case in order to avoid the disqualification of the office from the case. The employee is tainted because he or she has a conflict of interest in the case.

Choice of Venue See Venue.

Chose in Action The right to recover something through a lawsuit.

Citation A reference to any material printed on paper or stored in a computer database. It is the "address" where you can locate and read the material.

Civil Contempt See Contempt of Court.

Civil Fraud See Fraud.

Civil Procedure The body of law governing the methods and practices of civil litigation.

Closed Case File The file of a client whose case is no longer being worked on.

.e   A book or set of books that contains rules or .ws organized by subject matter. The state code, also called the *state statutory code,* is a collection of statutes written by the state legislature organized by subject matter.

Code of Ethics   See Canons of Ethics.

Code of Regulations   Laws written by administrative agencies organized by subject matter.

Cohabitants   Two unmarried people living together in the way that husbands and wives live together.

Cohabitation   Living together as husband and wife whether or not the parties are married.

Cohabitation Agreement   A contract made by two individuals who intend to stay unmarried indefinitely that covers financial and related matters while living together, upon separation, or upon death.

Collateral Attack   A nondirect attack or challenge to the validity of a judgment. An attack brought in a different proceeding.

Collusion   (1) An agreement to commit fraud. (2) An agreement between a husband and wife in a divorce proceeding that one or both will lie to the court to facilitate the obtaining of the divorce.

Comity   The court's decision to give effect to the laws and judicial decisions of another state as a matter of deference and mutual respect even if no obligation exists to do so.

Commingling of Funds   Mixing general law firm funds with client funds in a single account. More broadly, it means combining one's own funds with those to whom a fiduciary duty is owed. See also Fiduciary.

Common Law   Judge-made law created in the absence of other controlling law such as statutory law.

Common Law Marriage   The marriage of two people who have not gone through a ceremonial marriage. They have agreed to be husband and wife, lived together as husband and wife, and held themselves out to the public as husband and wife.

Common Law Property   Property acquired during the marriage in a state other than a community property state. Upon divorce, the parties are given an equitable, but not necessarily equal, division of such property. At one time, however, common law property was usually given to the party who had legal title to the property.

Common Representation   See Multiple Representation.

Community Estate   The community property of a husband and wife.

Community Property   Property in which each spouse has a one-half interest because it was acquired during the marriage, regardless of who earned it or who has title to it. (It does not include property acquired by gift, devise, or inheritance to one spouse only, which is the separate property of that spouse.) *Common law property,* on the other hand, is property owned by the spouse who earned it.

Compensatory Damages   Money that will restore the injured party to the position he or she was in before the injury or loss; money that will make the aggrieved party whole.

Competent   Using the knowledge, skill, thoroughness, and preparation reasonably needed to represent a particular client.

Complaint   A pretrial document filed in court by one party against another that states a grievance, called a cause of action.

Conciliation   The resolution or settlement of a dispute in an amicable manner. A Conciliation Service is a court-authorized process whereby a counselor attempts to determine if parties filing for divorce can be reconciled, and if not, whether they can agree on the resolution of support, custody, and property division issues.

Concurrent Jurisdiction   When two or more courts have the power to hear the same kind of case, each court has concurrent jurisdiction over such a case.

Condonation   An express or implied forgiveness by the innocent spouse of the marital fault committed by the other spouse.

Conducive to Divorce   Tending to encourage or contribute to divorce.

Confidence   A confidence is any information protected by the attorney-client privilege. A *secret* is any information gained in the professional relationship if the client has requested that it be held secret or if its disclosure would embarrass or be detrimental to the client.

Confidentiality   The ethical obligation not to disclose information relating to the representation of a client.

Conflict of Interest   You have a divided loyalty that actually or potentially places a person at a disadvantage even though you owe that person undivided loyalty.

Conflict of Law   An inconsistency between the laws of different legal systems such as two states or two countries.

Conjugal   Pertaining to marriage; appropriate for married persons.

Connivance   A willingness or a consent by one spouse that a marital wrong be done by the other spouse.

Consanguinity   Relationship by blood.

Conservator   A person appointed by the court to manage the affairs of an adult who is not competent to do so on his or her own.

Consideration   Something of value that is exchanged between the parties, e.g., an exchange of money for services; an exchange of promises to do something or to refrain from doing something.

Consortium   Companionship, love, affection, sexual relationship, and services that a person enjoys with and from his or her spouse. See Loss of Consortium.

Constitution   The basic legal document of a government that allocates power among the three branches of the government, and that may also enumerate fundamental rights of individuals.

Constructive Desertion   The conduct of the spouse who stayed home justified the other spouse's departure; or the spouse who stayed home refuses a sincere offer of reconciliation from the other spouse who initially left.

Constructive Trust   A trust created by operation of law against one who has improperly obtained legal possession of or legal rights to property through fraud, duress, abuse of confidence, or other unconscionable conduct. See also Trust.

Consumer Price Index   A monthly report by the U.S. Bureau of Labor Statistics that tracks the price level of a group of goods and services purchased by the average consumer.

Consummation   Sexual intercourse for the first time between spouses.

Contempt of Court   Obstructing or assailing the authority or dignity of the court such as by intentionally violating a court order. The purpose of a *civil* contempt proceeding is to compel future compliance with a court order. The purpose of a *criminal* contempt proceeding is to punish the offender.

Contested   Disputed; challenged.

Contingency   An event that may or may not occur.

Contingent   Conditional; dependent on something that may not happen.

Contingent Fee   A fee is contingent if the amount of the fee is dependent on the outcome of the case. A fixed fee is paid regardless of outcome.

Continuance   The postponement or adjournment of a proceeding to a later date.

Contract   An agreement that a court will enforce. The elements of a contract are offer, acceptance, and consideration. The parties must have the legal capacity to enter a contract. Some contracts must be in writing. See also Antenuptial Agreement, Cohabitation Agreement, Implied Contract, Separation Agreement.

Contract Cohabitation   See Cohabitation Agreement.

Conversion   (1) The unauthorized exercise of dominion and control over someone's personal property. (2) Once a judicial separation has been in place for a designated period of time, the parties can ask a court for a divorce on that basis alone. The latter is called a *convertible divorce.*

Conveyance   The transfer of an interest in land.

Co-parenting   Two individuals who share the task of raising a child. Usually, at least one of the individuals is not a biological parent of the child. Sometimes, however, co-parenting refers to two biological parents who have joint custody of the child.

Copulate   To engage in sexual intercourse.

Co-respondent   The person who allegedly had sexual intercourse with a defendant charged with adultery.

Corpus   The body of something; the aggregate of something.

Corpus Juris Secundum   A national legal encyclopedia.

Corroboration   Additional evidence of a point beyond that offered by the person asserting the point.

Count   A separate and independent claim or charge in a pleading such as a complaint.

Counterclaim   A claim made by the defendant against the plaintiff.

Court Opinion   The written explanation by a court of why it reached a certain conclusion or holding.

Court Rules   Rules of procedure that govern the mechanics of litigation before a particular court.

Covenant   A promise or agreement.

Coveture   The status of being a married woman.

Credit Clouding   To notify a creditor or credit bureau that a debtor is delinquent on certain debts.

Criminal Contempt   See Contempt of Court.

Criminal Conversation   A tort committed by having sex with the plaintiff's spouse.

Criminal Fraud   See Fraud.

Criminal Law   The body of law covering acts declared to be crimes by the legislature for statutory crimes, or by the courts for common law crimes.

Curtesy   The right of a husband to the lifetime use of all the land his deceased wife owned during the marriage (if issue were born of the marriage).

...ial Parent The parent with whom the child is ...g. The parent with physical custody of the child.

Damages Money paid because of a wrongful injury or loss to person or property. See also Aggravated Damages, Compensatory Damages, Mitigation of Damages, and Punitive Damages.

Decedent The person who has died, the deceased.

Deep Pocket The person or organization that probably has sufficient resources to pay damages if a judgment is awarded by the court.

Default Judgment A judgment rendered when the other side failed to appear.

Defendant The party against whom a claim is brought at the commencement of litigation.

Defense Allegations of fact or legal theories offered to offset or defeat claims or demands.

Defined-Benefit Plan A pension plan where the amount of the benefit is fixed but not the amount of the contribution.

Defined-Contribution Plan A pension plan where the amount of the contribution is generally fixed but the amount of the benefit is not.

Deposition A pretrial discovery device, usually conducted outside the courtroom, during which one party questions the other party or a witness for the other party.

Depository The party or place where something is stored.

Depository Library, Federal A library that receives certain law books from the federal government free (e.g., the United States Code), in exchange for which the library must allow the public to have access to those books.

Depreciation A decrease in value.

Derivative Actions A suit whose success is dependent on the success of a separate suit.

Descent Acquiring property by inheritance rather than by will; acquiring property from a decedent who died intestate.

Desertion One spouse voluntarily but without justification leaves another (who does not consent to the departure) for an uninterrupted period of time with the intent not to return to resume cohabitation. Also called *abandonment*. See Constructive Desertion.

Devise Land acquired by will. The person to whom land is given by will is the devisee.

Digest (1) Sets of books containing small paragraph summaries of court opinions. (2) A summary of a document or a series of documents.

Direct Attack A challenge to the validity of a judgment made in a proceeding brought specifically for that purpose, e.g., an appeal of a judgment brought immediately after it was rendered by the trial court.

Dirty Hands Wrongdoing or other inappropriate behavior that would make it unfair or inequitable to allow a person to assert a right or a defense he or she would normally have.

Disaffirm Contracts The right of a minor to repudiate and refuse to perform a contract he or she has entered.

Disbursement Payment.

Discharged Released; forgiven so that the debt is no longer owed.

Discipline Imposing correction or punishment.

Discovery Steps that a party can take before trial to obtain information from the other side in order to prepare for trial.

Disinterested Impartial; having no desire or interest in either side winning. See also Bias.

Dissipate Waste, destroy, or squander.

Distributive Share The portion of an estate that a person receives from a person who dies intestate, i.e., without leaving a valid will.

Divided Custody See Split Custody.

Divided Loyalty Representing a client when a conflict of interest exists. See Conflict of Interest.

Divisible Divorce A divorce decree that is enforceable in another state only in part. That part of a divorce decree that dissolves the marriage is enforceable (if the plaintiff was domiciled in the state), but that part of the divorce that ordered alimony, child support, or a property division is not (if the court did not have personal jurisdiction over the defendant).

Divorce A declaration by a court that a marriage has been dissolved so that the parties are no longer married to each other.

Divorce Kits A package of do-it-yourself materials containing standard forms and written instructions on how to obtain a divorce without an attorney.

DNA Deoxyribonucleic acid. A constituent of living cell nuclei.

Docket Number A docket is a list or calendar of cases to be tried or heard at a specific term of the court. Cases on this list are assigned a number.

Doctor-Patient Privilege The right of a patient to refuse to disclose any confidential (private) communications with his or her doctor that relate to the medical care. The patient can also prevent the doctor from making such disclosures.

Domestic Partners   Two persons of the same sex who live together in an intimate relationship, who register with the government as domestic partners, and who thereby acquire limited rights enjoyed by a traditional married couple.

Domicile   The place where a person has been physically present with the intent to make that place a permanent home; the place to which one intends to return when away. A residence, on the other hand, is simply the place where you are living at a particular time. A person can have more than one residence, but generally can have only one domicile.

Domicile by Choice   A domicile chosen by a person with the legal capacity to choose.

Domiciliary   One who is domiciled in a particular state.

Donee   The person who receives a gift.

Donor   The person who gives a gift.

Dower   The right of a widow to the lifetime use of one-third of the land her deceased husband owned during the marriage.

Draft   (1) As a verb, draft means to write a document, e.g., a letter, contract, or memorandum. (2) As a noun, it means a version of a document that is not yet final or ready for distribution.

Dual Divorce   A divorce granted to both the husband and the wife.

Durational Maintenance   See Rehabilitative Alimony.

Duress   Coercion; acting under the pressure of an unlawful act or threat.

Election against Will   Obtaining a designated share of a deceased spouse's estate in spite of what the latter provided or failed to provide for the surviving spouse in a will. A forced share of a decedent's estate.

Element   A portion of a rule that is a precondition to the applicability of the entire rule.

Element in Contention   The portion of a rule (i.e., the element) that forms the basis of a legal issue because the parties disagree on the interpretation or application of that element to the facts of the case.

Emancipated   Legally independent of one's parent or legal guardian.

Emolument   Compensation for services.

Encumber   To impose a burden, claim, lien, or charge on property.

Encumbrance   A claim, lien, or other charge against property.

Enoch Arden Doctrine   The presumption that a spouse is dead after being missing for a designated number of years.

Equitable Adoption   For purposes of inheritance, a child will be considered the adopted child of a person who made a contract to adopt the child but failed to go through the formal adoption procedures.

Equitable Distribution   The fair, but not necessarily equal, division between former spouses of property acquired during the marriage.

Equitable Estoppel   See Estopped.

Escalation Clause   A provision in a contract or other document that provides for an increase or decrease in the amount to be paid based upon a factor over which the parties do not have complete control.

Escrow   Property (e.g., money, stock, deed) delivered by one person (called the *grantor, promisor,* or *obligor*) to another (e.g., a bank, an escrow agent) to be held by the latter until a designated condition or contingency occurs, at which time the property is to be delivered to the person for whose benefit the escrow was established (called the *grantee, promisee, obligee,* or *beneficiary*).

Estate   (1) All the property left by the deceased. After being used to pay debts, this property is distributed to those entitled under the will or the laws of intestacy. (2) The amount or extent of one's interest in property.

Estopped   Prevented from asserting a right or a defense because it would be unfair or inequitable to do so.

Ethics   Standards or rules of behavior to which members of an occupation, profession, or other organization are expected to conform.

Et Ux   And wife.

Evidence   Anything offered to establish the existence or nonexistence of a fact in dispute.

Ex Parte Divorce   A divorce rendered by a court when only one of the spouses was present in the state. The court did not have personal jurisdiction over the defendant.

Exclusive Jurisdiction   A court has exclusive jurisdiction when only that court has the power to hear a certain kind of case.

Executed   Carried out according to its terms.

Execution of Judgment   The process of carrying out or satisfying the judgment of a court. Using a writ of execution, a court officer (e.g., a sheriff) is commanded to seize the property of the losing litigant, sell it, and pay the winning litigant out of the proceeds.

..or A person designated in a will to carry out terms of the will and handle related matters. If a .emale, this person is sometimes called an *executrix*. See also Personal Representative.

Executory Unperformed as yet.

Executrix See Executor.

Exemplary Damages See Punitive Damages.

Extradition The process by which a state or country turns over an individual who has been accused or convicted of a crime to another state or country.

Facilitation of Divorce That which makes a divorce easier to obtain.

Fact Particularization A fact-gathering technique designed to help you identify a large variety of questions you can try to answer through interviewing and investigation.

Fair Market Value The amount that a willing buyer would pay a willing seller for property, neither being under any compulsion to buy or sell and both having reasonable knowledge of or access to the relevant facts.

False Arrest An arrest of an individual without a privilege to do so.

False Imprisonment A tort with the following elements: (1) the defendant performs an act that completely confines the plaintiff within fixed boundaries set by the defendant; (2) the defendant intends the confinement; (3) the defendant causes the confinement; and (4) the plaintiff is either conscious of the confinement or is harmed by it.

Family-Purpose Doctrine The owner of a car who makes it available for family use will be liable for injuries caused while a member of the immediate family is using the car with the owner's consent for a family purpose at the time of the accident.

Fault Grounds Marital wrongs that will justify the granting of a divorce, e.g., adultery.

Federal Parent Locator Service (FPLS) See Parent Locator Service.

Fee Splitting (1) A single bill to a client covering the fee of two or more lawyers who are not in the same firm. (2) Giving a nonlawyer part of the fee of a particular client. The latter is often done as payment for making a referral of the client.

Fiduciary (1) As an adjective, pertaining to good faith, loyalty, trust, and candor; pertaining to the obligation to protect another's interest and to provide fair treatment. (2) As a noun, a person who owes another good faith, loyalty, trust, candor; a person who owes another an obligation to protect his or her interest and to provide fair treatment.

Filiation A judicial determination of paternity. The relation of child to father.

Filius Nullius The status of an illegitimate child at common law ("the son [or child] of no one").

Fixed Fee See Contingent Fee.

Flowchart An overview of the step-by-step process by which something is done.

Forced Share See Election against Will.

Foreign Divorce A divorce obtained in another state or country.

Forensic Pertaining to use in courts.

Formbook A practical treatise or manual containing standard forms along with checklists, summaries of the law, etc. See also Treatise.

Fornication Sexual relations between unmarried persons or between persons who are not married to each other.

Forum (1) The place where the parties are presently litigating their dispute. (2) A court or tribunal hearing a case.

Forum Non Conveniens The discretionary power of a court to decline the exercise of its jurisdiction when it would be more convenient and the ends of justice would be better served if the action were tried in another court.

Forum Shopping Seeking a court that will be favorable to you. Traveling from court to court until you find one that will provide a favorable ruling.

Forum State The state in which the parties are now litigating a case.

Foster Home A temporary home for a child when his or her own family cannot provide care and when adoption is either not possible at the present time or is under consideration.

Fraud Knowingly making a false statement of present fact with the intention that the plaintiff rely on the statement. The plaintiff's reasonable reliance on the statement harms him or her. See also Statute of Frauds.

Friendly Divorce A divorce proceeding in which the husband and wife are not contesting the dissolution of the marriage, nor anything related thereto. An uncontested divorce.

Front Loading Making substantial "alimony" payments shortly after the separation or divorce in an attempt to disguise a property division as deductible alimony.

Full Faith and Credit Clause "Full Faith and Credit shall be given in each State to the public Acts, Records, and judicial Proceedings of every other State." Article IV of the *United States Constitution.*

Garnishment A proceeding whereby a debtor's money or other property under the control of another is given to a third person to whom the debtor owes a debt.

Genetic Testing The analysis of inherited factors (usually blood) of mother, child, and alleged father to help prove or disprove that a particular man fathered a particular child.

Gestational Surrogacy The sperm and egg of a couple are fertilized in vitro in a laboratory, and the resulting embryo is then implanted in a surrogate mother who gives birth to a child with whom she has no genetic relationship.

Get A bill of divorcement in a Jewish divorce.

Gift The voluntary delivery of something with the present intent to transfer title and control, for which no payment or consideration is made. Once the item is accepted, the gift is irrevocable. The person making the gift is the *donor*. The person receiving it is the *donee.*

Goodwill The reputation of a business that causes it to generate additional customers.

Grantor A transferor; a person who makes a grant.

Gross Income The total amount received or earned before deductions.

Grounds (1) Acceptable reasons for seeking a particular result. (2) Foundation or basis for one's belief or conduct.

Guarantee A warranty or assurance that a particular result will be achieved.

Guardian ad Litem A special guardian appointed by the court to represent the interests of another.

Guardianship The legal right to the custody of an individual.

Harmless Without injury or damage.

Hearsay Testimony in court of a statement made by another out of court when the statement is being offered to assert the truth of the matter in the statement.

Heart Balm Action An action based on a broken heart, e.g., breach of promise to marry, alienation of affections, and seduction.

Heart Balm Statute A statute that abolishes heart balm actions.

Heir One who receives property by inheritance rather than by will.

Hold Harmless In the event of trouble, to relieve someone of responsibility or liability.

Holographic Wholly in the handwriting of a person.

Home State The state where the child has lived for at least six consecutive months or since birth if the child is less than six months old.

Homestead One's dwelling house along with adjoining land and buildings.

Hornbook A text that summarizes an area of the law, usually with commentary and extensive footnotes. See also Legal Treatise.

Hornbook Law Elementary principles of law often summarized in law books called hornbooks.

Husband-Wife Privilege See Marital Communications.

Illegitimate Child A child born when his or her parents are not married to each other.

Illicit Cohabitation Sexual intercourse between unmarried persons who are living together. See also Cohabitation.

Imminent Near at hand; coming soon; about to happen; immediate.

Immunity A defense that prevents someone from being sued for what would otherwise be wrongful conduct.

Impediment A legal obstacle that prevents the formation of a valid marriage or other contract.

Implied Contract A contract that is not created by an express agreement between the parties but is inferred as a matter of reason and justice from their conduct and the surrounding circumstances. A contract that is manifested by conduct and circumstances rather than words of agreement. A contract that a reasonable person would infer exists, even though there is no express agreement. Also called an Implied in Fact Contract.

Imputed Disqualification Something is imputed when it is forced upon or attributed to someone or something else. If, for example, a lawyer or paralegal causes a law firm to be disqualified, we have an imputed disqualification.

In Camera In the judge's private chambers.

Incest Sexual intercourse between two people who are too closely related to each other as defined by court cases or statute.

Inchoate Partial; not yet complete.

Incident to Closely connected to something else.

Incompatibility A no-fault ground for divorce that exists when there is such discord between the husband and wife that it is impossible for them to live together in a normal marital relationship.

Incorrigible Habitually disobedient and disruptive.

Indemnify   To compensate another for any loss of expense incurred.

Indemnity   The right to have another person pay you the amount you were forced to pay.

Independent Professional Judgment   Advice given by an attorney who is not subject to a conflict of interest. See Conflict of Interest.

Indigent   Poor; without means to afford something.

In Forma Pauperis   As a poor person. As such, certain filing fees are waived.

Inheritance   Property received from someone who dies without leaving a valid will. The state determines who receives such property.

Injunction   A court order requiring a person to do or to refrain from doing a particular thing.

In Loco Parentis   Standing in the place of (and able to exercise some of the rights of) parents.

In Personam Jurisdiction   See Personal Jurisdiction.

In Rem Jurisdiction   The power of the court to make a decision affecting a particular *res*, which is a thing or status.

Instrument   A formal document such as a will, deed, mortgage, or contract.

Intake Memorandum   A written report that summarizes an interview with a new client of the office. It normally contains basic facts on the client and on his or her legal problems. See also Interoffice Memorandum; Memorandum of Law.

Intentional Infliction of Emotional Distress   Intentionally causing severe emotional distress by extreme or outrageous conduct.

Intentional Torts   Torts other than negligence and strict liability, e.g., assault, battery.

Intercept Program   A procedure by which the government seizes designated benefits owed to a parent in order to cover the latter's delinquent child support payments.

Interlocutory   Not final; interim.

Interoffice Memorandum   A written report addressed to someone in the office where you work, usually a supervisor.

Interrogatories   A written set of factual questions sent by one party to another before the trial begins.

Interspousal   Between or pertaining to a husband and wife.

Intestate   Dying without leaving a valid will.

Intestate Succession   Obtaining property from a deceased who died without leaving a valid will. The

persons entitled to this property are identified in the statute on intestate distribution.

Intrafamily Torts   Torts committed by one family member on another.

In Vitro Fertilization   The surgical removal of a woman's eggs and their fertilization with a man's sperm in the laboratory.

Irreconcilable Differences   A no-fault ground for divorce that exists when there is such discord between the husband and wife that there has been an irremediable breakdown of the marriage.

Irremediable Breakdown   See Irreconcilable Differences.

Irrevocable   That which cannot be revoked or recalled.

Issue   (1) Everyone who has descended from a common ancestor. (2) A legal question. See also Legal Periodical.

Joint and Several Liability   More than one person is legally responsible. They are responsible together and/or individually for the entire amount.

Joint Custody   Each parent shares legal custody and/or shares physical custody, often over alternating, but not necessarily equal, periods of time. Also called *shared custody.*

Joint Representation   See Multiple Representation.

Joint Tenancy   Property that is owned equally by two or more persons with the right of survivorship.

Joint Venture   An express or implied agreement to participate in a common enterprise in which the parties have a mutual right of control.

Judgment Debtor/Judgment Creditor   The person who loses and therefore must pay a money judgment is the judgment debtor. The winner is the judgment creditor.

Judicial Separation   See Legal Separation.

Jurisdiction   (1) The power of a court to act in a particular case. (2) The geographic area over which a particular court has authority. See also Concurrent Jurisdiction, Exclusive Jurisdiction, In Rem Jurisdiction, Personal Jurisdiction, and Subject-Matter Jurisdiction.

Juvenile Delinquent   A young person under a designated age whose conduct would constitute a crime if committed by an adult.

Law Review/Law Journal   A law review is a legal periodical published by a law school. Also called a law journal. See Legal Periodical.

Legal Advice   Telling a specific person how the law applies to the facts of that person's legal problem or concern.

Legal Analysis   The application of rules of law to facts in order to answer a legal question or issue.

Legal Capacity   See Capacity.

Legal Custody   The right and duty to make decisions about raising a child.

Legal Encyclopedia   A legal encyclopedia is a multivolume set of books that summarizes almost every major legal topic.

Legal Issue   A question of law. See also Legal Analysis.

Legal Malpractice   See Malpractice.

Legal Periodical   An ongoing publication (e.g., published quarterly) that contains articles, studies, reports, or other information on legal topics.

Legal Separation   A declaration by a court that parties can live separate and apart even though they are still married to each other. Also called a *judicial separation*, a *limited divorce*, a *divorce a mensa et thoro*, and a *separation from bed and board*.

Legal Treatise   A legal treatise is a book written by a private individual (or by a public official writing as a private citizen) that provides an overview, summary, or commentary on a legal topic.

Legatee   A person to whom property (usually personal property) is given by will.

Legitimacy   The status or condition of being born in wedlock.

Legitimation   The steps that enable an illegitimate child to become a legitimate child.

Legitimize   To formally declare that children born out of wedlock are legitimate.

Letter of Authorization   A letter that tells the recipient that the office represents the client and that the client consents to the release of any information about the client to the office.

Letter of Nonengagement   A letter sent by a lawyer to a prospective client explicitly stating that the lawyer will not be representing this person.

Levy   To seize in order to satisfy a claim.

LEXIS   A legal database for computer research.

Liabilities   That which one owes; debts.

Lien   A security or encumbrance on property; a claim or charge on property for the payment of a debt. The property cannot be sold until the debt is satisfied.

Limited Divorce   See Legal Separation.

Living Apart   A no-fault ground for divorce that exists when a husband and wife have lived separately for a designated period of consecutive time.

Long Arm Jurisdiction   The power that a court obtains over a nonresident defendant who has such sufficient purposeful contact with the state that it is fair and reasonable for the state to adjudicate a dispute involving the defendant.

Loose-Leaf Service   A law book published as a three-ring binder containing pages that can be inserted and removed with relative ease.

Lord Mansfield's Rule   The testimony of either spouse is inadmissible on the question of whether the husband had access to the wife at the time of conception since such evidence would tend to bastardize (i.e., declare illegitimate) the child.

Loss of Consortium   A tort action for the loss of or the interference with the companionship, love, affection, sexual relationship, and services that the plaintiff enjoyed with his or her spouse before the latter was wrongfully injured by the defendant.

Loss of Services   A tort action for the loss of or the interference with the right of a parent to the services and earnings of his or her child because of the wrongful injury inflicted on the child by the defendant.

Lucid Interval   A period of time during which a person has the mental capacity to understand what he or she is doing.

Maintenance   Food, clothing, shelter, and other necessaries of life.

Majority   A designated age of legal adulthood in the state, usually eighteen.

Malice   Animosity; the intent to inflict injury.

Malicious Prosecution   A tort with the following elements: (1) to initiate or procure the initiation of legal proceedings—civil or criminal, (2) without probable cause, (3) with malice, and (4) the proceedings terminate in favor of the person against whom they were brought.

Malpractice   Professional wrongdoing. Legal malpractice normally refers to negligence by an attorney.

Manual   A practical treatise often containing standard forms along with checklists, summaries of the law, etc. Sometimes called a *Practice Manual*. See also Treatise.

Marital Communications   Those communications between a husband and wife while cohabiting. According to the privilege for marital communications, or the husband-wife privilege, one spouse cannot disclose in court any confidential communications that occurred between the spouses during the marriage.

Market Value   See Fair Market Value.

Married Women's Property Acts   Statutes removing

all or most of the legal disabilities imposed on women as to the disposition of their property.

Marriage   See Ceremonial Marriage, Common Law Marriage.

Martindale-Hubbell   The *Martindale-Hubbell Law Directory* contains a listing of the names and addresses of many of the practicing lawyers in the country. It also has a feature called the "Martindale-Hubbell Law Digest" that contains brief summaries of the law of every state.

Mediation   The process of submitting a dispute to a third party (other than a judge) who will help the parties reach their own resolution of the dispute.

Memorandum   A memorandum is any writing or notation sent to a person or to a file. It can be a highly formal and lengthy document or a simple one-line note. The plural of memorandum is *memoranda*.

Memorandum of Law   A written explanation of how the law applies to a given set of facts. See also Intake Memorandum.

Meretricious   Pertaining to unlawful sexual relations; vulgar or tawdry.

Meritorious   Having merit; having a reasonable basis to believe that a person's claim or defense will succeed.

Microfilm   Reels or cassettes that contain images or photographs that have been greatly reduced in size. Many law books and periodicals have been placed on microfilm.

Migratory Divorce   A divorce obtained in a state to which one or both of the spouses traveled before returning to their original state.

Minimum Fee Schedule   A list of fees announced by the bar association that an attorney *must* charge, at a minimum, for designated services rendered. Charging lower than the minimum would be unethical. (Today, however, minimum fee schedules are illegal.)

Minor   Someone under the age of majority in the state, which is usually eighteen.

Miscegenation   Mixing the races. The marriage or cohabitation of persons of different races.

Mitigating Circumstances   Facts that in fairness justify a reduction in damages because of the conduct of the aggrieved party.

Mitigation of Damages   Steps the aggrieved party could have taken to lessen the amount of injury or harm caused by the wrongdoer.

Model Rules of Professional Responsibility   See Canons of Ethics.

Mortgage   An interest in land that provides security

for the performance of a duty or the payment of a debt.

Multiple Representation   Representing more than one side in a legal matter or controversy. Also called joint representation and common representation.

National Conference of Commissioners on Uniform State Laws   See Uniform Laws.

Necessaries   The basic items needed by family members to maintain a standard of living. These items can be purchased and charged to the spouse who has failed to provide them.

Neglect   The failure to provide support, medical care, education, moral example, discipline, and other necessaries.

Negligence   Unreasonable conduct that causes injury or damage to someone to whom you owe a duty of reasonable care.

Nisi   Not final; interim.

No-Fault Grounds   Reasons for granting a divorce that do not require proof that either spouse committed marital wrongs.

Nonage   Below the required minimum age to enter a desired relationship or perform a particular task.

Noncustodial Parent   The parent with whom a child is not living.

Nonengagement   See Letter of Nonengagement.

Nonmolestation Clause   A clause in an agreement that the parties will not bother each other.

Notes to Decisions   Small paragraph summaries of court opinions that have interpreted a particular statute. These paragraphs are printed after the text of the statute within annotated codes.

Nuisance   An unreasonable interference with the use and enjoyment of land.

Obligor/Obligee   The person who has an obligation is the obligor. The person to whom this obligation is owed is the obligee.

Offer   To present something that can be accepted or rejected.

Open Adoption   An adoption in which the natural parent maintains certain kinds of contact with his or her child after the latter is adopted.

Operation of Law   Automatically because of the law. A result occurs by operation of law when it happens because the law mandates the result, not because a party agrees to produce the result.

Opinion   See Court Opinion.

Order to Show Cause (OSC)   An order telling a person to appear in court and explain why a certain order should not be entered.

Outstanding Unpaid.

Palimony A nonlegal term for payments made by one nonmarried party to another after they cease living together, usually because they entered an express or implied contract to do so while they were living together or cohabiting.

Paralegal A person with legal skills who works under the supervision of an attorney or who is otherwise authorized to use those skills.

Parens Patriae Parent of the country, referring to the state's role in protecting children and those under disability.

Parental Alienation Syndrome A disorder suffered by some children at the center of a custody dispute. They idealize one parent while expressing hatred for the other, even though the relationship with both parents was relatively positive before the dispute.

Parent Locator Service, State A state government agency that helps locate parents who are delinquent in child support payments. If the search involves more than one state, the Federal Parent Locator Service (FPLS) can help. The FPLS also helps in parental kidnapping cases.

Partition The dividing of land held by joint tenants and tenants in common. The division results in individual ownership.

Partnership A voluntary contract between two (or more) persons to use their resources in a business or other venture, with the understanding that they will proportionately share losses and profits.

Paternity Fatherhood.

Payee One to whom money is paid or is to be paid.

Payor One who makes a payment of money or who is obligated to do so.

Pecuniary Pertaining to or consisting of money.

Pendente Lite While the litigation is going on.

Per Curiam By the court. A court opinion that does not name the particular judge who wrote it.

Peremptory Challenges The elimination of a prospective juror during *voir dire,* which is the jury selection process. No reason need be given.

Periodic Payments A payment of a fixed amount for an indefinite period, or the payment of an indefinite amount for a fixed or indefinite period.

Personal Jurisdiction The power that a court obtains over an individual after proper service of process on him or her. The court's power to render a

decision that binds the individual defendant. Also called *in personam jurisdiction.*

Personal Property Movable property; any property other than real property. Also called chattels.

Personal Representative An executor or administrator of the estate of the deceased. Someone who formally acts on behalf of the estate of the deceased.

Petition A formal request that the court take some action. A complaint.

Physical Custody The parent with whom the child actually lives has physical custody.

Plaintiff The party bringing a claim against another.

Pleadings Formal documents that contain allegations and responses of the parties in litigation. The major pleadings are the complaint and answer.

Pocket Part A pocket in the inside back cover of some bound volumes. In this pocket you will find pamphlets that update the bound volume.

Polygamy The practice of having more than one spouse at the same time, usually more than two.

Post-Nuptial After marriage. See Separation Agreement.

Practice Manuals See Manual.

Practice of Law Assisting another to secure his or her legal rights. See Unauthorized Practice of Law.

Prayer A formal request.

Premarital Agreement See Antenuptial Agreement.

Premises (1) Lands and buildings. (2) The foregoing statements; matters stated earlier (in consideration of the premises).

Prenuptial Before marriage. See Antenuptial Agreement.

Preponderance of Evidence A standard of proof that is met if the evidence shows it is more likely than not that an alleged fact is true or false as alleged.

Present Value The amount of money an individual would have to be given now in order to produce or generate a certain amount of money in a designated period of time.

Presents, These This legal document.

Presumption An assumption of fact that can be drawn when another fact or set of facts is established. The presumption is *rebuttable* if a party can introduce evidence to show that the assumption is false.

Presumptive Created or arising out of a presumption; based on inference.

Primary Authority Any *law* that a court could rely on in reaching its conclusion, e.g., a constitutional provision, statute, regulation, ordinance, other court opinion.

Primary Caregiver Presumption The primary person who has taken care of the child should have custody.

Privilege A benefit, advantage, or right enjoyed by an individual.

Privilege against Self-Incrimination The right to refuse to answer questions that directly or indirectly connect the individual to a crime.

Privilege for Marital Communication See Marital Communications.

Probate A court proceeding at which a will is proved to be valid or invalid.

Probation Restricted and supervised living in the community in lieu of institutionalization.

Procedural Law Laws that pertain to the technical steps for bringing or defending actions in litigation before a court or an administrative agency. An example would be the number of days within which a party can request a jury trial in a divorce case after the complaint has been filed.

Proctor A person appointed for a particular purpose, e.g., protect the interests of a child.

Professional Responsibility See Canons of Ethics.

Pro Hac Vice For this particular occasion.

Proof of Service A statement that service of process on the defendant has been made.

Property Division The distribution of property accumulated by spouses as a result of their joint efforts during the marriage. Sometimes referred to as a property settlement.

Pro Se On one's own behalf; not using an attorney.

Pro Se Divorce A divorce obtained when a party represents himself or herself.

Prosecute To commence and proceed with a lawsuit.

Protective Order A court order directing a person to refrain from harming or harassing another.

Provocation The plaintiff incited the acts constituting the marital wrong by the other spouse.

Proxy Marriage The performance of a valid marriage ceremony through agents because one or both of the prospective spouses are absent.

Psychological Parent An adult who is not legally responsible for the care of a child, but who has formed a substantial emotional bond with the child.

Public Assistance Welfare or other forms of financial help from the government to the poor.

Public Policy The principle inherent in the customs, morals, and notions of justice that prevail in a state. The foundation of public laws. The principles that are naturally and inherently right and just.

Punitive Damages Money that is paid to punish the wrongdoer and to deter others from similar wrongdoing. Also called Exemplary Damages.

Putative Alleged or reputed.

Putative Spouse A person who reasonably believed he or she entered a valid marriage even though there was a legal impediment that made the marriage unlawful.

QDRO See Qualified Domestic Relations Order.

QMCSO See Qualified Medical Child Support Order.

Qualified Domestic Relations Order (QDRO) A court order that allows a nonemployee to reach pension benefits of an employee or former employee in order to satisfy a support or other marital obligation to the nonemployee.

Qualified Medical Child Support Order An order, decree, or judgment issued by a court that orders medical support or health benefits for the child of a parent covered under a group health insurance plan.

Quantum Meruit "As much as he deserves." Valuable services are rendered or materials are furnished by the plaintiff, and accepted, used, or enjoyed by the defendant under such circumstances that the plaintiff reasonably expected to be paid.

Quasi Community Property Property acquired by the spouses when they lived in a non-community property state before moving to a community property state. If they had acquired it in a community property state, it would have been community property.

Quasi Contract A contract created by the law to avoid unjust enrichment.

Quasi Marital Property Property that will be treated as having been acquired or improved while the parties were married even though the marriage was never valid.

Quitclaim A release or giving up of whatever claim or title you have in property. You are turning over whatever you have, without guaranteeing anything.

Real Property/Real Estate Land and anything permanently attached to the land.

Realize To obtain something actually, rather than on paper only.

Reasonable See Unreasonable.

Rebuttable Presumption See Presumption.

Recapture Rule The recalculation of a tax liability when the parties have improperly attempted to disguise a property division as alimony through front loading. See Front Loading.

Receivership The court appointment of someone to control and manage the defendant's property in order to ensure compliance with a court order.

Reconciliation The full resumption of the marital relationship.

Recrimination The party seeking the divorce (the plaintiff) has also committed a serious marital wrong.

Regional Digest See Digest. A regional digest contains summaries of opinions written by courts in a designated cluster of states. The full text of the opinions is found in the corresponding regional reporter for the digest.

Regional Reporter The volumes that contain the full text of opinions from courts within a designated cluster of states.

Regulation A law enacted by an administrative agency.

Rehabilitative Alimony Alimony for a limited time until the payee can get back on his or her feet and become financially self-sufficient. It is also known as *durational maintenance.*

Remand To send back for further proceedings.

Remedy The method or means by which a court or other body will enforce a right or compensate someone for a violation of a right.

Remise To give up or release.

Reporters The volumes that contain the full text of court opinions.

Reprimand A form of public discipline by which an attorney's conduct is declared to have been improper, but that does not limit his or her right to practice law.

Request for Admissions A request from one party to another that it agree that a certain fact is true or that a specified document is genuine so that there will be no need to present proof on such matters during the trial.

Res A thing or object; a status.

Rescission The cancellation of something.

Residence The place where someone is living at a particular time. See also Domicile.

Res Judicata When a judgment on its merits has been rendered, the parties cannot relitigate the same dispute.

Respondeat Superior An employer is responsible for the conduct of employees while they are acting within the scope of employment.

Respondent The party responding to a position or claim of another party; the defendant. See also Appellee.

Restatement of Torts A treatise written by the American Law Institute that articulates or restates the law of torts.

Restitution An equitable remedy in which a person is restored to his or her original position prior to the loss or injury. Restoring to the plaintiff the value of what he or she parted with.

Restraining Order A form of injunction initially issued ex parte to restrain the defendant from doing a threatened act.

Resulting Trust A trust implied in law from the intention of the parties. A trust that arises when a person transfers property under circumstances that raise the inference that he or she did not intend the transferee to actually receive any interest in the property. See also Trust.

Retainer (1) The contract of employment between lawyer and client. (2) Money paid by a client to ensure that a lawyer will be available to work for the client. (3) Prepayment or deposit against future fees and costs of representation.

Right of Survivorship When one owner dies, his or her share goes to the other owners; it does not go through the estate of the deceased owner.

Rules of Professional Responsibility See Canons of Ethics.

Sanctions Penalties or punishments of some kind. (The word *sanction* can also mean approval or authorization.)

Secondary Authority Any *nonlaw* that a court could rely on in reaching its conclusion, e.g., an article in a legal periodical, a treatise.

Second-Parent Adoption The adoption of a child by a partner (or cohabitant) of a natural parent who does not give up his or her own parental rights.

Secret See Confidence.

Security Interest An interest in property that provides that the property may be sold on default in order to satisfy a debt for which the security interest was given.

Self-Incrimination See Privilege against Self-Incrimination.

Separate Maintenance Court-ordered spousal support while the spouses are separated.

Separate Property Property totally owned by one spouse; noncommunity property.

Separation See Legal Separation, Separation Agreement.

Separation Agreement A contract between spouses who have separated or who are about to separate in which the terms of their separation are spelled out, e.g., support obligations, child custody, division of property accumulated during the marriage. The agreement may or may not be later incorporated and merged in a divorce decree. Also called a post-nuptial contract.

Sequester To remove or hold until legal proceedings or legal claims are resolved. The noun is sequestration.

Service of Process Providing a formal notice to the defendant that orders him or her to appear in court in order to answer the allegations in the claims made by the plaintiff.

Settlor See Trust.

Severable Removable without destroying what remains. Something is severable when what remains after it is taken away can survive without it. The opposite of severable is essential or indispensable.

Severally Individually, separately.

Sham Pretended, false, empty.

Shared Custody See Joint Custody.

Shepardize To use the set of law books called *Shepard's Citations* to obtain specific information about a document, e.g., whether an opinion has been overruled, or whether a statute has been repealed.

Sole Custody One parent has physical and legal custody.

Solemnization The performance of a formal ceremony in public.

Solemnize The verb for solemnization.

Sole Proprietorship A form of business in which one person owns all the assets.

Solicitation Asking or urging someone to do something.

Specialization The development of experience and expertise in a particular area of practice.

Specific Performance A remedy for breach of contract that forces the wrongdoing party to complete the contract as promised.

Split Custody (1) One parent has legal custody, with physical custody going to each parent during alternating periods when the child lives with him or her. (2) Each parent receives sole custody of at least one sibling with visitation rights as to the other siblings.

The latter definition is also referred to as *divided custody.*

Standard Form A frequently used format for a document such as a contract, complaint, or tax return. The form is designed to be used by many individuals, often by filling in blanks that call for specific information commonly needed for such documents.

Standing The right to bring a case and seek relief from a court.

State Parent Locator Service (SPLS) See Parent Locator Service.

Statute An act of the legislature declaring, commanding, or prohibiting something.

Statute of Frauds The requirement that certain kinds of contracts be in writing in order to be enforceable, e.g., a contract for the sale of land; a contact that by its terms cannot be performed within a year.

Statute of Limitations The time within which a suit must be brought. If it is brought after this time, it is barred.

Statutory Code See Code.

Stepparent A person who marries the natural mother or father of a child, but who is not one of the child's natural parents.

Sterility Inability to have children; infertile.

Stipulation An agreement between the parties on a matter so that evidence on the matter does not have to be introduced at the trial.

Sua Sponte On its own motion.

Subject-Matter Jurisdiction The power of the court to hear a particular category or kind of case; its authority to make rulings on certain subject matters.

Subpoena A command to appear in court.

Subscribe To sign at the end of the document.

Substantive Law Laws that pertain to rights and obligations other than purely procedural matters. An example would be the right to a divorce on the ground of irreconcilable differences.

Substituted Service Service of process other than by handing the process documents to the defendant in person, e.g., service by mail.

Succession Obtaining property of the deceased, usually when there is no will.

Summary Dissolution A divorce obtained in an expedited manner because of the lack of controversy between the husband and wife.

Summons A formal notice from the court served on the defendant ordering him or her to appear and answer the allegations of the plaintiff.

Supervised Visitation Visitation by a parent with his or her child while another adult (other than the custodial parent) is present.

Surety Bond The obligation of a guarantor to pay a second party upon default by a third party in the performance the third party owes the second party.

Surrogate Mothers A woman who is artificially inseminated with the semen of a man who is not her husband, with the understanding that she will surrender the baby at birth to the father and his wife.

Survivorship See Right of Survivorship.

System An organized method of accomplishing a task that seeks to be more effective or efficient than alternative methods.

Talak "I divorce you." Words spoken by a husband to his wife in a Moslem divorce.

Tangible Having a physical form.

Tax Basis One's initial capital investment in property. An adjusted basis is calculated after making allowed adjustments and deductions to the initial capital investment, e.g., an increase in the basis because of a capital improvement.

Tenancy by the Entirety A joint tenancy held by a husband and wife. See also Joint Tenancy.

Tenancy in Common Property owned by two or more persons in shares that may or may not be equal, with no right of survivorship. Each tenant in common has a right to possession of the property. See also Right of Survivorship.

Tender Years Presumption Young children are better off living with their mother than with their father.

Termination of Parental Rights A judicial declaration that a parent shall no longer have a right to participate in decisions affecting the welfare of the child.

Testament A will.

Testate Dying with a valid will.

Testator The person who has died leaving a valid will.

Tort A civil wrong that has caused harm to a person or property for which a court will provide a remedy. Conduct that consists of a breach of contract or a crime may also constitute a tort.

Tort Immunity One who enjoys a tort immunity cannot be sued for what would otherwise be a tort.

Transferor/Transferee The person who transfers property is the transferor; the person to whom property is transferred is the transferee.

Transitory Divorce A divorce granted in a state where neither spouse was domiciled at the time.

Treatise Any book written by a private individual (or by a public official writing in a nonofficial capacity) that provides an overview of and commentary on an area of the law. Hornbooks, manuals, and formbooks are treatises.

Trespass Wrongfully intruding on land in possession of another.

Trimester Three months.

Trust When property is in trust, its legal title is held by one party (the trustee) for the benefit of another (the beneficiary). The creator of the trust is called the settlor.

Unauthorized Practice of Law Performing functions that only attorneys are allowed to perform. Violating the state statute on who can practice law. Engaging in legal tasks without attorney supervision and/or without special authorization to engage in such tasks.

Unconscionable Shocking to the conscience; substantially unfair.

Uncontested Not disputed; not challenged. See also Friendly Divorce.

Undertaking A promise, engagement, or enterprise.

Unemancipated Legally dependent on one's parent or legal guardian.

Unethical Conduct See Canons of Ethics, Ethics.

Unfit Demonstrating abuse or neglect that is substantially detrimental to a child.

Uniform Laws Proposed statutes written by the National Conference of Commissioners on Uniform State Laws. The proposals are submitted to state legislatures for consideration.

Uniform System of Citation The bible of citation form—also called the *blue book*. See Citation.

Unjust Enrichment Receiving property or benefit from another when in fairness and equity the recipient should make restitution of the property or provide compensation for the benefit even though there was no express or implied promise to do so.

Unreasonable That which is contrary to the behavior of an ordinary, prudent person under the same circumstances.

URESA Uniform Reciprocal Enforcement of Support Act.

Venue The place of the trial. When more than one court has subject-matter jurisdiction to hear a particular kind of case, the selection of the court is called *choice of venue*.

Verification of Complaint A sworn statement that the contents of the complaint are true.

Vested Fixed so that it cannot be taken away by future events or conditions; accrued so that you now have a right to present or future possession or enjoyment.

Viability   The stage of fetal development when the life of an unborn child may be continued indefinitely outside the womb by natural or artificial support systems.

Vicariously Liable   Being liable because of what someone else has done. Standing in the place of someone else who is the one who actually committed the wrong.

Visitation   The right of a noncustodial parent to visit and spend time with his or her children.

Void   Invalid whether or not a court declares it so.

Void ab Initio   Invalid from the time it started.

Voidable   Invalid only if a court declares it so.

Voir Dire   Jury selection.

Waiver   The relinquishment or giving up of a right or privilege because of an explicit rejection of it or because of a failure to take appropriate steps to claim it at the proper time.

Ward   An individual, often a minor, under the care of a court-appointed guardian.

Welfare   See Public Assistance.

WESTLAW   A legal database for computer research.

Will   A document that specifies the disposition of one's property and provides related instructions upon death.

Words and Phrases   A multivolume legal dictionary published by West. Most of its definitions come from court opinions.

Work Product, Attorney   See Attorney Work Product.

Writ of Execution   See Execution of Judgment.

Wrongful Adoption   A tort seeking damages for wrongfully stating or failing to disclose to prospective adoptive parents available facts on the health or other condition of the adoptee that would be relevant to the decision on whether to adopt.

Wrongful Birth   An action by parents of an unwanted deformed child for their own damages. The defendant wrongfully caused the birth.

Wrongful Life   An action by or on behalf of an unwanted deformed child for its own damages. The defendant wrongfully caused the birth.

Wrongful Pregnancy   An action by parents of a healthy child that they did not want. The defendant wrongfully caused the birth. Also called *wrongful conception.*

Zygote   A cell produced by the union of two gametes before cleavage.

INDEX